FIGHTING
the Second
CIVIL WAR

A HISTORY *of* BATTLEFIELD PRESERVATION
and the EMERGENCE *of the* CIVIL WAR TRUST

BOB ZELLER

BOOK DESIGN *by* Jeff Griffith Creative
MAPS *by* Steven Stanley
FONTS: Minion for body face, Hoefler Titling and AT Sackers Gothic for headlines,
and Bodoni Ornamental for inital caps.

Library *of* Congress Cataloging-in-Publication Data
Zeller, Bob.
Fighting the Second Civil War / BOB ZELLER

Library *of* Congress Control Number: 2017937478
★ ★ ★ ★
ISBN (paperback): 978-0-9988112-0-8
ISBN (hardcover): 978-0-9988112-1-5

The paper in this book meets the guidelines for permanence
and durability of the Committee on Production Guidelines
for Book Longevity of the Council on Library Resources.

COVER PHOTO: Devil's Den Witness Tree, Gettysburg National Military Park, Pa.
by Dan Thompson, DanandHolly.com
BACK COVER PHOTO: Chancellorsville Battlefield, Fredericksburg & Spotsylvania
National Military Park, Va., *by* Theresa Rasmussen

Table of Contents

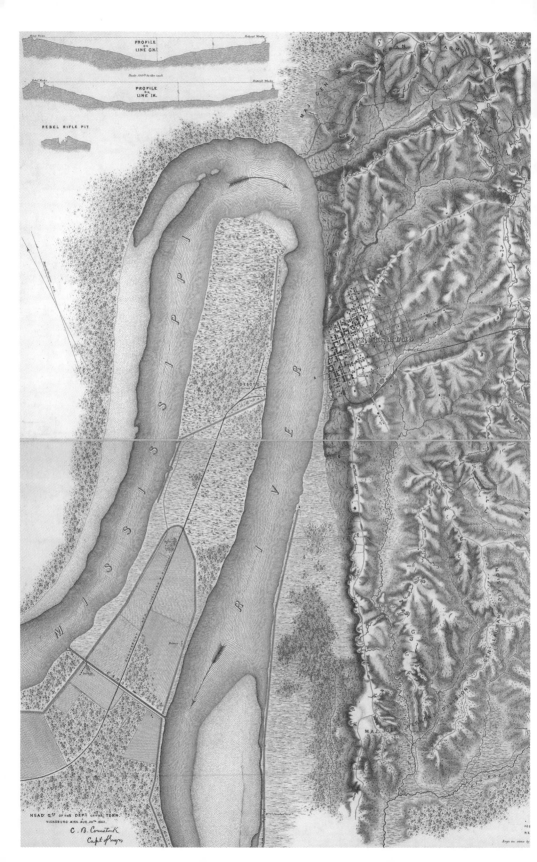

List of Acronyms

ABPP	American Battlefield Protection Program
ACHP	Advisory Council *on* Historic Preservation
ABPF	American Battlefield Protection Foundation
APCWS	Association *for the* Preservation *of* Civil War Sites
APVA	Association *for the* Preservation *of* Virginia Antiquities (now Preservation Virginia)
BGA	Battle Ground Academy
BSF	Brandy Station Foundation
CBA	Chantilly Battlefield Association
CWPT	Civil War Preservation Trust (2000-2010)
CWT	The original Civil War Trust (1991-1999)
CWSAC	Civil War Sites Advisory Commission
CVBT	Central Virginia Battlefields Trust
DRCC	Delaware *and* Raritan Canal Commission
FSNMP	Fredericksburg *and* Spotsylvania National Military Park
GBPA	Gettysburg Battlefield Preservation Association
IAS *or* **Institute**	Institute *for* Advanced Study
ISTEA	Intermodal Surface Transportation Efficiency Act of 1991
NPS	National Park Service
NWPCCA	Northwest Prince William Citizens Association
PGCB	Pennsylvania Gaming Control Board
PED	Piedmont Environmental Council
PMD	Planned mixed-use district
SBC	Save *the* Battlefield Coalition
SHAF	Save Historic Antietam Foundation
Society	Princeton Battlefield Society
STFB	Save The Franklin Battlefield
SHPO	Virginia State Historic Preservation Office
Trust	The Civil War Trust (2011-present)
TPL	The Trust *for* Public Land
UDC	United Daughters *of the* Confederacy
VDOT	Virginia Department *of* Transportation

"We leave you our deaths. Give them their meaning.

We were young, they say. We died. Remember us."

—ARCHIBALD MACLEISH
The Dead Young Soldiers

Battle of Antietam, 1862
Sharpsburg, Md.
ALEXANDER GARDNER
LIBRARY OF CONGRESS

560

FOREWORD

by O. James Lighthizer

 HIRTY YEARS ago, a Civil War academic scholar, five National Park Service battlefield historians and two Civil War buffs convened a meeting in a Fredericksburg restaurant to create an organization whose sole mission would be to buy and preserve the war's battlefields.

Development of the Chantilly battlefield in Fairfax County, Virginia, triggered the meeting. The growth-minded county had turned a blind eye to its own history —a heritage it had previously honored.

As they created the Association for the Preservation of Civil War Sites (APCWS), the 27 people who attended that first meeting knew all too well that the National Park Service battlefield parks, as well as state and local parks, as fine as they were, did not include the vast majority of battlefield acres on which young American men by the thousands fought and died for the causes in which they believed.

West of Fredericksburg, most of the Chancellorsville battlefield, including the field of Stonewall Jackson's legendary flank attack, remained privately owned and in imminent threat of development. The battlefield around Salem Church had already been lost. The story was the same at every significant battlefield of the Civil War. Some were more threatened than others, but most of America's own hallowed ground was not preserved.

Before the national movement was organized, there were the Jerry Russells and the Annie Snyders of the world, out there howling in the pre-movement wilderness. Local battlefield friends groups, supported by Civil War Round Tables and other heritage groups, took on the fights against developers. Some even began saving land.

The founders of APCWS, with little more than the spirit of volunteerism and a willingness to work, began chipping away at the mountain of preservation opportunities and challenges. APCWS had no money to start with, but the first three saves were donations, which underscored the need for their mission. People gave them land to keep it preserved.

Through tireless effort and with the support of thousands of Civil War buffs across the nation who joined the cause as APCWS members, these preservation pioneers began to build a record of success. By 1990, the APCWS had saved more than 660 acres at eight different battlefields.

Interest in the Civil War soared that fall with the airing of *The Civil War* documentary mini-series by Ken Burns. In 1991, Congress created the Civil War Sites Advisory Commission to study and rank the battlefields, their condition and the potential threats. The original Civil War Trust was created, as well as the National Park Service's American Battlefield Protection Program (ABPP).

For the next nine years, the APCWS and the original Trust warily co-existed, sometimes working together but mostly at odds and sometimes at war. Both groups became saddled with financial problems. The APCWS had begun buying battlefields on credit, and found itself smothered by more than $6 million of debt.

When I joined the board of the Civil War Trust in July 1994, it was obvious the two groups needed to be one. It wasn't easy, but the Trust and the APCWS finally merged in late 1999 into the Civil War Preservation Trust (and now, once again, simply The Civil War Trust). I was asked to lead the new organization and eagerly accepted the opportunity. I saw it as a chance to make a real difference in the movement.

The two groups, despite discord, had done a good job. In 12 years, they had saved more than 6,000 acres at almost 50 battlefields in 14 states, preserving hallowed ground from Gettysburg, Pennsylvania to Glorieta Pass, New Mexico.

My challenge, and the challenge I presented to my staff and our vast, loyal membership, was to transform good work into greater achievements. Together, during the past 18 years, we have pushed ourselves and our organization to be the best we could be. In this ceaseless quest to improve, we have become better in all facets of our mission. We are better at evaluating and prioritizing battlefield acquisition opportunities. We are better at using easements to protect historic ground. We are better at working with local organizations and forging a strong partnership with the ABPP. We are better fighters when preservation efforts become battles. We are better lobbyists on Capitol Hill, better fundraisers, better at Civil War history and education, and better custodians of our donor dollars.

I am proud of our sparkling reputation as an efficient, reliable and thrifty non-profit organization, with seven straight years (and counting) of four-star rankings for accountability, integrity and sound fiscal management by Charity Navigator, the nation's leading charity evaluator. Only two percent of more than 8,000 charities evaluated earn this distinction.

On the eve of the 30th anniversary of the founding of APCWS and the organized national battlefield preservation movement, we have saved more than 45,000 acres at 132 battlefields in 23 states. This noble labor includes more than 600 transactions—mostly fee-simple real estate acquisitions—with a total value of more than $300 million. And in 2014, we heeded the call to expand our mission to help preserve battlefields of the Revolutionary War and the War of 1812. We started a new organization, *Campaign 1776*, and have begun saving hallowed ground from the battlefields of those wars.

This narrative chronicles our work up to now, early 2017. But our duty is to become greater still, to use our experience, dedication and passion to sharpen our skills in all aspects of our mission. The need calls for nothing less. As many as 200,000 acres of core battlefield land are still privately owned and could be developed. Only about a third of major battlefields such as Chancellorsville, the Wilderness and Spotsylvania have been preserved. The battle of Cedar Creek in Virginia covered 20,000 acres. We managed to save about 640 acres in more than a dozen acquisitions since 1996, spending about $5.4 million. That leaves only 19,360 acres to go.

Our efforts have been uplifted time and again by our fabulous, generous members who have given us tens of millions of dollars over the years. Donors large and small rise to the call by the thousands for nearly every campaign, and remind us how many care enough to reach into their personal treasure on our behalf. Our board trustees have not only donated millions of dollars, but countless hours providing oversight and guidance, demanding accountability and making final decisions.

Our 30-year history is anything but smooth. Politically and emotionally, we have been fighting a second Civil War, with new battles being fought over the same battlefields. We have engaged in exhausting, frustrating preservation fights that often last longer than the Civil War itself. And too often we were fighting among ourselves.

These were times that brought drama, tension, sadness and exhilaration to our mission and a level of human emotion that makes for good storytelling. But I need to make two very important points. First, nearly all of our acquisitions and transactions—which total more than 550 in the first 30 years of the organized national battlefield preservation movement—have been routine, if not delightful, negotiations in which everybody won. Week after week, we close on deals, always working with willing sellers—deals that ruffle no feathers whatsoever. Second, almost always, our saves are team efforts. The list of organizations and agencies with whom we have partnered to save land would fill pages. The ABPP is a primary partner, overseeing federal funds that have been appropriated for battlefield preservation since 1998.

Many states with battlefields have been strong partners. Regional groups such as the Central Virginia Battlefields Trust and local groups such as Franklin's Charge and the Save Historic Antietam Foundation, to name but three, have done great work,

As hard as we work, we know the real sacrifice came from those citizen soldiers by the tens of thousands who gave their lives and shed their blood on American soil in this great experiment of democratic government. Hand in hand with preserving their battlefields, it is their story we tell—one of the greatest stories ever told.

We honor their memory best by preserving their battlefields and the history enshrined in those original landscapes, which show us how terrain influenced the deadly struggles, and allow us to see, in our mind's eye, what these battles must have looked like. Preserved battlefields are the foundation of our growing education and history initiatives on the internet, in classrooms and at the historic sites themselves.

Our mission is encased in the heritage of our country's most traumatic event, and how the Civil War set the United States on the path to become a bastion of freedom and the greatest power in the world. Yet, we are reminded frequently ours is a fragile democratic republic only as strong as the competency of its citizens. To know history is crucial to good citizenship. Who are you? Where did you come from? What do you stand for? We can answer questions with greater clarity when we preserve places where history was made.

The story of The Civil War Trust and the emergence of a national organized battlefield preservation movement is a story worth telling. I know of no heritage land preservation organization in the world as successful as the Trust. The amount of land saved, the amount of money spent, the number of members involved—no organization has accomplished what we have.

Our story is full of dreamers, schemers and true believers—volunteers seeking donations by the dollar in glass jars at Civil War reenactments, victories grabbed from the jaws of defeat, miraculous saves, and the heartbreak of losses, both heritage and personal. And in the background, quietly and always humming along, is our preservation generator and the steady process of saving more battlefield land.

As I look to the future, I see new frontiers in literally reversing development—one of the most exciting new initiatives in my time as president. Few things are more satisfying than buying developed properties, razing or moving post-war structures and returning a battlefield landscape to its wartime appearance. We did this at Gettysburg, buying Lee's Headquarters and returning the stone house to its wartime setting. We have done it at Antietam. And we joined local preservationists in Franklin, Tennessee, who pioneered this strategy, buying properties lot by lot and house by house, including a pizza parlor or two, to recover part of a core battlefield from a city and create a historic park.

I relived the best and worst moments of my life while reading this narrative of our preservation history. Others will, too. But I stand proud of our history. Together, despite the inevitable conflicts, we built something from nothing. It grew from the start and has kept growing. The APCWS started saving land in 1988 and the organized movement has saved land each and every year since. In our quest to always get better, to always achieve more, we developed a land preservation assembly line, with deals closing faster than our goal of one a month and a steady stream coming down the line. We developed successful new techniques in fund raising and innovative ways to present Civil War history.

But let me step aside so you can start reading a success story like no other. ★

PROLOGUE

★

N APRIL 22, 1987, Donald C. Pfanz, a National Park Service historian at Petersburg National Battlefield in Virginia, sat behind a typewriter and composed a two-page letter that is the documentary fountainhead of the organized, national Civil War battlefield preservation movement.

That spring, it became clear that most of the Chantilly battlefield in Virginia was lost and Stuart's Hill at Manassas had been conceded to impending development. Pfanz reached a breaking point. He expressed his outrage in a letter, not to local officials, newspaper editors or legislators on Capitol Hill, but to fellow historian Brian Pohanka, who was deeply involved in the struggle to save a tiny piece of Chantilly. Something had to be done, he wrote.

Pohanka agreed, and out of that exchange came a meeting in Fredericksburg, Virginia, in July 1987 to organize the Association for the Preservation of Civil War Sites (APCWS), the first national Civil War battlefield preservation movement. Four years later, the original Civil War Trust was founded. After eight contentious years, which included some cooperation and a lot of disputes, the boards of both organizations forced a merger in November 1999, to become the Civil War Preservation Trust, and in 2011, once again, the Civil War Trust.

That this all began with a letter makes perfect sense. Before the creation of APCWS, if you cared about battlefield preservation, you typed or wrote letters to make your views known, licked the postage stamps for the envelopes and sent them by "snail mail." You wrote letters because Jerry Russell in his Civil War Round Table Associates newsletter asked you to in his one-man preservation campaign from Arkansas.

Annie Snyder, the heroine of Manassas battlefield preservation before APCWS came into existence, wrote letters and pleaded with others to write them, too. Snyder was a dynamo who became nationally famous and, in today's terminology, "went viral" when she shed tears on national television during a Congressional hearing as she listened to eloquent testimony about the sacrifices of those who fought in the war.

A party at her Pageland Farm at Manassas was often an envelope-stuffing affair. The more letters and calls a public official received, the more likely he or she was to pay attention. Letters, phone calls and telegrams were the most effective lobbying tools for concerned citizens, although in 1980 long-distance phone calls and telegrams were far more expensive than a 15-cent first-class stamp.

But go back a century. After the war, the first saviors of battlefields were veterans themselves, who pushed Congress to memorialize the places where they fought. The first five battlefield parks, all administered by the War Department, were Chickamauga and Chattanooga in Georgia (1890), Antietam (1890), Shiloh in Tennessee (1894), Gettysburg (1895) and Vicksburg in Mississippi (1899). In 1933, when the National Park Service took over ownership and management, there were 11 national military parks, 10 battlefield sites and assorted monuments, memorials and cemeteries. But early preservation efforts projected a decidedly Union bent, and Southern battlefields that were witness to Confederate defeats, such as Champion Hill in Mississippi, were forgotten, if not ignored.

Gradually, grass roots support for battlefield preservation grew. The first Civil War Round Table was established in Chicago in 1940, spawning a movement that led to the creation of scores of Round Table discussion groups across the country. From the beginning, Round Tables provided anchors of support for the APCWS, and their members formed the core of a growing APCWS membership. Supporters began to organize at individual battlefields, with the Kennesaw Mountain Historical Association of Georgia (1948), the Wilson's Creek National Battlefield Foundation of Missouri (1950) and the Gettysburg Battlefield Preservation Association (1959) leading the way. A dozen or more friends groups existed when the APCWS was founded in 1987. Today, more than 100 such groups support and help preserve individual battlefields, working closely with the Civil War Trust.

Before 1987, Russell could stir up enough trouble to force the transfer of an NPS official who angered him, but his efforts did not include buying battlefield land. The purpose of the APCWS, from the start, was to acquire battlefield land. It was a heady goal for its founders, who had no money.

The APCWS's first save in 1988 was a donation—8.55 acres of "The Coaling," a Shenandoah Valley battle site at Port Republic, Virginia. The next two saves were donations as well. Soon, cash began to flow in as the membership grew, and it launched its first matching fund campaign.

The original Civil War Trust was created in 1991 at the behest of Secretary of the Interior Manuel Lujan, who was mesmerized by story-telling Civil War history lectures delivered by National Park Service Chief Historian Ed Bearss. That year, the Congressionally authorized Civil War Sites Advisory Commission began a comprehensive study and evaluation of Civil War battlefields, with support from the American Battlefield Protection Program established the same year under NPS.

The Trust was formed in the mold of the wildly successful Ellis Island-Statue of Liberty Foundation, which tapped into corporate giving and collected $700 million over the years to preserve and restore those New York City landmarks. The Trust's dream of corporate support for battlefield preservation, however, was dashed by the war's causes and controversies, especially slavery.

The Trust then became a membership organization, sparking immediate conflict with APCWS. Then the Trust was given control, along with ABPP, of allocating about $6.2 million in U.S. Mint commemorative coin profits for battlefield preservation. The APCWS, now aggressively buying battlefields on credit, demanded funds to meet looming deadlines, and when rebuffed, declared war and took the fight to Capitol Hill in an unsuccessful effort to pry loose the coin program's profits.

The movement has saved land through weak economic times and strong. Both groups acquired multiple tracts of new battlefield property in the 1990s, despite their respective financial problems, and through the real estate market's ups and downs. Since the merger, Trust President O. James Lighthizer has led a unified, revitalized Trust, pushing his staff to expand the boundaries of success in all facets of the preservation arena—budget efficiency and transparency, education, fundraising, internet presence, land acquisition, media relations, partnerships and political advocacy. The success in the movement's first three decades has been nothing short of phenomenal.

As of the spring of 2017, on the eve of the 30th anniversary of the founding meeting of the APCWS, the Trust and its forerunner organizations have saved more than a quarter billion dollars' worth of land. The more than 45,000 acres saved at 132 battlefields include the most famous sites, such as Gettysburg, Antietam and Shiloh, to lesser-known places such as Palmito Ranch in Texas and Peebles Farm in Virginia.

But conflict, controversy and bitter struggles have also marked the first 30 years of the national Civil War battlefield preservation movement. A century after the war itself, old battlefields felt the pressure of urban and suburban growth. Some were already all but gone, such as the battlefield at Franklin, Tennessee, and the field before Marye's Heights in Fredericksburg, Virginia, both covered by residential streets and businesses.

The preservation fights at Manassas, and those at Gettysburg, Chancellorsville, Brandy Station, the Wilderness, Franklin, Morris Island, South Carolina, the Revolutionary War battlefield of Princeton, New Jersey, and others, have been, unlike the battles, bloodless affairs. But they were costly, with millions of dollars spent on both sides of most of the fights. And they required extraordinary dedication by preservationists, many of whom were and continue to be volunteers to the cause. And they often left emotional scars.

The controversy over the Disney's America theme park and its proximity to Manassas, Virginia, split the APCWS and caused a war within a war, fraying unity and friendships alike. The fights to preserve the Brandy Station battlefield in Virginia, which stretch through the entire 30-year history of the organized national movement, also pitted preservationists against other preservationists.

Through the strife and struggle, though, the nuts and bolts of battlefield land acquisition has continued as a primary mission. Guided by the report of the Civil War Sites Advisory Commission, the Trust prioritizes battlefield land acquisition opportunities and routinely exceeds its aim for an average of one purchase a month. It casts a broad net, saving land at the most famous battlefields, but also reaching far beyond those to include lesser-known fields of conflict such as Devil's Backbone in Arkansas (10 acres), Ware Bottom Church in Virginia (two acquisitions, 21.5 acres) and Davis Bridge in Tennessee (five acquisitions, 858 acres). Most transactions include three, four or five partners, including ABPP, state preservation agencies, regional or local preservation groups and, of course, the consistently loyal local preservation groups and the generous Trust membership, now exceeding 47,000 members, with more than 200,000 other supporters, who know their donation dollars will be matched several times over by funding from other partners. The Trust's partnership with ABPP, and the ongoing participation of the federal government and the direct appropriation for battlefield preservation it has approved since 1998, have been vital to the success of the movement.

In a narrative where nearly every chapter could be a book unto itself, the history of the movement is, by necessity, a broad-brush examination. For every acquisition listed in this story, dozens go unmentioned. For every anecdote used, countless others must remain unprinted. For every major donor and trustee named here, scores must remain unnamed, unfortunately.

From the battle to save Brandy Station to the fight to stop a Walmart Supercenter at the Wilderness battlefield, the preservation convulsions that have shaken the history of the movement are a dramatic backdrop to the steady, quiet drumbeat of acquisitions, tract by tract, battlefield by battlefield.

Our history is often messy, as with any human experience. Moments that participants would rather forget illuminate the story, such as the wholesale firing of hostile, anti-merger APCWS staff members after the merger with the Trust. Even the greatest Civil War battlefield preservationists of our time, such as Lighthizer and former National Park Service chief historian and tour guide extraordinaire Ed Bearss, have their naysayers and critics.

There are times of sheer exuberance, as when the gavel fell on Lighthizer's successful bid at a downhome country auction to buy the Widow Pence Farm on the Cross Keys battlefield in the Shenandoah Valley in 2000, or when the Trust closed on the complex, unique and record-breaking $12 million purchase of the Slaughter Pen Farm at Fredericksburg in 2006.

And there are moments of fear, as when the bulldozers went to work at night under spotlights at Chantilly, Virginia, or when they appeared at the Oak Ridge railroad cut on the Gettysburg battlefield.

Here, then, is a history of a national preservation movement—a movement so many thousands have supported for decades. It begins at the overgrown site of two forgotten monuments behind a house in Fairfax County, Virginia, and a discovery more than three decades ago. That discovery brought three men together to sound the alarm about the desecration of the Chantilly battlefield and prompted Donald Pfanz to write a letter, perhaps the most consequential letter of all the millions of letters written in the service of Civil War battlefield preservation. ★

CHAPTER
ONE

Desecration at Chantilly

N 1986, behind a plain, one-story home on West Ox Road in Fairfax County, Virginia, a pair of small, granite monuments sat side by side at the edge of a wood line, almost hidden by the tall grass and weeds growing around them.

The stones were enclosed by a low, rectangular fence of granite posts and pipe rails. The tiny memorial site, once tidy and treasured, was now so overgrown, it appeared abandoned to the FBI agent who noticed it one summer day on a run through the woods.

Clark B. "Bud" Hall found that running helped relieve the stress of a career devoted to the pursuit of con men, gangsters, Mafioso, and a rich trove of other shady, dangerous characters. He was a unit chief in the FBI's Organized Crime Division at the Washington, D.C., headquarters and had developed a keen observational eye during an intense tour of duty in Vietnam as a U.S. Marine Corps combat patrol leader. He used that skill effectively during his 16 years at the bureau.

A student of the Civil War, Hall knew the moment he saw the memorial site that it was connected to that conflict—a connection he confirmed on closer examination.[1] Carved in the back of one stone was the name "Kearny" and on the other was "Stevens." Each was affixed with a bronze plaque. One said, "Major General Philip Kearny killed on this spot, September 1, 1862." The other said: "Here fell Major General Isaac Ingalls Stevens with the flag of his Republic in his dying grasp. September 1, 1862."

Two Union generals killed at the very same spot on the same day? Preoccupied with the two monuments, Hall continued his four-mile run that took him past Fair Oaks Mall and onto forest trails near West Ox Road.[2] What happened there? What battle was fought there? More importantly, how could he not know about a significant Civil War site this close to home? His curiosity ran wild.

Hall had a fondness for the dashing Confederate cavalry general J.E.B. Stuart.

He was more than an armchair reader. Most weekends, the decorated Marine combat veteran could be found in Culpeper County at his favorite battlefield, Brandy Station, roaming the pristine but unmarked field of conflict with wartime maps, figuring out how the war's greatest cavalry battle had played out on June 9, 1863. Southern blood—Confederate blood—ran through his veins. He grew up on a Mississippi cotton farm, and two great-grandfathers and a half dozen great-uncles served in Barksdale's Mississippi Brigade, as well as the Army of Tennessee.[3]

Hall knew the date of the deaths of the two generals, September 1, 1862, was right after the Second Battle of Manassas (Bull Run) and just before Confederate General Robert E. Lee marched his Army of Northern Virginia into Maryland, which culminated in the Battle of Antietam on September 17. Back at home, he checked his library and soon learned that Kearny and Stevens had died in the Battle of Chantilly, or Ox Hill as the Confederates called it. Both fell that September 1 during a rain-soaked Union attack on the Confederate flank of General Thomas "Stonewall" Jackson following the crushing federal defeat at Second Bull Run two days earlier.

Hall began knocking on the doors of residents living near the monuments. He called county officials to ask questions. Who owned these monuments, he wondered, and why were they sitting forgotten and half hidden behind someone's house? "I was convinced now that these guys were forgotten—tragically," he recalled.[4]

Unbeknownst to Hall, another Civil War enthusiast, Edward T. Wenzel, a topographic map compiler with the U.S. Geological Survey, also developed an interest in the mysterious monuments. Wenzel was visiting his neighbors in nearby Vienna, Charlie and Isabelle Wiggs, in 1985, chatting about history, which all enjoyed.

"You know, Kearny and Stevens were killed right up there at Ox Hill," Wenzel said. "I read that there are monuments to them on the battlefield. I've got to find those monuments one day."

"Oh, we know where they are," Isabelle Wiggs replied. Wenzel's ears perked up. A week or so later, they took him there.[5]

They turned off two-lane West Ox Road and drove up a narrow dirt driveway to a small white rambler at the top of the hill. "The two monuments were behind the back yard of the house, next to the woods," Wenzel recalled. "It was kind of trashy. The weeds were tall. Lying here and there was a rusty truck rim and some other vehicle parts. But you could find the monuments; you could see them easy enough. And having observed them, that piqued my interest and I started looking for information and reading up on the Battle of Chantilly."[6]

The combatants may have remembered the battle more for the violent, late-summer thunderstorm that pelted them than for the deaths of two courageous Union major generals. It was a small battle by Civil War standards, inflicting 1,500 casualties, two-thirds Yankees. Yet, for a bloody two hours, a man fell every five seconds as about 15,000 of Stonewall Jackson's Confederates fended off the attacks from about 6,000 determined Yankees.[7]

With the Union Army in retreat after being routed at Second Manassas, Lee sought to exploit his advantage. He sent Jackson's men on an end run to interdict the Union line of retreat. It could have been the prelude to the capture of Washington, but two understrength Union divisions were dispatched to first attack Jackson.

General Isaac I. Stevens, 44, a Massachusetts native who graduated at the top of his West Point Class of 1839, won respect, honors and promotions for gallantry in the Mexican War, where he was severely wounded in the foot in the climactic battle for Mexico City. He wrote in his war diary of the gallant and daring reconnaissance missions of his comrade and friend, "Capt. (Robert E.) Lee."[8]

Stevens was deeply shaken by the crushing Union defeat at Second Manassas and was determined to make up for it. When he met a line of Confederate skirmishers, he at once attacked and dispatched a lieutenant to seek support. Several generals declined the request without orders. But General Philip Kearny thundered, "By God, I'll support Stevens anywhere!"[9]

Kearny was the son of a founder of the New York Stock Exchange. At age 21, he inherited a fortune of more than $1 million, but swore off a business career for the military life. Three years older than Stevens, Kearny left one arm in Mexico after it was mangled by grape shot and had to be amputated after he led a daring cavalry attack at Churubusco during the Mexican War.

Kearny's daring bravery set a striking example. He led his soldiers into battles during the Civil War's Peninsula Campaign in southeast Virginia with exhortations such as, "I am a one-armed Jersey son-of-a-gun, follow me!" and "Don't worry, men, they'll all be firing at me."[10]

As the lines formed for battle, the skies grew darker under a massive summer thunderstorm. Lightning and thunder signaled nature's intent to join the fray. On foot and wearing a Panama hat, Stevens led his men on the attack up an open slope toward the Confederate line at the edge of a forest. The first Rebel volley slammed Stevens's son, Hazard, to the ground with hip and arm wounds. The general stopped briefly to check on him, but pushed on.[11]

"That hat will be the death of him," First Lieutenant Samuel N. Benjamin remarked to another officer. "The sharpshooters will hit him in the head."[12]

As the colors went down and the assault stalled in the face of murderous fire, Stevens grabbed the flag of the 79th New York and shouted, "Highlanders, my Highlanders, follow your general!"[13]

The skies opened up, and a cold, driving rain blew into the faces of the Confederates. As Stevens reached a fence line at the edge of the dense woods, a bullet ripped through his head. He fell dead, his blood mixing with rain in the muddy Virginia soil where his monument would be placed. "He still firmly grasped the flagstaff, and the colors lay fallen upon his head and shoulders," wrote Hazard.[14]

As Stevens's shattered force withdrew, Kearny and his men attacked. Kearny's soldiers warned the mounted general that a Rebel skirmish line rested just to his front, but he angrily ignored them and rode forward into the gloom and a fatal encounter with the enemy.

A Confederate recalled the moment: "General Kearny asked in a quiet way: 'What troops are these?' Possibly a half-dozen responded, 'the 49th Georgia.' He quietly remarked, 'All right,' and turned his horse in the opposite direction. Someone exclaimed, 'That's a Yankee officer!' Then, 'Halt!' rang out from a dozen voices, when the General threw himself forward on his horse … Major Pate, of the 49th, was standing just behind the line. He ordered, 'Shoot him. Fire on him,' as possibly a dozen or more rifles, as one explosion, rang out."[15]

A single minie ball slammed into Kearny's rear end, tore through his torso and stopped in his chest. He fell from his saddle, convulsed briefly and lay still in death in a cornfield a hundred yards or more west of where his monument sits today. Dripping-wet Confederates searched Kearny's sodden, blood-stained uniform for souvenirs, all soon returned on the orders of General Lee, who gave the corpse to Union forces the following day under a flag of truce. Lee later wrote a personal letter of condolence to Kearny's widow.[16]

The Confederates stopped the Yankee assault, inflicting twice as many casualties as they received, but the battle ended their threat to intercept the Union retreat to Washington. The Battle of Chantilly, or Ox Hill, was a stormy, bloody exclamation point to Second Bull Run. But Chantilly was squeezed into obscurity by the larger battle that preceded it and the events that followed—Lee's first invasion of the north culminating in the Battle of Antietam just two weeks later.

Hazard Stevens survived the war and returned to Chantilly in 1883 with another Union veteran. The battlefield was then largely owned by John N. Ballard, a Confederate veteran who had lost a leg serving with John S. Mosby. The men walked around Ballard's farm, identified the spot where Stevens had fallen, marking it with a pile of boulders and, later, a white quartz stone.[17]

In 1915, Ballard deeded a small plot of land where Stevens fell as a place for monuments "commemorating the death of any Confederate or Federal soldier who

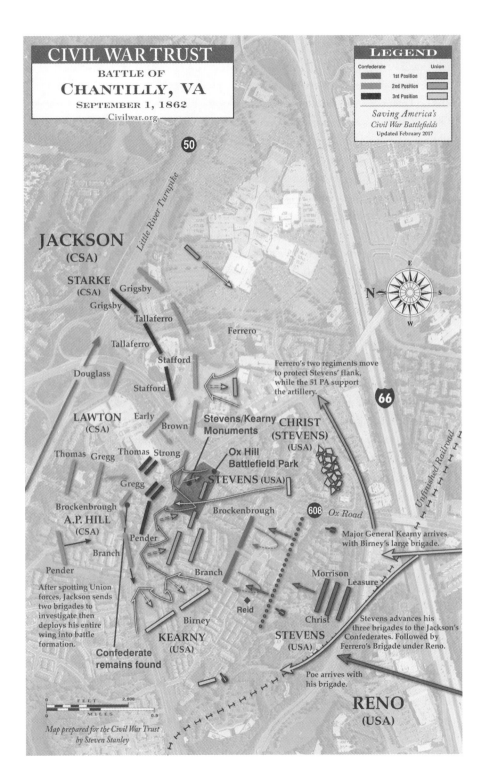

CIVIL WAR TRUST
BATTLE OF
CHANTILLY, VA
SEPTEMBER 1, 1862
Civilwar.org

50

Little River Turnpike

JACKSON
(CSA)

STARKE
(CSA)   Grigsby
Grigsby
Tallaferro
Ferrero
Tallaferro
Stafford
Douglass
Ferrero's two regiments move
to protect Stevens' flank,
while the 51 PA support
the artillery.
Stafford
66

LAWTON   Early
(CSA)   Brown

Stevens/Kearny
Monuments   **CHRIST**
(STEVENS)
(USA)

Thomas Gregg   Thomas Strong   Ox Hill
Battlefield Park
Gregg   STEVENS (USA)

Brockenbrough   Brockenbrough   608   *Ox Road*
A.P. HILL
(CSA)
Pender   Major General Kearny arrives
with Birney's large brigade.
Branch

Pender   Branch   Morrison
Leasure
After spotting Union
forces, Jackson sends
two brigades to
investigate then
deploys his entire
wing into battle
formation.   Reid   Christ   Stevens advances his
three brigades to the Jackson's
Confederates. Followed by
Ferrero's Brigade under Reno.
Birney   **STEVENS**
Confederate   **KEARNY**   (USA)
remains found   (USA)
Poe arrives with
his brigade.
RENO
(USA)

Unfinished Railroad

FEET   2,000
MILES   0.5

*Map prepared for the Civil War Trust
by Steven Stanley*

[27]

fell" at Chantilly, along with a narrow, pedestrian right-of-way down to Ox Hill Road. The battlefield still looked much as it did at the time of the battle when veterans on both sides gathered for a solemn ceremony on October 2, 1915, to dedicate new monuments to Stevens and Kearny. Six trustees, three from New Jersey and three Virginians, were appointed as guardians of the land and the monuments.[18]

By the 1930s, pine trees were encroaching on the abandoned pasture where Stevens charged and a few new houses appeared here and there, but the area remained largely rural. On the 100th anniversary of the battle on September 1, 1962, Fairfax County held a commemorative program at the memorial stones. Nationally known Civil War scholar Virgil Carrington Jones, author of *Gray Ghosts and Rebel Raiders*, was master of ceremonies. A century had passed, but the Battle of Chantilly's place in the history of Fairfax County was still well remembered.[19]

By then, the ever-expanding Washington, D.C., metropolitan area was beginning to replace the county's old farms and woodlands with housing developments, offices and businesses. The Capital Beltway was finished in 1964, the same year *Civil War Times Illustrated* magazine reported, "The opportunity to study (the Battle of Chantilly) on the ground is liable to vanish at any time under the crunching tracks of bulldozer and road grader. Parts of the battlefield remain as they were in 1862, but within the present decade the woods and open fields likely will give way to houses and service stations."[20]

In the late 1970s, the sprawling Fair Oaks Mall went up just east of the battlefield. The land occupied by the extreme left of Jackson's battle line at Chantilly was scraped clean and paved into a mall parking lot. The Kearny and Stevens monuments languished from inattention and became difficult to find, hidden as they were by brush and trees behind one of the houses that had gone up along West Ox Road in the 1950s. A Civil War tour guide described how difficult it was in the mid-1980s to find the memorials, even from West Ox Road:

"After going past six houses, on your left in .7 mile you will see an old fence line running back from the road for about 200 yards. It is 30 yards north of a brick house which has a small white house 50 yards behind it. Twenty feet on the north side of this white house are monuments. They are almost impossible to get to because of the difficulty of stopping" along congested, two-lane West Ox Road.[21]

In the summer of 1986, months after Wenzel's neighbors had taken him to see the monuments, and at a time he was studying Lieutenant Colonel Robert Ross Smith's *Ox Hill, The Most Neglected Battle of the Civil War*, he noticed something new. "I was going up Route 50 and I looked over and saw townhouses under construction and bulldozers clearing land," Wenzel recalled. "And I said to myself, 'Oh, my God. Those townhouses are awful close to where that battle was fought.'" The bulldozers had exposed the raw, orange clay earth for several hundred yards south of Route 50. Wenzel was certain the grading had intruded into the site of the cornfield where Kearny had fallen. The Fair Ridge townhouse development was enveloping the entire Confederate right flank in the battle of Chantilly.[22]

During the next nine weeks, from late July through September 1986, Wenzel called or visited everyone he could think of—civic associations, Civil War Round Tables, Smith, county officials, local historians, National Park Service historians and residents—to inquire about construction at the battlefield. Wenzel had never typed, so he took notes and wrote letters in the hand-printed style of a map draftsman. It was tedious to craft but easy to read. He would write hundreds of notes and letters this way in the following years.[23]

The more research he did, the better he began to understand the full scope of the tragedy that was befalling the battlefield. From county documents, Wenzel learned that massive new office buildings and a hotel were to be built by Centennial Development Corp. on a wooded tract north of the Kearny and Stevens monuments and that a new four-lane road, Monument Drive, would be built on top of the Confederate line of battle within 30 feet of the stones.[24] He learned that the county "hoped" to move the monuments to a new two-acre "historic park" proffered by Centennial that would be within the office-hotel complex, 270 yards behind the Confederate battle line. The park would be maintained and interpreted by Centennial, not by the county.[25]

How had Fairfax County government approved a massive development destined to destroy its only significant Civil War battlefield, then pushed responsibility for a lip-service memorial park onto the developer? In 1979, the county asked the National Park Service (NPS) if it was interested in acquiring the Chantilly battlefield. The answer was no.[26]

The park service traditionally focused on wilderness parks and had not even been responsible for Civil War battlefield parks until 1933. There were many other battlefields to consider and the position of the NPS was that all of them could never be saved, at least by the federal government. Zoning laws and land use regulations are the domain of local governments, which can do as they wish with unprotected historic sites.[27]

"When the county learned the NPS wasn't interested, that was the green light for development," Wenzel said. "The idea that if the federal government couldn't save the historic battlefield, that maybe the county should preserve it on their own—that was not on the table."[28]

Wenzel visited the county's Heritage Resources Branch, which was under the county's Office of Comprehensive Planning, the very office that was planning development. The person in charge, a "historic preservation planner," could provide no documents or memos calling for the preservation of the battlefield. She was defensive, and told Wenzel that her four-person office was underfunded, understaffed and "too small to keep up with the county's developers."[29]

Wenzel's next visit was to his county supervisor, Kate Hanley. He brought battle accounts and maps. She recommended that he talk to the History Commission because they were the historical advisors to the Board of Supervisors. She promised to send rezoning information and minutes of board meetings pertaining to Ox Hill.[30]

Wenzel went to the next History Commission meeting and was astonished to discover that the chairman and many of the commissioners were not familiar with the Chantilly battle. One commissioner said it was too late to do anything and the county was lucky to get two acres from Centennial.[31]

The only remaining Virginia trustee of the monuments was Robert Ross Smith, the retired lieutenant colonel formerly with the Office of the Chief of Military History of the U.S. Army. Wenzel had read his battle account, and on August 20, 1986, he called him. "What did the county's historical groups do to fight the rezonings at the battlefield?" Wenzel asked.

"They did nothing." Smith replied. "I think they were more interested in Colonial history than the Civil War."[32]

Of the supervisors, he knew that two favored a county-owned park. Smith was not up-to-date on the townhouse development, but heard they wanted to move the monuments to a two-acre "historic" park.[33]

Another of Wenzel's calls went to John J. Hennessy, the former NPS historian at Manassas National Battlefield Park who had moved to Albany to work for the State of New York. "I bet I talked with him for over an hour," Wenzel recalled. "We talked about the whole state of preservation and development in northern Virginia. The mindset of the people. The transient nature of the population. The foreign element. All these people, including politicians, who don't care one way or the other. They have no grounding in the local history. They're from someplace else. The strength of the developers, the lobbying, the pressure to develop. The pushing. And the need for an umbrella group to organize history-minded people, Civil War enthusiasts and preservationists.[34]

"There's a guy who lives down your way in Alexandria," Hennessy told Wenzel. "His name is Brian Pohanka. Call Brian. He's closer to the situation." Wenzel and Pohanka had the same kind of conversation, and Pohanka promised to help.[35]

Brian C. Pohanka was a true believer—a man who lived Civil War history as intimately as anyone in the 20th century could. Born in Washington, D.C. in 1955, Pohanka became consumed by the conflict during the Civil War Centennial and was researching at the National Archives by his teens.

"I saw the battle lines in those books and took my toy soldiers and set them up the same way," he told a battlefield preservation group in 2004. "I saw the connection between the men and the land."[36]

Elegant and formal, as one would expect of a disciplined Union officer, Pohanka trimmed his mustache and beard in the "Imperial" style of the 19th century. As a living historian, he was captain of the 5th New York Infantry, the colorfully dressed Zouave unit. In 1986, he was working full-time for Time-Life Books as the senior researcher, writer and adviser for its 27-volume Civil War series.[37]

In September 1986, Hall began researching the Kearny and Stevens monuments as well as the greater battlefield. He soon learned of the trusteeship that controlled the monuments and the land that Ballard had deeded for them. The original trustees had died by the 1960s, so new trustees were appointed. Four of the six new trustees were still alive in 1986, but they were elderly and not living in the area.[38]

Smith had lived in Fairfax County for many years before retiring to West Virginia. Smith told Hall he remained keenly interested in the monuments and their preservation. After being named a trustee in 1961, Smith said he tried time and time again to generate interest in the county, only to discover no one seemed to care. The trustees sought in vain to have the county create a battlefield park around the monuments, Smith said, but the county's History Commission, Heritage Resources Branch, Office of Comprehensive Planning, Park Authority and Board of Supervisors ignored his efforts, passed the buck or ducked responsibility. Smith said he had "at least a full linear foot of Ox Hill papers" going back to 1959 documenting his efforts to save the battlefield, but the county wanted development, not a publicly owned battlefield park that would cost money and take land off the tax rolls.[39]

The site might look abandoned, but any suggestion by the county that the trustees did not care was "a real slap in the face for my 25 years of fighting the problem," Smith wrote Hall in a 1986 letter.[40]

Hall could not bear the thought of neglected monuments. On Sunday, September 21, 1986, he cleaned up the site, mowed the grass with a hand mower and painted the rails with flat, black spray paint. Hall wrote in his journal, "I took photos for the trustees and also of the road, Monument Drive (don't you love it?), from the west of the markers heading directly (and inexorably) in this direction. Also, I took photos of the 'cornfield' area—now bulldozed ground."[41]

Hall made it his mission to maintain the memorial, and when he showed up with his mower, Anna Menge, a widow who lived on the adjoining parcel on West Ox Road just south of the monuments, would often visit with fresh-baked cookies. He would sometimes sit in her kitchen and listen as she told stories in her thick Eastern European accent about growing up in a small village in the "Old World." Hall would share what he was learning about the monuments, the battlefield and the developments that were taking over the land.[42]

Hall and Wenzel still did not know each other, but on September 23, two days after Hall's Sunday clean-up mission, Wenzel called Barbara Carton, a reporter at *The Washington Post*, who had been writing articles about development in the area. "Are you aware there's development now that's going in on top of a Civil War battle-field right here in Fairfax County?" he asked Carton.[43]

"No, I didn't know that," she replied. He briefly outlined the issue. "Let me check with my editors and I'll get back to you," she said. A week later, Carton interviewed Wenzel at the *Post*'s Fairfax office and, two days later with a *Post* photographer and Wenzel saw the monuments, the nearby staked and graded roadway that would soon be Monument Drive, and the building site where the Milton Company's Fair Ridge townhouse development was going up.[44]

"Fairfax is 400 square miles of real estate," Wenzel told her. "That's over 250,000 acres. Couldn't we have saved 40 acres?"[45]

The story ran on October 6, 1986. Wenzel recalled how he saw it: "On my way to work, I went by the 7-Eleven to get a paper. And I sat in my truck and pulled out the Metro section and paged all the way through it and never saw anything. Well, shoot, I looked at the Style section. Could she have put it in the Style section? I looked there and didn't see it there either. I said, 'Well, maybe it just didn't get in the paper today.' So, as I was tossing the paper over on the seat to drive off, I flipped it over. And there on the front page, right below the fold, was a photo of Stonewall Jackson with a story headlined: 'New Developments in the Battle of Chantilly.' I said, 'What the hell, it's on the front page!' And it was a good article. I was amazed. I was totally amazed. Well, that one story lit the fire under everything. I mean, all day long, for the next several days at work, people were calling from everywhere, asking what they could do. The *Post* story was picked up by the AP and local papers jumped on it."[46]

The firestorm was not a result of the desecration of the battlefield, but of a single sentence in the article's 13th paragraph, well after the story had jumped inside to page A-6.

"Recently, town house developers unearthed the brittle bones of a soldier and a brass uniform button that identified him as being from South Carolina; nobody has decided what to do with the remains, so they are in a cardboard box in the office of the Northern Virginia Medical Examiner James Beyer," Carton wrote.[47]

The bones had been unearthed by relic hunter Ron Blevins, a Vietnam veteran and Fairfax resident who gained permission from the developer's site preparer to search the freshly scraped ground for Civil War relics with his metal detector.[48]

The bulldozers had already cut the topsoil down about a foot when Blevins hunted on a Sunday afternoon in August 1985. Calling it a day, he began walking back to his car. "For some reason, I still had the machine on and I got a weak signal," he recalled. "So I stopped and dug down and found a South Carolina state seal button. I got another weak signal. It was another button with fragments of cloth still attached."[49]

Then he saw the distinctive curvature of a rib bone. Blevins knew that most of the Confederates killed at Chantilly were buried where they fell. Most had later been exhumed and moved to Fairfax Cemetery. "But they missed a few of them, and this was one they missed," Blevins recalled. He pondered what to do. He doubted he could reach anyone in time to stop the next morning's excavation work. He felt certain the discovery would generate interest.[50]

Blevins looked down at the unknown Confederate's grave, about 30 inches deep, and said, "They're damn sure not going to build a condo on you." He began carefully exhuming the remains. It was the most personal Civil War preservation project anyone could ever undertake. Blevins became emotional as he moved the dirt. "This guy had been killed right there and buried in a field grave," he recalled. "All of his comrades' remains had been exhumed and honored. But he had been left there and nobody knew about it."[51]

Much of the skeleton was still there, and when Blevins uncovered the skull, it was obvious what had happened. The South Carolinian had been hit in the face. The skull was shattered below the eyebrow. Moments later, Blevins found the .58 caliber Yankee bullet that had killed him. He also found some small buck and ball, a few white glass shirt buttons and a total of 10 South Carolina uniform buttons. The next day, Blevins turned over the remains to the Fairfax County Medical Examiner's Office.

After the police cleared the find as of no criminal concern, the bones, the buttons and the bullet were put in a box and placed on a shelf in the county morgue. "They put them up on a shelf and forgot about them," Blevins said. "And nothing happened for about a year."[52]

When the *Post* reported that the remains of a South Carolina soldier were sitting forgotten on a shelf in a Virginia morgue, a furor erupted among the South Carolina delegation on Capitol Hill. Two days later, one of South Carolina's Congressmen, Butler Derrick, announced that the unnamed soldier would be returned to the state and given a proper burial.[53]

The remains were placed in a coffin draped with a Confederate flag. On November 23, 1986, in front of the war-damaged statehouse in the South Carolina capital of Columbia, the soldier was honored with tributes and prayers. To the strains of "Dixie" and "Bonnie Blue Flag," the coffin was placed on an old wooden wagon and drawn by a horse that became skittish in traffic and had to be replaced by six pallbearers, who finished the journey to Elmwood Cemetery.[54]

After the singing of "Dixie", the loudest Rebel yell was said to have come from Thaddeus P. Raines Jr., 71, a true Confederate son, whose father fought in the same brigade as the unknown soldier. "He could have known him well," said Raines.[55]

"It was really gratifying to see him go back home after all that time," Blevins recalled. "I consider it one of the best things I've ever done."

In mid-October 1986, a week or so after the *Post* article was published, Wenzel and Pohanka were working to set up a meeting with county officials and the developers. Their priority was to preserve the monuments at the original site and salvage a piece of the battlefield. Bob Burgess organized the meeting. Burgess was the administrative assistant for John F. "Jack" Herrity, Chairman of the Board of Supervisors of Fairfax County, a pro-development politician who took charge of the board in 1976 and paved the way, almost literally, for the transformation of a semi-rural landscape into the sprawling suburbs of metropolitan Washington.[57]

Burgess was, of course, looking out for Herrity, but in a phone call told Wenzel the monuments were safe because they could not be moved unless the trustees agreed. Bud Hall, their representative, had said "they'd be moved over his dead body." Burgess asked Wenzel if he knew Hall. Wenzel said no.[58]

"Well, you need to get in touch with him," Burgess said. "He's been calling us regularly and sending us stuff. You need to talk with him." He gave Wenzel Hall's phone number.[59]

"I didn't know him and he didn't know me," Hall recalled. They arranged to meet in person at Hall's townhouse on October 26. Hall was wary by nature, but he quickly realized he and Wenzel shared a common passion and concern about the battlefield at Chantilly. They agreed to work together.[60]

Hall had independently tracked down Smith and the other trustees. The county never contacted them about the plan to move the monuments to Centennial's planned park. Horrified by Hall's news, the trustees had gladly designated Hall as their official representative with the county. They controlled a mere wisp of land, but the tiny, 50-by-100-foot parcel had been carved from the farm of the one-legged veteran John Ballard in 1915 for the sole purpose of creating a Civil War memorial. Hall sent sharp letters to the county, opposing any change of location for the monuments and demanding to know why the county believed the monuments could be moved without the consent of the trustees.

Wenzel introduced Hall to Pohanka, and the two hit it off. Hall could see his own martial traits in Pohanka and came to recognize him "as one of the most principled men" he ever knew. Pohanka, who died in 2005, "had unyielding views about issues he believed in, and these irresolute beliefs were not subject to negotiation or compromise," Hall recalled. The three became a team.[61]

"You talk about three angry guys," Wenzel recalled. "We just couldn't believe what the county was doing. This was one of the wealthiest counties in the United States and they knew full well it was a historic site and nobody was doing anything about this. It was a time when I didn't get much rest."[62]

The sought-after meeting with county officials and Centennial was finally arranged by Herrity's office, through Burgess, and scheduled for October 31. Hall, Pohanka and Wenzel attended, as did several other preservation-minded citizens.

Using a large, hand-drawn map of the battlefield that also showed the planned development, the three explained the history of the battle and the monuments and made the case that any historic park should be established at the existing memorial site. It was common sense, and Centennial agreed. The company announced they now owned the land adjacent to the monuments on the south side, known as Parcel 6. This was the heart of the open field in front of the Confederate battle line over which Stevens and his men had charged. Centennial said it would consider using Parcel 6 for an "Ox Hill Battlefield Park" instead of the previously approved location. It was only 2.4 acres, but more than nothing and far better than moving the memorials to a fake "historic" park.[63]

Supervisor Audrey Moore, who had long supported a Fairfax County-owned park, suggested that perhaps the county should consider "putting money into it" and becoming directly involved by increasing the size of the park. It was the very idea Smith had fruitlessly espoused for decades. The problem now was that almost no battlefield land was left for the county to acquire, although one contiguous piece —Anna Menge's property (known as Parcel 5)—had not been purchased by developers. The acquisition of Parcel 5 would take years of meetings, petitions, public hearings and negotiations, but the effort would eventually succeed.[64]

Wenzel, Hall and Pohanka organized themselves as the Chantilly Battlefield Association (CBA) in late 1986, fighting to save what they could of a battleground where more than 1,500 Northern and Southern soldiers had fallen. The new association rode the wave of indignation that followed the *Post* article as the controversy over the shelved remains of the South Carolina soldier kept the story in the news for a couple of additional months. The association received a boost from a hard-hitting story in the *Fairfax Journal* that placed blame for the fiasco squarely on the county's politicians and planners. But the development projects were already underway, and the association's strongest and only real leverage was the trusteeship of the memorials.

The formal correspondence between the preservationists and Fairfax County was polite on both sides, but it was often a different story in public meetings. Herrity had ruled the board for more than 15 years with a single-minded, authoritarian style. He despised the preservationists butting in as much as they despised him and his blind support of development. Both sides made that quite clear on occasion.

Herrity called the dispute a "hysterical historical" issue and publicly mocked it. When preservationists asked distinguished historian Virgil Carrington Jones to speak on the history of the battle at one supervisor's meeting, Herrity kept interrupting.[65]

Herrity walked out of another meeting, terminating it, when Wenzel criticized the head of the county's ineffective Heritage Resources Branch, part of the county's Office of Comprehensive Planning. Hall likened such oversight to the veritable fox guarding the hen house.[66]

At yet another contentious board meeting, Hall remembers that Herrity growled, "What do you care about where a couple of Yankees got shot in the ass?"

"That outraged Brian," Hall recalled. "Outraged him! And another supervisor, Tom Davis (who would later become a U.S. Congressman), to his credit, said, and I'll never forget it, 'We have people coming in here all the time, petitioning this board, for something that will enrich themselves. Or do something for themselves. All you three are trying to do is call attention to a threatened piece of battlefield. And you should be commended for that. And I commend you for that.'"[68]

Herrity did care about preservation when it came to something more personal to him, Hall said. "At the intersection of West Ox Road and Warrenton Turnpike," Hall recalled, "there used to be a country-and-western honky-tonk. It was a dilapidated old log building called Hunter's Lodge. And Herrity got behind a drive to save this building, which was going to be torn down. It was a popular honky-tonk and dance hall, and he'd gone there many times as a boy.[69]

"So he had a radio call-in show—the chairman's call-in show—and he got behind this kick to save this honky-tonk, which was less than a mile south of the battlefield. From my office at FBI headquarters, listening on the radio, I called in. I said, 'Mr. Chairman, this is incredibly interesting that you are throwing your considerable weight and reputation behind the salvation of a country-and-western dive. Could you tell us—the listeners—what you did to save the Chantilly battlefield, where young Americans fought and died?"[70]

"He sneered, 'Well, I know who this is!' And he started cursing on the phone at me. 'I know who this is—Chantilly battlefield people!' But he wouldn't answer my question, and they cut me off."[71]

Pohanka responded to a letter from Herrity's office in 1987 with an ever-so-polite response articulating why he, Wenzel, Hall and Civil War enthusiasts were fighting to save what they could at Chantilly.

"You know, we are not trying to rabble rouse or stir up trouble in our efforts to preserve Chantilly battlefield and other county historical sites," Pohanka wrote. "We care very deeply about these places and the lessons they teach us and hopefully will continue to teach generations yet unborn. Brave men, worthy men, caring men, fought and died and suffered here. Their sacrifice should never be forgotten, for if it is, we lose something of what it means to be an American. Surely economic growth and development can coexist with history. To ensure that it does is the challenge local government must face."

But at the top of the copy he sent to Hall, Pohanka included this handwritten note: "Bud: I know it's impossible to shame this miserable bastard into doing justice to anything worthwhile, but thought I should respond to his letter nevertheless. Brian."[72]

Late one night, Mrs. Menge (as Hall always called her) looked out her kitchen window and saw bright spotlights and bulldozers by the monuments. She called Hall and shouted in a panicked voice, "They're digging up the markers!"[73]

What they were digging, actually, was Monument Drive, extending it through the woods and just yards from the monuments. Hall, Wenzel and Pohanka met there early the next morning. Centennial's representative would not meet their gaze or speak with them, but Centennial had a county permit to dig the road. There was nothing they could do to stop it. Later that day, Hall informed Menge. He recalled, "Having witnessed oppressive government intrusiveness in her youth, this kind old lady then broke down into heavy tears. So, my heart was broken twice in the same day."[74]

For its part, Centennial Development was offended by the harsh criticism aimed its way. In June 1987, the developer was referred to as "greedy" in a letter to the *Fairfax Journal*. In response, Centennial President David L. Smith wrote that they were trying to work with the county and the preservationists to save something of the battlefield. "We have already incurred significant costs as a result of our voluntary commitment to historic preservation," Smith wrote. "We have redesigned our original master plan, taken the time to respond to citizens' concerns, and agreed to design and construct a monument park. We have done this voluntarily to respond to a civic need in a responsible manner. Instead of being called 'greedy,' Centennial Development Corp. should be recognized for its commitment and sense of responsibility to the community."[75]

Hall had nothing but contempt for the developer and the county, but as Wenzel saw it, the county was at fault, not Centennial. The developer was trapped in the county's habit of requiring "proffers," or concessions, in return for the right to develop. In demanding that Centennial build *and maintain* a "historic park," the county was refusing to take responsibility for its own history. "They were pushing off the history of the county to a developer. And it's not the developer's job. They're not in that business," Wenzel recalled.[76]

The county's attitude began to change in the latter half of 1987. Herrity was up for reelection. September 1 marked the 125th anniversary of the Battle of Chantilly (Ox Hill), and the association held a ceremony at the Kearny and Stevens monuments. Pohanka eulogized the soldiers and their sacrifices and a battlefield being destroyed by "greed and ignorance." He said he was "proud of what has been accomplished" to save at least a tiny part of Chantilly, but also felt "sadness and shame because more wasn't done sooner."[77] In the crowd stood Herrity, a sight that disgusted Hall. He knew the only reason Herrity was there was because Audrey Moore was present and the election was two months away.

When Moore, whose campaign for slower growth gained strong support, defeated Herrity in November 1988, the county became amenable to a county-owned battlefield park. Ultimately, the monuments and 4.8 acres were saved, a tiny fraction of the 500 acres on which the battle was fought, but this slight acreage preserved the ground of Stevens's fatal assault. Centennial donated about 2.4 acres (Parcel 6 and fragments) to the county in 1989, and the county acquired the adjacent 2.4-acre Parcel 5, Anna Menge's property, in 1994. Three years later, the Board of Supervisors conveyed the 4.8 acres to the Fairfax County Park Authority.[78]

After it was certain the monuments would not be moved and the historic park would be established, Hall and Pohanka left more and more of the Chantilly Battlefield Association responsibilities to Wenzel. He continued the struggle, turning it into one of the missions of his life. With Wenzel advising, prodding and pushing at every step, the park authority in 2008 dedicated the Ox Hill Battlefield Park, 22 years after the controversy began.

What began as a confrontational relationship with the county gradually become cooperative, "but it was never easy," Wenzel said. "There was always some kind of problem." But the preservationists were being heard. Wenzel served on the citizen's task force for master planning the park and continued to exhaustively research the battle. In fact, Wenzel wrote the text of most of the interpretive signs and markers now on the battlefield. Wenzel is proud of the Ox Hill Battlefield Park, even as he recognizes the preservation battle as mostly a defeat. "We saved what we could save," he said.[79]

Hall has never been to Ox Hill Battlefield Park. "I was sickened by the experience," he recalled. "Just completely sickened and disgusted people would be this way. It was my first lesson. To this day, I've never visited the park. I've never visited the markers again. I've been invited a ton of times by Ed and others to come back and speak, but I've never been back again. Never. I'm not going back. I want to remember it the way it was when I was running through the woods and came upon those two markers. The fact that someone would despoil that setting is still very hard to deal with. I drive past the area today going into D.C., and avert my glance. I don't look over there. I don't look at it. I just drive by."[80] ★

CHAPTER
TWO

*Birth of the Association for
the Preservation of Civil War Sites*

S THE CHANTILLY controversy reached a peak in the autumn of 1986 with the reburial of the unknown Confederate casualty in his native South Carolina, a development threat in Manassas, Virginia, that festered as an ever-growing possibility now bordered on inevitability.

Prince William County, just southwest of Fairfax County, had put development on a fast track along the Interstate 66 corridor next to the Manassas National Battlefield Park. In April, county supervisors approved a proposed 85-foot building near the entrance to the battlefield park. Three months later, they gave the go-ahead for five more office buildings, each 100-feet tall. The park service sent up helium balloons at the end of 100-foot cords; observers could see the balloons from all across the battlefield.[81]

During the Battle of Second Manassas, General Robert E. Lee posted his headquarters at Stuart's Hill, a wooded prominence about a mile west of Henry House Hill and today's visitor center. The 542-acre undeveloped, mostly wooded tract had been threatened by a proposed Marriott Corporation theme park in the 1970s and was now owned by the Hazel/Peterson Companies, Inc., which had filed to rezone the land for a $100 million-plus mixed-use development.[82]

"Such a shame," thought Donald C. Pfanz, a National Park Service supervisory historian at the City Point Unit of Petersburg National Battlefield. *Somebody needs to do something,* he kept telling himself. On a research trip to Fredericksburg in April 1987, Pfanz made a point of speaking to Robert K. Krick, his old boss, the Fredericksburg National Military Park chief historian. Pfanz bemoaned the fate of Chantilly battlefield and asserted that a national effort needed to be initiated to try to prevent this sort of thing from happening.[83]

In Krick, Pfanz had a sympathetic but skeptical ear, hardened by years of bitter experience. As much as it distressed him, Krick believed it was only a matter of time before thousands of acres of undeveloped battlefield land would be transformed into housing tracts or other developments, even next to National Park Service (NPS) battlefields. Each NPS battlefield has an official boundary, established by an Act of Congress, that outlines the extent of the land deemed to be historically significant. The law prohibits the NPS from acquiring land outside the boundary. At most battlefields, especially Fredericksburg and the central Virginia battlefields, the NPS owned only a portion of the land within the historic boundary. The rest was privately owned. Moreover, significant parts of battlefields were still outside federal boundaries and thus not even considered officially historic. As suburbia expanded in places such as Chantilly and Fredericksburg, rapacious growth was gobbling up hallowed ground as relentlessly as kudzu and fire ants spread through the South. Krick never suffered fools gladly, but as a federal bureaucrat, he often had to hold his tongue and try to ignore the ever-widening encroachment.[84]

When Pfanz expressed the need for a national preservation organization, Krick suggested Pfanz write to Pohanka, saying that Pohanka "had expressed similar concerns and agreed it would be nice if such an organization existed," Pfanz recalled. "Although (Krick) doubted such an organization could succeed, he promised to lend his support to any efforts I might make in this regard."[85]

Krick was concerned that any new grassroots organization whose reach was as wide as the entire realm of Civil War battlefields would bite off more than it could chew. "My position was that we could not, as a nascent organization, deal with anything sort of beyond our long rifle shot," Krick recalled. The scope, in Krick's view, should be limited to Virginia battlefields. There were enough threats in Virginia alone without taking on, say, the massive challenges at other southern battlefields or those in the more-distant Western Theater.[86]

On April 22, 1987, Pfanz typed a two-page letter to Pohanka. This document is the wellspring of the modern Civil War battlefield preservation movement. "The organization I envision would consist of a small, but active group of members divided into local chapters based on geography and answerable to a single, central committee," Pfanz wrote. Its aim would be "to preserve battlefield land by direct purchase, donations, scenic easements, rezoning, and the creation or extension of parks, if possible, before they are imminently threatened with development."[87]

Pohanka was instantly supportive. "This is exactly what I have in mind," Pohanka wrote in a brief note to Hall and Wenzel days later. "There is no doubt about it. We MUST do this. I will write Pfanz and let's all of us put our thinking caps on and make a list of people we ought to contact. Perhaps we can meet and begin to get established."[88]

"The sooner organizers of the group could meet, the better . . ." Pfanz wrote back to Pohanka on May 6. They agreed that any new organization should focus on eastern battlefields. "We might wish to limit the early organizational meetings to one or two dozen key people. Any more and nothing would get accomplished." Pfanz included a list of possible founding members embracing a mix of park service people, leading authors and historians. The list began with NPS Chief Historian Edwin C. Bearss and included historians John J. Hennessy and William A. Frassanito, preservation gadfly Jerry L. Russell, Civil War scholar/author Dr. Gary W. Gallagher and NPS historians Krick, A. Wilson Greene, and Dennis E. Frye, who had co-founded the Save Historic Antietam Foundation the previous year. The latter four would become founders of the new preservation organization, with Gallagher serving as president.[89]

No one had a longer record fighting for battlefield preservation than Russell, an Arkansas public relations specialist and political campaign manager who was president of the Little Rock Civil War Round Table, a Civil War discussion group he helped create in 1964. Four years later, Russell founded Civil War Round Table Associates to bring together round tables nationwide, largely through a newsletter he wrote and published. The Chicago Civil War Round Table, founded in 1940, was the first, and hundreds of others followed. After the Gettysburg tower went up in 1974, Russell changed the focus of his umbrella organization and his newsletters to outspoken battlefield preservation.[90]

For a dozen years, Russell was a strong but lone voice for preservation. His typed, single-spaced newsletters, mailed out every month or so, typically ran a dozen pages and never failed to include pleas to write representatives and senators or local officials to oppose one of the wide range of preservation threats for which he raised red flags. By 1987, Russell and his corps of letter writers had helped defeat plans for low-rent housing at the Petersburg battlefield, forced the rerouting of a railroad spur at Fredericksburg, stopped a radio tower at Wilson's Creek, halted a plan for an amphitheater on the battlefield at Prairie Grove, and forced the transfer of an NPS superintendent at Kennesaw Mountain. Gregarious, silver-bearded and sporting a crew cut, Russell possessed a ready smile but a ruthless pen for those who failed to meet expectations. No voice of moderation, he reveled in a widely recognized persona as an outspoken, combative preservationist, unsparing with the critical lash. More than a few folks in the Civil War community were wary of him, including Pfanz.[91]

"I had added Jerry Russell's name to the list as one whose past services to the cause of preservation merits inclusion," Pfanz wrote to Pohanka. "I would be wary about allowing him to take too large of a role in the organizations, however. He would make an invaluable ally, but his temper and his 'shoot from the hip' personality might do more damage than good in a position of leadership."[92]

Arkansas was too far removed for Russell to play an active organizational role, although his newsletter voiced strong support and generated donations as well.

One evening in May 1987, seven men gathered in the small living room of Greene's Fredericksburg home. Most were already close friends or associates. Gallagher had journeyed the farthest, driving 263 miles from State College, Pennsylvania, where he was a professor at Penn State University. The eight-hour round trip was the first of many he would make on behalf of the APCWS. Frye, Krick, Pfanz and

Pohanka attended alongside a friend of Krick's, Richmond attorney John P. "Jack" Ackerly III, a Civil War enthusiast. Greene brought in extra chairs; Frye sat on the upstairs steps.

"We knew each other very well," Frye recalled. "We could be very frank and honest with each other. For example, four of us, Will Greene, Gary Gallagher, Bob Krick and myself, had worked very closely together doing numerous battlefield tours over the years. And we would go on battlefields in the Valley and other places, giving these programs, where there was nothing but private property. So, we were very aware of the dangers to these sites. And all of us were very passionate. Of course, Bob Krick at Fredericksburg had witnessed the incremental destruction of the battlefields there, and it just ate him up. It was so hard for him to sit there and watch his battlefields disappear. That area, of course, was a nuclear bomb blast of development. I mean, they were losing battlefield property there faster than anywhere else."[93]

Everyone was excited about starting a preservation organization and they decided to have a larger, open meeting at a Fredericksburg restaurant, inviting anyone who was interested. In his commanding fashion, Krick said they first needed to decide among themselves what must be done.

"If we just go to this restaurant with no plan in mind and 50 to 100 people showing up, it's going to be chaos and we're not going to get anything done and the whole thing is going to collapse," Krick said. "So, what we need to do is to, between ourselves, decide what we want this group to do, how we're going to do it, select a slate of people to run this group, and then when we get to the meeting, instead of throwing these things up for discussion, you know, tell the group this (is) what we want to do and then essentially have the group ratify it."[94]

That's what they did. Krick took charge of the meeting, so someone suggested he be president. He was based in Fredericksburg, after all, and his professional purview included a cluster of the most threatened Virginia battlefields.

"Absolutely not. I ought not to be an officer at all," Krick said.[95]

Frye, Greene, Krick and Pfanz were all NPS employees, and Krick cautioned against any government employee taking the presidency of the new group, lest it be seen as an arm of the NPS. They decided Gallagher would be president and Krick agreed to serve as vice president. Pohanka would be secretary. Greene agreed to manage the newsletter. Ackerly would handle incorporation and legal matters.[96]

On July 18, 1987, at Arbuckle's Restaurant overlooking the Rappahannock River in Fredericksburg, after a $10 dinner of stuffed chicken, salad and "rice pilov" (sic), the Civil War historians and enthusiasts who filled the small meeting room finished dessert and settled in for the meeting. Several founding members, tugging on memories of more than a quarter century ago, recalled that the room was packed with 50 or 60 people. Pohanka's minutes, however, record 27 in attendance. Among them were four members of the Eastern Pennsylvania Civil War Round Table who had driven from the Allentown area, at least a five-hour drive through Philadelphia, Baltimore and Washington, D.C.[97]

Pohanka rose to explain why this first "Battlefield Preservation Dinner Meeting" had been called. He spoke eloquently of the loss of the battlefields at Chantilly and at Salem Church, just west of Fredericksburg, and emphasized the importance of trying to save what remained by establishing a non-profit organization to acquire battlefield land—to save it.[98]

Then Pfanz spoke, and explained that a smaller group met earlier at Greene's home and established a "steering committee," with Gallagher in charge, to bring the organization into existence. Krick stressed the organization "was in no way to be misconstrued as an organ of the National Park Service," Pohanka reported in the minutes. Krick said the new organization was not designed to compete with or supplant local battlefield preservation groups, such as the Save Historic Antietam Foundation.[99]

Gallagher was introduced as president and led a general discussion of current preservation issues. Pfanz recalled: "I remember that one of my suggestions was that as a condition of membership, every member had to write at least three letters a year to their congressman. It was quickly shot down. But that's what I grew up with and that was my mentality."[100]

Ed Wenzel was at the meeting representing the Chantilly Battlefield Association with Pohanka. But Wenzel had another organization in mind when he spoke. "I described the activities of The Nature Conservancy and suggested we meet with them to seek guidance and perhaps model ourselves on their highly successful organization," Wenzel recalled. Greene and others met with The Nature Conservancy officials at Rosslyn Plaza in Arlington, Virginia, some months later. "They advised that a broad-based membership would raise far more than corporate donors," Wenzel recalled. "Of the tens of millions they raised in 1986, they said 94% was from individuals. Only six percent came from corporations."[101]

It confirmed the virtue of a tactic the leadership had settled on even before the Arbuckle's meeting. In a planning document, the steering committee set its initial, "six-month goals" as incorporating, gaining tax exempt status, approving bylaws, holding an initial board meeting and "immediately upon above, go hard for members" and "get out an initial good newsletter."[102]

So as not to have the steering committee appear completely dictatorial, Krick had suggested at the planning session that the entire group at the restaurant meeting decide on a name for the new organization. At Arbuckle's, "the discussion on that topic went around and around, with dozens of choices being put forward and just as quickly shot down," Pfanz recalled. "After 30 minutes or more of discussion, I suggested the awkward name, "The Association for the Preservation of Civil War Sites . . ."[103]

It was modeled after the acronym APVA, the Association for the Preservation of Virginia Antiquities, founded in 1889 as the first state-wide preservation organization in the United States (now named Preservation Virginia). "After many name rejects, APCWS seemed like a real winner," Wenzel recalled. In any event, ". . . the group voted to adopt it, not because it was a good name but because everyone by then was tired and wanted to get home," Pfanz recalled.[104]

Wenzel accepted Pohanka's invitation after the meeting to join the APCWS steering committee, which would become the board of directors. Merlin E. Sumner, a former president of the Chicago Civil War Round Table who had resettled in Petersburg and opened a book shop, also was invited to join the steering committee and became treasurer.[105] As the committee members tackled the many tasks of starting a non-profit organization, their goal from the start was to preserve battlefield land through purchase, donation or other means. In this sharply focused aim, APCWS saw itself as different from other Civil War battlefield groups, and was organized as a national organization.

By September 6, 1987, when the steering committee met again and formally became the board of directors, the APCWS had been incorporated in Virginia and had applied to the Internal Revenue Service for tax exempt status as a non-profit organization. Membership dues were set at $20 annually, with a $10 student rate. Their new bank account contained little more than spare change.[106]

"None of us had any money," Gallagher recalled. "One of the key characteristics of the people who were involved early on is that they had absolutely no financial resources. None. So, there was no money in the room, but there was a great deal of interest in this ground that we knew, even before Chantilly, was under threat."[107]

Gallagher stressed the need for money at the September 6 meeting. He said that by December 1, every steering committee member should "have made some contacts with potential contributors to the association, and be able to present the names of two or three private individuals willing to contribute 5,000 to 10,000 dollars."[108]

Threats and opportunities soon emerged, demanding attention. The farmer who spent his life farming the famous wheat field at Cedar Mountain had died, and 150 acres in the heart of that pristine battlefield was for sale. At North Anna battlefield in Hanover County, Virginia, someone had applied for a permit to quarry some 200 acres of the battlefield to a depth of 400 feet.[109]

Krick revealed the potential availability of a portion of the historic Harris Farm, where the last action of the battle of Spotsylvania occurred on May 19, 1864. Here, a Confederate force in search of the Union line ran into Union artillerists who were fighting as infantry, including the First Massachusetts Heavy Artillery. They repelled the Rebels in a short but fierce fight.

"The owner of the land is considering selling all or part of the 144 acres to a development company, but seems willing to donate five or more acres to be preserved, including the 1755 farmhouse and the monument to the First Mass. Heavy Artillery," Krick reported.[110]

At Manassas, the development of the 542-acre tract at Stuart's Hill next to the Manassas National Battlefield Park loomed, although construction had not started.[111] As APCWS organized and gathered information on potential acquisitions, board members, in Russell's mold, wrote letters. "We didn't have a penny, of course, so we weren't going to be buying anything anytime soon," Gallagher recalled. "We didn't have the money to get a little promotional flyer made, or the initial stationary. So we didn't. Some people came forward—some of our members—and wrote the kinds of checks that let us get going. And (Civil War artist) Don Troiani was a friend right from the beginning. He did this logo for us at the beginning."[112]

"We just stumbled along for starters," recalled Krick. "We didn't know what the hell we were doing and we weren't doing a great deal."[113]

In late fall 1987, Gallagher drafted a letter to potential supporters announcing the start of a national membership campaign in January 1988. "A major fundraising effort will follow," he wrote, "We have already identified a number of sites and hope to have won protection for the first of them before the end of next year."[114]

Born of nothing but a good idea, the APCWS began to grow. The all-volunteer board consisted of Ackerly, Frye, Gallagher, Greene, Krick, Pfanz, Pohanka, Sumner, Wenzel and Alan T. Nolan, an attorney and noted Civil War historian. With no full-time employees, no money to speak of and an admittedly clunky name and acronym, the nation's first national Civil War battlefield preservation organization tried to make up in hard work and enthusiasm what it lacked in resources. For the first time, a national organization of historians, Civil War buffs, NPS employees and others was working on behalf of preservation. Even in seemingly simple acts such as trading information and getting the word out about threats, they soon made progress, more than ever previously accomplished. Everyone involved was invigorated as they worked tirelessly for a common cause.

The APCWS began its membership drive with the new year and by the middle of January, the first envelopes were arriving at P.O. Box 1862 in Fredericksburg. On January 16, 1988, the new board met again at Greene's house in the historic, once war-torn city.[115]

In two weeks and two days, 60 people became members and the APCWS now had $2,437 in the bank. The amount of work was multiplying by the week. This small, passionate, energetic band was a working board in every sense of the word.[116]

Ackerly reported that tax-exempt status was a work in progress, but it was far enough along that soliciting money was legal. Krick agreed to look into getting bulk mail permits with the U.S. Postal Service. Greene agreed to assemble and edit the first newsletter, which Krick would mail out in June from Fredericksburg. Sumner said he would put the newsletter mailing list on his home computer and print address labels. Pohanka took on the taxing job of preparing the membership cards and mailing them out to the new members along with the APCWS's glossy, color brochure. Krick led the membership drive, with the goal of 1,500 members by July 1, and 2,500 by the end of the year. Gallagher promised to write an article about the new organization for the *Civil War Quarterly*, the magazine of the Civil War Society. Frye agreed to organize a fundraising and informational booth at that summer's massive reenactment to commemorate the 125th anniversary of the Battle of Gettysburg. Everybody did something.[117]

At board meetings, members first spent a couple of hours hashing out the many administrative details—the membership drive, the treasurer's report, fundraising results, new projects, outreach and other matters. This amounted to a full meeting in and of itself. Then the board turned to battlefield preservation issues, and everyone knew they were just getting started. Not that they minded. This was their mission and it was urgent. The need to preserve battlefield land could not wait until the APCWS was fully developed.[118]

"It was real exciting," Ackerly recalled. "We would go from 10:00 o'clock in the morning until 4:00 o'clock in the afternoon. We'd have working lunches—box lunches—and there wasn't any slack. Gallagher ran a tight meeting. He didn't let people tell war stories or digress too much."[119]

At the January 1988 meeting, assignments were doled out among board members to produce reports about threats or land-buying opportunities at a dozen different battlefields in the region. The reports included a map of the area showing the threatened or target land, the market value, the name of the landowners and whether they were inclined to sell the property, or agree to an easement to preserve the land.[120]

Krick said he would handle the Virginia sites: Cedar Mountain, Cross Keys, Mine Run, Port Republic, and Rappahannock Station. Ackerly raised his hand for McDowell, Virginia. Greene took North Anna, Virginia, and so on. Board members and several trusted associates divvied up the battlefields. Chris Calkins, an NPS historian at Petersburg, Virginia, was assigned Five Forks and Reams Station. Calkins had a knack for, as he put it, "brokering battlefield land."[121] He joined the APCWS board later in 1988.

Chantilly Battlefield Association co-founder Bud Hall was another trusted APCWS associate. As a J.E.B. Stuart devotee, Hall's first love and primary interest was the sprawling cavalry battlefield at Brandy Station and the battle of June 9, 1863—the largest cavalry battle of the war.[122]

As he fought for Chantilly, Hall felt fortunate that Brandy Station was deep in the Virginia countryside, 60 miles from Washington, removed from burgeoning development. Suburban sprawl reached Manassas in Prince William County, but Brandy Station was beyond Prince William *and* Fauquier counties. Plenty of rural or semi-rural land would be developed before bulldozers reached Culpeper County, he thought. Still, Chantilly's destruction made Hall wary, and Brandy Station soon appeared on the APCWS radar.[123]

Near the end of the January 1988 meeting, Pohanka spoke of a rumor that Hall had mentioned about the potential sale of core Brandy Station battlefield land at Fleetwood Hill "to business interests." Hall was on top of the situation, Pohanka said, and promised to report any news.[124]

Had he been present, Hall would have reassured the board members that it was not the first time he had heard rumors of the possible sale of Fleetwood Hill, the scene of deadly charges and countercharges during the climax of the battle. But there *had* been real estate activity on another part of the battlefield, he would have told them. A married couple from California recently bought one of the large farms on the battlefield. It wasn't unusual, however, for a wealthy outsider to buy rural property for a horse farm, Hall would have said.[125]

As APCWS board members headed home from Fredericksburg that Saturday evening in January, they were energized with the steady progress they were making and how well the organization was taking hold in the Civil War community. New memberships arrived daily, feeding the bank account dollar by dollar. They were analyzing battlefield preservation needs and opportunities, setting priorities and getting a handle on what they needed to do to save land.

Less than two weeks later, on Thursday, January 28, 1988, bombshell news exploded at Manassas. In a surprise move, Hazel/Peterson Companies changed its development plans for Stuart's Hill. It would now team up with the nation's largest shopping mall builder to build William Center Mall, one of the region's largest malls, as the centerpiece of the office and residential development. The site of Lee's headquarters at the Second Battle of Manassas now seemed destined to be the site of a 1.2-million square foot mall, 560 new homes and 1.7 million square feet of office space.

The following morning, *The Washington Post*'s front-page headline read "Huge Mall Planned at Manassas." The *Post* reported that it was a done deal, the land had been rezoned in 1986 and "no public hearings or additional action by the supervisors are expected."[126]

The news sent shock waves through the fledgling preservation organization and its supporters, including Hall. But if Hall entertained any thoughts about becoming involved in the fight against William Center, those thoughts evaporated in a matter of days.

In early February 1988, Hall learned that another farm on the Brandy Station battlefield, adjacent to the first, had been sold to the same California couple, Lee and Joan Sammis. Hall was alarmed. Just who was this couple? Long before internet research was commonplace, it was a simple matter for Hall to do a background check at FBI headquarters. In short order, a stunned Hall learned Sammis was a real estate developer based in Irvine, California, with a large and active branch office in northern Virginia.

The information shook Hall to his core. *Not Brandy Station*, he thought. Not yet. How could this be possible? Hall knew that by buying the farms in the names of him and his wife, Sammis was doing his best to move quietly, under the radar. Hall felt his stomach churn as dread and anger welled up.

It would be decades before that feeling disappeared for good. ★

CHAPTER
THREE

War at Manassas

 T'S WAR," screamed the headline above the *Potomac News* story after more than 225 protesters crammed into the small auditorium of the Manassas National Battlefield Park on a Friday night to protest the planned construction of a massive mall next to the park.[127]

In a "collective display of outrage," *News* reporter Clint Schemmer wrote, the throng voted on the spot at this February 5, 1988, meeting—a week after the mall announcement—to sue the developers and the Prince William County Board of Supervisors.[128]

For almost two years, the county, local advocacy groups and the developer, Hazel/Peterson Companies, had negotiated proffers and other issues related to William Center, a planned, mixed-use development of offices, homes and stores proposed for a 542-acre tract adjacent to the NPS park. The tract included Stuart's Hill, where Confederate General Robert E. Lee established a headquarters during the Battle of Second Manassas.

Now, out of the blue, the developer decided to add "William Center Mall," one of the largest malls in the country, making a big project far bigger. The pro-development Board of Supervisors approved adding the mall without public comment and announced it would not review it, despite the uproar.[129]

Over the weekend, the protesters raised more than $5,600 to fund the lawsuit. On Sunday, February 7, someone hung an upside-down American flag—the symbol of distress—on posts planted along Interstate 66 to hold a sign heralding the new development.

The dispute was soon being called the "Third Battle of Manassas."[130] Francis F. Wilshin (1901-1990), the former superintendent of the Manassas Battlefield Park, would have chuckled. *Third* battle of Manassas? Try "eighth," or "ninth," Wilshin would have said. So many "third" battles of Manassas had been fought over preservation of the battlefield in the 20th century, who could keep track?[131]

Wilshin was park superintendent from 1955 to 1969, an assignment that encompassed the Civil War Centennial. A native of Virginia, he was an avid student of the Civil War. One of his grandfathers served in J.E.B. Stuart's Confederate cavalry; the other was a blockade runner, defying the Union Navy's blockade of southern ports.[132]

As a battlefield tour guide, Wilshin was of the same mold as the next generation's Ed Bearss, the National Park Service (NPS) chief historian emeritus known as the preeminent living guide for his dramatic and deeply knowledgeable battlefield tours. Like Bearss, Wilshin served at Vicksburg National Military Park, preceding

Bearss by almost two decades as the park historian. In 1955, as Wilshin took over as superintendent at Manassas, Bearss began his NPS career at Vicksburg.[133]

At Vicksburg in the 1930s, Wilshin's tour groups sometimes included elderly Civil War veterans of the battle. He never forgot a 94-year-old Illinois veteran who gently fingered the lettering on the stone memorial that marked where his regiment fought, calling out the names of one fallen comrade after another, asking if their names were carved on the memorial. Invariably, they were.[134]

"And it was a thrill to stand there and watch him as he looked about the field trying to readjust the memory that he had of that battlefield with what he was seeing now in its peaceful state," Wilshin recalled years later.[135]

Wilshin engaged park visitors in conversation, always asking if they had Civil War ancestors, and if they did, whether they retained any old letters. From these queries, he amassed an impressive archive of soldier letters that personalized his lectures.[316] He favored the Battle of First Manassas (Bull Run) over the second and a consequence was that the preservation of the Second Manassas battlefield lagged for years, Bearss said. Wilshin "believed he was from the Southern aristocracy," Bearss recalled, and freely expressed his points of view. Once, Wilshin was riding with fellow NPS employee John Luzader and his wife in a car pool, Bearss recalled. "John is liberal, but his wife is very liberal, and Francis was not. Francis used to read the paper on the way in every day, and he'd always be talking about the 'nigras' in Washington. Mrs. Luzader finally got her craw full of it and they kicked him out on the side of the road and ended the car pool."[137]

At Manassas, Wilshin had many responsibilities as superintendent but none he loved more than giving tours. Whether it was for 50 people or just one, he walked the battlefield in his NPS uniform—complete with a tie and the traditional, wide-brimmed, Stetson-style, felt hat—and made his guests feel as if they were living the battle.

One local woman vividly remembered her first tour with him. It was a quiet weekday in early 1957, and she was his only guest. "He was very articulate, very dramatic, and he would take me to a part of the park and say, 'This is where General Bee stood, and Private So-and-so was behind him, and he heard him say this to that.'" Wilshin would play the role of the private, and then Bee. "When you took a tour of that park with Francis Wilshin, you were there," she recalled. "I mean, nothing was left to your imagination. I was just standing there with my mouth open, I was so awed and overwhelmed."[138]

That woman was Annie Snyder.

Anne Delp Snyder lived on a farm next to the battlefield with her husband,

Pete, an airline pilot, and their six children. She worked the farm – milking the cows, clearing rocks, stringing fence line—while raising her flock of kids and immersing herself in local volunteer activities.

She had lived next to the battlefield for six years, just a short walk from the unfinished railroad line and famous "Deep Cut" in the Battle of Second Manassas (Bull Run). Until her tour with Wilshin, all of it had escaped her notice. "To me, the Civil War was just a name in a history book," she recalled.[139]

Snyder was instantly transformed into a loyal battlefield supporter. She had a take-charge attitude, unmatched energy, savvy organizing and political skills, a deep devotion to personal public service, an unending tolerance for writing letters, and a tendency to break into tears at emotional moments. These traits and qualities would eventually make her internationally famous as the grassroots leader in the struggles against William Center and Disney's America.

Snyder was a battle-hardened preservation veteran immersed in her biggest fight, William Center, as the organized national preservation movement was getting started in 1987-88 with the founding of APCWS. Her preservation work, and that of Wilshin before her, provided a blueprint for how to fight on behalf of battlefields. Many of their tactics are still used today, including the tried-and-true letter writing, now mostly accomplished by email.

Born in Pittsburgh and educated at the University of Pittsburgh, Anne Delp followed the footsteps of her attorney father and headed to law school when World War II broke out. Her only brother joined the Marines, and when the Corps decided to recruit women for various non-combat tasks to "free a Marine to fight," she was selected as one of the 10 women in the first Officer Candidate Class at Mount Holyoke, Massachusetts.[140]

Her first assignment, in New Orleans, involved recruiting other women, and she quickly learned about public relations, tact and the art of persuasion. "That was probably one of the most difficult jobs I ever had, because most of the men—brothers and fathers—were like my father," she said. "They didn't want their women to join the Marines or any branch of service. But I guess the theory was that they could see I was a fairly nice gal and the Marine Corps was not going to make prostitutes out of (women), which seemed to be a common belief in those days."[141]

And to those men who thought a woman in uniform was "an easy make," Snyder left "a trail of black eyes down there." But she also met Maj. Waldron Peter Snyder, a Marine aviator fresh from the Pacific. They married in 1946 and had six children in quick succession, a boy and then five girls.[142]

Her dream was to raise her kids on a farm, and in 1951, the Snyders bought a spread in rural Prince William County they named Pageland Farm. Six years later she took Wilshin's tour, then learned that Confederate General Stonewall Jackson's right flank had stretched across Pageland as the Battle of Second Bull Run began on the morning of August 29, 1862, that a Confederate field hospital had been established there, and that some of those who died there were probably still buried in her pastures.[143]

The farm was only a part of all she undertook. Her husband, a commercial airline pilot, was often away, so she threw herself into community activities of every stripe with indefatigable enthusiasm and energy. In the 1950s, when her children were in school, she served "on myriad committees in the PTA," the Parent Teacher Association, and was a charter member of the first county-wide PTA council.[144]

Snyder lost a bid to serve on the school board because she opposed Virginia's then-segregated schools. She worked on a campaign to build a local, central library. She served on legislative committees for the local farm bureau and fought "several, tough, hard, time-consuming campaigns" to keep favorable tax rates for farmers.[145]

She was a charter member of Prince William County's first Citizens Association and at least four other local groups. "I attended so many board meetings over the years that in the days when we sat on hard benches, my only claim to fame was that I was the only citizen in the county who had callouses on her derriere . . ." she wrote in a 1989 letter to the *Washington Post*.

Who watched the kids? "No one," she wrote. "I took them with me."[146]

In the spring of 1957, just weeks after Wilshin gave Snyder her first tour, he called to ask for help. The State of Virginia announced it was going to build the new Interstate 66 right through the heart of the Manassas battlefield, replacing the existing Lee Highway, called the Warrenton Road during the war.

It was a major 19th-century thoroughfare and the Union troops marched west on it in 1861 to confront the Confederates on July 31 in the war's first major land battle, the Battle of First Manassas (Bull Run). Thirteen months later, the Battle of Second Manassas was fought on both sides of this same road. Throughout the war, the Warrenton Road remained a key artery, as it is today, choked with traffic as it narrows to two lanes through the battlefield with a stop light midway.

The plan developed by the Virginia Department of Highways in 1957 called for Interstate 66 to replace Lee Highway on the same basic right of way. Implications to the battlefield were staggering. The road was to be widened to 300 feet, destroying the original landscape around Stone Bridge as well as the Stone House. An exit was planned for the intersection with Sudley Road, Route 234, with a cloverleaf that would carve into Henry Hill and other battlefield land.[147]

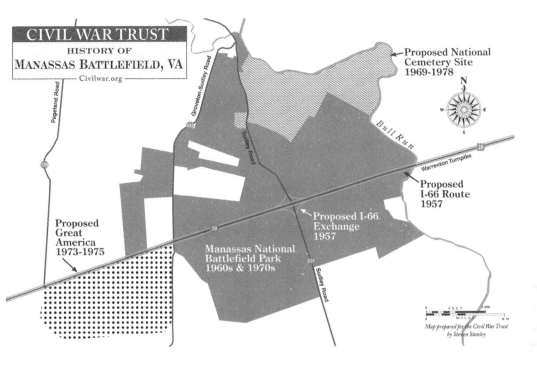

Proposed National
Cemetery Site
1969-1978

Proposed
I-66 Route
1957

Proposed I-66
Exchange
1957

Proposed
Great
America
1973-1975

Manassas National
Battlefield Park
1960s & 1970s

Map prepared for the Civil War Trust
by Steven Stanley

"When that was proposed, I just knew right off what a terrific impact it would have on the park in tearing up our lands..." Wilshin recalled years later.[148]

The NPS, right up to Director Conrad Wirth, expressed its grave concern. State agency officials agreed to lay out their plans in a public meeting at the visitor's center on March 12, 1957, in the electric map room, which was crammed with citizens, local leaders, park service representatives and state officials. A highway department official explained how vitally important—"absolutely essential"—it was to build the new interstate through the battlefield on the existing Lee Highway.[149]

Why?

It was less expensive.

Citizens submitted letters of protest. Some read them at the meeting. Wirth's letter was read. "And they were still determined to go ahead," Wilshin recalled. "They were just like a horse with a bit in its teeth; nothing was going to stop them, come hell or high water."[150]

That very night, The Civil War Round Table of Washington, DC, held its regular meeting. Wilshin was a charter member. Famed Civil War author Bruce Catton was the speaker. Some 300 members attended—a packed house.

"I was fresh from the (highway) meeting," Wilshin recalled. "So I asked for five minutes to alert the group to the situation. I really poured it on. I remember how excited I got. I was too close to the mike and I was talking too loud, and I said, 'Gentlemen, how fortunate it is you are coming to Manassas this spring because never again may you ever expect to see these fields in their unspoiled state. Robinson House Hill, where Hampton's Legion made its gallant stand—they're going to carve it up. Henry Hill, where one gallant wave of Union attackers swept after another, is going to be mutilated beyond recognition. And Chinn Ridge, where the issue of the campaign was decided—they're going to take 60 acres off for an interchange. And where the New York Monument area is, where the state of New York just spent $50,000 to acquire the land, they're going to almost completely despoil it! Here, gentlemen, is a clear case where we should take an adamant stand and like the Greeks at Thermopylae, like the French at Verdun, say, 'They shall not pass!'"[151]

After the applause tailed off, the Round Table members composed a letter on the spot to the 80 or so Round Tables around the country, asking that not only the Round Tables but individual members write letters of protest to their Congressmen and the Virginia Department of Highways.[152]

Wilshin asked his local supporters, including Snyder, to write. "He had everybody writing to Congress and flooding them, and here I was, a local citizen who he had trapped," she recalled. But the idea that they "would put a highway down the Warrenton Pike and divide the park in half for all time was just unthinkable. So, he was the one who got me started in my first letter-writing campaign for the park."[153]

Wilshin attended civic meetings and gathered support from local leaders, including the mayor and town council members in Manassas and members of the Prince William County Board of Supervisors. He drummed up local newspaper stories. And on March 24, 1957, the story went national, with NBC anchor Chet Huntley of the *Huntley-Brinkley Report* reporting on the controversy during his half-hour *Outlook* program.[154]

The highways department proposed an alternative plan. Wilshin and the NPS abhorred that plan as well. Years later, Wilshin recalled how the department buckled under the pressure.

"They said, 'Well, what will you permit us to do?'"

"We replied, 'Now you're talking turkey. Go either to the north or to the south, but preferably to the south.' And that's where they finally went. Now they skirt our park lands, bringing the visitor right to our door and don't mar our historic terrain," Wilshin recalled."[155]

While succeeding in fighting off that threat, Wilshin ignored park service custom, where neutrality was the watchword. Instead, he had led a highly organized, effective public campaign to pressure the Department of Highways to change plans.

But when Wilshin organized another opposition campaign in the next major preservation struggle at Manassas, it cost him. This fight over whether to build a national cemetery on the battlefield started in January 1969 and would continue for years. Representative William L. Scott, the Republican who represented Virginia's eighth Congressional District, which covered Manassas, filed H.R. 1357, a bill to create a National Cemetery on the grounds of the park.[156]

Arlington National Cemetery was almost full, necessitating a new cemetery, and Scott reasoned that no better place of honor existed than the battlefield in his district. A World War II veteran on the House Committee on Veterans' Affairs, Scott had surveyed his constituents and gained support for the proposal. The key challenge was persuading the National Park Service.[157]

In February 1969, NPS Director George Hartzog said he would support the measure if the cemetery was created on 500 acres of "moderate historical significance" within park boundaries, but still privately owned, northeast of the park along Bull Run. The following month, Scott revised and resubmitted his bill.[158]

The Department of the Interior supported Hartzog's proposal, although Chief Historian Bearss disputed Hartzog's historical assessment. Bearss described the land as having "at least as high a degree of historical significance" as areas already in the park.[159]

To Wilshin, it was not just the land's historical significance. The proposal "was absolutely averse to the whole concept of park development," he said. "Those lands, once they are established, as we in the Park Service understand, are inviolate. They are preserved forever, for the use for which they were committed, and established."[160]

Again, Wilshin took the fight to the local community. This time his own superiors disagreed, but his passion for preserving the battlefield would allow him to do nothing less.

Scott pointed out that national cemeteries existed at Gettysburg, Antietam, Vicksburg and other Civil War battlefields, and he did not see why Manassas should not have one. "But those cemeteries in other Civil War battlefields were *Civil War dead!*" Wilshin exclaimed. Scott argued, "To me, there's no inconsistency in burying today's veterans along with those of other wars."[162]

Snyder was a local Republican who had worked hard to get Scott elected in 1966. She and her husband were both Marine veterans and her initial reaction to the proposal was favorable. "Well, you know, we could be buried in our own backyard, on land we loved," she told her husband. "Annie, you can put a cemetery anywhere. You can't change the location of a battlefield," Pete said. "You know, you're right," she replied.[163]

Snyder became an opponent, and she and another local cemetery opponent, Gilbert LeKander, a Congressional aide, formed Friends of the Park in March 1969. Wilshin provided precise data on how the cemetery would affect the park, and Snyder made sure these facts were added to the many letters she helped get to Capitol Hill.[164]

Scott howled in protest to NPS, which defended its man, arguing that Wilshin had only acted as an official observer and answered citizen's questions. Then NPS heard that Wilshin had blasted the Congressman in public at a Manassas supermarket, sparing no measure of colorful language.[165]

Thus ended Francis Wilshin's tenure as superintendent of Manassas National Battlefield Park. After almost 14 years at the helm, he was transferred to Washington in April 1969 and shuffled to a shared office in the Historic Preservation Office. His office partner, and new boss, was an up-and-coming young NPS historian named Ed Bearss, who had been promoted to Washington from his Vicksburg assignment.[166]

"At that time, I was a team leader, and he was under me," Bearss recalled. "He was put there to let him get a little more time—a couple of years—and then he could retire. He was very opinionated and could be very boring. He was working for me at the time he got kicked out of the car pool."[167]

With Wilshin gone, Snyder and LeKander battled on, wording their messages carefully to avoid upsetting veterans. "There is no need to do grave injustice to an established memorial to our heroic veterans of the past to accommodate the needs of our gallant veterans of today," Snyder wrote in a white paper for her organization, renamed the Save the Battlefield Committee."[168]

LeKander's presence on Capitol Hill "was really very key," Snyder recalled, "because he was on the Hill where he could go and talk to anybody in Congress, practically on a first-name basis. He was highly respected, and we managed to—that legislation never got out of Congress into the Senate. We held it back."[169]

But Scott kept the cemetery proposal alive both as a Congressman and after he was elected to the Senate in 1972 as Virginia's first Republican senator since Reconstruction. "Year after year he would introduce that legislation, and year after year, we would defeat it," Snyder said. "That was a real, real tough fight."[170]

With help from LeKander, Congress eventually passed legislation that established a new national cemetery at the United States Marine Corps Base at Quantico. The cemetery fight was her first real preservation battle, Snyder recalled. She had written letters to help Wilshin fight the interstate highway. But in the struggle to stop the cemetery, she became a leader, refining strategies learned from Wilshin that she would use in every preservation fight to follow.[171]

"I operate very much the same in any battle," Snyder recalled in a 1993 NPS oral history interview with historian Joan Zenzen, author of Battling For Manassas: The Fifty-Year Preservation Struggle at Manassas National Battlefield Park. "I think it's very important to have public support. That's your first goal—to get public support. We aimed always to enlist the support of as many people as we could, not just here, but all across the country.

"So my first act in every battle was to make sure the story got out. I would write letters to all the Civil War Round Tables. I would just send out hundreds of things ... I always tried to get the national papers, and I found the best way to do that was to encourage the local press to write as many stories as they could about it. I would always have the names and telephone numbers of every person I thought could either substantiate what I said or be more authoritative ... to make it as easy as I could for the press to call these people. And another big help has always been that every major newspaper in the country, I've found, has a Civil War buff on the writing staff. That is very, very helpful.

"Once you get people who want to help, then the important thing is to have something for them to do. I've found that one of the best ways to get people involved is to give them a petition. From those petitions, you get your larger volunteers, future volunteers—the ones that help stuff envelopes, write letters, hold the auction sales and the fundraisers. I think you have to make the job not only possible for each person to do within their time frame and their limitations and their abilities, but you also have to make it fun. You have to have jobs that they can do in 10 minutes that they might even possibly enjoy doing. We found when we had letter-writing campaigns, or letters to stuff and mail, and we'd have everybody over and everybody would sit around the dining room table and do it, they enjoyed that, and it was fun."[172]

This was the essence of the Annie Snyder playbook, which adapted and expanded Wilshin's methods. Today, with the decline of newspapers, the rise of the internet and the overwhelming influence of social media, the playing field has changed. But the most basic formula for fighting a preservation battle from the grassroots level remains the same—get the word out in any and every way possible, mobilize as much protest as possible, become actively involved in the political and governmental processes and keep up the heat.

The next battle at Manassas began in 1973, when the Marriott Corporation announced at a February 14 press conference its intention to build a $35 million Great America theme park and other development projects at Stuart's Hill, the same land that would be fought over in the William Center battle more than a decade later. County supervisors at Marriott's press conference enthusiastically endorsed the project. Marriott announced that it hoped to break ground on the 513-acre tract in two months.[173]

Stuart's Hill had been a command center for Lee and a key signal station during the Battle of Second Manassas. It is unclear why it was named after the Confederate cavalry commander General J.E.B. Stuart, although he may have briefly napped or placed artillery there. Most significantly, on the battle's third day, Maj. General James Longstreet concealed his 30,000 men in the hidden depths of the woods at the foot of the hill's east side before sending them on the attack to crush the weakened Union left wing on Chinn Ridge and Henry Hill, triggering a Union rout.[174]

Stuart's Hill was not part of the NPS park, nor even in the Congressional mandated historical boundary, despite recommendations and efforts over the years to include it within the boundary. Although the land was significant in interpreting and understanding the Battle of Second Manassas, no combat had occurred there. Parts of the battlefield where fighting took place were always a higher priority. The Prince William County Board of Supervisors, eyeing development potential and tax dollars, staunchly opposed efforts to expand the park to land where no combat occurred. Marriott had obtained options to buy the 513 acres from 10 different property owners, but those options expired on April 7, 1973.[175]

Marriott executives looked at the large tract they had assembled and saw two million people a year flocking to the amusements and attractions of six historic zones—a New England seaport, a French market in New Orleans, the Southwest, the frontier Yukon, a rural town and the Midwest at the turn of the 20th century.[176]

What they saw as a complement to the battlefield—one that would enhance the appeal of the park by bringing more visitors to the area—preservationists viewed as a horrible intrusion. A tough fight loomed. Many citizens favored a new, local, family attraction, while county leaders and business people welcomed the anticipated economic boost from tourism revenues and the expanded tax base in a county that had more than doubled in size during the previous decade.[177]

Known as the "Four Horsemen" as in the biblical Four Horsemen of the Apocalypse, four of the five county supervisors, led by Chairman Ralph Mauller, supported the project. On February 16, two days after Marriott's announcement, the board voted 4-1 to approve and sign a letter of intent promising to provide the necessary services, highway access and all the permits for the theme park.[178]

A few days later, citizens opposed to the project formed the Battlefield Community Civic Association. Their temporary president, citing "many prior commitments," accepted the position only after being pressured by other members.[179]

Pageland Farm was silent. Snyder was 4,000 miles away in a hospital bed in Switzerland, recovering from a badly broken leg after a skiing accident. Even without the accident or the stress of preservation fights, Snyder's health was always a concern because of her diabetes. It was months before she was back in action. Snyder recalled, "The spark plug and the true leader of that fight was a woman named Memory Porter."[180]

Porter and LeKander created a new organization, a coalition of local grassroots groups they named the Prince William League for the Protection of Natural Resources, to fight the project, particularly the proposed rezoning of the land from agricultural to commercial. One of the most intrusive aspects of the $35 million project was a tower that would soar 350 feet above the landscape—taller even than the 307-foot Gettysburg Tower. Nearby would be several other 100-foot structures.[181]

Six hundred people came to the public meeting Porter and LeKander organized at a school on February 21, 1973. David L. Brown, Marriott's vice president in charge of theme parks, promised to appear then canceled at the last minute. Despite the lack of hard information, the crowd was eager to discuss the ramifications of the park. Sentiment was about evenly divided among those opposing, supporting and undecided.[182]

"I've tried to adopt an impartial attitude towards the location of the park," LeKander told the group. "My co-chairman, Mrs. Wesley Porter, is not at all impartial. She has been developing background information on the park and finding out about such things as the effect on Orlando, Florida, as a result of Disney World locating near there, and sewer, water and taxes."[183]

Manassas National Battlefield Park Superintendent Russell Berry, attempting to maintain neutrality, declined to support or oppose it, prompting local Civil War Round Tables to complain to Congress. The House Subcommittee on National Parks and Recreation scheduled a hearing on whether the Great America park would harm the NPS park. On March 30, four days before the hearing, several Congressmen, including Representative John Seiberling (D-Ohio), toured the battlefield with NPS's Berry, Marriott's Brown, Mauller and others.

"Don't you think it's incongruous to have an amusement park right next to the battlefield?" Seiberling asked the board chairman.

"Well, this particular park is more of a cultural nature that would add historical value . . . It's supposed to depict Great America and the American tradition," Mauller said.

Replied the Congressman: "What bothers me is that you have an authentic piece of American history here and they want to create something that's fake!" The hearing room on Capitol Hill quickly filled with supporters and opponents on April 3. "We intend to honor or celebrate the great things that make the United States," Brown testified. He said the corporation would be a good neighbor and would work with the community "within any kind of reason."[185]

Porter and LeKander argued the theme park would create traffic problems and bring even more development that would compromise the NPS park and the remaining green space in the area. The government should acquire the tract to save and protect it, they said. NPS Director Ronald H. Walker testified, but did not take a stance, which displeased theme park opponents, preservationists and some members of Congress.

Marriott faced other major hurdles. The county was trying to satisfy its promises and Marriott's needs, but sewer capacity was far short of what was needed, and there was no guarantee enough could be provided. A host of other challenges remained, including the arrangements for a new exit off Interstate 66. On March 16, two and a half weeks before the Congressional hearing, the Virginia State Water Control Board denied every county request to pave the way for the project. The board said if it had approved the requests, it would have violated water pollution laws and jeopardized "the future development of all of Northern Virginia."[186]

Despite this setback, the Prince William County Planning Commission on April 3, the same day as the Congressional hearing, recommended approval of the necessary rezoning and a special use permit, but enumerated a list of conditions: Marriott had to ensure adequate access roads, protection of water quality and the planting of trees to provide a buffer from the battlefield park.[187]

Time was of the essence—Marriott's options to buy the land expired on April 7. Two days before the deadline, the supervisors voted unanimously in favor of Marriott's proposal, rezoning 335 acres for the theme park and 178 acres for a light industrial park.[188]

The Prince William League for the Protection of Natural Resources sued the county, alleging supervisors failed to properly advertise the meeting and then failed to give opponents ample time to speak. Almost 90 people had attended, but the county allowed only nine opponents and 12 supporters to address the board.[189]

The lawsuit further delayed the project, although Marriott purchased the 513 acres. In January 1974, the county's lawyers told the board that the county had failed to properly advertise the meeting by giving only 15 days' notice instead of the state-mandated 19 days, so the rezoning and special use permit were probably invalid.[190]

This threw into question previous zoning changes, so the supervisors sought relief from the state legislature, asking for special legislation to validate all improperly advertised zoning changes. The League rebuffed that effort when Porter persuaded the legislature to exempt any zoning cases then under litigation, defeating Marriott's high-paid lobbyists. The *Washington Star-News* article was headlined, "The Lady Fells a Giant."[191]

By January 1974, Snyder was back in action. Her letter-writing campaign generated the usual flood of protest letters to the county, but there seemed to be no record of them. She began calling and asking questions, and learned that about 1,000 letters of protest to the county had not been included in the public record for consideration by the supervisors. When she demanded to see the letters, she was at first refused, then only allowed to look at them while being monitored. She had to copy anything she wanted from them by hand.[192]

In the fall of 1974, the lawsuit against the county was still being litigated, but that was not the most significant hurdle Marriott faced because it could simply reapply for rezoning. Far more challenging were the issues of sewer capacity and a new Interstate 66 interchange. Marriott came up with an innovative solution for the sewage problem—a zero discharge system that would treat the park's wastes on site, aerate the effluent and use the water to irrigate nearby hay fields.[193]

And in November 1974, when state and federal highway authorities approved a new interchange next to the planned park, it appeared that Marriott had conquered all the thorny problems and could build the park. "Major Obstacle to Marriott's Plan Removed," read the sub-headline in *The Washington Post* story.[194]

In fact, that approval sounded the death knell for Marriott's Great America park. It stipulated that Marriott alone would have to pay the estimated $4 million cost of the new interchange. More significantly, it demanded an environmental impact report for the interchange as was required for all such federal projects.[195]

Marriott had delayed the opening of the park from 1976 to 1978, and the environmental impact statement would take at least another year to complete. The company quickly lost interest in the project. Marriott was building theme parks in California and Illinois, too, and officials said they intended to focus their efforts on those projects until they were "well off the ground." Great America at Manassas went on the corporate back burner.[196]

The county tried to entice Marriott to refile its application for rezoning and a special use permit, but the company did not act. By December, company officials were telling reporters it was "very doubtful" the park would be built, and in March 1978, the company announced it had formally written off all associated costs.

Stuart's Hill had been spared for the time being.[197]

In 1975, legislation was introduced to expand the Manassas National Battlefield Park's boundaries. From the start, Stuart's Hill was excluded. The Marriott proposal was still a potential, though comatose, project. The county was dead-set against including that land within the boundaries. And there were still parts of the battlefield proper that needed to be brought within the boundaries.[198]

Stuart's Hill remained outside the Manassas boundary expansion bill when it passed in 1980. The land was still zoned agricultural, but that was no hindrance to a county bound and determined to see development and to opportunistic developers who were more than eager to build. The manifestation of that in the mid-1980s was the William Center controversy, another so-called "Third Battle of Manassas," the fight that became Annie Snyder's Gettysburg. ★

CHAPTER
FOUR

Epic Fight Over William Center

HAT STUART'S HILL survives today as part of the Manassas National Battlefield Park is nothing short of miraculous, but the campaign to save it led to a pyrrhic victory. The $135 million it cost to save the 542-acre tract in 1988 dwarfs the cost per acre of nearly every other battlefield land purchase in the Trust's history.

Almost 30 years later, the man at the center of the storm, developer John Tilghman "Til" Hazel, Jr., reflected: "As a public citizen, I'm very unhappy the way it happened because the public shouldn't spend its money that way. As the owner of the land and the developer, I was very pleased. Being absolutely brutal about it, we made a better deal the way it ended up than if we had developed it."[199]

The tract was always an unfavored stepchild at Manassas because no fighting occurred there. Yet it was crucial in interpreting the Battle of Second Manassas because of the climatic, victorious Confederate charge that was launched from there. After Marriott Corporation was thwarted in building its proposed Great America theme park and the land was excluded from a Manassas battlefield boundary expansion in 1980, the county slated it for development as an office park in its 1982 comprehensive plan.

The state of Virginia considered building its Center for Innovative Technology on part of the tract, but eventually picked another spot. In 1985, the Centennial Development Corporation, which had developed much of the Chantilly battlefield, purchased the entire tract from Marriott and announced plans to build a technology office park, only to back out before year's end because of the cost.[200]

The county had enthusiastically supported both development plans. It seemed almost desperate for develoment, as evidenced by a decision in November 1985 to increase the allowable height for buildings in commercial zones from 45 to 70 feet.[201]

In the spring of 1986, the Hazel/Peterson Companies obtained an option on the parcel, which had grown from Marriott's 513 acres to 542 acres. Hazel/Peterson asked the county to consider rezoning it from agricultural to a planned mixed-use district (PMD). A mixed-use development combined corporate offices, retail space and housing in an integrated arrangement. The Hazel/Peterson Companies were pioneers when it came to suburban development and PMDs, and their showpiece was the 657-acre Fair Lakes development in Fairfax County southwest of the Chantilly battlefield.

Mixed-use developments appealed to buyers and were lucrative. As partner Milton Peterson said, developers build what they can sell. "See, the whole thing in sales and marketing is making people feel good about themselves," he told *The Washington Post* in 1991. "Everybody, when they come to the suburbs, they want the trees and bunnies and birds, okay. And that's why we put two swans out there and feed the damn ducks so all the friggin' geese and ducks come around and people say, 'Gee, I work out in a place where they have paths and running tracks, ponds, birds. Do you have a running track where you work?'

"We're trying to make a person here feel as though he's going to drive in the country and his office just happens to be one of those little buildings off in the woods next to the birds and the bunnies, all right? And that's what he feels. Yes, a city in a garden."[202]

The county approved the PMD zoning for the Stuart's Hill tract in April 1986. A month later, Hazel/Peterson announced plans to build William Center, which would consist of an office park of about 275 acres, a residential section with 975 townhouses, apartments and single-family homes, as well as a small shopping center. William Center would be the "catalytic agent" for commercial development along the I-66 corridor in Prince William County, Hazel declared.[203]

"I knew the site and had for a long time," Hazel recalled. "And when Milt (Peterson) and I saw the site and realized that Prince William County wanted to use it for development and for commercial real estate, we bought it. We had no anticipation that anybody would ever connect it to the Manassas battlefield because it was not really part of the Manassas battlefield."[204]

Hazel, a Harvard-educated attorney, was one of the most powerful and prolific developers in the Washington, D.C. area.[205] He became a developer after realizing he could do as well or better than the builders he represented. Hazel and Peterson teamed up to build 900,000 square feet of office space on the McLean boundary of Tyson's Corner that is now the home of the National Intelligence Center. Hazel was responsible for much of the development in northern Virginia in the late 20th century, as well as a good bit of the philanthropy. He has been a key supporter of George Mason University, helping it grow from its original home in a repurposed, eight-room elementary school building to an institution with 34,000 students on a sprawling campus in Fairfax County.[206]

Hazel lived on a farm at Broad Run, Va., near Thoroughfare Gap and cherished his memories running his father's farm as a teenager. But he bulldozed countless farms in northern Virginia for his many developments. His career as a developer focused on growth and prosperity, and if critics wanted to call it sprawl, that was fine with him. "I'm very proud of suburban sprawl," he said in 2010. "Suburban sprawl is where most of America lives. Most of America doesn't want to raise a family on the 10th floor or the 20th floor of a high rise. Most of America likes to live on a quarter-acre lot. And I am very proud of sprawl. And to the extent that I have been involved in what is called sprawl, I'm proud of it.

"I'm a very traditional Virginian and think that to be a Virginian, you need to be committed to the general welfare of the community and the society. You need to be committed to what people need to prosper, and you need to do that in a civil, deliberate, unafraid way. What people need are schools, roads, shopping areas, housing and infrastructure. Secondly, I thought growth was a good thing and I do think growth is a good thing and will forever think growth is important. Because if you deal with people properly and you provide for growth, prosperity will be the product."[207]

At Harvard, Hazel majored in American history. Despite his deep Virginia connection, the Civil War elicited mixed feelings. "It's very depressing to me because it took so much energy and so many lives lost and so much destruction for reasons that should have been avoided," Hazel said in early 2017. "It's just too depressing, and I'm also distressed that it's become in the public imagination that it was nothing but a war for slavery when in fact it involved much more than that. It was much more than slavery that kept people involved and willing to fight and lose 300,000 people."[208]

At the same time, it fascinated him. Hazel considered the area at the unfinished railroad cut at Second Manassas, where Confederate General Stonewall Jackson massed his men and fought off repeated Union assaults, to be "the most interesting battlefield that I think I've ever seen. It looks just like the day when he left it. Nothing happened to it in those last 150 years." Hazel restored a circa 1830 building on his land that has the names of two Union soldiers scratched in the plaster in the attic. "They were bivouacked there in November 1862 on the way from Antietam to Fredericksburg," Hazel said. "We've got their records from the Union army and they both survived the war and were discharged at the end of the war."[209]

Stuart's Hill is almost due south of the heart of the unfinished railroad cut, on the opposite side, or south side, of Lee Highway. To Hazel, the land didn't seem special and wasn't even "particularly pretty." He knew no fighting had occurred there and since the tract had been excluded from the 1980 Manassas battlefield federal boundary expansion, it was clear that NPS had no interest in acquiring it.[210]

To avoid trouble, Hazel/Peterson in June 1986 began meeting with Rolland Swain, superintendent of the Manassas National Battlefield Park, to discuss ways to minimize the development's impact on the park. This led to a number of proffers, or negotiated concessions. Hazel/Peterson pledged to create an extended buffer zone along Lee Highway, limit the height of buildings to 45 feet, provide $2.25 million toward a new Interstate 66 interchange, route traffic away from already congested

Lee Highway and construct storm water retention ponds to limit drainage from the new development to prevent flooding.[211]

When the Northwest Prince William Citizens Association (NWPWCA, of which Snyder was a member), raised questions and objected, Hazel/Peterson offered more concessions. It reduced the number of planned housing units from 975 to 560. The company agreed to contribute $150,000 to help mitigate the impact on public schools, contribute acreage for a fire station, build a community trail system, a community swimming pool, tennis courts, and a ball field.[212]

Snyder's diabetes was causing problems and she largely stayed in the background of a debate whose result appeared to be a foregone conclusion. The object of the citizens association was to "make the best of a bad situation," she said, and "to mitigate the impact" of the project.[213]

In light of the proffers, the NPS and the NWPWCA came out in favor of the PMD rezoning and the William Center project. The land was going to be developed, or so it seemed, and Swain and Snyder both believed they had gotten the best possible deal. Swain was criticized for his stand, most aggressively by Jerry Russell, who urged in his Civil War Round Table Associates newsletter that the park service transfer Swain to a place where he would "not need to be sensitive to history." That prompted the NPS's Bearss to write Russell a three-page letter defending Swain against his "unwarranted attack."[214] None of it mattered, really. Even the preservationists agreed Stuart's Hill would be developed.

In the last week of January 1988, Hazel/Peterson's spokesman and public relations vice president Robert C. Kelly dropped by the park and casually informed park officials of a change of plans. The William Center project would now feature, on top of Stuart's Hill, the "William Center Mall," a 1.2-million square foot regional shopping plaza with five department stores.[215]

The story broke on January 28, 1988, when Hazel/Peterson filed a site plan with the county that included a mall built by the nation's leading mall builder, the Edward J. DeBartolo Corporation. DeBartolo was better known as the owner of the San Francisco 49ers National Football League team. This startling news blindsided everyone. "It was almost like reading, 'Hitler Invades Poland,' that's how shocking it was," said Brian Pohanka.[216]

Even Hazel/Peterson's strongest county boosters were surprised, not that it affected their unwavering support. Board Chairwoman Kathleen Seefeldt wondered about the impact of traffic. But the financial prospects for Prince William County looked dazzling.[217]

"It excites me in the sense that we're no longer going to stand in the shadow of

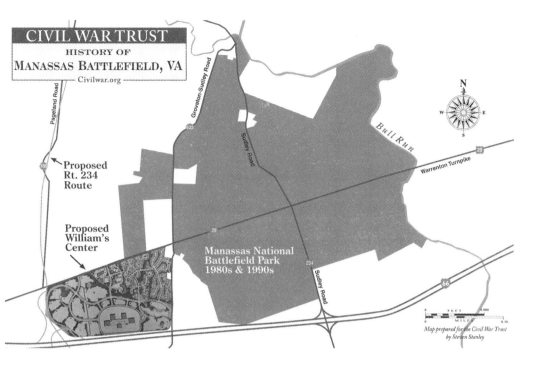

Pageland Road

Groveton–Sudley Road

Sudley Road

Bull Run

29

Warrenton Turnpike

Proposed
Rt. 234
Route

Proposed
William's
Center

Manassas National
Battlefield Park
1980s & 1990s

Sudley Road

234

66

Map prepared for the Civil War Trust
by Steven Stanley

Fairfax County," said supervisor Robert L. Cole.[218]

Other participants in the proffer negotiations felt deceived and were outraged. Swain felt Hazel/Peterson had been playing a "bait and switch game."[219] The mall idea was a bolt out of the blue, Hazel said, and did not become part of the project until the DeBartolo Company approached them with the proposal. The mall would bring office tenants, he said.[220] Adding the mall "seemed totally appropriate," Hazel recalled in 2017. "It was typically appropriate to build a retail mall and surround it with commercial development."[221]

But what about the proffers? It seemed as if all of the concessions to lessen the impact of the original project had been cast aside. The massive change of plans and the new project's sheer enormity sparked instant protest.

"We'll fight it with everything we've got," Snyder declared. "It would destroy western Prince William and it would destroy the battlefield."[222] But she had precious little ammunition. A mall was not excluded in the new zoning regulations for a planned mixed-use development zoning district. The county favored a privately financed project on private land. What was there to contest?

Washington Post columnist Jonathan Yardley cynically mocked Snyder's seemingly pitiful cry in the wilderness. "But, madam, right though you certainly are, your 'everything' is nothing," Yardley wrote. The supervisors were "hand in glove" with the developer. And developers, "with the cash and the clout," are the ones who own the country.[223]

But the tide of opposition was rising. Snyder's phone was ringing off the hook, and when Ed Wenzel called her, she complained bitterly about the Hazel/Peterson double-cross and said three different attorneys had left messages offering their help. Pohanka and Wenzel were busy helping organize the APCWS, which they had just helped co-found, but they were also active members with Snyder of NWPWCA.[224]

They decided to start a new organization to fight the mall and held the organizing meeting for the Save the Battlefield Coalition (SBC) on February 1. More than 100 local and national Civil War groups and other historical, conservation and preservation organizations soon joined.[225]

As for legal help, "you need to consider this attorney named Tersh Boasberg," Wenzel told Snyder. "Brian Pohanka and I saw him speak at a public hearing in Alexandria last November, and he was outstanding." Wenzel agreed to call Boasberg.

"Ah, so you want to save a battlefield," Boasberg said with dramatic flair when Wenzel called on February 2. "Well, let me tell you something. You happened to hit the right preservation lawyer because I named my son Jeb." Boasberg became the SBC attorney.[226]

Meanwhile on Capitol Hill, Congressman Mike Andrews saw the front-page news in *The Washington Post* and it struck a nerve. Days earlier, the Democrat from Houston had taken a tour of Manassas battlefield with historian Frank Vandiver. Andrews' office in the Cannon House Office Building was next to the office of Representative Robert Mrazek (D-N.Y.), a fellow Civil War buff.

Andrews walked into Mrazek's office and showed him the *Post* article. They contacted Snyder and offered support. The next step was not immediately ascertained, and there was no guarantee that any remedy was feasible.

"I remember talking to Rolland Swain," recalled Boasberg. "He said, 'No, I don't think you're going to win this one.' I said, 'Well, the odds are long.' And the odds were ridiculous against us."[227]

On February 5, 1988, after Prince William's supervisors said they would not review the proposed mall or conduct a public hearing, Snyder organized a meeting of her own. This was the "collective display of outrage" at the park visitor center. Bearss spoke, as did John Hennessy. A national treasure was at stake, Hennessy told the packed room, and if the mall was built, it would be "the greatest disaster to befall any of our Civil War sites in our lifetime."[228]

Despite working for the New York State Preservation Office in Albany, Hennessy became immersed "up to my ears" in the Virginia preservation battle with the full support of his superiors, who saw the relationship to preservation in their state.[229]

Snyder, casting aside health concerns, threw herself into this project like none before. Rising at 4 a.m., she entered her upstairs study, switched on her computer and pressed on with the fight long before the sun rose.[230] She fired off letters to Civil War Round Tables and anyone else who might have an interest, encouraging people to protest to their Congressional representatives. She wrote potential mall anchor stores, such as Bloomingdale's and J.C. Penney & Co., requesting they not open a store at William Center.

The SBC president was Betty Rankin, another local resident who gave her all. Snyder and Rankin were the two most prominent faces and voices of the SBC. To assist Boasberg and the other attorneys, coalition members patiently listened to hours of public hearing tapes for telling information and copied scores of planning documents. Many others, including Hennessy, plunged into the fight. "There were probably two dozen of us who were intimately involved with it and everybody spent hundreds of hours on that thing," Hennessy said. "It was writing background materials, reviewing documents, writing responses to documents, you know, all those sorts of things."[231]

Boasberg, meanwhile, enlisted the pro bono assistance of two high-powered Washington law firms. Shea & Gardner, with partner Benjamin Boley, handled the overall legal theories, while Beveridge & Diamond, experts in environmental law, represented the coalition on environmental issues, which became the focus of the preservationists' initial attack. The coalition filed suit against the project and demanded a temporary halt to any construction because of concerns of disturbing the streams and wetlands that were protected under the federal Clean Water Act.[232] The suit contended that at least 50 areas of wetlands existed on the property. How did they know?

"We had to do a little recon patrol through the middle of the Williams Center tract," recalled Wenzel. "They were looking for wetlands, and of course (Hazel/Peterson) had posted 'No Trespassing' signs all around that property. But (fellow SBC board member) Ray Wotring and I snuck onto the property on a Saturday and we went up the water course that flows through there, Young's Branch, taking pictures and marking aerial photographs."[233]

On February 17, Boasberg placed a call to Jody Powell, former press secretary to President Jimmy Carter, then a partner in the Ogilvy & Mather public relations firm. "I had met Jody Powell a few months before at some party, and I knew he was a great Civil War fan," Boasberg recalled. "I didn't know how much. So I called him up and I said, 'I have the keys to heaven for you. Would you like to hear how you're going to get there?'

"And he said, 'Yes, I would like to hear.'

"And I said, 'Okay, here's what you have to do. You've got to volunteer to help us organize the publicity, the whole PR campaign, for Annie Snyder.' Well, that was a big order. And I said, 'And you gotta do it free.'"

Powell, who had 10 ancestors in the Confederate army, agreed. "That was a great coup," Boasberg said, "Because he was absolutely fantastic. I mean without him, it would've been impossible."[234]

Powell tapped his vast network of media contacts, including Washington-bureau reporters from media outlets nationwide. Newspapers carried stories of the 'Third Battle of Manassas' for months, adding to the intense local coverage.

The Washington Post had a young reporter, John F. Harris, on the story. "He was gung-ho, a great reporter," Boasberg said. "He says, 'You'll never beat Til Hazel. Those guys have got too much on their side.' And I said, *'You just watch us.'* So, he was fascinated as this battle went on, and wrote about it virtually every week. And that was terrific coverage." (Harris became the *Post*'s national editor before co-founding Politico.com.)[235]

Powell arranged for powerful Representative Morris Udall (D-Ariz.) to tour the Manassas battlefield in late March. Pohanka, crisply dressed in a Union officer's uniform, joined Snyder to help lead the tour.[236] Soon, other influential organizations publicly opposed the project, first the National Parks and Conservation Association and then the National Trust for Historic Preservation.[237]

Andrews and Mrazek, meanwhile, consulted with Boasberg and decided the best strategy was to attack the project on its plan to create a new interchange for Interstate 66. The Congressmen wrote Transportation Secretary James Burnley asking him to block the interchange on the grounds that federal law prevented construction projects adversely affecting historic sites or parkland. Burnley agreed to look into it.

But the young Congressmen wanted to take more drastic action. They wanted the government to condemn the land and take it. "Personally, I think that's the approach we should pursue over the long term," Mrazek said at the time. "I can't predict the success of that and can't say it would be approved." The odds would be long, he acknowledged.[238]

Hazel/Peterson hired a Spotsylvania historian, Dr. James A. Schaefer, to conduct a historical review of the tract. Recalled Hazel, "He looked it all over for a week or two and said, 'I don't think this has any real connection to Second Battle of Manassas. I'm in favor of what you're doing.'"[239]

But when Schaefer became aware of the mall after reading a protest letter by Wenzel to the editor of the Fredericksburg *Free-Lance Star*, he became an opponent, expressing a "keen sense of betrayal" over the switch. Schaefer wrote to the coalition that he would "be pleased to assist in the struggle to prevent this outrage against our national heritage."[240]

The matter of whether any fighting occurred at Stuart's missed the point, the preservationists argued. "What made the William Center project so horrific and so objectionable to Civil War folks, besides the fact that the tract had Lee's headquarters, was that it occupied the entire southwest quadrant of the intersection of Lee Highway and Groveton Road, which is at the very center of the Second Manassas battlefield," recalled Wenzel. "Can you imagine the impact on the park with that entire quarter of the pie densely developed with residential and commercial development, spewing people and traffic into the heart of the battlefield?"[241]

Shea & Gardner kept up the pressure, questioning the legality of the project and imploring Secretary of the Interior Donald P. Hodel in a letter, hand-delivered on March 3, to intervene and stop the project. The following day, the law firm sent a letter to the director of the Prince William County Department of Development Administration, insisting that the preliminary site plan be disapproved.[242]

On March 23, 1988, Hodel expressed his concerns about the mall and particularly the increased traffic, echoing NPS Director William Penn Mott's concerns. However, Hodel declined to take a firm position or intervene.[243] Mott and Hodel met with county, state and federal officials, the state highway department, Hazel/Peterson, Congressional representatives and others to negotiate a compromise.

Mall opponents received another boost on April 13 when the *Potomac News*, a Prince William County paper, reported that its telephone poll of Virginians revealed that 57 percent of respondents favored a federal government takeover of the land, with 19 percent opposed.[244] The poll was the first of many on Civil War battlefield preservation issues conducted by Brad Coker, a young pollster, and his company, Mason-Dixon Polling and Research, still assists the Trust today.[245]

How much did it help that mall opponents were winning the public relations battle? On April 28, 1988, Hodel and Mott announced they had reached a compromise with Hazel/Peterson. The mall would be relocated to a lower elevation, making it less visible from the battlefield park. A portion of Stuart's Hill would feature park service interpretive displays (flanked by two-story buildings). The NPS would support building a much-needed highway bypass around the park with a major interchange for William Center. But the Save the Battlefield Coalition had been excluded from negotiations. Snyder, Rankin and other SBC leaders were outraged. Subsequent meetings that included the coalition produced little, and the SBC eventually formally opposed the plan.[246]

Mrazek took a new, more aggressive approach. In early April, he slipped language into a supplemental appropriations bill for the U.S. Department of Transportation that prohibited federal funds from being used to plan, design, or construct arteries into or out of any development within the three federal highways that surrounded the William Center tract.

"Lo and behold, it passed scrutiny," Mrazek recalled. "You know, there's a lot of language in an appropriations bill. This one got away. And when it became law, it raised a big ruckus. Stan Parris (R-Va.) took the floor and raged about the fact that we had done this end run and he was going to work to see it overturned, and that's not the way Congress was supposed to do its work." The measure still had to face Senate consideration, but "it made clear that we had serious intentions to stop" the project, Mrazek said.[247]

On May 4, hundreds filled the Stonewall Jackson High School auditorium in Prince William County to oppose the project in a meeting called by county officials. That same day, Andrews and Mrazek introduced H.R. 4526, a bill to require the federal government purchase the entire William Center tract for the Manassas National Battlefield Park.

"We're optimistic, but we can only do our best," Mrazek said at a press conference. "We're junior members and on the other side are some very powerful members and a very powerful developer."[248]

The Hazel/Peterson companies responded with iron-fisted resolve. "We are determined to develop that piece of property," said company spokesman Kelly. "We're not interested in selling it. We've been developing in Northern Virginia for 25 years and we will be developing here for 25 more."[249]

Andrews and Mrazek needed 218 co-sponsors for a hearing. By late afternoon, they had more than 50, and soon had more than enough. "I remember going to Newt Gingrich (R-Ga.) at the time and Newt signing on to the legislation and going to Bob Dornan (R-Ca.), who had the office on the other side of me, a very conservative Republican, and he signed on," Mrazek recalled. "And once we started getting Republicans... we really started to build a bipartisan consensus that this was something important, that we needed to do this to protect the battlefield."[250]

But under H.R. 4526, protection would not be immediate. Even if the bill passed, Congress would have to allocate money for the purchase. The 542-acre tract was said to be worth more than $70 million, even if Hazel paid only about $12 million for it three years earlier.

"Sixty to seventy million? That would be quite a profit for three years. I don't know if a federal judge would go for that," Mrazek said at the time.[251]

Hazel/Peterson had sold about 30 acres at the eastern side of the tract to a home builder, NV Homes (now NVR, Inc.) owner Dwight Schar. "We sold him the part closer to the battlefield for residential use because we were using that as a buffer between the commercial development and the battlefield," Hazel recalled.[252]

On May 6, the county issued permits to allow road work for William Center. The sound of bulldozers and earthmovers began to fill the air near Stuart's Hill. As Schar began constructing roads for his residential development, Hazel/Peterson began laying sewer lines under Interstate 66 to extend to the tract. Four days later, Snyder sent a letter to Prince William County Executive Robert Noe Jr., asking him to "stop the bulldozers" while the issue was debated.[253]

Noe replied: "You ask something we simply cannot do: You ask the County to 'stop the bulldozers' at William Center while discussions are under way. The County cannot revoke permits lawfully issued, and will not ask Hazel-Peterson to give up the benefits those permits confer."[254]

Around that time, Snyder received a call from Patrick Brennan, a Chicago music producer who volunteered to help in the fight. She talked about the importance of the battle for 15 minutes before he could say much of anything. "I finally told her I was already on board, but I wasn't sure how I could be helpful," Brennan recalled.[255]

"What do you do for a living?" Snyder asked.

"I'm a musician and recording studio owner, and I run a music production company that writes jingles and TV music," Brennan said.

"Oh, you must know people in Hollywood," she replied.

"Well, I'm in Chicago," he said. Snyder persisted. He had to know someone in Hollywood, she said. Brennan thought it wouldn't be that hard to make a few cold calls. He agreed to try. A few days later, he happened to see a photo of actor Charlton Heston at Gettysburg, peering across the field of Pickett's Charge. Brennan left a message with Heston's agent and a few days later, the in-a-hurry, all-business agent called back. Brennan gave his spiel.[257]

"When I finished, he asked why I had thought of Mr. Heston." Brennan recalled. "I described the picture I saw." Brennan sent the agent the SBC press packet Snyder had provided. When Brennan called Snyder to report that he had reached Heston's agent, "of course, she started crying," he recalled. "I discovered she cried a lot." Hearing that Brennan was a liberal, she began calling him "my little Communist."[258]

A personal letter from Heston, dated May 18, 1988, arrived in Brennan's mail. "The Civil War is the watershed experience," the actor wrote. "The preservation of the ground where it happened is vital. To put a shopping center where Manassas was fought demeans the men who died there. Please see this doesn't happen."[259]

Brennan called Snyder and read her the letter. This time, she *"really* cried," he recalled. They released Heston's letter and it became news. When Jackie Judd of ABC News interviewed Brennan, she told him the entire California delegation had changed their votes to support federal acquisition because Heston's letter had persuaded his old friend, President Ronald Reagan.[260]

At the tract, trees and bushes fell before bulldozer blades as red earth was turned. The first wide avenue was cut from Groveton Road. Then on May 25, Representative Frank Wolf (R-Va.), trumped Andrews and Mrazek by introducing even bolder legislation, H.R. 4691, to allow the government to take immediate possession through a rarely used "legislative taking," compensating land owners afterward. The maneuver had been used three times before; twice to save redwood trees in California to establish Redwood National Park, and once to acquire land across the Potomac River from Mount Vernon being used for an amusement park.[261]

Andrews and Mrazek enthusiastically supported Wolf's measure, as did Parris, despite being known as a close Hazel ally. Staunchly opposed, Interior Secretary Hodel fired off a letter to Capitol Hill that same day saying Wolf's bill was "not the answer" and his compromise plan should be adopted. Hodel attacked Democratic (but not Republican) supporters of Wolf's bill by sending blistering letters to their hometown papers. "Andrews ought to be ashamed of himself because he is playing politics with the future of Manassas Battlefield" simply "to gain media attention," read Hodel's letter in the May 27 *Houston Chronicle.*

By June, Hazel/Peterson recognized it was losing the public relations battle. "Frankly, we can't get through the fog of the emotional reporting on this issue," complained spokesman Kelly. Nevertheless, the developers counterattacked launching a public relations and lobbying blitz, mailing literature explaining the William Center project and extolling its economic virtues to 50,000 residents in Prince William County and all 535 members of the House and Senate. Hazel took the fight to Capitol Hill, visiting key members of Congress, including Andrews and Mrazek.[262]

"Til Hazel came to our office with his staff and with a big three-dimensional model of his project," Mrazek recalled. "And one of his aides, with a pointer, showed where everything was going to go, and that Lee's headquarters on the battlefield was going to be protected. It would have been protected, except that it would have been surrounded by a parking lot."

Mrazek was self-deprecating, acknowledging he was a junior member of Congress. "But I just want you to know that I'm going to continue to oppose you," he said. Hazel chuckled, Mrazek recalled, and in a cordial, gentlemanly fashion said, "Well, you just go ahead and do what you have to do."[263]

On June 21, 1988, the House Subcommittee on Parks and Public Lands held a hearing on the two bills. Snyder was among those who testified. "The disgrace is not only that the citizens of Prince William County and of the nation are victims of bait-and-switch tactics by an unscrupulous developer, but that our local governing body condones it, willingly denying due process to the people they represent," she said. Thankfully, it was no longer a local issue, she said, and "it is reassuring to know that Congress will determine what shall be done in the national interest."[264]

As Jody Powell began his brief remarks, Snyder sat in the first row, just behind him. Television cameras focused on him also captured her. "On that little hill, Mr. Chairman, history is palpable," Powell said. "You can see it and feel it, a blood-soaked piece of Virginia countryside." Tears filled Snyder's blue eyes, streamed down her cheeks and rolled past her quivering lower lip, all captured on camera and broadcast to the nation.[265] The moment was so vivid, when Snyder's old friends are asked about her today (she died in 2002), they almost always first recall the moment she cried in that Congressional hearing.

On July 12, preservationists scored another victory when the Senate approved legislation to bar an Interstate 66 interchange at William Center.[266] Four days later, on a hot and humid Saturday, with temperatures soaring to more than 100 degrees, mall opponents held a massive rally at the battlefield park. More than 5,000 people attended, among them Senator John Warner (R-Va.), who was moved by the show of support for the park and promised to introduce legislation in the Senate to save the Stuart's Hill part of the tract.[267]

Recalled Hazel: "Snyder and the TV cameras were whipping up the whole big uproar, and they whipped it up to a fever pitch and got the Senate and Congress all wound up, and they ended up with the taking thing." Sometime that summer, Hazel went to Capitol Hill and visited then- Representative Richard Cheney (R-Wyo.), who told him the game was up. "Dick Cheney put it all in context when he told me the day I visited with him that it had gotten so much publicity and so much TV coverage, there wasn't anything they could about it," Hazel recalled.[268]

By then, however, construction was well underway and progressing at a fast pace. "By the summer of 1988, I had accepted the fact that ultimately we would be prohibited from developing," Hazel recalled. "Accordingly, I pressed an effort to begin development and pressure the citizens and government to do what they intended to do without delay. By that time, it was obvious that the effort would include acquisition by the feds and delay was not in our best interest."[269]

Each day brought sounds of heavy equipment and evidence of new work. On June 23, neighbor Irma Peterson began keeping a construction journal. She documented the ongoing work as crews erected floodlights and labored deep into the night, grading land and using explosives to blast a sewer tunnel under Interstate 66.

Monday, June 27: "Working in tunnel 5 p.m.—3 a.m. Three workers. Blasting on during day."

Tuesday, June 28: "Working back in woods."

Wednesday, June 29: "Laying curbs and blacktop, also seeding, bulldozing back in woods."

On July 11, she counted 27 dump trucks entering the tract in a little over an hour as heavy grading progressed. In early August, she recorded that blasting at the tunnel continued past 5 p.m. On August 9, drilling started at 6 a.m. They were still working at 11:45 p.m., she noted.[270]

"While Congress piddles, Rome burns," Snyder complained to the *Washington Times*. Her acerbic comment was a bit too rough even for her own coalition's attorneys. Boasberg associate Charlie Lord sought to distance the coalition from Snyder's remarks, noting that she "had not been well," the *Times* reported. Snyder, in a subsequent interview, said she was "depressed" with how the struggle was going.[271]

Other animosities surfaced in the stress of the intense struggle. Hennessy was in the lobby of the park visitor center with Pohanka one day at the height of the battle. "Brian was introduced to Rolland Swain, the superintendent, a very mild-mannered kind of guy, and (Brian) refused to take his hand," Hennessy said. Pohanka thought the NPS was missing the mark. "I'd never seen anything like that," Hennessy said. "But Brian was just as intense as could be, and no one believed more deeply."[272]

Senator Warner's proposed compromise, stipulating as it did that at least the Stuart's Hill portion of the tract be saved, put him on the side of preservationists. That conversion helped sway others. The fight was almost over. On August 10, after a four-hour debate during which liberals and a small group of conservatives attacked the legislation, the House voted 307-98 to approve H.R. 4526, the bill introduced by Andrews and Mrazek, amended to include Wolf's language for an outright legislative taking. The measure moved to the Senate, where Senator Dale Bumpers (D-Ark.), chairman of the Senate Subcommittee on Public Lands, National Parks and Forests, championed the cause.[273]

The key Virginia players paraded before Bumpers' subcommittee on September 8 to testify. Hazel railed against "no growth" opponents and stressed the $23 million in expected tax benefits, calling William Center a "quality project" that would "make a little money on the way." Hazel said the Interior Department's compromise plan was a "win-win." Hodel also opposed the taking and said he would recommend that President Reagan veto the measure.

Dr. James M. McPherson testified, invited by Bumpers, who had just read McPherson's Pulitzer Prize-winning history of the war, Battle Cry of Freedom: The Civil War Era, published in 1988. McPherson said Stuart's Hill had "the same kind of historical significance as Seminary Ridge does." Two Confederate field hospitals had stood on this land, he said, and "probably hundreds of Confederates and some Union soldiers [were] buried on this property." Snyder testified, presenting a petition signed by 75,000 people.[274]

Bumpers's bill made it through committee, setting the stage for one of the most dramatic moments of the struggle. On the evening of October 7, in the final hours of the 100th Congress, as senators returned to the Capitol after dinner, Bumpers rose on the Senate floor to debate the legislation with a lesson in history.

Bumpers spoke of how Longstreet deployed all 30,000 of his men in the woods below Stuart's Hill to prepare for the great counterattack on the third day of Second Manassas. The Arkansas senator's sense of drama rivaled the performances by the best Civil War battlefield guides.

"You go down there right now and you will see where Longstreet had his men deployed behind all those trees down there . . ." Bumpers said, using maps to illustrate his remarks. He did not want take his grandson to the park "10 years from now" and try to tell him about the battle in the face of a sea of development. Bumpers surmised how that might go.

"He says, 'Well, Grandpa, wasn't General Lee in control of this war here? Didn't he command the Confederate troops?'"

"Yes, he did."

"Well, where was he?"

"He [was] up there where that shopping mall is."[275]

Recalled Mrazek: "I remember walking over there and watching the debate. And he was so eloquent. He was magnificent. And he won."[276]

When Senator James A. McClure (R-Idaho) sought to undercut support, his remarks had the opposite effect. "There is not a single battlefield free" from the pressures of development, McClure told his fellow legislators. The vote was 50-25 in favor of legislative taking.[277]

To avoid a presidential veto, Andrews had the bill attached to a much-larger tax bill, but that was no guarantee of success. House and Senate conferees began wrangling not over the legislative taking, but elements of the tax bill. On the eve of adjournment, negotiations broke down, but at 1 a.m. on October 22, 1988, the bill passed. It had made it through Congress "with the legislative equivalent of seconds to play," wrote Harris in *The Washington Post.*[278]

That did not stop construction. That same day, workers labored all day on Schar's first three homes. They worked on the 23rd, a Sunday, and each day the following week, including a half day Saturday. On November 2, when the bill arrived at the White House, Peterson wrote in her construction log: "Chopping trees along Groveton Road . . . Pumping water out of one of the house basements."[279]

On November 7, 1988, as the bill awaited presidential consideration, Peterson noted heavy bulldozing and more tree cutting. "John Machol from the Corps of Engineers came out, took pictures but said nothing could be done," she wrote. The work continued almost right up to the moment President Reagan signed the bill on November 10. Indeed, Peterson's log reported that day that a "light work force" was still working on the three homes, even though the structures would soon be removed.[280]

Two days later, Snyder, Boasberg and about 100 followers joined in a victory gathering on the William Center tract. It was emotional for all of them to finally walk around the land that Hazel/Peterson's burly guards had blocked access to throughout the year. But overhead, the engine of a small plane droned as it circled Stuart's Hill again and again, dragging a banner that read: "FEDERAL TAKING OF PRIVATE LAND—UNAMERICAN."[281]

"I didn't do that," Hazel recalled. "I was very pleased. What happened is the federal government made us an offer, we contested it, it was adjudicated in the Court of Claims and within a week or two after the adjudication, we got the check. It was very healthy. We were well paid.

"The day we got the check, my wife and I were at the airport on our way for a week or two in Europe. We were going to tour up in the Baltics. And I got a call from Milt, who had gotten the check that day, and all I could think of was how nice it was to celebrate that going to Europe—to make a deal that pays off like that."

Hazel/Peterson and its associates received about $135 million from the federal government for the land, almost twice the anticipated amount, pushing the definition of "staggering." Even preservationists, in celebrating the victory, had to admit that the price came with quite a hangover.[282]

The land cost almost $250,000 an acre, compared to an average of about $6,630 an acre paid by the Civil War Trust and its forerunner organizations for 42,500 acres from 1988 through 2015. With so much actual battlefield land to save, today's Civil War Trust focuses almost exclusively on buying land where fighting occurred.[283]

Stuart's Hill is now part of the Manassas National Battlefield Park, but not on the tour. The park's administrative headquarters, Stuart's Hill Center, is on the hill itself. On the eastern side, the NPS removed Schar's three homes, but retained the road and created a picnic area.

"I was in there a couple of months ago," Hazel said in February 2017. "My wife and I went down and walked the Stonewall Jackson positions at Second Manassas and ended up walking over and seeing the land that we bought. Really, most of it has been abandoned. The park service has a picnic ground back there where Dwight built the roads that were going to serve his subdivision. They put picnic benches back there and the rest of it is growing up in bushes."

The legislative taking at Manassas would have profound implications on the movement. Preservation-minded leaders in Washington, energized by the victory but unhappy with the cost, began talking about protecting battlefields without legislative takings.

Preservationists learned invaluable lessons, particularly about using the vast web of federal environmental, transportation and historic preservation laws to make them work the way they were designed to work, and how to use them to thwart or slow developments.

A few years after the fight, Brennan, the Chicago music producer, was visiting the battlefield and dropped by Snyder's farm. "Someone answered the door and I explained who I was," Brennan recalled. "He went upstairs and I heard Annie laugh really loudly. When she bounded down the stairs and saw me, she started crying and said, 'How's my little Communist?'"[284] ★

CHAPTER

FIVE

Land-Buying Spree at Brandy Station

N 1984, Bud Hall was promoted and transferred from the Kansas City FBI field office to headquarters in Washington, D.C. He thought his new position as a unit chief in the Organized Crime Section might require even longer hours than his field office work, where he was on the job nearly every weekend as the organized crime and surveillance supervisor. "When mob guys were out and around, we were out and around," Hall recalled.[285]

Hall was startled and delighted to learn that in Washington, everyone left headquarters at 5 p.m. Friday with no thought of returning until Monday morning. It was almost as if you were not allowed to work on the weekends. Though surprised, he had no intention of bucking the system.

With weekends free, and living in the heart of Civil War country, Hall indulged his passion for history, especially that made by the legendary Confederate cavalry commander General J.E.B. Stuart. He began spending many weekends at Brandy Station in Culpeper County, Virginia.

Hall was the eighth child born to Cluster and Mary Elizabeth Hall. His mother died while giving birth to him. He grew up on a hard-scrabble cotton farm in Neshoba County, Mississippi, a place that gained national infamy when three civil rights workers were murdered there during "Freedom Summer" of 1964.[286]

What the Hall family lacked in material wealth, it made up in heritage. His great-grandfather, Charles Harold Hall, was a sergeant in Barksdale's Brigade and his photograph hung on the wall with photos of Lee, Jackson and Stuart.

Fascinated by his great-grandfather—whose likeness glowered from above the mantle—Hall saw a "tough-looking dude" who was every bit as tough in real life. Charles Hall was shot and wounded on the second day at Gettysburg when Barksdale's Brigade charged the Peach Orchard. Captured and imprisoned at Fort Delaware, he escaped, rejoined his unit and survived the war, surrendering at Appomattox. Hall asked his father about Sgt. Hall, but Cluster Hall offered little in response. A farmer of few words, Cluster Hall nevertheless was a serious reader whose bookshelf included Lee's Lieutenants and R.E. Lee, both by Douglas Southall Freeman, and both of which Bud Hall read as a teenager. Stuart became his hero.[287]

To Hall, Mississippi was a place from which to escape. He joined the Marine Corps and spent 16 months in Vietnam in 1965-66. He served as a machine gun patrol leader in the more-dangerous northern part of South Vietnam. Shaken and emotionally battered, Hall came home with a deep abhorrence of war, and a profound respect for those common Americans in all wars—young men whose sense of duty compelled them to risk all and sacrifice life itself in the butchery of combat.[288]

On Hall's first trip to Brandy Station in 1984, he motored south in his Chevy El Camino on U.S. 29/15, the James Madison Highway, until suburban development finally gave way to the rural countryside of northern Virginia, with its broad, green, rolling plains spreading west toward the Blue Ridge. He passed through the battlefield without knowing it and pulled into the small, unincorporated town of Brandy Station, a stop on the Orange and Alexandria Railroad during the war. The tracks belong now to Norfolk Southern and the trains still pass, but no longer stop.

Nothing read "Brandy Station Battlefield," but just west of town, on the two-lane Brandy Road—the old road to Culpeper—he saw a lone Virginia state historical marker.[289] "Opening of Gettysburg Campaign," the title said, followed by, "On this plain Lee reviewed his cavalry, June 8, 1863. The next day the cavalry battle of Brandy Station was fought. On June 10, Ewell's corps, from its camp near here, began the march to Pennsylvania."[290]

But where was the battlefield? "I had a hard time finding it," Hall recalled 30 years later. He had maps—he had been a map instructor his final year in the Marine Corps. The battle was known by the Confederates as the Battle of Fleetwood Hill, and Hall's first aim was to find Fleetwood Hill itself. The hill was marked on maps, but he was not finding it. He looked around in despair. He didn't observe *any* notable hills. "I guess I was expecting to see Mt. Vesuvius," he recalled. "I drove around for some time, looking for the battlefield."[291]

Hall spotted an elderly man, stopped and introduced himself to Ray Bailey, a grocery store proprietor. "Where is Fleetwood Hill?" Hall asked.[292]

"You see that over there, son? That's Fleetwood Hill," Bailey said, pointing to a modest rise of land.[293]

"It was not very impressive," Hall recalled."[294] Fleetwood Hill stretches north and south for about two miles between the Rappahannock River and Culpeper. All of the ridge was camped on and fought over at one point or another during the war, but the southern section of the hill is particularly historic. The old Carolina Road—a primary artery during the Civil War (but a tight, two-lane road today)—crosses the hill near its southern terminus, providing easy access to the open land at the top of the hill and on its gentle slopes.

Hall drove the road to the crest and found an old stone monument—just what he was looking for. It was atop an embankment on the south side of the road. A set of nine stone steps led up the earthen bank to the memorial.[295]

"Battle Of Brandy Station," the monument's plaque says. "This is Fleetwood Hill. The crucial position finally occupied by the Confederates." The monument was dedicated in 1926 by the United Daughters of the Confederacy.[296]

The Battle of Brandy Station, fought in the hills and hollows just east of the town on June 9, 1863, was the Civil War's largest cavalry battle, with 12,000 Union soldiers, mostly horsemen, in a spectacle of combat with Stuart's 9,500 Confederate troopers. A month after crushing the Army of the Potomac in a decisive victory at Chancellorsville, Lee was on the move, massing his Army of Northern Virginia in Culpeper County. General Joseph Hooker, the Union commander at this point, knew Lee was up to something and sent the Union cavalry under General Alfred Pleasonton, with some supporting infantry, toward Culpeper. Lee ordered Stuart's cavalry to take positions along the Rappahannock River, just east of Brandy Station, to protect the army and to shield its march to the Shenandoah Valley, where he would head north and invade Pennsylvania. It was the first move of the Gettysburg campaign.

Before dawn on June 9, the Yankees attacked across the Rappahannock River and caught Stuart's men by surprise. It nearly cost Stuart the battle. For 10 hours, the mounted fighting raged across a broad expanse of more than 4,000 acres. As the battle reached a climax with chaotic charges and countercharges across Fleetwood Hill, Stuart's brilliant generalship helped save the day for the Confederates. They held the hill. The dashing Virginian had won again. Union forces withdrew back across the river. But the aura of superiority Stuart and his men gained during the war's first two years had all but disappeared. The Union cavalry proved at Brandy Station that it was a capable and fierce fighting force.

Hall's first visit whet his appetite. The battlefield was all but unmarked, but it was pristine. It became his passion. He began to study every aspect of the battle. He hunted for maps, battle accounts, and wartime photographs. Having overcome his brief, initial confusion, Hall found his bearings and used his analytical skills to reconcile primary source accounts with battle maps. He drew new maps as he obsessively sorted out the movements and compiled the details of this complex, wide-ranging, mounted battle in which topography played such an important role.[297]

The more he learned, the closer he became to the land and its history. He assembled a storehouse of knowledge—not only the movement of the forces, but the personal stories of the troopers who fought there. Starting with Ray Bailey, Hall made a point of introducing himself to local residents. He developed a network of friends who informed him of local happenings, and came to know most of the farmers who spent their lives cultivating land once the domain of antebellum Virginia plantations.

Hall discovered the significance of little-known details of the battle, such as the fighting on Yew Ridge, and how Union General John Buford, upon being stymied in his initial assaults, shifted his point of attack toward a stone wall that divided two farms about a mile from the ridge. His mounted horsemen attacked dismounted Confederate horsemen behind the wall time and again, with human and equine casualties piling up on the blood-soaked ground before the rock barrier. One fourth of the men killed in the battle fell near the stone wall. Some are still buried there.[298]

At Brandy Station, about 20,000 soldiers clashed in a spectacle of combat that harkened back to the Middle Ages, with slashing sabers glinting in the sunlight as mounted men rode wild-eyed horses galloping headlong toward each other. The swirling fury of eye-to-eye combat at Brandy Station was succinctly if gruesomely illuminated by the words of New Jersey officer Thomas Kitchen: "My sabre took him just in the neck . . . and the blood gushed out in a black-looking stream."[299]

For two years, Hall roamed the farms and fields of the battlefield with unbounded joy, exploring every hill and hollow with a sense of discovery and fascination. Then came the fateful run through the woods at Chantilly in mid-1986 when he discovered the Kearny and Stevens monuments. That fight, which consumed his weekends and sapped his energy, had trampled his free-spirited Civil War pastime. But development was not yet an issue at Brandy Station and Hall was thankful for that.

"I had no expectation that there would ever be a threat down there," Hall recalled. "It was too far away. There was this little Podunk airport there, but you would never see an airplane take off or land. I couldn't figure out for the life of me why an airport was there. So, I wasn't worried about the airport even."[300]

Hall's idyllic relationship with Brandy Station began to change in November 1987, when a local farmer told him, "Bud, I've sold my farm to a fellow from California." The 500-acre farm was just north and west of St. James Church, the center of the battlefield and its bloodiest ground. The famous stone wall is on the farm.

The sale of the farm to Lee Sammis and his wife, Joan, didn't raise red flags with Hall. Wealthy, out-of-state folks often bought picturesque northern Virginia farms in the area. Hall told Pohanka about the sale, who reported the news to the APCWS board during the meeting of January 16, 1988, and promised to stay on top of any developments.[301]

But when Sammis and his wife bought a contiguous 500-acre farm on the battlefield on February 11, 1988, Hall's investigative senses heightened, even more so upon discovering Sammis was a major developer—not only in California, but the Washington area.[302]

Development at Brandy Station? How could this happen, when suburbia was still two counties and 35 miles away? Hall soon learned that Sammis had purposely hopscotched over Fauquier County, whose many wealthy horse farm owners had

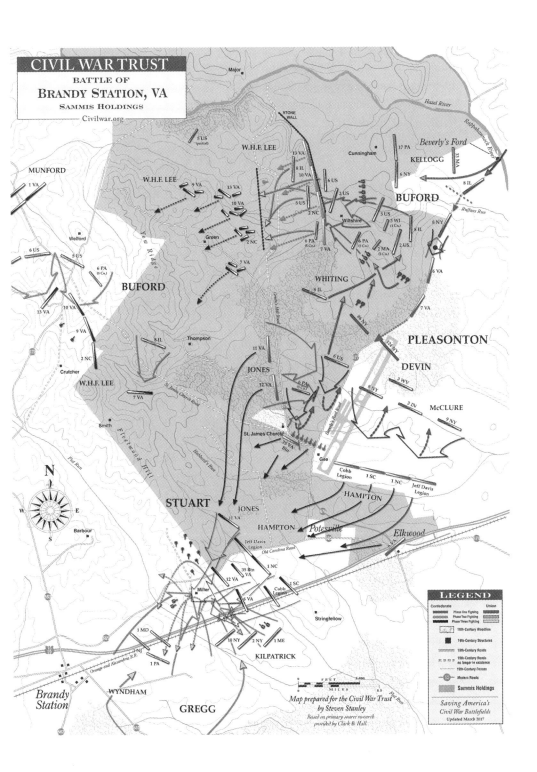

CIVIL WAR TRUST
BATTLE OF
BRANDY STATION, VA
SAMMIS HOLDINGS
Civilwar.org

already put into place restrictive development standards that Culpeper County did not have in its comprehensive plan.[303]

The timing could not have been worse for Hall. In Washington, he was deeply immersed in investigating the Iran-Contra scandal. In January 1987, Congress had formed a criminal investigative agency, the Office of Special Investigations, and hired Hall away from the FBI to help run it. The staff of 21 was made up mostly of FBI, CIA and Secret Service agents. "I was number two in that office," Hall said. "And in 1987, I was appointed chief investigator of the 'Select Committee To Investigate Covert Arms Transactions with Iran,'" otherwise known as Iran-Contra.[304]

At Pohanka's invitation, Hall appeared before the APCWS board at its next meeting on May 15, 1988, its fourth board meeting. He brought maps showing farm boundaries on the battlefield and outlined the impending threat. He spoke eloquently about the battlefield, his work, and the relationships he had with local farmers. The presentation was so impressive, board members broke out in "hearty applause" once he was done. Near the end of a four-hour meeting, they approved adding Hall to the board as a "welcomed addition."[305]

Hall told the group he had arranged to meet Sammis on the battlefield on May 30. Sammis was joined by his son-in-law, G. Scott Gayner, the project manager. Hall explained he was there on behalf of the APCWS board and that the land Sammis owned was in the heart of the Brandy Station battlefield. He said the organization wanted to know his plans and wanted to work with Sammis to preserve as much as possible.

"Well, I'm going to farm the property," Sammis said.

"Mr. Sammis, you didn't come here from California to buy these acres to farm them," Hall replied. "Give us a little credit."

"I know you people," Sammis sharply replied. "I've had trouble with you people before." Sammis had battled with Native American preservationists on a California development project.[306] Sammis finally allowed that he hoped to build half-million-dollar "country estates" for horse owners. At one point, he asked Hall what the APCWS would think if he named the project "Brandy Station."

"I must have given him a quick and vicious look as he immediately said, 'I thought so,'" recalled Hall.[307]

The conversation was edgy but not overtly hostile, with both men emphasizing that they wanted to work together. "Bottom line: I didn't like him and I trusted him less, but we left the session howling each other's praises," Hall reported to APCWS Vice President Krick in a letter. "I'm going to write him a nice letter on APCWS letterhead and stay in close touch . . . I left with the distinct impression he is fearful of our clout; so we'll exploit that a little."[308]

On the heels of Hall's meeting with Sammis came the 125th anniversary of the battle of Brandy Station on June 9. The day before, the *Culpeper Star-Exponent* published Hall's letter to the editor—one of his first public statements about an impending crisis. No one, including Sammis, had said a thing about developing land on the battlefield. But Hall wrote: "It is clear the future of the Brandy Station Battlefield is in serious jeopardy." He asked readers to write their elected officials and urge them to save the battlefield. But he took a conciliatory tone, noting that discussions were taking place with developers and property owners to save portions of the historic site.[309]

The following month, *The Culpeper News* published a front-page feature on the APCWS. Hall said the organization wanted to save the pristine battlefield, but accomplish it through cooperative efforts with local government and developers. "We're not interested in fights," Hall said. "We've had enough fights."[310]

As Sammis bought more and more land, the situation become ominous to Hall. On July 21 came news that Sammis bought the Presque Isle Farm, known locally as the Willis Farm, a state-of-the-art dairy farm with more than 1,500 acres on the battlefield, for $4.6 million.[311]

A resident of Newport Beach, California, the ambitious Sammis had opened a satellite office in northern Virginia in 1981 and in seven years became a leading developer of Washington area office and business parks. In 1988, he was the 14th-largest developer in the United States, and the 65 employees of Lee Sammis Associates in Virginia managed 13 active office and business park projects: two in Reston, two in Chantilly, two in Herndon, three in suburban Maryland, and one each in Dale City, Manassas, Richmond and Sterling.[312]

One of Hall's first preservation efforts at Brandy Station, in July 1988, was to seek official recognition of Brandy Station battlefield for its historic significance. Hall spoke before the Culpeper County Planning Commission, which was more receptive to preservation efforts than the Board of Supervisors. At Hall's urging, planning commissioners asked the county staff to consider a historic overlay district, though nothing came of it.[313]

On August 2, 1988, Hall appeared before the Culpeper County Board of Supervisors to speak on behalf of the APCWS about preserving the battlefield. As Hall described the battle and the need to save the land, the supervisor closest to the speaker's podium glowered at him the entire time, he recalled.

That year, a gypsy moth invasion was big news throughout northern Virginia. "As surely as the gypsy moth hordes are today moving south and devouring our vegetation, then just as surely the bulldozers are also moving south from Fairfax County," Hall said at the hearing. "And please hear this: These instruments of development are now poised at the entrance of this battlefield."[315]

In September, Sammis paid $4.1 million for 600 acres comprising the Spillman farm, which had not changed hands in more than 60 years. Now Sammis owned more than 3,100 acres on or near the battlefield and his rapport with the preservationists had deteriorated from tenuous to hostile.[316]

On October 24, Hall was twice denied permission to take a group from the Friends of Culpeper on a tour of the battlefield on land owned by Sammis. Five days later, Don Stockton, a local resident who was keeping a detailed diary of ongoing events, took a flight over the area. Stockton had always wanted to see the battlefield from the sky. He was stunned.

"I noticed a new road being bulldozed on land to the west of the runway" of nearby Culpeper Regional Airport," Stockton wrote in his diary for October 29, 1988. "No wonder Sammis wouldn't let us tour the property."[317]

Hall had seen the deep construction gouge during one of his unauthorized visits. It cut across the top of Yew Ridge, not far from the stone wall that Buford's troopers had charged. Hall found no permits for the work and complained to the county. A county planner responded that it was a common, honest mistake and that Hall was blowing the situation out of proportion.[318]

To Hall, the surprise appearance of the road was a replay of the dead-of-night construction of four-lane Monument Drive just a few feet from the Kearny and Stevens memorials. "I'd seen this before, okay?" he recalled. "And so then it was war to the knife."[319] Except the only recourse seemed to be to call the media and try to drum up support. "This is a rapidly deteriorating situation," Hall told the *Richmond Times-Dispatch*.[320]

Gayner, the project manager, dismissed the brewing controversy, asserting that the new road restored an existing farm lane, a claim Hall hotly disputed. Gayner said the only plans for the land were for farming. "We've expressed our cooperation to that group," he said, "All we've gotten back is a lot of grief."[321]

On November 2, the same day Congress sent the William Center taking legislation to the White House for President Reagan's signature, Sammis filed deeds in the Culpeper County clerk's office to add another 765 acres to his holdings, buying the Woolfrey farm and other parcels.[322] From 1987 to 1990, Sammis bought more than 5,300 acres of land at Brandy Station—an area covering the morning phase of the battle. Fourteen separate purchases cost him $21.2 million.[323]

Hall realized he would need more firepower. In December 1988, he called Tersh Boasberg, the attorney so helpful in the Stuart's Hill fight. On December 29, Hall gave Boasberg, Wenzel and two others a tour of the parts of the battlefield he still had permission to walk, such as Fleetwood Hill.[324]

Boasberg knew with the ink barely dry on the William Center measure, Congress would never take this land as they had Stuart's Hill. The anticipated price tag at Manassas was too high, and although Brandy Station was the war's biggest cavalry battle, it was not well known outside of Civil War circles. This rural, inactive railroad station was not in a national media market. "How in the hell are we going to save this?" Boasberg asked himself, but he stifled his doubts and offered his help on the spot.[325]

Sammis gave Culpeper County officials and the media a personal tour of some of his Washington area properties on January 26, 1989, "in an effort to show he's not such a bad guy after all," wrote reporter Judith Bowman, who was on the tour for the *Culpeper Star-Exponent*.[326]

The group visited five properties, including the Lafayette Business Center in Chantilly, where Sammis had restored the circa-1850 Hutchison House while developing the farm it used to preside over. This property earned Sammis a 1987 distinguished service award from the Fairfax County History Commission for outstanding contribution to historic preservation.

"It looks like something out of Williamsburg, that's the quality of restoration," gushed Culpeper Chamber of Commerce executive director Jim Witherspoon, without noting that a modern, two-story office building sat on what used to be the home's backyard, not 25 feet from the back door.[327]

To conclude the tour, Sammis took everyone to Brandy Station. A devoted family man by all accounts, Sammis spoke of his son-in-law, Gayner, purchasing a small farm in Culpeper County several years earlier. "We just fell in love with it," Sammis said. The area "sort of found us."[328]

Sammis told the group he planned to build Elkwood Downs, a development promising to be "The Gateway to Culpeper County," featuring residences, shops, and a corporate business park. He gave each of the attendees a leather-bound, gold-embossed, personalized copy of the preliminary plans for "a mixed-use community in which residents can ride a bicycle to work."[329]

Preservationists learned of the plans by word-of-mouth and stories in local newspapers. At the suggestion of Boasberg and Hall, local history buffs, farm owners and residents, including B.B. Mitchell III and Joe Troilo, who owned land on the most historic part of Fleetwood Hill, gathered informally in December to organize opposition to the project.

Boasberg suggested that the opponents create a local organization. By February 1989, they were forming the Brandy Station Foundation, which would incorporate in March using $1,500 of a $2,500 grant from APCWS—one of that organization's first grants—to pay the costs of incorporation. Under Mitchell's leadership, the foundation quickly became active and aggressive. Hall joined the Brandy Station Foundation (BSF) board in early 1990, initially declining because he was not a local resident.[330]

Boasberg recognized that formal historic designations from the state and federal governments were important. While it would not stop the development, an official historic designation would create more hurdles for the developers and potential legal inroads for the preservationists.

Hall pulled together the history while Boasberg prepared applications to nominate the Brandy Station battlefield and nearby Hansbrough's Ridge, the pristine site of the Union Army winter encampment of 1863-64, for listing on the Virginia Landmarks Register and, in turn, the National Register for Historic Places. Boasberg submitted applications for nomination of some 3,000 acres of Brandy Station as a historic landmark to the Virginia State Historic Preservation Office (SHPO) at the Virginia Department of Historic Resources, and to the National Park Service for National Register listing.[331]

The county supervisors were not pleased and voted 5-2 to send a letter to the NPS "strongly" opposing the nominations. No action was ever taken on the National Historic Landmark application, Hall recalled. But the National Register effort would play a major role in the Brandy Station saga.[332]

The nomination applications prepared by BSF and Boasberg failed to define the entire battlefield as required by governmental guidelines, recalled Bryan Mitchell, then deputy director of the Virginia Department of Historic Resources. The SHPO began its own study to determine the extent of the entire battlefield.[333]

BSF's nomination was flawed because it included Sammis's land and that of BSF members and supporters, but not the land of other landowners who might oppose historic designation. It was a significant omission, Mitchell recalled, because any site or area nominated had to have the consent of a majority of property owners to be listed on the National Register. No property owner consent was required by Virginia for listing on the state register.[334]

As the preservationists sought formal recognition of the historic site, the developer began disputing the history of his property. In February 1989, Sammis hired a local historian who contended that the most significant battle action occurred not on Sammis's land but on adjacent land that was now the county airport. Hall was mortified that anyone, much less a historian, would twist historical fact. He'd never heard of a historian "trying to move the battle of Brandy Station from where it occurred," Hall told the *Free Lance-Star*.[335]

In October 1989, almost two years after Sammis's first farm acquisition, he submitted a proposal to the county for the core development of Elkwood Downs—a business complex on 1,475 acres with 252 acres set aside for historic preservation.[336] The county supervisors took almost a year to decide the attendant rezoning request.

At the end of October, the Virginia State Board of Historic Resources approved placing 13,903 acres of the Brandy Station battlefield on the Virginia Historic Register—more than four times the land nominated by BSF—based on the SHPO's battlefield boundary study. Some affected landowners protested the new Virginia register determination as the Commonwealth submitted the National Register nomination to the NPS.[337]

The supervisors vowed to continue "business as usual," but it was a slow process.[328] The planning commission set a public hearing on the rezoning request for November 8, but postponed it to January 10, 1990, then March 14, then April 12.[339]

At the hearing, Sammis and an associate spent an hour extolling the virtues of the project. Fourteen different work sessions with county planners had forged a plan that was a "fair, well-considered solution for all involved," Sammis said, including the preservation of what had now grown to 265 historic acres. Most of the 32 speakers opposed the project and voiced concerns about historic preservation, congestion, cost, traffic and water use. Hall talked about history that would be destroyed. The hearing ended about 11:20 p.m. with commissioners announcing they would vote on May 9.[340]

On that day, the planning commissioners voted 5-3 to recommend that the county deny the rezoning request. The magnitude of the project was just too big, Vice Chairman Robert Kenefect stated, and various issues, such as historic preservation, traffic, sewer needs and wetlands protection, were not adequately addressed.[341]

When Hall, Pohanka, BSF board members and a crowd of several hundred reenactors, residents and politicians gathered on Troilo's Fleetwood Hill property to commemorate the 127th anniversary of the battle on June 9, 1990, no one was hailing the action of the planning commission as a victory. They knew the supervisors would have the final say.

Pohanka, dressed in full Union blue, was as passionate as he was formal while being interviewed by *The Washington Post*. "Some kid a hundred years from now is going to get interested in the Civil War and want to see these places," he said. "He's going to go down there and be standing in a parking lot. I'm fighting for that kid."[342]

Hall was dismissive of Sammis's offer to preserve 265 acres, a generous amount and worthy compromise to some. "If you've got isolated pockets of preservation, you've got nothing," Hall said. "You would have an artillery position overlooking warehouses."[343]

Boasberg's work at Manassas and now Brandy Station had made him keenly aware of the many unprotected battlefields of the Civil War, and on April 8, 1990, *The Washington Post* published on the front page of its Outlook section a long essay under Boasberg's byline that outlined the problem and described some of the threatened battlefields.

"What is badly needed is a strong federal initiative—a United States Civil War Sites Commission—to take charge and bring all interested parties together..." the essay said. The commission would identify threatened lands and work with Congress and other parties "to established permanent guidelines and mechanisms for protecting these irreplaceable parts of our heritage."[344]

The Interior Department and its National Park Service agency had a new boss, Secretary of the Interior Manuel Lujan, Jr., who was appointed to replace Donald Hodel by President George H. W. Bush in February 1989, after serving 20 years on Capitol Hill as a Republican Congressman from New Mexico. Lujan knew next to nothing about the Civil War, but his appointment came four months after the government took the Stuart's Hill property, which now fell under his control. Enough Manassas-related matters were crossing his desk that he wanted to learn more. The teaching job fell to National Park Service Chief Historian Edwin C. Bearss. No one was better equipped to do it.

Born in 1923, Bearss grew up on a ranch along Sarpy Creek in isolated, southeast Montana. In sixth, seventh and eighth grades, he rode six miles on horseback to school. Usually, he would pick up an older student and his younger brother would pick up two younger students to horse-pool to the one-room Sarpy School where one teacher oversaw 14 students in grades one through eight. Bearss hated math but loved history and was named Montana's history student of the year as a senior. After graduation, he hitchhiked around the country, seeing for the first time the Civil War battlefields and historic sites that fascinated him.[345]

Bearss joined the U.S. Marine Corps during World War II, enlisting in April 1942 at age 19. By July, he was fighting in the South Pacific at the Solomon Islands, Guadalcanal and the Russell Islands. In the Battle of Suicide Creek at New Britain on January 2, 1944, his unit was sprayed by a hidden Japanese machine gun nest. Bearss went down.

"Rather badly wounded," he would recall almost 70 years later. "I'm shot through the left elbow, which destroys two of three nerves that run to your lower arm. Gives me a stiff elbow. Shot through the shoulder, which I still have no motion in the right shoulder where the humerus goes into the socket." Bearss lay exposed, but quiet, for at least an hour. "Then I try to get up, and they open up. They see motion and fire back, and that's when they hit me in the foot and across the butt."[346]

He tried again and managed to make it to cover as bullets screamed six inches above his head. Scant protection from a slight incline gave him a life-saving, unforgettable lesson in the importance of terrain in combat. He learned in the most intimate and personal way that preserving the original battlefield landscape is important in interpreting and teaching the history of a battle.

"I can remember every moment as vividly today as it was on the second day of January 1944," Bearss recalled in 1992. He was in and out of rehabilitation hospitals for two years and three months and spent countless hours of his recovery reading Civil War history, including Lee's Lieutenants. After earning a B.S. degree at the School of Foreign Service at Georgetown University and an M.A. in history from Indiana University, Bearss was hired by the NPS in September 1956 as historian at Vicksburg National Military Park.[347]

There, Bearss and two others discovered the sunken remains of the U.S.S. Cairo, one of the first Union ironclads and the first warship to be sunk by a remotely detonated mine. The mud-covered vessel went down in the Yazoo River on December 12, 1862, during the Vicksburg campaign, and was still nearly intact as Bearss led the effort to retrieve and preserve it. During the Civil War Centennial, he played a key role in the creation of Pea Ridge National Military Park in Arkansas and Wilson's Creek National Battlefield in Missouri. He led NPS preservation efforts at Fort Donelson, Stones River, Fort Moultrie, Richmond-area battlefields and the Eisenhower Farm at Gettysburg.

Bearss began giving battlefield tours and off-site lectures as soon as he became the Vicksburg historian. In one of his first speeches in Clinton, Mississippi, in 1956, he relied on notes. After 20 minutes, "they start going to the bathroom and they don't come back," he recalled. He never used notes again. He has a good memory; not photographic, he says, but it seems so when you ask him about a battle—any battle—and he begins reeling off dates, names, detailed battle descriptions, telling anecdotes and providing his overall analysis.[348]

By 1959, Bearss was on the "banquet circuit" of Civil War Round Tables, mesmerizing audiences with dramatic presentations with detail and insight, sprinkled with gossipy tidbits and frank opinions. If a general was a philanderer, Bearss told you so with a twinkle in his eye.[349]

On a battlefield tour, his voice rises and falls as he speaks in present tense, pausing or holding onto words for dramatic effect. Never still, he carries his swagger stick in the crook of his lame left arm, emphasizing facts and pointing out locations.

"I copied some people I have great admiration for—certain professors in college that you learn are effective," Bearss said. His favorite was a course on the history of the Western world taught by Georgetown Prof. Carroll Quigley, who years later was Bill Clinton's most memorable college professor.[350]

Bearss's physical endurance is legendary. He never considered himself handicapped by his war wounds, which in fact drove him to be as fit as possible. He never took a sick day in 41 years with the NPS. Bearss gave up to nine tours a day at Vicksburg in the 1950s, and he recalled with delight how he would challenge high schoolers to a foot race up the circular stairs of a 90-foot battlefield observation tower (since removed). "I raced their best athletes up the tower and in three years never lost once," he recalled.[351]

Summoned to Lujan's office in 1990, Bearss gave him a "core, 101 class" about the battles at Manassas. After an hour, Lujan said, "Can you come back?" Recalled Bearss: "I have at least seven hours—seven meetings—with Secretary Lujan. The second meeting he brings his wife. Then the bureau chiefs start coming, and the assistant secretary. The land management people start coming. So, he is *captured*." [352]

Lujan became a Civil War battlefield preservation supporter, and on July 21, 1990, at Manassas National Battlefield Park, on the 129th anniversary of the Battle of First Manassas, he announced the creation of the American Battlefield Protection Plan. Relying on Bearss's expertise, the Interior secretary identified 25 threatened parks in 14 states and called for a coalition of private foundations, preservation groups and government at all levels to join together to buy the threatened battlefields or to protect them through zoning restrictions. He also called for the creation of a commission to prioritize battlefields and their threats, and said he would ask Congress for $15 million to fund the program and battlefield acquisitions.[353] Virginia Republican Senator John A. Warner joined Lujan at the announcement and urged Lujan to help sort out the 14 different battlefield protection bills being considered on Capitol Hill.[354]

Bud Hall asked if he would give the secretary a tour of Brandy Station. "Absolutely," he said. "It would be my pleasure." After Lujan's remarks at Manassas, he hopped in his limousine for the drive to Brandy Station, where Hall gave him a tour. "We're obviously overjoyed that the federal government is getting involved," Hall told the *Richmond Time-Dispatch*.[355]

Lujan's announcement and his visit to Brandy Station failed to sway the Culpeper County Board of Supervisors, which had considerable support for development of the battlefield site. On August 21, the Culpeper Chamber of Commerce Board of Directors voted unanimously to support Sammis's rezoning request.[356] Four days later, The *Culpeper Star-Exponent* joined the chorus, urging the board of Supervisors to approve the rezoning. "Mr. Sammis has been exceptional in his planning and in his reaction to public concerns," the paper editorialized.[357]

The preservationists fought back with full-page ads in the *Culpeper News* on September 6 and 7. "Brandy Station Now Faces An Enemy Far Worse Than The Union Cavalry: A Developer From California," read the ad on September 6, 1990. That same month, the NPS completed a mapping project of historic resources at Brandy Station and recommended that 1,262 acres of the battlefield be preserved at four separate sites where the battle was fought.[358]

The supervisors' public hearing on September 19 devolved into a free-for-all featuring more than 80 speakers. Hall began his remarks reciting the names of soldiers who paid the ultimate price at Brandy Station: "Benjamin Efner, Issac Ward, Virgil Brodrick, John Shelmire, George Williams . . . They came, they fought, they never left," he said. "And I'm here to tell you that most of them are still buried at what is now called Elkwood Downs."[359]

Five hours into the hearing, "the verbal rockets' red glare" had become "dizzying," the Fredericksburg *Free-Lance Star* reported. A man who said he was a descendant of a Rebel soldier supported the rezoning, claiming that Robert E. Lee and the Confederates were fighting for economic freedom. A Civil War reenactor from California presented the supervisors with 2,000 signatures supporting the preservation of the battlefield.[360]

One Sammis ally called the battlefield supporters "pseudo-preservationist" hippies who were cynically exploiting the men who fell there. Three Culpeper High School seniors with shaved heads announced they were bound for military service, but they would have nothing to come home for unless the county approved projects such as these and the jobs they offered.[361]

That Sunday, September 23, 1990, Ken Burns presented the first of nine episodes of *The Civil War* on PBS. The 11-hour, 30-minute series became the most-watched program on public television with 13.9 million viewers tuning in to the first episode and more than 40 million Americans watching later ones.[362]

On Monday, September 24, as episode two opened with Julia Ward Howe writing the *Battle Hymn of the Republic* at the Willard Hotel in Washington, the Culpeper County Board of Supervisors met to decide the future of the Brandy Station battlefield. Hall put a fresh tape in his VCR to record the television show and headed down U.S. 29/15 to learn the fate of his beloved land. He knew the winds of change were blowing that fall, and was resigned to the outcome. As expected, the supervisors approved the rezoning request—the largest in the county's history—and cleared the way for Elkwood Downs corporate park. The vote was 5-2.[363]

"Mr. Sammis won the first engagement," a grim Hall told a reporter. "The outcome of the battle is yet to be determined. We're optimistic in that we are not without resources and enthusiasm."[364]

Preservationists struck back on October 22. With J.E.B. Stuart IV of Richmond, great-grandson of the famous Confederate cavalry commander, at the forefront, the Brandy Station Foundation and local landowners filed suit against the Culpeper County Board of Supervisors to block the rezoning. The suit charged that the "intensive and massive development" violated the county's comprehensive development plan and would impinge on the property rights of its neighbors, threaten the local water supplies and create potentially dangerous traffic conditions.[365]

The APCWS recommended compromise, urging Boasberg and the BSF to acknowledge that Sammis had the right to develop the land and consider a reasonable package of concessions to secure the protection of a meaningful portion of the battlefield.[366]

Boasberg went in the other direction. He stepped out on a limb, alleging that the project violated the constitutionally guaranteed "right of heritage" of Stuart and local land owners. "It's novel and imaginative, and to my knowledge, the first time this has been claimed," said Boasberg.[367] He also knew that the lawsuit might delay development. Unlike Hazel at Manassas, Sammis did not begin construction at Elkwood Downs while the suit worked its way through the local courts.

"This is having a damaging effect on us," said Michael Armm, Sammis's new project director at Elkwood Downs, as lawyers wrangled over motions and procedures five months after the suit was filed. "In addition to the cost of litigation, we should be doing extensive marketing and securing financing at this point. None of that can happen until the zoning issue is cleared up."[368]

On Capitol Hill, Congress joined Lujan in his battlefield preservation movement and in November 1990 approved legislation to create the Civil War Sites Advisory Commission, a 15-member panel formed to identify significant Civil War battlefields and sites, determine their relative importance and condition, assess threats and recommend ways to preserve them. Out of Lujan's American Battlefield Protection Plan came the American Battlefield Protection Program (ABPP) in 1991 under the NPS, which included staff support for the new commission.[369]

Lujan expressed regret that Culpeper County had rezoned Brandy Station in an October 1990 letter to Board Chairman Jack E. Fincham, and in January 1991, the

Interior secretary became directly involved. He met with county officials to discuss ways to protect the battlefield.[370] He urged them to build a coalition of public and private interests to find solutions and suggested further meetings.[371]

The following month, on February 28, the NPS announced that it concurred with Virginia's report that 13,903 acres at Brandy Station were historic and eligible for listing on the National Register of Historic Places. This was more than four times the 3,000 acres originally requested by BSF and more than 10 times larger than the 1,262 acres of core battlefield land that an NPS mapping project had recommended for preservation just six months earlier. The key phrase was "eligible for listing." It could not be listed because federal law required that a majority of property owners support the historic designation.

Eligibility for the National Register was a victory, but too big a victory. "It was a massive hunk of land," Hall recalled, sure to generate land owner protests and renewed complaints of government overreach. "On the one hand, I felt validated, but on the other hand, it was dicey," Hall recalled. "It was a reach. I thought it would cause us problems. And it did. It gave the other side a weapon they could use against us."[372]

Another force was at work, though, that would have a far bigger impact than government. The country had undergone a recession that started in July 1990 after Iraq's invasion and occupation of Kuwait sent oil prices skyrocketing. Its impact was evident in April 1991 when William Bryant, a land speculator in Culpeper County, gave up his option to buy Hansbrough Ridge, the Union winter encampment site. He told Hall: "I'm not going to make any money. I got you crazies to worry about. I'm getting out of here."[373]

In July 1991, a local judge ruled the Brandy Station Foundation's lawsuit against the county would go to trial. It was unwelcome news for Sammis. "You cannot find investors who are willing to come in with a lawsuit hanging," Armm said.[374]

The court ruling was the last good news the preservationists would receive for many months as one after another, setbacks would stymie them until all that remained was vain hope and some mighty stubborn people. ★

CHAPTER
SIX

Puppet Master

 N MAY 11, 1988, the Association for the Preservation of Civil War Sites (APCWS) vice president and the National Park Service (NPS) historian Robert K. Krick took a day of annual leave and drove from Fredericksburg, Virginia to Capitol Hill to visit Congressman Bob Mrazek. The meeting was at Mrazek's request.

Krick had never heard of the liberal Long Island, New York Democrat until Mrazek called seeking his expertise.[375] As Krick waited outside Mrazek's office while the legislator met with a gay rights group, he wondered how Mrazek got interested in the Civil War and battlefield preservation.

"When I walked into his office, here was a virtual life-size blowup of Henry Kyd Douglas, of all people, who was on Stonewall Jackson's staff," Krick recalled. "He's just crazy—he still is—for Kyd Douglas. And he really wanted to save the battle-fields."[376]

A week earlier, Mrazek and fellow representative Mike Andrews (D-Texas) made news when they introduced H.R. 4526 to have the government seize the Stuart's Hill tract at Manassas. Krick had not seen the news and learned of the legislation directly from Mrazek. The congressman, however, was quite familiar with Krick, having read his books and learned of his preservation efforts. Andrews joined them and they asked how they could help in the Manassas fight. Krick promised to send them an assortment of maps, files, articles and references.

Krick saw in Mrazek a potential Capitol Hill champion for fulfilling his urgent desire to expand the authorized federal boundaries of the Chancellorsville battle-field, which is under the jurisdiction of the Fredericksburg and Spotsylvania National Military Park. Much of the battlefield land was privately owned and in the path of suburban sprawl spreading west from Fredericksburg. Expanding the authorized boundary to include this land would be a step toward protecting it; the government would at least be allowed to buy the site if the opportunity arose and money was available.

Krick invited Mrazek to Fredericksburg to show him crucial Chancellorsville battlefield land about 10 miles west of the city that was still privately owned and outside of the boundary. Krick's favorite of all the war's battles was the three-day struggle at Chancellorsville on May 1-3, 1863, widely considered Robert E. Lee's greatest victory. Some of the battlefield was owned by the NPS and well preserved, but some of the most important battlefield land was unprotected, including the site of Stonewall Jackson's epic, late-afternoon flank attack along both sides of Route 3 on the second day of the battle.

"Knowing now that I was a passionate advocate for battlefield preservation, he invited me to come down to take a visit," Mrazek recalled. "And of course, he was very salty and very funny and incredibly knowledgeable. And he just brought it alive for me."[377]

Krick took Mrazek to Wilderness Church in the heart of the second day's battlefield. As the cars and trucks whooshed by on Route 3, Krick told the story of how one of the greatest attacks of the Civil War had unfolded on the gently sloped fields before them.

In late April 1863, Union General Joseph Hooker marched the greater portion of the Army of the Potomac across pontoon bridges on the Rappahannock and Rapidan Rivers, concentrating his massive force at Chancellorsville. On May 1, Hooker advanced toward Fredericksburg to confront Lee and the Army of Northern Virginia. But Lee came out of Fredericksburg and attacked first, slamming into Hooker's forces, stopping his advance and prompting him to turn back to Chancellorsville.

The next day, Lee and Jackson, living up to their reputations for bold action, decided Jackson would lead his entire Second Corps on a seemingly impossible end run around the right flank of the Union army. Some 28,000 butternut soldiers tromped 12 miles or more on May 2 via narrow, winding dirt wagon roads through dense forests on a roundabout march that concluded back on Route 3, but now west of and behind the Union army.

Late that afternoon, Jackson's screaming Rebels kicked down Hooker's back door, pouring out of the woods on both sides of the road and overwhelming the Union Eleventh Corps as its men were settling in for dinner at their camp around the Wilderness Church. That evening, the great victory was diminished when Jackson fell mortally wounded after being shot accidentally by his own men while reconnoitering a position. He died eight days later.

The site of the flank attack was the most significant and important land on the

Chancellorsville battlefield, Krick told Mrazek, but the NPS owned only a single, 34-acre tract near the church. The rest of it was privately owned and outside the congressionally approved boundary of the battlefield. NPS could not buy—could not even accept for free—any land outside the boundary.

"You know, we really need to expand these boundaries if we're going to protect the most critical sites," Krick said. Mrazek was eager to help, but how? Krick knew how, but as a mid-level NPS employee, he was in no position to push or promote legislation affecting the NPS or anyone else.

"I'm not supposed to talk . . . my *boss* isn't supposed to talk . . . my *boss's boss* isn't supposed to talk to a member of Congress without permission of the director of the park service," Krick recalled. "I was about 12 grades below where I'm even supposed to be aware of their existence."[378]

Krick was well aware that stepping out of line at a bureaucracy like the NPS could quietly but swiftly lead to unpleasant consequences, such as reassignment to a remote outpost like the isolated Dry Tortugas National Park, a 70-mile boat trip from Key West, Florida, a threat he heard a year into his assignment at Fredericksburg. NPS had given right-of-way to Virginia to widen Route 3 to four lanes through the Chancellorsville battlefield, deciding "it would be okay to give up about 10 acres of park service land right where Stonewall Jackson was mortally wounded," Krick recalled. "I raised what hell I could as a very young man. And someone from the agency called me and said, 'Do you want to go to the Dry Tortugas?' But it didn't happen."[379]

Krick had 16 years at the NPS when Mrazek contacted him, and he knew how to be discreet while establishing a close working relationship with the Congressman. Krick provided Mrazek with a wealth of material, including detailed geographical information needed for the boundary expansion legislation.

"Bob, you're going to be the puppet master here, and I'll be your puppet," Mrazek told Krick. "Give me my marching orders for introducing the legislation that will expand the boundaries in a way that would effectively protect more of the battlefields, particularly the northern Virginia battlefields."[380]

Krick knew the NPS was a "big parks, geysers and waterfalls" bureaucracy.[381] With limited Congressional appropriations for land acquisitions, the massive natural parks such as Yosemite and the Great Smoky Mountains came first. The most popular battlefield park, Gettysburg, was far down the list compared to all NPS parks. (The park was 77th in 2014 in visitation, with about 1.02 million visitors, compared to the Great Smoky Mountains at number one with more than 10 million visitors).

Although a relatively junior member of Congress, Mrazek was on the

Appropriations Committee and found himself with the power to get boundary expansions and other preservation-related measures passed into law. "During the Reagan presidency, year after year, we could not get authorization bills passed," Mrazek said. "So, there was no Interior Authorization Bill. There was no Transportation Authorization Bill. At the end of the budget cycle, we simply came together as appropriators and did it all in these continuing resolutions. It focused far too much power in the Senate and House appropriations committees, but if you were a member at the time, it really enabled you to accomplish a number of different things."[382]

Although a relatively junior member of Congress, Mrazek found himself with the power to get boundary expansions and other preservation-related measures passed into law. With Krick guiding, Mrazek set about to expand the boundaries on the Chancellorsville battlefield. Krick believed the second day's battlefield at Chancellorsville—the scene of Jackson's flank attack—was "priority one and two and three and four and five and everything else." [383] But what was a reasonable expansion? Jackson's troops had attacked on both sides of Route 3, then known as the Orange Turnpike. "We were sure we couldn't take that whole sweep, or if we did, we couldn't get anything at any of the other three battlefields," Krick recalled. "So, we decided to take just one side, and the way the road is configured, the north side made far more sense as regards to history, interpretation, management and so on. So, we just took that half. Whether we could have gotten both halves, I don't know. We wound up getting everything we asked for. I wish we'd asked for more."[384]

On February 6, 1989, Representative D. French Slaughter Jr., the Virginia Republican whose 7th district included Spotsylvania County, introduced H.R. 875 to expand the boundaries of Fredericksburg and Spotsylvania National Military Park. The legislation proposed to add some 2,000 acres to the park's authorized boundaries, primarily at Chancellorsville, on the north side of Route 3, where Krick saw the most pressing need. The new boundary also included considerable acreage east of Chancellorsville, including a 100-acre farm where McLaws stood firm in front of Hooker's army while Jackson's men made their famous march. H.R. 875 also added substantially to Wilderness battlefield's boundary, especially along the shoulders of the Orange Plank Road. The bill included minor boundary adjustments at the Fredericksburg and Spotsylvania battlefields.[385]

Slaughter fronted the bill and Mrazek pushed it through the legislative process. Mrazek's staff member Ann Bennett "ran interference everywhere and always," Krick recalled.[386] Far from avoiding Capitol Hill, the mid-level NPS bureaucrat would sit in Mrazek's offices and use his telephone and stroll across the street to do research at the Library of Congress, which he did "50 times in a couple of years there." If Krick needed to see the Congressman himself, Mrazek would do the asking and the visit was always considered strictly about historical matters.

"Every time something came up where he wanted to talk to me or I wanted to talk to him, he'd have his secretary knock out a letter that said, 'Mr. Krick, I want to talk to you about some things of history that interest me. Please come up here,'" Krick said, "So it was him asking me, and you can't turn that down."[387]

The NPS under the Republican administration of President George H. W. Bush was officially opposed to the boundary expansions, leaving Krick in a tight spot. At least twice, the agency sent Bearss to Capitol Hill to testify against the measures. The NPS chief historian tipped Krick off about his mission, and Krick told Mrazek.

Krick recalled a 1989 session: "Bob [Mrazek] would put maps up in the subcommittee hearings, and he'd say, 'Well, here's the existing boundaries, and here are the red and blue arrows where Jackson attacked the Yankees. Ed (Bearss), tell us what happened here.' And Ed would tell everyone about the battle there. And Bob would say, 'Well, this is about as important as this, isn't it?' Ed would say yes. And Bob would say, 'But the park service is against this?' And Ed said, 'Yes, I've been instructed to tell you…'"[388]

Krick generated letters of support for the legislation from key scholars and leaders in the Civil War community, and watched from the sidelines as the legislation faced and then cleared each set of new hurdles. Once, Krick received a demoralizing call from Bennett, who was disconsolate. H.R. 875 was "dead in committee," she said. Fortunately, the obituary was premature.[389] "There were ups and downs," Krick recalled. "And at that point, she was just distraught about the state of the bill. But within a few days they got it back on track."[390]

H.R. 875, "The Fredericksburg and Spotsylvania County Battlefields Memorial National Military Park Expansion Act of 1989," passed the full House of Representatives on July 18, 1989. On August 4, Virginia Senators John Warner and Charles Robb, a Republican and a Democrat, plus Arkansas Democratic Senator Dale Bumpers, introduced companion legislation, S. 1559, in the Senate. The boundary expansion bills had not "a comma's difference between the two of them," Krick recalled.[901] But that was no guarantee of success.

In mid-August, Krick received "a great flurry of phone calls" from Capitol Hill "asking me to generate support letters at once." He drummed up almost 50 letters in two days. Through the fall, Mrazek, Krick and many others in the Civil War community worked the Senate, and the boundary bill passed on November 22, 1989. Then the measure had to pass a conference committee, where a small number of Senate and House legislators reconcile the bills from the two chambers but are not particularly bound by those bills.[392]

"We literally would not have gotten that legislation if Bob had not had that as one of his special hobby horses," Krick recalled. "He sent Ann Bennett over to the conference committee, and she sat outside the door. And on the very last day of the session . . . she finally had her inning. And it became law."[393]

Krick estimates that the 1989 boundary expansion "got more than half of what we should reasonably hope for and want" of the flank attack part of the Chancellorsville battlefield.[394] But Krick's work was not done. Mrazek was ready and eager to expand other boundaries and to provide money through legislation to save battlefield land.

"So, I grasped the bit and rode around with it for about three years, acquiring whatever boundary expansions we could convince just a couple of professional staffers on Capitol Hill made good sense. That's all it took," Krick said.[395]

In 1990, with Krick providing direction, Senator Jim Jeffords (R-Vt.) and Mrazek pushed another bill through Congress to expand the boundary at the Wilderness battlefield to include the "Fawn Lake" property, a single tract of 456 acres near the unfinished railroad bed where Confederate General James Longstreet made his renowned flank attack of May 6, 1864. That land was eventually purchased and is part of the national park at the Wilderness battlefield.

That same year, Krick helped Jeffords champion legislation that directed the NPS to conduct a comprehensive study of the Shenandoah Valley Civil War battlefields and sites as part of Public Law 101-628, the same law that established the Civil War Sites Advisory Commission. The Valley study led to the establishment of the Shenandoah Valley Battlefields National Historic District in 1996 and creation of the Shenandoah Valley Battlefields Foundation in 2002.[396]

From his perch on the Appropriations Committee, Mrazek kept the money coming in, time and again adding line-item appropriations to mammoth spending bills and giving millions of dollars to the NPS to buy land within federal battlefield boundaries at Fredericksburg, Antietam, Gettysburg and other battlefields.[397]

Krick considers the 1989 boundary expansion that included the flank attack battlefield at Chancellorsville to be his most important contribution to the cause of Civil War battlefield preservation. But it took nearly a decade for the expansion to yield results in protecting the ground over which Jackson's men advanced.

In October 1998, the park acquired a 40-acre tract where Jackson's Rebel troops poured out of the thickets as they launched their assault. Since then, more flank attack property has been preserved and added to the park. Today, save for a single privately owned tract, visitors may follow Jackson's advance from the area where the flank attack began to the spot more than a mile to the east, near the Chancellorsville Visitor Center, where the legendary Confederate general was mortally wounded by his own men.

As Krick worked behind the scenes on Capitol Hill, he served in his more visible role as vice president of APCWS, helping manage the fledgling organization as it grew. By May 1988, less than a year into the enterprise, the amount of work was becoming overwhelming. "The outlandish workload borne by some of the Board members prompts the suggestion that the Board be expanded at the next meeting in July," Krick wrote in the minutes of that month's meeting.[398]

The APCWS only had about $20,000 in the bank and was in no position to hire anyone. But two years earlier, board member and NPS historian Will Greene had befriended a wealthy New York investment banker, Richard Gilder, after giving a tour of Fredericksburg battlefield to Gilder and his friends. Greene called Gilder about APCWS.

Greene well remembers Gilder's reaction when he got his first taste of the workings of the APCWS. "We were going through what our organization was about and what we were trying to do and he was listening to all this," Greene recalled, "and he told us, 'You all are thinking like a bunch of school teachers. You're thinking much too small.'"[399]

Gilder offered a challenge grant: if APCWS could raise $50,000 between May 30 and December 31, 1988, the Gilder Foundation would match that amount. This became the board's top priority, and with the prospects of a much bigger budget, the board authorized Jack Ackerly to begin "a very preliminary search" for a paid director.[400] Board members went to work canvassing their 900 members and the country's Civil War Round Tables. By the end of the year, the APCWS had raised $67,508.42, and banked more than $117,000 when Gilder's $50,000 matching donation arrived.[401]

The Gilder challenge required minimum donations of $250 and 145 generous donors stepped up. But the APCWS was just as energetic pursuing spare change of passersby. Members set up information tents at Civil War reenactments and other events. On a table of saw horses and three 2x10 planks of wood, they placed a large, empty water cooler bottle, which slowly filled with change and bills.[402]

APCWS took no leadership role in the fight against William Center, but actively supported the cause. "Development Threatens Manassas Battlefield" roared the lead headline in the first *Hallowed Ground* newsletter, published in June 1988, to rally the growing membership to the cause. The first issues were far from the slick magazine of today. It was a newsletter of a few pages with design and printing donated by member Robert Younger, publisher of Morningside Books, which specialized in reprinting out-of-print Civil War books.

On October 17, 1988, the APCWS acquired its first battlefield land, 8.55 acres of "The Coaling," the key Union position on the Port Republic battlefield in the Shenandoah Valley. On June 9, 1862, during Stonewall Jackson's Valley Campaign, outnumbered federals held a strong position at the site. In the campaign's climatic fight, the stubborn Yankees lost then retook the hill before finally succumbing to another Confederate attack, losing five guns, a thousand men and control of the Valley.

The Lee-Jackson Foundation, whose aging leadership saw the APCWS as a long-term protector of the land, donated The Coaling, named for the charcoal furnace located there. Ackerly volunteered many hours overcoming "various legal complexities" of the title transfer, according to APCWS board meeting minutes.[403]

For 20 months, the APCWS had operated without a paid staff or office. It was an all-volunteer operation managed and built solely by board members, each donating professional expertise and countless hours of time. Many administrative duties were handled by Greene, and a consensus was forming that he should become the organization's first executive director and first paid employee.

At the March 1989 APCWS board meeting, Greene said he would be willing to seek a leave of absence from the NPS to run the organization, and the board promptly voted him interim executive director. The proposed annual budget of $100,000 included $40,000 for Greene, $18,000 for an assistant, $6,000 for rent and $4,000 for equipment, featuring an IBM AT class, 40 MB computer.

In January 1990, Greene became permanent executive director and opened the organization's first office in a 750-square foot, two-room annex at the back of a rambling building at 613 Caroline Street in downtown Fredericksburg.[404] Greene's tenure was to be one year, coinciding with his official leave of absence as historian at Fredericksburg and Spotsylvania National Military Park. Greene stayed on in 1991 after the NPS extended his leave of absence another year.[405]

In May 1989, the APCWS scored its second save by taking title to 1.5 acres of the Harris Farm on the Spotsylvania battlefield, including a prominent stone monument to the 1st Massachusetts Heavy Artillery, which suffered heavy losses at the farm in a Confederate attack on May 19, 1864. The land was donated by Agnes McGee, who had joined APCWS as a life member. She lived on the property in the Harris House, built around 1755, and had farmed the land for decades.[406]

That summer, APCWS made its first outright purchase, negotiating contracts to buy about 10 acres of the Petersburg battlefield in two purchases totaling $24,000. The land was at the intersection of White Oak and Claiborne Roads, 12 miles southwest of Petersburg and was the position of the extreme right flank of the Confederate line around Richmond and Petersburg at the end of the war. Here, on March 31, 1865, bitter fighting occurred in the Battle of White Oak Road. The entrenchments and a gun emplacement were still well preserved and visible.

Toward the end of 1989, Gilder offered a $35,000 challenge to be matched in a five-month campaign. When the membership raised $47,552, Gilder added a $25,000 bonus, bringing the total proceeds to $107,552.[407]

In 1990, with Greene at the helm, the APCWS became more effective in saving land and helping others save it. It allocated small grants to help local preservation groups, including additional assistance to the Brandy Station Foundation, $1,000 to to the Shenandoah Valley Civil War Foundation, $5,000 to the Cedar Creek Battlefield Foundation, and $5,000 to the New Market Battlefield Park and Virginia Military Institute to help buy 20 acres of that battlefield.[408]

In July 1990, APCWS paid $22,500 for 7.24 acres of critical battlefield land at Bentonville and a month later donated it to the State of North Carolina to be incorporated into the state battlefield park. The objective of acquiring battlefield land then giving it to a governmental entity continues today.

In August, the APCWS made its biggest purchase yet, acquiring 50 acres of the Hatcher's Run battlefield in Virginia for $65,000 from a timber company. Confederate General John Pegram was killed in action at Hatcher's Run as Confederate forces fought a fierce battle in February 1865 against Union troops trying to capture the South Side Railroad and isolate parts of the Confederate army.[409] In early December, the organization announced it had saved the battlefield at McDowell, Virginia, in the Shenandoah Valley, purchasing 126.4 acres for $64,000 to preserve the place where Stonewall Jackson had the first in a string of victories in his Valley Campaign.[410]

Independent of the work of the APCWS, a separate action in 1990 saved hundreds of crucial acres at several battlefields, including a site no less significant than the "Bloody Cornfield" at Antietam. On July 2, 1990, the Richard King Mellon Foundation of Pittsburgh and the Conservation Fund announced that they were purchasing and planning to donate several battlefield sites, including the Cornfield at Antietam and tens of thousands of acres of wildlife habitat to the U.S. government as part of the largest federal land donation up to that time. The donation included two additional parcels at Antietam, 266 acres at Gettysburg, 135 acres of the Wilderness battlefield in Virginia and 930 acres at Five Forks, where Lee lost 40 percent of his shrinking army in April 1865.[411]

The APCWS strengthened its board in 1990 with the appointment of well-connected Richmond attorney Carrington Williams, a courtly, quintessential "Virginia gentleman" and devoted student of the Civil War. Before joining, Williams lobbied pro bono on behalf of the organization for preservation initiatives in the Virginia legislature. Dr. James McPherson, Princeton professor and the 1989 Pulitzer Prize-winning author of Battle Cry of Freedom: The Civil War Era, joined the board in May 1991.[412]

Meanwhile, the APCWS began conducting membership drives, and member rolls increased from about 1,500 members in 1990 to more than 4,100 in 1991. Greene reported that one mailer went out to 35,000 addresses, generating 850 new members.[413]

In 1991, the APCWS gave the Cedar Creek Battlefield Foundation a $32,500 interest-free loan as well as a $100,000 challenge grant spanning four years. A $15,000 matching grant to the Save Historic Antietam Foundation helped preserve the Grove Farm. Later in 1991, with help from the Kansas City Civil War Round Table, APCWS expanded to the Western Theater, purchasing 38.75 acres for $42,600 at Byram's Ford battlefield near Kansas City, Missouri. It also saved its biggest tract yet, 194 acres of Fisher's Hill battlefield in the Shenandoah Valley for $111,000.[414]

There was no shortage of other possibilities. The board discussed at least eight or 10 potential acquisitions at every meeting. In July 1991, 18 possible battlefield purchases were discussed.[415]

One battlefield never listed in the APCWS "property updates" was Brandy Station, although Bud Hall reported on the development dispute at nearly every meeting. Hall received enthusiastic support and President Gary Gallagher more than once came to Culpeper County from State College, Pennsylvania, to attend meetings and support Hall and battlefield preservation efforts.

But the thousands of acres amassed by Lee Sammis were not for sale. Even if they had been, the cost would have been out of reach for the APCWS. The new organization was still getting comfortable with five-figure deals and had negotiated its first six-figure purchase with the Fisher's Hill battlefield acquisition in Virginia. Sammis had paid $21.2 million for the 5,300 acres he owned at Brandy Station.[416]

As a cavalry battle, the Brandy Station clash covered some 4,000 acres, far more territory than most Civil War battles. The entire field of operations spanned almost 22 square miles. An NPS mapping project had recommended in September 1990 that a total of 1,262 battlefield acres be preserved at four separate combat sites.

The Brandy Station Foundation's suit to block the county's rezoning of Sammis's battlefield property was still being considered by the court in early 1991 when the NPS announced that 13,903 acres in and around Brandy Station were eligible for listing on the National Register of Historic Places.

The area was so large that it reached into Fauquier County. A backlash began almost immediately. Sue Hansohn, a local realtor, organized and founded Citizens for Land Rights with funding from Sammis. "It's our turn to speak," said lands rights member Cindy Thornhill.[417]

"While most residents feel some areas of Brandy Station deserve recognition, they disagree that it is necessary to protect an area the size of Manhattan," wrote Alice Menks, the president of another group, the Virginians for Property Rights, in a letter to *The Washington Post*.[418]

Both Virginia U.S. Senators expressed concern about the designation, and how the decision was made. "The eligibility area of 14,000 acres does not, in my opinion, appear to be made on any reasonable standard," Senator John Warner complained in July 1991.[419]

The NPS began revisiting its decision in early 1992. For four months, it accepted input from interested parties, examined new materials and reexamined the historical record. On May 1, 1992, the NPS reaffirmed its earlier determination.[420]

By then, however, the preservationists had lost an important battle on another front. Unlike the National Register, the Commonwealth of Virginia did not have any owner-consent provisions in its historic designation process. In early 1992, two northern Virginia lawmakers sponsored a bill in the Virginia legislature that would allow Sammis and nearby landowners to revoke the Virginia Historic District designation from their land.[421]

Outraged preservationists called the measure a "developer relief act," but that did not stop it from sailing through the Virginia State Senate and House of Delegates. On April 6, 1992, Democratic Virginia Governor L. Douglas Wilder signed the bill. Supporters hailed the measure as a way to throttle the power of the SHPO in the historic designation process; opponents argued that it set a dangerous precedent by allowing property owners themselves to decide whether their property was historic, rather than the record of history.[422]

Secretary of the Interior Manuel Lujan, meanwhile, requested a meeting of all parties involved at Brandy Station in hopes of working out an acceptable compromise. It happened on April 8 at Sammis's Elkwood Downs offices on the Brandy Station battlefield just northwest of St. James Church. Hall was there, as was Sammis, Boasberg, Culpeper County officials and other BSF leaders. Bearss was there representing the NPS. Hall was already wary of Bearss, whom he knew casually. The NPS chief historian had made no effort to help the Brandy Station Foundation. Deputy Interior Secretary Knute Knudson, who had arranged the meeting, was in charge.[423]

Knudson asked Hall to give an overview of the battle—a task he always loved.

"I stood up and started to explain the significance of the battle," Hall recalled. "Ed stood up beside me. He cut me off and in that dramatic voice said, 'Brandy Station! Not very important!' Ed then took over the historical narrative from this amateur historian, me, and proceeded to denigrate the significance of the Battle of Brandy Station for about 10 minutes. After his delivery—and rejection of the battle's importance—whatever I had to offer in opposition fell entirely on deaf ears. I was more dead in the water than I've ever been in any meeting, before or since, put in my place by the chief historian of the National Park Service. I could not have been more stunned."[424]

After the meeting, which produced no solution, Hall went up to Bearss and said, "If you were trying to be helpful, you weren't." Bearss did not respond, Hall recalled.[425] Bearss said in 2016 that he did not remember the meeting. "I would have never said it's not very important," Bearss said of the battle. "I'm much more cautious than that. But I might have said there are more important sites."[426]

The episode came on the heels of Hall discovering that Bearss had been frequently communicating with Sammis and Elkwood Downs officials about the National Historic Register process and working to obtain a compromise that would save part of the battlefield but allow the development. Bearss's name appeared repeatedly in Elkwood Downs letters, memos and reports obtained through the discovery process after BSF filed its lawsuit.[427]

A June 29, 1990, Elkwood Downs memo reviewed a compromise deal involving Bearss of which BSF was unaware and not party to. "We believe that a deal can be struck with Ed . . ." the memo said.[428]

Sammis, in a "Memo to File" on September 4, 1990, thanked people and agencies who had helped him. He mentioned Bearss, "with whom we have worked for many months, and met with many times, both in his offices in Washington, and on site, for his help in doing 'field checks' and helping us understand what the Park Service is trying to achieve, and again, to put this matter in perspective."[429]

Another memo describing the "History of National Park Service Involvement" said Bearss "was active in working with Mr. Sammis and his associates on configuring the Sammis development plan so that it would fit in and work with the designation of the most historically significant areas."[430]

"Ed was great," recalled Michael Armm, Sammis's Elkwood Downs project director. "He did a number of tours for us. Ed would show us which areas were critical. Largely, the proffers [preservation concessions] were set up on what Ed pointed out to us about the history and not really on what Bud (Hall) said. I can't tell you how many times I went up to the National Park Service to meet with Ed and others and with the keeper of the National Register to sit down and work on the proffers.[431]

Hall considered Bearss's cooperation with Sammis a betrayal. A member of the APCWS advisory board, Bearss did not offer the same help to the preservationists. He had toured the battlefield with Sammis, but not the BSF. He had no contact with the Brandy Station preservationists. And when Bearss so explicitly put him in his place at the meeting at Elkwood Downs, Hall recalled, "then I knew we had been bought and sold down the river.[432]

Hall's life—framed in the context of a veteran federal investigator—was painted in black and white—no gray—with only comrades or enemies, honest men or corrupt ones, good guys or bad guys. Fellow Marine or not, Bearss had betrayed the cause, Hall believed, then blindsided and humiliated him.

But Hall never called Bearss to either ask for help or to criticize his actions. "I don't know why I didn't do that," Hall recalled. "Because I would have asked, 'Why are you meeting with these guys and not us?' It bothered me tremendously that the chief historian of the National Park Service was lending his title, his name and his presence to the other side, and we were not privy to what was being said or decided. Tersh and I talked about it a lot. Tersh just shook his head. He was complaining about it as much as I was. He knew a snake was in the woodpile."[433]

"I didn't do anything to throw any water over it," Bearss said of the Brandy Station preservation effort. His role was limited to the NPS evaluation of the National Register nomination, he said, because as chief historian, he was in charge of the landmarks program. But he was not the decision maker. The designation of almost 14,000 acres as being eligible for the National Register was made higher up the NPS ladder, as such decisions always were. Bearss recalled talking with Sammis only once. His attitude was the same as it was in other difficult negotiations—try to reach a compromise. "My feeling was that they should work it out—that it could be worked out," he recalled.[434]

Of Bud Hall, Bearss said, "I found him dedicated. I found him very determined, well-organized, and he's also a Marine so we have some simpatico there. I've met him, and he's always been civil, but I knew he wasn't one of my admirers."[435]

Bearss said he and Boasberg got along well. Boasberg said he remembered nothing negative about Bearss's involvement. "The only time I called Ed was once or twice at the very beginning" to ask about the significance and some details of the battle, Boasberg recalled. "It was one of the first calls I made. Ed was quite cooperative. He said Brandy Station was important," not on the level of Gettysburg or Antietam, but nonetheless the war's largest cavalry battle and one where the Northern cavalry became the equal of the Southern cavalry. Boasberg said the call reassured him that he was not wasting his time fighting for Brandy Station.[436]

Conflicting memories aside, the spotlight shifted back to the local court in Culpeper County as the foundation's lawsuit came to trial in the summer of 1992. On July 16, one year and nine months after the preservationists filed the case, the court ruled against them, affirming that the rezoning of Sammis's land was legal, that Culpeper County had conducted a careful and proper evaluation, and that its decision was reasonable.

"This case is not about the preservation of a battlefield," wrote Circuit Judge Lloyd C. Sullenberger, but whether the county acted properly in a rezoning case. "The judiciary must not . . . substitute its judgment for that of the governing body," he wrote.[437]

Hall was unsurprised and undeterred. His professional life was as tumultuous and demanding as ever. On Capitol Hill, he had completed the Iran-Contra investigation and was managing the investigation of the Senate Ethics Committee inquiry about the Savings and Loan scandal involving Charles Keating and five U.S. Senators. He was transferred to Atlanta for several months, then to Denver, to handle classified Congressional investigations. "I would come back and forth to Brandy Station, back and forth, back and forth," he recalled.[438]

He knew the political and economic forces arrayed against him were powerful. Preserving Brandy Station was personal for Hall and these were times of some of his greatest despair. But Hall was certain of one thing: He would not stop. He would be a relentless voice on behalf of hallowed ground. If Sammis or his team made a presentation, Hall would be there to argue the other side. He would fight to save the entire Brandy Station battlefield.[439]

On September 15, 1992, about two months after the court ruling, the U.S. Department of the Interior made a stunning, unexpected announcement: Secretary Lujan had revoked the NPS's finding that more than 13,000 acres at Brandy Station were eligible for the National Register of Historic Places. An Interior spokesman said the eligibility designation "was somewhat premature in that it had drawn a lot of concern, so we're going to withdraw it at this point."[440]

Just five months earlier, the NPS had reaffirmed Brandy Station's eligibility after a thorough, four-month review. Within days of the announcement, rumors of a back-room deal were confirmed. To save his own Civil War battlefield preservation initiative, Lujan had sacrificed Brandy Station's eligibility for the National Register. ★

CHAPTER
SEVEN

Birth of the Original Civil War Trust

ORE THAN two years had passed since that July day in 1990 when Manuel Lujan toured Brandy Station with Bud Hall, and agreed that the Civil War's largest cavalry battlefield was a top priority for preservation.

Lujan's announcement that day of a program to save Civil War battlefields had led to Congressional legislation that established the Civil War Sites Advisory Commission, which in 1992 was busy with its mandate to document, catalog and assess the nation's battlefields. Commission members included Bearss, Mrazek, Ken Burns, Dr. James M. McPherson, and Howard Coffin, a Civil War historian/author and staff member for Senator Jim Jeffords (R-Vt.). The chair was Dr. Holly A. Robinson, historian for the National Park System Advisory Board.[441]

Hall had been overjoyed when Lujan visited Brandy Station. The secretary had one question after another, mostly about the history of the battle, but also about the exact acreage and cost of the farms Sammis bought.[442] The tour was one of the most satisfying Hall had ever conducted. It gave him hope. At least the federal government wasn't rabidly opposed to preservation of the battlefield, and might even play an influential role in trying to save it.

Now, in September 1992, Hall felt blindsided and betrayed by Lujan. Far from fighting to save the battlefield, the secretary had revoked his own agency's formal determination that the land over which two gigantic mounted forces had clashed on June 9, 1863, was eligible for the National Register of Historic Places.

What had happened? The scarcely hidden truth was that back-room politics had gotten in the way. Lujan knew that getting Congress to create a study commission was one thing; appropriating money to buy battlefields was another. The former Congressman soon decided that a private foundation would be a better way to raise money. After all, when President Ronald Reagan asked Chrysler Chairman Lee Iacocca to head a private foundation to raise funds to save and preserve Ellis Island and the Statue of Liberty in 1982, American citizens and corporations initially contributed a staggering $350 million, and ultimately more than $700 million.[443]

Lujan's vision was to save far more battlefield land at many more places at a fraction of the cost of the Ellis Island project. He asked J. Roderick Heller III, a member of the Civil War Sites Advisory Commission, to chair the foundation. Heller was a Harvard-educated corporate lawyer and turnaround specialist in Washington who was leading a revitalization of the National Housing Partnership. Heller's family had 23 great-grandfathers or great-uncles who fought in the Civil War (nine survived), and he eagerly accepted the honor, treating it as a second job.[444]

On May 13, 1991, in a ceremony at Arlington House, Robert E. Lee's residence and the centerpiece of Arlington National Cemetery, Heller announced the creation of the American Battlefield Protection Foundation to raise $100 million to buy and save more than 60,000 acres at major Civil War battlefields. The foundation, renamed the Civil War Trust in June 1992, was a private entity.[445]

"Our initial, main focus is to raise the funds for other Civil War groups and make sure we purchase the sites," Heller said. Interior Department spokesman Steve Goldstein endorsed the private initiative, saying, "This is an avenue for corporations . . . who have an interest in the Civil War to donate to a nonprofit." The announcement was hailed in the Civil War community and endorsed wholeheartedly by the still-young APCWS.[446]

"We were excited about this," recalled Dennis Frye, APCWS co-founder and board member. "Because the APCWS board knew that we didn't have corporate connections and probably never would have corporate connections. We saw the founding of the Civil War Trust as complementary to our efforts. APCWS was a grassroots organization that was dependent upon small donors . . . If corporations came to the table and provided millions of dollars, we could save thousands of acres of ground. And so our hope was that we could perhaps be in a consulting role . . ."[447] This initial spirit of cooperation was sealed when several key APCWS leaders—Gary Gallagher, James McPherson, Richard Gilder and Carrington Williams—joined the foundation's board.

The new foundation had offices in Washington at the National Housing Partnership, which Heller headed, and he personally provided the interim budget. But it struggled with start-up issues and staff turnover.[448] In December 1991, Heller hired an experienced leader, Grae Baxter, as executive vice president. Baxter had served in the administration of President Jimmy Carter as an assistant commissioner in the Department of Health, Education and Welfare and then received a law degree at Georgetown University.[449] Baxter had no background in history, but was a confident leader. After the first president departed only months into the job, Baxter was promoted to Trust president. She ambitiously doubled the initial goal of $100 million. The new goal, "simply stated, is $200 million by the year 2000 . . ." with $100 million by 1996, reported the foundation's strategic plan of March 24, 1992.[450]

Simultaneously, Lujan backed legislation to create a Civil War Commemorative Coin Program through the U.S. Mint that was projected to deliver $20 million of the first $100 million. Foundation board member Richard Moe of the National Trust for Historic Preservation shepherded the bill through Congress. The Mint would produce the coins, and profits from their sale would be distributed by the Trust for preserving battlefields through a grants program administered by the American Battlefield Protection Program (ABPP). As the commemorative coin bill worked its way through Congress in 1992, the Civil War Trust ran into a brick wall with corporate fundraising.

"It did not work," recalled Lester G. "Ruff" Fant, former chairman of the Trust. "And the reason it did not work was the Civil War, then and maybe now, was controversial. If you were a company that wanted to appeal broadly to consumers, like Coca-Cola, you're worried about being identified with slavery, you're worried about a lot of things, and it just seemed a little risky to give money to it.

"Ellis Island is a really feel-good thing," Fant said. "Everybody who went through there is an immigrant. They all came to this country, they all lived in this country and their descendants lived in this country. But the Civil War had a very different legacy and it affected people in a very different way. And for that reason, the consumer-oriented corporate America was not interested. Period."[451]

Even with no corporate funding, the Trust could bank on the commemorative coin funding—if it passed. But in September 1992, the program became a bargaining chip. U.S. Senator Malcolm Wallop of Wyoming, the ranking Republican on the Senate Energy and Natural Resources Committee and an outspoken land rights advocate, told Lujan that if he wanted to see the program approved, he had to revoke the National Register eligibility for Brandy Station.[452]

Bearss described the role Lee Sammis played: "Mr. Sammis had contacts with Senator John Seymour of California. Senator Seymour, a member of the Republican minority, works with . . . Wallop. Senator Wallop, through his staffer Jim O'Toole, who is an ex-park service person, takes the position that he is going to put on hold the coin legislation unless the determination of eligibility is rescinded. The secretary is very interested in getting the coin legislation passed. So the secretary makes the political decision, and I think a wise decision, to rescind the determination."[453]

When Lujan withdrew Brandy Station's eligibility, Congress promptly approved the coin program and the legislation was signed into law by President George H.W. Bush. Trust President Grae Baxter was left to explain the decision to the media. "What Interior has tried to do is come up with a solution that wouldn't do permanent damage to any preservation efforts, either Brandy Station or the coin bill," Baxter told the *Richmond Times-Dispatch*'s Christine Neuberger. The battlefield simply had to go through the process again to regain federal historic recognition, Interior officials said.[454]

Boasberg's contacts at Interior privately told him they had to "temporarily sacrifice" Brandy Station, and urged him to reapply. Boasberg put on a strong face for the media. He sympathized with Lujan, who "must have been under enormous political pressure" to reverse eligibility after fully examining the property—twice.[456]

Boasberg said he planned to launch another campaign to get the property listed. "I'm confident we will get it," he said.[457] But no one has ever reapplied. Lujan's reversal remains in effect; Brandy Station is not listed as being eligible for the federal historic register.

Meanwhile, the recession of 1990-91 was taking its toll. Hall heard rumors from Culpeper County officials and landowners that Lee Sammis was undercapitalized, overextended and might not survive. "You guys just need to hang on," Bob Kenefect, the supportive planning commissioner, told Hall.[458]

By 1992, Sammis wanted to resume face-to-face talks with the preservationists. A week after Lujan reversed the Brandy Station designation, Boasberg agreed to meet with Sammis and two associates at Sammis's office in northern Virginia.

"You better pack heat when you go in there," Hall jokingly warned Boasberg.[459] Sammis was "your typical, hard-nosed Greek businessman," Hall recalled. "He was accustomed to getting his way. He was big and brawny, and there was a hint of evil in those twinkling blue eyes of his. I called them 'hitman' eyes. But I was never intimidated by him. I gave as good as I got. He was like Lyndon Johnson – he would try to hover over you and he liked to invade your body space. I'll never forget him asking me one time: 'What do you want? What do you *really* want?' I told him, "I want you to leave this battlefield alone, and I want you to go home."[460]

The meeting between Sammis and Boasberg on September 19 began "with Lee going through his litany of hate: Bud Hall, Tersh Boasberg, National Park Service and all the others who were in a massive conspiracy to deny him his Constitutional right to pursue the American dream," Boasberg wrote in a memo four days later.[461] Sammis complained that the preservationists wanted all of his property and did not want him to develop on any of it. "That's not true at all," Boasberg argued. "We just want sensitive development."[462]

Sammis cut to the core: What would the preservationists pay for the St. James and Cunningham farm areas, key battlefield sites within the 1,500 rezoned acres? Boasberg said he had no money, but had access to money and, if necessary, could start a national fundraising effort.

"He was anxious to try to get some settlement, I think, but reluctant to give up very much," Boasberg wrote. Ultimately, nothing came of these negotiations.[463]

Lujan decided to appoint a committee to "settle" the Brandy Station issue. He asked Heller and the Civil War Trust to intercede and serve as mediator. The hope was that the Trust could work in the "maze of conflicting interests," as Heller put it.[464]

Heller saw this as a no-win role for his organization. The Trust was just getting

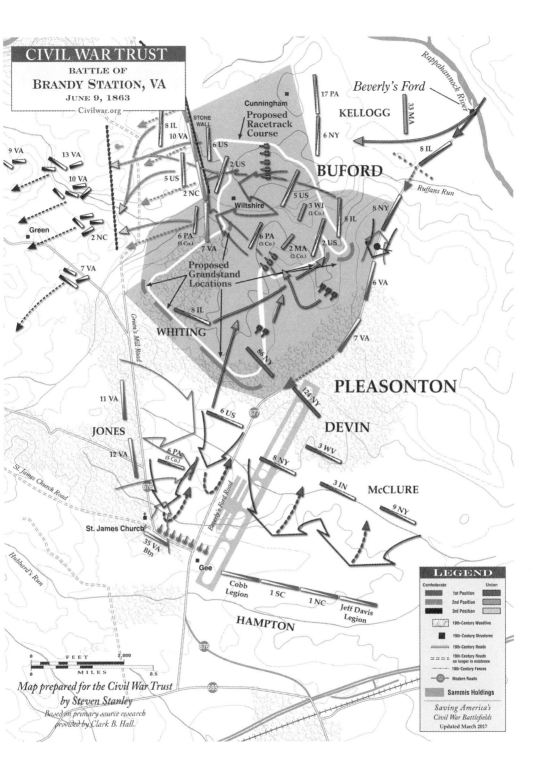

Rappahannock River

Beverly's Ford

17 PA

33 MA

KELLOGG

6 NY

8 IL

8 IL

10 VA

STONE
WALL

Cunningham

Proposed
Racetrack
Course

6 US

2 US

BUFORD

Ruffans Run

9 VA

13 VA

10 VA

5 US

2 NC

Wiltshire

5 US

3 WI
(1 Co.)

8 IL

8 NY

Green

2 NC

6 PA
(5 Co.)

7 VA

6 PA
(5 Co.)

2 MA
(2 Co.)

2 US

7 VA

Proposed
Grandstand
Locations

6 VA

8 IL

WHITING

7 VA

86 NY

11 VA

PLEASONTON

JONES

6 US

677

124 NY

DEVIN

12 VA

6 PA
(5 Co.)

8 NY

3 WV

St. James Church Road

676

3 IN

McCLURE

St. James Church

35 VA
Btn

Beverly's Ford Road

9 NY

Hubbard's Run

Gee

Cobb
Legion

1 SC

1 NC

Jeff Davis
Legion

HAMPTON

676

685

Map prepared for the Civil War Trust
by Steven Stanley
Based on primary source research
provided by Clark B. Hall.

FEET   2,000

MILES   0.5

started, but already saving land. It had donated $35,000 to a local Kentucky preservation group to save 19 acres of Mill Springs battlefield and was closing on the purchase of 56 acres, for $440,000, of Harpers Ferry battlefield that included Stonewall Jackson's position on School House Ridge.[465]

Reluctantly, Heller acceded to Lujan's request and Baxter began discussions that evolved into negotiations with Sammis about buying portions of Brandy Station. Baxter agreed to sign a confidentiality agreement about her discussions.[466]

In December 1992, in another indication of Sammis's funding troubles, Elkwood Downs decided to put 600 acres of one its properties, an 860-acre farm, up for auction, keeping 260 acres for development.[467] Five months later, in May 1993, came the bombshell news: Sammis was bankrupt. Elkwood Downs filed for bankruptcy under Chapter 11 reorganization statutes. Sammis and Armm, his project manager, laid the blame directly at the feet of battlefield preservationists and no-growth local residents. Asked by a reporter how and why it happened, Armm recalled the three words Boasberg had uttered to the *Civil War News* in 1991 after hearing the gratifying news that their lawsuit would to go to trial: "This kills 'em."[468]

The real purpose of the lawsuit, Armm said, was to cause delays. On that point, Boasberg agreed. If the only thing the lawsuit did was buy time—months of time—it had served its purpose. Boasberg "lost the case, but won a great deal," Sammis said.[469] And there were other costs as well, he complained. The project, he said, had "a big black cloud over it" until the two sides could compromise.[470]

More than four years had passed since Sammis bought his first farm. He had spent millions, but had done no marketing whatsoever of Elkwood Downs "because we knew it was useless," Sammis said. "There wasn't a lender in the world or a user in the world who would look at us. There wasn't a way in the world we could be viable as an industrial park with the (historic) designations. We finally just reached the end of our rope. The financial outgoing of constantly defending ourselves... was disastrous."[471]

"I'm not going to go away," Sammis said. "And I think we still have enough property left to do some of these things" in the proposed project.[472]

Recalled Armm: "The lack of compromise was the most frustrating thing. Lee figured, 'Okay, you're upset about this, Bud. You've got your followers and you have this following of no-growthers who now love hanging their hat on this historic aspect. You won't give us a compromise, so that's what's killing the whole thing. Let's just sit down and make a compromise. Let's work on the proffers. Let's work on the set-asides.' And that just never worked for them."[473]

So, the long struggle continued, and in fact, was soon to intensify. The preservationists' dogged campaign and the counterattack by Sammis and supportive local landowners was exemplified by two separate events that took place on June 23, 1993.

In Washington, the National Trust for Historic Preservation announced that Brandy Station battlefield, threatened by "haphazard commercial sprawl," had been named to its 1993 list of "America's 11 Most Endangered Historic Places."[474] That same day, 110 miles to the south, in Richmond, the board of directors of the Virginia Department of Historic Resources voted to remove the Brandy Station and nearby Bristoe battlefields from the Virginia Historic Register. The removal came after affected land owners formally complained, invoking the new state law approved in 1992 that allowed them to overrule a historic designation.[475]

In July 1993, members of the Civil War Sites Advisory Commission (CWSAC) gathered on the steps of the Lincoln Memorial to unveil their report on the state of Civil War battlefields. The commission identified and studied 384 principal battlefields in 26 states. It found about a third of them were already lost to development. Of the 232 judged to be in good or fair condition, about half were or would likely be threatened with development in the next decade—"disappearing under new buildings, parking lots and highways."[476]

From Cold Harbor in Virginia to Port Hudson in Louisiana; from Mobile Bay in Alabama to Glorieta Pass in New Mexico, battlegrounds judged to be "Class A Battlefields," with a "decisive influence on the outcome of the war," sat largely unprotected.[477]

"The battlefields are the surviving landscape of the war," McPherson said in a short speech at the ceremony. "They are, indeed, hallowed ground . . ."[478]

The CWSAC recommended spending $93 million to save land at the 50 most significant battlefields, with the federal government contributing $70 million in grants over seven years, matched by funds from states and non-profits. U.S. Senator Dale Bumpers (D-Ark.), who had championed the legislative taking at Manassas, promised a new bill to authorize the spending, but agreed that it would be difficult with Congress focused on cuts and the deficit.[479]

An appropriation never came out of that effort, but the commission's report became the guide for Civil War battlefield preservation and continues today as the primary source for setting Trust acquisition priorities. Grae Baxter hailed the "voluntary, non-adversarial approach" that was now the "strategy of choice" in preservation in a *Washington Post* commentary. "Such a cooperative system is already working at Brandy Station in Culpeper County," she wrote.[480]

The "cooperative system" lasted about one more week. The multi-party negotiations that included Sammis, Baxter and Boasberg continued that summer, but by then Boasberg had become deeply concerned. In June, Sammis filed the proposed Elkwood Downs bankruptcy reorganization plan with the court. The plan included the proposed sale of 683 acres for $3.4 million to Benton Ventures, Ltd., a company headed by New York businessman James Lazor, who intended to build a world-class automobile road racing track. The facility would be designed to attract the Formula One World Championship—the world's premier auto racing series—and revive the dormant United States Grand Prix.

The land in question was Sammis's first farm purchase in 1987, where the battle of Brandy Station opened. When Boasberg asked Baxter about the proposed sale at a meeting on July 22, she said she had signed a confidentiality agreement and could not provide any further information. But she told Boasberg that the Trust saw it as better to save at least some of the battlefield instead of losing all of it. The plan was to let one farm go in a compromise that would save another historic farm at the center of the battlefield.[481]

"This kind of 'Sophie's choice' —the loss of Button to save Spillman—causes the Foundation severe problems," Boasberg wrote to Baxter in a follow-up letter. Don't give up on either property just yet, Boasberg wrote. "He's in deep trouble," Boasberg said of Sammis. "It seems to be that our best chance is now, with Sammis in extremis, to see how much he'd take for both . . ."[482]

When Hall learned of the race track plans, he requested a meeting with Lazor, who met him on the battlefield on August 13. Hall took Lazor to Buford's Knoll, where Union General John Buford had commanded his troops during the morning phase of the battle. Hall told Lazor that his track would carve a course around the knoll and alongside the historic stone wall where a Confederate defensive line cut down the attacking Yankees. A quarter of the men killed at Brandy Station fell there.

"That's where your track is going to go," Hall said.

"Yes, you've got that right," Lazor said. He was defiant, Hall recalled. "Mr. Hall, you might not like it, but we'll build our race track here. Whether you like it or not, we're going to build it here," he said.

"You know what? I'll take that action," Hall replied. "You're *not* going to build your race track here. And we'll see who's right."[483]

On September 8, 1993, Benton Ventures filed its race track plans with the Culpeper County Planning Commission and formally unveiled the $15 million project. "World-Class Motorsports Complex," the press release headline read. "Businessman Pledges Commitment to Historic, Environmental Issues."[484]

More than 65 percent of the 515-acre tract would remain undeveloped, Lazor said in the release, and the track would be "tailor-fit . . . right into the natural contours of the land with minimal disturbance to the existing pristine wooded and grassy land. We're also pleased to maintain the adjacent land's integrity and will continue to work with officials from the Civil War Trust, the National Park Service and the Commonwealth and the County to ensure that our plan is as sensitive as possible to their valid and important concerns."[485]

The Brandy Station Foundation saw the project as a complete disaster – "perhaps the most invasive project ever proposed in Culpeper County," Boasberg and foundation director Arthur B. Larson wrote in a 27-page transcript of their testimony before the planning commission on October 13.

The track, Boasberg argued, would subject county citizens to "explosive noise, huge traffic jams and environmental pollution." Its construction would expose the county to "serious financial risks" and would "seriously devalue residential properties for miles around." He asked the commission to deny the Benton Ventures' request for the special use permit to allow the track or to delay it until more information was available about specifics of the project. Forty people spoke at the public hearing; 36 in opposition.

Meanwhile, word spread through the Civil War community that the threat at Brandy Station was once again imminent. Hall described it as an "unmitigated disaster."

"There is terrible news from Brandy Station," Jerry Russell wrote in his September 1993 *Civil War Round Table Associates Newsletter*. His article hit the Civil War Trust and Baxter far harder than it did the race track. He accused the Trust of being "involved up to its ears in a deal to rescue the bankrupt California developer, Lee Sammis."[486]

Baxter was trying to find a solution that was acceptable to all sides and allowed some of the seemingly inevitable development supported and approved by the county. "The issue is what do we do in the face of this in order to preserve as much of the battlefield as possible," she said.[487] The BSF, Hall, and most preservationists, however, favored an all-out war to stop the project altogether.

Russell believed Baxter's efforts provided Sammis and the county with legitimacy and the out they needed to present themselves as responsible to all citizens. Under intense pressure from leading preservationists to declare its opposition to the race track, the Trust's executive committee released a "Statement of Principles" on September 27: "We deeply regret the possibility of a racetrack on a portion of Brandy Station battlefield and certainly express our opposition in principle to the race track project."[488]

But the Trust also recognized "that community decisions are at the core of the preservation process" and thus would not "become deeply involved in local decision-making."[489] The organization said it wanted to continue to work with everyone involved "to preserve as much of the Brandy Station battlefield as possible . . ."[490]

Hall was as angry as Russell about Baxter's strategy. He arranged to meet with Baxter at her Washington, D.C., office. He could barely contain himself as he stood and, in his words, "did 99 percent of the talking."

"Grae, this will never happen," he said. "*Don't buy into this.* You'll come out of this with serious egg on your face. We'll stop at nothing."[491] Baxter was flustered by his intimidating approach, but replied, "Well, we're going to go forward with this."

"You're gonna lose this battle," Hall said. "We'll see to it. You're going to lose this battle."

Hall recalled: "I came unglued. I thought she was engaged in a conspiracy. I felt that I was in the presence of someone who had personally betrayed our cause. This was the kind of thing we'd been fighting all along—not standing up for principle. Grae Baxter didn't know the battle. She had no personal, emotional connection to Brandy Station, yet she was making decisions about Brandy Station."[492]

"They demonized me," Baxter recalled of her harshest opponents. "They demonized me on the basis of no facts. It's a holy war for some of them. There's almost a zealotry involved. You either agreed with them or you're the enemy. I am all about solving problems, getting things done, moving forward. And I did nothing that wasn't supported by the board of trustees.

"I remember being utterly shocked. Bud Hall was abusive to me. Bud Hall was a bully. And I have never been in a professional environment where people behaved like that. And I was very disappointed, because he's a bright guy. And I don't disagree with what his personal passions are. But where I disagreed was, we had to look at the bigger pictures, and they viewed it as a battle to the death."[493]

Hall took his complaints in writing to Civil War Trust Chairman Rod Heller, who, along with his board, defended his executive director. "We did support her," Heller recalled. "She was our choice. And I certainly supported her down the line and I think the board did as well. And so she was by no means out there by herself. But inevitably she bore the burden. I think some of the animus was directed at Grae as a woman, which was unfortunate. We were pacesetters in that regard. But it certainly made Grae's life more difficult and it also impeded her future effectiveness."[494]

The criticism of the Trust was intense. Annie Snyder decried the Trust's action as "betraying their trust by lending their officers to promote" the desecration of the battlefield.[495] Pohanka wrote Heller, warning him that "whatever good will the Trust has generated within the Civil War community will be severely jeopardized if this proposed 'Motorsports Complex' receives anything other than the scorn and vehement opposition it so clearly deserves."[496]

No one was more strident than Russell. When Heller wrote him on October 28 to criticize his harsh attitude toward Baxter and point out inaccuracies, Russell responded with a three-page, single-spaced letter that concluded with a "formal request to see the tax records of the Civil War Trust for 1991 and 1992 and whatever records are available for 1993."[497]

Trust Board Member Howard A. Hillman wrote Russell a sharper letter, criticizing his "caterwauling," his "skulking diatribe" and his "repugnant" all-or-nothing tactics. "Your writings show no gallantry and on balance, are cowardly," Hillman wrote.[498]

Russell responded to Hillman's "totally unreasonable letter" with a six-page screed of his own, declaring, "All or nothing tactics may be 'repugnant' to dilettantes-come-lately like you, but folks who are committed to Civil War battlefield preservation understand that many times 'all or nothing tactics' are the only hope to protect the battlefields."[499]

To Boasberg and his fellow preservationists, Lazor's project appeared to be a speculative pipe dream. Boasberg developed contacts in the racing community who told him Lazor was largely unknown in the sport and his chances for success appeared to be extremely long at best. Although Formula One racing was an international phenomenon, the sport held only modest interest in the United States, as the record showed. From the 1980s through the early 1990s, the United States Grand Prix bounced from Long Beach, California to Las Vegas to Detroit to Dallas to Phoenix and finally ceased to exist after 1991. Homegrown NASCAR racing was on the rise, and the nation's leading motorsports series already ran two races a year on road racing courses. But Lazor had no chance for a NASCAR race, because the sport was well represented if not overexposed in Virginia, with four major annual NASCAR races.

Lazor pressed on as the planning commission endorsed the application in December. In January 1994, as the Culpeper County Board of Supervisors prepared to rule on the special use permit, Boasberg made another plea to Heller and Baxter, telling them "we have a chance to win if we pull out all the stops. Now is the time to express the Trust's unequivocal opposition to the race track."[500]

On January 21, Baxter adopted the hardcore preservationists' stance. In a three-page letter to board Chairman Jack E. Fincham, Baxter said the track project "challenged to the limit" the Trust's ability to have a respectful and conciliatory negotiation. "It was difficult to imagine a more repugnant and intrusive use," she wrote. The track, she said, was a "dead end" for the county.

She asked the supervisors to disapprove it "as an inappropriate and destructive use of historic and beautiful land . . ."[501] The Trust asserted that it would not negotiate to purchase any land as long as the track was planned, effectively removing the organization from the Brandy Station controversy.

On February 1, 1994, the county board of supervisors voted 5-2 to approve Lazor's race track. He acknowledged he still faced challenges, including purchasing the land from Sammis, but expected to begin construction of a 3.1-mile paved road racing course in early April.

"Some people obviously don't want this track, and I can understand that," Lazor said. "But it will be built here. Sorry to the preservationists and whatever they think. There's not going to be any major hurdles . . . "[502] ★

CHAPTER
EIGHT

Disney's America

OR A WOMAN whose mastery of the media and public relations had made her the best-known of all Civil War battlefield preservationists, Annie Snyder was determined to keep her family life private. She was usually available at her Pageland Farm, next to Manassas National Battlefield Park. But when it came to her family's annual ski trips to Colorado, Snyder considered herself off limits.

She rarely relaxed her guard, but in 1990 she slipped and gave her Copper Mountain phone number to a *Washington Post* reporter. More than a year later, the phone rang while the family was there and Snyder found herself being interviewed by a different *Post* reporter, who obtained the number through the other reporter.[503]

So, in early October 1993, while she was talking with Jody Powell just before another Colorado trip and he asked for her Copper Mountain number, she said no.

"That's my refuge," she told him. "And it won't be if my number out there becomes common knowledge."[504]

Powell worked hand-in-hand with Snyder after his Washington public relations firm, Powell Tate, had jumped in to lead the media fight against William Center. They became fast friends. Powell wanted to know if Brandy Station battlefield was high on her list. She said yes, she was helping Bud Hall by writing protest letters and generating more letters from others.

Powell changed the subject. "There's someone I want you to talk with," he told her. "I can't tell you who it is now, but it's very important that he talk with you."[505]

"I'll be glad to talk to whomever you want me to talk to," she told him from Pageland, "but I'll be returning to Colorado in a week or so."[506]

Snyder and her husband, Pete, arrived in Colorado on November 8 to discover that Powell had been trying to reach her. She called his office a couple of times and finally, reluctantly, left her Colorado number. Powell called within the hour.

"The people I told you I wanted you to talk with are from Disney," Powell said. They wanted to build an American history theme park in Haymarket, about seven miles west of the Manassas battlefields. And they had hired Powell Tate to do the public relations work.[507]

Powell told Snyder that the Disney Company had bought about 3,000 acres, including the large Waverley Plantation, along Route 15 just north of Interstate 66. Snyder was incredulous. "What a beautiful piece of land that is," she said. "And that's on a two-lane highway. Billions will have to be spent to improve the road system." Powell suggested that buses and rapid transit could handle a good bit of the extra traffic.

Powell said Disney would be holding a press conference in a few days. He said he would FedEx the formal announcement to her. "I want you to know that if you decide to oppose the project, it will not diminish my affection for you," he said.[508]

On one level Snyder could sympathize with Powell. It must have been uncomfortable for him to drop this bombshell on the preservationists he had come to know and admire in the William Center fight. But Orlando next to Manassas? "I was so stunned I hardly knew what to say," Snyder wrote a few weeks later in a letter to Jerry Russell. "I told him I had worked for 40 years to retain the semi-rural status of western Prince William and now it looked as if all I had done was save the land for things like Disney."[509]

Powell could take some solace in that he had reached her before she was blindsided by the news, which broke that morning with a *Wall Street Journal* bare-bones report that Disney planned an "America" theme park somewhere in Virginia. The following day, November 9, *The Washington Post* narrowed it to Prince William County and the next day pinpointed the location.[510]

County officials were euphoric. "I'm going to Disney World!" exclaimed Claude "Brad" Bradshaw, an aide to Supervisor Bobby McManus, in whose district the park was to be built. Snyder was out of touch, carving paths through white powder in Colorado, so Save the Battlefield Coalition President Betty Rankin was the first to speak out. "People from Disney need to come forward and lay their cards on the table," she said. "We shouldn't be reading bits and pieces of speculation in the paper. . ."[511]

Disney had not yet gone public, but details emerged from their "private" briefings on Capitol Hill. The short distance from the theme park to Manassas National Battlefield Park was cited as a good thing because it "would be close to another prominent historic landmark," the *Post* reported.[512]

"I think people have learned a lesson to keep away from the battlefield," Bradshaw said. "But something tells me there is a lot of other land in the county outside it."[513]

On November 11, Disney confirmed the obvious, announcing its plans for "Disney's America" in simultaneous press conferences in Richmond and Manassas. Besides the theme park, the development would include 2,500 homes and two million square feet of commercial space. Disney said the $650 million project would employ 2,700 people. The "unprecedented investment in Prince William County and the Commonwealth of Virginia" was expected to generate $40 million in new revenues between 1993 and 1998, the company said, and over 30 years could produce more than $680 million for Prince William County and $1.18 billion for the state.

Disney's best creative minds, the Imagineers, came up with a layout that would allow park visitors to absorb the American experience. After entering at Crossroads USA, visitors would circle Freedom Bay, traveling to nine "Territories" aboard an

1840s-style steam-powered train to experience the broad tapestry of American history from 1600 to 1945.[514]

A replica of Independence Hall would be the centerpiece in President's Square, while the Native American Territory would feature a Powhatan village and a Lewis and Clark Expedition raft adventure ride. At a Civil War fort, visitors would experience the everyday life of a soldier. Reenactors would do battle daily and a Circlevision 360 movie would feature battlefield scenes. In a nighttime spectacular, the *Monitor* and *Merrimac* (*Virginia*) would fight again, every evening, in Freedom Bay.

The difficulty of mixing thrill rides with real history without compromising either proved to be one of Disney's thorniest issues. In the Industrial Age town of Enterprise, a planned high-speed thrill ride through a 1900s steel mill—complete with an escape from a vat of molten steel—was abandoned out of concern that it would trivialize the manufacturing process and taint the true history of the steel era.[515]

Disney's America represented the next step in CEO Michael Eisner's quest to expand the reach of the venerable entertainment company. After transforming Paramount Studios into a box office hit factory, Eisner had taken over at Disney in 1984 and turned it into one of the most profitable in the country. Seemingly anything he touched, or put his mind to, turned to gold.

For Eisner, "there was no project during my first decade at Disney about which I felt more passionate than Disney's America … " Eisner said he loved history and saw the park as a logical and public-minded extension of the company's interest in children, American heritage and education.[516]

When Eisner called Virginia Governor-elect George Allen in early November 1993 to give him advance notice, he was tickled to find Allen vacationing at Disney World with his family after his landslide election victory. Allen was delighted and told Eisner it was just the kind of project he wanted to bring to Virginia. Allen promised his full support, as did many others.[517] But despite the giddiness of state and local politicians and business owners, Disney's America faced trouble from the beginning.

By the time Disney announced the project on November 11, the *Post* had moved on to reaction stories, and its next-morning headline read: "In Disney's Grand Plan, Some See a Smoggy, Cloggy Transportation Mess."[518]

Another *Post* story that day grabbed most of the attention. A Disney executive out of Orlando, Scott Stahley, had worked "under cover befitting a secret agent" for more than two years to keep his land acquisition mission a secret, lest land prices skyrocket in a speculation boom. Identifying himself as "Scott Roberts," Stahley told local real estate agents he was from Phoenix and represented a "confidential trust," the *Post* reported. He used untraceable phone numbers, mail drops and dummy companies. He talked knowledgably about the Phoenix Suns pro basketball team—then headed home to Orlando. He used purchase contracts and options rather than risk the paper trails of outright purchases, the paper reported.[519]

The first opponents of Disney's America were not Civil War battlefield preservationists, but wealthy farm owners in Virginia hunt country. Some of the richest families in the country owned horse farms in the gently rolling hills of northern Virginia, just west of where the theme park was to be built. Many landowners feared the beautiful countryside would be marred forever by the park and collateral development it would bring, as it did in Orlando. "The setting was so beautiful that I began to wonder how local residents would feel about our building a theme park there, no matter how much of the land was preserved," Eisner wrote in his autobiography *Work in Progress*.[520]

Five days after the news broke, Charles S. Whitehouse, co-chairman of the Piedmont Environmental Council (PEC), a regional conservation organization, invited other local landowners to his impeccably groomed 90-acre horse farm in northern Fauquier County to organize against Disney and to formulate an opposition strategy. They decided to launch a campaign to generate negative publicity, but to refrain from direct attacks on the popular entertainment company. William Backer, the recently retired New York ad executive who came up with "Things go better with Coke," suggested a campaign around the slogan, "Disney, Take a Second Look."[521] Although the PEC's nine-county region did not include Prince William County, the organization became the most visible and vocal group against the project.

One of the most influential early skeptics was National Trust for Historic Preservation President Richard Moe, who had just published The Last Full Measure, an acclaimed regimental history of the First Minnesota Volunteers. In an essay "Downside to 'Disney's America,'" published on *The Washington Post* op-ed page on December 21, 1993, Moe did not explicitly oppose the project, but raised concerns about sprawl, the impact on genuine historic sites, and the potential for unauthentic history. "Can George Washington co-exist with Mickey Mouse?" Moe asked. "Can the meaning of the Civil War be conveyed next to a roller coaster?" Given the "countervailing pressures of authentic history on the one hand and sustained commercial success on the other…" Disney, Moe suggested, "should at least attempt to enlist some real historians—people like James McPherson and Shelby Foote on the Civil War…"[522]

A month later, on January 20, 1994, Allen asked the Virginia legislature to approve Disney's request for $137 million in state-backed bonds for highway improve-

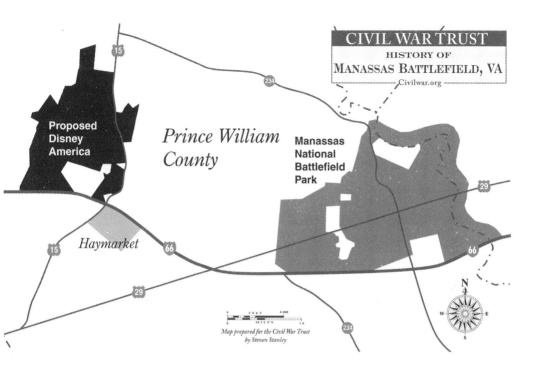

Proposed Disney America

Prince William County

Manassas National Battlefield Park

Haymarket

ments—primarily the widening of Interstate 66 near the park and construction of a new interchange—and $21 million for highway signs, advertising and other costs. Allen promised to "kick down any hurdles" to get the legislation passed quickly.[523] Disney's hope was to take care of all government approvals and preliminary measures in 1994, begin construction in 1995 and open the park in 1998.

As Disney mounted an intense lobbying campaign, newly hired PEC attorney Chris Miller and colleague Hilary Gerhardt moved to Richmond to be on the scene daily. It was a challenge to drum up opposition to the Disney project, which enjoyed widespread support in both houses of the Virginia legislature.[524] Miller brought in Mike Siegel, an economist who specialized in fiscal impact analysis, to testify at state hearings. Siegel raised his eyebrow at the big numbers Disney had cited in trumpeting the park's economic benefits.

It was "circus atmosphere" at the hearings in Richmond, Siegel recalled, as Disney brought in supporters by the busload. "Of course, this being my field, I realized that much of this was wrong and was really not much more than basic propaganda," Siegel recalled, He warned PEC and Miller promptly retained him as a consultant.[525]

Disney's revenue projections "didn't even attempt to quantify what the costs were supposed to be" to state and local governments, Siegel said. "And they overestimated revenues ... grossly overestimated revenues. We would give a net analysis. Well, Disney didn't do a net analysis. They did a gross analysis and then their gross analysis was grossed up. So it wasn't even really what we would call an economic or fiscal impact analysis. It was basically just a piece of propaganda to be used in a marketing campaign to generate a big number that looked impressive."[526]

Disney built support wherever it could and stayed in close touch with its long list of supporters. Its onsite staff met local groups with a friendly, neighborly approach, sent newsletters to 100,000 area households and financed and coordinated efforts of local pro-Disney groups. Disney met with officials from area museums and historic sites to brief them on how the park would present history and precisely as Moe suggested, it sought the help of prominent historians.[527]

Shelby Foote, the writer and historian who became a celebrity after his matchless Southern drawl, intellect and courtly manner were put on full display in Ken Burns's *Civil War* in 1990, turned Disney down flat. "I don't want to run them down," Foote said, "but I'm afraid they'll do to American history what they did to the animal kingdom—turn chipmunks and all the rest into chittering little lovable things. Well, a chipmunk can bite your hand damn near off. I worry about simplifying history; it's such a complex thing."[528]

McPherson also rejected Disney's advance. But his situation was more complicated. He was the vice president of the APCWS, and soon after he joined its board in 1991, the organization developed a strong and amiable working relationship with Disney Channel President John Cooke, a key Eisner lieutenant.

Cooke had become friends with Will Greene after taking battlefield tours with him. When Greene mentioned APCWS's plans to produce a corporate fundraising video, Cooke told him Disney would do it at no charge. At the APCWS board meeting of July 20, 1991, at Tyson's Corner, the board listened in on speaker phone as Cooke repeated his generous offer. "He asserted that videos must be both informative, dramatic and entertaining," the minutes reported. "He even promised a narrator of the stature of Richard Dreyfuss for the videos."[529]

Cooke said he could begin filming that fall. All the APCWS had to do was provide scripts and historical expertise. "The Board was delighted at the offer of the Disney Channel to help us in a major way . . . and could see no negative aspect," read the minutes. The 1991 teleconference ended with the board members "effusively" thanking Cooke.[530]

The videos were listed on the agenda and discussed at the next four board meetings. Ultimately, the project was scaled back to one seven-minute video that the board saw for the first time at its March 1992 meeting. The board "was very impressed with its quality . . . " the minutes said.[531] But the video was never mentioned again and seems to have been infrequently used, if ever. Today, Greene, Gallagher and Frye have no memory of it.

Disney reappeared on the APCWS radar in 1993 when the popular and influential Carrington Williams began teasing his fellow board members with hints of an impending surprise. "Something big is coming," Williams would say. "Something *really* big is coming. And it will benefit the Civil War. It will be an opportunity to highlight Civil War history and Civil War battlefield preservation."[532]

After the news broke, Disney officials formally approached Greene and asked the APCWS to be historical consultants. Greene informed the board members, who began debating the issue in a flurry of letters, phone calls and discussions.

"When it first came out, people were cautious, wanting to know more information, including us," Greene recalled. "Before it was controversial, it was intriguing and it raised all sorts of questions. And so we went about this in a very methodical, cautious way. It wasn't like when we first heard about it, we'd all jumped on the bandwagon and said, 'Oh, this great.' It was a very carefully considered position that we took."[533]

Supporters argued that APCWS would shape Disney's presentation of the Civil War in a genuine and authentic way. In exchange, Disney promised a large cash donation for the purchase of battlefield land, thus benefiting APCWS's primary mission. Disney would give APCWS a presentation area in the new park, and would contribute in some material way to Manassas National Battlefield Park.[534]

APCWS board members considered the proposals during a six-hour meeting on February 5, 1994, in the press room of the Fredericksburg *Free Lance-Star*. Disney would pay the APCWS $250 an hour—120 hours for $30,000 plus expenses—for its help during the next three months. Greene reported that he had met with Jody Powell and Disney's America Project Director Mark Pacala, and expressed his concern "about the content of the project, its impact on land prices and Civil War sites in northern Virginia and its competition with real historic attractions," the minutes reported.[535]

After spirited discussions, the board approved the contract, with McPherson and Howard Coffin opposing it.[536] The minutes do not mention dissent or opposition, only a final note that Greene "will keep us apprised on this matter."[537]

"There was serious discussion of the pros and cons about our relationship with Disney," Greene recalled. "There was no naiveté on our part in that we understood that Disney was going to be using us as a PR tool. We were not naïve about that. We considered all the reasons to oppose Disney. The only one that we could come up with was that it was going to create a public relations challenge with our membership to explain what was really going on and the benefits to battlefield preservation of entering into this agreement with them."[538]

News of the contract caused an immediate uproar in the Civil War community and shattered the unity that had existed since the founding of APCWS. When Greene called Annie Snyder to tell her, "I really lost my cool," she said. "So you're going to make money off Disney to save Civil War battlefields, and destroy Manassas in the process," she snarled.[539]

Snyder told journalist Deborah Fitts: "It's very unfortunate that APCWS permitted themselves to be used in this manner. It was a serious mistake. Disney is certainly making prostitutes of many."[540]

"I think Will Greene honestly believes this is not a sellout, that it's not an endorsement of the Disney project—and he's wrong," Jerry Russell said. "It is a sell-out. It's an attempt by Disney to co-opt the Civil War movement. APCWS has crossed the line to the ranks of the enemy."[541]

Civil War book publisher and APCWS member Tom Broadfoot, who had shared his mailing list with the APCWS, said the decision was "beyond stupidity, it's unbelievable," adding, "As far as I'm concerned, the integrity of APCWS has been totally compromised by this decision." He said he intended to tell his customers that the APCWS was now "nothing more than a paid bed partner" with Disney.[542]

Greene was resolute in his defense: "Make no mistake," he said. "The association has certainly not been 'bought and paid for' by Disney." And preservation, he said, would benefit "rather handsomely" from a direct donation of Disney cash to buy battlefield land.[543]

Gallagher and founding board member Brian Pohanka clearly struggled after their initial support of Disney and its promise of money for battlefield land. Gallagher called it a "good, if not perfect, bargain." Said Pohanka, "You've got to pick your battles." That area was doomed to development in any event, he said, and Disney may be "not stoppable." He added, "If we can get millions of dollars for preservation out of Disney, the sacrifice would be worth it."[544]

Gallagher recalled how Disney's efforts to court him turned him off instead: "I got a full court press from John Cooke … He wined and dined us. My ex-wife was from South Pasadena. We were out there all the time when we were married. Twice they sent a limo over to pick us up and took us to the Bel-Air Hotel and to the special table in the corner. And you know, leaning over with just the most, you know, 'We're really serious about this. We really love history.' Well, of course they didn't! They didn't want a public relations nightmare.

"The idea that they were going to really do the history of slavery? No one would go! What are they going to do? Are they going to show people being whipped? It was such a crock. It's a complete crock that they would do history the right way. I would say if they did the history right, no one would go. And so, they would not do history right."[545]

McPherson refused an invitation to be Disney's historical consultant and was opposed from the start. He regretted the APCWS approval. He had "grave reservations" about the impact of Disney on Manassas and other battlefields and saw "great danger" in a Disney treatment of American history—an "artificial and probably sanitized version..."[546]

Other board members were just as avidly for it, including Williams and another recent addition, Tom Richards, who had headed The Nature Conservancy. Dennis Frye was an enthusiastic supporter. On April 8–11, 1994, Frye and five others, including Greene and Pohanka, visited with Disney's Imagineers at Epcot Center in Orlando.[547] Together, they explored how to present the Civil War without sanitizing it. Frye and Pohanka told the Imagineers about the trove of "incredible photographs, these stereo photographs," that were an untapped visual resource. "We talked about the types of things that Disney could do with 3-D using historic resources. And to teach about photography. And to show the Antietam photos," Frye recalled. "And they were very excited about the type of presentation we were making to them. It was a remarkable, energizing, creative period—one of the most creative periods of my life."[548]

The APCWS support, announced on February 14 in a Disney press release, could only help the company as legislation was considered by the Virginia Senate and House of Delegates. The PEC's Miller and Gerhardt tried to rally opposition, but the votes were not there. Disney had blunted the attack of its opponents by using their wealth and status against them, depicting the PEC and its influential supporters as snobby, not-in-my-backyard elitists. A $163 million support package, nearly all the company had asked for, sailed through the state Senate 35–5 and the House of Delegates 73–25 on March 12. Miller and Gerhardt left Richmond in defeat.[549] The war appeared to be lost. Disney was on the fast track for local governmental approval to begin building the park in 1995.

"It was really the county government that had the keys," economist Siegel recalled. "And the county government was, again, all in, fully in, with Disney. They were going to approve anything that the Disney Company wanted them to approve. And quite frankly, there was nothing I could say or anybody else could say that would cause them to not do so. There was no path to victory. It was going to be a loss. We were going to lose. The state was going to give them the money, and we were going to lose."[550]

But fresh opposition emerged. A new organization to fight Disney, *Protect Historic America*, was created in the spring of 1994 by journalist Nick Kotz, public relations specialist Julian Scheer and others. Support came from a stunning range of notables ranging from conservative television commentators Pat Buchanan and Mary Matalin to consumer advocate Ralph Nader on the left. Actor Robert Duvall, who owns northern Virginia horse farm land and had worked on a Disney production in 1992, openly attacked the company as greedy. Dozens of top historians and scholars joined *Protect Historic America*, including David McCullough, Burns, Foote and the venerable historian C. Vann Woodward, one of the most influential historians of the post-World War II era. McPherson, turning his back on the APCWS entirely, agreed to be president of *Protect Historic America* and worked hard, writing four articles and appearing on television and radio. Bud Hall was on the board and Gallagher joined the organization's advisory panel. Both McPherson and Gallagher remained on the APCWS board.[551]

Kotz consulted with Moe, who threw the power of the National Trust for Historic Preservation behind the opposition. On May 2, the National Trust took out a full-page ad in *The Washington Post*, imploring Disney to seek another location. Nine days later, *Protect Historic America* held a press conference at the National Press Club in Washington, where its historians scathingly denounced the project. "We have so little left that's authentic and real," said McCullough. "To replace what we have with plastic, contrived history ... is almost sacrilege." In just weeks, *Protect Historic America* became a powerful and influential player—a national voice against Disney – because of its all-star lineup of endorsers.[552]

Despite the opposition of Gallagher and McPherson, a majority of the APCWS board remained unswayed in their support for Disney, voting at its May 6, 1994 meeting to continue the contract to provide historical consulting services for the proposed theme park.

That board meeting, at the Holiday Inn in Midlothian, Virginia, came just five days before the first *Protect Historic America* press conference denouncing the project. It was Gallagher's final meeting at the helm. Tom Richards was taking over as chairman as part of a new system of rotating chairmen.

In November 1993, the APCWS had changed its bylaws to make the Board of Directors the Board of Trustees. Greene's title was changed from Executive Director to President, and the board was headed by a chairman and vice-chairman. As Richards took over, Gallagher remained as a board member, but it marked the end of an era. Gallagher had been the only president/chairman of the APCWS since its founding almost seven years earlier.[553]

At the May 6 meeting, the Disney controversy continued to dominate discussions, and Coffin remembers being lobbied beforehand. "I was taken to breakfast, as I remember it, by Carrington and Will and perhaps Tom Richards," Coffin recalled. "They wanted me to go along with taking the money from Disney, and I told them I wouldn't do it and I thought it was the wrong thing to be doing."[554]

The board meeting that day lasted more than six hours. Most of the time was spent debating the Disney contract. The air was thick with tension. The debate was polite, but deep discord burned under the surface. Close personal friends Greene and Gallagher in particular had engaged in many long, often-tense conversations in the weeks before the meeting. Even after the long debate, the vote was not close: 11–4 in favor of renewing the contract. The minutes do not include the vote breakdown or say who was at the meeting, but McPherson, Gallagher and Coffin cast three of the four "no" votes and Pohanka, having become an opponent, probably cast the other. After the vote, Greene revealed that Disney had donated $100,000 to the APCWS for land preservation.[555]

Controversy or not, Greene put the Disney money to use. "I met the Disney people one Friday evening (in 1994) at a restaurant near Dulles Airport and they handed me a check for $100,000," he recalled. "I immediately went to Dulles to get on a plane to fly to Mississippi to meet with the people who were trying to preserve Brice's Cross Roads battlefield. They didn't know us from Adam."[556]

To reinforce the message that the APCWS was a serious and effective preservation organization, "at one point during the discussion I pulled out this check," Greene recalled. "I said, 'Here's a $100,000 check that could be used to help buy this battlefield,'" Greene said. Two years later, working with the local group, Brice's Cross Roads National Battlefield Commission, the APCWS bought 798 acres at Brice's Cross Roads, and the $100,000 Disney donation indeed went toward that purchase.[557]

The Disney's America controversy was barely on the radar at the Civil War Trust. The only mention is in the board meeting minutes of July 8, 1994, under "Other Business" where Richard Moe of the National Trust described "the full impact which Disney's America would have on one of the most important historic areas in the United States." The board took no action or official position on the project.[558]

The national media spotlight on the Disney project intensified. Eisner did himself no favors. "I'm shocked because I thought we were doing good. I expected to be taken around on people's shoulders," Eisner told *Washington Post* reporters and editors during a June visit. "It's private land that is not in the middle of a historic area...It's not in the middle of a battlefield." He said the "concept of reviewing a movie before the script is written or reviewing a book when you've only got the table of contents is pretty shocking to me." He savaged the historians of *Protect Historic America.* "I sat through many history classes where I read some of their stuff, and I didn't learn anything. It was pretty boring."[559]

Protect Historic America promptly placed an ad in the *New York Times* that republished Eisner's quote about the historians under the headline: "The Man Who Would Destroy American History."[560] Eisner would write that the opposition spurred him on, even if the fight extended the project's time schedule. As at Brandy Station, the preservationists would use every potential roadblock, from lawsuits, to demands for environmental impact reports, to public protests. If they could not stop the development, they would at least slow it down, all the while continuing the drumbeat of negative publicity, which they believed would affect a publicity conscious company like Disney.

The Disney Company was rocked in 1994 by other events. On April 3, Frank Wells, Eisner's top lieutenant, the Hyde to his Jekyll, died in a helicopter accident while skiing. On July 15, a month after his Washington visit, Eisner underwent emergency, quadruple-bypass heart surgery after suffering shortness of breath.[561]

Eisner was back at work by early August, but on the 29th he received a sobering report: Disney's America would lose money. Fighting the opposition was costly and the delays were adding to the cost. Refinements necessary to make the historical attractions acceptable increased projected costs by 40 percent. Revenues were down at Disney parks, and it appeared that projected ticket prices for Disney's America would need to be lower. After more analysis, a projected nine-month open season had been scaled back to eight months. On top of all that was the ongoing torrent of negative publicity led by *Protect Historic America.* On September 15, 1994, "after two weeks of soul searching," Eisner pulled the plug on his dream.[562]

For the PEC's Miller, the morning after the news broke remains his most memorable moment in preservation. "The television trucks came to my house in Arlington and did a 4:30 a.m. interview," he recalled. "And, you know, after living in complete tension and losing almost every debate in terms of the decision process for nine months, to have that announcement and be on camera, with your neighbors wondering what the hell was going on...that was pretty fun."[563]

Miller, such a central figure in the fight, cannot recall a thing about APCWS's role. "For the life of me, I don't remember them," he said. But the impact Disney had on APCWS was profound.[564]

"It almost killed the organization," Frye recalled. "I mean, the knife was right at the heart. And it almost penetrated. The rift was so deep...it didn't look like we were ever going to be able to unify again." Disney opponent Ed Bearss recalled that it got to the point that "Will Greene asked me not to do tours for him."[565]

"It was really the end of the group that had founded APCWS," recalled Gallagher. APCWS was "completely split."[566] When the APCWS board voted to renew the Disney contract May 6, Gallagher returned to Penn State to write one of the most difficult letters he ever typed. He took his old and close friend, Greene, to task over his handling of the Disney affair. Gallagher accused Greene of misrepresenting the attitudes of other trustees in an effort to generate full support for the consulting contract. He criticized Greene for "churlish" responses to Disney opponents, including Annie Snyder. "She has been a major figure in battlefield preservation and should not be treated as a cranky old woman," Gallagher wrote. He took Greene to task for describing Disney opponents as "the lunatic fringe" at the board meeting – "a direct slap at the four (opposing) directors who were then in room."[567]

Gallagher knew the letter would strike Greene as harsh. "Yet I believe the issues to be so important that I risk a rift with an old and valued friend," he wrote.[568] And indeed, that rift occurred. Greene felt betrayed when Gallagher's initial support for the project turned to strong opposition. "We drew lines, and it took *years* to repair that breach," Gallagher recalled. "And it has not been repaired for others. Never was. Never was."[569]

Greene's detractors extended well beyond the APCWS trustees who opposed Disney. "He became the fall guy, and he became the guy that everybody blamed," Frye recalled. "How dare anybody—*anybody*—in the Civil War community possibly support Disney? And Will became the public figure who was just assassinated... because he was willing to support this monster. So, it created a leadership chasm. It created personal animosity. And Will was done at APCWS. He was a lightning rod for everything bad. And I felt so badly for him because he didn't deserve it."[570]

Jack Ackerly and other APCWS trustees—Ackerly counted at least seven—had other issues with Greene's leadership. At the August 20, 1994, board meeting that followed the Disney contract renewal, a sometimes-contentious discussion ensued about whether Greene was taking too much power for himself and not properly informing or including trustees in decisions.[571]

"All these things were happening where I thought Will Greene was doing too much on his own without getting clearance from the board," Ackerly recalled. "And I was very vocal about a bunch of things. I had a list of things."[572]

Most of the trustees supported Greene. In February 1994, when the Disney contract was first approved, the board increased his salary from \$40,000 to \$56,000. On November 12, the board gave him another raise—to \$65,000. His salary began low but jumped more than 38 percent in his most divisive, controversial and final year as president.[573]

Ackerly's complaints led Richards to appoint a special committee to evaluate the concerns. They met on December 3, 1994, with Ackerly mailing in advance a four-page letter listing his questions and criticisms.[574]

Two days later, Greene announced that he had accepted an offer to become executive director of Pamplin Historical Park to develop a state-of-the-art Civil War museum and visitor experience for Robert B. Pamplin, Jr., a wealthy Oregon businessman and APCWS supporter. Pamplin had purchased a large tract of land outside Petersburg, Virginia, owned by his ancestors during the war. It was "The Breakthrough," a particularly historic part of the Petersburg battlefield, complete with extant trenches, where Union troops had first broken through Confederate defenses on April 2, 1865, to end the siege of Petersburg. Pamplin had contracted with APCWS for interpretive help, then decided to build his own park and museum.[575]

"My departure for Pamplin Historical Park had nothing to do with Disney," Greene recalled. "My decision was almost entirely one of going to an opportunity that I thought was too good to pass up. The opportunity to create a world-class historical park from scratch is obviously something that almost no one in my field gets to do. That was my primary motive. It had nothing to do with Disney. I didn't flee APCWS."[576]

Chairman Richards concurred in a 1995 letter to *The Civil War News* criticizing its coverage of the resignation: "To suggest that the board or any part of board pressured Greene into resigning is simply untrue."[577] But Greene agrees that APCWS's involvement with Disney was "enormously controversial. I still bear the scars from what was, in many ways, the most difficult and painful year of my career."[578]

The board accepted Greene's resignation in a special meeting on December 10, 1994, then passed a resolution expressing its "deep appreciation for his invaluable services." As an APCWS founder, as its first paid executive director and then president of APCWS, Greene had led the transformation of an all-volunteer, grassroots group into a professional, highly effective land preservation organization with six full-time employees, including separate positions for real estate, membership, administration, programs and outreach.[579] Its membership, the bedrock of APCWS, had grown from about 1,500 when he took over in 1990 to more than 9,400, with a 57 percent increase in 1994 alone, the year of the Disney controversy.[580] He had saved land each year he was in charge, preserving more than 2,100 acres in eight states valued at more than $2.7 million. And in the troubled year of Disney's America, Greene had engineered arguably the greatest save of his presidency—Malvern Hill near Richmond, Virginia—raising more than $1.5 million to buy 519 then-unprotected acres of the final battlefield of the Seven Days' Battles.[581]

Greene remained on the board for another year. The board appointed Frye, another strong Disney supporter, as interim president and invited Jody Powell, another Disney ally, to become a trustee, an invitation Powell accepted.

The APCWS pushed on without pause in its mission. Frye provided his usual passion, energy and dedication, but something had been lost. The founders created APCWS in a common cause, imbued with a common spirit. They forged an even tighter bond in the relentless parade of challenges they faced as a result of their dedication. The mission would continue and the organization would evolve, but in the wake of Disney's America, the camaraderie among the original founders was torn asunder. Sides were taken by people who shared a common passion and a common goal, and a sense of perspective was lost in the process.

As intensely as some of the trustees opposed Greene for his support of Disney, each of them saw in themselves what he saw in himself when, years later, he reflected on that time and said, "I was never so dedicated to anything in my life as I was to the survival and then growth of that organization and its effectiveness in achieving its purpose of saving battlefields."[582] ★

CHAPTER
NINE

Victory at Brandy Station

N THE SPRING of 1994, as the nation's leading historians joined *Protect Historic America* and prepared their public relations assault against the Disney's America history theme park, Brandy Station Foundation (BSF) attorney Tersh Boasberg added his voice to the anti-Disney chorus. "What we're talking about is not only Disney and 6.3 million visitors a year, we're talking about the kind of Disney-related development you see at Anaheim and Orlando," he told *America's Civil War Magazine.*[583]

But the fight to save the battlefield at Brandy Station absorbed most of his time and energy. It was more than a fight. It was a war, now into its sixth year, with defeat for the preservationists always seemingly just over the horizon, as it was that spring.

Lee Sammis had seen his plans for an office park and residential development held up by preservationists. After an economic downturn, Sammis was forced to declare bankruptcy to reorganize and refinance. The court had yet to approve his bankruptcy plan, but it included selling 515 acres in the heart of the battlefield to New York entrepreneur James Lazor to build a Formula One auto race track.

On February 1, 1994, the Culpeper County Board of Supervisors approved the project and Lazor announced that construction would begin in early April, vowing that "it will be built here. Sorry to the preservationists and whatever they think."[584]

Boasberg knew that the race track property included wetlands, though they were insignificant. Still, to alter wetlands, Lazor needed a permit from the U.S. Army Corps of Engineers. Normally it was a formality, but Boasberg planned to aggressively oppose the permit and contest every point. He knew the best he could expect, though, was to slow the process, so he also planned a bold strategy to buy the land right out from under the developers. Not only would he snatch the race track land from Lazor, he intended to purchase all 2,300 acres of Sammis's land that comprised the battlefield, or more than two-thirds of what Sammis still owned. If he could come up with $5.6 million, Boasberg's offer would be competitive with the Sammis and Lazor offer. The bankruptcy court, on behalf of Sammis's creditors, would be obligated to accept the best offer.[585]

With millions on his mind, Boasberg did not even have enough to pay the foundation's legal bills. Arnold & Porter, a high-powered Washington law firm, and attorney Dan Rezneck provided hundreds of thousands of dollars' worth of pro bono services. But in fighting the unsuccessful BSF lawsuit, the law firm had incurred $67,000 in out-of-pocket expenses that needed to be reimbursed. It had been almost two years since the foundation lost the trial. But Boasberg knew he needed to pay the outstanding bill to ensure Arnold & Porter's continuing good will and assistance if he was to entertain any hope of successfully pursuing the purchase of the battlefield, especially if he hoped to win over the bankruptcy court.[586]

"We have so few people we can lean on; and we desperately need Arnold & Porter's services," Boasberg wrote to a foundation donor who had provided key financial assistance in the past. Could she, her brother and her sister each contribute $10,000? "Also, if there were any way your father or (another relative) could contribute, it would be really terrific," he wrote. "Please let me know what might be possible."[587] Boasberg, in a 2016 interview, could not recall whether this particular effort yielded a donation. But he did manage to pay Arnold & Porter, he recalled.

That spring, Charles Seilheimer, a wealthy Fauquier County businessman, and other anonymous landholders decided they wanted to stop the track. They told Boasberg they were willing to commit $3.6 million to buy and preserve battlefield property.[588]

Boasberg was thrilled. He redoubled his efforts to find $2 million more. The Civil War Trust had been a player but was no longer involved, having taken the position that it would not purchase land if a race track was planned. Boasberg turned to the Association for the Preservation of Civil War Sites (APCWS), then deeply embroiled in the Disney's America controversy. On May 27, 1994, just weeks after *Protect Historic America*'s historians rained criticism on Disney and a divided APCWS voted to renew its controversial consulting contract with the company, Boasberg made his pitch to APCWS President Will Greene in a three-page memorandum titled "End Game at Brandy Station."[589]

"We must raise an additional $2 million," Boasberg wrote. "Can APCWS borrow this? The $2 million and trustee Seilheimer's $3.6 million will give us $5.6 million, which our creditor-ally feels will be the amount necessary to buy out the Sammis creditors and convince the Bankruptcy Court to go with our plan … "This is really an opportunity of a lifetime to save Brandy Station … "[590]

The APCWS had followed the Brandy Station fight from the sidelines. Now it jumped into action. In a special board meeting on July 11, APCWS trustees approved the request to seek a $2 million loan, with at least four trustees as guarantors. An anonymous donor promised $500,000—a record for a single APCWS donation.[591]

On July 14, Boasberg offered Sammis $5 million for six farms totaling 2,322 acres that comprised most of his battlefield holdings. The court urged Elkwood Downs to consider the offer carefully. Five days later, Sammis's attorney turned it down, stating that Lazor was willing to pay twice as much per acre for the land he wanted.[592]

The next day, July 20, APCWS and BSF announced the offer in a press conference, calling it the largest private effort ever to preserve a Civil War battlefield. They said they submitted a cash proposal to the bankruptcy court, and despite Sammis's rejection, were confident it would eventually be accepted by the judge. A hearing was set for September 19.[593]

Benton Ventures posted signs showing the location of the soon-to-be-built race track and placed stakes in the ground to outline the route of the 3.1-mile road course.[594] As Boasberg prepared for the crucial September 19 hearing, the prospects of success still appeared hazy. He needed backup. On Friday night the 16th, backup seemed to arrive when Boasberg's phone rang.

"What's the status of the Brandy Station battlefield?" the caller asked, identifying himself as a businessman from Potomac, Maryland. "In three days, I expect that it will be sold to build a race track," Boasberg replied.[595]

The caller said he was strongly opposed to the track and wanted to buy the land and donate it as a battlefield park. He said he would receive a lot of money around October 15 from overseas investors in a U.S. development company. The man said he was willing to donate a large sum.

"It was absolutely incredible," Boasberg recalled. "I thought at the time I had a savior, a knight in golden armor. I remember I was stunned. I was just stunned. It came totally out of the blue."[596]

There was no time to lose. Boasberg arranged to meet at the man's home on Sunday, the eve of the bankruptcy hearing. Boasberg drove down into Virginia, where the prospective savior said he lived, and was stunned. The man lived in a trailer. He'd just been divorced, he explained. "It wasn't trash, but a trailer?" Boasberg recalled."[597]

Still, the man impressed Boasberg with his knowledge of the battle at Brandy Station. He asked Boasberg not to judge him by his surroundings; his modest home had been the family's weekend hideaway. He assured Boasberg that he had the money. He promised to be at the courthouse the next morning with a certified check.[598]

Boasberg departed, somewhat reassured. His "knight in shining armor" would be the surprise up his sleeve at the next day's hearing. With his funding, the foundation could offer $6,000 per acre, $1,000 more per acre than Benton Ventures and

Lazor were offering.

"The guy never showed up," Boasberg recalled. "And still to this day I don't know who this guy was. But it was typical of the unbelievable ups and downs that happened during that fight."[599] Boasberg doesn't remember it, but he went into the hearing and still said BSF could now offer $6,000 per acre. The judge agreed it was a "substantial amount of money," and postponed his decision for several days.[600]

On September 26, 1994, the bankruptcy judge rejected BSF's offer and approved Sammis's reorganization plan, including the sale of 425 acres to Lazor and Benton Ventures for $5,000 per acre. The judge said he almost always accepted the highest offer, but noted that the funds promised by Boasberg's savior were still unavailable.[601]

Around this time, Bud Hall and Boasberg learned that the primary investor in Benton Ventures was B. Thomas Golisano, the wealthy founder and president of Paychex, Inc., and a former business partner with Lazor. Golisano also happened to be the Independent Party's candidate for governor of New York.

Hall called the Rochester newspapers and minced no words. "It's odd to me that (Golisano) has an interest in despoiling a nationally significant historic battlefield in Virginia," he told the Rochester *Times-Union*.[602]

"I don't see it as interfering with anything," Golisano said, defending the project. "I think from a marketing enterprise it's a great concept. It's a great location. It's going to create some jobs."[603]

As the preservationists launched a letter-writing campaign, Hall wrote directly to the gubernatorial candidate, explaining that New York had more Union cavalry units in the fight at Brandy Station than any other state. Golisano's enthusiasm as a financial backer disappeared, Hall said. "There was an immediate reaction," Hall recalled. "He wanted no part of this thing. One of his staff members told me, 'We're not going to do this.'" That decision, however, would not be reported for months.[604]

By the end of October, though, Lazor had purchased 425 acres, a smaller tract than originally planned, for $2.1 million. The pending U.S. Army Corps of Engineers wetlands permit was all that stood between Lazor's bulldozers and the battlefield. The wetlands at Brandy Station were insignificant, but Boasberg opposed the permit at every turn. Benton Ventures had filed its plan with the U.S. Corps of Engineers in early 1994. Boasberg countered with a formal protest opposing the permit, and in late May, followed up with a seven-page, point-by-point letter on why it should be denied.[605]

Since this was a federal process, the Advisory Council on Historic Preservation (ACHP), an independent federal agency, was required to conduct a "Section 106" historic preservation review before the Corps could issue a wetlands permit. When

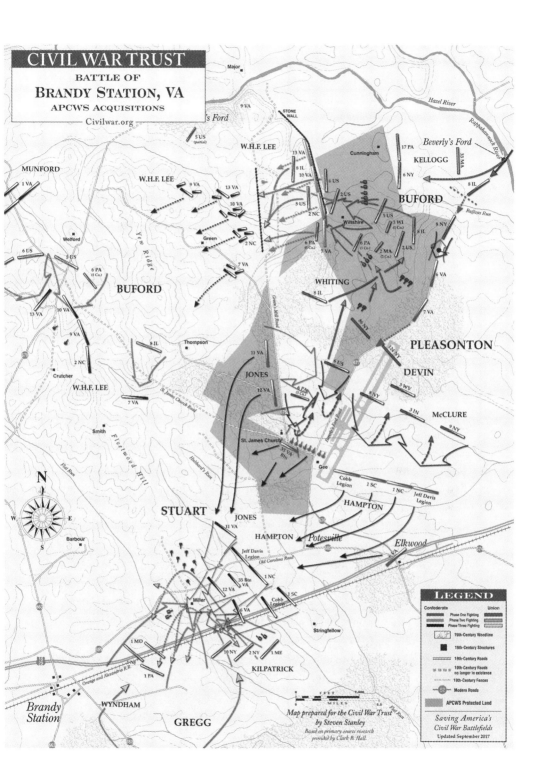

CIVIL WAR TRUST

BATTLE OF
BRANDY STATION, VA
APCWS ACQUISITIONS
Civilwar.org

Major

Hazel River

STONE WALL

9 VA

's Ford

Beverly's Ford

W.H.F. LEE

Cunningham

17 PA

KELLOGG

33 MA

6 NY

13 VA

8 IL

6 US

8 IL

10 IL

2 US

BUFORD

Ruffins Run

MUNFORD

W.H.F. LEE

9 VA

13 VA

3 US

5 US

Wiltshire

5 US

1 VA

10 VA

2 NC

6 PA

6 PA

2 MA

2 US.

Welford

Green

7 VA

6 PA

6 VA

6 US

5 US

2 NC

WHITING

7 VA

6 PA

8 IL

7 VA

13 VA

10 VA

9 VA

BUFORD

8 IL

Thompson

11 VA

JONES

6 US

PLEASONTON

DEVIN

2 NC

Crutcher

7 VA

12 VA

6 PA

8 NY

3 WV

3 IN

McCLURE

9 NY

W.H.F. LEE

Smith

St. James Church

35 VA

Gee

Cobb Legion

1 SC

1 NC

Jeff Davis Legion

HAMPTON

STUART

JONES

11 VA

HAMPTON

Potesville

Elkwood

Jeff Davis Legion

Old Carolina Road

1 NC

35 Btn VA

12 VA

1 SC

Cobb Legion

Miller

6 VA

Stringfellow

1 MD

10 NY

2 NY

1 ME

1 PA

KILPATRICK

N

Barbour

Brandy Station

WYNDHAM

GREGG

Map prepared for the Civil War Trust
by Steven Stanley
Based on primary source research
provided by Clark B. Hall.

LEGEND

Confederate		Union
	Phase One Fighting	
	Phase Two Fighting	
	Phase Three Fighting	

19th-Century Woodline

19th-Century Structures

19th-Century Roads

19th-Century Roads no longer in existence

19th-Century Fences

Modern Roads

APCWS Protected Land

*Saving America's
Civil War Battlefields*
Updated September 2017

Benton Ventures closed on the property in October 1994, the "Section 106" review —a methodical, step-by-step process—was only getting underway. Unless Lazor decided to begin construction without the permit, a decidedly risky move, Boasberg knew he had a few more months to work with.[606]

Four months later, in January 1995, the Corps developed a tentative plan to approve the permit with various environmental stipulations and considerations, including an archaeological review in construction areas and a promise from Lazor to build the complex "with respect for the significant features of the landscape, including the historical features." On January 17, the Corps formally asked the ACHP to sign off on the plan.[607]

Boasberg went back into battle, firing off letters to the council's chairman, vice chairman and public members demanding a full and careful Section 106 review. Hall developed a nine-page "Impact Analysis." Boasberg wrote a 14-page battle plan that summarized the historical significance of the land, the impact of the track, traffic and noise issues and every potential problem he could think of. No question was too small to consider, even "the smell of burning tires and the dust from the car exhausts."[608]

Ultimately, BSF's formal comments in opposition to the permit became a 77-page, bound document. In mid-February, the ACHP responded to the Corps and suggested a public meeting in April to hear all viewpoints because the permit faced significant opposition.[609]

Boasberg was running out of time and options. He and Hall reached out, once again, to the APCWS and its new president, Dennis Frye. As Frye recalled, "I think they both had pretty much thrown their hands up in the air and said, 'It's done. We're finished. We've lost.' They were very desperate. But I think they thought, 'Well, you know, let's just go make one more request and see if we can get any kind of positive response from Dennis.'"[610]

Boasberg and Hall do not recall being that desperate, but in mid-March came an alarming new development. Hall trespassed on Lazor's battlefield land and discovered, to his dismay, that the new owner had destroyed "40 historic cedar trees ... and a historic roadbed within the boundaries of the battlefield site."[611] Also destroyed—burned by the local fire department for a training exercise—was a pre-war overseer's house. And 50 yards of a historic stone wall had been damaged. Boasberg sent two letters to the Corps, along with Hall's photographs, complaining about the destruction and calling for a formal investigation, alleging that the destruction made it impossible for the ACHP to complete a proper review.[612]

"I never stopped going on the battlefield, even after Sammis told me not to go on the property," Hall recalled. "I was on the battlefield with my camera almost every week. I'd park my car off the battlefield in a hidden locale and I would walk on the battlefield, staying at a tree line as much as possible, just like I did in the Marine Corps in Vietnam."[613]

As Lazor began preliminary work, the first public indication appeared that Benton Ventures was in a financial bind. The Maryland engineering firm Greenhorne & O'Mara filed a mechanic's lien in mid-April, claiming $297,540 in unpaid bills for surveying and site work.[614]

"It happens. It's not really an issue," Lazor said. It was simply a disagreement over "what the values of the services rendered are." Construction would begin in May. "We'll soon have large vehicles out there moving dirt," he said.[615]

"I thought to myself, 'No, you will not,'" recalled Hall. "'I'll go stand in front of your bulldozers if I have to.'" It had become personal for him. "But it had become personal for me a long time before that," Hall recalled. "I made sure he knew I was a federal investigator and not without resources. I was crazed … obsessed … a zealot."[616]

On April 27, 1995, news came that Golisano, Lazor's one publicly known financial supporter, had backed out. "I divested myself of this months ago," Golisano said. "It was a business decision. It has nothing to do with the Civil War, which I don't feel like reliving—even though I think the wrong side won."[617]

Once again, Lazor acted unperturbed. "It really isn't news," he said. "Shareholders come and go in companies all the time. There are a lot of people with deep pockets. This project is not based on one individual."[618] Lazor admitted that the letter-writing campaign to Golisano had had an impact, and said that was a reason he wouldn't identify his other backers—"investors who prefer not to go through what Tom did" because of the preservationists' "guerilla tactics."[619]

BSF kept up the pressure on the Army Corps of Engineers, filing a 32-page report in April on "issues that need to be resolved" regarding the wetlands permit.[620] But in mid-May, after the ACHP completed its review, the Corps decided to grant Lazor the wetlands permit. The agreement still included a lengthy list of conditions, but the Corps determined that any environmental impact of the track would be minimal and Benton Ventures had not intentionally done any significant damage to the property. Once again, development of Brandy Station battlefield appeared imminent.[621]

Boasberg and the BSF then filed a lawsuit against Benton Ventures asking for an injunction to block construction of the race track. The plaintiffs were 24 property owners, including B.B. Mitchell and other BSF board members, who claimed the track would be a massive intrusion on its neighbors, bringing air, water and noise pollution. In a private memorandum, however, Boasberg said the actual reason for the suit was to buy time and to "force Lazor to lower his price and take a reasonable amount to 'get out.'"[622]

At 6:20 a.m. on May 19, Lazor awoke to a process server knocking on his door serving him with injunction papers. "There are much more enjoyable ways to wake up," he told a reporter. "Enough is enough."[623]

But with Golisano out of the picture, Lazor's ability to proceed appeared diminished. Rumors that he was out of money gave Hall, Boasberg and the Brandy Station preservationists a reason for cautious optimism. Boasberg was in touch with landowners who had committed their land to Sammis or Lazor and they "now realize that the racetrack is very doubtful and that the Civil War groups represent the best deal for these properties," Boasberg wrote to Frye on May 24. "That's a real sea change!"[624]

Frye and the APCWS, particularly trustee Carrington Williams, became more actively involved after Frye met with Boasberg and Hall. On June 1, 1995, Boasberg and the APCWS jointly offered Lazor $2.1 million for his 425 acres of the battlefield —the same price he paid Sammis. "The intent is to make him whole as to what he's paid," Boasberg said.[625]

Lazor rejected the offer the next day. "It's not even in the ballpark of what we've invested," he said. "We're not trying to be selfish, but we have costs that we should be reimbursed for. I want to recoup our investment."[626]

That same month, two more liens were filed against Benton Ventures, one for almost $200,000 of road and sewer work, and another for about $33,000 for excavation.[627] The Corps' permitting process dragged on through the summer, prime construction season, as preservationists continued to file long, detailed arguments about why the permit should not be issued. On August 11, the Corps granted the wetlands permit, but by then, the special use permit had expired, sending the project back to the Culpeper County Board of Supervisors for approval.

The BSF launched a new assault on August 23, filing suit against the Corps challenging the wetlands permit and seeking a reversal. Lazor called the action "a travesty of our legal system."[628] He vowed to begin construction in the fall. The suit would not delay things, he said. "It's sort of like that mosquito that's flying around you when you're camping," he said. "You just hope it will land and you can hit it."[629]

But Lazor was out of money. He had missed payments on far more than engineering bills. On September 15, 1995, Elkwood Downs announced that it was foreclosing on the property it had sold to Benton Ventures. In a statement, Sammis said that for "reasons beyond its control," Benton Ventures was unable to pay its bills, and owed about $1.5 million. "It's been quite a long period of time that they've been in default," said Elkwood Downs Vice President Michael Armm.[630]

Lazor tried to minimize the setback, acknowledging that Elkwood Downs was "exercising its business rights" but also claiming he had the funds available to build the track. "Our intention is to still build the project," he said. And Sammis said it was not the end of his effort to exercise his "legitimate development rights."[631]

Newspapers were reporting that the race track was all but dead. Hall told the Fredericksburg *Free Lance-Star* the foreclosure "leaves opportunities for preservationists," adding, "We're going to try to take advantage of the opportunities."[632]

Frye called Armm in late September. To distance the APCWS from the hard feelings and disagreements of the Disney episode, Frye had authored a column for the *Civil War News* in the second month of his interim presidency emphasizing the organization's accomplishments. "APCWS *delivers* success," he wrote.[633] Frye made acquiring more battlefield land his number one goal, and Brandy Station, still in limbo and under great threat, became a priority.

"I'd like to meet with you and I'd like to talk about buying Lee Sammis's battlefield," Frye told Armm. They met and Armm agreed to arrange a face-to-face meeting with Sammis.[634]

"We met at Tyson's Corner near Dulles airport at a hotel," Frye recalled. "And I was in the presence of Lee Sammis. Now, I remember preparing myself for this, thinking, 'Well, will I be intimidated? Will I be thrashed? Is he going to yell and scream at me? Because we certainly have done a lot of yelling and screaming at him. Is he going to treat me with any respect at all?' As it turned out, Mr. Sammis took a liking to me. He didn't thrash me. He didn't yell at me. He didn't criticize me. He said, 'So, you want to do a deal?'"[635]

They talked for hours, much of it about family and personal interests. "We spent that whole afternoon building a relationship," Frye said. "And all of a sudden, I was in Mr. Sammis's car, and we were on our way into Washington D.C. Same day. Right to Capitol Hill. He instructed Michael Armm to get on the telephone and make a few calls and we drove right up onto the plaza on Capitol Hill, right behind the rotunda, and parked there. And I thought, 'Oh, man, I am definitely in the presence of power.'"[636]

The trip included visits to a senator's office and to the Interior Department to discuss opportunities for federal dollars to help with a potential sale to the preservationists. "So, all of this happened in the course of one day. And Sammis says, 'We're going to do a deal with you guys. We're going to make this happen.'"[637]

Recalled Armm: "Carrington Williams was the solution. It wouldn't have happened without him. Carrington just had a really great way about him. He was a true gentleman. He was always kind in conversation. He was always easy to talk to. Dennis and (APCWS Director of Real Estate) Bob Edmiston did a lot of the legwork, because they were the day-to-day staff. But Carrington immediately jumped right in and got very, very involved. That's when we finally got somebody who said, 'Look, we're not going to fight you. We're not going to battle with you. If it doesn't work, we're going to leave you alone.'"[638]

In late September 1995, Sammis agreed in principle to sell 1,543 acres at Brandy Station for about $6 million, with half due at closing. "It took a while, of course," Frye recalled. "We had to negotiate. It wasn't inexpensive. We had to figure out sources of funding. I think Mr. Sammis had tired of the controversy. He had moved on to other things. He obviously had purchased the land for investment purposes to make a good return on his money—a fairly quick return—and that hadn't happened. And so he was ready to depart."[639]

Unlike other preservationists, Frye found Sammis to be an affable and straightforward businessman, and enjoyed a friendly relationship. Together, Frye and Sammis worded a sensitive letter that Sammis sent to Culpeper County officials and the local newspaper. They explained that Sammis needed to divest and although the preservation organization he was selling land to had fought him and the county, he had negotiated a fair deal and saw the potential for APCWS to develop heritage tourism in Culpeper County.[640]

After nearly another year of negotiations, on August 5, 1996, APCWS and Elkwood Downs agreed to a price of $6.2 million for 1,543 acres of Sammis's land, including most of the sites of the heaviest fighting. Ultimately, APCWS acquired 570 acres and protected another 116 acres with a conservation easement. It was, at that time, the largest privately financed battlefield preservation acquisition in American history.[641]

Preservationists agreed that Brandy Station ought to be saved, but the deal was not universally hailed and prompted lively debates among APCWS trustees and others. Recalled Gallagher: "I remember Bob Krick would say, 'What about millions for Jackson's flank attack area at Chancellorsville? Which is more important, Jackson's flank attack, or this cavalry battle? How about millions for the ground opposite the Sunken Road at Antietam? Is Brandy Station as important as that?'"[642]

Frye was nervous at the contract signing and in a rush. "I had never signed a deed that big," he recalled. "Nobody in the Civil War community had ever done that and I knew that we would be responsible for it."[643]

"The closing took place at a local attorney's office in Culpeper," Armm recalled. "Dennis had an appointment that he had to get to back up in D.C. A ton of papers had to be signed. Finally, Dennis had signed everything. He said, 'Look, I've got to go.' He left and Carrington stayed to make sure the closing got completed. All of a sudden, Carrington realized there was one more paper that Dennis needed to sign. Carrington was not a young man. And I can still see Carrington grabbing this paper off the table and literally running down the street after Dennis to catch him."[644]

Five weeks later, on September 12, the APCWS held a press conference under brightening gray skies at Robert E. Lee's Arlington House at Arlington National Cemetery. "This is almost a surrealistic event," Hall told a reporter. Armm and Sammis were there, as was Robert Kenefect and other Culpeper County officials, Bearss, Boasberg, Frye, BSF's B. B. Mitchell and APCWS Chairman Tom Richards.[645] "Gradually the realization has begun to sink in," Mitchell said. It was a "dream come true."[646]

Frye's remarks, wrote Deborah Fitts in the *Civil War News*, were "ringing off the large Doric columns that surround the portico" of Lee's home as he declared, "The Civil War community has its chance to make history by saving history."[647]

"I never quite envisioned this day," Sammis told the gathering. "It's a damn shame things got off course for an extended period of time. Admittedly, it hasn't always been a smooth path, but the evolution has been fruitful and we have developed some close relationships with some wonderful people along the way." Said Armm, "The APCWS folks have been a pleasure to work with."[648]

In a photograph taken that day in front of one of those Doric columns, six men who waged the struggle, on both sides, stood in their suits and ties, shoulder to shoulder. On the left were Mitchell and Frye. Richards and Armm stood on the right. And in the middle, a beaming Lee Sammis stood next to Bud Hall.

Hall's face is blank. He is neither smiling nor frowning. His appearance is that of someone who has been through a lot. For eight years, the fight consumed much of his time and energy and the stress and worry had worn him down. Soon after the press conference, he went back to the battlefield. "I remember going out to Buford's Knoll, by myself, and standing on Buford's Knoll, realizing that it was now ours," Hall recalled, "and that I didn't have to sneak on there anymore, didn't have to trespass to get out there, didn't have to meet James Lazor or Lee Sammis."[649]

Hall had named it Buford's Knoll; his meticulous research had led him to conclude beyond any doubt that this was the prominence—the one that afforded the best overall view of the battlefield—that Buford had come to as the battle opened on June 9, 1863, to assess the situation. Hall wondered what the crusty Union cavalry commander would have thought, not to mention J.E.B Stuart. He let himself believe they would have been proud of what he had done and how hard he fought for the land where so many of their young troopers had shed blood.

He saw the preservation struggle as nothing less than "the forces of good triumphing over the forces of evil." But with feelings of vindication, euphoria and "sweet justice" was "terrible sadness that it had ever gotten that far, that a board of supervisors could care so little, that we had been betrayed by our own."

Hall knew from then on that his battlefield tours would not only feature the story of the battle, but also the story of the battle to save the battlefield. "Every time I take a tour up there now—and I have over the years taken dozens and dozens of tours up there—I let people know that they're standing on ground that was to be developed, but that a group of citizens came together and said, 'No, thank you. We don't want that to happen.' And we prevailed in the end. Brandy Station is, through a lot of blood, sweat and tears, a success story."[650]

Although Sammis, who died in 2013 at age 82, is smiling in the group photo at Arlington House, he paid a price, too. "It took a lot out of him, it really did," recalled Armm. "There was a lasting effect after what he went through. This was a big project for Lee. It wasn't just a small bump in the overall portfolio. He had really set his sights on this. He loved the idea of doing something at this scale not in an urban area—a lifestyle community that was a combination of residential, commercial and industrial and was well-planned out.

"The fight—all the opposition and being dragged through court—was very strenuous on Lee. It almost was the beginning of the end of his career. It was sort of like the perfect storm. The markets were changing, Lee was getting on in years, and I think going through that experience and expending the energy that he did had a really profound effect on him. I'm not just talking financially. I think it took some happiness out of him."[651] ★

CHAPTER

TEN

The Coin War

HE GROVE FARM, where President Abraham Lincoln posed after the battle of Antietam for one of the most famous photographs of the Civil War, fans out along Shepherdstown Pike, just outside Sharpsburg, Maryland. A long, tree-lined driveway leads to the 200-year-old, elegant brick house that is visible in the photo.

Dennis Frye lived on a 19th-century farm about five miles southeast of Grove Farm, and his route to his National Park Service (NPS) office at Harpers Ferry National Historical Park took him past the historic site. Though not part of the battlefield, Grove Farm is an elemental part of the Antietam story.

"Every time I drive by the Grove Farm, I fondly think of the (original) Civil War Trust," Frye recalled. "In the mid-to-late 1980s, Sharpsburg was on the verge of becoming a commercial Gettysburg. Its entire western end, denoted by the Grove Farm, was destined to become a strip mall." The Trust deserves credit for assisting Save Historic Antietam Foundation (SHAF) in saving Grove Farm, Frye said. In 1991, the Trust contributed $100,000 toward the purchase of 40 acres of the farm to give the privately owned farmhouse a preservation buffer.[652]

In the spring of 1992, Frye went back to the Trust for help at nearby Harpers Ferry, West Virginia. As with Grove Farm, Frye approached the Trust in his role as a NPS historian, although he was also a co-founder and a board member of the Association for the Preservation of Civil War Sites (APCWS).

Fifty-six acres of School House Ridge on the Harpers Ferry battlefield, a patch of rolling meadowland that abutted the NPS's Harpers Ferry National Historical Park, was for sale in bankruptcy court. A developer had planned to build up to 180 houses and townhouses where Confederate General Stonewall Jackson had massed some 15,000 men—three divisions—during the clash at Harpers Ferry on September 12-15, 1862. Jackson met Union commander Brig. General Julius White at School House Ridge to discuss terms when the Union force of 12,000 surrendered.[653]

Frye could have presented the preservation opportunity to the APCWS, but it had never spent that much; the $440,000 price was twice that of any previous purchase. He thought the Trust could better handle the purchase because it was expecting to generate millions in corporate donations. SHAF had just successfully partnered with the Trust to save Grove Farm. Frye wanted the new preservation organization to succeed, and a distinctive save like the land at School House Ridge would enhance its reputation.[654]

Frye had hoped for beautiful spring weather when he showed School House Ridge to the Trust board and staff in 1992, but a hard rain that morning had him wet and worried. If his presentation had to be cut short in the face of the elements and this key tract got away, another developer could easily show up with a new set of plans.

"Since it had been raining so hard, I was distressed that we would not be able to physically visit the site so they could visualize the grave danger of development in the middle of the battlefield," Frye recalled. "I knew if the Trust's board saw it, they would buy it. I just knew it. But I also knew that if they didn't witness it, our chance was lost. The forecast was not good for a break in the weather, so I thought we were doomed. Lo and behold, just before we visited, the clouds broke, the skies opened and the sun shined brightly. The whole panorama of Bolivar Heights and School House Ridge appeared majestic, with steam rising from the green fields. It was as if spirits were rising and inviting the board to make history on this battlefield."[655]

The Trust purchased the property from Jefferson Security Bank in Shepherdstown, West Virginia, for $440,000, in partnership with the National Park Trust, a land conservancy.[656] The two saves brought to the Trust by a founding APCWS board member seemed to presage a bright and effective partnership between two preservation organizations with precisely the same goal—saving Civil War battlefields.

The APCWS was almost four years old when the original Civil War Trust was created in 1991 as one of the battlefield preservation initiatives of Secretary of the Interior Manuel Lujan. The organization was formed in May 1991 as the American Battlefield Protection Foundation and later renamed the Civil War Trust. APCWS President Will Greene told his board the new organization's role was "still murky."[657]

"Will suggested that it may replace our fundraising efforts," the minutes of the May 3, 1991, APCWS board meeting reported. "Will indicated that the foundation plans to raise millions for the purchase of battlefield property." If that happened, it could change the entire course of battlefield preservation and profoundly affect the mission of the APCWS, which "might be revised in the future to emphasize our fact-finding and deal-making skills," the minutes said.[658]

By July, the APCWS had become an enthusiastic supporter of the Foundation. After all, the APCWS was beating the bushes for money just to close six-figure deals; the Foundation was promising tens of millions of dollars. Three APCWS board members—Gary Gallagher, Jim McPherson and Carrington Williams—were appointed to the foundation's board. The APCWS passed a motion formally expressing its partnership with the foundation. Board members discussed and prioritized potential sites that the two organizations might save together. "Gary said that there was no doubt the ABPF (Foundation) will raise a lot of money," read the minutes of the July 20, 1991, APCWS board meeting.[659]

The foundation renamed itself the Civil War Trust in June 1992, and when the corporate fundraising campaign failed, the Trust decided to become a membership organization, bringing the first dark cloud over the relationship. Grassroots membership was the heart and soul of the APCWS, and board members were deeply troubled that they would have to compete with the Trust for members. In July 1992, Gallagher, McPherson, Williams and Greene met with Trust Chairman Rod Heller and President Grae Baxter in Washington. It was a friendly meeting, but Greene made it clear the APCWS intended to continue building its membership and raising funds. Heller said a consultant had advised the Trust to become a membership organization, but promised to continue "close cooperation" in acquiring land.[660]

In September, a Trust board member recommended during a board meeting that the Trust be "the exclusive fundraiser" for battlefield preservation. Williams reported this distressing news at the September 19 APCWS board meeting and said he had "strongly objected to this strategy" at the Trust board meeting. Greene reported that he had received no communication from the Trust in two months. But there was little to do but try to forge a reasonable working relationship. Greene and Baxter resumed discussions and the two organizations made some progress in the following months, mutually approving a memorandum of understanding.[661]

Discussions continued, but little was accomplished. Greene reported to his board in July 1993 that he had "cordial relations" with Baxter, but was "still attempting to engage the Civil War Trust in a serious discussion on partnership on preservation."

The report was far less positive in November. It had become clear to the APCWS that "the CWT (Trust) seeks to compete with us in every activity, despite promises reiterated over the years by Baxter and Heller." If things didn't change, APCWS board members (hereafter known as trustees) Gallagher, Williams, McPherson and Richard Gilder might have to resign from the Trust board "to avoid conflict of interest."[662]

On February 5, 1994, McPherson told his fellow APCWS trustees that he was leaving the Trust's board. The other three had already resigned. "Apparently, they (Trust) have decided that they do not wish to have us as a collaborator; rather they plan to compete with us directly in all respects," the meeting minutes reported. The board also decided it had better cover its flanks on Capitol Hill. The APCWS created a political arm—an "Ad-Hoc Committee on Congressional Liaison," chaired by trustee Representative Bob Mrazek, to "seek to influence Congressional action" on funding decisions for battlefield preservation.[663]

The Disney matter kept APCWS preoccupied through the rest of 1994, but in 1995, when Frye became president, Heller was one of the first to call and congratulate him. Frye had good rapport with the Trust, having brought them the Grove Farm and School House Ridge acquisition opportunities. Heller invited Frye to Washington several times for dinner at the exclusive Metropolitan Club. "Rod was a gracious host and I had wonderful meals there with him," Frye recalled. "And we had some really good, heart-to-heart talks about our visions for Civil War battlefields and how we could approach battlefield preservation together as two organizations, perhaps joining as one. And we had not just one meeting, there were numerous meetings," including a half-dozen in 1995 alone, he said.[664]

Frye thought the two organizations ought to be merged into one and continued conversations with Heller and Trust leaders in 1995 and later years, even as relations became ever more strained. "Tom Richards (APCWS chairman) and I believed that a merger was in the interest of both organizations. So, one of my first goals became merger," Frye recalled. Members on both boards supported a merger. Some of the nation's top Civil War scholars were on *both* boards. It just made sense to bring the two organizations together.[665]

But the APCWS and the Trust had fundamental differences that prevented any real progress in merger talks. The rumor at APCWS was that the Trust was awash in red ink. Frye heard in early 1995 that Trust debt exceeded $700,000. It was true. On December 31, 1994, The Trust's fund balance had a deficit of $701,988. Frye saw no value in a merger if the APCWS had to help pay that off.[666] The APCWS was amassing debt too, however, and the Trust was equally averse to helping pay off APCWS debt.

The divide between the two groups exploded into all-out conflict in 1995 over the disbursement of millions of battlefield preservation dollars generated by the sale of U.S. Mint Civil War commemorative coins.

"Now the war begins!" Frye declared in a fax to APCWS Chairman Tom Richards on September 11, 1995. It would be a brief and bloodless affair, save for hurt feelings and mangled egos, destined to conclude with a legislative showdown on the floor of the U.S. Senate between some of the nation's most powerful senators – virtually all of them ardent preservation supporters.

The Trust had the responsibility for disbursing the coin profits under a competitive grant program supervised by the NPS's American Battlefield Protection Program (ABPP). Frye accused the Trust of unreasonable delays, and worse.[667]

"Considering this fondness for the Civil War Trust, what made me wage war against them during my tenure as ACPWS president?" Frye asked. "Simple. First, it became a CWT interest to destroy APCWS as APCWS threatened CWT through larger-scale battlefield preservation. Second, CWT refused to release coin dollars to

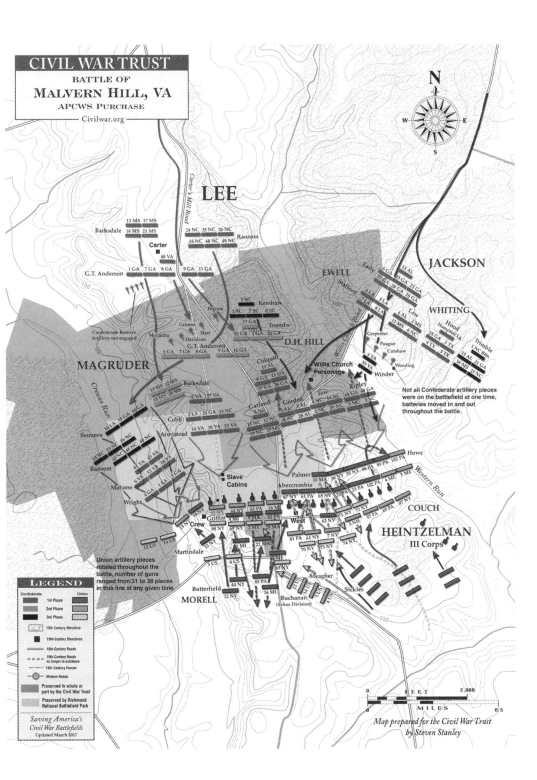

CIVIL WAR TRUST
BATTLE OF
MALVERN HILL, VA
APCWS PURCHASE
— Civilwar.org —

LEE

Barksdale 13 MS 17 MS
18 MS 21 MS

24 NC 25 NC 26 NC
35 NC 48 NC 49 NC
Ransom

Carter
48 VA

G.T. Anderson 1 GA 7 GA 8 GA 9 GA 11 GA

JACKSON

EWELL

Stafford

Early
6 GA 19 GA 23 GA
21 VA 28 GA 28 GA
6 LA 9 LA
8 LA

WHITING
Hood
Hampton Lg.

Law
1 AL 2 MS
11 MS 6 NC

Carpenter
Poague
Cutshaw

4 VA
33 VA
Winder

Wooding

Trimble
1 NC Bttn

18 GA 4 TX
4 GA 5 TX
15 AL 21 GA
16 MS 21 NC

3 SC
2 SC 7 SC 8 SC
Kershaw
17 GA
Toombs
13 GA 2 GA 20 GA

Pegram
Grimes
Hart
Davidson
McCarthy
G.T. Anderson
1 GA 7 GA 8 GA 9 GA 11 GA

D.H. HILL

Willis Church
Parsonage

Not all Confederate artillery pieces
were on the battlefield at one time,
batteries moved in and out
throughout the battle.

Confederate Reserve
Artillery not engaged

MAGRUDER

Crenes Run

13 MS 17 MS
Barksdale
18 MS 20 MS
9 VA 57 VA
2 LA 24 GA 14 NC
Cobb
14 VA 38 VA 53 VA

Colquitt
13 AL
6 GA 23 GA
27 GA 28 GA
Garland
5 NC
Gordon
3 AL 5 AL
13 NC 12 NC
Tew
26 AL
23 NC 20 NC
Ripley
48 GA 44 GA
1 NC 3 NC
30 NC 1 NC 3 NC

Semmes
10 LA 53 GA 10 GA
32 NC 28 NC 16 NC
35 GA 15 NC 10 GA
Armistead

Ransom
41 VA 49 VA
12 VA 1 EA 16 VA

Mahone
3 GA 1 EA 1 LA

Wright

Howe
98 PA 55 NY 96 PA 93 PA 102 PA

Palmer
10 MA 36
61 PA 65 NY 23 PA 102 PA 4 ME
67 NY
Abercrombie
71 NY 57 NY
62 NY
5 NH
74 NY

COUCH

Slave
Cabins
Crew

12 US 14 US

81 PA 61 NY 7 NY
70 NY 73 NY

Griffin
44 NY 83 PA 16 ME
4 ME
88 NY 69 NY 2 ME 9 MA
1 ME
22 MA

West

HEINTZELMAN
III Corps

Martindale
3 US
4 US

Union artillery pieces
rotated throughout the
battle, number of guns
ranged from 31 to 38 pieces
in this line at any given time.

44 NY 83 PA
16 MI

Butterfield
12 NY

MORELL

Meagher

Buchanan
(Sykes Division)

Sickles

LEGEND
Confederate   Union
1st Phase
2nd Phase
3rd Phase
19th-Century Woodline
19th-Century Structures
19th-Century Roads
19th-Century Roads
no longer in existence
19th-Century Fences
Modern Roads
Preserved in whole or
part by the Civil War Trust
Preserved by Richmond
National Battlefield Park

Saving America's
Civil War Battlefields
Updated March 2017

0   FEET   2,000
0   MILES   0.5

Map prepared for the Civil War Trust
by Steven Stanley

acquire battlefield land in immediate danger. Both of those causes were worth waging war over."[668]

The commemorative coin program, a Lujan initiative approved by Congress in 1992 when he withdrew Brandy Station battlefield's National Register eligibility, came to fruition in 1995. That March, the Mint began selling 3.3 million legal tender Civil War battlefield commemoratives, consisting of 300,000 five-dollar gold coins, a million silver dollars and two million half dollars. If every coin sold, the program would generate $21.5 million for battlefield preservation. Based on past commemorative coin releases, however, the Mint anticipated that only about 40 percent would sell, or about $8.6 million.[669] Ultimately, the program generated only about $6.2 million, nonetheless a sizeable sum for battlefield preservation.

Frye was troubled by rumors that the Trust intended to use coin funds to help pay off its administrative debt. Rather than complain directly, Frye used a more powerful weapon, asking for help from Representative Frank Wolf, a Virginia Republican and strong supporter of APCWS, whose district included a half-dozen major battlefields. Wolfe sent a letter to Secretary of the Interior Bruce Babbitt, appointed by President Bill Clinton to replace Lujan in 1993.

"I have recently learned that the Civil War Trust has accumulated about $700,000 to $1 million of administrative debt and am concerned that the surcharges from the sale of the coins may be used to retire the Civil War Trust's debt," Wolf wrote. "This is not the stated purpose for the use of those funds."[670]

The Trust gave assurances that it would not spend coin funds for administrative debt or costs. But the problem for Frye soon became that the Trust wasn't spending the coin funds at all. The APCWS had been clamoring for a commitment of funds even before the program started. In one of his last acts as APCWS president, Will Greene wrote the Trust on December 8, 1994, the day before he resigned, requesting a firm commitment of funds for APCWS acquisitions at the battlefields of Malvern Hill/Glendale and Brice's Cross Roads. That commitment was not forthcoming.[671]

By late June 1995, the Trust had taken in more than $4 million in coin funds but had allocated none of it. Under the program's rules, the Trust reviewed and evaluated the various grant requests from APCWS and other local preservation organizations and recommended grants of varying amounts. Coin proceeds were considered federal funds, which meant governmental oversight. The review and certification of the Trust's work fell to the NPS's American Battlefield Protection Program (ABPP).

Frye was ready, eager and almost desperate for coin proceeds, but soon learned that money would not be available until November or December at the earliest. At the top of the APCWS preservation list was the Third Winchester battlefield, also

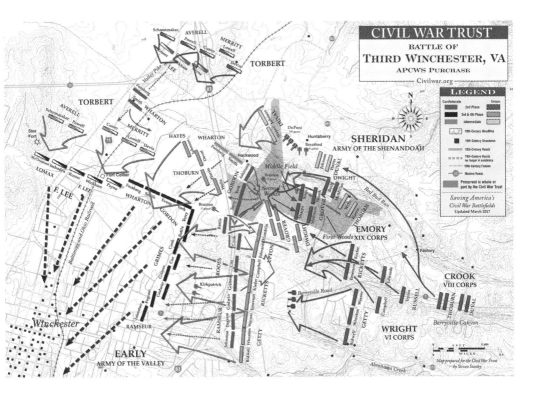

known as Opequon, the largest and most hotly contested of all the Shenandoah Valley battles, inflicting more than 9,000 casualties. The APCWS requested $500,000 in coin funds for a down payment on 222 acres in the heart of the battlefield. Frye said the deal was threatened if they could not get funding by August 16.

The battlefield at Malvern Hill was also a top priority. Without $500,000 in matching coin funds by the end of 1995, the APCWS stood to lose a $100,000 corporate grant for Malvern Hill. The organization also asked for a $250,000 grant for Glendale, $150,000 for Cedar Mountain and $1 million for Brandy Station.[672]

The response from the Trust was: Slow down. When the board met July 5, 1995, "we decided that the only appropriate course of action at this time was to defer action until later this year," the Trust's executive vice president, Edgar M. "Matt" Andrews told Frye in a July 6 letter. The Trust wanted to consider the "full range of preservation options" from "all potential partners" and the extent of their needs was "not yet fully identified," wrote Andrews (who replaced Grae Baxter as president in mid-1994). "Especially disturbing is the low level of (coin) sales in the Civil War preservation community. We may be forced to leverage the available funds to a much greater degree than originally anticipated, or develop other strategies to conserve available resources."[673]

Frye was enraged. "This letter of rejection will make you boil," he wrote to historian Holly Robinson, who had chaired the Civil War Sites Advisory Commission, as he informed friends and associates of the Trust's decision. "What arrogance! They have $5 million in the bank, yet they tell us how disturbed they are at the failure" of the coin program to generate more.[674]

Congress intended the money for battlefield acquisitions. The APCWS was facing critical deadlines on purchase agreements. Some $5 million was available. And the Trust wanted to hold the funds for more than six critical months? Frye went back to Capitol Hill to see Wolf and others. By July 12, he had a strategy: Get Congress to "strip the money from the Civil War Trust bank and have it placed in the APCWS coffers."[675]

On July 17, Wolf sent a letter to Heller, asking him to reconsider the APCWS requests. That same day the Trust formally invited applications for a "first round of grants" and set an October 25 deadline. Frye issued a three-page press release on July 20 about the immediate threat to Third Winchester. The *Richmond Times-Dispatch* and others ran a story.[676]

To head off further escalation of the conflict, Wolf pulled the two parties together. On August 1, Frye and Andrews met for five and a half hours with Wolf and hammered out a statement of cooperation, with the Trust promising a $500,000 loan for Third Winchester and "accelerated consideration" for several other battlefields. Frye and Andrews jointly signed a statement that said they expected the agreement would be "the cornerstone for new cooperative and joint efforts between our organizations."[677]

"There was no negotiation," Frye recalled, despite the length of the meeting. "Congressman Wolf ordered the Civil War Trust to release the money. The Congressman looked Matt Andrews in the eye with very little discussion and said, 'You will release immediately $500,000 to preserve the Third Winchester battlefield. Do you have any questions?' Well, of course, Matt made a minimal defense because he knew he couldn't take on the Congressman. He was in a pretty poor position to try to defend the Civil War Trust position, and he really didn't and he couldn't."[678]

Even after the meeting, Frye questioned whether APCWS would receive the Third Winchester money. "If the Trust reneges on these agreements (which is highly likely, considering their dreadful past), then move forward with the legislation," he wrote in a memo.[679] The money arrived in time.

Six days after the meeting, Frye approached Vermont Senator Jim Jeffords, another APCWS supporter, asking him to write a letter to the Trust requesting the names of its potential projects, grant amounts, the Trust's guidelines for considering projects and an assurance that coin money was being spent only on land purchases. The APCWS was "smoking the Trust out of their self-imposed cave," Frye wrote. Jeffords sent the letter on August 11. Frye also arranged for Virginia Representative Thomas J. Bliley, Jr., to request $500,000 for Malvern Hill, $250,000 for Glendale and $150,000 for Cedar Mountain.[680]

Heller responded to Senator Jeffords on August 23 with the Trust's guidelines and procedures and reported that the Trust had received 44 grant applications with funding requests totaling more than $9 million, and thus far had received slightly more than $5 million in coin revenues.[681]

Since requests exceeded revenues, the Trust was obligated by law and fairness to consider all applications, Heller said. The ABPP agreed. In fact, in the wake of the meeting with Wolf, when the Trust forwarded the expedited grant request to ABPP for Third Winchester funding more than two months before the Trust's own deadline for applications, the agency balked.

The Trust's emergency action to assist on Third Winchester created a situation where "we will likely end up funding those applications that were first in line and not necessarily the most worthy applications," Jan Townsend, the ABPP director, told the Trust in an August 15 letter. While the ABPP had approved the emergency allocation for Third Winchester, that process had to stop. "If we continue the current process, the results will likely be less-than-satisfactory battlefield preservation," Townsend wrote. To be fair to all applicants, the Trust needed to wait until after the deadline to review and submit applications for coin money funding to the ABPP.[682]

Heller underscored this point in his response to Jeffords, saying the Interior Department had "specifically requested" the more thorough but slower approach.[683] The APCWS and its Congressional allies kept up the pressure. Bliley sent another letter to Heller on September 1, requesting $500,000 for Malvern Hill by October 15—before the application deadline. Frye sent his own letter on September 5, calling Malvern Hill such a historically significant and pristine battlefield that saving it would be a "win-win-win scenario" for the Trust, the APCWS and the federal government, even if the ABPP had to sidestep normal bureaucratic procedures.[684]

A few days later, Frye received a letter from Andrews rejecting the APCWS appeal for emergency funding for Malvern Hill because "the need does not appear to be so urgent and extraordinary as to justify consideration" before the deadline.[685]

Rejection was one thing, but Frye was infuriated that Andrews's letter contained elements of a pre-prepared letter—apparently the letter the Trust had prepared for unsuccessful grant applicants. Frye scorned the response as a "form letter," and noted that the Trust's only reply to Bliley's letter was a "cc" of this "form letter."[686]

Around the same time, Frye received another letter from the Trust—a full-on form letter—that made him even angrier. It was a membership fundraising letter, seeking donations to save the Third Winchester battlefield, which the APCWS had saved. "We need your immediate assistance … " the Trust's letter began. "After negotiations with the Civil War Trust and another preservation group, the developer has agreed to sell these 222 acres. That's why we have acted to save the battlefield at Winchester, for if we don't do it, no one else will. Time is critical, so please respond right away."[687]

To Frye, the letter implied that the *Trust* was buying the property. "Third Winchester is *APCWS* property," he said. "It is an APCWS acquisition. It is an APCWS deal. APCWS did all of the negotiation. Our name is on the deed. The Civil War Trust does not own one square inch of the Third Winchester battlefield."[688]

This was when Frye declared: "Now the war begins!"[689] He went back to Capitol Hill—to the U.S. Senate—and began working his connections with Republican Senators Pete Dominici, Phil Gramm, Jim Jeffords and Trent Lott. The plan they helped hatch, according to Frye, was to "insert a line in one of the banking bills and it would become law. Done. Money comes to us."[690]

On October 27, 1995, the Senate adopted a banking bill that included a stealth amendment to the Civil War Battlefield Commemorative Coin Act. The surprise addition, offered by Dominici, Jeffords and Lott, required that the Civil War Trust pay $5.3 million from coin proceeds to the APCWS for acquisitions at 10 different Civil War battlefields in five states.

Andrews and Trust board members were shocked by this end run. They immediately went into crisis mode. Staff and board members were told to call their contacts on Capitol Hill. Trust staff notified the other grant applicants, telling them they were in danger of being shut out of the coin money. O. James Lighthizer, who joined the Trust's board in July 1994, remembers receiving a harried phone call from Trust Vice President Elliot Gruber saying, "They're trying to steal our money!"[691]

Ed Bearss, who had retired the previous month after 40 years at the NPS, recalled, "Now it's war to the knife and war to the hilt between the Trust and APCWS."[692]

"It was an extraordinary flanking movement around the Trust's open and competitive process … " Andrews wrote in a Trust newsletter whose publication was delayed by the crisis. "It would have summarily eliminated 19 of the 29 projects under consideration for funding." *Coin World*'s Beth Delsher wrote a scathing editorial, calling the APCWS move a "cowardly venture that can only be described as despicable. It must be stopped."[694]

It was stopped, but only after "many harrowing hours of telephoning, letter writing and meetings on Capitol Hill by the Trust's staff," Andrews wrote in the newsletter." Senator Dale Bumpers, an ardent preservationist, ended the APCWS's sneak attack in early November after objecting to the elimination of the safeguards and competitive selection process established for the coin program.[695]

"We got within a whisker of making it happen," Frye recalled. "It almost happened. And at the very last moment, Dale Bumpers stopped it. But we got within a cat's whisker of having that money transferred over APCWS. I knew how to play the political game. And I think this petrified the Civil War Trust, because here I am, roaming around on Capitol Hill. For heaven sakes, I'm just a little puny, rinky-dink, park service employee who shouldn't know anything about how to work Capitol Hill."[696]

The chasm widened between the Trust and APCWS. "I write this letter to you more in sorrow than in anger to relate how our own battlefield preservation colleagues have tried to discredit and undermine the work of the Trust and divert its resources for their own purposes," Andrews wrote to the Trust's membership. "We have won the battle. However, a tremendous toll in unity and trust has been exacted." The battle had been waged, Andrews said, amidst "a cacophony of cynicism and irresponsible rhetoric."[697]

Julie Fix Udani, the Trust's manager of education programs, had been at the Trust since 1993, but her work had nothing to do with the troubled relationship with APCWS. All she knew was "there's two groups. It's no big deal. They do their thing and we do our thing," Udani recalled. She learned otherwise during a 1995 ABPP education conference.

"Ed Bearss got up and spoke in his inimitable style about telling good stories and being accurate and walking the ground. And he was fabulous," Udani recalled. "And then I got up and talked about our Civil War Explorer program, and: 'It's a computer. Isn't that exciting? It can store so much information. And we're working with the Genealogical Society, so people can look up their ancestors … ' Then I sat down.

"And then Dennis Frye got up, and instead of talking about education programs from his perspective, he attacked the Civil War Trust and the Civil War Explorer program and talked all about how we were trying to take people away and we were threatening the jobs of the Civil War historians and how they can't be replaced by a computer. It was horrible. It was a personal attack. And he went on for easily 20 minutes about it, to the point where after the session was over, the ABPP organizers came up to me and apologized for his behavior."[699]

Frye recalled that he criticized Udani "because she was talking about things that were not battlefield preservation. I don't remember exactly what she was talking about, but it seemed to me it was some kind of tourism program that they were going to implement. Now I understood what they were trying to do—same thing I wanted to do, broaden the appeal of the organization to a broader audience. Excellent. Good. But that was going to be paramount to buying battlefield land. It was the wrong direction at the wrong time. We needed to be committing our resources and their resources to preserving battlefields as quickly and immediately as possible."[700]

Despite the chronic strife, the two organizations couldn't divorce, not only because of their mutual preservation mission, but because the Trust continued to administer the coin funds. For the most part, the APCWS and Trust maintained a professional demeanor. Occasionally, a sense of camaraderie and goodwill prevailed, as it did at the APCWS annual conference in Nashville, Tenn., in April 1996. The APCWS held its banquet at nearby Spring Hill, which was practically Heller's back yard. Afterward, Chairman Richards extended "a heart-felt thank you" for Heller's gracious participation—a "splendid example of what our two groups can accomplish through cooperative efforts." The Trust extended an invitation to Richards the following year to join its board; there is no record that he accepted.[701]

In mid-December, the Trust had good news for the APCWS. The grant applications had been evaluated, and it had recommended ABPP approval of a $419,000 grant for Malvern Hill, including an extra $66,000 requested by APCWS after the original application. The approval allowed the APCWS to secure a $100,000 Cabell Foundation grant that, combined with $1.2 million contributed by members, allowed the APCWS to complete the purchase two years ahead of schedule.[702]

"Ready for a wonderful Christmas present?" Frye began his letter to the Trustees. Frye's full-page letter of thanks to Andrews included, "Your assistance allows us all to claim victory in our efforts to save these hallowed grounds."[703]

Less than a week later, Frye lost his Christmas spirit. The Trust's year-end, fundraising appeal to members, which he received, read as if the Trust had been the driving force to save Third Winchester. "Your contributions also helped us leap into action just two months ago, when the site of the Third Battle of Winchester was threatened by zoning (for) residential subdivisions," said the form letter signed by Andrews. "We had to work fast. And thanks to you, we were able to rescue 222 acres of this pristine site in Virginia."[704]

It was even worse than the Trust's earlier Third Winchester form letter. The APCWS went unmentioned. "The Trust owns none of this battlefield," Frye angrily said at the time. "It provided 20 percent of the purchase price as the down payment, and APCWS is responsible for the remaining $2 million." Any donations made to the

Trust because of its Third Winchester appeal should be used to help the APCWS pay down the debt on that land "and not go back into their bank to compensate themselves for the $500,000 that they've spent (in coin funds) on this project," he said.[705]

On January 30, 1996, the Trust announced the grant winners, distributing $2.046 million for nine battlefield preservation efforts in seven states. Counting the $919,000 for Third Winchester and Malvern Hill, the Trust distributed less than half of the more than $6 million collected in coin sales.[706]

Two of the nine projects, Brice's Cross Roads in Mississippi and Spring Hill in Tennessee, were spearheaded by the APCWS. The other seven grantees included the Cedar Creek Battlefield Foundation, which teamed with the Trust to save 158 acres, and the Georgia Civil War Commission, which saved 1,200 acres at Resaca, in part with $500,000 in coin money.[707]

Brandy Station was conspicuous in its absence. Frye and Lee Sammis had agreed in September 1995 to the sale of 1,543 acres at Brandy Station to the APCWS for $6.2 million. Frye and the APCWS, as well as Boasberg and the Brandy Station Foundation, had applied to the Trust for a $1 million emergency grant from coin funds. Not only was emergency money not allocated, no money was granted. Heller told the board both Ed Bearss and former board member James McPherson were advising the Trust in the grant funding process, and reported that "Ed Bearss said that it was not as historically significant as other battlefields; Jim McPherson disagreed," reported the Trust board meeting minutes of November 2, 1995. The Trust's concerns kept Brandy Station off the list; this omission bothered Frye as much as the other grants pleased him.[708]

In early March 1996, with a Brandy Station financing deadline looming, he turned on the public spotlight. Frye contacted *The Washington Post* suggesting a story on the need for coin money to help buy Brandy Station and the Trust's failure to grant it. But the *Post's* story on March 10, 1996, put the spotlight on the larger issue. A war for supremacy was being fought by the APCWS and the Trust—a fight "for the mantle of battlefield savior"—and the *Post* reported that key players were none too happy.[709]

"Right now, we should be building bridges instead of tearing them down," said the ABPP's Townsend. "It's tough to fathom that egos would get in the way," said Sammis, who vowed to "go ahead and develop our property" if the groups could not raise the money.[710]

Brandy Station funding boiled down to the same difference in philosophy that had prevented a merger. The APCWS wanted money for Brandy Station and wanted it now. "Every day the money stays in the bank is a day of lost opportunities," Frye said. The Brandy Station deal stood to fall through if the APCWS did not receive the requested $1 million in coin money from the Trust. The Trust's concern, Heller told the *Post*, was that the APCWS was overextended after trying to save too many battlefields at once, and that Brandy Station was too expensive.[711]

Upset by the tone of the article, Frye and the APCWS scrambled to spin a more positive angle, citing the APCWS's public appreciation for the grants for Malvern Hill and Third Winchester. In a letter to the editor, Richards chided the *Post* for suggesting APCWS was competing for the "mantle of battlefield savior." "We already wear this mantle with great pride," Richards wrote.[712]

Even before the *Post* article was published, however, Frye and the APCWS had begun to explore another funding strategy—a bold, new way to finance the purchase of battlefields. This strategy would allow the APCWS to make some of its biggest saves yet, but would also bring some of its biggest headaches. ★

CHAPTER
ELEVEN

Big Money, Big Problems

 N EARLY 1996, investment banker Frederick J. Zavaglia, a dedicated APCWS member and Civil War reenactor with the 8th New Jersey Infantry, began talking to a colleague about a Wall Street partnership with the Civil War battlefield preservation movement.

"The preservation movement just seemed to be a very natural extension to what I was doing as a reenactor, so I naturally gravitated toward it," Zavaglia recalled. "As I learned more and more about it, I tried more and more to get close to it." He unsuccessfully applied for a job at APCWS, but became friends with Dennis Frye and instead found himself appointed to the board of trustees in January 1997.[713]

Zavaglia worked for NatWest, an international financial firm based in England with a marketing arm in New York City. He believed that if the APCWS could issue revenue bonds, it could lighten its debt load and save more battlefields. His colleague, Gregory LiCalzi, recognized the unique idea, but remained skeptical. "While I certainly understood Fred's desire to create a financial vehicle APCWS could use to periodically borrow low-cost funds for its real property acquisitions, my initial reaction was that this appeared to be too ambitious a transaction for such a small organization to successfully undertake," LiCalzi said. For that and other reasons, "I doubted any institutional investor or bank lender would tackle this financing,"[714]

Still, it was potential business, and on February 14 LiCalzi sent Frye a letter suggesting NatWest create and implement a "cost-effective, tax-exempt, revenue bond financial program" to optimize the organization's borrowing power and lower its interest rates.[715]

APCWS had made its first purchases with cash. After a few years, it began buying land with a sizeable down payment and paying the balance within a year or two. The Third Winchester battlefield property in Virginia, offered at $2.5 million in 1995, required $500,000 down and 10 years of payments at about 10 percent interest to pay off the balance of $2 million. For Spring Hill battlefield land in Tennessee, the APCWS put $350,000 down and secured a 10-year loan at 8.5 percent to pay the $850,000 balance.[716]

"Through the NatWest offer, interest costs can be reduced to between 3.5-4.0%," or less than half of what we pay, Frye reported. That got the APCWS board's attention. Richards, Frye, Director of Real Estate Bob Edmiston and trustee Carrington Williams met with Zavaglia and LiCalzi in Washington on March 5, 1996.[717]

The proposal involved a complex arrangement, but basically a bank would provide the up-front cash to APCWS to pay off the Third Winchester debt and to buy Brandy Station outright. The APCWS bank debt would be financed through the sale of tax-exempt, low-interest revenue bonds. To issue the bonds, APCWS had to have a local government conduit, which it found in the Industrial Development Authority of the town of Culpeper, Virginia.[718]

Williams used his considerable influence, negotiating skills and charm to overcome hurdles the APCWS faced, not the least of which were chronic problems within the operating budget. Although most banks and financial institutions "showed a disinterest bordering on apathy," LiCalzi wrote in *Hallowed Ground*, three banks expressed interest and, ultimately, NationsBank agreed to underwrite a $5.4 million bond issue. In January 1998, the APCWS successfully sold its tax-exempt bonds at an interest rate of 3.5 percent. Bond revenues paid off Third Winchester and most of the Brandy Station and Cedar Mountain purchases.[719] Coin money also helped buy Brandy Station, as the Trust in 1997 finally approved a $500,000 grant.

Zavaglia's idea came to fruition, and "really made it much easier for us to make the payments on the different deals that we had structured," recalled Frye, who had become APCWS president in 1995. "The board adopted this concept with very little controversy. Our board by this time had transitioned to a board of business people. I had worked very diligently to change the board from a board of passionate historians to a board of professional business people. And that was very, very important to do. The bond issue would never have been achieved if we were still the original board of historians. We would've been frightened to death. This did not scare businessmen. They understood debt, and they understood how debt could be used. So, we were saving battlefields, using debt very creatively, wisely ... with risk, yes, but now with the Wall Street bonds, we reduced our risk."[720]

The bond issue was one of many changes in an organization in transition. In the spring of 1996, the APCWS relocated from Fredericksburg to Frye's hometown of Hagerstown, Maryland, which offered office space almost rent-free on the town square. The March 2, 1996, board meeting was the last for several trustees, including founders Gary Gallagher, the first president/chairman, and Will Greene, the first paid employee.

The APCWS had come a long way since the 1987 dinner meeting at Arbuckle's Restaurant, where a few friends haggled over a name and debated how to get money. Gallagher and Greene had sacrificed far more than countless hours on the "messy road to overall success," as Gallagher described it. He realized he was "completely burned out."[721]

"But it was much more complicated than that for me because I became head of the history department at Penn State in the middle of all of this as well, which just upped my level," Gallagher recalled. "And then Religious Studies was put under me. And then Classics was put under me. And so I had, overall, 100 faculty I was responsible for there. I just didn't have the time to do what I had. And it had become something that didn't really need me anymore, I thought. It had moved beyond the stage where it needed any one of us individually."[722]

Long meetings, countless tasks, disputes, controversies and the demands of leadership had taken their toll. Greene and Gallagher could and did take great satisfaction in their accomplishments and the battlefields saved. Gallagher would never forget the thrill in 1991 when APCWS managed to come up with $110,000 to save 194 acres that comprised the key ground at Fisher's Hill in the Shenandoah Valley. "Every time I drive past it on Interstate 81 in fact, and look at the cut on Little North Mountain where the power lines go through—that tells you exactly where the Confederate line was—still, every time I drive past there, I think about the work we did to get that ground," Gallagher recalled. "I get a lot of satisfaction from that."[723]

As Gallagher, Greene and others left the board that day, new trustees joined, including Cincinnati businessman Alan E. Hoeweler and New Jersey attorney and publishing executive Norman B. Tomlinson, Jr. Almost immediately, Frye approached Tomlinson about upgrading the modest APCWS newsletter, *Hallowed Ground*, first published in June 1988. Tomlinson agreed to finance and produce *Hallowed Ground* as a full-color magazine, and the first issue was published in January 1998.[724]

In his initiative to change the board, Frye recruited a number of wealthy and influential men and women. Jody Powell and Frank Bracken, former Deputy Secretary of the Interior under President George H.W. Bush, came from the national political scene. Bankers Zavaglia and LiCalzi from New York joined, as well as educator Mary Munsell Abroe from Chicago, who continues today as a trustee.[725]

From Richmond, Frye recruited well-connected attorneys C. Hobson Goddin and Daniel T. Balfour. From Alabama came banker Paul W. Bryant, Jr., son of the legendary football coach "Bear" Bryant, and Birmingham attorney Henry Simpson.

Each would later serve as chairman. From Mississippi came attorney and banker John D. Haynes, a fraternity brother of Senator Trent Lott. Austin, Texas, attorney Daniel M. Laney was another Frye recruit. Nearly all were deeply devoted students of the Civil War with ancestors who fought in the conflict.[726]

In the battle to come, some of Frye's Southern recruits, including Bryant, Haynes, Laney and Balfour, would fight hard for merger. Northern trustees Zavaglia and Hoeweler would fight just as hard against it, giving the dispute a taste of the same North-South divide as the war itself.

But first, the "Yankees" had another target—Frye himself. Hoeweler had become vice chairman at the same March 15, 1997, board meeting where Zavaglia, Haynes and Bryant were named to the board. At the next meeting, on July 26, Zavaglia was appointed secretary. Zavaglia and other trustees began to take a dim view of some of Frye's actions.

An APCWS initiative was installing interpretive signs at some of the battlefields it had saved. Everyone supported that. But one of Frye's proposals was to start a Guide Service at Antietam battlefield, and another was to help stage the 135th anniversary reenactment of the Battle of Antietam. Neither proposal was universally popular with the trustees.

Frye also faced chronic financial problems. APCWS was plagued by administrative budget shortfalls and weak accounting practices. One fundraising event had done the exact opposite. A seven-day Delta Queen cruise in July 1996 had lost about $70,000 despite an all-star lineup of speakers and tour guides.[727]

A brief, happy moment came at the January 23, 1997, board meeting, when Chairman Richards reported: "The Association is not bankrupt. In fact, APCWS has experienced its greatest year ever," with net income of more than $1.7 million.[208] But the APCWS was losing money; it suffered a net loss of $83,000 during the first quarter of 1997, despite a mandate from the board that past November to cut 1997 operating expenses by $100,000.[729]

While fighting the coin war with the Trust, Frye was trying to manage employees who were coming in late and leaving early, frustrating those working full days and more.[730] In October 1996, Frye instituted a "Tour of Duty" agreement for work hours, compensatory time, sick leave and annual leave that each staff member was required to sign. If an employee went "AWOL," their paycheck was docked for the number of hours they were absent without permission.[731]

Frye's biggest problem was with one of his top lieutenants, Bob Edmiston, Director of Real Estate. Edmiston, who died in 2004, was hired by Greene in 1994. He did a good job, Greene recalled, and served effectively as the organization's point man on land acquisition.

During Ed Wenzel's years-long effort to have Fairfax County establish Ox Hill Battlefield Park, Edmiston appeared at a hearing in 1994 to support the county's proposed acquisition of a small parcel for the park, which it approved. Afterward, Wenzel thanked Greene and APCWS for the support, writing that Edmiston's "eloquent remarks demonstrated the concern and support of a nationwide organization and we were delighted to have him on the speakers list."[732]

"Bob and I were great friends," recalled Zavaglia. "Bob was a very capable guy. He had a sixth sense for knowing where property was and under what kind of threat it was. He carried most of that around in his head."[733]

But Edmiston developed a habit of working short days. Frye disciplined him, but he and other staff members sometimes found Edmiston playing solitaire and video games on his computer.[734]

Frye's "Tour of Duty" reports, however, came off as heavy handed, along with other accountability measures he instituted. Ruth Hudspeth, hired by APCWS in 1998 as a part-time bookkeeper and today the Trust's chief financial officer, recalled that Frye installed a sign-in board for employees to mark upon leaving or returning to the office. "He decided that wasn't good enough, so he made a book that, even when they went to the bathroom, they had to sign in what minute it was and how long they were in the bathroom," she recalled. Frye doesn't remember doing anything that strict.[735]

The beginning of the end of Frye's presidency began in January 1998 with the election of Alan Hoeweler as the new APCWS chairman. Frye enjoyed warm and strong support from departing Chairman Tom Richards and together they decided Hoeweler was the perfect candidate to take over. A Cincinnati businessman, Hoeweler was a former president of the Friends of the National Park at Gettysburg and a founding member of the Perryville Battlefield Preservation Association in Kentucky.[736]

Frye's honeymoon with Hoeweler would not last long. Almost immediately, Frye felt Hoeweler wanted to be chairman *and* president, closely monitoring day-to-day activities, handling press queries and being the public face of the APCWS.[737] But Frye had management problems and Hoeweler had the support of the board. "We had to make a change from Dennis. We all realized that," recalled the late trustee Henry Simpson.[738]

"Dennis has a lot of enthusiasm – tremendous enthusiasm—but not good on dollar and cents," Ed Bearss observed. "My saying about Dennis: Dennis has great passion, but as a businessman, he could go broke running a whore house in Pearl

Harbor during World War II."[739]

In February, just weeks after his election, Hoeweler began stripping Frye of his management responsibilities, turning them over first to Zavaglia and later to Edmiston. Frye was assigned to handle "development," or fundraising.[740]

The transition was difficult. Two employees continued to come in late and leave early, and Frye believed Hoeweler and Zavaglia, now allied with Edmiston, would overlook the problem. On March 23, 1998, Frye wrote Zavaglia a three-page memo describing the problem in detail. He said Edmiston's practice of routinely coming in late, and sometimes not at all, was why he had implemented increasingly strict work schedule rules.[741]

Frye could see that Hoeweler supported Edmiston. Frye explicitly told Zavaglia that he could not support Edmiston as staff supervisor. In addition to his attendance problems, "Bob on many instances spent much of his day playing computer games," Frye wrote. "I received so many complaints from staff that I had to have the games removed."

On April 24, 1998, Hoeweler formally announced the leadership changes, telling trustees in a statement that under Frye's management, "the APCWS has not produced the effective organization we need to meet the significant operational challenges of the next few years." He appointed Edmiston as chief operating officer to handle day-to-day operations and assigned Zavaglia to oversee the transition.[743]

Edmiston presented the treasurer's report and described the overall financial condition as a "precarious situation." Zavaglia told the board that "only recently" had steps been taken to correct the problems. Expenses had exceeded revenues by $95,158 in 1997. To solve the problem, APCWS would have to raise $2 million in 1998 and every year for some time to come.[744]

Frye was angry and hurt by Hoeweler's statement (which misspelled his name "Fry"), but accepted the demotion and agreed to the "collective conclusion" (Hoeweler's words) that change was necessary. Frye, however, fought back subtly when he told the board at the April 24 meeting that one of the tasks taken from him was setting the program for the annual conference, which had occurred in March. Mike Yost "questioned the apparent [financial] loss the conference was to show." Attendance had been lower, Frye pointed out.[745]

In July, the *Civil War News* and the Hagerstown *Morning Herald* reported Hoeweler was highly critical of APCWS involvement in the Antietam battle reenactment that had taken place nine months earlier. The APCWS, with board approval, though not unanimous, had partnered with local officials to stage the three-day extravaganza, which drew some 12,500 reenactors and an estimated 100,000 spectators. Frye saw APCWS participation as an expansion of its education and outreach mission. He had worked "ridiculous hours," as described by one participant, and APCWS had earned more than $75,000 from the event as well as a 10 percent increase in membership.[746]

Hoeweler said the event was a distraction and not worth the staff time spent on it. "We should have realized what was happening," he said. "We couldn't afford it." He accused local officials of backing out of their commitment to the event and failing to compensate the APCWS. "That's not our job to promote Hagerstown," he said. Frye and another board member had conflicts of interest when they served on the local reenactment committee, he said.[747]

Hoeweler's belated criticism blindsided nearly everyone, including Edmiston, who tried to minimize the damage, telling the paper, "We don't want to think anyone in the community was not appreciated." Local officials were shocked and furious. In a scathing editorial, the *Herald* schooled Hoeweler in the art of public relations. Even if Hoeweler's accusations were true, the newspaper wrote, "what good can possibly come out of making a stink about it now, almost a year after the event?"[748]

In the aftermath of the public relations fiasco, the APCWS executive committee decided at its July 8 meeting that it needed a press policy because "at this time, no one on staff is capable of credibly performing the function." On a voice vote, without dissent, the organization designated Hoeweler as the APCWS spokesperson, "stipulating that no other individual Trustee or member of staff is authorized to speak with the press."[749]

Frye was at the meeting, but missed the discussion and vote. He would explain later that he stepped out for water and ice to relieve a sore, dry throat. Two days after the meeting, Frye delivered a letter he wrote to the *Herald* editor and sent Hoeweler a detailed memo.[750] Frye's letter attempted to counter any public perception of a leadership rift. He wrote that Howeler's reorganization had "my full endorsement" and "I am relieved to be relieved of my day-to-day management responsibilities."[751]

Hoeweler and Zavaglia were furious. "What are you doing!?" Zavaglia emailed Frye. "The EC [Executive Committee] unequivocally formulated a press policy. You ignored. Before the policy could even be used, you trashed it. You are either insubordinate or no longer capable of making the basic distinctions required of a professional who is involved with normal business discourse."[752]

Hoeweler acknowledged Frye's heart was in the right place, but asked, "Why would you go against the Executive Committee's desires in such a blatant manor (sic)? It baffling (sic) why you are undermining me."[753]

Frye was profusely apologetic. "I missed this part of the discussion. I am so sorry if I have disappointed you," he emailed Hoeweler on July 10.[754]

Three days later, Frye was deeper in Hoeweler's doghouse. The APCWS chairman received a scathing letter from trustee Susan Saum-Wicklein's husband, Mike, a Frye supporter, taking Hoeweler to task over the public relations fiasco. Hoeweler believed Frye was behind Wicklein's letter and peppered him with questions about Wicklein's access to the APCWS office and its records.[755]

Frye answered Hoeweler's questions point by point. "The impression that I am undermining you is wrong," he wrote. "I am not leading any forces against you." He volunteered to come to Cincinnati at his own expense to discuss the matters of contention. "You do not have my story, my perspective nor (sic) my thoughts," Frye wrote. "I only request the opportunity to share these with you."[756]

Even as he wrote, Frye knew that no amount of effort on his part would repair the breach. Fault did not matter; he served at the pleasure of the board. On July 23, 1998, Frye resigned as president and trustee in a letter to Hoeweler. "Eleven years ago, seven of us set (sic) in a living room and dreamed of saving our Civil War heritage," he wrote. "Bulldozers and earthmovers were hauling our battlefields to the dump, and we seemed powerless to prevent it. The organization has accomplished so much, and I am humbled to be associated with its many successes. Now is the proper time to turn this 'creation' over to the next builder. Frye offered Hoeweler his continued services "if you feel they may be of value."[757]

At the lowest moment of his life, Frye put on a good face and told the media his departure was not acrimonious. Within a week, APCWS hired him as a consultant to work with federal and state governments on legislative issues.[758]

If measured only by the amount of land saved, Frye's presidency established impressive new standards, including 1,563 acres at Brandy Station, 831 acres at Brice's Cross Roads, 222 acres at Third Winchester, 158 acres at Cedar Creek and 97 acres at Sailor's Creek. These were complemented by a string of acquisitions or partner acquisitions beyond the mid-Atlantic, including Griswoldville and New Hope Church in Georgia, Camp Wildcat and Mill Springs in Kentucky, and Davis Bridge, Spring Hill and Roper's Knob in Tennessee.[759]

But Brandy Station cost $6.2 million; Third Winchester was more than $2.5 million; the price tag at Spring Hill was $880,000, and Brice's Cross Roads was $600,000, to name the most expensive. Making the monthly payments on these debts was an enormous challenge. Local partners shared some of the burden, but at the end of 1998, APCWS was servicing nearly $7 million of debt, including $5.45 million on the bond issue, with a principal payment of $480,000 due on January 1, 1999.[760]

As chief operating officer, Edmiston's approach was molded by the massive financial burden. New saves slowed to a trickle. "Simply because we do not announce a new battlefield purchase several times a year does not mean we have become less active," Edmiston wrote in a "Message from Headquarters" in *Hallowed Ground* in spring 1999. "Paying over three-quarters of a million dollars in debt service is preserving battlefields. If the debt cannot be retired, the battlefields will yet be lost. The days of an all-out, go-for-broke fundraising campaign to make an outright purchase of most remaining battlefields are over."[761]

Austin, Texas, attorney Daniel M. Laney, who joined the board in 1998, recalled, "I got involved in it and found out pretty quickly there were really serious financial difficulties because in doing some pretty good work, the APCWS had really stretched itself thin. We were just kind of dead in water. We weren't raising any money and we didn't have any momentum. We had just sort of ground to a halt at that point. Basically, the whole thing had stagnated over the debt."[762]

There were other problems, too. Edmiston, who led the APCWS staff from July 1998 to December 1999, did not run a strict office. Recalled Hudspeth, "There were a lot of things that happened there that made it just a very casual office to the point that it was not businesslike at all. They'd go down as a group to go visit a site and it was really bad, because they would come back and they knew the [local] bartender's name. And that's what they were talking about, instead of the site that they had gone to visit."[763]

Dana Shoaf, now editor of *Civil War Times*, was hired as Director of Education in the spring of 1999. He considered it his dream job. "I was incredibly passionate about preservation, and I still am," he said. "And I thought, 'Man, this is really what I got into history to do ... to go out and get in touch with history, to kind of feel and taste and smell history and at the same time to save it.' I was just thrilled that I got this job."[764]

Shoaf prepared to edit and produce his first *Hallowed Ground*. He began learning how to lead battlefield tours, figuring out the other responsibilities of his job and determining how he could best contribute. He soon realized that the pace at APCWS was decidedly laid back, and the tone was set by Edmiston.

"I was very fond of Bob Edmiston," Shoaf recalled. "I actually learned a lot from him ... But, Bob would get in between nine and ... usually closer to 10 in the morning. And he would go in his office. And I'd go in there to talk to him, and he'd be playing solitaire, you know? And I kept thinking to myself, 'Gosh, he's running the organization. There has to be more for him to do than that.'"[765]

Ironically, the same scene occurred at Civil War Trust offices under the late Matt Andrews. "Listening to bluegrass. Taking care of his personal business. Putting with

golf. And solitaire," recalled Bonnie Repasi, hired as administrative assistant in 1992
—one of the Trust's first employees. "And then when it was time to get to work, it
was always fast and furious and the last minute. Because he wasn't a self-starter. He
did a task well, but he wasn't creating work."[766]

Once, Andrews went to Tennessee to present a check to Woody Harrell, the influential Shiloh National Military Park superintendent. Harrell had "knocked himself out" planning a tour to show Andrews the park's land problems and discuss
projects they could jointly work on, recalled Ed Bearss. "And Matt says, 'I gotta take
a break. I'm going to play golf,'" Bearss said with a laugh. "That story got all over the
park service fast."[767]

Leadership came from Vice President of Development Elliot Gruber, hired by
the Trust in July 1993. Gruber had been Director of Development and Marketing at
the National Parks Conservation Association, where he built membership, solicited
large donations and forged partnerships with regional and local groups.

"My strategy from the beginning was that if we were going to be a nationally
recognized Civil War preservation organization, we needed to work extremely closely and develop partnerships with, one, those Civil War preservation organizations
around the country, and then, two, those kinds of, say, historic councils or heritage
councils around the country," Gruber recalled.[768]

The Trust had begun its first educational programs in April 1993, when President Grae Baxter outlined a vision "of a national Civil War Heritage Trail—a voluntary network of public, private, local, state and federal sites—as the conceptual
framework and best inspiration for fund raising…"[769]

When Gruber came on, he threw much of his considerable energy into developing the education programs. He hired Julie Fix Udani as education director, renamed
the program, "Civil War Discovery Trail" and developed ties with dozens of historical sites and organizations. Gruber knew relationships would expand the Trust's
reach and influence. In 1995, the Trust published the Civil War Discovery Trail Official Guidebook and by the following year, the book had gone into three printings
and sold more than 26,000 copies.

Gruber "was a good teacher, a great mentor, wonderful boss and a fun guy
to work with," recalled staff member Melissa Meisner Sadler, who is still with the
Trust."[770]

"I just remember the enthusiasm," said staff member Bonnie Repasi, who also
still works for the Trust. "His mind was working at times faster than anyone else's
was working."[771]

As the Trust developed the Civil War Discovery Trail, Gruber turned to Ed

Bearss for historical help. "Some were little, little sites that most people hadn't heard of. And, literally, it was a brain download from him," Gruber recalled. "It was, 'Here are the yeses and here are the nos' from Ed Bearss, over several days. And I just said, 'Thank you, thank you, thank you.' It was amazing."[772]

The original Trust also launched a Civil War Explorer System, with interactive, multi-media computer presentations inside kiosks at select battlefields, but the program failed to take hold.[773] "It was a kind of big version of the battle apps that the Trust has now," Repasi recalled. "It was a little bigger than us — it was a little before its time — so we didn't have the support for it. But it was a good idea."[774]

A $30,000 grant from the History Channel in 1997 was used to develop the Trust's first website, *www.civilwar.org*, which went live that August. At the November board meeting, the staff proudly reported that the site had received more than 10,000 hits; by the following spring, it had more than 100,000 hits a month.[775]

But the Trust, as with the APCWS, had chronic financial issues, including a persistent operating fund deficit. The Trust's failure to attract large corporate donors compounded the problem and by the end of 1994, the organization's deficit totaled $777,000. A year later, it had been reduced more than half, to $327,000, but the problem persisted.[776]

Sometimes the Trust called upon one of its wealthy directors for a bailout, as it did in April 1996, when an unnamed Trust director guaranteed half of a $375,000 prime interest rate loan from Riggs National Bank in Washington so the Trust could finance some of its debt.[777]

In February 1997, Lester G. "Ruff" Fant III became the Trust's chairman and immediately demanded changes, improvements and more accountability from Andrews. "When I got in and got my hands on the organization, I found that it was in very poor shape," Fant recalled. "We had to borrow money from a board member to pay the payroll. The problem was that the coin money could only be used to buy land. And so we had to pay our overhead. We had this Civil War Discovery Trail and a book was published with that, which was a very successful thing. But it's not free."[778]

Repasi had been asked to take over some bookkeeping duties after the departure of a finance administrator. She became so uncomfortable with the work, she resigned in 1996. "There was just a lot of not okay things going on at the Trust financially," Repasi recalled. "I was young and I was afraid I was going to be held responsible for some of these things. I felt like there was a lot of misuse of money." She had no accounting background but could tell that money for preservation acquisitions was being used on administration. "It became the kind of problem that I couldn't live with," Repasi recalled. "I didn't see an end to the cycle of money problems."[779]

Fant dismissed Andrews after about a year. Gruber well remembers Andrews's last day in the early spring of 1998. "He took me into his office and he said, 'We have $20,000 in the bank, we have about a hundred or so thousand dollars of expenses, and here is a stack of bills that haven't been entered.' And he said, basically, 'Good luck. See you later.'"[780]

Thus began "the most stressful time period I've ever had in my professional career," Gruber recalled. "It was keeping the lights on. There were agreements that were signed by Matt that were unknown to the board and to anybody else. I had to go talk to direct mail firms, I had to go talk to creditors." Trust records show that in October 1997, the total number of "aged payables," or unpaid bills, was four pages long and just shy of $130,000.[781] One minute Gruber would be on the phone asking a member for a donation. The next minute, he'd be fending off an angry creditor, pleading, "Don't take us to court."[782]

Several staff members resigned shortly before Andrews was dismissed, so the Trust was down to three employees—Gruber, Udani and Melissa Meisner Sadler, hired that year as executive assistant. "It was like, 'Guys, we gotta band together and figure out how we're going to get this done,'" recalled Gruber. "And we did. The board helped significantly…"[783]

Both organizations sputtered forward in their shared mission of saving battle-fields. But the APCWS Board of Trustees and Civil War Trust Board of Directors were composed of strong, successful, wealthy and powerful members who shared a deep passion for Civil War history. These men and women would look beyond conflicts to forge a new future. But before a pact would be sealed, discord would reach new heights and heads would roll. ★

CHAPTER
TWELVE

The Merger

HE IDEA of a merger between the Association for the Preservation of Civil War Sites (APCWS) and the Civil War Trust (Trust) was suggested almost as soon as the Trust was created in 1991. The two organizations held meetings about their mutual roles in Civil War battlefield preservation as early as 1992, when a possible merger was discussed by the APCWS's Will Greene and the Trust's Grae Baxter. Dennis Frye continued the dialogue with Trust Chairman Rod Heller when Frye took the helm at APCWS.

On February 10, 1995, while Frye was still interim president, four members of each organization, including Heller and Jim Lighthizer from the Trust and Tom Richards, James McPherson and Carrington Williams from APCWS, met to informally discuss a merger. The different philosophies, as well as some mutual mistrust and hostility, proved insurmountable.[784]

Relations reached new lows later that year during the coin war, but to many on both sides, the ongoing discord was pointless and counterproductive. Taking their problem to Capitol Hill and forcing preservation-minded legislators to choose sides was unwise and they were complaining about it. Something had to change. APCWS trustee John D. Haynes and Trust board member Lighthizer had developed a strong working relationship as heads of their respective organization's legislative affairs committees. Haynes, a Mississippi attorney involved in the efforts to preserve Brice's Cross Roads, was a Frye recruit who joined the APCWS board in January 1997.

Lighthizer had joined the Trust's board in July 1994, while he was Secretary of Transportation for the State of Maryland, where he helped pioneer the use of ISTEA (Intermodal Surface Transportation Efficiency Act of 1991, or "Ice Tea") funding to save Civil War battlefields as transportation enhancements.[785]

His interest in the Civil War had been ignited by reading Michael Shaara's Pulitzer Prize-winning Civil War novel The Killer Angels on a Nags Head vacation in the summer of 1983. "It lit something that can best be defined as between a passion and an obsession," Lighthizer recalled.[786]

Lighthizer and Haynes forged a partnership, presenting a united front on Capitol Hill on behalf of the APCWS and Trust. Their first objective in 1998 was to secure a direct federal appropriation to save battlefields.

The initiative to secure direct federal funding was begun by the APCWS in 1997 by Frye and trustee Howard Coffin. With help from Coffin's boss, Vermont Senator Jim Jeffords, they sought direct funding for APCWS battlefield land acquisition through an amendment to the Land and Water Conservation Fund, a standing fund of revenues from gas and oil drilling leases used for conservation and recreation projects nationwide.[787]

Frye's presidency brought massive debt to the APCWS, and he saw a direct federal appropriation as salvation. If successful, the legislative effort could relieve much or all of the $5 million debt incurred by acquisitions, including Brandy Station and Third Winchester. Better yet, it would give APCWS funds outside the control of the Civil War Trust and unencumbered by the vicissitudes of the sale of commemorative coins. It would also give the APCWS a huge edge over the Trust. Most importantly, it could save a lot more land.[788]

On August 19, 1997, Frye contacted Haynes to seek support from Senator Trent Lott (R-Miss.). Lott and Haynes were fraternity brothers in college, and Lott agreed to help, although the original idea of seeking $75 million was reduced to $50 million before the amendment was introduced and cut to $25 million as it was debated on Capitol Hill in September. As the legislation progressed, the APCWS agreed to commit $5 million as matching funds, and Frye periodically faxed out alerts with requests for members to lobby their Congressmen.[789]

"We're close—very close," Frye faxed Jerry Russell on September 22, 1997, after the Senate passed the amendment, moving it forward to a Conference Committee of House and Senate members.[790] There the effort died. Congressman Ralph Regula (R-Ohio), an Interior Committee co-chairman, was dead set against any measure that would award federal money to private entities to purchase land. Eventually, Congress appropriated $272 million to the Interior Department for priority land acquisitions—described in The Washington Post as "one of the biggest splurges" of land buying by the federal government in years. From that funding pie, NPS spent $11.1 million at six NPS battlefields, including the heart of Monocacy National Battlefield, the Roulette Farm next to the Sunken Road at Antietam National Battlefield and property at Gettysburg, Fredericksburg, Spotsylvania and Stone's River.[791]

Although it was a victory for preservation, it did nothing for battlefields outside the NPS net, such as Brandy Station. It brought no money to APCWS. So, in February 1998, Frye and Haynes started anew. This time their goal was a more modest $6.6 million, with $4.2 million to pay off the outstanding debt at Brandy Station and Third Winchester. This time, the Civil War Trust was involved from the start.[792]

Frye and Haynes invited the Trust to join because "we believed it would be helpful to have Senator Dale Bumpers on board, and his connections were with the Civil War Trust," Frye recalled.[793] On February 10, Frye contacted the Trust's Elliot Gruber to inform him of the $6.6 million goal and identify the battlefields likely to benefit from the anticipated funding. Gruber's response—expressing a desire to "integrate our plans into an effective strategy"—was a positive sign.[794]

"It was so crucial that we went up to Capitol Hill as one entity," said Haynes. "We could sell the message as a united front and there wouldn't be any debate … "[795] Recalled Lighthizer, "John Haynes and I were working those halls together, but he was the lead horse, I can tell you that. It wasn't me. I helped. But he was the lead horse. That changed the ball game. One of the keys to the game was bringing government in as a partner."[796]

As they walked the long corridors of Congressional office buildings, Haynes and Lighthizer also talked about how a merger would benefit both organizations and be a huge boost to the mission, even though the cultures were entirely different.

The APCWS, reflecting Frye's nature and leadership, had become brash and aggressive by 1996, willing to take risks and assume significant debt to save battlefield land *now*. The Trust was cautious and conservative, some would say to a fault. Then again, it had little choice given the government's strict bureaucratic regulations in disbursing funds for land preservation, including coin proceeds.

As former Trust Chairman Fant recalled, the APCWS just before the merger "would have 16-hour board meetings with yelling and screaming and threatened fist fights and everything else. And we had very Episcopalian board meetings. Everybody was respectful. We had issues, but we discussed them in a respectful way." Some of the APCWS (trustees) preferred the calmer environment over "this Wild West culture that at times, I think, prevailed on their board," Fant said.[797]

While working together on Capitol Hill, Haynes and Lighthizer organized a meeting to discuss merger with members of both boards at Episcopal High School in Alexandria, Virginia, on March 14, 1998. Afterward, both organizations created merger committees to mutually share financial and management information and to schedule more discussions.[798]

Haynes quietly took charge. "Haynes was the wizard," Lighthizer recalled. "He was the guy. He was the brains behind the merger. He was the manipulator. He was the schemer. He was the planner. He was the strategist. I remember joking with (APCWS Trustee) Paul Bryant once. I said, 'We're all puppets. John is just pulling the strings.' He stayed in the background. But he's the one who manipulated the whole merger process. John was key on the Hill and he was key to the merger. He's one of the unsung heroes."[799]

Trust board members had plenty of questions, but did not oppose a merger. However, a core of opposition formed and hardened within the APCWS, including Zavaglia, Hoeweler, Edmiston and most of the APCWS staff, which had a highly skeptical view of the Trust from past clashes. During an April 3, 1998, teleconference of the board's executive committee, Zavaglia cast the sole "no" vote on a resolution to form a special merger committee.[800]

To Zavaglia, the Trust appeared to be trying to absorb the APCWS into its operation when the APCWS had established itself as the clear leader *and* innovator in battlefield land preservation. "I think the bond funding was one of the major accomplishments of the APCWS," Zavaglia recalled. "I think it's one of the most overlooked ones, too. The idea of a member-based, private, nonprofit actually accessing the capital markets on a tax-exempt basis to preserve land that was not going to produce anything is astounding. At any other time, it would have been considered crazy."[801]

Zavaglia and the opponents worked to convince trustees that a merger would mean the APCWS would vanish, absorbed into the Trust. Even worse, it threatened the APCWS's bond financing arrangement with NationsBank, they said, and could force the organization into bankruptcy.[802]

Henry Simpson became a trustee in April 1998. "The first meeting I went to was in Lexington, Kentucky," Simpson recalled in 2012, a year before his death, "and I told Paul Bryant, 'Listen, I thought I was going to join something and decide what to do with other people's money.' We were up until midnight talking about whether we were bankrupt or not. It was a financial mess. We were heavily in debt as a result of Brandy Station, and it was coming out of that."[803]

On the legislative front, however, the APCWS and the Trust were working in perfect harmony. By May, the organizations had hammered out a joint priorities list for their 1998 campaign for funding, and Haynes and Lighthizer were back on Capitol Hill pitching a proposal for $6.5 million.[804]

On May 22, the two met with Bruce Evans, the staff member who ran the House

Interior Appropriations Subcommittee. Frye was there, too, eager to continue pursuing this effort despite the ignominy of his demotion, which Hoeweler had orchestrated the month before.

Evans left them all slack-jawed. He told them $6.5 million *wasn't enough*. He "asked us to submit additional projects," Frye wrote to the APCWS trustees on May 26. "In addition to our priority list, he wanted another $5 million in projects!"[805] The trustees revised their priority list, added more battlefields and increased the request to $12.5 million, with the two organizations agreeing to nearly match the federal appropriation with $11.78 million in donations and matching funds.

The measure gained steam. Lott turned to Senators Frank Murkowski and Ted Stevens, Republicans from Alaska, for support—"two very powerful men who controlled most of the land issues in the Senate. And they became supporters of money for battlefield preservation," Frye recalled. "You've got to give Lee Sammis some credit here for helping to plant the seed in Senator Murkowski's office. And, of course, Senator Jim Jeffords. He sang with Senator Lott in the men's quartet—they had a Senate quartet—and so they were very close."[806]

At the suggestion of Lott's office, Haynes and Lighthizer sought a $10 million appropriation to benefit 24 sites in 10 states. "They said it shouldn't even come up on the radar screen," Frye recalled.[807] But after breezing through the Senate, the appropriation stalled. It came up on the radar—Regula's radar—and became stuck in the House Conference Committee in September because of his opposition. "He continued to demand NO dollars for this purpose," Frye wrote in a memo to Hoeweler.[808]

In October 1998, a budget deadlock worked to the preservationists' advantage. "All the incompleted appropriations bills were lumped together into a 4,000-page document, and our good friend Senator Lott was one of the key negotiators," Frye wrote to Hoeweler. "Regula's influence remained strong, however, and our $10 million request was shaved to $8 million." The preservationists also had to promise a two-to-one match in privately donated funds, or $16 million. It was a challenge, but still a huge victory. "For the first time in the history of the United States Congress, it has established funding for non-federal Civil War battlefield sites," Frye wrote.[809]

Hoeweler was not impressed. He said he and other trustees saw the effort as promoting "what they foresee as a dead end." Hoeweler wanted to know, "Are we spending our hard-earned money to forward the cause of all preservation groups or just APCWS?" He also asked: "At what point must we call off this campaign?"[810]

Frye and Haynes were alarmed at Hoeweler's response, and polled the trustees to make sure their joint effort with the Trust on Capitol Hill would not be damaged by a lack of support from the board, especially now that $8 million had been secured.[811]

"Why should it ever end?" Frye asked trustee Daniel M. Laney rhetorically in an email. "As long as we can continue to successfully obtain money from Capitol Hill, why should it end? APCWS should delight in this type of success."[812]

The APCWS never took official action opposing the $8 million federal appropriation, Frye said. There is no indication that it was ever formally discussed after Frye briefed the board on details of the new legislation at a contentious board meeting in November 1998. Zavaglia was skeptical of the initiative and questioned "how much more effort the APCWS should devote toward the advocacy of legislation that appears to have, at least on the surface, more obstacles to funding than funds."[813]

At the same meeting, Zavaglia also complained that the Trust had not responded in a timely manner to APCWS requests for information and failed to act on promises. Zavaglia said he thought it would be irresponsible to continue with the merger.

A "lively discussion" ensued, with several trustees, including Laney and Haynes, defending the Trust and arguing that the dialogue should continue. After a few minutes, Hoeweler asked for an end to the debate and said he would call the Trust and ask for an explanation.[814]

APCWS records that survive in the Civil War Trust archives contain no complete or formal minutes from the final APCWS board meetings in 1999, reflecting the chaos within the organization as the drumbeat for merger became louder, along with vehement opposition.

In early 1999, Hoeweler decided that the APCWS was not going to merge with the Trust. No record exists of this in the incomplete APCWS archives. It was reported in the minutes of the Civil War Trust board meeting of February 25, 1999, when Chairman Fant told his board that "the merger was called off by APCWS Chairman Alan Hoeweler." The minutes added, "We will continue to work with APCWS but the likelihood of renewing merger talks is unlikely."[815]

For APCWS Trustee Haynes, the "most pivotal point in the merger" came as opponents were arguing at a meeting that it could threaten the APCWS's relationship with its bond underwriter. Haynes is uncertain of the date, but recalled: "Paul Bryant, who was sitting in the back of the room at Hagerstown, kind of raised his finger up to his heart to get the chairman's attention. And Paul basically told him that if NationsBank did not want the letter of credit for $7 million, there was a bank in Alabama that would be glad to have it. The bluff was them trying to stop the merger by that threat: 'Well, we're going to be forced into bankruptcy.' And Bryant killed it by saying, 'Well, if they don't want the seven-million-dollar guarantee, I'll move it to Alabama.' Which he did. Guaranteed it himself."[816] Bryant's promise reassured many trustees, but did not sway the opponents.

Haynes and fellow trustees Laney, Bryant, Simpson and others sensed that a majority of the board favored merger. The showdown came on April 23, 1999, at the board meeting held in conjunction with the annual conference in Richmond.

"It was a horrific conference," recalled Ruth Hudspeth. "The hotel was falling apart. There was no food there. The tours were wonderful, but everything else … " The hotel had a construction project going on and "it looked like they had a giant garbage bag over the front of the hotel," recalled Laney.[817]

Hudspeth was sitting outside the board meeting as an angry Zavaglia walked out. "Is the meeting over with?" asked Hudspeth. "No," he told her. "I made my point. I threw my stuff across the table and I'm leaving."[818]

Recalled Hudspeth, "We were at a place where there was not a restaurant. A half a block away was a bar that had a restaurant. He went down to the bar. Bob Edmiston went down to the bar. The auditor went down to the bar, because they had presented the financials, and a couple of the employees went down to the bar. And then the chairman of the board left, and he went down the bar. And they were all down at the bar having their own private meeting."[819]

The vote was not close. The board voted 15–4 to resume merger talks with the Trust, and reduced the merger committee to three trustees—Laney, Williams and Simpson—all supporters of the merger. Although no APCWS records exist for the meeting, Lighthizer reported at the Trust's board meeting of May 21 that the AP-CWS board had overruled its chairman and merger talks were back on.[820]

The new APCWS merger committee spent countless hours with their counterparts working through endless details. During a June 2, 1999, APCWS executive committee teleconference (for which minutes exist), Laney reported good progress and "nothing but cordial, prompt and meaningful cooperation from the Trust's merger committee." Laney spoke of "the intriguing possibility of a vibrant new combination."[821]

Hoeweler said he appreciated "talks were finally progressing and looked forward to being kept up to date and to the formal report," the minutes said. The update was brief and noncontroversial.[822] The fireworks began soon enough.

Later in the teleconference, Laney questioned Zavaglia's recommendation to hire an accountant as a staff member rather than continue contracting for his services. Given APCWS's precarious financial condition, Laney thought hiring a fundraiser was far more important than a finance officer. Laney questioned whether AP-CWS was fulfilling its role. The association "had lost a great deal of its passion for preserving the battlefields," he said, and "there was a major disconnect brewing with the membership." Laney cited the disastrous Richmond convention as evidence.[823]

Zavaglia disagreed. "He blamed certain departed employees of the Association for its current plight and for the problems with the annual convention," the minutes said.[824]

"Stop blaming people no longer with the Association for every current ill," Laney said, according to the minutes.[825]

Zavaglia hotly challenged Laney. Both Laney and trustee Frank Bracken called out Zavaglia on his demeanor, with Laney saying he "would not be intimidated by Fred's method of arguing."[826]

"Fred then declared that the whole idea of merger discussion with the Trust was a worthless enterprise," the minutes said.[827]

As far as the original APCWS founders were concerned, the merger was anything but worthless. In fact, it was essential. "In many of the (APCWS) accomplishments, we have been aided by The Civil War Trust," they wrote in an open letter unanimously supporting the merger. "We believe that the combination of these two dedicated groups will allow the (preservation) effort to proceed in harmony and to accomplish goals together neither could achieve if acting independently ... " It was signed by Gary W. Gallagher, A. Wilson Greene, Robert K. Krick, Donald C. Pfanz, Brian C. Pohanka, Dennis E. Frye, Edward T. Wenzel and John P. Ackerly, III.[828]

On June 13, the merger committees of the two organizations met in Annapolis. After a few hours, "we had everything ironed out," recalled Lighthizer. "We agreed to merge, we had the name done and we had the logo done." At that point, the APCWS's Carrington Williams stood up and said, "I support this merger. But I'm only going to vote for it under one condition. And that is that Jim Lighthizer be president of the group." Recalled Lighthizer: "I don't think I'd even talked to him about it."[829]

The merger was now on a fast track. Before a key July 24 board meeting, APCWS trustees continued their efforts to convince merger opponents to relent in hopes of securing a unanimous vote. On July 23, Simpson faxed a letter to Zavaglia explaining some of the financial details. "Any sophisticated banker is going to be overjoyed by the merger of the two entities," Simpson wrote.[830]

But Edmiston's emails make it clear how deeply entrenched the APCWS opponents were. "Haynes keeps saying crap like 'big things are going to happen and you're (me) going to be a big part of it,'" Edmiston wrote to Zavaglia on July 13. "These guys are off their rockers."[831]

"Give 'em hell!!!" Edmiston emailed Zavaglia and Hoeweler on July 14. Later that day, under the subject of "that goddamn merger," Edmiston wrote: "Just had a conversation with Laney. WATCH HIM LIKE A HAWK IN YOUR MEETING

FRIDAY!! His last comment to me was to be sure I got 'on the right side of this' because they (whoever 'they' is) were 'going to the wall on this.' I reminded him that there were those on the other side ready to do the same ... I know you and Fred have had conversations about this matter being a coup. There is no longer any doubt."[832]

Recalled Laney, "we had the votes and we wanted to try to bring everybody around and make it as close to unanimous as possible so there would be as few hard feelings as we could manage. I remember telling Bob that we had the votes, that we were serious about this and there was no going back. It was basically a last-ditch attempt to bring everybody along. But as you can tell from what he wrote, they were going to go down swinging."[833]

In Hagerstown, the APCWS staff became mired in turmoil and stress. "On Monday, it would be that the merger was off," Hudspeth recalled. "By Friday afternoon, the merger was back on. They'd all be depressed, go home over the weekend, then come back and do this again. This went on for months."[834]

"Here I come, Mr. Idealistic," recalled Dana Shoaf of his hiring at APCWS in the spring of 1999. "And then, all of a sudden, I start hearing there's issues. And the board is mad at each other. And there was this internal tension."[835]

One staff member left, saying "she just couldn't take it anymore," Hudspeth recalled. "She said they would have all these plots, they would be on their computers, looking up Jim Lighthizer, trying to find out anything they could about him, about the organization."[836]

At the July 24, 1999, board meeting, the APCWS merger committee presented a "Merger Memorandum" along with a strong recommendation that its report be accepted. "The merger memo is detailed and its conclusion is clear and unambiguous," Laney wrote in a cover letter. A merger was in the best interests of battlefield preservation, he said, and was "the last, best chance we will ever have to assemble a coalition that can save the most of our precious and irreplaceable Civil War battlefields."[837]

The board had approved merger discussions, but Haynes knew it might not be so easy to persuade everyone to accept the report and its recommendation for merger.

The APCWS had established a remarkable record from nothing but a sense of mission and hard work. It was the leader in battlefield preservation, not the Trust. "I think a lot of the staff and some of us, including me, thought we were abandoning ship for no good reason," Zavaglia recalled. "There was a sense that certain board members were selling out. There was a good deal of loyalty between the board and the staff, and there were no guarantees about the staff and what was going to happen to them. I thought we had accomplished so much and had been so innovative in our approach, particularly with the bond issue, that too many people were willing to pack it in too early and not be innovative enough to think outside the box."[838]

Haynes made sure he had the votes before the meeting. "John Haynes is tremendously astute at the political process and he was tremendously effective in getting things back on the right track," recalled Laney. "Paul Bryant provided leadership and the financial muscle. He was the one who was willing to stick his neck out financially. That gave us a lot of tools to get things done. We worked politically to bring everybody on our board along and everybody in the Trust along and managed to convince an overwhelming number of the (trustees) that merger was only thing that made sense. People like Carrington Williams and Henry Simpson were just outstanding providing liaisons between the two boards."[839]

Bearss, though not actively involved, said Williams played a crucial role. "I don't know what would have happened if they hadn't Williams there to boost that," he recalled.

No record exists of the vote at the July 24 APCWS board meeting, but participants remembered that it was again 15 votes to accept the merger report and two or three against.[840]

The following day, Zavaglia resigned as APCWS trustee and treasurer.[841] "I'm sure the Southern boys will not lose any sleep over the news," Zavaglia wrote. "But it must be clear to them and to the Trust that the vote for merger was not unanimous and that I, for one, have the courage of my convictions."[842]

On September 19, the Civil War Trust board met to debate the merger. It was a long meeting and trustees had plenty of questions. Minutes of the discussion fill six, single-spaced pages. But in the end, the trustees voted unanimously to approve.[843]

Four days later, on September 23, the APCWS board met to vote on the merger itself. No formal minutes survive, but Edmiston's handwritten notes provide a blow-by-blow snapshot of a fierce, verbal firefight between Laney (D.L.) and Hoeweler (AEH) as the chairman fought the merger to the end:

D.L.:	"Board approved merger report."
AEH:	"I'm not going to do that."
D.L.:	"Not your decision, it's board decision."
AEH:	"Then you'll have to remove me."
D.L.:	"Can't unilaterally go against board."
AEH:	"Impeach me."
AEH:	"Won't sign something that was ramrodded through a board that didn't read the papers."

D.L.:   "We followed will of the board. Follow direction of board or step aside."

AEH: "This stinks."[844]

Hoeweler "had basically gotten outmaneuvered through the political process," Laney recalled. "We had the votes. He thought he was going to use extra-constitutional measures to do what he wanted to do, and I was the one who said that you can't just unilaterally defy the will of the board."[845]

On November 12, 1999, 22 Civil War Trust board members and APCWS trustees gathered in McLean, Virginia, at the offices of McGuire, Woods, Battle and Boothe, the law firm of Carrington Williams, to formally merge. Nine more joined by telephone. The meeting began with a brief joint session. The roll was called for the Trust, followed by the APCWS. The Trust then conducted a final, brief board meeting and approved the articles of merger with their final amendments. The APCWS trustees repeated the process. With no opponents present, the APCWS vote was unanimous.[846]

Both final meetings took a total of 18 minutes and, at 9:55 a.m., Williams convened the first meeting of the new organization – The Civil War Preservation Trust. The Trust's former chairman, Ruff Fant, nominated the APCWS's Williams as chairman and the Trust's Lighthizer as president and the new combined board approved.[847]

Williams read a letter from Hoeweler, who apologized for not attending and explained that he was out of the country. He said his absence should not be construed as not supporting the new organization, that the concept of merger was a good one, and that "acres of land saved would be the criterion by which to judge the success of the new organization."[848]

Laney, representing the merger committees, spoke eloquently of how the "long, difficult struggle for merger evolved into a struggle for the soul of APCWS, which had finally been won." He concluded, "Mr. Chairman, I am just pleased to death to report that our work is done."[849]

Williams introduced Lighthizer, who told the new board that he saw his duties in two categories: manager/administrator and outside salesman. He said he didn't accept the challenge lightly, but was confident that he could overcome any obstacles.[850]

At 53, Lighthizer was only too eager to take on this new challenge. He had been the county executive of Anne Arundel County, Maryland, from 1982 to 1990, and then Maryland Secretary of Transportation from 1991 to 1995, but his professional life had stalled. "I worked for a very good law firm called Miles & Stockbridge," he recalled. "The problem wasn't the company. The problem was the type of work. I was making more money than I'd ever made. And I had some pretty good clients. But I just didn't like it. I was mucking around chasing people up and down the halls. Some of them used to work for me. It was demeaning."[851]

When Williams suggested he take over and lead the merged organization, Lighthizer thought, "God, that's a great idea. I'd like to get the hell out of what I'm doing and I'll be happy to take a pay cut. I'll do it. I want to do something fun again."[852]

It was anything but fun at first.

Even after the APCWS unanimously approved the merger, Laney recalled, "A lot of the staff members just had the idea that they really didn't need to follow the direction of board and that somehow all of this was going away."[853]

The APCWS staff would find out soon enough who had the power. Tempers would flare and tears would spill on a day that became known as "Bloody Monday." ★

CHAPTER
THIRTEEN

Bloody Monday

FEW DAYS after the boards of the Association for the Preservation of Civil War Sites (APCWS) and the original Civil War Trust voted to merge on November 12, 1999, the president-to-be of the renamed Civil War Preservation Trust (CWPT) drove to Hagerstown to meet the APCWS staff.

Jim Lighthizer knew his visit probably would be met with hostility, considering the icy reception he received when he telephoned the Hagerstown headquarters. The APCWS office was a wellspring of anti-merger sentiment despite the board's overwhelming support. Lighthizer expected the meeting to be awkward since the man he was replacing, Bob Edmiston, was a leader in the merger fight and technically still in charge of the office.

The anti-merger sentiment did not exist at the Trust office. Elliot Gruber supported merger, and attrition had shrunk his staff to only two employees in mid-1998. Lighthizer was purposefully non-confrontational during his first meeting with the APCWS staff. "I wanted to get a feel for them and let them get a feel for me," Lighthizer recalled. "I just wanted to size them up. I already knew the Trust staff pretty well and had my opinions of them." At the same time, he was wary, knowing how hard the APCWS staff had fought the merger.[854]

APCWS was a grassroots organization, at least in the beginning, while the Trust, founded on a $200 million dream by powerful officials and executives, exuded an air of superiority. To opponents of merger, the Trust seemed to naturally expect the APCWS to be folded into the seemingly more prestigious organization. This infuriated APCWS leaders and members who felt *they* were the ones saving land. And when the Trust's $200 million fundraising dream evaporated, it became a membership organization, muscling into what the APCWS considered its domain. Then came Frye's coin war and the Trust's tight-fisted hold on the money.

Although Frye was deposed by APCWS Chairman Alan Hoeweler, both Hoeweler and Bob Edmiston, Frye's successor, shared Frye's hostility toward the Trust, as did the staff. Frye, however, had favored merger before the coin war and favored it afterward, joining his fellow APCWS founders in supporting merger when talks became serious. His former staff at APCWS did not agree, nor did Hoeweler or Frederick Zavaglia.[855]

In that first meeting with the new boss-to-be a few days after the merger, the APCWS staff, which numbered about a dozen, was "absolutely, with a couple of exceptions, just belligerent," Lighthizer recalled. "Belligerent to me, belligerent about the merger, like it was going to be on their terms. And the people weren't working hard."[856]

Hudspeth, however, had connected with Lighthizer instantly and already was his confidant by the time of his first face-to-face meeting with the staff. She was relieved to finally have someone in authority listen to her, because she had plenty of improper activity to tell him about. "She educated me to a lot of what was going on," Lighthizer recalled. "I remember going to a budget meeting. Now to have a budget meeting in November, knowing you're merged and I'm taking over on December 1, I thought somewhat remarkable. They were doing a budget for the APCWS and there wasn't going to be any APCWS in two weeks. And they were spending $2,200 to buy APCWS diamond pins, knowing that it's not going to be there in two weeks."[857]

The diamond pins were to be given to top-tier members for their loyalty and generosity. When Hudspeth had challenged Edmiston on the expenditure, he told her the merger wasn't going to happen. "And even if it does, our members are going to know they are APCWS members," she remembers him saying. Hudspeth also challenged several purchases Edmiston had made on an APCWS credit card, including a diamond necklace and a trip to London. He promised to pay it all back, but nothing happened, even after she'd mentioned it to the treasurer and auditor. The debt eventually was satisfied from Edmiston's remaining vacation time after his dismissal, Hudspeth said.[858]

Gruber recalled that APCWS had a "very extensive section" in its bylaws prohibiting nepotism. "They went through chapter and verse, more than I've seen in most other non-profit organizations," he said. And yet, Edmiston's daughter worked for APCWS, as did Shoaf's wife.[859]

On December 1, 1999, Lighthizer became president of the new CWPT. Two days later, on Friday December 3, he went to Hagerstown to fire Edmiston. At six foot six and some 300 pounds, Edmiston dwarfed him. And given the open hostility demonstrated by Edmiston and the staff, Lighthizer decided he'd better have backup. Lighthizer arranged for Carrington Williams to join him, but the new CWPT chairman was stuck in traffic. Lighthizer waited for a while, but decided he could not put it off any longer. He asked Hudspeth to arrange for a Hagerstown city police officer to be stationed at the building.

As Lighthizer headed up to Edmiston's office on the third floor, Hudspeth looked out the window. "The city police had sent this little police girl down there to protect Jim!" she recalled, laughing. Edmiston, however, was "a gentle giant" and accepted his fate without rancor.[860]

Lighthizer and Gruber returned to Hagerstown the following Monday, December 6. Beforehand, he and Gruber met with Hudspeth at the Sheraton Hotel on Dual Highway. Over breakfast, Lighthizer asked Hudspeth to take charge of the office. "I don't trust any of the other ones that are left there right now, and a lot of them are not going to be there by the end of the day," he told her.[861]

Lighthizer had had enough of the truculent APCWS staff. He was in no mood for conciliation as he started the staff meeting promptly at 9 a.m.[862]

"Boys and girls, it is a new day," Lighthizer announced. "I'm going to be primarily down in the office in Rosslyn, and the first thing you need to know is that your new boss is Ruth Hudspeth. If you want to leave the office, you need her permission. You can't just go wandering out into the field.

"Two, you're not going out in pairs. This is not a duet. If you've got something to do and need to leave the office and Ruth approves it, you go individually. Third, pass down all credit cards, all phones—company credit cards, company phones, pass them down right now."

"Well, my phone is upstairs," a staff member said.

"Fine, we'll wait," Lighthizer said. "Go get it."

When he returned, Lighthizer continued, "Credit cards will be handed out on an as-needed basis, as well as cell phones. It's a new day, and you're going to work 40 hours a week, and you're going to work it in your office. You're not going to work it in your car or out on the sidewalk or at home. If you have an overnight trip, you go to Ruth. She'll give you a credit card, you come back, you give her the receipts and there better not be any bar bills on there."[863] Then he said, "There's a number of you I'd like to talk to after the meeting."[864]

Lighthizer recalled, "They were belligerent, they were sullen—it was almost an outright mutiny."[865] Gruber agreed. "Anything he said about those experiences, trust me, they were not exaggerations," Gruber recalled. "I was in there and I have never witnessed people curse, people use four-letter words, all sorts of things … And even tell him, 'Well, you can't do anything. You're just the president.' And Jim goes, 'You're right. I am the president. You are on my staff, and I can decide if you are going to remain on my staff.'"[866] Some of the cursing came from Lighthizer, who did not tamp down his tendency to use profanities in conversation.

Lighthizer went into an office and Gruber went into the board room, and each evaluated APCWS staff members one by one. Lighthizer recalled one staffer brought out an employment contract. "We asked if there were any contracts, and your organization answered no," Lighthizer said.[867]

"Well, that wasn't my job to answer yes," the staff member said.

"Yeah, but you're an employee of this organization, and you knew this question had been asked, and you let them answer it falsely."

"Well, that was their problem," the staff member said.

"Well, it's your problem now, because you're fired," Lighthizer snapped. Lighthizer recalled that the CWPT had to pay a considerable sum to void the contract.[868]

Gruber called in Shoaf's wife, Heidi Campbell-Shoaf, the receptionist. As Hudspeth recalled, "Elliot called her in and said, 'I don't know what you do, but you're fired.' She said, 'What?' And he said, 'Yes. You have such a bad attitude, we can't have you as the face of our organization. You're fired.'"[869]

"So, she came out crying," recalled Dana Shoaf. "And this infuriated me because this had been handled so poorly. Because he didn't find anything out about her education or anything. Heidi has a master's degree in history… She's no slouch. Neither one of them took the time to see what she could do."[870]

"I remember I looked for Elliot," Shoaf recalled. "I went after him, so to speak, in the office and I confronted him and he kind of literally halfway stepped behind Ruth Hudspeth. I was so mad." Shoaf wanted to take a swing at Gruber, but restrained himself.

"Why are you firing all the APCWS people?" Shoaf hollered at Gruber.

"I'm just doing what Jim told me to do," Gruber said.[871]

Recalled Shoaf, "It was very apparent to me from the interaction from the very beginning that we were being made to feel like we had done something wrong. That we were, to put it in a simplistic term, a bad organization that had not been run properly. And (Lighthizer) was there to clean house. He was making it rough and not very friendly. He came in swearing, and taking stuff from us, and scowling and scaring the hell out of us."

Shoaf said it was difficult to act positively in the face of this level of mistrust and hostility. "You could just tell that this was a takeover, and we were on the outs, for whatever reason. Before this merger, we had been so made to feel like the Trust was not our friend," he said. "And then it started so badly. And after your wife is fired in such a manner, you know, it didn't do anything to make me want to work with them very much."[872]

By lunch time, Hudspeth recalled, Edmiston's daughter had become tired of waiting for the inevitable. "Would you please tell them that if they're going to fire me, to fire me now. I don't want to sit around in this office anymore," she told Hudspeth, who went to Gruber.

"Well, Elliot, you're going to fire her," Hudspeth said. "Let's just get rid of her now." Gruber said okay, "So I went back to her and I said, "Okay, you can go."[873]

Lighthizer and Gruber fired eight or 10 APCWS staff members that day, Lighthizer recalled. Of those that remained, within six months, all but two had been fired or left on their own volition.[874]

Pam Davis, an APCWS staffer who continued with the merged organization for many years as membership coordinator, went in to Lighthizer and said, "Can you at least give me a little bit of notice when you're going to fire me? Because I have some bills that I need to pay." Lighthizer told her he was not firing her.[875]

Dana Shoaf was not fired because, as Gruber recalled, the Shoafs had a baby and had just bought a house. But Shoaf said he was never made to feel welcome and believed he was given tasks and deadlines that set him up for failure. He soon resigned and returned to the magazine world with his old employer, PrimeMedia. The job of his dreams had dissolved into a nightmare.[876]

"I'd been there nine months," he recalled. "I hadn't been a part of anything that had occurred before. And if I may say so, I'm not exactly a slouch either. If he'd have given me a chance, I'd probably still be there. Because I had some ideas about things I wanted to do. I probably stayed there a month after the merger, I guess. It was extremely painful to me, and when I left, Heidi picked me up and I took my last box of stuff the last day I walked out of there, and I broke down in tears in the car. You know? I said, 'This wasn't supposed to end like this. I was gonna come here and save battlefields and do the right thing.' And I said, 'I don't understand what happened here. I don't understand why we were all lumped up as bad people. And why this approach was taken.'"[877]

After Bloody Monday, the bond among ex-staff members at APCWS remained strong. The former staff would reunite for dinner from time to time, and in the spring of 2000, several months after the merger, Hudspeth and Davis went to one of the dinners in Frederick, Maryland. The get-together became a "gripe session," Hudspeth recalled, and both she and Davis left early. But one thing she will always remember about that dinner: "They had a picture of Jim Lighthizer on the wall with darts in it."[878]

Bloody Monday had been a messy affair. Though perhaps inevitable, it made reconstruction challenging. "When the old APCWS and the Civil War Trust merged, a lot of people didn't feel that it was a merger, but more of a takeover," recalled Robert Lee Hodge, a longtime preservationist and well-known Confederate reenactor pictured on the cover of author Tony Horwitz's Confederates in the Attic. "When the merger was all done and finalized, only like two people from APCWS were left. Some of the treatment was a little rough, and just the way some of these things were handled was a little rough."[879]

Although the APCWS staff was all but eliminated, that wasn't the case for trustees. All APCWS trustees and Trust board members who attended the merger meeting became members of the new Civil War Preservation Trust Board of Trustees. The new chairman, the APCWS's Carrington Williams, had developed a warm relationship with the Trust's Lighthizer, which made the transition that much easier.

But distrust of the merger had spread to APCWS members who may not have known any of the leaders personally, but who took pride in the growth and success of APCWS. The new CWPT took great pains to make those members feel that APCWS was a full partner. Several days after Bloody Monday, Lighthizer called Frye, thanked him for his support and asked him if he would return to the Hagerstown office and call major donors to explain the merger and let them know he fully supported it. "I soon found myself back in my old office," Frye recalled. "It was a weird feeling." He spent about a week there, personally reassuring loyal APCWS supporters.[880]

The issue of *Hallowed Ground* magazine that arrived in APCWS members' mailboxes in the winter of 2000 looked the same in design and presentation. The logo looked almost the same. The name at the very top of the cover, in small type, was no longer "Association for the Preservation of Civil War Sites," but "Civil War Preservation Trust" and the issue was identified as "Vol. 1, No. 1." (It was the third Vol. 1, No. 1 in *Hallowed Ground's* history, and the second in three years.)[881]

Readers first came upon a letter from former APCWS and now CWPT Chairman Carrington Williams, who directly addressed his old flock:

"To the many loyal friends and supporters of the former APCWS. You have carried us a long way in the last twelve years, and you should be justly proud of it. Your record includes forty-six Civil War sites saved or partially saved in twelve states, a growing constituency, a reputation for accomplishment, an enthusiastic response when the calls went out for money to save battlefields, and obtaining the first tax-exempt bond issue for financing battlefield acquisitions in known history, at about 3% interest."[882]

Williams succinctly summarized the case for merger and provided a point-by-point rundown of what the APCWS stood to gain with phrases such as "elimination of confusion," "avoidance of competition" and "better acceptance by Congress." He concluded, "We on the merged board will continue striving to save battlefields, to merit your confidence and enthusiasm."[883]

Below his message was an excerpt of the July 1999 letter in which the original APCWS founders jointly expressed their support for the merger. Readers then turned the page and found a letter from Lighthizer that focused on the future and outlined preservation challenges. Printed beside it was another article revealing a bold goal put forth by an energized, combined board of trustees determined to show the strength of its unity.[884]

"Trust Board Vows to Save 2,000 Acres in Year 2000," read the headline. In its first board meeting of the year on January 22, trustees set the bar high. Two thousand acres was 20 percent of the entire total acreage saved by both organizations in their combined history. But, as Lighthizer pointed out, "If we can save 2,000 acres in our first year, imagine what we can do when we're up and running. It will illustrate just how strong we are now that we've merged."[885]

The era of two like-minded organizations struggling to coexist was over. Now a single organization, no longer encumbered by competition or turf wars, could pursue saving battlefields without distraction. Lighthizer spent a good bit of the year 2000 reorganizing and addressing the massive debt inherited from the APCWS. Fortunately, he could tap into that new $8 million Congressional appropriation to help reduce the obligation.

In April, Lighthizer and Williams met with federal officials, who determined that CWPT was eligible to receive $2.76 million of the appropriation to match funds already spent on preserving battlefields. Williams and others had been working hard in Richmond, too, and the result was a similar sum appropriated by the Commonwealth of Virginia. The combined amount of $5.5 million paid the $4.8 million in bond debt, the old organization's largest obligation.[886]

"By early fall (2000), CWPT will have gone from about $7 million in debt in the beginning of the year to about $700,000 in debt," Lighthizer told the board on April 28.[887] In fact, by that October, the debt had fallen to $462,000.[888]

The new staff was in constant flux in 2000. At the April 28 board meeting, trustees learned that three employees had departed and one key hire had backed out after accepting the job—a "very disappointing setback," Lighthizer reported. At the same meeting, trustees learned that Lighthizer had hired a political fundraiser named David Duncan to become Director of Membership and to work on fundraising. Lighthizer hired James Campi, Jr. "to conduct public relations efforts and to solicit for foundation grants," the September 27 board meeting minutes reported.[889]

Campi was a 14-year political communications specialist who had most recently served as a Congressional press secretary and media director for another non-profit organization, Citizens Against Government Waste. He read an article in *The Washington Post* about the merger, contacted CWPT and handled media relations as a volunteer from March through September 2000 until he was hired.[890] These two men would play crucial roles in the coming years, helping Lighthizer transform the merged groups into one efficient, effective, award-winning non-profit organization.

Duncan was not the first choice of the board's personnel committee, but Lighthizer saw potential that the committee did not. For one thing, Duncan was persistent in his job quest, even though he already had an established career. He was a successful political fundraiser for a direct mail company headquartered at Tyson's Corner. But Civil War history was in his blood. He was a native Virginian, and three of his great-great grandfathers fought for the Confederacy, serving in the 54th and 57th Virginia Infantry regiments. Duncan became captivated listening to Civil War books on tape during his daily commute from Burke, Virginia. He became a member of the original Civil War Trust. With his $25 annual membership came direct-mail fundraising flyers. He read one and said to himself, "I can do this better. I can help these people."[891]

Duncan knew he would rather raise money for the Civil War Trust than for politicians. "What if I could actually get paid to do something that I really am passionate about and care about?" he asked himself.[892]

Duncan contacted the original Trust in 1999, told them he was a professional fundraiser, and offered to help, even to volunteer. But he could never get anyone to call him back except Melissa Meisner Sadler, the executive assistant, who would say, "Yes, we've got your information. It's a busy time …" Duncan also applied to the APCWS in Hagerstown. He received a membership package in response. Both organizations ignored him, which was fortuitous, since both organizations were in chaos.[893]

When Duncan saw the same *Washington Post* article about the merger as Campi, he decided to try again in the age-old tradition of preservationists—by letter. "I wrote Jim Lighthizer a fundraising letter selling myself and just said, 'Jim, you don't know me from Adam, but I've spent the last 14 years putting money in politicians' pockets. Now, I want to help you save Civil War battlefields.' I sent the letter to him Certified Mail, so he had to sign for it. And then, two days later, I got a phone call from Elliot Gruber, saying, 'Hey, come on in and talk. Jim wants to talk to you.'"[894]

After several interviews, and the thumbs down from the personnel committee, and after agreeing to a salary substantially less than what he was making, Duncan was hired. "I started on March 20, 2000, which is Jim's birthday," Duncan said. "I always tell him every year, I'm the best birthday present he ever got."[895]

Duncan's impact was immediate. With the skill of an experienced, professional letter writer, he infused his fundraising letters with the passion of a Civil War buff. The new organization sent out its first three fundraising mailings in 2000, hoping to pull in $185,000. Duncan's letters brought in more than $485,000. It cost the CWPT only eight cents to raise each dollar, and the membership response rate was almost twice the national average. Duncan was promptly promoted to Director of Membership and Development.[896]

"David's writing and his communication skills are the fundraising basis for everything that we have. Jim is out talking to the leaders and getting the big donations, but the appeals and member acquisition letters that David writes are the reason that we have what we have today," Hudspeth said.[897]

In March 2000, Lighthizer hired Noah Mehrkam as a jack-of-all-trades. The year before, Mehrkam had walked in the APCWS door in Hagerstown, a "long-haired, hippie-looking kid" from Harpers Ferry who said he'd like to volunteer to help, Hudspeth recalled.[898]

A protégé of Dennis Frye, Mehrkam was smart, eager and hard-working. Soon Lighthizer had him working to answer a key question: Exactly how much and what land did the merged organization own? As he compiled the inventory, Mehrkam became fascinated with the real estate acquisitions. By the fall of 2000, he had been promoted to Director of Battlefield Preservation.[899]

Even in the transitional, debt-reducing year of 2000, the new Civil War Preservation Trust (CWPT) shattered its goal of saving 2,000 acres, amassing 2,421 acres in 23 acquisitions at 18 battlefields in eight states. CWPT averaged almost two acquisitions a month, and the total acreage in 2000 alone exceeded the total of 2,398 acres saved by the two organizations combined during the previous three years, 1997 to 1999.[900]

The CWPT worked with local groups and preservationists to save the 135-acre Davis Tract on the Manassas Battlefield, scene of some of the heaviest fighting during Second Bull Run and the most significant battlefield land not owned by the NPS.[901] It helped save 570 acres at Resaca, Georgia, and secured a historic easement protecting 315 acres at Kernstown battlefield in the Shenandoah Valley. At Fox's Gap at South Mountain, Maryland, the CWPT helped save 136 acres. In Virginia, it picked up 258 more key battlefield acres at Brandy Station, saved more than 300 acres at Cedar Creek, and helped save 245 acres at Malvern Hill.[902]

But none of the acquisitions in 2000 were quite as exciting as the 51-acre farm the CWPT bought at Cross Keys, Virginia, in June. For Lighthizer, it became personal, and it came as a bolt from the blue in a phone call from Bob Krick.

In April, Krick had driven to the Shenandoah Valley to give a tour at Cross Keys. The battle at Cross Keys was one of the climactic clashes in Confederate General Stonewall Jackson's brilliant Valley campaign. Krick knew the land well, having walked it time and again while figuring out and establishing where the battlefield was. Before Krick studied the maps, read the battle reports and walked the land, nobody in modern times really knew what had happened at Cross Keys.

The battle's fiercest fighting occurred around the Widow Pence house. Krick

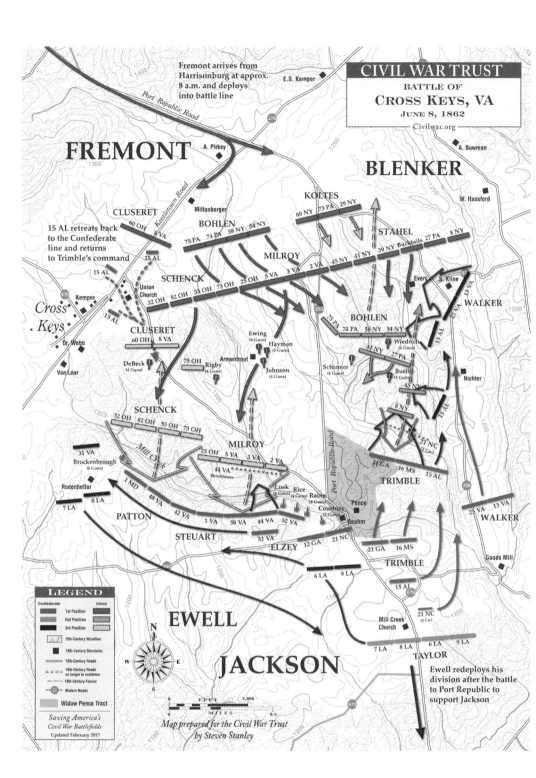

Fremont arrives from
Harrisonburg at approx.
8 a.m. and deploys
into battle line

E.S. Kemper

CIVIL WAR TRUST
BATTLE OF
CROSS KEYS, VA
JUNE 8, 1862
Civilwar.org

Port Republic Road

A. Pirkey

A. Bowman

FREMONT

BLENKER

W. Hansford

CLUSERET
60 OH
8 VA

Miltonberger

BOHLEN
75 PA 74 PA 56 NY 54 NY

KOLTES
68 NY 73 PA 29 NY

STAHEL
39 NY Bucktails 27 PA 8 NY

15 AL retreats back
to the Confederate
line and returns
to Trimble's command

Keezletown Road

15 AL

MILROY
2 VA 45 NY 41 NY

SCHENCK
25 OH 5 VA 3 VA

15 AL

Union
Church

SCHENCK
32 OH 82 OH 55 OH 73 OH 25 OH 5 VA 3 VA

Evers
S. Kline

WALKER

Cross
Keys

Kemper

BOHLEN
75 PA 74 PA 58 NY 54 NY

15 AL

Dr. Webb

CLUSERET
60 OH 8 VA

Ewing
(4 Guns)

Wiedrich
(4 Guns)

Hayman
(4 Guns)

41 NY

27 PA

15 AL

Van Lear

DeBeck
(4 Guns)

75 OH

Armentrout

Rigby
(4 Guns)

Johnson
(4 Guns)

Schirmer
(4 Guns)

Buell
(4 Guns)

Nichter

45 NY

SCHENCK
32 OH 82 OH 55 OH 73 OH

8 NY

15 AL

MILROY
25 OH 5 VA 3 VA 2 VA

21 NC
(2 Co.)

31 VA
Brockenbrough
(4 Guns)

44 VA
Skirmishers

21 GA 16 MS 15 AL

Rodenheffer

1 MD

Lusk
(4 Guns)

Rice
(4 Guns)

Raine
(4 Guns)

TRIMBLE

7 LA 8 LA

48 VA

42 VA

Courtney
(2 Guns)

Pence

Beahm

PATTON

1 VA 58 VA 44 VA 52 VA

STEUART

31 VA

ELZEY 12 GA 21 NC

WALKER
25 VA 13 VA

21 GA 16 MS

Goods Mill

TRIMBLE

6 LA 9 LA

15 AL

EWELL

LEGEND

Confederate   Union
         1st Position
         2nd Position
         3rd Position

19th-Century Woodline
19th-Century Structures
19th-Century Roads
19th-Century Roads
no longer in existence
19th-Century Fences
Modern Roads

Widow Pence Tract

Saving America's
Civil War Battlefields
Updated February 2017

N
W   E
S

Mill Creek
Church

21 NC
(2 Co.)

JACKSON

FEET
2,000

MILES
0.5

Map prepared for the Civil War Trust
by Steven Stanley

TAYLOR
7 LA 8 LA 6 LA 9 LA

Ewell redeploys his
division after the battle
to Port Republic to
support Jackson

[218]

was well acquainted with the home's residents, Mary Catherine Jarrels and her husband, Warren. Mary Jarrels had lived there since 1921. "First time I walked into her yard, she had no idea it was on the battlefield," Krick recalled. "And I still wasn't sure it was the Widow Pence house in that early day. I remember walking into the little kitchen and smelling something good frying and I said, 'Oh, that smells good.' And she said, 'Well, I'd invite you to stay for dinner but you young people wouldn't appreciate it. I'm frying dandelion greens from the yard.' They had a pretty primitive lifestyle. The only water in the house was caught on the roof and poured into a cistern in a lean-to."[903]

During his trip to Cross Keys that April, Krick knocked on the front door once more.

"I'm glad to see you, Mr. Krick," Mary Jarrels said in her quiet, direct country manner.

"Oh, well, I've always appreciated the chance to walk on this ground," Krick replied. "It's so historic. And I love taking people on it."

"Well, I don't know if you will be able to do that anymore," she replied quietly. She and her husband were moving into a retirement home in nearby Harrisonburg, she said, and the Widow Pence farm would be sold at auction in about a month.

"Thank goodness I was out there on a tour," Krick recalled, "Nobody would have even known about it, I suppose." He called Lighthizer immediately and said a "really important piece" of the Cross Keys battlefield was soon to be auctioned. Word was that a developer would be bidding.[904]

Lighthizer investigated and found that the Widow Pence Farm had been appraised for $205,000. He contacted the Jarrels and offered to buy it at the appraised value, but they said no, they'd auction it in June. Lighthizer at that time had no available money with which to buy it. But he managed to secure a $200,000 loan from his friend Pat Noonan, president of the Conservation Fund. Lighthizer knew he had a good chance of securing federal battlefield preservation funds through an ABPP matching grant, but not before the auction.[905]

Unexpectedly, Lighthizer received a call from a Harrisonburg orthopedic surgeon, Irvin Hess, who was interested in the property. Hess had family connections to the battle and his ancestors had owned the adjoining farm.[906]

"I want to buy it to preserve it, but if you're going to buy it, that's fine with me," Hess told Lighthizer.[907]

"I'll make you a deal," Lighthizer replied. "Let's go in 50-50. You own it and I'll own the development rights. So you'll own a piece of property with a pre-war house, a pre-war barn and real history. You'll own it, you just won't ever be able to develop it."

"Okay, I'll do that," Hess said. "I'll go up to 175 grand, that's all my half can go."[908]

Carrington Williams became keenly interested. "Jim, we've got to have that property … We've *got* to have that property," Lighthizer recalled Williams saying.

"Well, let's drive out there," Lighthizer told him. "We've got Irvin's $175,000. We've got a $200,000 loan from Noonan. Let's go buy the thing at the auction." The hammer was to fall on June 17, 2000.[909]

Lighthizer recalled: "It was one of those country auctions that was a social event where everybody comes. There must have been a couple of hundred people there. Everything is for sale. And the auctioneer goes through the house, room to room. He sells the stove, he sells the old Coke bottles, he sells the silverware, he sells everything. And at the end of the day, the culmination, the height of the day, the crescendo, is he auctions off the property."[910]

When going through old homes, Lighthizer has a habit of running his hand across the top of door frames "to see if anything is up there." As he walked through the Widow Pence house, he reached above one door frame, felt a piece of metal and pulled down a chunk of shrapnel from the Civil War. He wondered for a moment whether he should keep it. "I can't do that," he said to himself. "I'll just come back and get it after we buy it." He put it back up on the door frame.[911]

As the auction for the property started, only two in the large crowd became active bidders—Lighthizer and an agent representing the developer. As the price soared above the appraised value of $205,000, the auctioneer went to $500 increments. "So, the two of us were just raising our fingers, back and forth," Lighthizer recalled. Lighthizer was ready to spend all $375,000 if he had to. The auctioneer reached $225,000 … $250,000 … $260,000 … $270,000. The developer's agent dropped out at $288,000 and the auctioneer's hammer fell.[912]

"Now come on up here and tell this crowd what you plan to do with this property," the auctioneer told Lighthizer.

Lighthizer took the microphone and announced, "This property is going to be preserved forever as a Civil War battlefield." The crowd erupted in applause and cheers, and Lighthizer felt goose bumps breaking out—a moment he still savors. A few minutes later, Lighthizer went back to the door frame holding the piece of shrapnel. He reached up there and felt around. It was gone.[913]

But he had the property, and Duncan had a project he could sink his teeth into —raising money to pay off the Conservation Fund loan. Duncan decided this direct mail appeal, his third for the CWPT, needed more than just a well-written letter.

"I've got this idea," Duncan told Lighthizer. "I'd like to put a color map with the letter that shows our members what they're buying in context with the rest of the battle." The target property would stand out in yellow, and the land already saved would be in blue. Overlaid would be a battle map showing troop movements and positions during the battle. In one glance, a member could see the target property and its significance. The problem for the cash-strapped CWPT was the expense of a full-color map.

"Jim, a black-and-white or a two-color map is going to cost five cents per copy," Duncan said. "This is going to cost nine or 10 cents per copy. So that is a big expenditure."

"Let's give it a shot," Lighthizer said. "Let's do it."[914]

Duncan turned to Steve Stanley, a talented graphic designer and mapmaker. "I had seen some examples of his work not long after I started at the Trust, and asked him if he could do one for Cross Keys, with the tract we were buying shown in yellow," Duncan recalled. "When I saw it, I knew we had to use it."[915]

"I remember thinking it was a good idea," Lighthizer said. "It turned out to be a *fabulous* idea. It changed everything. Because it dramatically increased the response rate from our members. And we paid that property off in 90 days. We paid our $144,000 off in 90 days. They could see exactly what they were buying and they could see it in context of the battle. So, they could see they were adding value. And it revolutionized our direct mail. That's a huge milestone in this organization's history."[916]

"We've done hundreds together since then," Duncan said, "and the 'look' of those maps is a strong branding element for our members now—they expect to get a map, and they love them and collect them."[917]

Hess and his wife, Nancy, were at a medical conference and could not attend the auction. But they threw themselves into the time-consuming, expensive restoration of the Widow Pence house, which cost several times more than the $144,000 they spent on property. By all accounts, it was a magnificent restoration.

"It has been restored and it's just the way it was at the time of the battle – the house, the barn and the property," said Lighthizer. "So, that was our first victory. Carrington and I were beside ourselves with joy. We were just ecstatic. And that got us rolling. It had a lot of ramifications. It gave us credibility with the Bob Kricks of the world."[918]

Under Lighthizer's direction, Mehrkam began developing a systematic process to identify and rank acquisition opportunities using the Civil War Sites Advisory Commission report as a guide. "We were trying to get more targeted," Mehrkam recalled. "We were saying, 'Let's plan this out. Let's go out and identify and map certain areas of the most important battlefields, and then go approach those property owners.' So, that's what I spent all my time doing; identifying sites, getting control of those sites, working with our team to figure out how we were going to pay for the acquisition, and then getting those acquisition dollars in, be it grant money or foundation money."[919]

Before the merger, the Trust and the APCWS, despite the discord, had jointly helped pay for acquisitions nearly every year throughout the 1990s. The 40-acre Grove Farm purchase at Antietam in 1991 was a Trust initiative, using coin funds, and APCWS pitched in $15,000. The Trust in 1992 helped APCWS buy about 39 acres at the Byram's Ford battlefield in Missouri. The following year, each group paid about half of the cost of 256 acres at Port Hudson, La.[920]

After the merger, the CWPT actively sought partners to help share the cost of acquisitions, and used those partnerships to enhance the fundraising appeals to members by stressing that each dollar they donated was matched several times over. The CWPT also refined and enhanced an efficient working relationship with The American Battlefield Protection Program (ABPP), which began controlling the disbursement of battlefield preservation funds through a competitive grant program after Congress began approving matching fund appropriations in 1998.[921]

During Mehrkam's six years at CWPT, from 2000 to 2005, the CWPT saved 15,011 acres of battlefield land in 155 transactions—an average of 2,500 acres a year. In 2004, Mehrkam's biggest year, the CWPT saved 3,603 acres in 35 transactions, almost three a month.[922]

"The most fun was … it was not the government grants. Those were pretty tedious," Mehrkam recalled. "It was not the late hours around Christmas trying to get deals closed, and working 18– to 20–hour days to get all the stuff done. The most fun was putting those pieces of the puzzle together at a battlefield" while acquiring different parcels.[923] Mehrkam and Lighthizer also put more emphasis on acquiring historic conservation easements and letting the land remain in private ownership.[924]

Gaining the trust of hostile landowners was particularly satisfying to Mehrkam, "especially the tougher they were."[925] Lighthizer had told him, "Look, you can read books about negotiations, but I will tell you one thing: Nobody is going to sell you their land unless they like you and trust you."[926]

The Trust usually buys land at market prices, even expensive properties. The demand for land by developers leaves no option. This hard truth made the save of 127 key acres of the Bristoe Station battlefield in 2002 particularly notable. The acquisition didn't cost a cent.

The land around Bristoe Station, Virginia, like other battlefield land in rapidly growing suburban areas, became too expensive for the CWPT to buy in the boom years before the recession of 2008. The battle at Bristoe Station on October 14, 1863, was an ill-considered assault by Confederate General A.P Hill that earned him the rebuke of General Robert E. Lee, who scolded, "Well, general, bury these poor men and let us say no more about it." Some 2,000 men, including 1,300 Confederates, fell in a brief but fierce battle as about 17,200 Confederates attacked a Union force less than half its size, but well protected behind the railroad embankment near the station. The Confederates were mowed down.[927]

In 2001, Centex Homes planned to build 520 dwellings and 175,000 square feet of office and commercial space on 341 acres at Bristoe Station. The tract's long southern border was adjacent to the still-existing railroad tracks and at the core of the battlefield.[928]

In an early meeting with Prince William County planners, Lighthizer described the historical significance of the property and said a large number of Confederate graves were still there. Lighthizer said he wanted 130 out of the 341 acres preserved.

"Boy, that's an awful lot," one of the planners said. "I don't think they'll go for it."[929]

When Lighthizer and Mehrkam met with officials from Centex, one of the nation's largest homebuilders, "they were going to put houses all over the 340 acres," Merkham recalled. "And they said, 'Over here, we've got a little two-acre parcel where you guys could put a little museum.'"[930]

"Jim looked at me and I looked at him. And he said to them, 'Guys, we're not in the museum business. We're in the land business. What about this?' Lighthizer drew a line across the map encompassing the huge swath of acreage he sought. "Okay, there's the important battlefield," he said. "That's the 'museum' to us— just leaving the land in place and preserving it."[931]

Lighthizer proposed that Centex be allowed to build the same number of homes, but on 213 acres. The county agreed to the idea. Mehrkam told the developers: "How would you like to *not* have to build and extend roads and water and sewer over this whole property?"[932]

It wasn't a bad deal for Centex. "You don't want houses to be next to the railroad track anyway," Lighthizer argued. "We can make this into a history park that becomes an amenity in the neighborhood."[933]

It helped that the Centex attorney was a Civil War buff, and that Centex had a record of civic responsibility and a long-standing relationship with The Nature Conservancy. The attorney "was a very influential lawyer—a big zoning lawyer for that part of Prince William County," Lighthizer recalled. "You could do business with the guy. And in the end, as long as they got their lots, they were happy."[934]

The CWPT formally accepted ownership of the land in 2004. "We got 127 very expensive acres that would not have been able to be acquired by the Trust at that time on the open market," Mehrkam said. "Everybody had to live with some tradeoffs, but it became a very good model in a very hot housing market to preserve high-cost land."[935] The CWPT acquired an additional 6.2 acres of the battlefield that same year from another landowner.

As time passed, Mehrkam put together ever-more-complicated deals. "I'll always remember the conversations, particularly with Ruth Hudspeth and [Chief Operating Officer] Ron Cogswell, about the creative financial structures I would come up with," Mehrkam recalled. "Ron would say, 'Now, explain this to me one more time. Tell me how this works again.' It was to make sure everything was above board. There were projects where it wasn't unusual to have a half-dozen different pots of money coming in. And that's not exactly the easiest deal in the world to get closed."[936]

In 2002, the CWPT was shocked and deeply saddened by the sudden loss of Carrington Williams, the first chairman of the merged organization. He drove "a little red sports car—not something you'd expect from an 83-year-old man," Lighthizer recalled, and was on Route 50 in northern Virginia, on July 22, 2002, when his car was rear-ended and his leg was violently slammed in the crash. Williams went to a hospital emergency room for treatment and was released. More than a week later, Williams awoke at night with terrific pain in his leg and was admitted to Inova Fairfax Hospital.[937]

On August 3, Lighthizer called Williams to see how he was doing. Williams told him about the severe leg pain. "But he said his knee was not the problem," Lighthizer recalled. "He said, 'I can't breathe.' Within an hour or two he was comatose, and within a day he was dead." Blood clots that formed in his leg after the injury broke free and obstructed his lungs, leading to a fatal heart attack.[938]

Williams had been a quiet, genial leader at APCWS, contributing in countless ways. He had lent a steady, unifying hand during the merger negotiations. "He was a paragon of polite decency," recalled Lighthizer. "Everybody loved him. He believed in historic preservation absolutely, but he was also very pro-growth."

Williams was founding chairman of the Shenandoah Valley Battlefields Foundation, and in 2004, the foundation installed a wayside exhibit at the Widow Pence Farm at Cross Keys in Williams's memory. It was a time for reflection as Lighthizer stood by the new exhibit with Irvin and Nancy Hess and told the story of the auction. Lighthizer described how he'd found a piece of shrapnel above a door frame while inspecting the house on the day of the auction but left it there, only to find it gone after the sale. "And I saw her give a look at her husband, but she never said anything," Lighthizer recalled.[939]

By then, the Widow Pence home had been restored, and the Hesses had invited local residents in for a look. One visitor paid particular attention to a display case in the house—a mini-museum where the Hesses kept all the artifacts found on the property. He came to Nancy Hess with the piece of shrapnel. "I found it during the auction," he said. "But you all have done such a wonderful job here, I want you to have it back."[940]

Nancy gave the piece of shrapnel to Lighthizer. He had it framed, and it hangs on the wall of his office in Washington, D.C. ★

CHAPTER FOURTEEN

Standing Up for Chancellorsville

N JANUARY 2002, just after the merger, Civil War Preservation Trust President Jim Lighthizer reported to his trustees that the CWPT was running smoothly, having shed all baggage left in the wake of the tumultuous unification.

It had saved another 2,121 acres in 2001, bringing its 2000-2001 total to 4,400 acres. And the American Battlefield Protection Program (ABPP) of the National Park Service (NPS) had a bigger battlefield preservation fund than ever, with a new $11 million appropriation for the next three years, ready and waiting for CWPT land acquisition grant applications.[941]

When Jim Campi was hired in September 2000 as Director of Policy and Communications, he became the CWPT's point man on Capitol Hill. His first assignment was to lobby for and secure a new federal appropriation of funds for battlefield preservation and extend the success that John Haynes and Lighthizer had engineered in 1998 with an $8 million appropriation.[942]

It was a tougher challenge because George W. Bush was president, and his administration was dedicated to cutting federal spending. In the face of an austerity mandate on Capitol Hill, Campi lined up bipartisan support to *increase* the appropriation to $11 million for 2002–2004. He arranged for a dozen senators and 68 representatives to express their written support. Supporters included the chairmen and ranking opposition members of both the House and Senate Interior Appropriations Subcommittees.[943]

"I ought to have a copy of that authorization bill framed here in my office," Campi recalled, "because that really is one of the biggest accomplishments we have had as an organization. That authorization paved the way for a program that helped save more than 27,000 acres nationwide."[944]

Campi could breathe a bit after the new federal appropriation was approved in the fall of 2001. But in 2002, he became embroiled in his first intense preservation battle. News had come from Fredericksburg in June that Dogwood Development Group of Reston, Virginia, headed by developer Ray Smith, planned to build a massive, mixed-use development of homes and businesses along Route 3, the old Orange Turnpike (now called Plank Road), in the heart of the first day's battle at Chancellorsville.

The Battle of Chancellorsville on May 1–3, 1863, is widely considered to be Confederate General Robert E. Lee's greatest victory. The tone was set on the first day, when Lee's army, squeezed between two massive elements of the Union Army of the Potomac commanded by General Joseph Hooker, attacked the advancing federal forces instead of fighting defensively. Stalled and sapped of confidence, Hooker withdrew, giving up the initiative. The next day, General Stonewall Jackson's famous flanking march and attack caused a Union rout. On a third, bloody day of fighting, Hooker's campaign was crushed, although it took several more days for the Union army to fully withdraw.[945]

The heart of the first day's battlefield had been a dairy farm for most of the 20th century. In 2002, the open fields and pastures looked much as they did more than 140 years earlier, when a country at war with itself made the landscape a stage for the bloody spectacle of warfare. The new development, called the "Town of Chancellorsville," was to be a densely packed, mixed-use development on 788 acres with 2,350 homes, some 10,000 residents and more 2.4 million square feet of office and commercial space.[946]

"I think we're doing the right thing," said developer Smith. The mixed-used development was a perfect fit with the county's vision for growth. The area had been designated a "Primary Settlement Area," exactly the place for Smith's self-proclaimed "smart-growth" project, with stores and offices intermingled with homes. The project encouraged more walking and less use of automobiles. Smith also planned to preserve 34 acres, where he claimed all the fighting took place, and donate it to the county for use as a park.[947]

The size of the project was unlike anything Spotsylvania County had ever seen. "It was like dropping a bomb on the Chancellorsville battlefield," Campi recalled. "You would not have recognized the battlefield if this project had been approved and built."[948]

Bob Krick, Gary Gallagher and other top Civil War historians had feared this threat as the Fredericksburg area grew. They had watched Salem Church, part of the third day's battlefield, become surrounded in the 1970s and 1980s by a glut of fast food restaurants, auto parts stores, banks, grocery stores, steakhouses and more. But they had no organized means with which to fight the sprawl. The first day's battlefield was just a couple of miles farther west, and now, as they had long dreaded, the specter of development had arrived.

The first direct threat had its genesis in January 1995, when Fredericksburg funeral home owner and businessman John T. Mullins bought two adjacent farms on Route 3 in the heart of the first day's battlefield. Mullins paid about $563,000 for the 297-acre Orrock farm, and less than two months later, paid $2.2 million for the 500-acre Ashley Farms, where dairy cows had grazed for some 60 years. "We plan to continue operating it as a farm … " Mullins said of Ashley Farms, raising beef cattle and growing soybeans, hay and corn.[949]

That same year, to address local traffic woes, the Virginia Department of Transportation (VDOT) began developing plans for a Northwest Outer Connector—a four-lane bypass that would connect I-95 north of Fredericksburg with Route 3 west of the city. The new highway and interchange were bound to spur growth wherever they were placed. Several routes were being considered, including one right through the Mullins property.[950]

By 1997, Mullins had decided to develop. That October, the Spotsylvania County Planning Commission approved Mullins's plan for 225 lots on the property. A year later, commissioners approved a special use permit for a golf course along Route 3. And in December 1999, a lame-duck board of supervisors approved Mullin's request to rezone the eastern 55 acres along Route 3 from agricultural to commercial for an office and commercial park.[951]

The county's "Primary Settlement Area" designation was ideal for Mullins's proposed development. The National Park Service expressed its concerns, and local preservationists protested the planned development of the battlefield at a public hearing on the rezoning request on November 23, 1999. But the push for growth eclipsed the voices of protest. The rezoning was approved the following month.[952]

About this time Lighthizer became aware of the threat and Krick drove him out Route 3. "We went to this vast expanse of field," Lighthizer recalled, "and Bob said, 'See that, Jim, that's 700 or 800 acres. Half of it is the first day of Chancellorsville. And one guy owns it and he wants to develop it.'"[953] Lighthizer stood thinking, "Well, there's no way we'd ever be able to afford that."[954]

Mullins, meanwhile, had yet to fire up the bulldozers. He had grown frustrated by bureaucratic hurdles, especially the lack of a decision on the outer connector route. Local officials favored a proposed route through Mullins's land; the state favored a route east of his land. The decision was still pending in October 2001 when Mullins announced that he was walking away from it all. "We've been a yo-yo for about six years, waiting for VDOT to make a decision," Mullins told the Fredericksburg *Free Lance-Star*. "We're definitely going to sell it."[955]

By the spring of 2002, Dogwood Development had an option to buy Mullins's land. On June 21, Smith revealed his ambitious plan for the "Town of Chancellorsville" mixed-use development when he filed a request with the county to have the zoning changed to allow for much denser development than Mullins's plan. Dogwood's purchase of the land hinged on approval of the development and the first hurdle was rezoning.[956]

The CWPT was better positioned in the spring of 2002 to face the Chancellorsville threat than in 2000, when Krick first showed Lighthizer the land. Lighthizer decided to visit Smith to see if more of the first day's battlefield could be preserved.

Smith began by disputing that any widespread fighting took place on the land, Lighthizer recalled.

"Are you going to save any of it?" Lighthizer asked.

"I'm going to save 34 acres here in this swale," Smith replied, according to Lighthizer. "I'll sell you anything you want for $40,000 an acre. But I tell you, it's a done deal, we're getting our zoning."[957]

"I said, 'Hmmm. Well, is there any way we can compromise on this?' And he said, 'Nope.' So I said, 'Okay, gotcha. See you later.'"

Lighthizer returned to Washington and announced, "Guys, we gotta go to war." He turned to Campi and said, "Go get 'em."[958]

Campi knew they were in for a tough fight when six of the seven county supervisors refused to talk with Lighthizer. But Campi had a few months to prepare. Smith's zoning change request first had to be considered by the county planning commission, which meant a final decision by the supervisors was unlikely before the fall.[959]

Campi began organizing local anti-growth forces and battlefield preservationists to form the Coalition to Save Chancellorsville Battlefield. Coalition members ranged from the National Trust for Historic Preservation to the Concerned Citizens of Spotsylvania.[960]

On a hot July 31, 2002, coalition members and supporters gathered on the front lawn of the old Salem Church to announce the organization's creation and intent. Photographs of the event captured a background of commercial sprawl.

Campi had fretted over every detail of the press conference and found plenty to worry about. "It was probably the least well-choreographed news conference we ever did," he recalled. A large sign threatened to blow over in the breeze so David Duncan held it up while speakers took too long with their remarks.[961]

The shortcomings did not matter. "Clearly, there was an energy there," he recalled. "There was great press turnout. We had helicopters from a couple of the TV

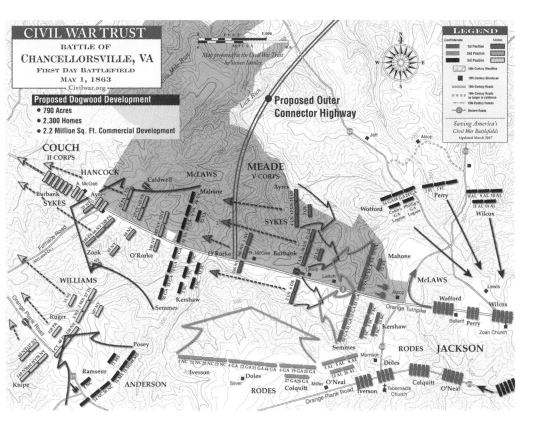

stations. It was chaotic, but the result was terrific."[962]

One of the speakers Campi invited was reenactor and preservationist Robert Lee Hodge. An APCWS loyalist, Hodge still resented the wholesale firings in the wake of the merger, but when Campi called, Hodge agreed to speak. "In 10 years," Hodge told reporters at the event, the Mullins property "will be as ugly as Fairfax."[963]

John Hennessy was acting superintendent of the Fredericksburg and Spotsylvania National Military Park. NPS employees are supposed to maintain neutrality in local matters, but Hennessy stuck his neck out. He had already been quoted in the *Free Lance-Star* sharply questioning the project. Before the press conference, Hennessy led coalition members on a battlefield tour to get them fired up about its history.[964]

The next day, a photo of Hennessy leading the tour was splashed across the front page of the *Free Lance-Star*, accompanied by a story about the formation of the coalition. Hennessy was quoted saying the degradation of the historic land was "an outcome we cannot blithely accept."[965]

Smith complained to a congressman, and suddenly Hennessy faced trouble at the NPS.[966] "From what I understand, I could have easily ended up in Tuzigoot," Hennessy recalled. (Tuzigoot National Monument in Arizona, like Dry Tortugas National Park in Florida, is widely considered in the NPS to be a punishment assignment). "Fortunately, I did not end up there," Hennessy said. "There was some real positive intervention somewhere above me in the organization and that eventuality did not happen. We did foresee that this was going to be an ugly battle. And we did foresee that at some point we, the park service, would probably be shut down as public advocates for the battlefield. I probably played that role to a greater extent than I ever had before."[967]

Many organizations joined the coalition and there was no longer a shortage of protest voices. Campi was ultimately in charge of a tight-knit leadership council, working hand in hand with Kevin Leahy of the Central Virginia Battlefields Trust, a regional preservation organization, Caroline Hayden of the Spotsylvania Preservation Foundation, and Henry "Hap" Connors, Jr., a local resident who worked at the National Trust for Historic Preservation.

Campi sensed the project's size and density were the main objections, so he commissioned a local poll, turning to Mason-Dixon Polling and Research and Brad Coker, whose preservation-related polling projects dated to Til Hazel's William Center at Manassas in the 1980s. On August 29, Campi released the results: 66 percent of those polled were against the Dogwood Development project, and 63 percent believed the county was growing too fast.[968]

Campi tailored his strategy to the audience. Spotsylvania residents saw a campaign that differed from the national campaign. Local flyers, press releases and other opposition efforts focused overwhelmingly on growth issues created by the development, including tripling the traffic on Route 3, with an estimated 70,000 vehicle trips a day in and out of the new "town."[969] The national campaigns zeroed in on the history – the destruction of the first day's battlefield at Chancellorsville.

Orchestrating any preservation fight is more than generating opposition. "It's taking that energy (of the protesters) and putting it in productive places," Campi said. "Trying to convince people that writing angry rants online isn't the best use of their time. Getting them in front of the policy makers that make the decisions. Putting together events. Connecting the various groups.[970]

"And the idiosyncrasies of some of the partners we've got to work with, the jealousies … we set that aside. So often in grassroots fights where I've seen groups defeated, the number one reason is infighting. We always focus on the big picture. And the big picture is winning."[971]

As the coalition focused its efforts on the planning commission, which scheduled a hearing on the Dogwood development for November 8, 2002, some coalition participants were busy on another front. As members of the Committee of 500, a local political action committee, they were striving to elect a development opponent to an open seat on the Spotsylvania County Board of Supervisors.

The special election was set for November 7 and Republican Robert "Bob" Hagan had announced his opposition to the Dogwood project. His opponent had not taken a position. Hagan swept to victory with 64 percent of the vote.[972] The following day, the planning commission heard more than three hours of testimony. Normally, it delayed a vote on a contentious project until the following meeting, but at half past midnight, the commission broke precedent. It recommended approval of the rezoning and a development plan for 1,995 homes and 2.2 million square feet of stores and offices.[973] Some in the crowd booed and hissed. "Shame on you!" shouted one woman.[974]

"I think that was the watershed moment," Campi recalled. "We knew we were probably going to lose with the planning commission. But it was the way the commission handled the vote and fact that they treated the opponents so badly, such as making them wait until late in the evening to speak. It left everyone feeling like they were being railroaded. And that was the moment, I think, that our movement really started to take off. There was a real backlash—almost immediately—with press coverage, letters to the editor, editorials, political cartoons ... " Within a week, an apparent defeat "had been transformed into a victory," Campi recalled.[975]

The coalition built momentum. "Almost every story you would see was favorable to us," Campi recalled. "We had a great network of people involved. Which meant that every time our opponents tried to do something, we could jump on it quickly. Probably my favorite instance of that was when we found out that they were doing this lopsided poll—a push poll. So, before they could even get the results of their poll out, we were in press, beating the hell out of that poll and how lopsided it was. Ultimately, they probably end up paying 10 grand for a poll that did them no good whatsoever, because we turned it around on them."[976]

In December, the coalition attacked the developer's economic impact forecasts, asserting that the economists who prepared it used accounting gimmicks to overplay the benefits of the project and grossly underestimated the actual costs of new schools and county services. To analyze the developer's figures, the coalition turned to preservation veteran and economist Michael Siegel, who had exposed the inflated economic projections for Disney's America theme park. The developer's economists defended their work, but the coalition again had the edge.[977]

The Dogwood development was not the only vexing issue for the Spotsylvania supervisors that winter. Far more board turmoil was generated by infighting over whether to fire the county administrator, which led instead to the sudden resignation of supervisor Tricia Ledwell, who stalked out of the board meeting of November 26, 2002.[978]

The board decided at its December 10 meeting to appoint, not elect, Ledwell's replacement. It asked for interested candidates to submit their resumes with a petition containing the signatures of 125 voters in their supervisorial district. With the coalition's full support, Hap Connors applied, submitting 1,700 signatures on his petition.[979]

When the supervisors met on January 14, 2003, to decide who would join them on the board, Campi and nearly 200 others gathered outside, holding candles to memorialize the soldiers who died at Chancellorsville and quietly demonstrating their opposition to the Dogwood development. Some demonstrators wanted to storm the administration building to disrupt the meeting.[980] Absolutely not, said Campi, who insisted on keeping the show respectful. He assembled everyone at the far end of the parking lot, with the historic Spotsylvania Court House building, built in 1839, as the backdrop. He arranged for cookies and hot cider as refreshments.[981]

No one expected the supervisors to fill the open seat with the ardent preservationist Connors, co-leader of the coalition. A friend quipped to Connors in the parking lot, "It'll be a cold day in hell before the supervisors put you on the board."

Connors smiled and said, "Well, it *is* snowing."[981]

The snow created a sublime scene. "It was the prettiest protest I've ever seen," wrote *Free Lance-Star* columnist Larry Evans.

Brian Pohanka rose to speak. In 1998, at age 43, Pohanka had been diagnosed with cancer and had lost an eye in the surgery to eradicate it. But he had recovered and was more than happy to help Campi and the CWPT at the vigil. Pohanka stood "as erect as a soldier on a parade field," wrote Evans. He spoke of just one of the men who had died on that first day's battlefield, a 21-year-old Union officer named William James Temple.[984] Temple could have stayed out of the war, Pohanka said. Both of his parents had died and he was the guardian of his five brothers and a sister. But he saw it as his patriotic duty to fight for the Union, and he died on that first day at Chancellorsville.

"This is about people like William Temple, who fell there, who shed their blood there for their ideals," Pohanka said as the snow began to fall harder. Quoting Union General Joshua Chamberlain, Pohanka said, his voice rising, "Willing to die, we will not be forgotten. *They will not be forgotten!*" A wave of applause rose from the crowd.[985]

Shortly after 11 p.m., near the end of a long meeting, the supervisors went into closed session to consider the four qualified candidates. They soon emerged. Quietly, unanimously, they appointed well-spoken, likeable Hap Connors to the board.[986]

As it was, whomever the supervisors chose, it was going to be a preservation-minded replacement. It was a matter of those 125 signatures. "What the candidates quickly found out was that people were asking what their position was on the development," Campi said. "And if you said you were for it, you didn't get a signature. By that time, we had built up so much opposition to this development, that none of the people who supported it could get enough signatures to be considered."[987]

Although the tide seemed to be turning, the developers launched a telemarketing campaign to sway public opinion. An organization named The Spotsylvania County Landowners Association released its own poll indicating that 62 percent of residents favored the project. The coalition attacked the poll as flawed and excoriated Dogwood's "slick" ads and "11th hour desperation tactics."[988]

When a landowners association's flyer claimed preservationists were akin to Yankees invading from the North, the coalition responded with its own flyer, headlined, "Exactly who is the outsider?" with an image of Dogwood Development's Reston, Virginia, address from the telephone book.[989] All the while, the coalition kept up the pressure with a national letter-writing campaign and national media coverage on the proposed desecration of the battlefield. Campi allowed himself to be cautiously optimistic.

On the afternoon of March 26, 2003, the supervisors met to consider the rezoning application and the fate of the development. The debate lasted for more than seven hours as some 300 people filled the board room. Raucous cheers followed the remarks of those opposing the project. They outnumbered those in favor by three to one.[990]

Campi sat in the audience with the other coalition leaders as the hours dragged by. Hodge was there, too, as was Pohanka.

"Thanks so much for coming," Campi told Pohanka. "You certainly don't need to be here. We're going to be here for hours, and you're not going to get much time to speak."

"I just wanted to be here," Pohanka said.[991]

It was well past midnight before the supervisors finally voted. It was 6-0, with one abstention, against the rezoning and the project.

"We were just stunned for a minute—that it was unanimous," Campi recalled. "This quiet went over the audience, and then this huge cheer went up."[992]

But the fight was far from over. Not a single acre of the battlefield site had been saved. Virtually all of it remained threatened and open to development. Although Dogwood abandoned its project, Mullins still had the right to build a commercial center of offices and stores on the rezoned eastern 55 acres and to build 225 homes on a portion of the rest. He was ready to sell to a developer.

On April 7, Lighthizer arranged a meeting with Mullins, who offered to sell it for $40 million. The assessed value was $5.6 million.

"This is so far out of the realm of reality that it's almost laughable," Lighthizer told a reporter.[993]

"Everybody has had their chance," said Mullins. An announcement about the development of the property was imminent, he said. Only a single bureaucratic hurdle remained before he could begin building. He needed a permit from the Army Corps of Engineers, required under the Clean Water Act, to allow stream crossings in six places.

The coalition appealed to the Corps to include the potential impact on historic resources within its scope of inquiry, as it had done at Brandy Station in the permitting process for the race track. The coalition argued that the Corps was required to do that as a custodian of the National Preservation Act. But on October 21, 2003, the Corps approved the permit, giving the green light to the development. "We're not surprised, but we're clearly disappointed," Campi told the *Free Lance-Star*.[994]

By then, Campi's focus was back on county politics. Local preservationists and slow-growth activists "weren't satisfied, nor should they have been, in just beating back the development. They wanted to get involved in local politics," Campi recalled. He helped lead the effort, strictly as a volunteer, using his annual leave to clear time to work on the campaign.

On November 4, 2004, with all six seats of the board up for election, a slate of slow-growth candidates swept to victory in five of six races. The biggest upset was the defeat of development supporter, longtime supervisor and board chairwoman Mary Lee Carter. "That's the one thing they said couldn't be done, and we did it," said Leahy of the Central Virginia Battlefields Trust.[995]

Turning the board upside down would have a tremendous impact on the preservation battle. But it did not immediately change anything. The entire battlefield was still threatened. In January 2004, Toll Brothers, Inc., a nationwide builder of luxury homes, bought 30 building lots, or about 90 acres, from Mullins for $2.73 million, and in June, the company paid $3 million for 123 more acres, with options to buy hundreds more. The company announced plans to build 225 luxury houses.[996]

By July, the Toll Brothers bulldozers were carving new roads on the least historically important north side of the property. But some of the land the company had bought or optioned was in the heart of the battlefield along Route 3.

"There are indications that they're interested in working out a compromise," Campi said.[997] With the shift in power from pro-growth to slow growth on the board of supervisors, the preservationists had political muscle in Spotsylvania County. The Outer Connector highway plan had never gotten off the drawing board and was all but dead by 2004. And the board began considering withdrawing the "Primary Settlement District" zoning classification for the first day's battlefield and instead making it a "Rural Development District." That could be a fatal blow even to the relatively small, 55-acre commercial development that Mullins first planned.

"So tell us—how does well and septic strike you, Mr. Mullins?" the *Free Lance-Star* asked rhetorically in an August 27, 2004, editorial. "The county has made no bones about its plans: If Mr. Mullins cuts a deal with preservationists … he will get water and sewer for his commercial visions. If he balks, he may not."[998]

Into the picture came Tricord Homes, a local development company founded and run by brothers Mike and Doug Jones and cousin Craig Jones. The trio believed they could develop in the county and help it grow while being good stewards of the land and establishing a positive relationship with the community. They approached Hagan, who put them in touch with Campi and Lighthizer.[999]

Since Mullins seemed determined to sell his property to developers, Tricord sought to buy the property from him and then sell the crucial battlefield acres to the CWPT. The shift in power on the board of supervisors paved the way for the unique arrangements that saved the first day's battlefield. In simplest terms, the battlefield land—the acreage along Route 3—was saved, and the rest was developed. The negotiations were complex, involving multiple partners, and lasting for weeks, but Mullins finally agreed to sell 227 acres to Tricord for $12.5 million, including the acreage for the commercial center as well as the rest of land he had not already sold to the Toll Brothers.[1000]

Tricord then sold about 140 acres of Route 3 frontage—the heart of the battlefield—to the CWPT for $3 million. Tricord needed a denser development on the remaining 87 acres to make the project financially feasible. The county approved the requested rezoning and project in November 2004, and Tricord developed "Retreat at Chancellorsville," a 300-unit, age-restricted subdivision that included a church and an assisted living facility.[1001]

A year later, after extensive negotiations, the CWPT secured a final victory, paying the Toll Brothers $1 million for 75 acres it owned along Route 3 extending 950 feet from the highway.[1002] The "carrot for the developer," as Campi put it, was county approval for more density—33 more homes—in the Toll Brothers development on the remaining land it owned.[1003]

Today, suburban sprawl along Route 3 out of Fredericksburg continues for almost five miles—a succession of strip malls, big box stores, gas stations, fast food restaurants and all manner of other businesses. But after the light turns green at the intersection with Spotswood Furnace Road, motorists pass open land and rolling pastures.

For two miles, the land remains undeveloped, preserved as hallowed ground. Dividends go beyond saving the land, however, as the green oasis provides a respite from dense suburban development and visual clutter. No one had fought harder for these unmeasurable payoffs than Campi.[1004]

"Jim Campi is probably the best operative for battlefield preservation who has ever walked the earth," said Hennessy. "He is just really good at what he does on the local level, and the muck and grinding of getting things done. I'm not sure how he does it, because it's stressful, it's an exhausting thing. But he's just amazing."[1005]

Not only did the preservationists and local anti-growth activists stop development of the first day's battlefield at Chancellorsville, they changed the entire focus of growth in that area. "The county ultimately decided to relocate its focus on development to the I-95 corridor and not out Route 3 (at Exit 30)," Hennessy said. "So, you've seen tremendously intense development along there, especially down at Exit 126. It has had far-reaching implications for Spotsylvania County. The fact is, downtown Spotsylvania, which was envisioned to be on the eastern edge of Chancellorsville battlefield, is now someplace else. And there's no understating how important that is."[1006] ★

CHAPTER
FIFTEEN

Defeats and Victories at Gettysburg

ISTORIAN William A. Frassanito could not believe his eyes as he approached the Oak Ridge Railroad Cut from the direction of Gettysburg College on a clear and cold Pennsylvania afternoon, January 15, 1991. Perched atop the northeast edge of the cut sat a bulldozer.

"What is *that* doing there?" he said to himself with considerable alarm. Thus began a three-year ordeal that kept his life tied in knots and led to one of the greatest battlefield losses of the modern preservation era.[1007]

Frassanito at the time was writing about the Oak Ridge Railroad Cut for his next book, Early Photography at Gettysburg, published by Thomas Brothers in 1995. The Oak Ridge Railroad Cut on Seminary Ridge is one of two railroad cuts on the northwest edge of Gettysburg. It is much larger and deeper than the more famous McPherson Ridge Railroad Cut a quarter mile west. More than 200 Confederates were trapped and captured at McPherson Ridge, where a fierce fight occurred.

The Oak Ridge Railroad Cut is not part of any battlefield tour and in modern times has been obscured by a line of trees. The hellish combat in this railroad cut on the first day of the Battle of Gettysburg was well documented by the combatants, but not as well by historians.

In Early Photography at Gettysburg, Frassanito planned to publish vintage photographs from 1863 and 1867 that showed just how prominent and visible the Oak Ridge Railroad Cut was on the Gettysburg wartime landscape. The cut was a gaping hole that bisected the final defensive line of the Union First Corps at Seminary Ridge on the afternoon of July 1, 1863, and became the focal point of heavy fighting. Its ultimate envelopment by Confederate forces resulted in the largest mass capture of Union troops at Gettysburg.[1008]

On that January day in 1991, "I was heading from my apartment in town out to my mother's house and just to reconnect with the vibrations of the railroad cut, I decided to go back there and revisit the cut before I started writing about it," Frassanito recalled.[1009]

A bulldozer was not the reconnection he expected. The unmanned machine had not torn up anything at the railroad cut but was ominously prepared. Frassanito was a member of the Gettysburg Borough Planning Commission and on the board of the Gettysburg Battlefield Preservation Association (GBPA), founded in 1959 and one of the oldest local battlefield preservation organizations.

Frassanito was aware of a land swap involving the railroad cut that had taken place the previous September. The National Park Service had traded to Gettysburg College 7.5 acres of battlefield along the eastern base of Oak Ridge Railroad Cut in exchange for a historic easement that prevented construction of buildings on 47 acres of battlefield land owned by the college and used as athletic fields.[1010]

The trade had been sought by the college so it could move a line of railroad tracks away from campus and onto the 7.5-acre tract along the base of Oak Ridge. The terms of the swap took more than three years to negotiate and included public briefings. Frassanito knew that some trees at the base of Oak Ridge might be removed as part of the swap, and he could see that trees were being cut. But neither the college nor NPS had mentioned that the relocation of the railroad line would involve massive excavation that would chop off and round off the northeast corner of the railroad cut.[1011]

The NPS had officially asserted that the swap would have no adverse impact on known historic resources. NPS Chief Historian Ed Bearss had signed off on the project and in November 1989 had taken a tour of the site as part of the approval process. There was no mention of excavation on the tour.[1012]

From his mother's home, Frassanito called historian Kathy Georg Harrison's office at the Gettysburg National Military Park. "They had no idea why there was a bulldozer on top of the cut," Frassanito recalled. No one at the historian's office was aware that the plans called for bulldozers to destroy the northeast corner of the cut. They were shocked. Within days, "we found out what was going on," Frassanito said. By then, bulldozers had begun tearing down the corner of the embankment.[1013]

The land swap, Frassanito learned, not only involved moving the railroad line to the base of Oak Ridge, but called for a new, 90-degree westbound connection to the east-west rail line that runs through the cut. Because trains can't make sharp right turns, the installation of the connection "necessitated this massive destruction of the northeastern portion of the railroad cut, which of course was very sensitive battleground," Frassanito said.[1014]

Frassanito and GBPA Executive Director Walter Powell were among the first and most vocal critics. They complained bitterly that the excavation plan to destroy the northeast corner of the railroad cut had never been divulged to the public. The map that had been shown to the planning commission by the college depicted the movement of the tracks to the base of the ridge, they said, but did not show the spur line that would have to slice through the corner of the cut. They complained that the NPS had failed in its responsibility to protect its own historic ground. Their complaints fell on deaf ears.[1015]

In late January or early February, not long after excavation began, Bearss was alerted to the destruction by John O'Donnell, an aide to Representative Peter Kostmayer (D-Pa.), who wanted the chief historian to go to Gettysburg with him and the congressman. Bearss said O'Donnell never called back. He also said he did not investigate "because I was waiting for Mr. Kostmayer to lead the expedition up there. The park service is somewhat of a 'you go when the task force is going.' I was led to believe with John that there would be a number of us going up, and John never called me back."[1016]

Around that time, Bearss saw in print that the NPS was saying the land had no historical significance. He called other officials to complain, but did not formally object in writing, because he had learned from bitter experiences at Petersburg and Vicksburg NPS parks that it did not do any good.[1017]

"When the alarms began to sound, if there was anyone in the world in a position of authority who could have rushed to Gettysburg and come to the rescue, it was the chief historian of the National Park Service, Ed Bearss," Frassanito said.[1018]

Bearss did not visit Gettysburg until June 27, two months after the destruction was completed, and it was not to visit the cut, but to lead a pre-arranged battlefield tour for the college's Civil War Institute.[1019]

Fellow NPS Historian Robert K. Krick, now retired but familiar with how the NPS works, said Bearss had little to do with the issue internally. The chief historian position "has no clout whatsoever in an organizational sense," Krick said in 2016. In military terms, Krick compared the chief historian's job to that of a staff officer, not a line officer who makes decisions. Krick said Bearss had "infinitely less capacity to do anything … and his boss probably cared very little unless it was in *The New York Times*." Civil War parks represent a small fraction of the NPS system, and a myriad of tasks constantly flowed across the chief historian's desk, Krick said. "One of his jobs that month may well have been whether the Hoover Dam, which was then more than 50 years old, could be power-washed without National Register permission."[1020]

In any event, no one heeded the cries to stop excavating, even as the destructive nature of the work sometimes literally bombarded the area. Larson's Motel was sandwiched between the railroad cut and the Chambersburg Pike, next to Lee's Headquarters, and when workers started blasting, chunks of rock flew into the motel yard. Owner and Gettysburg Borough Planning Commission Chairman Andrew Larson "was just beside himself, complaining about all the destruction that was happening back there," Frassanito recalled.[1021]

By January 23, the planning commission and the borough's Historical Architectural Review Board had unanimously passed resolutions calling upon the borough council to seek an immediate halt to all excavation and conduct a full investigation of the land swap. Nothing happened.[1022]

There would be no last-minute preservation heroics at Oak Ridge Railroad Cut.

From January through April 1991, in Frassanito's words, "the public was forced to watch relentlessly—day after day, week after week, month after month—the most massive destruction of fully protected historic terrain in the 78-year history of the National Park Service. Nothing like this had ever happened before."[1023]

This was not to say the war's greatest battlefield had escaped commercial indignities and encroachments over the years. An unsavory legacy started long before the government's Gettysburg National Military Park was established in 1895. In 1869, the Katalysine Springs resort and spa was built on the first day's battlefield. It eventually came to include a four-story hotel that vanished from the landscape in a 1917 fire. In the 1880s, photographer Levi Mumper established a photography studio and souvenir stand in Devil's Den. It was purchased by photographer William Tipton and by the 1890s had become "Tipton Park," with several structures, including a restaurant, darkroom, dancing pavilion, horse sheds and swing sets for children. In those years, "there was a struggle over whether this would be a historic park or an amusement park," said Garry Adelman, the Trust's Director of History and Education and a Licensed Gettysburg Battlefield Guide.[1024]

The government condemned and took over Tipton Park in 1902, and the restaurant building was moved several hundred yards to a spot along Warren Avenue on the slope of Little Round Top, where it continued to operate under another proprietor until 1919. The government, meanwhile, used the battlefield for military purposes. The War Department, which managed the park until 1933, created a U.S. Army Mobilization Camp on the fields of Pickett's Charge during World War One and held tank exercises and artillery training on the battlefield into the 1920s. The military returned during World War II, establishing a German prisoner of war camp where Pickett's men charged. This brought multiple escape attempts and manhunts, featuring a particularly daring unsuccessful effort on July 3, 1944, the 81st anniversary of the charge.[1025]

Hand in hand with intrusions came preservation efforts, which began while the war still raged. Seventeen acres on Cemetery Hill became the Gettysburg National Cemetery, consecrated by President Lincoln on November 19, 1863, with his Gettysburg Address. In 1864, the Gettysburg Battlefield Memorial Association was created and began acquiring battlefield acreage. The dedication of the first two memorial stones on the battlefield proper, outside the cemetery, came in July 1878. One honors Union Colonel Strong Vincent, who fell on Little Round Top, and the other memorializes Union Colonel Fred Taylor, who fell in the Valley of Death. The memorialization era had begun, and in the following decade, more than 90 other memorials were installed, mostly for regiments and batteries, nearly all erected by Union veterans,

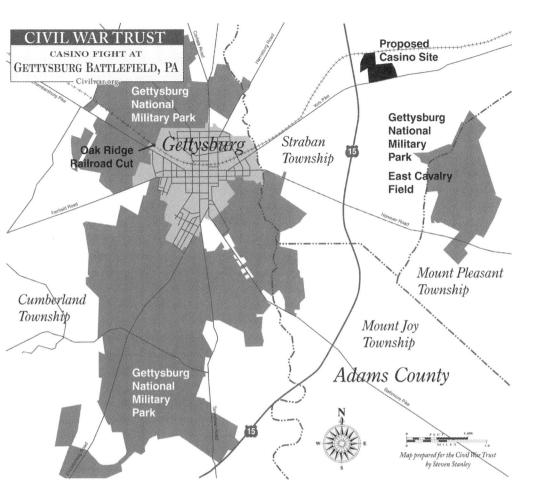

who held massive reunions at the battlefield. Today, more than 1,300 monuments, memorials and markers are in the park.[1026]

A federal national park at Gettysburg was first proposed in 1890, but it took five years for authorizing legislation to pass. On February 11, 1895, President Grover Cleveland signed the bill that established Gettysburg as the fourth federally established battlefield, behind Chickamauga and Chattanooga (1890), Antietam (1890) and Shiloh (1894). The Gettysburg park had a head start on land acquisition because the Gettysburg Battlefield Memorial Association turned over about 800 acres it had acquired since 1864.[1027]

The biggest 19th-century preservation fight at Gettysburg was waged over the construction of a battlefield railroad for tourists. The first railroad excursion line at Gettysburg was built in 1884. It featured Round Top Park, a recreation and amusement park, at its southern terminus—one of three amusement parks that operated on the battlefield in the late 19th or early 20th centuries. It had its own post office, "Sedgwick," which opened in 1886 and postmarked postcards by the thousands.

A more intrusive railway, the commercial Gettysburg Electric Railway project, was started in 1891 and in operation by 1894. The federal government sued to stop it, and the future of preservation at Gettysburg hinged on this legal fight. In a landmark decision on January 27, 1896, the U.S. Supreme Court ruled that the United States could condemn land for preservation, presaging the end of the electric railway as well as Tipton Park and the Land Syndicate, a battlefield land-profiteering venture bent on buying hallowed ground and selling it to the government at inflated prices.[1028]

In 1904, the park was declared semi-complete with 1,380 acres. The federal commissioners in charge declared that the acquisition of any further extensive parcels of land "would be a waste of public funds." The park today consists of more than 6,000 acres.[1029]

Encroachments, however, persisted through the 20th century. For many years, the Peach Orchard's neighbor across Emmitsburg Road was a Stuckey's restaurant. From 1925 to 1985, the Shields Museum sat on the first day's battlefield on Chambersburg Pike, near the McPherson barn.[1030]

Motels, businesses and the Colt Park subdivision pushed their way onto the northern edges of the battlefield where Pickett charged. Some 50 structures known as the community of Pinchgut existed for many years along Emmitsburg Road at Confederate Avenue. A junkyard came and went on Baltimore Pike near Power's Hill. Two little airports, modest as they were, once existed on the battlefield.[1031] Large chunks of battlefield to the north and northeast of the town were overrun by development, including the famous Camp Letterman tent hospital, part of which was on the site of a multi-story hotel.

The saga of The National Tower, a 307-foot observation tower built on privately owned battlefield land on the east flank of Cemetery Ridge, could be a book in itself. The gigantic steel structure was the creation of real estate developer Thomas R. Ottenstein, who opened his "classroom in the sky" in 1974 despite intense opposition from the NPS and others.[1032]

Ottenstein stood firm in the heat of media coverage, which included a CBS *60 Minutes* segment, and prevailed in court over all legal moves to stop him, in part by citing the other commercial enterprises on or next to the battlefield. Construction of the $2.5 million structure began in 1972, and it opened on July 29, 1974. For more than a quarter century, the National Tower dominated the skyline in Gettysburg and for miles around.[1033]

In 1990, Congress expanded the battlefield's federally legislated boundary, encompassing Ottenstein's land and opening the door for eminent domain condemnation proceedings. "This tower is coming down on my watch," U.S. Secretary of the Interior Bruce Babbitt declared on Earth Day, April 22, 1999. In December, the Department of Justice filed suit to acquire the property. In June 2000, the court granted the NPS ownership,[1034] and on July 3, 2000, the 137th anniversary of Pickett's Charge, artillery reenactors fired dummy charges toward the tower as real explosives simultaneously blew its legs out. Down came the tower in an enormous crash as a large crowd cheered from a distance.[1035]

After a six-year legal battle, the government paid $4.035 million for the tower and six acres of land in 2006. By then, Ottenstein was dead. He had died of prostate cancer at age 70 on August 3, 2000, one month after his classroom in the sky was destroyed.[1036]

The tower had been a blight on the landscape, but it did little damage to the land itself. The greatest destruction of the natural geography of the battlefield before the railroad cut debacle was during construction of the electric railway in 1893. As workers laid the railroad bed, a scene of devastation unfolded on Tipton's property near Devil's Den. "All along the line, in the vicinity of Devil's Den, there is heavy blasting and digging and filling, and great havoc is played with the face of the landscape," a witness said. "Huge masses of rock are displaced, great boulders are moved … and a wholly new appearance will be given to the famous field of carnage."[1037] That damage is evident today in Devil's Den as well as on the slope of Little Round Top.

Ninety-eight years later, heavy blasting returned to the battlefield, this time at the Oak Ridge Railroad Cut. Gettysburg College's actions in the 1990 land swap —especially its apparent efforts to hide the planned excavation from the NPS and the public, and its strident defense of the work once the destruction started—were deeply distressing to Frassanito and Gettysburg preservationists. Not only was Frassanito a Gettysburg College alumnus, the college in 1984 had presented him with its Distinguished Alumni Award. He also was an active participant in the college's Civil War Institute, directed by Dr. Gabor Boritt.[1038]

On February 1, 1991, as the railroad cut excavation progressed, Boritt assembled a meeting to "straighten this thing out." It included Frassanito, other local historians and three high-level representatives of the College, but not business manager William Van Arsdale, who knew more about the project than anyone else. Frassanito described the rich history of the site, appealing to their sense of heritage.[1039]

The meeting amounted to nothing. College officials continued to contend that the land was not of significant historical value. The college's representatives insisted they had done everything properly and if something had been done wrong, it was the fault of the NPS. Frassanito, Powell and others got nowhere. Frassanito felt like the entire bureaucracy had battened down the hatches and gone into cover-up mode.

"Denials, lies, refusals to release information, and gag orders were quickly implemented. The cover-up story aggressively promulgated by the NPS was suspiciously similar to the story then being promoted by the public relations office of Gettysburg College," Frassanito would later write.[1040] The NPS covered it up because of "the simple fact they were made fools of, and were perfectly willing to sacrifice one of the key terrain features on the Gettysburg battlefield to avoid the embarrassment of the truth."[1041]

In the fall of 1991, the GBPA filed suit in federal court to have the outrage exposed and the site restored. Erosion had become a problem, with runoff washing away even more of the embankment. The suit was dismissed by the court without a formal hearing. The dismissal was upheld on appeal.[1042]

Even after the battle was lost, Frassanito, Powell and others continued to press their grievances, demanding accountability from the NPS if nothing else. Why no thorough historical review, as required by the National Historic Preservation Act of 1966? Why was a mid-level NPS bureaucrat with no historic background the one to approve the land swap? Why were the implications of the land swap never plainly revealed during the long negotiation process?[1043]

They finally found an eager and outraged listener in Representative Michael Synar, (D-Okla.). On May 9, 1994, more three years after the excavation, Synar held a hearing of the House Natural Resources Subcommittee about the land swap and called the NPS and the college on the carpet. Synar's staff had investigated the incident and the well-informed congressman—the only legislator at the hearing—grilled the college officials and bureaucrats who faced him.[1044]

The swap had supporters, including Representative William F. Goodling (R-Pa.) whose district includes Gettysburg. "There were no backroom deals or cover-up ... " Goodling wrote to the subcommittee. "I know there are those who believe there is a grand conspiracy between Gettysburg College, the NPS and Members of Congress. I can assure the Members of the Subcommittee there was no conspiracy. I am convinced that both the College and the NPS are still fully confident they acted in the best interests of both the local community and the country."[1045]

But new NPS director Roger Kennedy did not agree. "It's useless for the director of the National Park Service to assert that this was not a mistake," Kennedy said in the most dramatic testimony from any of the 23 witnesses during the six-hour hearing. The cut was clearly historic and its destruction was "lamentable," he said. NPS policies and procedures on land exchanges were "inadequate" and would be fixed so that something like this never happened again.[1046]

Van Arsdale, the former business manager at Gettysburg College, faced some of the toughest questioning, given his key role in the land swap. Frassanito and others blamed him for masterminding a "calculated scheme" to hide the true nature of the project. Van Arsdale stood firm in its defense. "I am certain of one thing: each time that we were requested to provide information to a responsible park service official, we did so to the best of our ability," Van Arsdale testified. It was a "successful exchange," he said, "and I am pleased with the end result … "[1047]

The college submitted statements from two historians, neither a specialist in military history. Dr. Robert Bruce, professor emeritus of Boston University, had won the Pulitzer Prize for history in 1988 for The Launching of Modern American Science 1846-1876 and had collaborated with Boritt on two other works. Bruce wrote that the cut had "never been called to my attention as significant … " Harvard Civil War history professor Dr. William Gienapp said he had "never read anything about or seen any evidence substantiating the claim that an important action took place" there.[1048]

At the hearing, Frassanito and four other historians provided a history lesson on the importance of the action at Oak Ridge Railroad Cut during the first day's battle, using official reports, soldier accounts, maps and other primary sources.[1049] Bearss testified that he thought the excavation was an outrage, but confirmed that he did nothing to raise alarms after learning about it and did not formally object to assertions from the NPS that the railroad cut was not historically significant.[1050]

In a 2012 oral history interview, Bearss described the hearing with his well-known dramatic flourish, "Synar then opens the meeting at eight, and he hitches up his britches, and he says, 'There's going to be no recess to go to the bathroom. You'd better have good kidneys. There's going to be no recess for lunch. And you better, if you're on your own time out, you better leave someone here to take notes when you're not there.'"[1051]

Bearss recalled that it had been his understanding throughout the negotiations that the land swap "was not going to scar the area." But the park service "did not have the maps to show what was going to happen," he said. "I should have asked, 'Where are the maps?' They should have walked (us) through it. And no one did. And my dereliction would be I didn't insist on it."[1052]

After the hearing, Bearss recalled, the NPS bureaucrat who signed off on the land swap, a native of Gettysburg, "broke down and cried on the steps of the Rayburn House Office Building when we were leaving."[1053]

Frassanito would call the debacle "the great terrain robbery." The system was not broken, it was sidestepped, he said. "There is absolutely nothing wrong with the Federal, state, and municipal historic-preservation statutes as they currently stand," Frassanito wrote in a statement to accompany his testimony at the Synar hearing. "The disaster at Seminary Ridge resulted directly from a combination of mind-boggling incompetence, deceit, and the fact that these statutes, for whatever reason, were completely ignored by those charged with their enforcement."[1054]

The greatest tragedy of all, he wrote, was that even after it started, it could have been stopped. "The public caught this disaster in sufficient time to save the historic terrain," he wrote. "While incompetence may, perhaps, be excused in hindsight – the deliberate, cynical, and arrogant responses of both the NPS and Gettysburg College to the desperate pleas of the public and professional historians can never be condoned, forgiven, or forgotten."[1055]

After Synar's hearing, three outcomes were possible: complete restoration, mitigation, or no action at all. But the Oklahoma Democrat lost his primary that September. With his departure from Congress went hope for action. For the sake of constructing a little-used spur on the relocated rail line, the Civil War's greatest Civil War battlefield had been permanently scarred.[1056]

A more organized Civil War Preservation Trust (CWPT) would no doubt become involved in such a controversy today, but there is no mention of the railroad cut debacle in the minutes of the APCWS or the original Civil War Trust. The APCWS was four years old in 1991 and was busy buying land, including key battlefield acreage at Fisher's Hill. The Civil War Trust had just been founded. Frassanito did not recall that either organization actively supported the GBPA.[1057]

"We took on the struggle ourselves," Frassanito recalled. "We did everything humanly possible to expose this outrage. We sounded the alarm, we had people writing to their congressmen, and we sued in an effort to restore the site. But all of our efforts were thwarted by a federal agency in cover-up mode until Congressman Synar came to our rescue and forced the NPS to admit that everything the GBPA had been saying for three years was correct."[1058]

Today, the northeast corner of the railroad cut is a massive, rounded escarpment of huge gray boulders, held in place with wire mesh. Abandoned rail cars and other railroad debris litter the area. Frassanito does not expect the damage to the cut to be repaired. "We can only hope that NPS director Kennedy was successful in correcting the 'inadequacies' that contributed mightily to the evisceration of a unique terrain feature which had once been located safely within the protected boundaries of the national park," Frassanito said.[1059]

Fourteen years later, when a casino was proposed for Gettysburg, the CWPT wasted no time becoming involved in the fight. The project was proposed in the wake of Democratic Pennsylvania Gov. Ed Rendell's successful initiative to bring legal gambling to Pennsylvania so the state's gamblers could wager their money in-state. In July 2004, the Pennsylvania legislature approved allowing up to 61,000 slot machines at 14 casinos across the state in a controversial, dead-of-night vote.[1060]

Most were to be at existing race tracks, resorts or other pre-determined places, but two of the 14 approved casinos were designated to be "stand-alone" facilities in existing tourist areas.[1061] In April 2005, a group of investors led by local business leader David LeVan's company, Chance Enterprises, announced its intention to seek state approval for a $300 million Gettysburg Gaming Resort and Spa featuring a 3,000-slot gaming parlor, a 30,000-square-foot spa and a four-star hotel with 224 rooms. It was planned for 44 non-battlefield acres east of Gettysburg on Route 30 (York Road) at the U.S. 15 bypass.[1062]

LeVan was a local success story, a Gettysburg plumber's son who was chief executive officer at Conrail, Inc., from 1995 to 1998, retiring to his hometown to open and operate Battlefield Harley-Davidson and undertake good works for the community. He grew up on a battlefield farm sandwiched between Culp's Hill and Cemetery Ridge, and played war with his buddies on the battlefield itself.[1063]

LeVan "tools around town on a Harley with his ponytail blowing in the breeze," *The Hartford Courant* reported in 2006. He served as chairman of the board of his alma mater, Gettysburg College, and presided over a $100 million capital improvement program. He helped restore the Gettysburg train station where President Lincoln arrived in 1863 and raised money to restore and revive the Majestic Theatre just off the main square.[1064] LeVan told the *Courant* he proposed the casino project because he "could see the real potential from the economic impact … " As to the morality, he said, "I take the view that gambling is just another form of entertainment."[1065]

LeVan and his associates announced the project at a press conference in the Gettysburg Hotel ballroom on April 27, 2005. That morning, a local radio reporter told activist Mark Berg about the press conference. Berg attended and took a seat next to another local resident, Muriel Rice, and told her a bit too loudly, "I don't think this is a very good idea." An attorney for Chance Enterprises walked up to him and told him the session was only for reporters and he'd have to leave. Berg was escorted to the door.[1066]

No other citizens were kicked out, so Berg stood at the open door. They ordered him out of the hotel. He wouldn't go. "They tried to close the door, but I had my foot in the door and I kept it there so they couldn't close it," Berg recalled.[1067]

The hotel manager, whom Berg knew, showed up and sympathized with him, but said, "Just please do me a favor and leave." Berg complied. "I was, of course, a little annoyed at the whole thing," he said. "And I immediately went home and started working on a combination of things."[1068]

Berg reserved the meeting hall at the Adams County Agricultural and Natural Resource Center, put together a PowerPoint presentation on the problems of gambling and how they affected local communities, and on May 5 held a meeting of concerned citizens. More than 100 people showed up.

"Well, people were naturally very curious, and this meeting at the Ag Center was just packed," said Gettysburg resident Susan Star Paddock, who was involved from the start with her husband, Jim. About a week later, some 80 people showed up for a more serious organizing meeting at the Ragged Edge Coffee Shop, and from this meeting, the No Casino Gettysburg organization was created, with Susan Paddock as its president and Rice as vice president.[1069]

No Casino Gettysburg set up a table at a local antique fair and solicited signatures to petition the state not to approve the Gettysburg casino project. It was one of eight proposed casino projects vying for the two available "stand-alone" establishments. "The first day we set up, we got a thousand signatures in one day," Susan Paddock said. "It was unbelievable."[1070]

She and Jim developed lists of local businesses that were against the project. One list had businesses that were privately opposed; another had businesses willing to voice their opposition, including putting "No Casino" signs in their windows. Paddock set up a No Casino Gettysburg website and the organization began putting out a press release at least once a month lest the issue fade from the public eye.[1071]

They made presentations to the local Chamber of Commerce, Borough Council and Adams County Commission. Winning support with all of them was a challenge. The Chamber was clearly in favor of the project while the two local governmental entities seemed more split. Eventually they, too, came out in favor of the project.[1072]

The CWPT became involved soon after No Casino Gettysburg was formed. "We were pleased they existed because we knew we needed ground troops there," recalled Jim Campi. "The biggest concern we had was how close it was to East Cavalry Field, an area less than a mile away that the Trust had been very involved in preserving," Campi recalled. "Ultimately, we just could not see supporting gambling at Gettysburg. Initially, it looked like we were going up against a Goliath."[1073]

Although Campi had directed the Chancellorsville fight, No Casino Gettysburg "was more independent," he said. "They did their own thing and we did ours. But we provided a lot of support and there was constant communication."[1074] Campi helped organize a "Stop the Slots Coalition" that included No Casino Gettysburg and other local and regional opponents, such as Preservation Pennsylvania and national groups such as the National Trust for Historic Preservation.

The Pennsylvania Gaming Control Board (PGCB) in Harrisburg was tasked with deciding the winners and losers among the proposed projects. The Gaming Control Board was just getting organized, and a lawsuit over the constitutionality of the new gambling law had to be adjudicated first. The legal challenge was rejected by the Pennsylvania Supreme Court in late June 2005, but the court also established that local communities retained power over zoning in regard to casinos.[1075]

To ensure their presence was known, the Paddocks attended every PGCB public meeting in Harrisburg, no matter what was on the agenda. "We sat in the front row or as close as we could get to the front row in these T-shirts or sweatshirts that had 'No Casino Gettysburg,'" Susan Paddock said. "There was no public comment allowed in any of these meetings. So, we were absolutely silent. But we sat there and took notes about everything. And if they had some regulation about this or that they wanted comment on, we would comment on it."[1076]

After sitting quietly at every meeting for months, the Paddocks and other casino opponents came to have "a silent relationship" with board members, who soon became comfortable with these unthreatening, "very polite" protesters, Paddock recalled.[1077] Once, the chairman encountered Susan Paddock in the parking garage after the meeting and said, "You're falling down on your duty. You didn't come to our meeting." She told him she was in the back. From that hint of rapport, she realized their presence had made a difference.[1078]

To keep the issue active through periods of relative quiet, CWPT and No Casino Gettysburg took advantage of anniversaries and other occasions to hold rallies. On July 3, 2005, several hundred protesters gathered on the lawn at the Lutheran Theological Seminary for a Sunday evening "Solidarity with No Casino Gettysburg" candlelight vigil that included CWPT, the National Parks Conservation Association, the National Trust for Historic Preservation and the Friends of the National Park at Gettysburg.[1079]

While the casino proposal had significant local business and political support, it was different in the Pennsylvania state capital. In mid-July, the Paddocks received private encouragement from their Harrisburg contacts, who said that Rendell, a friend of LeVan's, actually opposed the project, as did most of the legislative leadership. "They saw it as political suicide," Susan Paddock recalled. But don't expect any public statements of support, they were told.[1080]

In mid-September, however, Rendell went public with his opposition, telling reporters: "I wouldn't want a casino two blocks from the Liberty Bell in Philadelphia and if it were my decision, I wouldn't want it anywhere close to the historic area of Gettysburg."[1081]

The following month, the CWPT rented a billboard on Route 30 that read, "Don't Gamble With Our Future!" They also gathered 33,208 signatures on petitions and letters opposing the project, tediously counted by hand by CWPT Grassroots Field Coordinator Mary Goundrey Koik, who was the organization's point person for many hearings and activities in Pennsylvania.[1082]

CWPT asked Brad Coker of Mason-Dixon Polling and Research to poll area residents. The results, released November 15, showed that 78 percent of those polled in a 10-county region around Gettysburg opposed the casino. Statewide, 65 percent of those polled opposed the project, 26 percent were in favor and nine percent were undecided.[1083]

"I think it shows beyond a reasonable doubt that this is a bad idea for central Pennsylvania," Campi told the *Hanover Evening Sun*.[1084] Casino investor Barbara Ernico countered: "We believe, when people hear about our project, they will rethink their position." [1085]

The anti-casino movement received another boost on November 22 when Pennsylvania State Representative Steve Maitland introduced a measure to ban any casinos from within 15 miles of an NPS battlefield or historic site. The bill was destined to die in the state senate in 2006, but not before receiving considerable publicity.

Four days before Christmas, Chance Enterprises submitted to local officials a "local impact report" predicting an average of almost 15,000 trips a day to the casino, but stating that it was unlikely the casino would adversely affect traffic, tourism, crime or the economy.

Campi called the report a "public relations device" and compared it to "an old-fashioned Christmas ornament"—pretty on the outside but hollow inside.[1086] Campi contacted another longtime CWPT associate, Michael Siegel of Public and Environmental Finance Associates, who had provided crucial economic analyses in the Disney and Chancellorsville fights. Campi put Siegel to work analyzing Chance's economic projections. Momentum seemed to remain with casino opponents, so much so that in January 2006, months before the public hearings about the project, Susan Paddock told *The Civil War News*, "We feel very hopeful."[1087]

In March 2006, the CWPT named Gettysburg as one of the 10 most endangered battlefields because of the casino threat, prompting LeVan to comment that it was amazing the battlefield went "to the top of the list overnight."[1088]

The fight became uglier as the Paddocks received death threats in the mail and by email. Other No Casino Gettysburg supporters received threats as well. Jim Paddock was pushed by an off-duty police officer at a press conference, who accused Paddock of doing the pushing.[1089]

"That ugliness was not one-sided," LeVan recalled. "There were plenty of ugly comments directed at me and my late wife, Jennifer. We also received anonymous threats and the one I remember most vividly was a letter that said, 'We can't wait until you die so we can come piss on your grave.'" The unsigned letter indicated it was sent by a Civil War legacy group, he said.[1090]

The casino proponents went after CWPT, attempting to get the Pennsylvania state attorney general's office to cancel CWPT's authorization to raise funds in the state. "We had to meet with the state attorney general's representatives to explain what we were doing, and to demonstrate we weren't doing anything illegal," Campi recalled. "It also made us more determined to defeat LeVan's casino plan."[1091]

The NPS and Gettysburg College took neutral stances, although the college's faculty members voted overwhelmingly to express their opposition.[1092] The Gettysburg Battlefield Preservation Association (GBPA) had changed in the 15 years since the railroad cut disaster; the board of directors remained officially neutral but lent tacit support to the project.[1093]

"They played into LeVan's hands, giving him a fig leaf to argue that preservation groups were divided on the issue," recalled Campi. "But the reality was that an overwhelming number of preservation groups opposed the casino. And that was the only organization that seemed to favor of it."[1094]

In the spring of 2006, the PGCB began holding hearings around the state. The three hearings on the Gettysburg proposal were April 5 and May 17 at the Gettysburg College student union building and April 7 in Harrisburg. On April 4, the eve of the first hearing, the CWPT released Siegel's analysis of the Chance Enterprises local impact report, which concluded that it was "erroneous, unreliable and misleading." Siegel said the Chance report exaggerated the amount of economic activity the casino would generate, the number of jobs it would create and failed to address a possible rise in crime.[1095]

Much of the Chance report focused on Vicksburg, Mississippi, where four casinos were built in the 1990s. The Chance report said the Vicksburg casinos had helped heritage tourism and brought more visitors to the battlefield. In Gettysburg, a "small but meaningful proportion of gamblers" would visit the battlefield, it said.[1096]

In fact, visitation at the Vicksburg battlefield "fell substantially," Siegel reported, and "continues to struggle" 13 years later to reach pre-casino visitation levels. The new report "confirms that a casino in Gettysburg is not just bad for history, it is also bad for business," CWPT President Jim Lighthizer said in a press release.[1097]

"I disagreed with Siegel's analysis and I think the history of gaming in Pennsylvania suggests otherwise," LeVan said in 2017. "All of the casinos in Pennsylvania are successful without any of the negatives that were thrown out. Crime and traffic have not been big issues and the success of the casinos is now well documented."[1098]

More than 300 people came to the first hearing, many wearing pro-casino or anti-casino T-shirts. As Susan Paddock spoke, 10 fellow casino opponents carried in cartons filled with petitions bearing 60,305 signatures. Twenty-six people spoke against the casino and eight in favor. The opponents outnumbered the supporters by about five to one at the Harrisburg hearing the following month.[1099]

In June, the focus of the struggle shifted to the local zoning board with jurisdiction over the proposed site. The Straban Township, Adams County, Zoning Hearing Board was to consider the request by Chance Enterprises to allow a special exception for commercial entertainment in a "commercial highway" zone. The issue got off to a particularly contentious start when Chance Enterprises challenged the impartiality of the top two members of the board, alleging that they had signed the No Casino Gettysburg petition. An Adams County judge decided that board Chairwoman Marcella Kammerer had to recuse herself, but Vice-Chairman Ed Gillespie did not.[1100]

The Straban zoning battle raged through the summer of 2006 and included five public hearings. Emotions ran high. During the fifth and final hearing on August 28, 2006, police issued a harassment citation to one casino opponent who kicked a casino supporter in the back.[1101]

On October 11, 2006, the zoning board decided in favor of Chance Enterprises, ruling that the casino was permitted in the commercial highway zone as long as the casino met 10 conditions related to signage, traffic and an adjacent park.[1102]

"It was just the most divisive, horrible thing for Straban Township," recalled Susan Paddock. "But it was exciting, too, because there was something every single day. Jim and I would wake up in the morning talking about the casino. It took over our entire lives. That's all we did. We stopped doing practically everything else."[1103]

On December 13, the gaming board held a final, three-hour hearing on the Gettysburg proposal at the State Museum in Harrisburg. Two busloads of casino backers came from Gettysburg, joining dozens of opponents as an estimated 300 people filled the museum hall. The decision was expected the following week, and after 20 months of struggle, LeVan was confident of victory, but so was No Casino Gettysburg.[1104]

The CWPT had spent countless hours fighting the project. "It was a wild time —with so many changed hearing dates and votes that we often had to do mailings, printings and phone calls at the last minute," Campi recalled. His filing cabinets were crammed with the paperwork of the campaign—sample opposition letters for both residents and businesses, heritage tourist talking points, mailings to historians, legislation material, petitions, opposition letters from Gettysburg kids and dozens of manila folders filled with news stories of the controversy. One newspaper alone, the *Evening Sun* of Hanover, reported that it had run more than 200 articles on the issue.[1105]

With little discernable support in Harrisburg, the Chance Enterprises Gettysburg casino proposal was doomed. On December 20, the Gaming Control Board announced the winners of 11 licenses. Developer and future president Donald J. Trump, who proposed a northwest Philadelphia casino, joined LeVan among the losers. Bethlehem and the Poconos won the stand-alone casino permits.[1106]

The board made no immediate comments about its decisions, but members later said opposition to the Gettysburg project played a role. But they were also concerned about the casino's ability to generate adequate revenues, particularly if nearby Maryland legalized slot machines.[1107]

Congratulatory calls poured into the CWPT's Washington office. "This is a great day for Gettysburg and for preservationists throughout the nation," Lighthizer said in a press release written by Campi. "By not allowing gambling to encroach on this famous town and battlefield, Pennsylvania has sent a clear message that it cares deeply for its historic treasures."[1108]

Campi and Koik headed from Harrisburg to Gettysburg for an afternoon champagne celebration at the Farnsworth House. "For those of us manning the fort in D.C., champagne will be served at 3 p.m. in the kitchen. Civil War songs will be sung," staff member Yvonne Barton announced in an email.[1109]

LeVan said he had no plans to appeal. "It's been a real long ride," he told the *Hanover Evening Sun*. "And, yeah, it was a difficult day, but I've had worse days…"[1110] It was a complete victory for the anti-casino forces, but LeVan was not one to take the defeat as ultimate surrender. He would be back. ★

CHAPTER SIXTEEN

Reclaiming the Franklin Battlefield

N 1996, a blue, craftsman-style house at 109 Cleburne Street in Franklin, Tennessee, with a broad front porch and triple dormers on the second floor, went on sale for $162,000.[1111]

To the casual observer, the "Blue House" at 109 Cleburne Street was just another house on just another street in Franklin. But Franklin attorney Julian Bibb wanted to buy it in the worst way. The unsightly presence of the backside of a strip mall as a next-door neighbor did not deter him. Bibb was president of the Heritage Foundation of Franklin and Williamson County and the Blue House sat on land that more than a century and a half ago had been the heart of a Civil War killing ground that rivaled any in that bloody war's history.[1112]

The Confederate frontal assault at Franklin on that beautiful Indian summer afternoon of November 30, 1864, was a spectacle larger than Pickett's Charge. With the sun's rays casting a fragile, golden light over the Tennessee countryside, 20,000 Confederates in General John Bell Hood's Army of the Tennessee swept across an open, gently sloping plain in a line two miles wide to make an all-out attack on a makeshift Union line.

Two divisions of Rebels, some 5,000 men, rushed toward a cotton gin that stood behind the Union line just off Columbia Avenue (then Columbia Turnpike) at the south edge of the town. The Carter cotton gin was to the battle of Franklin what the Copse of Trees was to Gettysburg's third day.

Confederate General Patrick Cleburne, one of six Confederate generals to die in the assault, was cut down before he reached the wooden structure. Cleburne's men continued to surge forward in the face of a murderous fire that included two Union guns firing triple canister. An artillery officer would never forget the cracking and popping sounds of breaking bones as the guns blasted clusters of men out of existence with every discharge. Hundreds of soldiers were killed or wounded around the cotton gin.[1113]

By the 1990s, the Franklin battlefield had been almost completely developed. The vast, open plain across which the Confederates advanced had filled with homes and businesses in much the same manner as the battlefield in front of the Stone Wall at Fredericksburg. Bibb and foundation executive director Mary Pearce still wanted that lot, though. "This is the *cotton gin*," he said to himself and others. "One day, this will be a big site to have."[1114]

"The Heritage Foundation didn't have any money," Bibb recalled. "But Mary Pearce and I talked our board into buying that house. We bought it from the owner with an owner's note. Then we just leased the house and paid our mortgage with the rent. We were holding it."[1115]

With the purchase of the Blue House, Franklin preservationists launched an initiative unlike any other in the battlefield preservation movement—the reclamation and restoration of a developed battlefield. Hand in hand with this achievement, however, have come stinging defeats. While the Heritage Foundation and other local preservation groups worked with the Civil War Preservation Trust to reclaim more land, the local Williamson County government constructed buildings on the battlefield, including a big county library just a few hundred feet from the Blue House lot.

"So, on one side of Columbia Avenue, you have buildings being torn down and buildings being moved as we reclaim part of the lost battlefield," said Pearce. "And on the other side, just up the street, you have the county building new buildings. That's just the truth."[1116]

The history of battlefield preservation in Franklin bespeaks almost a century of neglect, followed by a remarkable renaissance. Southerners bore no fond memories of the Confederate disaster at Franklin and little desire to preserve the scene of the tragedy. In 1899, when a Confederate Soldier Monument was dedicated on Franklin Square, the local United Daughters of the Confederacy (UDC) chapter also petitioned Congress to establish a battlefield park, but the effort went nowhere.[1117]

As the battlefield gradually became developed in the 20th century, the first fledgling preservation effort came in 1948, when Winstead Hill Ridge, where Hood's troops formed before the assault, was donated to the UDC. The land was preserved, later expanded and eventually became a city park. In 1971, the city bought and created another city park with 14.5 acres that included the remains of Fort Granger, a fort built in 1863 while Union troops occupied the city.[1118]

Downtown Franklin's transformation began with the creation in 1967 of the Heritage Foundation of Franklin and Williamson County, which was established after a historic house was demolished and replaced with a gas station. By 1984, when the Downtown Franklin Association was created to assist businesses, the city's core was thriving in the new, heritage-minded environment.

For many years, Franklin's Civil War heritage was focused on two antebellum mansions, the Carter House on Columbia Avenue in Franklin proper, which stood at the Union battle line, and Carnton, a plantation mansion outside of town that was at the right flank of the Confederate line's launching point. Carnton became a primary field hospital for the battered Confederates as they fell back after the disastrous charge. Its wood floors are permanently marked with large, ghastly spreads of blood stains left by wounded and dying Confederates. Its wartime owners, the McGavock family, helped tend to the wounded, and established a Confederate cemetery next to their mansion that holds the remains of almost 1,500 Southerners who fell in the battle.

Carnton fell into disrepair, but in 1977, local citizens formed the Carnton Association, restored the home and opened it for public tours. The Carter House, its bricks pockmarked with bullet craters, had opened to the public in 1953 after it was bought by the state of Tennessee.

The two wartime mansions operated independently and their leaders sometimes squabbled. When Pearce moved to Franklin in 1979, she remembers that "it was a lot about them being just beautiful, old homes that happened to have a Civil War history."[1119]

In 1989, as the Association for the Preservation of Civil War Sites (APCWS) was entering its second full year, Franklin Civil War enthusiasts formed Save The Franklin Battlefield (STFB). Three years later, the group saved its first land, acquiring an acre with an artillery lunette that was part of the Fort Granger complex.[1120]

The Heritage Foundation expanded its scope to embrace Franklin's Civil War heritage when it arranged and staged preservation conferences in 1992, 1993 and 1994 with local, state, and federal officials as well as the APCWS and original Civil War Trust. These included some of the first organized discussions about reclaiming part of the Franklin battlefield.[1121]

By 1994, Bibb had spent a decade leading or helping lead the Heritage Foundation as it transformed Franklin from just another Tennessee town into a charming, popular, history-rich destination. Bibb's Civil War roots were deep. His father's kin were Confederates; his mother's kin fought for the Union.

Growing up in Decatur, Georgia, in the 1960s, he would "walk down the river banks, looking for arrowheads," but also found minie balls and, once, even a soldier's belt buckle—discoveries "that would really light up your imagination," Bibb recalled. When the young graduate moved to Franklin in 1974, he knew that a battle had been fought there, but little else. That changed as the years passed and his interest in Franklin's Civil War history mushroomed.[1122]

In 1995, a year before the Blue House was offered for sale, development began to threaten Roper's Knob, an undeveloped, 994-foot peak overlooking Franklin from the northeast. The prominence held the well-preserved remains of a small Union fort built in 1862 after the army occupied Franklin and Nashville. Although fighting did not occur there, the fort was a vitally important signal station site for both sides, facilitating communication between Nashville and points south.

The Roper's Knob fort underscored the rich diversity of Franklin's Civil War history. In fact, *five* battles or engagements occurred at Franklin, including two in the spring of 1863 as well as clashes in September and December 1864, before and after the most famous battle.[1123]

Bibb and foundation members moved quickly to end the threat to Roper's Knob. "The Heritage Foundation, for the first time, stepped totally into the Civil War and bought 90 acres at the top of the hill," he recalled. "We stopped the rezoning and then bought it. We moved very quickly. We had a banker who loaned us the money with no collateral and no interest and off we went."[1124]

The foundation took an option to purchase the site in February 1996 for $438,500 and launched a campaign called "The Thousand Friends of Roper's Knob," to raise $100,000 locally in a thousand $100 donations. Help came from the state, too, through the Tennessee Wars Commission. The APCWS kicked in $5,000. A last-minute burst of donations leveraged $10,000 in matching funds from the original Civil War Trust to help secure the purchase.[1125]

During the campaign to save Roper's Knob, the Blue House went on sale. The house was built after the war on a lot two blocks north of its present location. When the city bought the property in the 1920s for a new high school, a Franklin resident considered the house distinctive enough to buy it and move it about 1,000 feet south to the then-vacant lot at 109 Cleburne Street. The attractive house was set back from the street, with a deep front lawn. But as Franklin grew, the neighborhood changed. A small strip mall went up on the northeast corner of Cleburne Street and Columbia Avenue, and the Blue House was adjacent to the mall's rear parking area and the dumpsters of a Domino's Pizza outlet and a Mexican restaurant.[1126]

The site's history was all but unknown to Bibb and other students of the battle. Their knowledge was limited to an early post-war map's placement of the Carter cotton gin on the Blue House lot.[1127]

As purchase negotiations continued for the house, a special task force that included Bibb spent seven months studying the feasibility of a battlefield park around

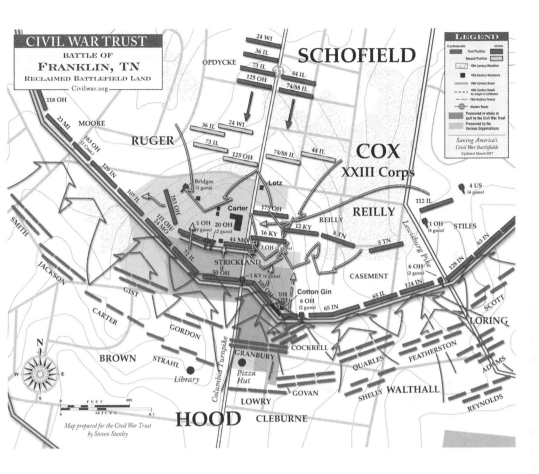

the Carter House and the nearby Blue House lot. With real progress being made, discussions turned to a strategy to reclaim more battlefield land. Bibb was authorized to begin negotiations to acquire the strip mall as well as a Pizza Hut across the street, on the southeast corner of Cleburne and Columbia, where the Confederate general fell.

The "dream plan" for a Franklin battlefield park on both sides of Columbia Avenue near the Carter House was introduced in late April, 1997. "Fifteen years ago, downtown Franklin was a dream," said Stephen Biggers, a local business executive who was on the task force. "A lot of people said then that downtown couldn't be revitalized, but it was. We think this dream can become a reality, too."[1128]

Less than two months later, on June 4, 21 local preservationists and community leaders gathered at the front porch of the Blue House for a ceremonial closing on that property. Goodwill abounded as praise and thanks were extended to the heritage-minded seller Roy Barker, who offered the property at an affordable price, as well as realtor Danny Anderson and attorney Bibb, who donated their professional services. It was "the first step" toward the foundation's goal "to develop a battlefield park … near the Carter House," reported the *Williamson Leader* of June 5, 1997.

The Blue House itself, with an impressive central staircase, original fireplaces and beadboard paneling, was bought by a preservation-minded Franklin couple, Sharon and John McNeely, for $7,500, separated into two parts and trucked 50 miles south to be rebuilt on their 25-acre, Tennessee country estate in Giles County.[1129]

Victory at Roper's Knob came on August 25, 1997, when the debt was paid off in full. As almost 500 celebrants looked on, Pearce lit the mortgage on fire and raised the flaming papers to the sky, declaring, "This year, we're burning the note on Roper's Knob. Next, let's burn the notes on Domino's Pizza and Pizza Hut sites!"[1130] It was an ambitious pronouncement; the foundation had only begun exploring purchase of those properties.

It was a summer of achievement for preservation in Franklin, mostly due to the work of Franklin's own preservationists. With only modest help from national preservation organizations, two different local groups were building impressive track records.

In 1998, after the county proposed an expanded community center just north of the Carter House on the site of the old Franklin High School, local preservationists worked out a land swap that moved the location of the new center farther from the house.[1131]

In June 2001, after eight months of negotiations, STFB made its second save, purchasing for $227,000 the 3.22-acre Collins Farm property, which was a killing ground in the battle as a division of Confederates charged across it under intense Union fire. It was also a field hospital after the battle.

The acreage at Collins Farm and Roper's Knob was eventually transferred to the City of Franklin to become new city parks.[1132] The city, rejuvenated by promoting its heritage, welcomed the preservation movement with open arms. Williamson County, however, was another story. In 2000, the county announced plans for two separate construction projects on battlefield land, triggering simultaneous preservation battles.

Bibb and Pearce already had experience fighting for preservation. Bibb and other foundation members had once literally faced off with bulldozers, forming a human circle around a stand of 150-year-old trees to prevent their destruction.[1133] Pearce had successfully stopped a city plan to allow light industrial development on Winstead Hill. She had also helped thwart a plan to build HUD housing around the Harrison House, a circa-1810 mansion about two miles south of Franklin on

Columbia Pike. (Columbia Avenue becomes "Pike" outside of Franklin.) Confederate General John Bell Hood convened his final meeting with his generals and staff officers at Harrison House before watching his 20,000 troops begin their awesome charge.

Pearce went to battle once again in early November 2000, when the Williamson County Board of Education announced plans to build an elementary school on hallowed ground almost directly across Columbia Pike from the Harrison House.[1134]

On both sides of the pike, open space spread a quarter mile north from the Harrison House to Winstead Hill Park. The board of education had its sights on a section of the undeveloped property on the eastern side of the pike, across from Harrison House. The targeted property was where 24-year-old Confederate General John Herbert Kelly was mortally wounded while leading his brigade in an assault during a small engagement on September 2, 1864. He died two days later at the Harrison House.

The owner of the land sought by the school board didn't want to sell, but the board planned to force the sale by starting condemnation proceedings. The board's plan touched off a months-long struggle, led by Pearce and Harrison House owner Pam Lewis. And it prompted the new Civil War Preservation Trust (CWPT) to get involved.

A second battle erupted in December 2000 when Williamson County made an 11th hour decision to build its new library in the heart of what had been the Franklin battlefield, less than 300 yards southwest of the cotton gin site. In 1864, Confederates had fallen in droves as they charged across this property, closing in on the Union line.

For months, the county had been planning to build the new library on Second Avenue in downtown Franklin. But late in the process, on December 14, 2000, the county commissioners decided to abandon the Second Avenue site in favor of purchasing the property of the Battle Ground Academy (BGA) on Columbia Avenue, two blocks south of the Carter House. To put it in historical perspective, the library site on the Franklin battlefield would be comparable to a library at Gettysburg on Emmitsburg Road in front of the copse of trees. The county's plan was not only to build a library, but to make the BGA campus home to a performing arts center, a county archives and other cultural attractions.

When the BGA was founded in Franklin in 1889, the original school building was constructed on the cotton gin sit—the Blue House lot. A 1902 fire destroyed the original building, and a new building was constructed several hundred yards south on the other side of Columbia Avenue. The entire area, which had been a killing zone when the assaulting Confederate army approached the Union line at the Carter

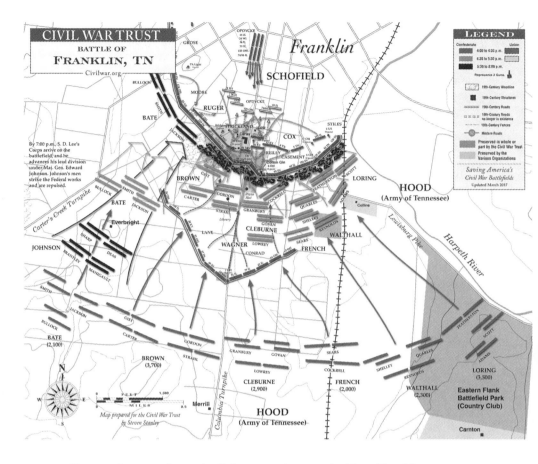

Map prepared for the Civil War Trust by Steven Stanley

House and cotton gin, gradually became crisscrossed with residential streets.

In 1996, the BGA moved to new facilities north of the center of town and made plans to sell the battlefield property. "The Battle Ground Academy needed to move and they needed the money from selling the old location," Pearce said. "They could sell it to someone else, such as a developer, and some were interested. But many Franklin citizens and some of the leaders had graduated from the academy. It was a beloved location. It was a way for BGA to turn the legacy over to the county government instead of a developer. It was a win-win, with everybody winning but battlefield preservation."[1135]

For months, Pearce had supported the county's plan to build the new library downtown. The sudden change to the BGA land, made at the December 2000 meeting, left her devastated. The next morning, she left to visit her son Steven in Atlanta for the holidays. "I remember crying all the way to the airport," Pearce said. "I was just bawling. I was exhausted. It was a heart-breaking loss, a crushing loss in my mind. I remember kind of being thankful that I was going to be gone for a few days."[1136]

But the fight had only begun. As preservationists lobbied the commissioners, wrote letters to local newspapers and campaigned against the library relocation, the Battle Ground Academy Board of Trustees voted in January 2001 to sell the Columbia Avenue campus to the county "for the site of the county's new library and other community facilities." [1137]

For the next few months, however, the school site controversy, rather than the library, dominated the headlines. In February, preservationists stood up one by one at a meeting of the Williamson County Board of Education and "bombarded" the board members with emotional appeals to relocate the school site. The new school, preservationists argued, would ruin the view from Harrison House and other nearby historic properties and forever mar the natural setting. Lewis spoke of being "economically stupid and foolish" with how far she had gone to restore and preserve the Harrison House, including lowering the property value by putting it under the protection of a historic easement.[1138]

The board was unmoved. By April it had condemned and taken possession of the school site. That month, CWPT President Jim Lighthizer visited Franklin for the first time and spoke at the April 14 meeting of the Tennessee Civil War Preservation Association.[1139] The CWPT was well past the merger difficulties and moving full steam ahead in 2001 on land acquisition and threat assessments. In February, CWPT issued its first Top 10 Endangered Battlefields list and gained great press coverage. Franklin did not make the top 10, but was on a secondary list of 15 other endangered battlefields.[1140]

In May 2001, the Heritage Foundation threw its weight behind the fight to save the school site. It guaranteed that it could find other land that met the board's criteria that would not have to be condemned and taken from an unwilling seller. It asked for a 30-day delay. As an alternative, it offered the board $350,000 to move the school behind a tree line that would protect the view from the road and the Harrison House.[1141]

The board rejected these pleas. It was ready to grade the land as soon as the farmer who had been renting it finished harvesting his hay.[1142] The foundation and preservation supporters came out in force to the board's June meeting, again asking for a delay. This time, on a seven-to-five vote, the board granted the preservationists two weeks to find another site, but wanted at least $1 million to cover costs incurred. As the foundation scrambled to respond, good news came in June on another front as the STFB announced its purchase of the Collins Farm.[1143]

CWPT became directly involved in the school site fight in early July 2001, as

Brad Coker and Mason-Dixon Polling and Research polled 502 registered county voters by telephone, asking whether they opposed or supported relocating the elementary school to another site. Seventy-eight percent favored relocating the school.[1144]

But the battle was lost at the school board's July meeting. For more than an hour, the preservationists again pleaded their case. The foundation said it had come up with at least half of the money to repay the county, but not $1 million. Work was already underway. The school building pad was complete and the new storm water pipes were on site. Although the land grading had uncovered shell fragments and other wartime relics, the board was unmoved. "If (the school) didn't move tonight, it won't," board Chair Jean Keith said.[1145]

Pearce told *Civil War News* she was in tears for nearly three days after the fight. "I don't lose many of these battles, and this one was particularly difficult," she said. "It makes me feel inadequate, like there was something I should have done differently." Pearce said the struggle "was like a roller coaster ride for much of the summer ... " Preservationists would gain a foothold, "only to be pushed back by requirements and aggressive deadlines."[1146]

If there was a silver lining, it was that the Heritage Foundation obtained preservation easements on hundreds of acres of undeveloped land around the new school —Winstead Elementary School—preventing further destruction of historic land.[1147]

The school battle was lost, but the library fight continued. The STFB August 2001 newsletter published the addresses of the county executive, the 24 county commissioners and the six trustees of the Williamson County Public Library system and urged its members to write and ask that the library site be moved.[1148] In mid-September, however, the county voted to spend up to $8 million to build the new library on the BGA land. Commissioner Lou Green defended the action, saying, "We are building a War Memorial Library on a battlefield."[1149]

Two commissioners were opposed to the BGA site for the library and in October offered a resolution to establish a battlefield park on the entire 12 acres of the old campus. The full commission limited public input to five speakers, then rejected the resolution. The commission offered a compromise plan to devote part of the BGA land for a memorial park, but did not waver on the library. In December, architects unveiled their plan for a two-story, 50,225-square foot library. By then, the threat had become a CWPT priority.

Franklin was one of the nation's "10 Most Endangered Civil War Battlefields" in February 2002 when the CWPT issued its second annual listing. Lighthizer and the STFB's Sam Huffman held a press conference at the Carter House on March 5.

"Franklin needs to stop paving over its history," Lighthizer said. "Putting up a few historical markers is not enough. We must preserve the hallowed ground where the dead of Franklin fought and bled."[1150]

A few days later, CWPT's Jim Campi and his wife, Jennifer, were visiting Jennifer's ailing grandmother in New Hampshire. Among the staff, Campi is famous for having vacations and time off routinely interrupted by urgent CWPT matters, and this time was no different. He received a call from actor and TV celebrity Ben Stein, whose television show, "Win Ben Stein's Money," was a popular Comedy Central staple. Stein, a strong advocate of battlefield preservation, had begun trading e-mails with Campi after seeing the CWPT's endangered battlefields list.[1151]

"He indicated he was going to be in the Franklin area and really wanted to do a tour," Campi recalled. "And I said, 'Well, I'll set it up. Would you mind if we have a reporter tag along?' He agreed to that, and did the tour." Working the phone in his hotel room, Campi made the arrangements. Stein toured Franklin on March 18, 2002.[1152]

"When I read that this site was in jeopardy, I was moved to make a contribution and come here," Stein said in a press conference at the Carter House. "Franklin will get some of Ben Stein's money. Franklin got $1,000 and it's about to get $1,000 more." He designated the contributions to go toward CWPT land purchases at Franklin.[1153]

Stein's Franklin visit was well-covered by the media. Dozens of newspapers across the nation published stories. But nothing changed on the county commission. On April 30, 2002, the commission voted 19–2 to build the library on the BGA site. Two days later, construction of the $9.5 million facility was underway.[1154] "For me, that was the lowest moment at Franklin," recalled Campi. "We just weren't making a lot of progress."[1155]

"There wasn't a well-developed plan of 'save it for the battlefield' then," recalled Bibb. "It was just, 'Don't put that there.' But the battlefield had been developed. They weren't tearing down the Carter House to build the library."[1156]

"We had good footing on battlefield preservation back then," recalled Pearce. "We had really gained some ground by the time the library was proposed. We were working hard and making huge headway. But the county's elected officials were not getting this vision. I tried with all my might to stop the library from being built on the BGA campus. We just simply did not have the political muscle with the county to make that happen."[1157]

In February 2003, Lighthizer visited Franklin for the third time in three years. The elementary school had opened the previous fall. The library was under construction. The CWPT had been involved from afar in two losing conflicts and Lighthizer was not happy with how the locals had fought the battles. No fewer than four independent local preservation-minded organizations existed in Franklin, but sometimes they operated at cross purposes.

Lighthizer met at the Carter House on February 21 with a group of about a dozen key local preservationists representing the four groups. "Get into politics or get out of preservation!" he bluntly told them. "Form a coalition and have a specific plan, like what parcels of land you want and what to do with them. You make your mind up and call me when you do."[1158]

Pearce, for one, might have taken offense when Lighthizer "read us the riot act," given all she had done and the successes she had helped achieve. But she agreed with him. "I thought it was deserved," she recalled. "Because we were losing with the county. And I thought it would engage a few more people in the fight. But I also think it was Jim Lighthizer selling *himself* on digging in here and helping us out."[1159]

After Lighthizer's visit, the CWPT went from helpful but distant friend to "gigantic partner," Pearce recalled. "And when Jim Lighthizer decides to become a community partner, the magic happens. He is compelling, he has an incredible staff, he has incredible wisdom and he has political connections."[1160]

The Franklin preservationists, however, had to endure another defeat, this time at the hands of the City of Franklin. In April 2003, just weeks after Lighthizer's visit, a developer asked the Franklin Planning Commission to rezone a 48-acre parcel of historic land from light industrial to commercial so he could build a 48,000-foot retail development that would include a Target store, a Kroger grocery store and other businesses.[1161] The property is on Columbia Avenue at the northern base of Winstead Hill. No fighting took place there, but much like Stuart's Hill in the Battle of Second Manassas, it was the launching point of the center of the Confederate line in its assault. From an overlook on Winstead Hill, the view of Franklin would be dominated by the shopping center.[1162]

Preservationists opposed the rezoning and city engineers expressed concerns about increased traffic, but the planning commission recommended rezoning by a vote of four to three and sent the request on to the City of Franklin Board of Mayor and Aldermen for three readings in the following three monthly meetings.[1163]

Although opposition intensified, the request sailed through the rezoning process. Several aldermen said they had heard from around 200 people and the tally was heavily in favor of rezoning. Another said his phone calls were running about 50-50. On July 8, 2003, the city's leaders voted five to three to rezone; the shopping center was built and soon open for business.[1164]

But the preservationists took Lighthizer's lecture to heart and began to do things differently. At least seven local organizations formed to create a coalition that fought the shopping center rezoning. The new group included the Heritage Foundation, the STFB, and the Carnton and Carter Houses. The different groups became comfortable working together.[1165]

The preservationists also became successful in politics, at least in the city. In the November 2003 election, three incumbents—the longtime mayor and two city aldermen—were swept from office by candidates who favored preservation and slow growth, one of whom was Pam Lewis. An incumbent alderman, staunch preservationist Ernie Bacon, was reelected.[1166]

During Lighthizer's March 2003 visit, one of his stops was at Carnton, where he and his wife received a tour from Nashville music producer Robert Hicks, the driving force behind the mansion's latest restoration and revival. The convivial Hicks was full of energy and the Civil War reverberated in his family's history. His ancestors hailed from Hicksville, Tennessee and several generations had married late in life, which gave him a grandfather born in 1860. When he sat at the elderly man's feet, he heard war stories from personal experience. Recalled Hicks: "My grandfather would say, 'Do you see over there? Over that hill, I saw the Union Army come to our farm.'"[1167]

Hicks, who lives outside Franklin in Williamson County at "Labor in Vain," a log cabin home exquisitely appointed with antiques, has long been enthralled with Carnton and its story. Built by slaves in 1826 for local politician Randal McGavock, Carnton had been at the center of 19th-century Tennessee politics since the days of Andrew Jackson. After the fateful battle of November 30, more than 6,200 Confederates lay dead, wounded or were missing, and Carnton was overwhelmed with casualties. The bodies of four of the six Rebel generals who died were laid out on the mansion's porch.

Hicks became involved in the Carnton Association in the early 1990s and was soon elected president. He embarked on a savvy restoration of the mansion that was both budget-minded and of the highest quality, and Carnton reopened for public tours in the late 1990s. Hicks felt proud as he gave the Lighthizers their tour, describing the restoration in detail and the resourceful strategies he had used to keep costs low.[1168]

As they stood at a window open to the Tennessee countryside, Lighthizer spoke. "Look, Robert, you've done a wonderful job saving this house. It's beautiful," he said. "But now you have to start looking outside this window. Now you need to step outside this house and *really* do something. Now you need to start dealing with land."[1169]

It was as if Lighthizer took "a bucket of cold water and threw it on me," Hicks recalled. But the phrases "you need to really do something" and "start dealing with land" kept repeating in his mind.[1170]

That summer, the financially strapped 110-acre Franklin Country Club adjacent to Carnton went on the market. Hicks knew if he didn't move quickly on the 110-acre property, Carnton itself would be threatened. A developer had bought the land for development but was operating the country club for now. He had wanted to reduce the golf course from 18 to nine holes and build 150 townhomes, some bordering Carnton's Confederate cemetery. But the developer changed his mind and now wanted to sell the land outright. Hicks knew he had to buy the country club, but had no idea how.[1171]

Hicks called local friends and preservation leaders to Carnton's porch, where the slain generals had lain. One of the attendees knew the developer socially, and Hicks learned that he had become fed up dealing with club members, prompting his decision to sell. The price was $5 million.[1172]

Hicks came up with a plan. "My plan was to go visit a friend of mine," Hicks recalled. "He was a descendent of the McGavocks." The friend was Rod Heller, founder of the original Civil War Trust. And with perfect timing, Heller and his wife Kay invited Hicks to a ball in Washington, D.C.[1173] Heller's grandmother was Hattie McGavock, the last of the McGavocks born and raised at Carnton. "I was always interested in Carnton because I'd heard the family stories," Heller recalled.[1174]

After the ball, Heller asked Hicks if he had any active projects. As Hicks recalled the exchange:

"Yes, I'm going to buy the golf course and we're going to convert it back into the battlefield," Hicks said.

"It's none of our business, but how much is that going to cost you?" Heller asked.

"He wants $5 million," replied Hicks.

"Where are you going to get that?"

"Well, I have some people I am going to ask to buy it, and they're going to buy it and hold it until I can put together a campaign to raise the money to buy it back from them," Hicks said.

"Well, that's fantastic," Heller said. "Again, it's none of our business, but could you tell us who that is?"

"Well," Hicks replied, "it *is* kind of your business. It's you all."[1175]

The Hellers were already aware of the threat to their ancestral home if the golf course was developed. After deliberating overnight, with Kay Heller in strong support, the couple agreed to buy it and hold it until the preservationists could buy it back from them at the same price. The purchase was formally announced in October

Chantilly Battlefield Association founders (from left) Ed Wenzel, Brian Pohanka and Clark "Bud" Hall stand at the Kearny and Stevens monuments on the Chantilly battlefield in November 1994. **CLARK B. HALL COLLECTION**

Pioneering preservationist Jerry Russell at the Civil War Preservation Trust 2002 annual conference in Chattanooga, Tennessee, where he was awarded the Edwin C. Bearss Lifetime Achievement Award. **CIVIL WAR TRUST**

Four of the eight founders of the Association for the Preservation of Civil War Sites (from left), A. Wilson Greene, Robert K. Krick, Gary W. Gallagher and Dennis E. Frye, on the Antietam battlefield during a June 1988 APCWS seminar.

GARY W. GALLAGHER COLLECTION

National Park Service historian Donald C. Pfanz, who wrote the 1987 letter that led to the founding of the APCWS and started the modern battlefield preservation movement. **CIVIL WAR TRUST**

The tireless preservationist, Annie Snyder, on the Manassas battlefield in 1988 during the William Center fight. **MANASSAS NATIONAL BATTLEFIELD PARK**

A 1988 aerial view shows grading and road building for development of part of the William Center complex at Stuart's Hill at Manassas.

MANASSAS NATIONAL BATTLEFIELD PARK

United States Treasurer Mary Ellen Withrow and Civil War Trust President Matt Andrews unveiled the U.S. Mint's Civil War commemorative coins at the battlefield at Mill Springs, Kentucky, in 1995. **CIVIL WAR TRUST**

In 1989, APCWS raised money from simple tents erected at battle reenactments by marketing T-shirts, selling raffle tickets for a Don Troiani print and soliciting coins and bills in a large glass water bottles. This effort focused on the emerging threat at Brandy Station. **CIVIL WAR TRUST**

From left, Civil War Preservation Trust trustees Paul Bryant, Jr., John Haynes and President Jim Lighthizer at the Chattanooga conference in 2002. **CIVIL WAR TRUST**

The preservation of the Widow Pence Farm at Cross Keys, Virginia, in 2000 was among the first significant preservation coups by the new Civil War Preservation Trust. **CIVIL WAR TRUST**

Celebrity Ben Stein helped CWPT preserve key tracts at Franklin, Tennessee, and headlined the Most Endangered Battlefields press conference in 2006. **CIVIL WAR TRUST**

Since 2001, the Trust has saved 442.5 acres at Monocacy battlefield— the "Battle that Saved Washington" near Frederick, Maryland, in 1864. **CHRIS HEISEY**

From left, National Park Service retired Chief Historian Edwin C. Bearss, former Secretary of the Interior Manuel Lujan, and History Channel vice president Libby O'Connell with Civil War Preservation Trust President Jim Lighthizer in 2006. **CIVIL WAR TRUST**

On January 14, 2003, snow fell on a candlelight demonstration against Dogwood Development Group's planned development on the Chancellorsville battlefield. "It was the prettiest protest I've ever seen," a columnist wrote. **CIVIL WAR TRUST**

Secretary of the Interior Dirk Kempthorne announced a $2 million government grant to help preserve the Slaughter Pen Farm battlefield at Fredericksburg on October 16, 2006. The $12 million acquisition was the most expensive in Trust history. **CIVIL WAR TRUST**

The preservation of the first day's battlefield at Chancellorsville demonstrated CWPT's willingness to work with developers, in this case Tricord Homes and Toll Brothers. Hundreds turned out for the 2005 trail opening. **CIVIL WAR TRUST**

Civil War Trust leaders at Antietam in 2008 included, from left, Director of Real Estate Tom Gilmore, Director of Internet Strategy Rob Shenk, President Jim Lighthizer, Director of Development David Duncan and Senior Vice President Frank Deluca. **CIVIL WAR TRUST**

Trust President Jim Lighthizer with Tennessee Representative Steve McDaniel (center), a tireless battlefield advocate, and Civil War Trust Chairman (2013-15) Mike Grainger (right) at Parker's Cross Roads, Tennessee. **CIVIL WAR TRUST**

The Civil War Trust has sponsored its annual Park Day since 1996, organizing tens of thousands of volunteers to help with maintenance at hundreds of battlefields and historic sites. Here, participants help restore a historic foundation at Fayetteville, North Carolina. **CIVIL WAR TRUST**

When a developer dug 1,900-foot utility trenches on land the Civil War Trust had preserved and donated to the National Park Service at Harpers Ferry, West Virginia, preservationists and the NPS cried foul. Before long, the developer was in bankruptcy.
CIVIL WAR TRUST

Tennessee Civil War Battlefield Preservation Association Executive Director Mary Ann Peckham with Civil War Trust Chief Policy and Communications Officer Jim Campi (center) and Franklin's Charge co-founder and best-selling author Robert Hicks, who brought his dog to a 2010 Trust event in Spring Hill, Tennessee. **CIVIL WAR TRUST**

In 2008, the CWPT helped preserve the last remaining privately held land on Morris Island, South Carolina, made famous in *Glory*, the Academy Award-winning 1989 Civil War-themed movie. **CIVIL WAR TRUST**

The fights against proposed Gettysburg casinos were grassroots scraps reminiscent of early APCWS days. From left, Alan Spears of the National Parks and Conservation Association with No Casino Gettysburg's Susan Paddock and the Trust's Mary Goundrey Koik along a Gettysburg parade route. **CIVIL WAR TRUST**

Since 2005, the Trust has preserved 272 acres at the 1861 battlefield at Wilson's Creek, Missouri. **CIVIL WAR TRUST**

Passing a "For Sale" sign on property the Trust had just purchased at Shiloh battlefield in April 2012, Trust President Jim Lighthizer could not resist updating the sign with a Sharpie, designating the property as "SOLD." **CIVIL WAR TRUST**

The late Henry Simpson, left, Trust chairman in 2011-13, joined country music artist and Trustee Trace Adkins, Gettysburg National Military Park Superintendent Bob Kirby and Pulitzer Prize-winning historian James M. McPherson in 2011 to announce the sesquicentennial fundraising program, *Campaign 150.* Trust members and others exceeded the $40 million goal by more than 30 percent. **CIVIL WAR TRUST**

After many years of waiting and negotiation, the Trust in 2013 finally acquired the crest of Brandy Station's Fleetwood Hill. By 2015, the Trust had removed the modern house, restored the hilltop and installed an interpretive trail. **CIVIL WAR TRUST**

In the Civil War Trust's high-profile effort to preserve Lee's Headquarters at Gettysburg, President Jim Lighthizer walked the property with CBS News correspondent Martha Teichner before restoration began in 2016. **CIVIL WAR TRUST**

Battlefield experiences remain the hallmark of the Trust's educational efforts. Here, Trust Director of History and Education Garry Adelman conducts a tour at Gettysburg in 2014 with longtime Trustee Dr. Mary Munsell Abroe (center), Trust Chairman (2015-17) Kirk Bradley (right), and others. **CIVIL WAR TRUST**

At the first of the Trust's many *Generations* events in 2015 led by Garry Adelman, a crowd of more than 250 family members and friends retrace the route of Pickett's Charge. **BRUCE GUTHRIE**

The Civil War Trust expanded its mission in 2014 to include battlefields of the Revolutionary War and the War of 1812, with President Jim Lighthizer announcing *Campaign 1776* at Princeton, New Jersey, on Veterans Day, November 11.

CIVIL WAR TRUST

The Civil War Trust staff in 2015. **CIVIL WAR TRUST**

2003 and the Hellers continued to lease the course to the club members.

"My only trick in the bag" was to ask the Hellers to buy the property, Hicks recalled. "We're very grateful, because they were the key to this vision I had. I don't know that we ever had another answer. They came through magnificently."[1176]

Heller, whose Washington, D.C., venture capital firm is named Carnton Capital Associates, spent childhood summers in Tennessee at a nearby farm. "We all just loved Tennessee," he recalled. "We were brought up in family history. It became clear that the land would be lost and developed unless someone stepped up. Obviously, my wife and I did. We said from the inception that we would sell it at our cost."[1177]

Hicks knew it would take a monumental fundraising effort to buy the property. He scheduled a lunch meeting with Franklin's preservation leaders and recommended that they formally organize as a single Franklin preservation fundraising group while retaining their individual identities. Hicks spoke eloquently and passionately about preserving Franklin's history. Bibb spoke up, "I can't think of anyone who should be heading this up more than Robert."[1178]

Hicks turned to Bibb and asked, "Julian, will you be my co-chair?" and Bibb agreed. Initially adopting the name Coalition for the Preservation of Historic Open Space, the group became Franklin's Charge the following year.

"Julian was the best partner to work with that I could have ever had," recalled Hicks. "And so, Julian and I led the organization. We began to add people to it. And we began to meet every Friday for the next year and a half. Every Friday." [1179]

It was always at the end of the work day, recalled CWPT staff member Mary Goundrey Koik, and while the meetings in Tennessee were highly productive, they also had a happy hour atmosphere and "it was a kind of torture" for the CWPT staffer in Washington who had to stay late Friday and listen in. When the night cleaning crew arrived, the staff would have to mute his speakerphone microphone lest those in Tennessee be overwhelmed by the noise of vacuums.[1180]

Despite the earlier setbacks, the Franklin preservation movement made an extraordinary comeback in 2004. In August, new Franklin Mayor Tom Miller unexpectedly announced the city's intention to buy the Pizza Hut at Columbia Avenue and Cleburne Street to reclaim the land where Cleburne fell.[1181] Miller had not run on a preservation platform, but after taking office, he helped lead the charge.

Miller's next recommendation, which he made just days later, was even more startling; If the preservationists could raise $2.5 million for the golf course next to Carnton, the city should match it.[1182]

To cap off that remarkable month, on Friday night, August 20, 2004, the Coalition for the Preservation of Historic Open Space was officially launched as Franklin's

Charge in a gala under a big white tent outside Carnton. Hicks knew top recording artists in Nashville and called his friends, Vince Gill and Amy Grant, for help. Before making his pitch, Hicks told Grant: "If you have a brain in your head, you'll hang up!" But once he explained in his typical storytelling fashion what he needed and why, "I was hooked," Grant said.[1183]

"Here in Franklin, we live in exciting times, indeed!" wrote STFB President Joe Smyth in the August 2004 newsletter.

At the Franklin's Charge party, Grant sang Joni Mitchell's *Big Yellow Taxi* and its famous lyric: "They paved paradise and put up a parking lot." Hicks told the audience Franklin's Charge had nearly $875,000 in pledges with which to match the city's challenge, including $500,000 from CWPT.[1184]

Country club members fought the preservationists in efforts that included an "open letter" to Gill and Grant, claiming, "They plowed paradise and put up a weed field." They criticized the preservation movement's aim "to destroy a community to manufacture a battlefield."[1185]

In early 2005, the CWPT commissioned another poll that showed that 61 percent of Franklin's residents approved of using public money to save the battlefield land at the golf course. Miller's proposal to help buy the country club won full support of the Franklin Board of Mayor and Aldermen, which proposed a $10 million bond issue to fund the country club purchase as well as acquisition of 200-acre Harlinsdale Farm, birthplace of the Tennessee walking horse, in northeast Franklin. Harlinsdale Farm also was the scene of several minor Civil War engagements.[1186]

As bad as the year 2001 had been for preservationists, the year 2005 was good. That spring, the city agreed to buy the Pizza Hut building and lot for $300,000. Later that year, STFB made the final mortgage payment on Collins Farm. Negotiations continued on terms of the golf course acquisition.

On November 30, 2005, the Pizza Hut building was torn down. It was a crisp and sunny morning, not unlike the day of the battle exactly 141 years before. A jubilant crowd of about 200 that included Lighthizer, Ed Bearss, Congressman Lincoln Davis and dozens of local preservationists gathered as Miller struck the first blow with a 10-pound sledgehammer. Lighthizer, Bearss and Davis took their turns. Then Miller hopped onto the seat of a backhoe, punched a hole through the roof of the building, and the demolition began in earnest. By sundown, the structure was down and all but removed. The property was well on its way to becoming one of the first pieces of the Carter Hill Battlefield Park.[1187]

Several days before the ceremony at the Pizza Hut, Franklin's Charge announced it had secured the $2.5 million needed to meet the city's matching offer for purchase of the Franklin County Club. During the Pizza Hut ceremony, Miller and Heller surprised the crowd by taking seats at a table and signing the contract to sell the acreage to the City of Franklin.

Earlier that morning, they had hammered out the final details of what had become a complicated $5 million transaction. In the end, the money for the country club's 110.78 acres came from several sources, including the City of Franklin, the Tennessee Heritage Conservation Trust Fund, the CWPT, the American Battlefield Protection Program and the Hellers, who gave $100,000.[1188]

Hicks, meanwhile, had poured his passion into another project—writing a novel about Carnton. Widow of the South was published on September 1, 2005, and in a rare publishing triumph, the first-time novelist's book became a *New York Times* bestseller that fall and brought thousands of new heritage tourists to Franklin and Carnton.[1189]

From 2007 to 2012, CWPT and Franklin preservationists, with ABPP assistance, acquired seven more parcels in the core battlefield area, including the strip mall on Columbia Avenue, the Cleburne Street property on the other side of the Blue House lot and a house and lot across the avenue.

"We're buying postage stamp-sized properties and putting them back together, weaving a story," Hicks said. "And we have merged the Carter House and Carnton into one organization called the Battle of Franklin Trust."[1190]

The various properties around the cotton gin site are being cleared, combined and transformed into Carter Hill Battlefield Park, which will occupy 20 acres. The park will include the Carter House as well as the nearby Lotz House, still bearing the dark blood stains of the wounded and dying on its wooden floors.

The 20-acre park is just the start. "In fact, the Franklin's Charge plan is to reclaim that entire Union line from the Carter House to Carnton," Campi said. "It's a big, hairy and enticing goal.[1191] But three links in that chain already exist. About three blocks east of Carter Hill park is the 3.22-acre Collins Farm, now a city historic park, and about 250 yards farther southeast, near Carnton, begins the 110-acre Eastern Flank Battlefield Park, the former country club.

Campi played such a key role navigating roadblocks at Franklin over the past 15 years, Hicks said he'd like to "build a statue to him on the battlefield." Time and again, "Julian and I and the rest at Franklin's Charge would be meeting, shaking our heads, and we'd call Campi and he'd say, 'Well, let me see. Let's try to figure out an answer. Oh yeah, you need to call so-and-so; you should talk with them.'"[1192]

Almost every recent issue of the STFB newsletter carries the headline "Update" as the City of Franklin, local preservationists, the Trust, and other entities work to restore the landscape into the Carter Hill Battlefield Park.

"For the old-timers here in Franklin and for so many of our long-time support-ers, this is almost too much to believe," reported the STFB newsletter of February 2014. In mid-2014, Franklin's Charge and The Battle of Franklin Trust announced a purchase agreement to buy the Lovell properties—1.6 acres of land with two houses in the heart of the battlefield along the west side of Columbia Avenue just south of the Carter House. In late 2014, the strip mall that the Trust had acquired and trans-ferred to the City of Franklin was razed. That same year, archaeologists precisely identified the Union line at the epicenter of the battlefield.[1193]

In May 2015, archaeologists found the original foundation of the cotton gin, which was constructed of "good, Middle Tennessee limestone," lead archaeologist Larry McKee reported. It was under the site of the Blue House. The Union line, they discovered, stretched east and west directly in front of the cotton gin.

In a bittersweet episode for many Franklin residents, the old Franklin High School gymnasium just north of the Carter House—all that was left of the old high school—was torn down in 2016 so the land could be incorporated into the battle-field park. New interpretive signs were installed at the emerging park, along with 19th-century-style cedar fences.[1194]

But a few hundred feet away, on the old BGA property, Williamson County kept developing. "They decided in 2014 that they were going to build a senior citizen's center there on core battlefield land," Pearce said. "The county still looks at it as cre-ating a balance. Our advocacy to get the county to stop building on core battlefield has not been so successful."[1195]

As 2017 began, the Williamson County Enrichment Center was still under construction on the site of one of the old BGA buildings. Another former acad-emy building, built in 1905, was being renovated into a Performing Arts Center, including a 300-seat theater. Both facilities were scheduled to open in the spring of 2017, and the Williamson County Parks and Recreation department launched a commemorative, personalized brick program for the two structures "built on the site of the original Battle Ground Academy campus where the rich history of the county has been preserved," the county's web page said. Nevertheless, the rich *Civil War* history of the county—and some of the most hallowed ground in the entire state—was developed in the process.[1196]

"The Civil War Trust has been the most incredible partner a community could ever have," said Pearce. "They have failed us never. But our advocacy to get the coun-ty to stop building on core battlefield? Not so much."

Despite Williamson County's intransigence, the preservationists have such a long track record of success, "the result is probably the most significant and certainly the most viable local preservation group—true preservation group—in America," said Lighthizer. "They're reclaiming scores of acres and dozens of properties. And they're creating a critical mass out of something that was gone and couldn't come back. And it is a miracle."[1197] ★

CHAPTER
SEVENTEEN

More Victories, More Losses

HE SPECTACLE of thousands of young Union soldiers advancing to their doom across an open plain to attack Confederates massed behind the stone wall at Marye's Heights in Fredericksburg, Virginia, on a cold December 13, 1862, was one of the most tragic of the Civil War.

Less well known was the almost simultaneous massive Union frontal assault about five miles south at Prospect Hill, a muddy plantation field. Prospect Hill was the main objective of the Union strategy, the "true battle for Fredericksburg," said historian Frank O'Reilly. Before the fighting ended, 9,000 Union and Confederate soldiers had fallen at a place the veterans called "the Slaughter Pen."[1198]

Development permanently altered the Marye's Heights battlefield in the 20th century as Fredericksburg grew, and today only the area along and to the rear of the Stone Wall is preserved. The Slaughter Pen and Prospect Hill, however, were well outside the city and remained unchanged.

Most of the land along the Confederate line at Prospect Hill was added to the Fredericksburg and Spotsylvania National Military Park in the 1930s.[1199] But at the southeast foot of the hill, the vast open field across which the Union soldiers attacked remained the privately owned dairy farm of John W. Pierson, consisting of about 250 acres in the 1970s. Pierson had deep family roots in Fredericksburg, but was "very unsophisticated," recalled APCWS co-founder Robert K. Krick, retired historian at the Fredericksburg and Spotsylvania National Military Park (FSNMP).[1200] Krick said Pierson would drive his farm equipment barefoot. "Bad idea, I thought, but the epitome of agrarian simplicity," Krick recalled. "His house was primitive beyond belief. He lived on millions of dollars of real estate, but existed as though beset by poverty."[1201]

Although it had been one of the bloodiest fields in the Battle of Fredericksburg, the Pierson Farm was not within the congressionally authorized boundary of the FSNMP and thus could not be considered for acquisition by the NPS. But, it was ripe for development. A railroad bed that separates Slaughter Pen Farm from Prospect Hill was the scene of furious, close-quarters fighting in 1862. It remains an active line today, with spurs on both sides of Pierson's property. The farm is beside a major road. A small airport sits on the farm's northeast border. The relatively level land was zoned for light industry. These features made the farm all the more valuable. "The only thing missing is a navigable port," CWPT President Jim Lighthizer quipped.[1202]

Pierson's "stubborn dislike for the airport saved the battlefield," Krick recalled. "They kept wanting either land or over-flight permission. He gave them none. John always wanted the battlefield saved. Fortunately, I persuaded him on two occasions in the '70s to sell the NPS bits of his farm." For "very modest prices," the park acquired tracts of 20 and 23 acres, respectively, in the southwest corner of the Pierson farm right along the railroad. "We simply leased them back to him for farming, and it was as if nothing had changed," Krick recalled. "But he would not do any further."[1203]

The Pierson farm, which the CWPT came to call the "Slaughter Pen Farm," attracted the attention of other preservationists. Mike Stevens, former president of Central Virginia Battlefields Trust (CVBT), quipped that the Slaughter Pen Farm was on CVBT's radar "long before CVBT even existed" because future members would visit so regularly with Pierson. "We recognized that this was hallowed ground in the truest sense of the word, the key to the battle of Fredericksburg and almost certainly still the resting place today for many of the brave men who fought and fell there," Stevens said. "It is quite literally sacred soil ..."[1204]

The battlefield survived a development threat in 1997 when the farm escaped becoming an auto auction venture only when the business decided to build on another property. There had been talk about putting a hospital there, but it also was built elsewhere.[1205] By 2003, the CWPT recognized the need to save the property, but also realized the challenge would be immense. The farm was valued at more than $10 million. The organization had never had any transaction that large.

By November 2004, when the CWPT inquired about the property, Pierson was in ill health in a home for the elderly. He had no children, so a niece was to be the sole beneficiary and executor of the estate when her uncle died. She was being hounded by a constant barrage of calls from developers and realtors wanting to know her plans for the acreage. CWPT backed off.[1206]

That fall, however, the Central Virginia Battlefields Trust scored a major preservation victory when it obtained a conservation easement on 104 prime industrial acres on Latimer's Knoll, just northwest of Slaughter Pen Farm on the other side of the railroad tracks. Krick had long ago named the area "Latimer's Knoll" for the teen-aged, VMI-educated, Confederate artillery captain, Joseph White Latimer, who placed five cannon just behind the crest of the open knoll that raked advancing Union troops with shells.

A Pierson relative, local resident and builder Tim Welsh, had purchased the property and other acreage there in 2003 with several partners. Welsh was contemplating what to do with it when he ran into a longtime acquaintance, CVBT founding member Johnny Mitchell, at a local John Deere dealership. Mitchell suggested a preservation easement for part of it. Welsh knew his property included hallowed ground, and Mitchell told him the easement would save it, giving him a tax benefit as well. They agreed within five minutes[1207]

"It was a quick, slam-dunk deal," Welsh told the Fredericksburg *Free Lance-Star*. It was a quiet deal, too. The newspaper did not report the "low-profile" deal until the following spring, some six months later.[1208]

In March 2005, Campi was alerted that the Spotsylvania County School Administration was working on a plan to buy 25 acres of Slaughter Pen Farm for a new elementary school. He worked with Coalition to the Save the Chancellorsville Battlefield veterans Kevin Leahy and Caroline Hayden to reorganize local residents into the Spotsylvania Battlefields Coalition, arranging tours of the property to prepare volunteers for another possible fight. Despite learning of battlefield preservationists' interest in the property, the administration scheduled a community meeting for early July.[1209]

Campi was vacationing at Chincoteague Island, Virginia when the call came. He purchased an extra-long cord so he could work on the patio and enjoy the seaside. He had a CWPT law firm send a Freedom of Information Act request "to show the county we already had a high-profile legal firm on board." Lighthizer sent a letter to members of the Spotsylvania Battlefields Coalition, calling out the preservation troops to attend a special community meeting set for July 14.[1210]

"This was on the heels of the Chancellorsville First Day victory (in March 2003), and all we needed to do was bark to get the school board to back down," Campi said. "They cancelled the meeting."[1210]

Pierson died at age 86 on September 1, 2005. His niece planned to sell the farm but wasn't keen on selling to preservationists. "I don't think she ever got over us stopping the school board," Campi said.[1212]

The farm, then totaling 208 acres, went on the market in December as the "Pearson Industrial Tract," priced at $12 million, or almost $60,000 an acre. Agent Alex Long, however, did not exclude preservationists from discussions. "In all honesty, we'll try to work with them, but cooperation is a two-way street," Long told the *Free Lance-Star*. "If it becomes shrill and nasty on the other side, that cooperation can be taken off the table as easily as it was put on the table."[1213]

CWPT's real estate director, Tom Gilmore, approached the realtor with proposals that included big benefits on estate taxes and other taxes because of the organization's status as a non-profit. But the niece "wasn't interested in any of that,"

Gilmore said. "She just wanted to sell it for full cash value and on a first-come, first-served basis, and didn't want to have to deal with preservationists at all. In fact, we assumed that she would not contract with us directly, even if we walked up and said, "We'll pay you $12 million for that."[1214]

Campi and his colleagues at CWPT already knew that "if we were going to save it, we had to pay developers' prices."[1215] The challenge was getting the seller to entertain a CWPT offer. They were concerned that the seller might sell to a developer at less than the asking price just to spite the preservationists. Lighthizer and Campi decided on a bold flanking maneuver, in military parlance, and contacted Tricord Homes, the Fredericksburg developers who partnered with the CWPT at Chancellorsville, to see if the company might be willing to purchase then sell the property to the CWPT.

Recalled Gilmore, "Jim arranged a call between me and Mike Jones, who was the principal of Tricord. We talked about how we could do it and I said, 'Well, if Tricord contracts for the purchase of the property and then has an assignability feature in the contract, we could do it.'"[1216]

Another challenge was persuading the CWPT's board to approve the organization's largest single purchase ever, and the ambitious fundraising effort that would have to follow. Where would the $12 million come from? Chief Operating Officer Ron Cogswell, now retired, remembered hearing small gasps from some of the more fiscally conservative board members as they contemplated the magnitude of the transaction.[1217]

The CVBT, whose members were so eager to save the property, promised to play a significant role in raising money and with Mike Stevens taking the lead, pledged a whopping $1 million. "That an all-volunteer group would make a seven-figure pledge profoundly impressed our board, and helped influence the decision to make the deal," Campi recalled.[1218]

The staff and trustees were tense before the purchase was consummated. "It was literally like giving birth over that period of time," recalled David Duncan.[1219]

Cogswell was not a regular church-goer, but one day when Gilmore told him the deal still hung in the balance, he went across the street from the CWPT's former offices on H Street to pray in New York Avenue Presbyterian Church, President Abraham Lincoln's preferred church. "I sat in the Lincoln pew and just asked for a good outcome at the Slaughter Pen Farm," Cogswell recalled.[1220]

Tricord secured a $12 million purchase contract on Slaughter Pen Farm in February 2006. On March 28, the CWPT announced that it had agreed to buy the property for $12 million with a closing date of June 15. Tricord's Jones agreed that the land was a "developer's dream," but said preserving it was more important.

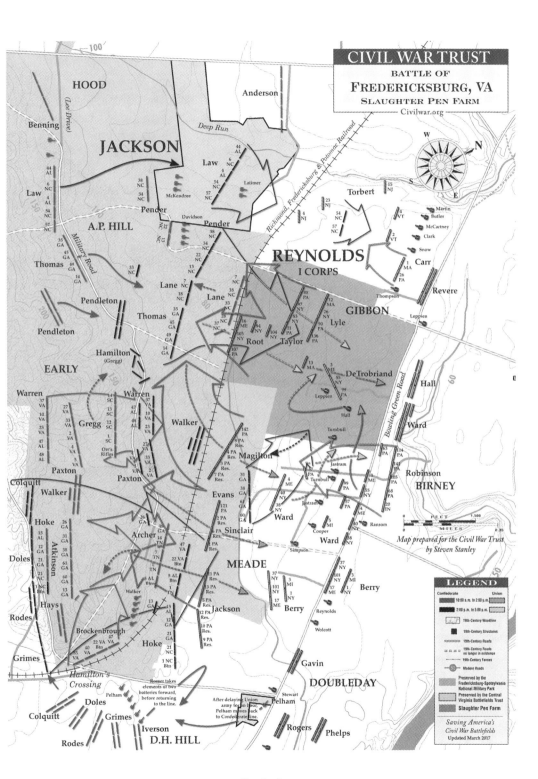

CIVIL WAR TRUST
BATTLE OF
FREDERICKSBURG, VA
SLAUGHTER PEN FARM
Civilwar.org

HOOD

Anderson

Benning

(Lee Drive)

Deep Run

JACKSON

Law

44
AL

6
NC

4
AL

54
NC

57
NC

Latimer

44
AL

38
NC

McKendree

Law

4
AL

54
NC

57
NC

34
NC

Pender

Davidson

A.P. HILL

Pender

22
NC

13
NC

38
NC

34
NC

22
NC

13
NC

Thomas

35
GA

45
GA

49
GA

14
GA

33
NC

Pendleton

Lane

7
NC

18
NC

35
GA

45
GA

49
GA

14
GA

Lane

7
NC

18
NC

33
NC

37
NC

Pendleton

Thomas

Root

107
PA

Hamilton
(Gregg)

EARLY

Warren

37
VA

10
VA

23
VA

47
AL

49
AL

Warren

14
SC

37
NC

13
SC

47
AL

12
SC

10
VA

2
VA

23
VA

1
SC

Gregg

Orr's
Rifles

Walker

142

5 PA
Res.

4 PA
Res.

3 PA
Res.

7 PA
Res.

Paxton

Paxton

Magilton

Colquitt

Walker

Evans

121
PA

38
GA

61
GA

6
GA

Hoke

26
GA

GA

15
AL

31
GA

12
GA

38
GA

21
GA

61
GA

1 NC
Btn

13
GA

Archer

26
GA

GA

14
TN

7
TN

1
TN

47
VA

22 VA
Btn

Sinclair

1 PA
Res.

5 PA
Res.

Doles

Atkinson

21
NC

5 AL
Btn

5 AL
Btn

2 PA
Res.

MEADE

Hays

Walker

13
GA

15
AL

12
GA

21
GA

21
NC

Jackson

12 PA
Res.

10 PA
Res.

9 PA
Res.

Rodes

Brockenbrough

47
VA

22 VA
VA

40
Btn

Hoke

55
GA

21
NC

1 NC
Btn

Grimes

Hamilton's
Crossing

Rosser takes
elements of two
batteries forward,
before returning
to the line.

After delaying Union
army for an hour,
Pelham moves back
to Confederate line.

D.H. HILL

Doles

Colquitt

Grimes

Iverson

Rodes

REYNOLDS
I CORPS

Torbert

15
NJ

23
NJ

54
NC

57
NC

4
NJ

4
VT

2
VT

Martin

Butler

McCartney

Clark

Snow

Carr

3
MA

1
MA

26
PA

Thompson

Revere

GIBBON

88
PA

16
NY

94
NY

11
PA

12
MA

Lyle

Leppien

Taylor

104
NY

55
PA

136
PA

16
ME

94
NY

13
MA

3
ME

DeTrobriand

Hall

99
PA

5
NY

Leppien

Hall

Ward

Turnbull

Jastram

Bowling Green Road

Hall

Ward

5
PA

4 PA
Res.

31
GA

63
PA

114
PA

14
PA

145
PA

Robinson

BIRNEY

4
ME

Turnbull

9
PA

57
PA

99
PA

55
PA

3
ME

63
PA

20
IN

Ward

Jastram

40
NY

38
NY

Cooper

5
MI

40
PA

Ransom

Ward

Simpson

37
NY

NY

3
MI

Berry

5
NY

101
NY

17
ME

17
ME

7
ME

3
MI

1
NY

Berry

Reynolds

Wolcott

Gavin

Stewart

Pelham

DOUBLEDAY

Rogers

Phelps

W

N

S

E

60

Hall

60

FEET   1,500

MILES

Map prepared for the Civil War Trust
by Steven Stanley

LEGEND

Confederate	Union	
		10:00 a.m. to 2:00 p.m.
		2:00 p.m. to 5:00 p.m.

19th-Century Woodline

19th-Century Structures

19th-Century Roads

19th-Century Roads
no longer in existence

19th-Century Fences

Modern Roads

Preserved by the
Fredericksburg-Spotsylvania
National Military Park

Preserved by the Central
Virginia Battlefields Trust

Slaughter Pen Farm

*Saving America's
Civil War Battlefields*
Updated March 2017

Richmond, Fredericksburg & Potomac Railroad

[283]

"Smart developers are interested in the community as a whole," he said. "We live here and we work here."[1221]

Lighthizer called it the "single most important piece of ground" related to the battle of Fredericksburg: "If you don't have this, you don't have the battle of Fredericksburg." He said a massive fundraising campaign would begin immediately. "We'll pass the hat around here in a minute," he told press conference attendees.[1222]

In his *Message from Headquarters* column in the summer 2006 *Hallowed Ground*, Lighthizer wrote that the CWPT was buying the farm without knowing how to pay for it. "I cannot tell you exactly how we are going to accomplish this unprecedented feat, primarily because we don't have $12 million," he noted. "This is the biggest challenge we have ever faced. Five years ago—heck, two years ago—we could not have even contemplated a project of this magnitude."[1223]

The CWPT confronted the challenge with innovation and creativity. The organization's largest deal ever was also one of its most complex as Gilmore took advantage of new and different financing opportunities. SunTrust Bank agreed to fund the whole transaction, although one of its top bankers quipped during a ceremony at the farm that he hoped no banking regulators were present. After all, SunTrust was financing a plan not to develop the property, but to *never* develop it.[1224]

But the CWPT had an excellent reputation with the bank going back to the days of the APCWS. And a key reason for SunTrust's decision to approve, which was made by the bank's highest officials, was the plan to take advantage of land preservation tax credits in Virginia.[1225]

Gilmore had explored the use of land preservation tax credits, a unique funding tool available only in Virginia. In the late 1990s, Virginia devised a way to preserve land by granting tax credits at a percentage of the value of a land donation. The credits could be sold by the landowner to taxpayers who could use the credits to offset state income taxes. Once the CWPT placed a conservation easement on the property, the land value instantly plummeted from $12 million to $2 million, creating $5 million in tax credits that the Trust could sell, and did so during the next three years to help pay down the loan.[1226]

To ensure the CWPT was eligible for the tax credits, it engaged the legal services of the law firm McGuireWoods, which agreed to provide pro-bono services. Through the help and expertise of attorneys Craig Bell, Christian Tennant and former Virginia Attorney General Bill Broaddus, the CWPT obtained a special tax ruling from the Virginia Department of Taxation to support the credits.

In addition to the tax credits and the CVBT's $1 million donation, the CWPT received a $2 million land acquisition grant from the American Battlefield Protection

Program (ABPP) to be matched by membership donations. Ultimately, nearly a half of the $12 million would be raised in private funds, mostly from CWPT members.[1227]

The acquisition of the 208-acre Slaughter Pen Farm closed on June 15, 2006, and remains to this day the largest battlefield land acquisition in history made by the private sector.

"Then, because we're a non-profit, we can do tax-exempt financing," Gilmore said. "So maybe six months after our acquisition, I went to SunTrust and talked to them about refinancing our outstanding debt after our tax credit reduction into a long-term bond issue. So, that's what we ended up doing with about $5 million in outstanding debt on the deal."[1228]

The size of the transaction, its complexity, the challenges of a reluctant if not hostile seller—all contributed to the sense within CWPT that it had broken new ground. "I think that was the defining moment for the Trust," Cogswell said. "It took the organization to a new level—just the challenge, the intricacies of it. We couldn't have done it without Tom Gilmore. But it was also the courage of Jim Lighthizer. And his maneuvering." [1229]

Along with the countless details, the legwork and the paper work of the negotiations, a human touch was warranted. Pierson's niece may not have wanted to sell to CWPT, but at closing her biggest concern was for the feral cats that lived at the farm. They remained the only residents.[1230] Lighthizer expressed a "what now?" sense of exasperation as he told the story to a *Washington Post* reporter, joking that he had "toyed with the notion of delivering a few feline corpses, like the horse's head in 'The Godfather,' to the uncooperative landowner's doorstep."[1231]

What actually happened was that Gilmore and his family cared for the cats. "We used to go to the Slaughter Pen Farm to feed the cats," Gilmore recalled. "Ultimately, we got a local animal league, who came in and caught most the cats and relocated them to farms in the area." Pierson's niece, he heard later, was pleased.[1232]

Slaughter Pen Farm was not the only priority for CWPT staff. Board meetings stretched four hours or longer, and the single-spaced minutes filled six, eight, even 10 pages or more. Most board members were big donors and all were expected to be hard workers, serving on active and involved committees, including Development, Education, Finance, Government, Preservation and Public Relations. Trustees put staff members through their paces with tough examinations and hard questions as a part of their oversight.

In 2006, the seventh full year after the merger, CWPT raised its own bar. The $12 million purchase of the 208-acre Slaughter Pen Farm was a record amount for one transaction, but in terms of land mass, it was only the second-largest save that year. At Port Republic, Virginia, CWPT added 219 battlefield acres.[1233]

Also in 2006, the organization saved hallowed ground spanning the entire field of operations of the Civil War, at battlefields large and small. CWPT saved the 106-acre Cunningham Farm at Gettysburg and 6.5 acres at Mine Creek battlefield in Kansas. It preserved the death sites of a controversial Union officer, Lieutenant John Rodgers Meigs, at Swift Run Gap in Virginia and Confederate Colonel Benjamin Franklin Terry of Terry's Texas Rangers near Rowlett's Station. At the Bentonville, North Carolina battlefield, it made three separate acquisitions totaling 299 acres. The CWPT also saved battlefield land at Shepherdstown, West Virginia; Perryville, Kentucky; Champion Hill, Mississippi; Wilson's Creek, Missouri; and Fort Donelson, Tennessee. In Virginia alone, it saved land not only at Fredericksburg and Cold Harbor, but Swift Run Gap, Fussell's Mill, Kelly's Ford, Totopotomoy Creek and Trevilian Station. The final tally for the year was 1,310 acres saved in 21 separate deals at 17 sites in nine states.[1234]

One of the most significant saves announced in 2006, and finalized two years later, was the purchase of the last privately owned part of Morris Island outside Charleston, South Carolina. This barrier island at the southern entrance of Charleston Harbor was the scene of the famous assault of the 54th Massachusetts against Fort Wagner (now underwater), immortalized in the Academy Award-winning 1989 movie *Glory*. Morris Island held some of the heavy Union guns that shelled Charleston during the war. The evidence of at least one emplacement remains visible today. Although a few summer homes appeared and disappeared over the years, the 840-acre island has long been uninhabited and accessible only by boat. Generations of Charlestonians loved having such a big, wild expanse of open, oceanfront land so close to their city.[1235]

The northern-most historic point was privately owned when Greenville, South Carolina developer Harry Huffman optioned some 126 acres in 2003 and decided to build houses. The preservation fight was led by Blake Hallman, an instructor at the Culinary Institute of Charleston. Like many Charlestonians, Hallman had camped on the island. He loved it so much he proposed to his wife there.[1236]

Hallman was a board member of the South Carolina Battleground Preservation Trust. He ignored naysayers who thought the organization was not strong enough or big enough to take on the fight and organized the Morris Island Coalition, bringing together a diverse collection of groups and entities. They included the City of Charleston, the CWPT, the Coastal Conservation League, the NAACP, Sons of Confederate Veterans, The Trust for Public Land (TPL) and even Surfrider Foundation's Charleston chapter.

The owners had no interest in selling to preservationists. "They said the preservation community had dropped the ball to purchase Morris Island several times" Hallman recalled. "And they were going to see what was going to happen with a developer purchasing the island."[1237]

Huffman was acquiring permits and had filed for zoning variances to allow new homes when Hallman and his coalition became involved. It began to fight at every step in the process. "That worked out pretty well in our favor," Hallman recalled.[1238]

"It was not financially feasible for the developer to move forward with only two homes," Hallman said. "So, he asked for it to be zoned for 120 homes. And the county told him no. Then he asked for to be zoned for 60 homes. And they told him no. So, then he asked for it to be zoned for 20 homes. And they said, 'That seems like a more reasonable number. Let's work on potential zoning for that number.'"[1239]

The coalition redoubled its efforts and worked to thwart a permit for 20 houses as the CWPT named Morris Island one of its 10 Most Endangered Battlefields in 2004. Huffman became frustrated with the slow process and made national headlines in January 2005 when he offered Morris Island for sale on eBay for $12.5 million. "It's sad to see such a priceless piece of American history put up for auction like some unwanted holiday gift," Campi told the Associated Press. "If the developer really wants to sell Morris Island, the preservation community is ready to buy. But to do so, he needs to stop the gimmicks and get down to real bargaining based on fair market value—not a $12.5 million pipe dream." The property had been appraised at $4.1 million in 2000.[1240]

A CWPT/Mason-Dixon poll confirmed that Charleston was strongly pro-preservation. Seventy-one percent of 400 registered voters polled supported preserving the island without development, while 77 percent opposed rezoning to allow 20 residences. Huffman decided not to renew his purchase option. Once again the preservationists approached the owners and once again they were rebuffed. Later in 2005, however, Edward R. "Bobby" Ginn III, a Florida resort developer, took an option to buy the island acreage.[1241]

Ginn was a native of Hampton, South Carolina, and he, too, had visited Morris Island while growing up. Hallman considered Ginn more of a threat than Huffman because Ginn had more financial resources. The CWPT and the coalition went on the offensive with the slightest hint of possible development. Campi issued a press release when Ginn took the routine step of recording the two plat maps noting his purchase.[1242]

"Just in time for the holidays, the Grinch has reared his ugly head outside Charleston Harbor," the release began. Ginn was frustrated by the negative publicity;

he had not even proposed a project. Ginn received a call from longtime Charleston Mayor Joe Riley, who said he wanted to let Ginn know as a courtesy that he was writing an opinion piece for the Charleston *Post and Courier* about the need to preserve Morris Island.

Riley had been mayor for more than 30 years, and led the revitalization of the moribund Charleston of the 1970s into the vibrant, leading cultural destination that it is today. Riley's former executive assistant, David Agnew, had become the new South Carolina advisory chairman for TPL, the preservation organization that had tried and failed to buy the property earlier. Riley urged Ginn to preserve the island. "You ought to talk with David Agnew," the mayor said.[1243]

Agnew believed he could "strike a chord" if he could just tell Ginn about TPL and its mission. They met in Agnew's King Street office and six weeks later had a deal. Of all the developers who had intentions of developing hallowed ground, Ginn may have been the most generous and amenable to historic preservation.

On February 2, 2006, Ginn closed on the Morris Island land for $6.8 million and agreed to immediately sell it to the TPL for only $4.5 million—an instant $2.3 million loss. TPL then sold the island to the City of Charleston to preserve in perpetuity. Ginn agreed to donate $500,000 for historical and archaeological studies and planning [1244]

"Bobby Ginn bought it and sold it to The Trust for Public Land at a loss, to his credit." Hallman recalled. "I consider that to be a real win-win for everybody. He did the right thing. He collected all the accolades due to him. The island was preserved, which is what the citizens wanted. And then the overwhelming majority said, 'Don't touch a thing. Leave it exactly as it is.' And so, we took that to heart, and that's the end result. It is in the exact same condition it was before."[1245]

Successes in 2006 came with threats and battles. At Harpers Ferry, West Virginia, a developer, Jefferson Utilities, Inc., had moved in with heavy machinery on an August weekend that was particularly busy for NPS staff. Without permits or notifications, the company cut a 45-foot wide swath and dug two 1,900 foot trenches across a NPS-owned historic tract at School House Ridge, a property purchased by the original Civil War Trust and donated to the NPS.[1246]

By putting water and sewer lines in place, the development company hoped to enhance its ability to have a 200-acre tract of historic land adjacent to School House Ridge rezoned to allow the construction of as many as 3,400 homes and 2.3 million square feet of commercial space. Outraged by the blatant desecration, the preservation community, led by the CWPT, went to war against Jefferson Utilities to thwart rezoning.[1247]

As the bulldozers excavated the trench, a preservationist took a photo of several of the developers, one of whom held up the middle finger of his raised left hand. David Duncan took full advantage, sending out a direct mail appeal with a special envelope inside that was labeled: "WARNING! OFFENSIVE IMAGE ENCLOSED! Open only if you want to see what a developer really thinks about protecting America's heritage at Harpers Ferry!" The appeal was unusually successful.[1248]

First, the developers tried to have the city of Charles Town, West Virginia annex the property, losing on a 4–3 vote in April 2007. Next, the developers lost their petition to the Jefferson County, West Virginia, Board of Commissioners to rezone the tract in a 3–2 vote. Stymied, Jefferson Utilities and its development partners filed for bankruptcy. The pipes laid by Jefferson Utilities became pipes to nowhere.[1249]

In September 2006, Lighthizer took a vacation to go hiking and camping in California's Sierra Nevada mountains with his 28-year-old son, Conor, a Baltimore banker and avid outdoorsman. Lighthizer and his wife, Gloria, married in 1976 and had two children, Conor and Meghan. He had three children by a previous marriage —sons Jim, Jr., and Robert, and a daughter, Patrice. The boys continued to live with him after his ex-wife moved to Massachusetts with their daughter.

Robert, or Bobby, named after Robert Kennedy, was an outstanding athlete who served honorably in the Army but struggled to find direction and fought depression. On February 17, 1993, Bobby filled his car with carbon monoxide and took his own life.

"It's nobody's fault," Bobby wrote in a note to his father.[1250]

Lighthizer struggled for years to cope. Bobby had covered his depression with an optimistic spirit and Lighthizer had not seen disaster coming. He visited Bobby's grave, usually alone, talking to his son as he paced, until he had traversed so many times a groove appeared in the ground.[1251]

Friends and colleagues noticed changes in Lighthizer. He grew more empathetic and less self-involved. He took more time with his family. He started a new pastime with Jim, Jr. and Conor. He called them "big boy hikes; together they challenged trails at the country's greatest parks, including the Grand Canyon, the Grand Tetons and Glacier National Park.

Jim, Jr. couldn't go on the 2006 trip to Kings Canyon National Park, so Jim and Conor were joined by Lighthizer's brother-in-law, Greg Voets. Conor was a Type 1 diabetic—the most serious type—but it had never stopped him from having an active, athletic life. Conor had run a marathon that year, an accomplishment that had filled his father with pride.[1252]

Conor did not feel well the day before the expedition, but insisted on going.

On September 4, after a long, steep horseback ride into the high country, the three started an hour-long hike in the early afternoon to their camp at Granite Lake, a remote lake at 10,600 feet. Halfway there, Conor became violently ill. When they reached the camp site, Conor was too weak to help pitch the tent. He could not hold anything down.[1253]

Now, in the high country, with no phone signal and the nearest ranger station a four-hour hike down the mountain, Conor was afflicted by a serious diabetes-related condition known as ketoacidosis, which can lead to severe dehydration.

At 6 p.m. Lighthizer proposed that he go for help. "Let's wait until morning," Conor said.[1254]

Conor battled through the night, weak, thirsty and confused. Lighthizer administered to him, catching only an hour or two of sleep. Conor wasn't in pain, but was so thirsty, he asked his father to inject him with water.[1255]

Conor weakened. "I can't see," he said.

"That's not good," his father said.

"No, it's not," Conor said.

At first light, Voets headed down the mountain for help. Conor hovered on the verge of unconsciousness as Lighthizer paced back and forth, "scared to death." At 10:30 a.m., Voets reached the ranger station. A helicopter was immediately dispatched. Five minutes later, back at Granite Lake, Conor died in his father's arms.[1256]

Lighthizer agonized over what he might have done differently, as he had done after Bobby's death. He had to stay busy and force his mind to think about other things. Lighthizer's passion for saving Civil War battlefields became one of his key survival tools. He threw himself back into that familiar routine. "You go on because you have no choice," he said.[1257]

A meeting of the CWPT board was scheduled for September 22 in Charleston, South Carolina. The news of Conor's sudden death left the entire staff devastated, and the office closed for his funeral on September 11. Afterward, at a reception at Lighthizer's home, Duncan pulled him aside.

"Jim, you know, this has been an awful lot on you," Duncan said gently. "A couple of trustees have mentioned to me that maybe we ought to postpone the board meeting."

"No, no, no," Lighthizer said. "We're not postponing it; we're having the board meeting."[1258]

Duncan realized his boss needed the meeting. "He still had to get ready, so he had to focus on his job, on the mission, and that was going to help him,"

Duncan recalled.[1259]

Conor had aspired to be a park ranger and died doing something he and his father loved. His tombstone, which has a mountain range etched into the granite above his name, reads, "You Ran a Great Race." In October, the family and several CWPT staff members, including Campi and Duncan, joined in a diabetes walkathon held in Conor's honor in Annapolis. And in November, Jim and Gloria Lighthizer decided to go ahead with a previously scheduled trip to Hawaii to celebrate their 30th wedding anniversary.

At the CWPT offices in Washington, the intense pace of the work commanded Lighthizer's full attention. Real estate acquisitions continued at a rate of almost two a month. The staff was fighting four battles at once—Harpers Ferry, the proposed casino at Gettysburg, a rezoning battle at Cedar Creek and a development threat at the Wilderness. But there were celebrations, too.

On October 16, Lighthizer led a ceremony at Slaughter Pen Farm with an all-star cast of federal and state officials, led by Secretary of the Interior Dirk Kempthorne, who announced the $2 million matching grant from ABPP. That the Interior secretary himself appeared "was an absolute coup for the CWPT," recalled Mary Goundrey Koik.[1260]

Several top Virginia state legislators, along with CVBT leaders, officials with SunTrust Bank and Tricord and a crowd of more than 150 attended this first public ceremony at the farm. The preservation of the battleground "is a model for conservation partnerships throughout the nation," Kempthorne said.[1261]

The year 2006 also marked the 10th anniversary of the Brandy Station purchase. For Bud Hall, who had fought so long and hard to preserve the battlefield, the years after the 1996 agreement were some of the happiest of his life.

Hall had found the love of his life, Deborah Fitts, in his quest to save Brandy Station. Fitts was a reporter for the *Civil War News*. The monthly newspaper had started as the *Civil War Book Exchange* in 1974. Peter and Kay Jorgensen, history buffs who published community newspapers, acquired the paper and in April 1989 published the first monthly issue of the revamped *Civil War News*, which focused on news and current events in the Civil War community as well as book reviews.[1262]

Peter Jorgensen's column, "Paging Through," usually focused on saving battlefields. Jerry Russell was an early columnist. Fitts, a newspaper journalist, saw one of the first issues, contacted the Jorgensens, and found herself with a job. Her first bylines appeared in the July 1989 issue, and she became the paper's primary reporter.[1263]

Hall and Fitts met at the 1990 APCWS annual conference. He gave her a tour at

Brandy Station and she interviewed him, which led to her first major article about the Brandy Station preservation fight in June 1990 under the headline: "Bud Hall Is Leader Of Efforts To Save Brandy Station Sites."[1264]

They shared an instant mutual attraction. Hall was taken by her attractiveness and personality. He asked Pohanka and John Hennessy to join her for a photograph just so he could have a photo of her. He asked her out. They traded ancestor stories and discovered that her great-grandfather, Private Henry Fitts of the 22nd Massachusetts, had been wounded and captured at Gaines' Mill, while his great grandfather, Sergeant Charles Hall of the 13th Mississippi, had been wounded and captured at Gettysburg. They became a couple.[1265]

Hall had a grown son and daughter from his first marriage, which ended in divorce. His second wife died of MS a few of years after they married in 1985. But Fitts was unlike any woman he had met; they were so like-minded, they rarely needed to explain things to each other or even talk.

"From the start, it was clear to me that she was not a dilettante about the Civil War," Hall recalled. "She knew more about the artillery of the Civil War than most artillerists. The two of us were simpatico in all respects. Never in my life had I ever seen two people bond like we did from the first time I met her."[1266]

On May 5, 2001, Hall and Fitts were married in a small ceremony at the Doubleday Inn in Gettysburg. They hiked New Zealand in the fall on their honeymoon.[1267] In 2002, they moved to the Berkshires in western Massachusetts, but that never stopped Hall, now both of them, from visiting Brandy Station, where the news had continued to be good. A key part of the battlefield that had remained in private hands throughout the Sammis era—a 258-acre farm considered to be "the hole in the donut" of the preserved battlefield—was bought by CWPT for $1.33 million.[1268]

But the southern end of Fleetwood Hill, arguably the most important part of the Brandy Station battlefield, remained in private hands. In 2001, Lighthizer had written the owners of the land, the Pound family, expressing the CWPT's interest in buying it. He outlined the tax advantages of selling to a preservation organization. Nothing came of it.[1269]

In his research on Fleetwood Hill, Hall had discovered that both armies had camped on its open southern slope several times during the war. Besides the epic cavalry battle, other fighting took place there. Hall documented so much military activity on Fleetwood Hill during that war, he could state unequivocally that "it was the single-most fought over, marched on and camped upon piece of land in American military history."[1270]

In January 2002, the Pound family sold its 17 acres on Fleetwood Hill to Tony Troilo, a Culpeper businessman and son of Joe Troilo, one of Hall's closest friends at Brandy Station. Joe and his wife, Bootsie Rosson Troilo, lived in a ranch home at the base of the hill. Tony had grown up there and raised his own family at the home. On Hall's first visit in 1984, he had introduced himself to Joe, who was just arriving home from church. "He was a wonderful guy," Hall recalled. "Joe loved the history at Brandy Station. He lived it and breathed it."[1271]

Joe was a Pennsylvanian who came to the area with the Civilian Conservation Corps in the 1930s and never left. He worked at the Rosson garage and became so well known for his precise auto alignments, Bear Alignment brought him to the Indianapolis 500 in 1963 and 1964 to help align the race cars.[1272]

In 1972, as chairman of the local Ruritan Club's Preservation of the Civil War Battlefield Committee, Joe Troilo had written his Congressman, Representative J. Kenneth Robinson (R-Va.), asking for official recognition of the Brandy Station battlefield and "a proper marking for this historical battle."[1273]

"On hundreds of occasions," Triolo wrote, "we have been stopped by tourist and sightseers who have asked us to point out particular spots of historical significance, such as Fleetwood Hill ... "[1274]

"When Tony bought Fleetwood Hill, Deb and I were relieved," Hall recalled. "We went down there and we both hugged Tony's neck."[1275]

"Nothing will ever happen here, Bud," he recalled Tony saying.[1276]

Hall was relieved, but by nature remained cautious. Announcing the sale to the Brandy Station Foundation board in a February 4, 2002, email, Hall recommended that "we take Tony at his word that he is willing to work with us" to preserve the hill as well as the pre-Civil War slave dwellings. For a time, all was quiet again with Brandy Station.[1277]

In August 2003, Hall learned that his old friend Brian Pohanka's cancer had returned and spread to other parts of his body. Pohanka cut back on speaking appearances to concentrate on fighting the disease and finishing his regimental history of the 5th New York Volunteers. Pohanka had no plans to attend the CWPT annual conference in Nashville in late April 2004, but staff members implored him to come. So, he went, although his health and stamina had declined considerably. He was honored there with one of the CWPT's highest awards, the Carrington Williams Battlefield Preservationist of the Year award.

By the fall, Pohanka was writing farewell notes to old friends, thanking them for their efforts on his behalf and for history. His email to preservationist and living historian Daralee Ota said he was not planning on "crossing the river" soon, but "my health situation is rather precarious."[1278]

Hall and Fitts had enjoyed a wonderful summer, although she was nagged by a continuing nasal infection. Antibiotics finally cleared it up, but Fitts's doctor sent her to an ear, nose and throat specialist who, on August 8, 2004, felt a tiny lump in her neck.[1279] Other tests brought the horrible confirmation of a dangerous and lethal adenocarcinoma cancer. Hall heard the diagnosis while awaiting a flight in Charlotte, North Carolina and flew back to Massachusetts that night.

Fitts had always been extremely active and healthy. She had exhibited no cancer symptoms. Doctors had determined that the neck tumor was not the primary source of the cancer, but could not discover what was.[1280]

Like Hall, Pohanka had found love and a devoted partner within the Civil War community later in life when he met Cricket Bauer, a reenactor, at an event in 1991. They were married in 1999, shortly after his first cancer diagnosis. In May 2005, Bauer called Hall, saying Pohanka wanted to see him. Hall went to Pohanka's historic 1888 home in Alexandria, Virginia, the Tower House.

"It was like a funeral parlor," Hall recalled. "All the lights were off." Pohanka had already lost one eye to cancer, and "light bothered Brian," Hall said. "Brian was in the back, sitting there behind his desk. I could hardly see him." Hall tried to keep the conversation upbeat until Pohanka spoke.

"Bud, I will miss this world and everything in it," Pohanka said. He said the word "miss" with profound heartache. Pohanka knew he was near the end, and his feeling was one of regret, not acceptance.

Hall left Tower House profoundly depressed. He had become the expert on his wife's cancer because she preferred knowing as little as possible. She did not take bad news well. So Hall studied everything he could lay his hands on about her disease. He found little to encourage him. "I knew more of her situation than anybody else," he recalled. "I could look at Brian and see what her situation could be."[1281]

Less than a month later, on June 15, 2005, Brian Caldwell Pohanka died. He was 50 years old. In his will, he left $1 million to the CWPT. *The New York Times* and his hometown *Washington Post* wrote lengthy news obituaries. The *Civil War News* paid tribute to Pohanka *and* to his wife.

"In the months before Pohanka's death, many friends came calling at Tower House in Alexandria, the couple's home," the paper reported. "They saw how Pohanka relied on Bauer, and what a tower of strength she was for him. On June 23, she presided over her husband's funeral, interment and memorial service. Dignified, calm and focused, she set a worthy tone for a day of tributes and remembrance."[1282]

The tribute was written by Fitts, who attended the funeral with Hall. By then, she had undergone radiation as well as more chemotherapy. More than 10 months had passed since her diagnosis and doctors still could not find the primary location of the cancer. Hall concluded that her treatment "was, in fact, mostly guesswork." [1283]

In early 2006, Hall was back at Brandy Station when he stopped at Joe Troilo's ranch home, as usual, to say hello. Troilo took Hall outside, and with tears in his eyes, told him that Tony was going to build "a really big house" on the crest of the southern slope. It was another smack in the gut. Hall felt bad for Joe, and betrayed by Tony. [1284]

But Tony had become fed up with Hall. He mistrusted Hall as much as Hall mistrusted him. As Hall recalled it, he spoke to Tony as the bulldozers were poised to scrape a level spot for the house.

"So you're going to build a house here?" Hall asked.

"Yeah, Bud."

"Tony, the hill you're building your house on is the most important part of the battlefield."

"I know, Bud, but it's my property. It's not yours."[1285]

As the house went up, "I was devastated—literally driven to my knees," Hall recalled. "And Deb told me, 'One of these days, Clark B, that house will be gone.' She always called me 'Clark B.'" Fitts said it with such finality, Hall recovered some hope. "It will come down some day," she said. "You will see, Clark B., you will see."[1286]

Once Troilo finished the house in late 2007 and moved in, Hall refused to go back up there. The crest of Fleetwood Hill became like Chantilly battlefield to Hall. He had to remember them as they were. He stopped visiting or taking tours to Fleetwood Hill.[1287]

Joe and Bootsie Troilo moved into the big, new home with their son and daughter-in-law. "My dad loved that house," Troilo recalled. In fact, building it was his father's idea, he said. "There were eight of us living there in the older house. My wife, Pat, and I had been talking about doing something. And we were all sitting around the dinner table—it was 2005—and my dad said, 'You know what, if I was you two, I would go right up there on the peak of that hill and I would build a house right there.'[1288]

"And Pat, and I looked at each other and we thought, 'Oh my God, has he just said that?' My dad just thought it was the greatest thing in the world. And he thought, too, that it was going to be a great thing that we were going to put a walking trail around it. He took pictures of that home while it was being built. I can see him riding around that field in his El Camino, taking pictures."[1289]

By 2007, Fitts had been fighting cancer for more than two years and it had spread to her liver. The previous October, almost two years after her first diagnosis, a doctor had finally found the primary location of the cancer. It was microscopic; no mammogram could pick it up. But it was breast cancer.[1290]

"What in the world did she do to deserve this?" Hall wrote in a private journal. "The irony is that I have done everything I can to make her happy, and now an insidious disease threatens to rob her of any future happiness and joy—and there is nothing anyone or I can do about it. But we refuse to give up. I think she is scared to death. I know I am. But I can't let her know of my fears."[1291]

Fitts and Hall consulted new doctors. They made one trip after another from the Berkshires into New York City—a seven-hour round trip in good traffic—for appointments at Memorial Sloan Kettering Hospital. No matter what doctors tried, no matter how much chemotherapy she endured, the disease spread. On July 16, 2008, Fitts went into severe septic shock and passed away early the next morning. Hall was alone with her, stroking and kissing her face. "As she passed away," he would recall, "Deborah never looked more beautiful or peaceful."[1292] ★

CHAPTER

EIGHTEEN

Fight Over The Wilderness Walmart

A T 7:30 A.M. on Wednesday, July 10, 2013, dignitaries and officials cut a ceremonial yellow ribbon and hundreds of waiting shoppers poured into the new Walmart Supercenter on Route 3 in eastern Orange County, Virginia.

The freshly paved parking lot was nearly full as customers joined county leaders and Walmart corporate leaders to celebrate the opening of the retail giant's 128,000-square foot store at Locust Grove. With it came 300 new jobs and a predicted $20 million annual economic benefit to the county.[1293]

The local Lake of the Woods Veterans Club color guard presented the colors before store manager Terralis Gibson welcomed the crowd and announced, "The long wait is now over. We are delighted that this Walmart in Orange County is now a reality … "[1294]

A costly, time-draining battlefield preservation struggle preceded the store's opening, but it was an afterthought in at least one news account. "People were also concerned about the original location of the Walmart," reported Charlottesville's NBC Channel 29. "Some thought the location would tarnish a Civil War landmark. The location has since been moved."[1295]

If only it had been that easy.

The original location was to be about seven miles east on Route 3, directly opposite from the NPS Wilderness Battlefield, but part of the battlefield as defined by the Civil War Sites Advisory Commission. Union General George Meade established his headquarters there and the area came to include a field hospital, a Union artillery position and a holding area for captured Confederates.[1296]

Despite the eventual selection of another location just a few miles farther west on Route 3, the fight over the Walmart became one of the most contentious, hard-fought battlefield struggles. It pulled in not only the Civil War Preservation Trust (CWPT) and local and regional preservation organizations, but the National Trust for Historic Preservation and the National Parks Conservation Association. Until it ended suddenly in a judge's chambers in Orange, Virginia, preservationists shared an all-too-familiar fear: This was a fight they stood to lose.

Long before the Walmart crisis, growth had spread west out of Fredericksburg and Spotsylvania County into neighboring Orange County, reaching the Wilderness battlefield. In 1967, the massive Lake of the Woods private community of single-family homes was developed off Route 3, just west of the NPS park. In the late 1980s, adjacent to the east side of the battlefield park, came the Lake Wilderness subdivision, which eventually grew to 860 residences. New businesses popped up along the road, especially around the intersection with Route 20 near the park's eastern entrance.

In 2004, the same year CWPT saved the first day's battlefield at Chancellorsville, it put Spotsylvania County on its Top 10 Most Endangered Battlefields list, warning that "its historic battlefields are under constant threat of the bulldozer." In 2005, it put the spotlight farther west, in Orange County, listing the Wilderness as one of the nation's 10 most endangered battlefields that year. "Development plans abound" around the busy Route 3/Route 20 intersection, the CWPT reported.[1297]

In 2006, Orange County conducted a Route 20 Corridor Study that recommended either widening Route 20 or rerouting it—directly through the site of Confederate General John Gordon's flank attack on May 6, 1864. The NPS, CWPT and others knew the battlefield would be severely affected if either proposal was adopted, and urged the county to pursue a new study. The county, by law, had to adopt the plan into its Comprehensive Plan. But in January 2007, at the urging of a half-dozen national and local preservation groups, the county, among other actions, added amendments to require special use permits for large commercial establishments.[1298]

Six months later, two local developers requested rezoning from agricultural to commercial 177 acres of privately owned land within the congressionally authorized boundary of the Wilderness battlefield—an area where more than 5,300 Union and Confederate soldiers fell during the battle. Their plan was to build "Wilderness Crossing," including a hotel and conference center, medical offices, fast-food and sit-down restaurants, a strip mall and warehouses.

The project faced overwhelming opposition from preservationists as well as locals. The Orange County Planning Commission recommended 7–0 to reject the rezoning after a packed hearing on July 17. The board of supervisors unanimously concurred on August 28.[1299] Rebuffed by the county, the owner of 63 of the 177 acres sold his land to the National Park Service (NPS) on December 19, 2007.[1300]

These preservation successes prompted the CWPT to award its 2008 Brian C. Pohanka Preservation Organization of the Year Award to the Friends of the Wilderness Battlefield. The defeat of Wilderness Crossing was "a tribute to the Orange County Board of Supervisors, which repeatedly rejected the development proposal," the CWPT reported in *Hallowed Ground*.[1301]

Despite three major accomplishments in 2007 at the Wilderness, new threats appeared in 2008 on other tracts. The developers who were thwarted in 2007 targeted land across Route 3, opposite the NPS park, and announced plans in the spring of 2008 for an even bigger "Wilderness Crossing" mixed-use development spread over 900 acres that would include retail stores, housing, office space, restaurants, retail stores, and recreational amenities in a "village configuration."[1302]

About the same time, rumors spread that a new Walmart Supercenter was coming to the area. When plans were submitted to Orange County in the spring of 2008 for an unnamed "big-box retailer" with adjoining "mini-box" neighbors on a 52-acre site adjoining the proposed Wilderness Crossing, it was an open secret that the big box would be Walmart. The 52-acre tract had been zoned for commercial development more than 20 years earlier and slated for economic development in county plans.[1303]

"We knew pretty early that the developer was Walmart. In response, we tried to open a dialogue with the county to encourage them to consider an alternate site," recalled Jim Campi. CWPT President Jim Lighthizer sent a letter to Walmart urging the same thing.[1304]

The county wasn't interested in putting roadblocks in front of Walmart. "They didn't want to press Walmart for concessions and take the slightest risk that they might decide to not build in Orange County," Campi recalled.[1305]

That summer, CWPT organized the Wilderness Battlefield Coalition. It consisted of local groups and regional groups—Friends of Wilderness Battlefield, Central Virginia Battlefields Trust (CVBT), the Piedmont Environmental Council (PEC), and Preservation Virginia; and national groups—National Parks Conservation Association, National Coalition for History, and the National Trust for Historic Preservation. The coalition began a public campaign urging Walmart to seek a nearby location that would not threaten the battlefield. PEC conducted a study that revealed eight other locations in Orange County that posed no threat to historic sites.

The controversy bubbled beneath the surface that summer and fall because Walmart had yet to formally file plans with the county. On October 21, 2008, Walmart officials met with Lake of the Woods residents. Officials answered the audience's written questions, which were mostly about project details and infrastructure issues such as traffic, parking, water and sewer. The location was of little concern.[1306]

In December 2008, Walmart applied for the special use permit required by the county for any retail stores larger than 60,000 square feet. The coalition generated strong opposition. In February 2009, the Vermont State Legislature, honoring the 1,200 1st Vermont Brigade soldiers who fell in the battle, passed a resolution condemning Walmart's plans. The Fredericksburg *Free Lance-Star* hailed the resolution and editorialized, "Battlefields can't be moved. Big boxes can."[1307]

Two hundred fifty-two historians, including Ken Burns, Gary Gallagher, David McCullough and James I. Robertson, joined James McPherson in signing a letter to Walmart's president and chief executive, Lee Scott, urging the company to find another site.

Walmart fought back. It released results of a survey of local residents on February 18, 2009, the day before the *Free Lance-Star*'s editorial, reporting that 61 percent of the 300 registered voters who responded supported the project.[1308] Three of five Orange County supervisors announced their support that month for the Walmart on the selected site.[1309]

In March, CWPT named the Wilderness one of its 10 Most Endangered Battlefields of 2009. Representative Ted Poe (R-Tex.) joined Representative Peter Welch (D-Vt.) on the floor of the House of Representatives to speak out against the project. The *Culpeper Star* added its editorial voice: "We've joined a long list of opponents…"[1310]

The county's support of Walmart stiffened. In April, the Orange County Board of Supervisors rejected a proposal by the Wilderness Battlefield Coalition to delay construction six months for a "Wilderness Gateway Study" to take a long-term, comprehensive approach toward development. The study was supported by the largest landowner in the area, the King family, who owned 2,000 acres, although not the Walmart site.

Opposition letters were filling the mailboxes of the supervisors, making some of them cranky. They voted 3–2 against a study, with the majority arguing it was a "delaying tactic."[1311]

One of the pro-Walmart supervisors was a history and Civil War buff. "Jim Lighthizer and I and a staff member met with him at his house," Campi recalled. "He was the guy who had been most sensitive on the board to preservation issues in the past. He was initially pretty friendly to us. But for whatever reason, he was absolutely 100 percent for Walmart. We tried to talk it through with him, and it was

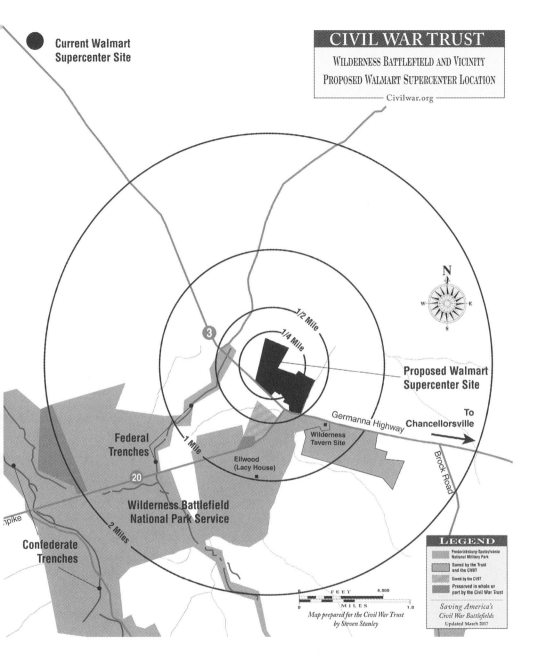

Current Walmart Supercenter Site

1/2 Mile

1/4 Mile

Proposed Walmart Supercenter Site

To Chancellorsville

Germanna Highway

Federal Trenches

1 Mile

Wilderness Tavern Site

Ellwood (Lacy House)

Brock Road

20

Wilderness Battlefield National Park Service

2 Miles

npike

Confederate Trenches

LEGEND

Fredericksburg-Spotsylvania National Military Park

Saved by the Trust and the CVBT

Saved by the CVBT

Preserved in whole or part by the Civil War Trust

Saving America's Civil War Battlefields
Updated March 2017

FEET 4,000

MILES 1.0

Map prepared for the Civil War Trust by Steven Stanley

a very cordial conversation, but we left there with a very clear understanding that he was all for Walmart. And it was pretty clear there wasn't any room for compromise, either."[1312]

The coalition kept up the heat. The 145th anniversary of the three-day battle began on May 5, 2009, a day after preservationists led by actor and Fauquier County resident Robert Duvall and Representatives Poe and Welch gathered on a rainy afternoon at the battlefield, a "cathedral of suffering," as Poe called it.[1313] From the porch of the recently restored Ellwood mansion to an umbrella-covered audience of about 150, Duvall recalled the battle against Disney's America. "Now," he said, "we have Walmart … with its deep pockets of cash."[1314]

Confusion about the NPS park's location complicated the issue. Many people thought the park started at the exhibit shelter at Saunders Field on Route 20, where the main NPS Wilderness Battlefield sign was, but that was in the middle of the park. (Former park Superintendent Russ Smith later moved the sign more than a mile east to the edge of park property). Another issue arose when the American Battlefield Protection Program (ABPP) updated the Civil War Sites Advisory Commission's original 1993 battlefields report and came out with a Wilderness map that showed a larger battlefield. Walmart supporters howled that they were being gamed.[1315]

"It was fascinating," recalled PEC President Chris Miller, "because you have the battlefield park across the road, but this site was clearly part of the core battlefield. This is where the headquarters for the Union tactical command was. They were sitting up on this high spot, surveying the battlefield. But it was outside the federally established park boundary in an area that was planned for growth by Orange County. The Walmart folks are sitting there going, 'What are you guys talking about?' From their perspective, they hadn't sited it inside the battlefield. But from the perspective of the Civil War Preservation Trust and National Trust, it was an important historic resource. From a landscape perspective, it would have a huge impact on people's perception of the battlefield going forward. And from our perspective, it was a disastrous place to site a major economic development."[1316]

On May 21, 2009, the Orange County Planning Commission conducted a public hearing on the project. About 200 people attended, and 73 spoke, stepping up to the microphone one by one. The sentiment was at least two-to-one against the project, and after four hours, the commissioners decided to recess and resume the hearing on June 11. The June session lasted more than three hours as commissioners questioned Walmart representatives and various government officials. They voted to reconvene a third time to address remaining questions and on June 26, following more testimony, the commission voted 5–4 in favor of the project and sent its non-binding recommendation to the board of supervisors. The supervisors scheduled the board's public hearing for July 27.[1317]

On Friday night, July 3, the supervisors called a sudden, special meeting and fired County Administrator Bill Rolfe on a 3–2 vote.[1318] Rolfe had emailed the supervisors and other interested parties, including the media, writing that it would be in the county's best interest to "broker a deal that keeps Walmart in the county" but moved it away from the battlefield.[1319]

"It was insane," recalled Campi. "All Rolfe had said was maybe the county should look at a compromise."[1320]

As the supervisors' public hearing approached, the *Virginian-Pilot* in Norfolk and the *Culpeper Star-Exponent* published editorials urging that Walmart be moved to a different site in the county. In a bipartisan show of support, Virginia's Democratic Governor Tim Kaine joined Republican Speaker of the Virginia House of Delegates William Howell to call for the same solution. They were soon joined by Democratic U.S. Senator Jim Webb.[1321]

Hours before the public hearing was to start on July 27, the board cancelled it. The county had failed to properly advertise the planning commission's public hearing in the legal notices of the local newspaper. The commission's hearing was voided, as was its 5–4 vote recommending county approval. The governmental approval process went back to square one.[1322]

The process became even messier in round two. On August 20, the Planning Commission held a properly advertised public hearing. Twenty-one of 33 speakers opposed Walmart's site. Eight of the 10 planning commissioners attended the hearing. No one changed their vote, but this time it ended in a 4–4 tie. The Code of Virginia establishes that a tie vote results in no official recommendation on the permit. The commission's by-laws, however, said absent a majority vote, the recommendation had to be denial of the permit.[1323]

That did not happen. The next night, August 21, six of the 10 planning commissioners reopened the meeting and voted 5–1 to recommend approval of Walmart's special use permit. Some of the commissioners who failed to attend said they had not been told of the meeting. The August 21 date had been legally advertised with the idea of using it as a backup date if the hearing required more time. Now it had become a mechanism to permit a re-do of the vote.[1324]

But after the tie vote on August 20, few people learned of the commission's sudden decision to meet again on August 21 for another vote.[1325] Campi found out at 4 p.m. on the 21st. No national wire service reporter was there to cover it, unlike previous sessions, and only one regional newspaper ran a story—six days later.[1326]

The Orange County Board of Supervisors took up the matter four days after the 5–1 planning commission vote and held its own seven-hour public hearing. Opponents had outnumbered supporters at the planning commission hearings; now 55 of the 102 public speakers supported the project. Walmart's Director of Public

Affairs, Keith Morris, said, "We've met and exceeded any requests and guidelines put before us by the community."

At 1 a.m. on August 26, 2009, the board of supervisors voted 4–1 to issue the special use permit for Walmart to build.[1327] Some supervisors sniped at the preservationists. In a pointed reference to the Vermont legislature, Commissioner Zack Burkett said he was "pretty sure the only troops that went through there were Yankee deserters."[1328]

Campi sat alone through most of the meeting to avoid being around anyone who might be the least bit disrespectful. After the vote, Campi allowed himself a slight, grim smile. He had known for months the coalition was going to lose and had plenty of time to prepare. The Washington law firm of Arnold & Porter, which had fought so effectively for Tersh Boasberg and the Brandy Station Foundation, was prepared. Campi thought, "They have no idea what we're going to hit them with next."[1329]

On September 23, Arnold & Porter filed a complaint against the county board of supervisors in the Circuit Court of Orange County alleging serious procedural errors and missteps. Plaintiffs were the Friends of the Wilderness Battlefield, the National Trust for Historic Preservation, and six local residents, five from Lake of the Woods.[1330]

The National Trust was selected by the coalition as the primary plaintiff because it had better legal standing than the CWPT, even though CWPT was managing the preservation fight and more actively involved.[1331]

The suit asked for a court order declaring the board's approval of the special use permit unlawful and stopping the county from taking further action. It alleged that the county's decision-making process and the decision itself failed to protect historic resources. It alleged that the zoning ordinance was unlawful because it failed to give reasonable consideration to encroachment upon historic areas. The county "brushed aside and gave inadequate weight to the substantial negative impacts of the Walmart project" that would result in the "desecration of hallowed ground," the complaint said.[1332]

The suit challenged the legality of the planning commission's 5–1 revote a day after the 4–4 tie. It also alleged the permit was unlawful because it illegally allowed an access road to be built on residentially zoned land.[1333] The county responded with a legal answer that the coalition had no grounds to sue. It challenged the legal standing of the plaintiffs, claiming they were not aggrieved persons. It said the plaintiffs didn't understand Virginia law; the matter was a "policy dispute" over a legislative decision involving no demonstrable harm or injury to the plaintiffs. The county asserted the lawsuit was a contrived effort "to prevent use of land that they do not own ... and the complaint was "a rambling set of allegations designed to try to avoid dismissal prior to trial."[1334]

Arnold & Porter's Robert Rosenbaum was the coalition's attorney. He had litigated a similar suit in Pennsylvania after a private company secured zoning to build a hotel, conference center and museum on a 78-acre privately owned tract within the boundary of Valley Forge National Historical Park. Rosenbaum had just retired at 69 years old, but agreed to take on the case pro bono. The CWPT later estimated the donated legal services would have cost more than a million dollars.[1335]

Rosenbaum was well equipped to take on the nation's largest corporation. "We're a huge law firm," he said. "We do this all the time." But the preservationists knew they faced an uphill battle they could lose. "The laws in Virginia make it almost impossible to overturn a zoning decision," recalled Rosenbaum. "We thought we had a good case, but against that standard it was going to be very hard."[1336]

Rosenbaum planned to argue that the county failed to properly evaluate the historic nature of the proposed Walmart site, but he knew that argument was less likely to sway a judge than the allegations that both the county and Walmart made serious mistakes in their zeal to bring Walmart to Orange County. He would not only spotlight the planning commission re-vote, but would argue that Walmart's traffic predictions were gravely flawed. Rosenbaum would argue that the county relied on an economic and fiscal impact analysis provided by Walmart that was faulty, misrepresentative and "just as phony as a three-dollar bill," recalled economist Michael Siegel, who was hired by the coalition to review it. "It just made stuff up. It made huge errors. The tables they presented made no sense because they had been assembled improperly. It was just an inept, incompetent report. It was good enough for Orange County and they liked it. But I took it apart."[1337]

Rosenbaum also intended to reveal that the county had acted without seeing a study which, as the county knew, had been requested by the Virginia Department of Transportation on the impact of traffic at the intersection of Routes 3 and 20, but that Walmart never gave the county or VDOT. During the discovery phase of the litigation, Rosenbaum learned that Walmart had in fact conducted the study and that it showed the intersection would be badly affected, according to Rosenbaum's traffic expert. Rosenbaum planned to argue that the county should have insisted on seeing the study before acting.[1338]

A key allegation was that the defendants purposely misrepresented and downplayed the historic legacy of the land.[1339] Walmart had hired a respected Fredericksburg archaeological consulting firm, Dovetail Cultural Resource Group, to conduct an archaeological study as part of the special permit process. Walmart reported that its study found that nothing of historic significance had happened on the land, Rosenbaum recalled.[1340]

Citing the study, Orange County Director of Community Development David Grover said there was "no evidence of encampments, movements of significance, or engagements on the subject site. The consultants retained by Wal-Mart have advised me that they have ... found nothing of significance" and nothing that would merit the land's inclusion in the National Register of Historic Places.[1341]

Virginia Department of Historic Resources Director Kathleen Kilpatrick, well known in the preservation community as a passionate defender of Virginia's history, issued a public letter "to set the record straight" after she heard the "nothing of significance" declaration.[1342] A Walmart Supercenter at the proposed site would have "a serious adverse effect both on the Wilderness Battlefield and on the National Park," she wrote to the planning commission. "Please be advised that the proposed Wal-Mart site is located entirely within the boundaries of the Wilderness Battlefield," she said, and "clearly eligible" for inclusion on the National Register of Historic Places.[1343]

Rosenbaum took a deposition from Dovetail President Kerri Barile, who said the archaeological study had uncovered evidence of a Civil War-era encampment and military activity. She testified that she had come to the planning commission hearing and wanted to speak to that point, but a Walmart lawyer said no.[1344]

Rosenbaum planned to argue that the site wasn't just a staging area, as Walmart and the county claimed. The Union army's headquarters area included the 5th Corps hospital. Dovetail also found evidence of an artillery encampment. Atop the small hill whose top was to be cut off and leveled for the Supercenter, a Union battery had unlimbered, anticipating a Confederate attack the next morning.[1345]

Scholar and Pulitzer Prize-winning historian James McPherson was prepared to testify that the Walmart site was "the nerve center of the Union Army" during this pivotal three-day battle involving some 185,000 troops. "This site is important for understanding the Battle of the Wilderness because of its centrality during the entire battle for Union troop movements on the roads through that intersection, artillery emplacements, infantry deployments, communications and care of the wounded," McPherson wrote in a nine-page preview. "Those three days of trauma in the Wilderness were the beginning of the end, even if the end was still eleven months in the future."[1346]

As the case moved through the legal system in 2010, NPS Director Jonathan B. Jarvis took the unusual step of supporting the lawsuit. Usually the NPS remains neutral in local legal or governmental land use issues. But Jarvis, in a January 2010 letter to Lighthizer, said the agency did not believe the county had "taken actions necessary to address our concerns." Jarvis wrote, "Hills would be leveled and roads widened so that the Piedmont landscape would be unrecognizable."[1347]

On April 30, 2010, the county lost the first showdown in court when Circuit Judge Daniel R. Bouton rejected its motion to dismiss the suit. Bouton tossed the National Trust out of the case, saying it had no standing, but allowed the suit to proceed with Friends of the Wilderness Battlefield and the six local citizens as plaintiffs. Later, Rosenbaum succeeded in forcing Walmart into the case as a defendant. A trial date was set for January 25, 2011.[1348]

"Walmart and the county fought tooth and nail," Rosenbaum recalled. "Some people say we never got to fight because we never had a trial, but we had to fight every step of the way."[1349] At one point, Bouton criticized both sides for a "contentious dispute over exchange of information" and told them to sit down and work it out.[1350] But the problem persisted.

"We had to fight with them for every document we got," Rosenbaum recalled. "We had to fight to take the depositions of the county commissioners. We were blocked every way they could block us. This is normal when two corporations are fighting with each other. Big corporations always fight like hell. But why would they want to put up this kind of scorched-earth defense if they had nothing to hide?"[1351] Rosenbaum knew he had some good material, but would it be enough?

The uneasy feeling persisted within the coalition as the case went to trial. Brad Coker of Mason-Dixon Polling and Research recalled, "That Wilderness Walmart situation had me concerned, because the economy was really bad, and the county was looking for the jobs, and Walmart had a lot of money to throw around, and could hire a lot of lobbyists and local lawyers. They were a formidable opponent. That was probably the biggest preservation win where there was a stronger possibility we were going to lose."[1352]

As pre-trial proceedings began on January 25, 2011, Bouton announced he was smothered with at least 16 motions and thousands of pages of supporting documents. "The material kept coming in," he said. Boxes and boxes of color-coded files were piled up around and behind him. It would take at least two days to hear the pre-trial motions, Bouton said.[1353]

Bouton started with the defendants' motion for summary judgment to dismiss the case. Orange County Attorney Sharon E. Pandak, leading a team of five attorneys, including two from Walmart, spoke for the defense. "This case is not about the Civil War or whether one likes Walmart," she said. "Very simply, this is a land-use case."

She spoke for an hour, attacking the preservationists and asserting that the county had been thorough and fair.[1354]

Now it was Rosenbaum's turn, and he relished the opportunity to unleash his own attack. But a Walmart attorney approached and asked if he would agree to a brief recess. The attorney needed to make some phone calls. "You really need to agree to this. This will be good for you," the attorney told him. Rosenbaum agreed to a recess.[1355]

The attorney returned and asked Rosenbaum for a recess for the rest of the day. "He told us they were considering abandoning the site as a store location but a final decision hadn't been made," Rosenbaum recalled. "He told me to come to the judge's chambers first thing in the morning." The judge agreed to the recess and adjourned until 9 a.m. the following day.[1356]

In Bouton's chambers the morning of January 26, Walmart attorneys agreed to drop the battlefield site as a Supercenter location as long as the announcement was made then and there and the suit was dismissed with no further proceedings. "That's not fair," Rosenbaum argued in chambers. "The county is leaving the public with this false impression about our case and the facts, and I'd really like the opportunity to respond publicly."[1357] But Walmart's legal team "absolutely insisted" that the case end right then and there, or there was no deal, Rosenbaum recalled. He consented. Back in the courtroom, only the judge spoke.[1358]

"The trial is not going to go forward," he said. "Walmart intends to relinquish its rights under the special use permit."[1359] Bouton then read a statement from Walmart: "We have decided to preserve the property near the Wilderness battlefield in Orange County, Virginia, that was approved by the Board of Supervisors for a new store. We will still buy the land, but not develop it." The retail giant also said it would "compensate the county for its legal and administrative expenses related to this project" and find a new location farther out Route 3.[1360]

As the courtroom emptied, Walmart spokesman William C. Wertz stood outside handing out copies of Walmart's statement. Wertz said the decision had been made in the previous 24 hours. "We tried to weigh the balance between preservation and economic growth and decided preservation needed to get the weight," he said.[1361]

The preservationists were ecstatic. "Sam Walton would be proud of this decision," Lighthizer said. Friends of the Wilderness Battlefield President Zann Nelson said her reaction was one of "pure joy."[1362]

"We were all prepared to try it," Rosenbaum recalled. "I thought for sure that Walmart would not want the PR nightmare of this fight. I thought they would have seen the light much sooner. But that didn't happen until it was clear that we had the team ready and the ammo in our guns and were ready for trial. And we were."[1363]

Orange County officials could not contain their bitterness. The county was "stunned and disappointed" at Walmart's decision, the county's press release said. "Forces from largely outside the County, using exaggeration, took advantage of the horrors of the Civil War to achieve their own goals. Concepts of private property ownership, which were well-understood by our ancestors at the time of the Constitution and the time of the Civil War, were forgotten by the Plaintiffs in their zeal," said the county's statement.[1364]

The press release misrepresented McPherson's attitude about the historic significance of the land and complained about "the economic damage created by those who brought the lawsuit," even though no store yet existed and there was every expectation that Walmart would build in the county. The CWPT (renamed Civil War Trust in 2011) had never seen a government press release so petulant and bitter; staff posted it on the civilwar.org website, where it remains.[1365]

By May 2011, Walmart had found a location 7.2 miles farther west on Route 3 and more centrally located in Orange County. At the annual conference, the Civil War Trust awarded Rosenbaum its Shelby Foote Preservation Legacy Award and presented its Carrington Williams Battlefield Preservationist of the Year award to the plaintiffs—the Friends of the Wilderness Battlefield and local residents Curtis Abel, Dale Brown, Sheila Clark, Susan Caton, Dwight Mottet and Craig Rains.[1366]

On November 8, 2013, Republican Governor Robert "Bob" McDonnell announced that Walmart had made a "generous and voluntary gift" of the original store site to the Commonwealth of Virginia. By then, the store had been open for five months at the new location and was bustling with shoppers. The preservationists, meanwhile, had made progress in healing the rift created by the controversy.[1367]

Less than two months after Walmart's surprise announcement, the Wilderness Battlefield Coalition began a cooperative effort with local officials, landowners and businesses to develop a blueprint for the Wilderness Gateway region's future development that balanced preservation, conservation and economic development. The study, completed and released in April 2012, "unequivocally demonstrates that preservation and development need not be mutually exclusive," said Project Manager Glenn Stach.[1368]

"We began by lobbing volleys at each other," said Orange County Board of Supervisors Chairman Teel Goodwin. "Now that the smoke has cleared, it is time to find common ground to meld a future that we all can share."[1369]

As Lighthizer saw it, the lesson for Walmart or any corporation or developer bent on building on hallowed ground "is that when a group like the Civil War Trust comes to talk to you, find out who they are. If they had done a Google search and seen the fights we were in at Gettysburg, if they'd seen the fight we won right down the street—five miles down the road—at Chancellorsville, they would have said, 'These guys are formidable. They can cause a lot of trouble. Let's talk to them.'

"They didn't do that," Lighthizer recalled. "But in the end, they recognized that this was not a good idea for them. They changed course and everybody ended up happy."[1370]

The story didn't end there, however. Never satisfied with just defeating a development proposal, the Trust recommitted itself to acquiring additional land near the intersection of Routes 3 and 20. Working with the CVBT and Friends of the Wilderness Battlefield, the Trust has helped save much of the land associated with the Wilderness Gateway area, in addition to the former Walmart location. ★[1371]

CHAPTER

NINETEEN

A Capstone Acquisition During Campaign 150

HE STAFF at the Civil War Preservation Trust (CWPT) was fully engaged in the Walmart battle in the fall of 2009 when a new threat reignited. David LeVan had not given up his dream of building a casino in Gettysburg. On November 25, 2009, LeVan announced a proposal for the Eisenhower Inn and Conference Center on Emmitsburg Road less than a half mile south of Gettysburg National Military Park's boundary. The gaming palace would feature 600 slot machines and dozens of table and card games.

Four months earlier, LeVan and his wife donated to the Gettysburg Foundation a scenic, historic and open space easement on 61 acres adjacent to the Gettysburg Museum and Visitor's Center.[1372]

"We were repeatedly asked to participate in the big news conference they held," Campi recalled. CWPT seriously considered the request to celebrate the protection of additional land at Gettysburg, but concerns about how LeVan might try to construe the organization's participation for other purposes led CWPT to decline.[1373]

The second casino fight started out much differently than the first. Though rebuffed in his effort to have the Trust be a part of the July preservation ceremony, LeVan told the Trust about the project in advance. "We and our coalition partners had two meetings with him to discuss this proposal before it came out," Campi recalled. But from the start, it was "almost inevitable" the Trust would oppose the project, Campi said. "It was just too close to Gettysburg and the battlefield."[1374]

As LeVan geared up for another run at the state gaming board, so did No Casino Gettysburg. Three years after the first casino battle, Susan and Jim Paddock shuddered at the thought of another drawn-out fight. Yet even as exhausted as the last fight left them, they did not hesitate to re-engage, joining once again with the CWPT and other organizations.[1375]

On August 31 and September 1, 2010, the Pennsylvania Gaming Control Board held public hearings at Gettysburg on LeVan's proposed project, which was competing with other proposals for a single available license. The Trust delivered petitions with 30,000 signatures asking that the board reject the LeVan license request. No Casino Gettysburg premiered a nine-minute, "all-star" video with a score by composer John Williams; appearances by historians Ken Burns and David McCullough, actors Matthew Broderick, Stephen Lang and Sam Waterston, and Susan Eisenhower, chairman emeritus of the (President) Eisenhower Institute at Gettysburg College. The video, produced and directed by New York City Creative Director Jeff Griffith, featured other Gettysburg residents and a powerful statement about the casino's likely impact on budget-strapped county support services.[1376]

"We also used this campaign to pioneer a number of new online and digital outreach tools," recalled Mary Goundrey Koik, CWPT's former deputy director of communications, who, with policy associate Nick Redding, was on the front lines of the fight. "This was where we learned how to use social media to mobilize people," she recalled. "That's how the movement found some of its most passionate volunteers. We also helped organize the Veterans for Gettysburg organization, which was one of our first explicit attempts to make the connection between historic and contemporary military service and sacrifice."[1377]

But the casino supporters were better organized, too. "We did the same strategy, but they had a much, more powerful pro-casino group than the first time and a much more vocal group," recalled Susan Paddock. Several local businesses supported the casino, convinced they could anticipate an influx of business for themselves. More casino supporters appeared at the public hearings and their testimony included false allegations that CWPT President Jim Lighthizer had a financial stake in another casino project under consideration. LeVan recalled that the allegations "did not come from us, but came out of a group we didn't have total control over."[1378]

The Pennsylvania Gaming Control Board was expected to announce its decision in December 2010, but it was unable to reach a consensus and postponed the decision. The delay was especially frustrating for CWPT staff. They would have to continue the casino fight into the new year at the same time the Wilderness Walmart fight was fully engaged. The suit to stop it was set for trial in late January 2011. It was a busy holiday season, but the tide shifted in January when Walmart sought a new location away from the Wilderness battlefield and settled the suit. In April 2011, the gaming board voted to award the casino permit to a large resort in western Pennsylvania. A Gettysburg casino project had received one board member's vote in 2006, but none in 2011.[1379]

As these two fights faded into history, Lighthizer and the staff could focus on important initiatives to shape the organization's future. Eleven years after the merger between its two predecessor groups, the nation's largest battlefield preservation organization announced a new brand identity, timed to coincide with the beginning of the Civil War's 150th anniversary.

Gone was a name usually reduced to a poorly recognized acronym—"CWPT" for Civil War Preservation Trust—refined and simplified to the Civil War Trust, or the Trust. The organization also redesigned its logo, an oval amalgamation of the Union and Confederate battle flags held over and adapted from the original 1987 Association for the Preservation of Civil War Sites (APCWS) logo. It was replaced by a graphic interpretation of two silhouetted soldiers respectfully bearing the flag

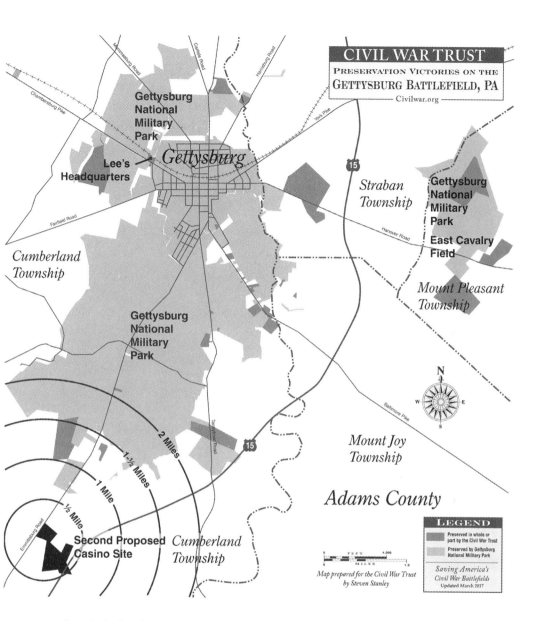

Gettysburg
National
Military
Park

Lee's
Headquarters

Gettysburg

*Straban
Township*

Gettysburg
National
Military
Park

East Cavalry
Field

*Cumberland
Township*

*Mount Pleasant
Township*

Gettysburg
National
Military
Park

Mount Joy
Township

Adams County

2 Miles
1-½ Miles
1 Mile
½ Mile

Second Proposed *Cumberland*
Casino Site *Township*

under which they fought, standing guard over a battlefield landscape. A new tagline summarizing the mission—"Saving America's Civil War Battlefields"—and a 21st-century necessity, the official www.civilwar.org website URL, were also added.

"After careful thought and deliberation, we determined that the time was right to modernize our image to better reflect the Civil War Trust's mission and to reach more Americans concerned about our shared heritage," said Lighthizer in the official announcement. "We hope that unveiling this change at such an exciting time—as the sesquicentennial stimulates interest in the Civil War and the hallowed battlegrounds where that conflict was decided—will also help generate greater support for battlefield preservation. After all, what better way to commemorate the great struggle between North and South than to save the historic landscapes of the Civil War for our children and grandchildren?"[1380]

Anticipating a major uptick in public interest in the months and years following the 150th anniversary of the April 12, 1861, bombardment of Fort Sumter, South Carolina, the Trust prepared itself for the unprecedented opportunity by announcing a campaign that seemed almost outlandish in its goals.

For the next 48 months, the Trust intended to take advantage of every possible battle anniversary to promote preservation and Civil War history. Well-timed land acquisitions, property transfers to the U.S. Department of the Interior National Park Service (NPS), new animated maps, new smart phone battle applications and local or regional anniversary events all became opportunities to enhance the Sesquicentennial of the American Civil War.

The anniversary era would feature new education programs for all ages, on the battlefields, online and inside classrooms. The Trust would sponsor a Civil War supplement with the Newspapers in Education program and would join publisher Houghton Mifflin Harcourt to sponsor the National Civil War Student Challenge, a trivia competition.[1381]

The crowning feature, though, was the Trust's most ambitious and longest-running fundraising campaign ever. On June 30, 2011, at the Lutheran Theological Seminary in Gettysburg, Lighthizer was joined by Trust Chairman Henry Simpson, country music star Trace Adkins, then the newest member of the Trust's board of directors, and James McPherson to announce *Campaign 150: Our Time, Our Legacy.*

The Trust aimed to raise $40 million in four years, using it to protect 20,000 more battlefield acres through acquisition or easement—a figure representing two-thirds of the 30,000 acres that had been saved in the entire history of the preservation movement to 2011. "The idea was to have a big, hairy, ambitious goal," Lighthizer recalled. "And raising $40 million was a big number. When we started, some of the board had trepidations that we could raise that kind of money. But, really, it's the story of an organization challenging itself with a difficult but realistic goal."[1382]

Members responded in their customarily generous fashion, and by the end of the first year—just a quarter of the way through the campaign—the organization had passed the halfway point, collecting $25.6 million, or 64 percent of the $40 million goal for the preservation coffers.[1383]

An early highlight in the four-year commemoration came in April 2012 at

Shiloh, Tennessee, where the Trust rolled out three preservation accomplishments. Neither the APCWS nor the original Trust saved land at Shiloh before the merger. But after the CWPT made its first save there in 2001—a modest two-acre purchase for $35,000—new tracts were added almost yearly. By 2012, the Trust had saved 524 acres in 17 different acquisitions.[1384]

On April 5, 2012, the day before the 150th anniversary of the first day's battle at Shiloh, Lighthizer and Trust Chairman Emeritus John L. Nau III joined Tennessee Governor Bill Haslam, Adkins and longtime Shiloh National Military Park Superintendent Woody Harrell for three major announcements. The ceremony included leaders of Tennessee's particularly effective Civil War Sesquicentennial Commission, other state and local officials and battlefield supporters.[1385]

Harrell, in one of his final official acts before retiring, accepted the transfer to the Shiloh park of 167 acres the Trust had amassed in three acquisitions during 2007 and 2008. The NPS had begun its own sesquicentennial initiative with a $5 million program to transfer more than 536 acres at Shiloh and three other battlefield parks to federal ownership.[1386]

The Trust also announced a $1.25 million campaign to pay for a 491-acre tract (ultimately 504 acres) along the Tennessee River on the southeastern part of the battlefield. The property had become a killing zone for retreating Union soldiers a few hours into the battle. "It was like shooting into a flock of sheep," a Confederate recalled. The large tract had been a top NPS acquisition priority for decades, and when the Trust sold it to the NPS, it was the largest addition to the Shiloh park since it was established in 1894.[1387]

Finally, Lighthizer announced that the Trust was closing on 267 acres about six miles southwest of the main battlefield. The area, known as Fallen Timbers, was the site of the final clash of the Shiloh campaign on April 8, 1862. In this single purchase, the Trust saved 75 percent of a small battlefield with a big history. Here, Confederate General Nathan Bedford Forrest was wounded and nearly captured after galloping headlong into a Yankee vanguard, helping thwart a Union advance.[1388]

The day after the announcement, Lighthizer, Nau, and staff members Koik and Redding took a quick driving tour of the Shiloh battlefield before heading to the airport. The route took them past the large tract at the southeastern corner of the battlefield that the Trust had just contracted to buy. It still had a large "For Sale" sign displayed.[1389]

"We stopped and all got out to look at the sign," Koik recalled. "I happened to have a 'Sharpie' in my bag. So, Jim Lighthizer and Nick and I actually marked "SOLD" over the sign in big letters. It was not the best handwriting, but Jim helped color it in, too."[1390]

For the Antietam Sesquicentennial in September 2012, the Trust unveiled a "digital trifecta." The web site, civilwar.org, debuted "Antietam 360," a series of 360-degree interactive photographs of the battlefield at eight key locations, an animated Antietam map and a GPS-enabled Antietam Battle App® smartphone tour, adding to a program begun two years earlier with a Gettysburg version that had since grown to include Fredericksburg, Chancellorsville and First Manassas. A web presentation on the Emancipation Proclamation was also introduced.[1391]

The Trust honored every battle anniversary possible during the Sesquicentennial. In 2012, it added more than 95 acres at Mill Springs, Kentucky, transferred 15 Trust-owned acres to Tennessee's Fort Donelson National Battlefield and announced a new campaign to buy a six-acre tract at Cedar Mountain, Virginia.

In 2013, the Trust announced a $720,000 campaign for its first three saves at Mississippi's Vicksburg National Military Park, securing six acres that year, followed by five more acres in 2014. Although the land was near the battlefield's famous Railroad Redoubt, it was next to Interstate 20 and zoned for commercial development. When the Trust held its annual conference in Vicksburg May 29 to June 2, it unveiled a new Vicksburg Battle App®, produced with the aid of the Vicksburg Convention & Visitors Bureau and Friends of Vicksburg National Military Park and Campaign. The Trust's 2013 acquisitions also included multiple purchases at the 1863 battlefields of Brandy Station, Chancellorsville and Gettysburg.[1392]

When the Trust reached its goal of $40 million in 2014, more than a year early, the board of trustees decided to raise the bar to $50 million. By the spring of 2015, the 150th anniversary of the war's end, *Campaign 150* had brought in more than $52.5 million.[1393] "We raised the money and exceeded our [original] goal by 25 percent, so it was a very successful campaign," Lighthizer said.[1394]

As for acquisitions, the Trust had saved more than 10,000 acres during the four-year sesquicentennial.[1395] "We didn't hit the acreage goal, which was a stretch goal to begin with," Lighthizer recalled. "The land cost more and we ended up spending more money. When it comes to land, it's all about money."[1396]

An acre might cost less than a $1,000, as it did at White Oak Road, an 1865 battlefield in rural Dinwiddie County, outside Petersburg, Virginia, where the Trust purchased 12.3 acres for $8,000 in 2013. Or it might cost $1 million per acre, as was the case for one of the greatest preservation victories in Trust history, the purchase and restoration of Lee's Headquarters at Gettysburg.

That transaction was not finalized in time for the 1863 battle's sesquicentennial, but on July 1, 2014, the Trust held a press conference to announce a fundraising campaign to help pay part of the $5.5 million needed to buy the 4.14 acre-tract. The property included the pre-war stone house that had been Lee's command post during the battle, as well as a motel and restaurant.

The Trust had long seen the property as high priority. "Not only was it historically very, very significant, but it had all the ingredients," Lighthizer recalled. "It had Gettysburg, the Kentucky Derby of battlefields; it had Robert E. Lee, the Clark Gable of generals, and it was a building, something tangible, something you could see and feel. And that's what made it by far and away the most well-known thing we'd ever attempted."[1397]

Trust Director of Real Estate Tom Gilmore negotiated with the owners for several years before reaching agreement to acquire the entire property. The tract had been commercially developed and was worth more than $1.3 million per acre, but the history of the old house and the intense fighting on the property made the expense worthwhile to the Trust.

Built in the 1830s, it was the home of the widow Mary Thompson in 1863, owned in trust for Thompson by Thaddeus Stevens, the intense abolitionist Republican congressman from Pennsylvania who hailed from Gettysburg, where he practiced law.

Due to its proximity to Chambersburg Pike, the Oak Ridge and McPherson Ridge railroad cuts and Seminary Ridge, the land around the house was the scene of the heaviest fighting on July 1 and, arguably, of the entire battle. After Confederate forces finally flushed out Union soldiers taking cover around the house, Lee established his headquarters there, and directed the battle as command staff tents and a field hospital sprouted up around him.

When the federal government established a national battlefield park at Gettysburg in 1895, the Thompson home, still privately owned, was not part of it. The Gettysburg Battlefield Memorial Association gave the park about 800 acres it had gradually acquired since the war, but this acreage, centered on Union positions, did not include the Thompson house.[1398] Confederate strongholds remained mostly privately owned, and commercial interests took advantage, especially along Seminary Ridge, where tourist cabins, diners and even a roller rink went up.[1399]

In 1904, the federally owned park was deemed semi-complete at 1,380 acres, with the battlefield commissioners declaring that acquisition of any further extensive parcels of land "would be a waste of public funds." This included the Thompson house.[1400]

Lee's Headquarters eventually became part of a popular commercial complex that included a restaurant and Larson's Motel. The Thompson house was converted to a museum and gift store. "The house had been covered up in plain sight," Lighthizer said."[1401]

The Trust's acquisition, to be sure, had its critics in Gettysburg. The township lost a viable business and the taxes it paid when the motel closed permanently. After the Appalachian Brewing Company brewpub vacated the restaurant building, however, it relocated to a downtown property with outdoor seating and far more foot traffic.[1402]

Most of the 70 or so people who attended a public forum on October 6, 2015, at the park's visitor center supported the Trust's plan to purchase and return the battlefield land to its wartime appearance, as outlined by Director of History and Education Garry Adelman and Chief Administrative Officer Steve Wyngarden. In response to concern for the Borough's tax losses, the Trust chose to make a voluntary payment in lieu of taxes. Moreover, the Trust pointed out that the hotel vacancy rate in Gettysburg was more than sufficient to absorb the closure of the motel.[1403]

Nostalgic critics mourned the loss of an important part of Gettysburg tourism history. Countless baby boomer Civil War buffs had stayed at Larson's Motel in the 1960s and 1970s when their parents brought them to the battlefield. The Trust promised to honor that history with interpretive signs that told both wartime and tourism stories.[1404]

As always, Trust members responded to the call for donations, contributing $4.5 million to the campaign. The Trust closed the deal on January 7, 2015, paying $5.5 million, including $1.5 million in grant proceeds funded by the American Battlefield Protection Program.[1405]

Restoration costs increased the overall project price to about $6 million, as the Trust began working with the Borough Council, Gettysburg's Historical Architecture Review Board and the Pennsylvania Historical and Museum Commission in the year-long approval process for storm water management, soil conservation and other required plan elements.[1406]

Following asbestos removal, the motel, restaurant and other structures were demolished in March and April 2016. Copper piping and fixtures were recycled. Asphalt parking lots were ripped up and hauled off. The old sewer and electrical systems were removed, upgraded and reinstalled.[1407]

The original landscape had been so disturbed by post-war grading and construction that only one Civil War artifact was uncovered during the restoration. After the sale closed, the owners generously donated to the Trust a trove of artifacts the museum had displayed, including original Thompson house relics. These included a chair that was in the house during the battle and a pair of outbuilding shutters pock-marked by bullets. All artifacts associated with the house were donated to Gettysburg National Military Park, while artifacts related to other battles were donated to relevant national parks, and artifacts with less certain provenance were sold to aid the restoration effort.[1408]

In May 2016, the three-month restoration of the land and the Thompson home was underway. "Most of our projects are demolitions or timbering, where we try to restore historic landscapes," said Matt George, the Trust's land stewardship manager, as the work progressed. "This is much more a restoration project. We're doing both in this case, and restoring the historic landscape as well as restoring the building on site."[1409] The historic contours of the land were restored using post-war survey maps created by civil engineer and former General Gouverneur K. Warren, who fought at Gettysburg. Twenty-four apple trees were planted in the spring of 2017 to recreate the historic orchard that existed at the time of the battle. A five-stop interpretive trail was created to explain the momentous events that took place in and around the home during the three-day battle.[1410]

Inside the house, post-war walls were ripped out, revealing an original fireplace. A historically accurate cedar shingle roof was constructed. A brick and earth berm around the building was removed, revealing two hidden basement windows. The original porch was rebuilt, in part by relying on visual information from Mathew B. Brady's 3-D photographs of the house in mid-July 1863. Other features visible in the Brady photos, including a garden and fencing—even a doghouse—were recreated.[1411]

"The historic photos connect us right to the scene in 1863," Lighthizer said. "Figuratively, you're looking through the same lens that Brady did more than 150 years ago. You can touch the same house he saw, and know what you're touching is the same house Robert E. Lee touched and saw, and where he made some of the most historically momentous decisions that were ever made—decisions that affected the course of our republic. People can relate to that. When they can see and touch things that were actually there, it adds another dimension to the experience."[1412]

On October 28, 2016, with the battlefield aglow in fall colors, some 700 people gathered outside the house for the official rededication and ribbon-cutting of the transformed acreage and restored house. "We restored the building—Lee's Headquarters—to the point where if Robert E. Lee rode up today on his horse, Traveller, he'd know where he was," Lighthizer told the audience.[1413]

It was the largest gathering in the Trust's history, exceeding any conference, banquet, announcement, protest, dedication or unveiling. Dozens of reenactors were there, along with many local, state and federal officials. But they accounted for only a fraction of the crowd. Before he stepped to the podium, Lighthizer studied the audience and wondered: *Just who are all these people?* His instincts told him it was a Trust crowd. So he asked: "Would you please raise your hand if you are a member of the Civil War Trust?" Nearly every hand went up.[1414]

"It was exciting to see that we were with a whole bunch of our fellow travelers," Lighthizer said. "These were members coming to celebrate something that they did, something they believed in, something very significant. And there was a tremendous amount of pride that they did this."[1415]

At Brandy Station, though, more controversy erupted as Sesquicentennial got underway. In the spring of 2011, bulldozers started scooping out land for a large pond at the base of Fleetwood Hill below Tony Troilo's big, new hilltop home.

A small perennial stream known as Flat Run ran across Troilo's Fleetwood Hill property, and a small watering pond was leaking. Troilo decided to install a small dam and expand the pond to more than 600 linear feet. He planned to install a small footbridge over the run as part of a battlefield heritage walking trail. He was exploring tax credits and "ready to give a deeded right of way for putting a walking path in," Troilo recalled. "We were talking with VDOT (Virginia Department of Transportation) about how far we needed to be off the road to put an asphalt walking path. That's how far we had gone with this." Troilo also said he was making arrangements to have a fire hydrant installed so local fire department pumpers could fill up from the pond.[1416]

Troilo saw nothing inconsistent with his use of Fleetwood Hill and its heritage. He built his new house on the footprint of a wartime home that stood on the hill throughout the war and survived until destroyed by fire in 1896. He had the right by zoning law to build five homes on the property, but had no intention of doing that. He said he never stopped visitors or tours from coming onto the property and, in fact, encouraged it.[1417]

Brandy Station's heritage was part of Troilo's family heritage; his mother had spent her life there. "My mother was born in 1922, and a family—the Matthews family—had lived here adjacent to Fleetwood Hill back to the early 1800s. My mother remembered listening to the Matthews men, who had been born around 1850, as they talked about General J.E.B. Stuart sitting in their house and eating with them. My father was always after my mother to tell people about this, but she kept it to herself."[1418]

Bulldozers began sculpting the lake along a 666-foot stretch of Flat Run around March 1, 2011, Troilo said. The county had raised no objections, and Troilo said he was unaware of any federal permitting requirements. He said he had enlarged the

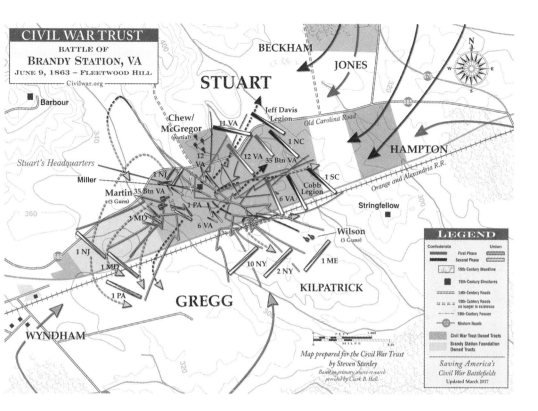

Barbour

BECKHAM

JONES

STUART

Chew/
McGregor
(partial)

11 VA

Jeff Davis
Legion

Old Carolina Road

1 NC

HAMPTON

12
VA

12 VA

35 Btn VA

Stuart's Headquarters

Miller

1 SC

Cobb
Legion

Orange and Alexandria R.R.

Martin 35 Btn VA
(3 Guns)

1 PA

6 VA

Stringfellow

1 MD

6 VA

Wilson
(3 Guns)

1 NJ

1 MD

10 NY

2 NY

1 ME

KILPATRICK

1 PA

GREGG

WYNDHAM

Map prepared for the Civil War Trust
by Steven Stanley
Based on primary source research
provided by Clark B. Hall

original watering hole in 2002 with no permits or complaints. But from the day he started work, Troilo said, someone was watching and taking photographs.[1419]

On May 6, 2011, Joe Troilo, 90, passed away at his son's new home. Bud Hall and Joe Troilo had been friends for years. Hall drove to Brandy Station to attend services for his old friend. Upon arriving, Hall said he was shocked to see bulldozers and the makings of the pond at Flat Run.

"Friggin' disaster," he emailed on May 9 to several Trust staff members. "Will send you pictures tomorrow (Think Lake Tahoe on the Brandy Station Battlefield)." Hall's emails indicated the work was a total surprise to him. He sent an email to the Brandy Station Foundation (BSF) asking, "Did anybody from BSF know about this ahead of time?"[1420]

Jim Campi advised Hall to call the Army Corps of Engineers to make sure Troilo had the permit required by the federal Clean Water Act. On May 11, Hall emailed Campi that he met on-site that morning with a Corps official who then went to speak with Troilo.[1421]

"He came the day we were having the wake service for my father," Troilo said. "The gentleman was very nice ... " They agreed to meet a few days later to discuss the issue.[1422]

The official later confirmed Troilo needed a Corps permit and was in violation of the Clean Water Act. The project would have to stop immediately and the stream would have to be restored. Troilo agreed to the costly repairs. But he was furious with Hall for filing the complaint.

"I got blindsided," Troilo recalled. "He never came to me and said, 'What are you doing?' He was out to get me, and he finally was able to capture me doing something."[1423]

Troilo confronted Hall in a pickup truck standoff on BSF property at Fleetwood Hill. He believe Hall or his associates had been watching the work since March, well aware that he was violating the Clean Water Act.

"He rolled down the window and glared at me," Hall recalled. "He was hot."[1424]

"Bud, you could have *told* me!" Troilo said. "I can't believe you didn't come to me and tell me first."[1425]

"Tony, you could have come to me," Hall replied. "You're the one who's at fault here. Tony, that's *Fleetwood Hill* you're digging up!"[1426]

Hall did not go to the funeral of his long-time friend lest he be unwelcome. He did not want to disturb the services. "It's something I regret to this day," Hall said.[1427]

In October 2011, Troilo signed a formal Memorandum of Agreement with the Corps admitting to the violation and agreeing to the restoration of the landscape at Flat Run, which he said cost him more than $230,000. As a further sign of good faith, Troilo donated a 3.1-acre parcel next to Flat Run to BSF.[142]

The following month, Troilo decided to sell the Fleetwood Hill property, including his four-year-old home, and resettle on other land he owned in Culpeper County. He wanted about $5 million.[1429]

"I got tired of dealing with Civil War people," Troilo recalled. "So, I said, 'You know what? Enough's enough.' And I just walked away from it."[1430]

In January 2012, "For Sale" signs went up along the border with U.S. 29 for Troilo's Fleetwood Hill mansion and acreage. Later in 2012, Troilo reduced the price to $4.2 million. By the fall, the Trust had become Troilo's best potential buyer.

In November, Troilo and his wife were driving to Georgia to celebrate his brother-in-law's birthday. As they passed Danville, Virginia, his phone rang. It was Trust Director of Real Estate Tom Gilmore, offering to buy the 61 acres Troilo owned at Fleetwood Hill, including the mansion, for $3.6 million.[1431]

"Let me think about it and call you back," Troilo told Gilmore. The Troilos discussed the offer. Tony was worried that the recent permitting violation might lead to problems with other potential buyers. About 45 miles later, in Greensboro,

North Carolina, he called Gilmore back and accepted the offer.[1432]

There was no rancor when the Trust announced the agreement in December. Troilo said it "made sense that this is where it really needed to go," while Hall said the family had been "wonderful stewards of the land."[1433]

Troilo lived in the house until the summer of 2014 before moving to another home just south of Brandy Station. That September, when heavy machinery returned to the property, it was sent by the Trust to tear down the mansion. Three months later, the hill was clear and ready for installation of interpretive trails and signs.

"What I feel is that justice prevailed," recalled Hall. "In spite of obstacles from many different corners, the Brandy Station battlefield is largely saved today. But we're not going to give up."[1434]

Troilo was philosophical. He was a willing seller and was paid for his property, but his overall experience with preservationists, Hall in particular, was unpleasant. His father always told him, though, to never love something that can't love you back. "You can love a dog, and a dog will love you back," Joe would say. But a house will never love you back, and this was true of his Fleetwood Hill mansion. The structure had been poorly built, Troilo discovered, with a list of problems that included improperly installed windows and a chronic water leak in the basement.

Still, he thought it was a shame the Trust tore it down. "The house was handicapped friendly," Troilo said. "It could have been a useful museum."[1435] ★

CHAPTER TWENTY

"A Hot Place" at Antietam

OR HALF A CENTURY, through hot summers and frigid winters, a simple battle monument made from three actual Union muskets, stacked in a triangle, stood on the Antietam battlefield near the Bloody Cornfield.

Its presence was distilled into three simple words on the side of a camp bucket hanging from the muzzles: "A Hot Place."

Veterans of the 90th Pennsylvania Volunteers had placed the unusual monument on the battlefield in the 1880s, and year after year it stood until time and the elements eased it into disrepair and the threat of vandalism or theft led Antietam National Battlefield rangers to dismantle it.

Descendants of the veterans of that regiment installed a new, all-metal monument in 2004 at the original location amidst a cluster of low boulders on the south side of Cornfield Avenue. The full inscription reads, "Here Fought The 90th Penna. (Phila) Sept. 17, 1862. A Hot Place."[1436]

As the fighting swept back and forth across the open fields between the cornfield and the Dunker Church during the morning phase of the Battle of Antietam, the regiment at one point defended that spot against an assault by a larger force of Confederates. The Pennsylvanians endured a "raking fire of grape, canister and shell," regimental commander Colonel Peter Lyle wrote in his official report two days later while nursing his own serious side wound. At one point, a vicious, bloody hand-to-hand fight broke out for possession of the regiment's battle flag. Seven Union men fell—two dead and five severely wounded—before Pvt. William H. Paul yanked the flag from the hands of a Rebel and sprinted away. He was awarded the Medal of Honor for his act.[1437]

Two days after the battle, with dead Confederates only then being buried by Union troops, photographer Alexander Gardner, working for Mathew B. Brady, came upon the small outcropping of rocks where the 90th Pennsylvania fought. Gardner's stereo photograph of the spot shows seven dead Confederates lying where they fell—stark truth that it was a hot place for both sides.

The background of Gardner's photo shows a section of this bitterly contested battlefield land that Save Historic Antietam Foundation (SHAF) co-founder Dennis Frye describes as some of "the bloodiest ground on the bloodiest day in American history."[1438]

In 2014, this land—a 44.4-acre triangular tract—was still privately owned. Sandwiched between the Dunker Church, Cornfield, West Woods and East Woods, this was the "epicenter tract" of the morning phase of the battle. It is mostly open farmland that was part of the D.R. Miller farm during and after the war. In 1880, Miller built a new, two-story house and barn along the pike, about 300 yards south of his wartime home.

Although the Antietam National Cemetery was established and dedicated in 1867, the Antietam National Battlefield would not be created for another 23 years. Established by an act of Congress in 1890, it was the second of five Civil War battlefields created in the 1890s.

Unlike the others, where large swaths of battlefield acreage were bought, Antietam was a low-budget enterprise known as the "Experiment at Antietam." The government purchased only enough land for rights of way for an automobile and buggy tour route. By 1895, the original creation was largely done. The government had bought only 17 acres, enough for a tour road and a few feet of land on either side. Five miles of macadamized gravel roads were built and more than 200 descriptive tablets were installed along the route. Most of these are still in place today, although in some places a road no longer exists.[1439]

When the NPS took over the jurisdiction of Antietam and other federal Civil War battlefields from the War Department in 1933, the Antietam park had grown to 65 acres, but was still mostly just the tour route. Preservation wasn't a pressing issue because the area remained rural. But intrusions had begun to appear. In addition to Miller's 1880 house on Hagerstown Pike, a house was built on the embankment beside Burnside Bridge. Another post-war dwelling along the Sunken Road became a sandwich and souvenir shop. In 1921, a windstorm or tornado flattened the Dunker Church and the new structure that went up on its foundation would house

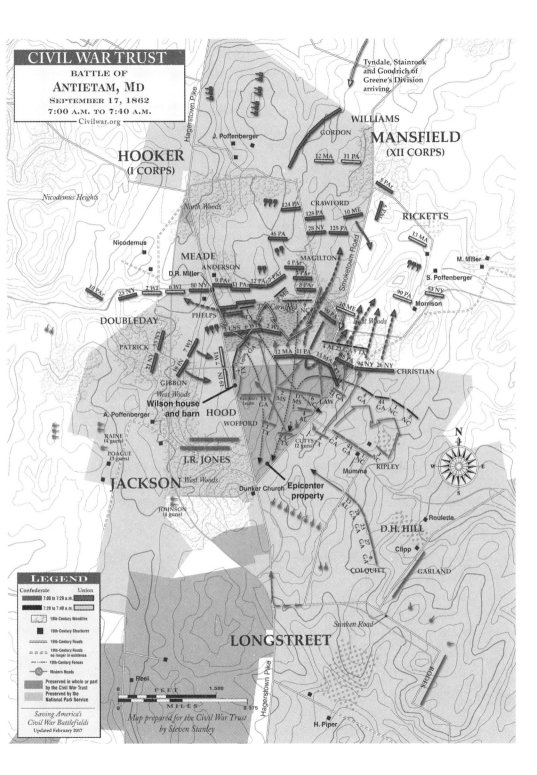

CIVIL WAR TRUST

BATTLE OF
ANTIETAM, MD
SEPTEMBER 17, 1862
7:00 A.M. TO 7:40 A.M.
Civilwar.org

Tyndale, Stainrook
and Goodrich of
Greene's Division
arriving.

J. Poffenberger

GORDON

WILLIAMS

12 MA   11 PA

MANSFIELD
(XII CORPS)

HOOKER
(I CORPS)

Nicodemus Heights

North Woods

124 PA

CRAWFORD

128 PA   10 ME

28 NY   125 PA

RICKETTS

13 MA

Nicodemus

46 PA

M. Miller

MEADE

ANDERSON

4 PA

MAGILTON

D.R. Miller

3 PAr   11 PAr   12 PA 7 PA   8 PAr

9 PAr

8 PAr

S. Poffenberger

90 PA   83 NY

10 PA   23 NY   2 WI   6 WI   80 NY

Morrison

DOUBLEDAY

PHELPS

The Cornfield   6
NC

90 PA

10 ME

West Woods

4 USS   6 WI   2 WI

TX

PATRICK   55 NY

12 MA   11 PA   13 MA   94 NY   26 NY

CHRISTIAN

21 NY   19 IN   7 WI

19 IN

GIBBON

West Woods

Wilson house
and barn   HOOD

Hampton's
Legion

GA

18
GA   2
MS   11
MS   6
NC   LAW

GA

44
GA   I
NC   3
NC

A. Poffenberger

WOFFORD

4
AL

RAINE
(4 guns)

TX

POAGUE
(3 guns)

J.R. JONES

CUTTS
(2 guns)   TX   GA   NC

GA

JACKSON

West Woods

Mumma

RIPLEY

JOHNSON
(4 guns)

Dunker Church   Epicenter
property

AL GA GA GA GA GA GA

D.H. HILL

Roulette

Clipp

COLQUITT   GARLAND

Sunken Road

LONGSTREET

Reel

FEET
0   1,500

MILES
0   0.375

Map prepared for the Civil War Trust
by Steven Stanley

H. Piper

Poffenberger's Lunch Room in the 1930s. The Lunch Room was removed after the lot was purchased by the Washington County Historical Society in 1951 and donated to the NPS.[1440]

"Mission 66," a 10-year improvement program in anticipation of the Park Service's 50th anniversary began in 1956. At Antietam, major improvements included the opening of a new visitor center and rededication of the Dunker Church—rebuilt on the original site using some of the original bricks, window frames and other materials—in conjunction with the battle's centennial in 1962. By 1975, the park had grown to 810 acres, its federally mandated limit.[1441]

But the battlefield also suffered its most significant and lasting scarring around this time. The State of Maryland built a bypass for Hagerstown Pike (Route 65) to ease battlefield congestion. Regular traffic was tangling with tourist traffic on the old Pike. But the state built the new road only a few hundred feet west, through the heart of the West Woods battlefield, cutting off much of the western part of the battlefield from today's battlefield tour route. Confederate Avenue, a major feature of the original tour route, was eradicated. Today, most park visitors experience the fierce West Woods fighting that raged on either side of the bypass with a single stop at the towering Philadelphia Brigade Monument, just off the Pike.

In 1985, a developer proposed building a shopping center at the Grove Farm on the western outskirts of Sharpsburg. President Abraham Lincoln met with Union commander Major General George McClellan at Grove Farm in early October 1862, posing with McClellan, George Armstrong Custer and other Union officers for an iconic photograph by Alexander Gardner. The Grove home, slightly visible in the photo, still stands. But the Grove Farm acreage had been divided into four parcels.

The Washington County, Maryland, Board of County Commissioners had rezoned land at the Grove farm to allow for the shopping center, seeking to keep residents' spending in the county rather than losing it to nearby Shepherdstown, West Virginia. A 10-home development was proposed for another of the four parcels.

The threat prompted Frye, Hagerstown Junior College history professor Tom Clemens and the Reverend John Schildt to create SHAF in March 1986. After a decade of court battles, the preservationists were victorious, acquiring all four parcels and saving the entire farm.[1442]

At the park itself, the NPS had begun adding land, expanding the original, narrow tour route. In 1960, however, to appease local farmers and residents who feared the park aimed to take their farms, Congress mandated that Antietam National Battlefield could add no more than 600 additional acres to the park. By 1975, the park had reached the acquisition limit and was now at 810 acres, with hundreds of crucial battlefield acres still unprotected.[1443]

In 1987, the same year he co-founded APCWS, Frye took Washington County commissioners on a battlefield tour. At Cornfield Avenue, with the Cornfield on one side and the epicenter tracts on the other, Frye told them that the bloodiest killing zone on America's bloodiest day was zoned agricultural. "That means the owner can build one house per acre," he said. The commissioners were shocked.[1444]

As Commissioner Richard E. Roulette told the *Potomac News*, "I personally didn't realize there were significant areas that weren't protected, like the Cornfield. There's no scenic easements there. It's not owned by the NPS. It's completely unprotected."[1445]

Owner Paul M. Culler said he had no plans to develop the Cornfield property, which he had owned since the early 1950s. The park service had offered several times over the years to pay him for a preservation easement, but he declined each time.[1446]

In 1988, however, Representative Beverly Byron (D-Md.) successfully pushed legislation through Congress to lift the acquisition restriction at Antietam. The following year, she negotiated a $1 million Congressional appropriation for land purchases.[1447]

In the 1990s, the park's biggest benefactor was the Richard King Mellon Foundation, assisted by The Conservation Fund, which made crucial acquisitions of several of the most important parts of the battlefield. In July 1991, the Foundation bought the 145-acre Miller Farm, including the Cornfield, and donated it to the park. That same year, the two groups paid $500,000 for a 151-acre tract of the West Woods, also donating it to the park. And in 1998, the Foundation and The Conservation Fund, with help from the original Civil War Trust, paid $660,000 for the 179-acre Roulette Farm, which borders Bloody Lane, and again transferred ownership to the NPS.[1448]

But these purchases fueled fires of discontent among skeptical farmers and landowners who were unhappy with the park's proposed long-term management plan, as well as a county proposal to institute zoning overlay zones. These zones would put limitations on development, deforestation and other activities that might alter the area's bucolic appearance. Local landowners wanted the rural feel to remain, but were concerned their community would become a government-owned tourist mecca. The most outlandish rumor held that the NPS had designated for purchase a 240-square-mile area between Antietam and Harpers Ferry, West Virginia.[1449]

Dozens of local protesters, some on tractors circling through the visitor center parking lot, met members of a federal advisory council who arrived to tour the battlefield on June 12, 1989. Signs read, "NPS is a developer!" and "NPS land acquisition is killing rural America." A child's sign asked, "Future Farmer?" The following day, the Washington County commissioners approved the Antietam overlay zones.[1450]

The State of Maryland then came up with a solution that satisfied preservationists and landowners. Through the Maryland Agricultural Preservation Foundation, the state in the mid-1980s began purchasing development rights by obtaining easements from farmers and landowners, allowing them to keep their land but protecting it from development. When Jim Lighthizer became Maryland's Secretary of Transportation in 1991, he put the program in high gear. The federal government had just approved the Intermodal Surface Transportation Efficiency Act (ISTEA), which in part was designed to acquire land or non-development easements to preserve scenic vistas as well as historic sites.

The opportunities stirred Lighthizer's imagination. Taking advantage of Maryland's existing program, he convinced the state to match federal ISTEA funding for preservation. Former Maryland Program Open Space Director H. Grant Dehart worked with landowners, preservationists and others at Antietam and elsewhere to prioritize easement purchases.

The acquisition of easements in favor of outright land purchases demonstrated a different and efficient use of federal funds for preservation, especially when matched by state funds and other sources. The approach allowed Lighthizer to expand the zone of preservation around Antietam far beyond the battlefield itself to include the many 19th-century farms and scenic viewsheds that gave the area its back-in-time character. Between 1991 and 2014, the programs Lighthizer championed protected 8,700 acres on 61 properties near the battlefield.[1451]

But at Antietam National Battlefield, the epicenter tract in the heart of the battlefield remained in private hands. In 1949, five-year-old Philip Craig "Ranger" Wilson moved with his parents into the home Miller built in 1880. Wilson graduated from Boonsboro High School in 1962, joined the Army and served in the Vietnam War, eventually becoming a long-hauler truck driver. He married Lilli Ann Souders of Sharpsburg in 1989 and they raised their three daughters in the house.[1452]

Living in the heart of the battlefield brought episodes of innocent trespassing and plenty of tourists asking questions, but as Lilli Wilson recalled, it also brought "many memories of sitting on the porch in the summertime and just watching the world go by." [1453] The battlefield's monuments were an ever-present reminder of the history in their midst, amplified by the booms from the park's weekend artillery demonstrations and quietly captured in the low voices of the reenactors who camped on their land, the pleasant smell of their campfires wafting past their farmhouse. Every year, on an early December weekend evening, during the annual battlefield luminary display, a vast sea of candlelight surrounded them as more than 23,000 candles flickered in honor of the soldiers who fell on that day—the bloodiest in American history.[1454]

The Wilson land was under a protective easement, but it was weak. Director of Real Estate Tom Gilmore established a rapport with the Wilsons, who regularly heard good things about the post-merger Civil War Trust from friends who had dealings with the organization. After Craig Wilson died in 2014, Lilli decided to sell the property to the Trust, believing that preserving the land would honor her military veteran husband's service. The sale closed in the summer of 2015 for $510,000. The Save Historic Antietam Foundation (SHAF) contributed $50,000, and the Trust paid the rest with the aim of restoring the property and eventually conveying it to the NPS.[1455]

"The old farm served us well, but there comes a time when you need to move on. My husband grew up there, he came home from the service there and he died there. I feel very fortunate to have lived there," Wilson told the *Herald-Mail* of Hagerstown.[1456]

Not long after the Trust held a celebration ceremony at the property on September 30, 2015, which Wilson attended, demolition specialists arrived. They tore down the barn, already in poor condition, and it was gone by early November. Lilli Wilson moved out in 2016 and the house was torn down as well, fully restoring the wartime appearance of the battlefield and the view at that site.

"It has completely changed the north end of the battlefield. The view is closer to what it was in 1862 than it has been for 100 years," said Antietam National Battlefield Chief of Resource Education and Visitor Services Keith Snyder. "The house was on one of the highest pieces of ground around there and you now have a 360-degree view of the entire morning action of the battle. You can even see the Pry House [McClellan's headquarters] from that spot."[1457]

In the heart of the East Woods, the Trust purchased a 5.6-acre parcel in 2015 not long after the owner erected a large, metal storage building near a post-war house. The Trust also successfully acquired a one-acre tract at the North Woods that was put up for sale at a public auction. And in 2016, the Trust purchased a 9.1-acre tract across three contiguous lots next to the Dunker Church and will continue to remove modern structures as it acquires more.[1458]

"Three post-war houses or structures on the battlefield came down in six months," Snyder said. "It's unbelievable how much has changed here in the last year."[1459]

As of 2016, the NPS park had grown to 1,937 acres. But preservation work remains to be done, including acquiring or preserving other privately owned tracts within the boundary of the park. But the battlefield is close to complete and is complemented by the historic feel of Sharpsburg, still a small town, its Main Street lined with homes that were witness to the 1862 battle.

Lighthizer is one of countless Civil War buffs who consider the Antietam battlefield their favorite. "To me, it always comes back to Antietam," Lighthizer said. "To be able to walk along Bloody Lane, or to walk along the bank of Antietam Creek from Burnside's Bridge to where nobody goes, where the Union troops crossed at the ford. And just to walk that path by myself when nobody is there is a special experience."[1460] ★

CHAPTER
TWENTY-ONE

Campaign 1776

I NOVEMBER 2014, with six months left in the Civil War Sesquicentennial, the Civil War Trust (Trust) launched a ground-breaking initiative that, for the first time, extended the national preservation movement to the battlefields of the American Revolution and the War of 1812.[1461]

Throughout the first 25 years of the modern battlefield preservation movement, sites of conflict from the Revolution and War of 1812 were the unprotected flanks. The U.S. Department of the Interior National Park Service (NPS) recognized that deficiency in 2007 with a formal report on the status of these battlefields. The NPS's American Battlefield Protection Program (ABPP) identified 243 significant combat sites from the two wars and urgently recommended that an organization modeled after the Trust be created to acquire and protect those lands.[1462]

These battlefields are fewer in number and smaller in scale than those of the Civil War. Many northeastern battlefields in urban areas—such as Brooklyn Heights, New York, and Trenton, New Jersey—have long since been developed, but others, such as Minute Man National Historical Park at Lexington and Concord, Massachusetts, still contain privately owned tracts with historic integrity that can be preserved.

The recession of 2008 and other factors stalled immediate action, but in 2013, ABPP formally asked the Trust to consider expanding its mission to include the country's earlier wars. The Trust staff had been weighing whether to expand its role since 2011, thanks to a pair of bills introduced on Capitol Hill: one to reauthorize ABPP's Civil War battlefield preservation funding at $10 million per year and one to authorize and create a separate $10 million per year program for protection of Revolutionary War and War of 1812 battlefields.

Chief Policy and Communications Officer Jim Campi believed that the two bills would ultimately be combined into a single $10 million annual appropriation for battlefields of all three wars. Thus, when the NPS request came, the Trust was ready to begin serious deliberations. Staff analyzed the recommendation, surveyed the membership, consulted major donors, and discussed the mission within the board of trustees as well as with top historians. "The reaction we received almost across the board was that the time had come to step up," recalled Campi.[1463] The grounds upon which these earlier battles were fought were just as hallowed as those of the Civil War, members declared, and just as important.

On Veterans Day, November 11, 2014, Lighthizer and the Trust launched their national preservation initiative, *Campaign 1776.*[1464] Just one month later, Campi's instincts were proven correct, as Congress passed the Fiscal Year 2015 National Defense Authorization Act, including authorization for a single $10 million fund to protect battlefields of the Revolutionary War, War of 1812 and Civil War. The new name of the program was the American Battlefield Land Grants Program.

"You don't say 'no' to your biggest partner," Lighthizer said, noting the NPS request. "And no one else is doing it. If we don't do it, it's not going to get done." He estimated that at least 10,000 to 15,000 acres of Revolutionary War and War of 1812 battlefields needed protection.[1465]

Campaign 1776 was unveiled in Princeton, New Jersey, with the imposing Battle Monument as a backdrop, specifically to announce a seven-week campaign to raise $25,000 toward the preservation of 4.6 acres of Princeton battlefield land adjacent to the Princeton Battlefield State Park. At Princeton, on January 3, 1777, General George Washington's thread-bare, shrinking army defeated the British regulars, forcing them to flee in retreat. It was the climax of the "Ten Crucial Days" that began with the Christmas night crossing of the Delaware River, which led to a progression of triumphs that concluded with the British surrender four years later.

The Princeton fundraising effort became *Campaign 1776*'s first success when the State of New Jersey completed the purchase of the 4.6-acre battlefield tract in April 2015. It was principally funded by the New Jersey Department of Environmental Protection's Green Acres program, along with the $25,000 from the Trust and help from local governments and private sources. The acquisition made it possible for the state to build a trail from downtown Princeton along Route 206 into the state park. The Trust's contribution also helped fund a ground-penetrating radar study and archaeological project.[1466]

The Trust's announcement at Princeton also meant joining a long-time battle with the Institute for Advanced Study (the Institute or IAS) over preservation of the battlefield. With three separate disputes between the Township of Princeton and IAS dating to the late 1960s, Princeton held claim to one of the longest-running, on-again, off-again struggles in the history of battlefield preservation. As *Campaign 1776* got underway, the unresolved dispute with the IAS focused on Maxwell's Field, arguably the most important part of the battlefield, where the "Washington's Charge" counterattack, personally led by General Washington, decided the battle's outcome.

For 11 years, local preservationists had fought an IAS plan to build 15 housing units on Maxwell's Field. A week before the launch of *Campaign 1776*, the Princeton Regional Planning Board approved the IAS project in a unanimous decision.

The IAS, an intellectual bastion of higher learning with great prestige and worldwide renown, was unlike any developer the Trust previously had faced. As one of the world's leading centers for theoretical research with 30 faculty members guiding the independent work of some 200 visiting scholars, the Institute embodies the intellectual inquiry that freedom and democracy nurture. Among its first scholars

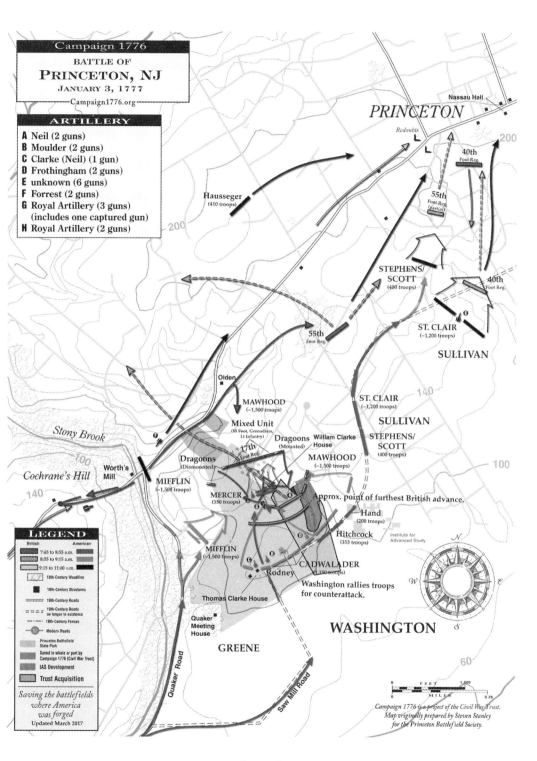

Campaign 1776

BATTLE OF
PRINCETON, NJ
JANUARY 3, 1777
Campaign1776.org

ARTILLERY

A Neil (2 guns)
B Moulder (2 guns)
C Clarke (Neil) (1 gun)
D Frothingham (2 guns)
E unknown (6 guns)
F Forrest (2 guns)
G Royal Artillery (3 guns)
    (includes one captured gun)
H Royal Artillery (2 guns)

LEGEND

British	American
7:45 to 8:55 a.m.	
8:55 to 9:15 a.m.	
9:15 to 11:00 a.m.	

18th-Century Woodline
18th-Century Structures
18th-Century Roads
18th-Century Roads
no longer in existence
18th-Century Fences
Modern Roads
Princeton Battlefield
State Park
Saved in whole or part by
Campaign 1776 (Civil War Trust)
IAS Development
Trust Acquisition

*Saving the battlefields
where America
was forged*
Updated March 2017

PRINCETON

Nassau Hall

Redoubts

40th
Foot Reg.

55th
Foot Reg.
(partial)

Hausseger
(410 troops)

STEPHENS/
SCOTT
(400 troops)

40th
Foot Reg.

ST. CLAIR
(~1,200 troops)

SULLIVAN

55th
Foot Reg.

Olden

MAWHOOD
(~1,500 troops)

ST. CLAIR
(~1,200 troops)

SULLIVAN

Mixed Unit
(55 Foot, Grenadiers,
Lt Infantry)

Dragoons   William Clarke
(Mounted)   House

STEPHENS/
SCOTT
(400 troops)

Stony Brook

17th
Foot Reg.

Dragoons
(Dismounted)

MAWHOOD
(~1,500 troops)

Worth's
Mill

Cochrane's Hill

MIFFLIN
(~1,500 troops)

MERCER
(350 troops)

Approx. point of furthest British advance.

Hand
(200 troops)

Hitchcock
(353 troops)

Institute for
Advanced Study

MIFFLIN
(~1,500 troops)

CADWALADER
(1,150 troops)

Rodney

*Washington rallies troops
for counterattack.*

Thomas Clarke House

Quaker
Meeting
House

GREENE

WASHINGTON

*Campaign 1776 is a project of the Civil War Trust.
Map originally prepared by Steven Stanley
for the Princeton Battlefield Society.*

FEET   1,000
MILES   0.25

were European mathematicians and physicists, most notably Albert Einstein, escaping spreading anti-Semitism of the Nazi party in Germany. The institute opened on October 2, 1933, and by the end of the month, Einstein had arrived in the U.S. and settled in Princeton, where he would live until his death in 1955. The Institute had an endowment of astronomical proportions: more than $740 million in 2014, according to IAS financial documents. As one local resident told Campi, IAS was spoken of in "hushed tones" in the tight-knit Princeton community.[1467]

The IAS established its campus in 1938 about a mile southwest of Princeton University on what had been a 450-acre farm next to the then-privately owned Princeton battlefield. The main building, imposing Fuld Hall where Einstein had his office, is a Georgian structure similar in appearance to Independence Hall in Philadelphia. Over the years, the IAS acquired hundreds of additional acres around the campus, including significant tracts of the battlefield.

Washington's victory at Princeton came during the darkest days of the American Revolution. Just six months after joyful colonists hailed the Declaration of Independence in July 1776, the words in that defiant document were hardly worth the parchment they were written on. A powerful British army had arrived to confront the rebellion, and the cause teetered on the verge of collapse.

The British routed Washington's army on Long Island in August 1776, and captured New York City in September. Back-to-back defeats at White Plains and Port Washington left Washington's army in desperate shape. The British occupied most of three colonies and were poised to capture Philadelphia, the colonial American capital.

With enlistments set to expire on January 1, 1777, Washington's demoralized force—reduced to about 5,000 ragged, ill-fed and ill-clothed soldiers after more than twice that number deserted—was about to disappear before his eyes. "I think the game is pretty near up ... " Washington wrote to his brother.[1468] Instead of accepting defeat, Washington went on a final offensive, crossing the half-frozen Delaware River in the rain and darkness of Christmas night, 1776 and routing the Hessians holding Trenton, New Jersey. He sidestepped an approaching British force and executed a freezing night march to confront another British force at Princeton.

The battle at Princeton on January 3, 1777, started disastrously for the Americans. A British regiment crushed the American left flank and mortally wounded General Hugh Mercer. On the brink of yet another defeat, Washington led a counterattack while mounted on a shirking, terrified white horse, advancing to within 30 yards of the British as he urged his men forward. In a brief and bloody climax to a battle fought on ice-hard ground in sub-freezing temperatures, Washington's men overwhelmed the Redcoats, who fled the field.

After the victory at Princeton, the tide began to turn. It took four long years, but with the surrender of the British at Yorktown, Virginia, in 1781, the United States finally gained its independence.

When *Campaign 1776* launched in November 2014, Maxwell's Field, the open plain of Washington's Charge, was almost unchanged despite more than two centuries of private ownership, most recently by the IAS. As well-regarded as the Institute was nationally and internationally, its local legacy included long, contentious battles with preservationists over historic lands. A plan announced in 2003 to build 15 faculty housing units at Maxwell's Field ignited the third such battle—the longest-lasting, most controversial of all.

The Princeton battlefield's first savior was Moses Taylor Pyne, the wealthy Princeton philanthropist largely responsible for transforming the small College of New Jersey into prestigious Princeton University. When development threatened the battlefield around the turn of the 20th century, Pyne twice stopped it by purchasing land.[1469] Long after his death in 1921, Pyne's land became part of the original 40-acre Princeton Battlefield State Park, which was dedicated on October 20, 1946, with more than 1,000 people on hand.[1470]

From the beginning, the park included the left side of the American battle line where Mercer was mortally wounded in a murderous British bayonet attack. But even though it has expanded, the park never encompassed the right side of the American line and Maxwell's Field, where Washington counterattacked. This was the land, about 22 acres, the IAS owned and decided to develop.

With the 2003 announcement, IAS embarked on its development plan with determination and unbending resolve forged by earlier preservation fights. At the end of the previous struggles, hard-won compromises were hailed as victories for all, even though IAS had been thwarted from developing anything. This time, it would forcefully assert its rights as a landowner, determined to build what was legally allowed by right, based on zoning. Once again, the Princeton Battlefield Area Preservation Society, known today as the Princeton Battlefield Society (the Society), prepared to fight.

The Society owes its very existence to the IAS's development zeal. It was formed in 1970 to confront the first IAS threat, which surfaced in the fall of 1969, when the Institute requested Princeton Township to rezone "the Weller tract," a 12-acre parcel at the southwest border of the state battlefield park, so it could build 10 faculty houses.[1471] The tract was clearly part of the battlefield, and the state expressed a desire to buy the land but did not allocate funding.[1472] The fight dragged on for years, finally ending in 1973 when the IAS agreed to sell the Weller tract and another property totaling 33 acres to the state for $335,000. The land was added to the battlefield park.[1473]

The second fight began in March 1983, when the IAS announced plans to build 400 to 600 housing units on 230 acres of land it owned along Quaker Road, southeast of the park and campus, hoping to make a $5 million to $8 million profit.[1474]

It was not battlefield acreage. The controversy centered on the impact to Institute Woods, a pristine old-growth forest beloved by the community that covered about 300 of 589 IAS-owned acres near the campus.[1475] Opposition was immediate and intense and the IAS abandoned the plan a year later.[1476]

The issue erupted again in 1990 when the IAS filed suit against the planning board to fight a planned downzoning of the Institute's 589 acres. During this dispute, the IAS rejected any suggestion of developing land near Fuld Hall, such as Maxwell's Field.[1477] Cluster housing there, the Institute argued, "would destroy the Institute's reflective tranquility at the heart of the campus."[1478]

In 1997, 14 years after it started, the struggle finally ended when the IAS accepted $13 million to give up development rights on all 589 acres. The Institute was credited with contributing $1.2 million to the preservation effort.[1479]

In the later fight for Maxwell's Field, the IAS would assert that its concessions in 1973 and 1997 underscored the Institute's "longstanding support for the Princeton Battlefield State Park, which it helped to create and expand." Not mentioned were the long, expensive battles and the compensation the IAS received for its concessions.[1480]

The IAS launched its effort to build on Maxwell's Field in February 2003. "The houses would be on the battlefield," argued Society President Jerry Hurwitz, one of several citizens and officials who protested the project at a planning board meeting that month. "To put housing on that field is to desecrate hallowed ground. This should be part of the battlefield park."[1481]

Borough Mayor Marvin Reed said the planning board could not prevent the IAS from developing the 22.5-acre tract consistent with its single-family residential zoning. Reed told Hurwitz the Society would need to buy the property or the development rights to stop the project.

"The Institute intends to develop this land for its faculty housing," IAS attorney Christopher Tarr said at the meeting. "It does not intend to sell it." Tarr pointed out that the IAS had allowed three quarters of the 800 acres it owned to be preserved.[1482]

It was the opening round in a 14-year drama. The project was stalled several times by various technical issues, including the size of the buffer zone between the park and the proposed new housing, and a dispute between the IAS and preservationists over the historical significance of the land. One state requirement was an archaeological study for which IAS hired Hunter Research, Inc. On a 4.8-acre quadrant of the 22.5-acre tract, in a limited search, the company's professional relic hunters uncovered 15 lead balls, 14 grape shot, lead flint wraps, a bayonet fragment, a ramrod holding and a portion of a cartridge box. The IAS hired another firm to complete the report. The second study covered the same ground and uncovered no artifacts, which prompted the IAS to claim the land was not battleground.[1483]

In November 2008, when ABPP released its report on the status and condition of Revolutionary War and War of 1812 battlefields, Princeton was listed as a Priority I site, meaning among the most historically significant and the most endangered.[1484]

ABPP funded an archaeological and mapping survey of the battlefield for the Society in 2011, producing 35 maps showing troop movements during the battle, which further documented the Institute's Maxwell's Field tract as the site of Washington's Charge. Three companies of Continental Marines had participated in the charge, and the U.S. Marine Corps suffered its first battlefield deaths here.[1485]

In 2011, eight years after the project was first proposed, the IAS submitted a revised development plan to the planning board. Construction that in 1990 the IAS had said would "destroy the reflective tranquility at the heart of its campus" was now a necessary part of "a true academic village" that would enhance the IAS as a tight-knit "community of scholars."[1486]

After four long hearings spread over three months, with impassioned arguments from both sides, the planning board approved the plan unanimously in March 2012. The following month, the Society filed suit in New Jersey Superior Court to block the project and appealed the planning board's decision to the Mercer County Superior Court. In June 2012, the National Trust for Historic Preservation named the Princeton battlefield to its list of America's 11 Most Endangered Historic Places. The IAS issued a statement saying it remained committed to its housing project.[1487]

The Society lost its suit against the planning board in June 2013 when a judge ruled that the board had acted reasonably. But to proceed, the IAS needed a waiver from the Delaware and Raritan Canal Commission (DRCC) because of the project's impact on stream corridors leading to the nearby waterway. Four votes were needed for approval, and the commission came up short with its 3–2 vote in favor in January 2014. The project was temporarily halted.[1488]

With the Trust now in the fray through its new *Campaign 1776* initiative, the preservationists intensified their publicity campaign. On Washington's Birthday in 2016, Lieutenant General Richard Mills (U.S. Marine Corps, retired) joined the Trust in announcing an alliance of veterans organizations in support of Princeton battlefield. On March 4, 2016, the new Save Princeton Coalition—in which national groups such the Cultural Landscape Foundation, the National Coalition for History and the National Parks Conservation Association joined long-term opponents like the Society and the National Trust for Historic Preservation—announced it had requested by letter that the IAS board of trustees reconsider its development plan. The full preservation community was ready to fight.[1489]

Meanwhile, the IAS had made more concessions, and its amended application won approval from the planning board in November 2014. But on January 21, 2015, after a full evidentiary hearing, the DRCC again denied the waiver necessary for IAS to proceed with the project. The vote was 3–2–1 in favor, but lacked the four votes necessary for approval.[1490]

Less than a month later, however, the DRCC conducted an unscheduled re-vote to allow a previously absent member to vote, which secured a 5–2 tally to approve the waiver. The member who had a change of heart would later apologize to Bruce Afran, the Society's attorney, saying, "When you get a call from the commissioner's office, you have to do what you have to do." The Society filed an appeal with the Superior Court of New Jersey, arguing that the second vote was illegal because no grounds existed to reconsider the first vote.[1491]

Lighthizer sought a meeting with IAS officials. His request was rebuffed, as were additional requests through third parties. As the Society pushed forward with appeals, heavy equipment arrived at Maxwell's Field in June 2015, a fence went up, and Jim Campi lost another vacation. Campi, who was managing the Princeton fight for the Trust, was in Downingtown, Pennsylvania, with his wife to visit family. He excused himself from socializing to help Bruce Afran and Jerry Hurwitz prepare the Society's request for a temporary restraining order. It was granted and construction came to a halt. The legal fight eventually reached the New Jersey Supreme Court, which, on November 24, 2015, rejected the Society's effort to permanently stop construction.

The coalition offered to buy the 22-acre tract for $3.3 million. IAS rejected the offer. The coalition increased the offer to $4.5 million, nearly 40 percent more than the appraised value. That, too, was rejected. In November, the IAS began clearing trees on the land and in December began grading and installing infrastructure. Its development plan had evolved to building seven single-family homes and eight townhomes on seven acres.[1492]

The coalition kept up the pressure publicly and privately. In April 2016, an article by Princeton alumnus and syndicated columnist George F. Will ignited a perfect storm of advertisements, editorials and news stories about the plight of Maxwell's Field. "It is especially disheartening that a distinguished institution of scholars is indifferent to preserving a historic site that can nourish national identity," Will wrote.[1493]

During this media storm, the Campis were attempting to vacation again, this time at Rehoboth Beach, Delaware. Almost like clockwork, the first major break occurred—a call from Princeton Battlefield Society attorney David Bookbinder indicating that IAS was willing to meet to discuss a settlement. Campi spent much of his vacation week preoccupied with helping make the meeting a reality.[1494]

Soon thereafter, Campi and Tom Gilmore, along with Trustee Tom Lauer, traveled to Princeton to quietly meet with IAS and its attorneys. Much like the Battle of Princeton itself, the issue was often in doubt. Progress was slow as talks dragged through the spring and summer.[1495]

Fortunately, a rapport developed, and the long months of meetings and confidential negotiations paid off. In a joint statement released December 12, 2016, IAS and the Trust announced an agreement—"a plan to significantly expand the land that will be preserved adjacent to the current Princeton Battlefield State Park while enabling the Institute to construct new housing for its faculty on its campus."[1496]

IAS could build 16 townhouses on the northernmost seven acres of the tract, substantially reducing the development footprint by replacing the seven single-family home lots with eight townhomes. The Trust, through *Campaign 1776*, agreed to buy the southern 14.85 acres of the tract and an important adjacent parcel with a modern house for $4 million, restoring and later conveying it to the state for inclusion in the battlefield park. A 30-foot wide vegetative buffer of about one-half acre, protected by easement, would shield the development from the preserved acreage and vice versa. Closing was scheduled for December 2017.[1497]

The acquisition would be the third-most expensive in Trust history, behind Slaughter Pen Farm ($12 million) and Lee's Headquarters ($5.5 million). Chief Development Officer David Duncan knew the tremendous effort a campaign of this scale would require, but he had resources.

In a quiet moment after the fall board meeting at West Point, New York, when the trustees had learned how close the Trust was to making a deal with the IAS, trustee Mary Munsell Abroe pulled Duncan aside. She turned to him with a smile, saying, "If we get Princeton, I'm all in."[1498] And she was, with a six-figure donation that helped end almost 14 years of conflict over the battlefield made famous by George Washington. Lighthizer told the Trust board the property was "easily one of the most historically significant we have ever tried to preserve."[1499]

In the meantime, the Trust's fledgling initiative had expanded to Massachusetts and in June 2015, *Campaign 1776* began raising $300,000 to purchase one acre of wooded land that was part of the "Parker's Revenge" battleground at Minute Man National Historical Park in Lexington and Concord. The project also included a $25,000 archaeological grant to Friends of Minute Man National Historical Park to study the Parker's Revenge site. *Campaign 1776* leaders joined grant recipients, NPS officials and the Society of the Cincinnati—the nation's oldest patriotic organization, founded in 1783 by former officers of the Continental Army—to announce the efforts.[1500]

The clash known as Parker's Revenge occurred on the afternoon of April 19, 1775, the first day of the Revolutionary War. Captain John Parker's Colonial militiamen had been ravaged by British regulars in action that morning on the Lexington Green. Eighteen of 77 militiamen had been killed or wounded, but Parker regrouped forces on a rocky hillside just west of Lexington. Despite having lost more than 20 percent of his men, Parker prepared to attack a force more than 10 times larger than his, the battalion of 700 British regulars returning to Boston from Concord.[1501]

Parker's ambush—his revenge for his dead and wounded at Lexington Green —bloodied and slowed the Redcoats and wounded a British colonel. His disciplined, coordinated attack was a key engagement in the series of skirmishes and ambushes that turned an orderly British march into a desperate retreat.

The Trust's fundraising campaign was successfully and acquisition of the acre of the Parker's Revenge site was completed later that year. The Trust transferred the property to the NPS in September 2016.[1502]

Parker's Revenge "took place right next to the park's Minute Man Visitor Center, where thousands of visitors begin their tour of the park," said park Superintendent Nancy Nelson as the archaeology project launched. "The Parker's Revenge area has escaped intense development over time, and all of us at the park are excited about what this long-needed archaeological project will reveal."[1503]

The general site of Parker's Revenge had been determined, but only a single, brief witness account was known to exist. Archaeologists used geophysical surveying, 3-D laser scanning, GPS feature mapping, ground penetrating radar and metal detection and excavation to comb the landscape for battle debris and musket balls, both dropped and fired, to determine more precisely where the two forces faced off and where the combat was most intense.[1504]

Lead archaeologist Dr. Meg Watters recruited a team of five Revolutionary War reenactors who donned rain slickers and heavy boots and began sweeping the ground with metal detectors. After unearthing several dozen pieces of metal garbage, they found the first musket ball. "It was like, 'Alright, here we go!'" Watters said.[1505]

Seventeen months later, fresh history was revealed in a 320-page report.

Researchers located the site of a farmhouse that was an important feature of the 1775 terrain, recreated the battlefield landscape and determined exactly what Parker's men could and couldn't see from various positions along the battle road. The earth gave up 29 British and Colonial musket balls (along with thousands of pieces of metallic trash spanning three centuries), the spatial pattern of which revealed where the forces were positioned.

The project included a thorough review of all available historical information and the use of modern analytical strategies, including "viewshed analyses" based on the locations of the balls and what Watters described as a "military tactical review event." In that exercise, historians, archaeologists, ecologists, veterans and military commanders gathered to study all available information, walk the field and jointly reach conclusions. This paved the way for a detailed account of an engagement that lasted only about 10 minutes.[1506]

As would be expected, Parker placed his men on an elevated slope above the road at the edge of forested land, giving them a clear view of the approaching British, while providing cover behind boulders and trees. From the British perspective, computer simulations and analysis that considered the 5'5" height of an average marching British soldier and the nine-foot height of a mounted British officer revealed that dips and rises in the land and other obstacles kept Parker's men well-concealed. When the British spotted them, they deployed a unit of closely spaced soldiers to flank the militia, only to be battered by a blast of colonial musketry from only 40 yards away. Then, the minutemen withdrew to continue the fight farther down the road. The project "enabled us to literally peel back time and expose the artifacts that tell the story," Watters said.[1507]

Volunteers from a dozen Colonial and British reenactment groups helped with metal detection, site preparation and other tasks. And on Patriot's Day, April 16, 2016, steeped with the vast trove of new information gained from the project, they held, for the first time, an accurate reenactment on the actual battlefield grounds.[1508] ★

CHAPTER
TWENTY-TWO

The Civil War Trust Today

★

URING THE RECESSION that began in 2008, several concerned trustees floated the idea of laying off the staff of the real estate department to save money. Trust President Jim Lighthizer was stunned by the suggestion. "That would be like turning the motor off to save fuel," he thought[1509] But it made him realize that although trustees approved each transaction, that didn't mean they fully understood the Trust's overall land acquisition strategy.[1510]

At the heart of everything the Trust does is a real estate deal. The Trust is there as a buyer, seeking willing sellers, offering to pay market value for battlefield property. The nucleus is the real estate department, headed by Director of Real Estate Tom Gilmore since 2005, assisted by Deputy Director of Real Estate Kathy Robertson and a small staff.

The Trust's strategy of a relentless parade of deals led Lighthizer to develop his "propeller" analogy. "Our business, like a propeller, has to run at a continuous rate. You can't have a burst of speed and then stop. If you do, that plane will fall out of the sky," Lighthizer said. "The propeller spins because we find deals and mail out solicitations and the cash comes in, which allows you to do the next deal. But the propeller has to keep spinning. [1511]

"The accounting is the simplest in the world," Lighthizer said. "How much is coming in? How much is going out? And how much money is in the bank? That said, the structures of many of our deals are insanely complex, with money coming from various sources. So that's very complicated. But in the end, from an accounting standpoint, it's strictly a cash flow business."[1512]

The Trust propeller spins at a rate of at least a deal a month, although the organization routinely exceeds this goal. "We'll sometimes have three deals in a month," Lighthizer said. "But we've got to have a quality deal every month of the year. And to do that in the real estate business, you've got to have a lot more deals in the pipeline. We need 30 to 40 deals cooking so we can get at least one a month."[1513]

"Sometimes we need more than one deal a month because we need to combine deals to make it more marketable," he said. "We have to have variety. We can't send three straight mailings on Brice's Cross Roads. The land needs to be historically significant *and* have the recognition that it is historically significant. We have to have the right matching money. We have to be aware of the politics of it. And we also have to have a product—an acquisition—that appeals to our customers."[1514]

To evaluate potential acquisitions for their historical value, the Trust uses Lighthizer's "200-Year Rule," "Will the visitor in 200 years have a meaningful history experience when they visit?" Five acres of a battlefield in the middle of a subdivision may be inexpensive, "but you'll never be able to explain and show the historical significance, so it would never meet the 200-Year Rule," Lighthizer said.[1515]

"In the end, it all comes down to needing a new product every month to feed this machine," Lighthizer said. "I call it the 'twenty-chickens-a-day alligator.' You feed it 20 chickens a day or it eats you."[1516]

From 2000 through 2015, the Trust completed 481 transactions, or an average of 30 a year. The "propeller" spun faster beginning in 2005, as the average jumped to more than 40 a year, with a record-setting 47 transactions in 2013.[1517] More than 85 percent of the 45,000 saved acres have been preserved since the 1999 merger. Prior to that, the Association for the Preservation of Civil War Sites (APCWS) and the original Civil War Trust had saved a combined 6,339 acres.[1518]

Another Lighthizer priority, exemplified at Antietam, is to finish battlefields. "At this stage of the Trust's maturity and development, we're looking to finish many battlefields, or what we also describe as 'substantially complete.' We want to check battlefields off."[1519]

The 1993 Civil War Sites Advisory Commission Report on the Nation's Civil War Battlefields is the guidebook that helps the Trust prioritize battlefield lands. Almost 10,000 armed engagements were documented during the war, from the smallest skirmishes to the biggest battles. The report, produced at the behest of Congress, identified 384 battlefields worth saving and outlined their boundaries.

Outright acquisitions—"fee simple" transactions that transfer ownership to the Trust—are the most common transactions. But the Trust also pursues conservation easements that protect land against development in perpetuity. Easements allow a farmer or other landowners to retain ownership and use their property while being compensated for relinquishing development rights.

If possible, the Trust seeks to sell the land to the National Park Service (NPS) or to the state to be incorporated into a park. But, as Gilmore said, "Sometimes we know we're going to be holding onto land for the long term."[1520] Such is the case with the remote McDowell battlefield, sandwiched between mountains deep in the Appalachian range 34 miles west of Staunton, Virginia. A four-hour clash at McDowell on May 8, 1862 felled 750 men in blue or gray as Stonewall Jackson defeated two brigades of Union troops advancing on the Shenandoah Valley from western Virginia.

In one of its first land purchases in 1990, the APCWS paid $65,159, all from member contributions, to buy 126.5 acres of the McDowell battlefield. The CWPT added another 26 acres in 2000 and 422 acres in 2007 and owns 574 acres, with another nine acres preserved by easement. Other tracts are owned by the Highland Historical Society and Shenandoah Valley Battlefields Foundation. The Trust has installed interpretive signs and a battlefield trail and will maintain the land until Virginia or the federal government is willing to establish a park.[1521]

As of early 2017, the Trust owned more than 8,600 acres of the 45,000 acres saved in the movement's history. The inholdings included more than 196 separate tracts spread among 70 battlefields in 17 states. At many battlefields, the Trust owned multiple parcels, including five different parcels of battlefield land at Antietam, seven at Shiloh and 10 properties at Gettysburg.[1522]

The Trust will also buy battlefield property and hold it while working with Congress to expand a battlefield's boundary. The NPS cannot buy or accept donations of land outside a battlefield's federally established boundary, but the boundary often doesn't include the entire battlefield. Following in the footsteps of Bob Krick and Bob Mrazek in the 1990s, the Trust has persuaded Congress to expand park boundaries at several battlefields, notably Petersburg National Battlefield. But the process is neither short nor easy.

To care for Trust-owned properties, Land Stewardship Manager Matt George oversees a network of allies and assistants who look after and maintain properties on the organization's behalf, including National Park Service rangers, state park employees, battlefield friends groups and local residents.[1523]

Gilmore took over real estate operations from Noah Mehrkam in 2005. Gilmore had enjoyed a career in corporate finance, but sought a change and was attracted to non-profit land preservation. Growing up in Waynesboro, Virginia, Gilmore remembers his grandmother telling family stories of Yankee depredations and how his great-great grandmother "threw down a sword to prevent the Yankees from taking bread off the table."[1524] He also has photos and correspondence from his great-great grandfather, a captain in the 31st Virginia Infantry.

Gilmore heard the Trust was looking for a real estate director and submitted his resume. He heard nothing, but sent a donation that was large enough to prompt a personal letter of thanks from Chief Development Officer David Duncan, who suggested they get together for lunch. The "thank you" lunch led to interviews and, ultimately, the job.[1525]

On his first day of work, November 15, 2005, Gilmore was asked to return the call of a land owner who wanted to sell his portion of the Glendale battlefield outside Richmond, but needed to close by the end of the year. "I was thrown into it on day one," he recalled. Gilmore's first transaction saved 43 acres at Glendale for $700,000, which included $200,000 in grant funding from the Virginia Civil War Historic Site Preservation Fund. In Gilmore's first full year, 2006, the CWPT saved 1,310 acres in 21 transactions, including Slaughter Pen Farm at Fredericksburg. [1526]

"I've been in a few different positions, but for the amount of land that we are trying to preserve, the number of transactions that we are looking at and the number of things at so many different places, it is definitely one of the busiest, most intense positions that you could possibly have," Gilmore said. "There's just so much that we're trying to get done in a relatively short period of time. It's been like that from Day One. And so, it's exhilarating."[1527]

Like Mehrkam before him, Gilmore cultivates and nurtures relationships. "They're making life decisions with respect to land that they've owned, in many cases, for generations," Gilmore said, "It really comes down to a matter of trust between everyone involved. And you need the technical expertise to be able to sit down with people and go through all their options.[1528]

"Fortunately, with the Trust, people have a lot of options with how they want to protect their property, through selling it, through conservation easement, through variances, donations, bargain sales, life estates, and sale-leasebacks. We've got good funding sources, and there are all sorts of things we can do. The goal, of course, is to preserve the property, but to minimize our cost and maximize the third-party sources, such as the federal and state grants available to acquire these properties."[1529]

Gilmore develops personal attachments to every deal, although feeding stray cats, as he did at Slaughter Pen Farm, is unusual. "They all have their own stories," he said, "There are so many situations and stories. They're all unique."[1530]

From 2006 through 2015, Gilmore's first decade, the Trust saved 21,167 new acres in 326 transactions, an annual average of 2,116 acres in 32.6 transactions. The single-year acreage record is 3,773.58 acres in 2012, while the benchmark for acquisitions occurred in 2013 with 47 closings on a total of 2,737.82 acres. At nearly *four* deals a month, the Trust almost quadrupled the one-per-month bar set by Lighthizer.[1531]

"We're only 30-some people, but when I think of how much we accomplished for our size organization, it amazes me," Gilmore said. "And how significant we are at the federal and state level with government and politicians and what we're able to accomplish. That's amazing for a small organization. People are fooled—people never know that we're as small as we are when they see us from the outside."[1532]

A few offices down from Gilmore at the Trust's headquarters on the ninth floor of an office building at 1156 15th Street NW in Washington, D.C., sits Duncan. His windows face busy 15th Street. A block to the east is Thomas Circle, honoring Union General George Henry Thomas, called "Slow Trot Thomas" but better known as "The Rock of Chickamauga."

Duncan's office is often empty while he travels to visit major donors and prospective donors alike. Establishing close, personal relationships is every bit as important to him as it is to Gilmore. "Some donors will be hurt if I stay in a hotel instead of staying with them in their homes," Duncan said. "The hard sell—the arm-twisting—doesn't work. So we don't do it. We rarely ask somebody specifically for a major gift. And if we do, we only do it generally after we have known that person for a long time and they are comfortable with us and we have established a personal relationship with them."[1533]

Big-money donors "are the hardest ones to find," Duncan said. "It is really, really hard work. It's almost always through a connection, either a board member knows them or knows somebody who knows them. And they do still pop up from time to time within our own membership. If I can meet 10 of those people over the course of a year and can get two or three of them to come on board, it is worth it. What you don't want is a guy who can give us a million dollars to give us $5,000 just so we'll go away. We'd rather they just keep their money and get to know us first."[1534]

Duncan writes the solicitation letters mailed under Lighthizer's name. "You've got to have the facts straight, because our members know the history backwards and forwards," he said. "I try and inject some of Jim's personality as well. Sometimes, you'll get a hint of his irreverence," he said. "I try to keep it as conversational while still being urgent and important. Direct mail should be a conversation. It is not a speech to a big group of people. It's a one-on-one message." The Trust generally sends 12 to 14 appeals a year for Civil War properties and several more for *Campaign 1776*. "We may squeeze another couple of extra ones in at the end of the year when most people are thinking about giving more money," Duncan said.[1535]

Duncan emphasizes how a donor's dollar is matched many times over by federal grants and other funding. His solicitation mailers encourage donors to "multiply the power of your generosity," such as a "$22.04-to-$1 match" to save 160 threatened acres at the Battle of Fort Ann, New York, and 24 acres at Sacket's Harbor, New York, in a January 2017 letter.[1536]

"David was able to sell it and make it kind of a cause-célèbre with our membership," Mehrkam recalled. "I really think it is something the membership almost expects now."[1537]

"I don't know if I was the originator of it, but to me it just made sense," Duncan said. "I think everyone enjoys having an instantaneous four- or five-hundred percent return on their donation dollar. It's something that differentiates us from just about any other non-profit. When it comes to buying land, a donor's dollar is almost always multiplied. We work very hard to make every dollar worth more than just a dollar."[1538]

Many grant programs, including the critical federal grant money administered by the American Battlefield Protection Program (ABPP), require matching funds. "Some of the state funds are like that as well," Duncan said. "We've got to put up a dollar to get a dollar."[1539] But that opens the door to the "multiply your dollar" fundraising strategy with the membership.

The ABPP administers the annual appropriation Congress has mandated for battlefield preservation since 1998 through its Land Acquisition Grant Program. The Civil War Trust is by far its most active partner. Forty of the 45 grants issued by the ABPP in fiscal year 2016 listed the Civil War Trust as the non-profit partner, accounting for $10.08 million of the $11.96 million awarded in preservation grants.[1540]

Annual funding for the ABPP grant program is the number one priority of the Trust's Policy and Media Department, led by Jim Campi. The program has provided federal matching dollars for hundreds of Civil War Trust land deals, including high profile acquisitions like the Slaughter Pen Farm and Lee's Headquarters. Since taking over the government relations shop at the Civil War Trust, Campi's team has successfully lobbied for more than $150 million in federal, state and local government grants for the Trust. "By leveraging government grants with the private dollars raised by David Duncan's team, we have accelerated our battlefield preservation effort beyond anything we thought possible around the time of the merger," Campi said.[1541]

In late 2001, around the second anniversary of the merger, Duncan established the Color Bearers, an elite group of members who contribute at least $1,000 annually. Duncan and Lighthizer had visited Thomas Jefferson's Monticello in Virginia, where they were encouraged to start a major donor group like the "Cabinet" of the Thomas Jefferson Foundation, owners of Monticello.[1542]

At the beginning of 2017, about 1,200 of the Trust's 48,000 members were

Color Bearers. "Without a doubt, they are the leaders," said Duncan. "They represent two-and-a-half percent of the membership and they contribute 50 percent of the revenue."[1543]

Duncan also established in 2002 an Honor Guard Society of members who include the Trust in their estate. By 2017, Deputy Director of Development Alice Mullis had tripled the society's membership to almost a thousand. Those legacy gifts "are going to be worth potentially tens of millions of dollars at some point down the road," Duncan said.[1544]

Around 2005, Lighthizer visited New York financier Richard M. "Dick" Cashin to thank him for his generous contributions. "If you really want to grow this organization, what you need is a revolving fund," Cashin told Lighthizer. The fund would be the Trust's own, in-house bank, allowing the organization to borrow money from itself to pay for urgent acquisitions, Cashin explained. The Trust would no longer have to wait for a fundraising campaign to succeed or a grant to be approved. It would have a mechanism to close on a deal that would fall through unless funds were immediately available.[1545]

In the early years after the merger, the Trust had purposely avoided taking on debt and was forced to decline several acquisition opportunities because it didn't have the money on hand to afford them. With a multi-million dollar revolving fund, that would no longer be a problem.

"I tell you what," Cashin said, "I'll put up a million dollars to get it started."[1546]

Lighthizer, startled and delighted, expressed his thanks, and said, "Let me do this, though. Let me go back and talk to the board and tell them they're going to have to match it."[1547]

The trustees more than tripled Cashin's donation and the revolving fund began with about $4.5 million. The fund is not an investment or an endowment; the Trust does not sit on money when more land needs to be saved. Like any bank, the fund has its rules, and money withdrawn is considered a loan—a zero percent loan. "Before we can borrow from the revolving fund, we have to have a replenishment plan and we have to pay it back within 36 months," Duncan said.[1548]

As the Trust saves more land at more battlefields, the achievements underscore the crucial role of education in its mission. "People have to care about preserving battlefields or they won't support us," said Director of History and Education Garry Adelman. "And caring starts with knowledge and understanding.[1549]

The Trust uses a "shotgun" approach to reach as many different people in as many ways as possible. "Our focus is to get out there on a lot of different fronts, to be in the classroom, to be on battlefields, to be in the media, to be on the web, to be in books, and to reach people in other ways," Adelman said.[1550]

A native of Chicago, Adelman had only a passing interest in history as a child. "On the last day of my sophomore year of high school, I happened to go in the library," he recalled. "I had a minute and picked up William A. Frassanito's book about Antietam photos (Antietam: The Photographic Legacy of America's Bloodiest Day). And, literally, I became obsessed with the Civil War right then and there. About five years later, I made my first trip to get Gettysburg—my first Civil War trip—and I was really obsessed thereafter."[1551]

Adelman graduated from Michigan State University and managed restaurants in Chicago for three years as he read about the Civil War "and used my scant vacation time to visit faraway battlefields." He moved to Gettysburg without a job at age 25 in 1992. While studying to become a licensed battlefield guide, he opened the Food for Thought Café and Coffee House just off the town square and began work on his master's degree in history at Shippensburg University. After stints at Thomas Publications in Gettysburg and History Associates in Rockville, Maryland, Adelman landed his "dream job" at the Trust in 2010.[1552]

When he took over, the education program featured an annual Teacher Institute as well as a "traveling trunk" of Civil War education materials based on what Adelman called an "outmoded" curriculum. "Now we have five traveling trunks, a popular field trip fund and a new and constantly updated free, downloadable curriculum," he said. "We have more Civil War lesson plans than anyone else, more short videos for teachers than anyone else, and a 'Teacher Regiment' where a thousand teacher 'soldiers' can share ideas as they move up through the ranks.[1553] Much of the work is funded by education-specific donations. In 2015, the Trust raised more than $500,000 for its education programs; five years earlier, it raised only $20,000.[1554]

"I had a teacher contact me who was applying to the Field Trip Fund we created," Adelman said. "She had already participated in our Teacher Institutes, has used our Traveling Trunk, and said she regularly used our lessons and "In4" videos in her classroom. That's wildly satisfying, because that one teacher, of the tens of thousands we reach each year, will in turn teach thousands of students in her career. Our broader mission to preserve battlefields, but we are helping to instill in children a passion for their history."[1555]

Adelman also developed the *Generations* program in a focused effort to have older people share their passion for history with younger people. As of early 2017, the Trust had held 10 events and had more planned.[1556] After the 2015 event, a participant emailed Adelman that program "was the best time my son and I have ever had together. The weekend together did much more than give us a wonderful

Civil War experience." A 2016 participant said the event prompted her grandson to ask for a Civil War uniform for Christmas.[1557]

"When I conceive events, my main goal is to open up what I call windows of understanding or recognition, where a participant will, even if just for a moment, grasp or understand something in a new way," Adelman said. "Different people connect with different windows, but I have found that recreating a known event on a battlefield to be the most effective."[1558]

At the summer 2016 *Generations* "Attack and Defend Little Round Top" event at Gettysburg, Adelman split the 200 attendees into Union and Confederate forces. "I was leading the Confederates, and as we approached, we could at last see through trees and spy the Union defenders on the rocky hill," he recalled. "A window opened for me at that moment and afterwards, participants on both sides agreed."[1559]

While the APCWS was initially created solely to acquire battlefield land, the original Trust made education a key component of its mission almost from the start. The Trust started a Civil War Discovery Trail that, by 1996, had enlisted 21 states and more than 350 sites in the program. The Trust also printed the Civil War Discovery Trail Official Guidebook, which quickly sold out. Eventually 33,000 copies were sold in three printings, including an updated guidebook with double the pages in 1996. A further update, Civil War Sites: The Official Guide to The Civil War Discovery Trail, is still in print. "There is now an online component that allows us to add sites regularly and keep the information more consistent," said former communications officer Mary Goundrey Koik, who continues to serve as the organization's editorial director. "It has maps that let folks get directions and find sites near each other. Now we're up to 600, including international sites."[1560]

In early 1996, the APCWS began working toward a presence on the emerging World Wide Web, and by spring 1997, under the guidance of Chairman Alan Hoeweler, it had a website. The original Civil War Trust was online by August 1997.[1561]

A decade later, the CWPT maintained an outdated web page. "It was a *terrible* website," former Trust webmaster Rob Shenk recalled. "We used to call that page the 'Blue Monster.' It was this dark, blue dungeon. It had a seven or eight-step donation process. I mean, you had to really want to give online."[1562] And measurably few members did.

Shenk was a master web developer who had honed his skills at AOL and eTrade. He also was a generous donor, so Duncan invited him to lunch. "I was a total prospect to him," Shenk recalled. "So, I fooled him and the legend is that I became less of a prospect and more of a cost." Shenk talked to Duncan about the website; Duncan invited him speak with the senior leadership. His impressive presentation led to the creation of a new position—Director of Internet Development and Strategy—in 2007.[1563]

Like Duncan and Gilmore before him, Shenk wanted to combine his profession with his personal interests and accepted a significant pay cut to do so. Shenk led a task force to redesign the website, keep it constantly updated with the Trust's new campaigns and add an ever-growing trove of cutting-edge historical presentations. Visitation soared from some 300,000 visits in 2008 to more than nine million in 2015. After Shenk streamlined the donation process, the Trust began to raise millions online. In 2015 alone, it raised more than $1.3 million online.[1564]

Adelman was impressed with the array of new content when he arrived in 2010, but noticed that little of it was tailored for novices. "So, I went back to basics," he recalled. "We started a simple Civil War Facts page which quickly became our most popular page. We followed up with short, four-minute productions on basic Civil War subjects called "In4" videos. We have more than 70 of these now, and they have been viewed by millions of people. We added animated map offerings that cover the entire Civil War and the whole Revolutionary War. These basic offerings are our most popular pieces and they both speak to public cravings for simple information."[1565]

The site features individual pages for 125 battlefields in 22 states and the District of Columbia with detailed articles, facts and links related to their history and preservation. Animated maps show the action unfolding as if from a hot-air balloon. In addition to the "In4" features, the site includes longer "War Department" videos that showcase the expertise of the nation's leading scholars and battlefield guides.[1566]

At the helm, Lighthizer runs a streamlined organization in relentless pursuit of excellence. "The objective is to always be challenging it to be better than it is right now," he said. "Part of my leadership philosophy is to always be pushing the organization to be better. You can never be satisfied. We never rest on our laurels, and that's a mind-set you get into, I never let up."[1567]

Many of Lighthizer's leadership principles are of his own making, but he isn't hesitant to borrow from others. Years ago, trustee Kirk Bradley introduced Lighthizer to Good to Great by business author Jim Collins. The Trust's operational model is now built around many of the concepts in the book.

"It's not just finding good people," Lighthizer said. "It's making sure you have the *right* people in the *right* positions. That's my most important job as CEO of the Trust; finding the right people, the best in their respective fields, making sure everyone is on the same page as to what we want to accomplish, and then getting out of their way and letting them do their jobs."[1568]

"We may be a non-profit," said Duncan, "but we run this place like a for-profit business, with high levels of rigor and accountability. Video gamers need not apply. I tell donors that we have five levels of rigor, which track our finances on a daily, weekly, monthly, quarterly and annual basis. On any given day, our key staff and the trustees know exactly where we are year-to-date against our budget, against our revenue projections and against where we were last year."[1569]

The Trust keeps a "laser-like focus" on preserving battlefields and does not stray. Good organizations may be good "at a lot of things," Lighthizer said, "but great organizations are the best in the world at just one thing. We get asked all of the time to help save Civil War prison sites, or campsites, or boat landings, or historic homes. As important as those things are, we have to turn them down. Or you end up diluting your efforts."[1570]

Admiral James Stockdale observed during his more than seven years as a Vietnam prisoner of war that captives who acknowledged the reality of their situation and still refused to give up hope fared best under the terrible conditions. The Trust leans heavily on the "Stockdale Paradox," which is also embraced in Good to Great. Trust staff are told to "confront the brutal reality of your situation but never lose faith that you will prevail in the end," Duncan said.[1571]

"When we started out, if you asked me if I ever thought we could raise over a quarter of a billion dollars in 17 years, I would have said, 'Hell, no,'" Lighthizer said. "But we did. I never thought like that. I never thought in terms of numbers. I just pushed to make us better. There were different goals along the way, and as we got better, we made the goals bigger."[1572]

Lighthizer described his staff and himself as workaholics. "You push people as far as you can push them," he said. "It's a delicate balance. It's almost a sixth sense that I've developed on when to back off. Most of the time, they need more help. And I give them help. But you stretch the staff as tight as you can without snapping it. Employees are an overhead expense, and when you have an overhead expense, it directly detracts from the money you can spend on the mission. That's why we're loath to add employees until we absolutely, positively need it."[1573]

"There are many reasons for the success of this movement, and there are many people who have contributed to that success over the years," Duncan said. "And Jim will seek to give others the credit for our success, but anyone who has even been halfway paying attention can see that everything changed when he took over the day-to-day management of the Trust in late 1999. Everything."[1574]

Behind the scenes, the Trust's large board of trustees not only oversees the organization and approves all real estate transactions, it helps evaluate properties, sets acquisition priorities and raises funds. Committees oversee the various functions, such as acquisitions, development, education, government relations, and the revolving fund. After the 1999 merger, members of both preceding boards were invited to stay on, and the board swelled to 35 members. It has remained large, with about 30 trustees.

"As I look around the room at these board meetings, I see people who are very, very talented and very, very busy people who have a lot of different talents, who have a lot of different kinds of interests, and they bring to the board a wide variety of backgrounds and a wealth of experience," said longtime trustee Mary Munsell Abroe, an Illinois community college history teacher who was on the APCWS board. "These are successful businessmen. There are lawyers. Like me, there's a teacher. They bring all of these different attributes that they can use to give back to the organization."[1575]

No trustee or chairman has been more important to the board and the organization in recent history than John L. Nau III. Since the 2000s, he has worked on Capitol Hill to reauthorize the annual federal appropriations for battlefield preservation administered by the American Battlefield Protection Program through its grants programs.

Nau is the president and chief executive officer of Silver Eagle Distributors, the nation's largest distributor of Budweiser products. He built the distributorship after switching to the beer business from Coca-Cola, where he started as a marketing trainee after serving in the U.S. Marine Corps. He joined the original Trust's board in 1998, remained on the post-merger CWPT board, rising to chairman, and continues today as a trustee and a major donor. He endowed the John L. Nau III Center for Civil War History at his alma mater, the University of Virginia, directed by Dr. Gary W. Gallagher. In 2016, he was also vice chairman of the National Park Foundation Board of Directors and a board member of the Baylor College of Medicine and Gilder-Lehrman Institute of American History.

"With John, it's even more than just the Congressional relations," said Duncan. "It's his total ability to work the halls of Congress and the Washington bureaucracy. He's always close to whomever is the director at the National Park Service. He's a Republican—he was President George W. Bush's chairman of the Advisory Council on Historic Preservation for many years—but he has an incredible ability to work with both sides. For a private individual in historic preservation, there is no one more connected to the federal government than John."[1576]

"No one has volunteered more of their time on behalf of the Trust's lobbying efforts than John Nau," Campi said. "He is a tireless advocate for battlefield preservation."[1577]

Trustees often step up individually with large donations to make the difference in a purchase. The list would fill pages, but includes longtime Trustee Dan Beattie and his wife, Peggy, lead donors for the 258-acre "hole in the donut" tract at Brandy Station in 2000 and other parcels as well. Norm Tomlinson, the successful publisher who financed the transition of APCWS's *Hallowed Ground* newsletter into a full-color magazine in 1998, is "the single most generous trustee for 15 years," Duncan said. More recently, businessman and Trustee Bruce Gottwald has donated generously to help the Trust acquire battlefield land around Richmond, Virginia, his home. Trustee Tom Lauer has taken the lead with *Campaign 1776* for the Revolutionary War. Like Beattie, Trustee William J. Hupp, a retired private equity manager from Chicago, took Brandy Station under his wing.

During the Trust's spring board meeting in Memphis, Tenn., in March 2013, the board was wrangling with the purchase of Fleetwood Hill at Brandy Station from Tony Troilo. The land had been on the market for most of 2012 and if sold to a developer, could have been subdivided for five more homes. But the Trust had announced a tentative agreement at $3.64 million in December. Now the trustees were struggling with how to come up with all of the money. The ABPP had awarded a matching grant of almost $1.8 million, leaving the Trust to come up with the remaining $1.84 million. The Commonwealth of Virginia helped with a $700,000 grant, but when the meeting began, the Trust was still $500,000 short.

Duncan was sitting at the staff table behind Hupp at the board table. "Here was a travesty at Fleetwood Hill that could have been multiplied by five," recalled Duncan. "I was thinking, 'This is going to be tough.' There was a lot of back and forth. And I remember Jim Lighthizer finally said, 'Well, if we can't raise the money, guys, we can't do it.' And the board almost tabled it."

The trustees took a break. As Hupp stood, he turned around to Duncan. "So, if I'm understanding this right, we need $500,000 to get this done," Hupp said.

"That's right," Duncan told him.

"I'll do that," Hupp said, holding up all five fingers on one hand.

The board is united in its passion for history and preservation. Each trustee's story is unique, but retired attorney and Board of Trustees Secretary William W. Vodra's path to board service began in the early 2000s, when he and his wife, Drusilla, decided to make a large gift to a worthwhile charity. They had been devoted members of the "Bearss Brigade" since the 1980s, traveling the country, even the world, to tour battlefields with the retired NPS chief historian and hear his unmatched commentary. "I think my wife and I have spent at least one full year, that's 365 days, on buses with Ed Bearss," Vodra recalled. "Over a course of 20 years,

I'll bet you we have done well over 300 of the 380 or 390 sites in the American Battlefields Commission Report with Ed."[1578]

The Vodras had given donations large enough to earn personal voicemails of thanks from Lighthizer. Eventually, Vodra recalled, Lighthizer "made sure he got through to me, and he thanked me profusely, and then said, 'Who the hell are you?' So we had lunch together and he asked me if I was interested in joining the board. I was getting to a point of looking at retirement, and something to do after I stepped down from the active practice of law. And this seemed like a fun project, so I signed on in 2005."[1579]

The expectation from trustees, Vodra said, is "time, treasure, or talent. Give, get, or get off." Vodra offered his legal expertise when the Trust was searching for effective pro bono legal help in the Wilderness Walmart fight and paved the way for representation by Robert Rosenbaum at Arnold & Porter, his old law firm.

"The board has changed remarkably since I came on," Vodra said. "Back then, the members essentially didn't have deep pockets and they weren't focused on money raising and this was not their biggest priority in life. The biggest change is that we've gone to people who are much more generous and much more financially successful in life. They've been in major corporations, they've been in major banks, they've been in venture capital, they've started up their own companies, a whole variety of things like that.

"We have three board meetings a year, and we've actually had a couple people turn us down for board membership because they don't want to commit to more than two meetings a year. So, we have a real talk-down, come-to-Jesus meeting with the candidate, saying, 'This is what we expect, are you willing to do that?' This is one that they really have to put in time and effort," said Vodra. In most cases, trustees are now expected to donate at least $10,000 a year as well as one, major six- or seven-figure gift during their time on the board.[1580]

The amount of work overseen by the board could easily lead to marathon, all-day board meetings, but much is handled in committees, streamlining the three annual board meetings to a half-day, "with the other half for tours and fun," Lighthizer said.[1581]

"The two things the board focuses on the most tightly are the finances and the land acquisitions," Lighthizer said. "The land is always the fun part. The Land Committee is always the chairmanship everybody wants. Every battlefield purchase is exhaustively analyzed, so when it comes up for final approval, it's never turned down by the board."[1582]

As the board discusses acquisitions and issues, "a general consensus evolves in an extremely collegial atmosphere," Lighthizer said. "As a practical matter, when a decision comes before the full board, it has already been decided. I can think of only one 12–11 vote in the history of the organization. Everybody is involved in anything significant and a genuine effort is made to accommodate all points of view. But you have to play well with others."[1583]

That said, "the board has gotten better, particularly in terms of generosity," Lighthizer said. Entering the 2016 holiday giving season, the 31 trustees had amassed more than $23.5 million in cumulative giving—more than 73 percent of that since 2010.[1584]

In 2015, Lighthizer asked a movement veteran, APCWS co-founder Gary Gallagher, to rejoin the board. Gallagher declined. He had traveled his entire life in the service of history, especially the first 10 years leading APCWS. The endless trips to and from State College, Pennsylvania—the rain and snow and the dead-stop traffic jams—had exhausted countless hours as surely as any work of scholarship, and taken a toll on his back.[1585]

Gallagher could not have been happier with the Trust's record. What it had done for battlefield preservation, and continued to do with ever-greater success, astonished him, and was extremely gratifying. He donated every year and made himself available for lectures, history videos and such, but "I really felt like I had done my major part in the first 10 years," he said, "I really thought any active role was behind me."[1586]

Gallagher resisted even when board member and former Chairman John Nau, who endowed Gallagher's professorship at the University of Virginia, asked. But the more he thought, the harder it became to say no. Preserved battlefields are a wonderful resource for teaching and research for a scholar such as Gallagher.[1587]

The Trust had transformed the "labor of love" he and his fellow historians had created into a land preservation success story. "I would not have forecast, as a member of the original board back in 1987, that the organization would be anywhere near where it is now," Gallagher said.[1588]

"We need you back," Nau and Lighthizer told him.[1589]

Gallagher knew the board was "light years from the one we had when the APCWS was just getting launched and we were starting to look for projects. There's a lot of wealth on the board and it is part of an organization that has a tremendous record, saving tens of thousands of acres and regularly taking on multi-million dollar projects."[1590]

Gallagher knew that the trustees shared a love of history, but most were CEOs, investment bankers, leading attorneys and top executives. Some had started their own companies. The board even had a couple of celebrities: musician Trace Adkins and NCAA championship-winning former Georgia football coach Vince Dooley. At least three board members had served the country in war and seen combat. Two were awarded with Purple Hearts, two with Bronze Stars.[1591]

Back in 1987, the APCWS founders were mostly professional historians; now only a single professional historian was on the Trust's board. At 93, Ed Bearss still carried the flag, travelling constantly to lecture and provide tours, always spreading the word of the mission to preserve hallowed ground.[1592]

"I'm not young anymore," Gallagher thought. "But I'm 30 years younger than Ed is. And they need at least a couple of historians."[1593]

The 30th anniversary of the organized battlefield preservation movement was approaching. Gallagher and the other founders could never have predicted the enormous success to come, certainly not during the years of discord. Now, more than 45,000 acres of hallowed ground—70 square miles—had been saved at 132 battlefields in 23 states. Still, the sobering reality was that so much remained threatened. As successful as it was, the Trust had work to do. Gallagher decided he could not resist the call back to service. In 2016, he became a member of the Board of Trustees of the Civil War Trust.[1594] ★

EPILOGUE

★

T AGE 16, Theodore Gerrish was mustered as a private into the 20th Maine regiment, commanded by Joshua Lawrence Chamberlain. Gerrish was wounded at the Wilderness. General Chamberlain was wounded six times and almost killed at Petersburg. But both survived the war to witness the Confederates stack their arms at Appomattox, where Chamberlain ordered Gerrish and his comrades to salute their vanquished foe.

Two decades later, the private and the general would write eloquently of the battlefield landscapes they and their fellow soldiers had consecrated with their blood. Gerrish expected the destruction of hallowed ground.

"That country must have changed, my comrades, since we were there," Gerrish wrote in his 1882 memoir, <u>Army Life: A Private's Reminiscences of the Civil War.</u> "Those rifle-pits we digged are now filled with earth; the breastworks are leveled down; the forts all dismantled. I presume we should hardly remember now at what points in the line our regiments fought, or where we buried our comrades."[1595]

Yet Gerrish also wrote, "I wish we could go down there again... I believe that we should derive an inspiration from the visit."[1596]

Gerrish's commander, Chamberlain, one of the most eloquent Civil War generals, concurred. "In great deeds something abides. On great fields something stays," Chamberlain said in a speech at Gettysburg on October 3, 1889, at the dedication of the Maine battlefield monuments. "Forms change and pass; bodies disappear; but spirits linger, to consecrate ground for the vision-place of souls. Generations that know us not . . . shall come to this deathless field, to ponder and dream . . ."[1597]

The Civil War Trust and its predecessor organizations have spent tens of millions of dollars in the past 30 years preserving the places—the battlefields—that both the general and private considered so important. The Trust's relentless parade of battlefield acquisitions passed 45,000 acres at 132 battlefields in 23 states in early 2017. That includes battlefields of the American Revolution and War of 1812, whose lands became part of the Trust's preservation mission in 2014 with the creation of *Campaign 1776*.

Since 1987, tens of thousands of loyal members and supporters have donated to the cause—everything from spare change dropped into a donation jar at an Association for the Preservation of Civil War Sites (APCWS) booth to game-changing, million-dollar donations.[1598]

That so many have given so much of their time and treasure over these past three decades to honor those who fought and fell on American soil would be welcome news to Chamberlain and Gerrish. The private peered into his crystal ball in 1882 and supposed that the United States of America in our time would "probably contain two hundred millions of people, and be the center of the world." Although Gerrish worried about the state of battlefields, he kept faith that the country would "always honor our memory and not forget us when we have vanished from its sight."[1599]

The Trust transforms old battlefields, some all but forgotten, into places of history and learning, reconnecting communities with their heritage and, ultimately, giving more meaning to the deaths of young Americans who perished there. The Trust almost always has partners in saving land, including local and regional preservation groups, state preservation agencies and the American Battlefield Protection Program of the National Park Service. At the heart of it all is the ongoing support and generosity of more than 47,000 Trust members.

Two decades after the war, Gerrish envisioned a return to the Virginia battlefields and the "the heights that encircle Fredericksburg," an expanse now filled with homes and businesses. Gerrish also wished to "cross the plains around the ruins of the old Chancellorsville house; then enter the Wilderness," where he and his comrades were "plunged into the depths of death . . ."[1600]

Today, because of the success of the Civil War Trust and the battlefield preservation movement, Gerrish could stand at the foundation of the Chancellor house and see the open plain to the west of the first day's battlefield at Chancellorsville. Four and a half miles farther west, because of the Trust's acquisitions, he would still see open fields around the Wilderness Church where Stonewall Jackson made his surprise flank attack on the battle's second day. In 2016 alone, the Trust acquired almost 1,200 new battlefield acres at Chancellorsville, increasing the total saved at the Wilderness and Chancellorsville to 1,546 acres, or more than two square miles of historic land.[1601]

Civil War Trust President Jim Lighthizer, at age 71 in 2017, has lost none of the zeal he brought to the position in 1999, in part because there's so much hallowed ground left to be saved. "A conservative estimate of the universe of significant battlefields that ought to be saved is about 200,000 acres in private ownership that will ultimately be developed," Lighthizer said. "I'm talking about core battlefields. So, it's like drinking out of a fire hose. It's a gargantuan area to try and save. If we save a fraction of it, we'll be happy."[1602]

Of the eight original founders of APCWS, only Brian Pohanka has died. Donald C. Pfanz, who wrote the letter to Pohanka that triggered the organization's creation, remained on the APCWS board for about a year before accepting a South Carolina NPS position and resigning from the board, "confident that the APCWS was in capable hands," he said. Pfanz, who has authored or co-authored five Civil War books, retired as NPS historian at the Fredericksburg park in 2013. "Although my role in creating the organization was modest compared to that of many others, nevertheless I view it as the greatest accomplishment of my life," Pfanz said.[1603]

Will Greene, APCWS co-founder and its first employee and executive director, retired on February 28, 2017, as executive director of Pamplin Historical Park. Greene developed the privately owned, 424-acre site of the "Breakthrough" on the Petersburg battlefield after leaving APCWS in 1994. The park features The National Museum of the Civil War Soldier, a cutting-edge museum where visitors experience a sense of the fury of combat, with the sound of bullets zipping past their ears as the floor shakes from the concussion of shell fire. Greene has also authored more than 20 published works on the Civil War and served on the board of the Institute of Museum of Library Services.

Co-founder John P. "Jack" Ackerly III, now a retired Richmond attorney, serves as president of the Lee-Jackson Educational Foundation. He served on the boards of the Shenandoah Valley Battlefields Foundation, the Museum of the Confederacy and the Stonewall Jackson House in Lexington. "I think it's amazing what they've done, you know, with the money they can command," Ackerly said in 2012.[1604]

Robert K. Krick, APCWS co-founder and vice president, retired in 2002 after 35 years with the National Park Service, 30 of them as chief historian at Fredericksburg and Spotsylvania National Military Park. Krick is secretary of Central Virginia Battlefields Trust, which he co-founded in 1996, lives in Fredericksburg and quietly works behind the scenes to facilitate more preservation at the Fredericksburg, Chancellorsville, Spotsylvania Court House, the Wilderness and other Virginia battlefields.

Krick's "puppet" on Capitol Hill, Robert Mrazek, retired from Congress in 1993 after serving five terms. He became a successful writer, and has published eight books—four novels and four works of non-fiction. He wrote and directed his own independent film, *The Congressman*, starring Treat Williams, which premiered at the Sarasota Film Festival in April 2016.

After resigning as APCWS president in 1998, co-founder Dennis Frye resumed his National Park Service career at Harpers Ferry National Park, where he works today as head of the Cultural Resources and Interpretation Division. He continues to serve on the board of the Save Historic Antietam Foundation, the local preservation organization he co-founded in 1986.

APCWS co-founder Ed Wenzel continues to work for Ox Hill Battlefield Park and document the history of the Civil War in Greater Fairfax County. On December

22, 2015, the Bull Run Civil War Round Table published his Chronology of the Civil War in Fairfax County, Part 1, a 618-page chronicle of skirmishes, engagements, battles and wartime events. Over the years, Wenzel's relationship with the county gradually transformed from adversarial to cooperative. In 2010, at the sixth annual Fairfax County History Conference, the Fairfax County History Commission presented Wenzel with its Lifetime Achievement Award.

Co-founder Gary Gallagher, the first president/chairman of APCWS, still teaches and serves as director of the John L. Nau III Center for Civil War History at the University of Virginia. He has several writing projects in progress, including a second book he is co-editing with J. Matthew Gallman (following Lens of War in 2015) that will offer interpretive essays by 28 leading historians who reflect on specific Civil War places.

Former APCWS Chairman Alan Hoeweler is owner of Aluminum Extruded Shapes, Inc., in Cincinnati, Ohio. He is chairman (emeritus) of the Aviation Hall of Fame in Daytona, Ohio, a former commissioner of the Perryville (Kentucky) Battlefield Commission and a former council member of the Village of Glendale, Ohio. He is fully supportive of the work of the Civil War Trust.

Former APCWS Treasurer Frederick Zavaglia regrets that the APCWS staff and organization were wiped out by the merger. "I'm relatively ambivalent about how it all turned out," he said. "I'm glad the merger didn't cause the complete collapse of the membership or the mission. I'm clearly glad that persisted, but I still think the merger was more medicine than either organization needed to become better at what they did. What they needed was to distinguish themselves from each other, not amalgamate. We'd taken great risks at APCWS and had pulled off something with the bond issue that nobody thought possible. It might have actually been a whole new model for private nonprofit preservation fundraising. It could have been a whole new paradigm."[1605]

Former APCWS Director of Education Dana Shoaf returned to the magazine world to become editor of *America's Civil War* and, in 2007, editor of the venerated grandfather of Civil War periodicals, *Civil War Times*. His wife, Heidi, is Daughters of the American Revolution Museum Director and Chief Curator in Washington, D.C.

Former Trust Executive Vice President and acting President Elliot Gruber remained in the non-profit world after leaving the Civil War Preservation Trust in the fall of 2000. He has worked with The Ocean Conservancy, the Gettysburg Foundation, United Way of the National Capital Area and, from 2013 to 2016, was president and CEO of The Mariner's Museum in Newport News, Virginia, home of the recovered gun turret of the USS *Monitor*.

Ed Bearss continues his active touring and speaking schedule out of his home in Arlington, Virginia, anticipating his 94th birthday on June 26, 2017. "I can't speak too highly of what has been accomplished," he said. "If you didn't have somebody like Jim Lighthizer, you would have to create somebody like him because he has objectives, he is dynamic and he believes in what he does."[1606] The Trust has honored Bearss by creating a lifetime achievement award in his name.[1607]

J. Roderick Heller, founder of the original Civil War Trust, spends much of his time at his Tennessee home at "Windemere," a former McGavock family estate adjoining Carnton. He authored a biography, Felix Grundy, Democracy's Lawyer, published in 2012 by Louisiana State University Press. In October 2016, his development company, Harpeth Associates, released plans for Harpeth Square, a $90 million mixed-use development occupying 10 blocks of downtown Franklin. The proposed project includes a high-end hotel and restaurant, 150 apartment homes, a four-story garage, 15,000 square feet of retail space and more than 3,600 square feet of office space, while preserving four historic buildings on the property. It would be the largest and most expensive development in downtown Franklin's history. Opponents cite traffic and overcrowding issues and object to a tax break request.[1608]

Julian Bibb, Mary Pearce and Robert Hicks continue to serve on the Franklin's Charge Board of Directors. Hicks's third novel, The Orphan Mother, was published in September 2016 by Grand Central Publishing.

The reclamation of the epicenter of the Franklin battlefield and restoration into Carter Hill Battlefield Park continues at a fast pace. By mid-February 2017, two houses directly south of the Carter House had been removed, restoring for the first time in more than a century the view of the Union line seen by Confederate soldiers in the final, bloody yards of their charge. That same month, Lighthizer was in Nashville to honor Tennessee and Governor Bill Haslam for becoming the first state to establish a permanent funding source to help protect its battlefields – the "Civil War or War Between the States Site Preservation Fund." Days earlier, Haslam dedicated $3.2 million to the state budget for the construction of a new visitor's center for Carter House and the new Carter Hill Battlefield Park.[1609]

In Gettysburg, David LeVan launched a third attempt to develop a Gettysburg casino in January 2017. "We've listened to those who were concerned about our previously proposed location," LeVan said in a news release. "That's why this project will be located 2.5 miles farther southeast, across a major highway and along the Maryland border." The planned Mason-Dixon Downs would include a harness racing track and would be constructed on land owned by Mason Dixon Country Club along the Pennsylvania-Maryland border, about three miles from Gettysburg

National Military Park.

LeVan disagrees with the argument that Gettyburg and gambling don't mix. "Elsewhere in Pennsylvania, the record is now clear as far as the coexistence of gambling and history," LeVan said, citing the Lady Luck Casino at Nemacolin Woodlands Resort near Fort Necessity National Battlefield and Valley Forge Casino Resort near Valley Forge National Historical Park. "In fact, the casinos promote the historical sites," he said.[1610] As of March 2017, the Trust had not taken a position on the proposal.[1611]

Five years ago, on the 25th anniversary of the founding of APCWS, the Trust gave three men its Edwin C. Bearss Lifetime Achievement Award: Tersh Boasberg, Ed Wenzel and Bud Hall. Now retired from law practice, Boasberg reflected on the preservation fights for Stuart's Hill at Manassas and Brandy Station: "Yeah, they were great, great battles. They were very, very significant and very memorable. And I take great pride in having them out there and having those two battles lead to the current Civil War Trust. I didn't have anything to do with that, but I think it's fair to say that these two contributed to that, and nothing could make me happier than to see this much Civil War property protected. It's just a wonderful feeling, vicarious anyway, of accomplishment and pride."[1612]

Boasberg's protagonist in the Stuart's Hill fight, Til Hazel, who was 86 in early 2017, lives an active retired life at 86 on his vast farm at Broad Run, Virginia. He and his brother's family own 5,000 acres. "I have become a member of the Civil War Trust," he said. "I've contributed to them in the last couple of years, and I've been impressed with the preparation that they make for their requests. They identify the pieces that are involved and the significance of the parcels and they have very good maps. And I think that's a good thing the way they do it.

"And I'm glad the Trust got involved in the Revolution," Hazel said. "They recently sent some appeals based on some of the lands in South Carolina and North Carolina in the Revolution, and that has been a neglected area until recently. What they're doing and what happened at William Center are entirely separate."

Michael Armm, the late Lee Sammis's Elkwood Downs project director at Brandy Station, remained with Sammis for 19 years. He lives in Culpeper, Virginia, and is senior vice president—director of acquisitions and development for The Hornbaker Group, an Alexandria, Virginia-based data center development and services company.

Tony Troilo sold his Fleetwood Hill mansion to the Civil War Trust for $3.6 million in 2012, only five years after he built it. "They paid me, it's theirs and that's the end of the story," he said. But animosity lingers in Brandy Station. "I hate to say this, but I've got to say it's the truth, but a lot of the people in this community have become anti-Civil War because of what happened to us. I still hear it—not as much today—but I bet you before the week is out, somebody will bring it up and say, 'What a damn shame it was that they tore that house down. Couldn't they have used it for something?' But time will heal that. You know what? Time will heal that."[1613]

Bud Hall frequently returns to Brandy Station from his home overlooking the Wicomico River, deep in the northern neck of Virginia, to give battlefield tours, sharing not only the saga of the war's greatest cavalry clash, but the story of the preservation of the battlefield.

Hall vows to curtail his work in preservation, but can't. Not completely. "Hundreds of acres of the battlefield around Yew Ridge and other places are still unprotected," he said.[1614] He also continues to work to preserve the pristine Union winter encampment on nearby Hansbrough's Ridge.

In 2015, the Trust joined with the Brandy Station Foundation and nine other organizations to create the Brandy Station & Cedar Mountain State Park Alliance and began lobbying for a new state park in Culpeper County. "Now we've got public support in Culpeper County, where we didn't have it before," Hall said. The alliance created a Facebook page to help spread its message. It soon filled with history posts, with no more devoted a contributor than Hall.[1615]

With Fleetwood Hill once again clear, the Trust in 2015 opened a trail with interpretive markers telling the story of the site in text, photos and maps. Hall once again feels comfortable coming there. His late wife, Deborah Fitts, would have been thrilled. But it is not the same for Hall without her. It never will be.[1616]

Hall made plans to move in 2017 from his Wicomico River home to a condominium in Richmond. He never considered moving to Brandy Station. "I think it has helped my credibility over the years not to be a resident," he said. But the trip to Culpeper County will be easier from the Virginia state capital, and Hall knows he will never stop going back to Brandy Station. ★

ACKNOWLEDGMENTS

★

ighting the Second Civil War: A History of Battlefield Preservation and the Emergence of the Civil War Trust was conceived by Director of History and Education Garry Adelman soon after he joined the Trust staff in 2010.

Garry commissioned me to research and write the history, starting with a project in 2011–12 to obtain more than 50 oral history interviews from the founders and leaders of the movement. In December 2012, we signed an agreement where I agreed to produce a 15-chapter narrative of about 80,000 words by mid-2014. Almost three years after the original deadline, we present a history that spans 22 chapters and contains almost twice as many words. It is only a broad-brush history of the modern battlefield preservation movement's first 30 years, but nevertheless goes well beyond Garry's initial vision and my own projections. I thank Garry for giving me the privilege of being its creator.

Historians hold themselves to a high standard when it comes to retelling the history of other times and people, as do the readers of their works. Fighting the Second Civil War puts the spotlight on living historians and history lovers and their preservation accomplishments, and it was gratifying to discover that they wanted their own history to be accurate and well-told. They were frank and open, sometimes painfully so, in recalling their experiences.

Using the oral histories and many other interviews, I sought to write a history in the mold of the storytelling style of the greatest Civil War tour guides of modern times, such as Ed Bearss and the late Francis Wilshin. The storytelling has been melded into the facts of the movement's history, which I assembled from countless documents, meeting minutes, news stories and other sources.

Archives are the lifeblood of historians, and I am particularly grateful to the preservation pioneers who opened their personal archives for my benefit. Clark B. "Bud" Hall, in addition to sharing his personal story in numerous interviews, loaded two foot lockers of Brandy Station records in my car around 2013. They spent a couple of years in my office. Edward T. Wenzel is a meticulous, prolific archivist who answered every question I posed with dates, times and hard facts. Dennis E. Frye copied a stack of documents four or five inches thick from his archives that documented his time as a board member and president of APCWS. From the archives of Robert K. Krick came valuable early documentation on the APCWS. Ed Bearss agreed to several interviews and also provided documents from his archives. Time and again I returned to these historians with follow-up questions. They were always helpful, as was Bryan Mitchell, who guided me through the intricacies of the nomination process for the National Register of Historic Places. These six men also contributed oral histories that were consulted or excerpted in this book.

From the Civil War Trust staff, Jim Lighthizer, Garry Adelman, Jim Campi, Ron Cogswell, David Duncan, Tom Gilmore and Ruth Hudspeth also contributed oral histories and patiently endured a parade of follow-up questions and emails. Their contributions brought life and color to the narrative.

I offer thanks as well for interviews granted by Mary Munsell Abroe, Jack Ackerly, Grae Baxter, Tersh Boasberg, Brad Bradshaw, Paul Bryant, Jr., Childs Burden, Chris Calkins, Howard Coffin, Brad Coker, Charlie Crawford, Pam Davis, Lester "Ruff" Fant, Gary W. Gallagher, A. Wilson Greene, Elliot Gruber, Blake Hallman, Paul Hawke, J. Roderick Heller III, John Hennessy, Irvin Hess, Robert Hicks, Robert Lee Hodge, John Howard, Chris Miller, Robert Mrazek, James M. McPherson, Noah Mehrkam, John L. Nau III, Libby O'Connell, Jim and Susan Paddock, Bonnie Repasi, Melissa Meisner Sadler, Stephanie Saul, Rob Shenk, Dana Shoaf, Mike Siegel, the late Henry Simpson, Mike Stevens, Julie Fix Udani and William W. Vodra.

Thanks as well to Michael Armm, Mark Berg, Julian Bibb, Ron Blevins, Patrick Brennan, H. Grant Dehart, William A. Frassanito, Sam Gant, John D. Haynes, John T. "Til" Hazel, Jr., Alan Hoeweler, Sam Huffman, Jerry Hurwitz, Kay Jorgensen, Daniel M. Laney, David LeVan, Tom Miller, Daralee Ota, Mary Pearce, Ron Perisho, Donald Pfanz, Tony Troilo, Stacey Watson and Frederick J. Zavaglia for sharing their recollections or providing information.

I am indebted to Jim Burgess at Manassas National Battlefield Park, Eric Mink at Fredericksburg and Spotsylvania National Military Park and Keith Snyder and Brian Baracz at Antietam National Battlefield for information or interviews.

My research was made easier because the movement's history is well documented by newspapers and periodicals. Of the many dozens of journalists cited in the notes, of particular distinction are the late Deborah Fitts, who covered preservation for the *Civil War News* from 1989 until shortly before her death in 2008, and Clint Schemmer, who has covered all 30 years of the movement as a journalist for several Virginia newspapers, currently the Fredericksburg *Free-Lance Star*.

To the Trust staff, I extend thanks to Mark Coombs, Patrick Farrell, Matt George, Tracey McIntire, Jon Mitchell, Alice Mullis, Samantha Ringer, Kathy Robertson, Roz Siegel, Kris White and Steve Wyngarden. Thanks as well to the Trust's cartographer Steven Stanley, designer Jeff Griffith, who designed this lovely book in record time, and my literary agent, John Silbersack.

Every writer needs a good editor, and I had a team of editors, most importantly my wife, journalist Ann Bailie, who volunteered dozens of hours reading the manuscript. She caught hundreds of mistakes and made at least as many improvements.

Garry enlisted Mary Goundrey Koik, whose encyclopedic knowledge of Trust messaging and crack editorial skills were essential to this narrative. Garry also brought on a "secret reader," who constantly impressed Ann and me with his expertise. He turned out to be a friend, whose name and contributions to this book shall remain unknown to all but a few of us. The editing team for the full narrative also included Garry, John Beshears, Jim Campi, Jim Lighthizer, Donna Weisner and Indexer Enid L. Zafrin. Special thanks to William W. Vodra, a key supporter of the project, who also reviewed the full narrative.

Bob Zeller
Lake Norman, North Carolina
March 10, 2017

★

APPENDIX
ONE

*Battlefield Land Preserved in Whole or in Part
by the Civil War Trust, as of March 1, 2017*

★

BATTLEFIELD	STATE	NUMBER OF TRACTS	NUMBER OF ACRES
Civil War			
Fort Blakeley	AL	I	67.27
Hog Mountain	AL	I	40.00
McGee House	AL	I	I2.6I
TOTAL ALABAMA:		**3**	**II9.88**
Devil's Backbone	AR	I	I0.I7
Elkins Ferry	AR	I	44I.86
Helena	AR	I	56.00
Prairie Grove	AR	2	270.33
TOTAL ARKANSAS:		**5**	**778.36**
Sand Creek	CO	I	640.00
TOTAL COLORADO:		**I**	**640.00**
Natural Bridge	FL	2	I09.74
TOTAL FLORIDA:		**2**	**I09.74**
Chickamauga	GA	3	I40.8I
Dallas	GA	I	64.37
Griswoldsville	GA	I	I7.33
Kennesaw Mountain	GA	I	3.78
New Hope Church	GA	I	4.83
Rocky Face Ridge	GA	2	926.II
Resaca	GA	2	I044.09
TOTAL GEORGIA:		**II**	**220I.32**
Mine Creek	KS	2	326.00
TOTAL KANSAS:		**2**	**326.00**

BATTLEFIELD	STATE	NUMBER OF TRACTS	NUMBER OF ACRES
Camp Wildcat	KY	1	263.72
Mill Springs	KY	18	685.93
Munfordville	KY	7	134.82
Perryville	KY	13	1025.99
Richmond	KY	4	365.62
TOTAL KENTUCKY:		**43**	**2476.08**
Fort DeRussy	LA	2	73.40
Mansfield	LA	4	421.17
Port Hudson	LA	1	256.00
TOTAL LOUISIANA		**7**	**750.57**
Antietam	MD	9	314.19
Monocacy	MD	3	442.50
South Mountain	MD	11	546.69
Williamsport	MD	1	3.50
TOTAL MARYLAND:		**24**	**1306.88**
Wood Lake	MN	2	240.00
TOTAL MINNESOTA:		**2**	**240.00**
Big Black River Bridge	MS	1	28.07
Brice's Cross Roads	MS	8	1335.80
Champion Hill	MS	7	475.96
Corinth	MS	9	783.20
Iuka	MS	1	57.98
Okolona	MS	1	77.31
Port Gibson	MS	2	644.09
Raymond	MS	2	105.65
Tupelo	MS	1	12.38
Vicksburg	MS	4	11.27
TOTAL MISSISSIPPI:		**36**	**3531.71**
Byram's Ford	MO	1	38.75
Fort Davidson	MO	1	40.58
Newtonia	MO	1	8.00
Wilson's Creek	MO	3	272.00
TOTAL MISSOURI:		**6**	**359.33**

BATTLEFIELD	STATE	NUMBER OF TRACTS	NUMBER OF ACRES
Glorieta Pass	NM	2	19.00
TOTAL NEW MEXICO:		**2**	**19.00**
Averasboro	NC	7	519.89
Bentonville	NC	51	1784.21
New Bern	NC	1	24.65
Wyse Fork	NC	2	114.75
TOTAL NORTH CAROLINA:		**61**	**2443.50**
Honey Springs	OK	2	83.75
Cabin Creek	OK	2	87.70
TOTAL OKLAHOMA:		**4**	**171.45**
Gettysburg	PA	32	982.70
TOTAL PENNSYLVANIA:		**32**	**982.70**
Fort Moultrie	SC	1	0.23
Morris Island	SC	1	117.70
TOTAL SOUTH CAROLINA:		**2**	**117.93**
Chattanooga	TN	5	106.35
Davis Bridge	TN	5	858.92
Fort Donelson	TN	11	314.26
Fort Sanders	TN	1	68.87
Franklin	TN	11	177.61
Johnsonville	TN	1	19.04
Parker's Cross Roads	TN	8	349.59
Shiloh	TN	25	1199.29
Spring Hill	TN	3	194.65
Stones River	TN	4	25.92
TOTAL TENNESSEE:		**74**	**3314.50**
Palmito Ranch	TX	1	3.00
TOTAL TEXAS:		**1**	**3.00**

BATTLEFIELD	STATE	NUMBER OF TRACTS	NUMBER OF ACRES
Aldie	VA	4	604.88
Appomattox Court House	VA	10	238.73
Appomattox Station	VA	1	45.00
Ball's Bluff	VA	1	3.22
Brandy Station	VA	15	2085.81
Bristoe Station	VA	2	133.41
Buckland	VA	1	90.51
Cedar Creek	VA	13	639.22
Cedar Mountain	VA	5	497.85
Chancellorsville	VA	14	1287.60
Cold Harbor	VA	7	51.64
Cool Spring	VA	2	1119.72
Cross Keys	VA	5	281.81
First Deep Bottom	VA	3	257.81
Fisher's Hill	VA	4	361.79
Five Forks	VA	1	419.47
Fredericksburg	VA	5	247.32
Second Deep Bottom	VA	3	41.81
Gaines' Mill	VA	8	341.26
Glendale	VA	15	679.48
Hatcher's Run	VA	4	387.20
High Bridge	VA	2	175.65
JEB Stuart Birthplace	VA	1	71.37
Kelly's Ford	VA	4	1234.34
Kernstown	VA	3	388.38
Lee's Mill	VA	1	5.87
Malvern Hill	VA	7	952.97
Manassas	VA	9	198.22
McDowell	VA	4	583.22
John Meigs Death Site	VA	1	0.50
Middleburg	VA	1	5.01
Mine Run	VA	2	689.99
New Market	VA	1	20.00
New Market Heights	VA	2	16.38
North Anna	VA	3	750.71
Breakthrough	VA	5	407.19
Peebles Farm	VA	2	87.87
Petersburg	VA	4	122.77
Port Republic	VA	7	946.86
Rappahannock Station	VA	6	855.84
Reams Station	VA	7	182.85
Sailor's Creek	VA	5	885.47

BATTLEFIELD	STATE	NUMBER OF TRACTS	NUMBER OF ACRES
Saltville	VA	I	106.90
Spotsylvania Court House	VA	2	4.63
Thoroughfare Gap	VA	I	109.00
Tom's Brook	VA	5	491.50
Third Winchester	VA	4	446.84
Totopotomoy Creek	VA	3	131.80
Trevillian Station	VA	12	1789.95
Upperville	VA	I	793.76
Ware Bottom Church	VA	2	21.51
White Oak Road	VA	12	903.06
Wilderness	VA	5	258.69
Williamsburg	VA	3	68.87
TOTAL VIRGINIA:		**251**	**23,523.51**
Corrick's Ford	WV	I	26.40
Fort Mulligan	WV	I	5.50
Harpers Ferry	WV	8	342.25
Rich Mountain	WV	3	57.00
Shepherdstown	WV	II	343.47
Summit Point	WV	2	454.61
TOTAL WEST VIRGINIA:		**26**	**1229.23**
TOTAL CIVIL WAR:	**21 STATES**	**595**	**44,644.7**

RevolutionaryWar

BATTLEFIELD	STATE	NUMBER OF TRACTS	NUMBER OF ACRES
Lexington-Concord	MA	I	1.00
Princeton	NJ	2	5.00
Brandywine	PA	I	10.40
Hanging Rock	SC	I	122.17
Siege of Charleston	SC	I	88.33
Waxhaws	SC	I	50.84
TOTAL REVOLUTIONARY WAR:		**7**	**277.74**

APPENDIX TWO

Members of the Boards of Trustees

NOTES

★

CHAPTER ONE

1   Clark B. "Bud" Hall interview with author, January 16, 2011.
2   Ibid.
3   Clark B. Hall oral history interview, Civil War Trust oral history project, January 16, 2011, Civil War Trust archives, Washington, D.C., transcript pages 1-5.
4   Ibid.
5   Edward T. Wenzel interview with author, January 16, 2011.
6   Ibid.
7   Wenzel, Edward T., "Facts and Significance of Ox Hill (Chantilly) – September 1, 1862," self-published paper. Page 1.
8   Ibid., see section on Mexican War in Volume I.
9   Joseph W. A. Whitehorn, "A Beastly, Comfortless Conflict: The Battle of Chantilly," *Blue and Gray*, May, 1987; page 48.
10   Stephen W. Sears, "A One-Armed Jersey Son-of-a-Gun," *Civil War Monitor*, Vol., 4, No. 1, Spring 2014, page 37; "Civil War Stories: A 150th Anniversary Collection," *The Washington Post*, (New York: Diversion Books, 2013).
11   Stevens, *Life of Stevens*, page 485.
12   Samuel N. Benjamin, letter to Hazard Stevens, May 2, 1877, Hazard Stevens papers, Library of Congress, from photocopy in archives of Ed Wenzel.
13   William Todd, The Seventy-ninth Highlanders, New York Volunteers in the War of Rebellion, (Albany, N.Y., Press of Brandow, Barton & Co., 1886). Page 220.
14   Stevens, *Life of Stevens*, pages 485-486.
15   Joseph W.A. Whitehorn, "The Death of General Kearny," *Blue and Gray*, May, 1987; page 53.
16   Ibid.
17   "Boulders and Quartz Stone – The Spot Where General Stevens Fell," battlefield marker at Ox Hill Battlefield Park, Fairfax County, Virginia., Park Authority.
18   "Ox Hill Battlefield Park General Management Plan and Conceptual Development Plan, Fairfax County Park Authority, pages 11, 15; Fairfax County Deed Book X-7, page 571.
19   Invitation and brochure on the "Commemorative Program Marking the Centennial of the Battle of Ox Hill (Chantilly)" September 1, 1962; from Clark B. Hall archive. The battle had long been known in Fairfax County by its Confederate name and today's park is named Ox Hill Battlefield Park, although the Union name, Battle of Chantilly is frequently used.
20   L. VanLoan Naisawald, "A Nasty Little Battle in the Rain – Chantilly," *Civil War Times Illustrated*, June 1864, page 11.
21   Joseph W.A. Whitehorn, "The General's tour of The Chantilly Battlefield and Environs," *Blue and Gray*, May, 1987, page 60.
22   Edward T. Wenzel oral history interview, Civil War Trust oral history project, January 16, 2012, Civil War Trust archives, Washington, D.C.; transcript page 6.
23   Ibid.
24   Ibid; see also pages 9-11.
25   County of Fairfax, Virginia, Staff Report, February 5, 1985, concerning application RZ 84-P-101 of Centennial Development Cora, page 12, under section "Ox Hill Battlefield Park"; Ed Wenzel correspondence with author, August 5 and 12, 2016.
26   Fairfax County Board of Supervisors Chairman John F. Herrity letter to Cecil D. Andrus, Secretary of the Interior, November 15, 1979. Copies in the archives of Clark B. Hall and Ed Wenzel; Notes of Wenzel phone call to Edwin C. Bearss, National Park Service, August 26, 1986.
27   Ibid.
28   Wenzel oral history.

29   Ed Wenzel correspondence with author, August 12, 2016, from Wenzel's notes of Elizabeth David meeting, July 29, 1986.

30   Wenzel oral history; Wenzel's notes of Hanley meeting, August 5, 1986, from his archive.

31   Wenzel correspondence, August 12, 2016, from his notes of History Commission meeting, August 6, 1986.

32   Ed Wenzel correspondence, August 12, 2016, with information based on his notes of August 20, 1986 conversation with Robert Ross Smith.

33   Ibid.

34   Wenzel oral history, transcript page nine, with additional material based on follow-up conversations between the author and Wenzel and his notes of phone conversation with John Hennessy, August 20, 1986.

35   Ibid.

36   Patricia Sullivan, "Brian Pohanka Dies; Civil War Historian, Film Adviser," (obituary) *The Washington Post*, June 17, 2005. Accessed at: http://www.washingtonpost.com/wp-dyn/content/article/2005/06/16/AR2005061601571.

37   Ibid.

38   Hall oral history, pages 5-6.

39   Ibid., Robert Ross Smith, December 11, 1986, letter to Ed Wenzel detailed in Wenzel e-mail to author, July 29, 2016.

40   Undated letter from Robert Ross Smith to Bud Hall written in October 1986, Clark B. Hall archive.

41   Clark B. Hall, "My Notes," handwritten entry for September 21, 1986, Hall archive.

42   Clark B. Hall email to author, March 9, 2016.

43   Wenzel oral history, pages 10-12; Wenzel correspondence, August 12, 2016.

44   Ibid.

45   Barbara Carton, "New Developments in Battle of Chantilly," *The Washington Post*, October 6, 1986, page A-1.

46   Wenzel oral history, page 12.

47   Carton, "New Developments," page A-6.

48   Author's interview with Ron Blevins, April 13, 2013.

49   Ibid.

50   Ibid.

51   Ibid.

52   Carton, "New Developments"; Blevins interview.

53   Associated Press, "Confederate soldier's remains are unearthed," as published in *The State* newspaper, Columbia, S.C. October 8, 1986. The soldier has not been identified, but Blevins has narrowed down the possibilities to about a dozen South Carolina casualties.

54   John Collins, "Unknown soldier rests," *The State*, Columbia, S.C. November 23, 1986,   page D-1.

55   Ibid.

56   Blevins interview.

57   Wenzel correspondence, August 12, 2016.

58   Ed Wenzel correspondence from his notes of conversations with Bob Burgess, October 17-24, 1986.

59   Wenzel oral history, page 16.

60   Hall oral history, page 6; Wenzel correspondence, August 12, 2016.

61   Clark B. "Bud" Hall email to author and others describing the qualities of Brian Pohanka, December 10, 2012.

62   Wenzel interview, January 16, 2011.

63   Wenzel correspondence, August 12, 2016, from his original notes of the October 31, 1986, meeting based on Hall's follow-up letter to Herrity dated November 6, 1986. In the archives of both Hall and Wenzel.

64   Ibid.

65   Hall oral history, page 12.

66   Ibid, Wenzel oral history, page. 24.

67   Hall oral history, page 7.

68   Ibid.

69   Hall oral history. page 12.

70   Ibid.

71   Ibid.

72   Brian C. Pohanka letter to John F. Herrity, Chairman, Fairfax County Board of Supervisors, March 10, 1987, Hall archive. Herrity died in 2006 at age 75.

73   Hall email, March 9, 2016. Hall remained in touch with Anna Menge until her death in 2002.

74   Ibid.

75   Letter to the Editor from David L. Smith, President, Centennial Development Corpage, *The Fairfax Journal*, June 22, 1987.

76   Wenzel correspondence, August 12, 2016.

77   "Chantilly Remembered?" Un-bylined article in *The Firing Line*, The Newsletter of Civil War Travel and Historic Preservation, No. 35, October, 1987, Time Capsule Publications, Manassas, Va., Wenzel archive.

78   Ed Wenzel email to author, December 30, 2016.

79   Wenzel January 16 interview.

80   Hall oral history, page 9.

CHAPTER TWO

81   Joan M. Zenzen, Battling For Manassas: The Fifty-Year Preservation Struggle at Manassas Battlefield Park, Chapter Nine, "Negotiations with Hazel/Peterson," (University Park, Pennsylvania, The Penn State University Press, 1998). Accessed at https://www.nps.gov/parkhistory/online_books/mana/adhi9c.htm

82   Lee Hockstader, "Hazel Proposes Prince William Project," May 10, 1988. Accessed at https://www.washingtonpost.com/archive/local/1986/05/10/hazel-proposes-prince-william-project/8ff31580-1e44-4b45-bc73-23353ac9b12c/?utm_term=.8b5aadad1eb2

83   Donald C. Pfanz, "A Brief History of the Origins of The Association for the Preservation of Civil War Sites," June 2011, narrative submitted as part of Civil War Trust oral history interview and appended to interview, pages 8-9 (see note 94).

84   Robert K. Krick oral history interview, Civil War Trust oral history project, February 22, 2011, Civil War Trust archives, Washington, D.C., page 7.

85   Pfanz, History of the Origins of APCWS, pages 8-9.

86   Krick oral history, pages 7-8.

87   Donald C. Pfanz letter to Brian Pohanka, April 22, 1987. Copy in author's archives provided by Pfanz.

88   Brian Pohanka note to Bud Hall and Ed Wenzel, April 29, 1987. Ed Wenzel archive.

89   Donald C. Pfanz letter to Brian Pohanka, May 6, 1987. Wenzel archive.

90   "Jerry Russell Is Leader In Saving Battlefield Sites," *Civil War News*, November-December, 1987.

91   Ibid.

92   Pfanz to Pohanka, May 6, 1987.

93   Dennis Frye oral history interview, Civil War Trust oral history project, February 15, 2012, Civil War Trust archives, Washington, D.C., pages 11-12.

94   Donald C. Pfanz oral history interview, Civil War Trust oral history project, June 22, 2011, Civil War Trust archives, Washington, D.C., page 3.
95   Krick oral history, page 7.
96   Ibid.
97   Brian Pohanka, "Minutes of a Meeting to Establish a Civil War Battlefield Preservation Organization," July 18, 1987; also "Battlefield Preservation Dinner-Meeting" flyer and agenda, Wenzel archive; Robert K. Krick email to the author, July 29, 2016.
98   Ibid.
99   Pohanka, Minutes.
100   Pfanz oral history and narrative, page 4.
101   Brian Pohanka, "Minutes of a Meeting of the Steering Committee of the Association for the Preservation of Civil War Sites, September 6, 1987, Wenzel archive; additional facts from Wenzel email to author, September 13, 2016.
102   Robert K. Krick, "Goals for the July 18th (1987) Meeting," organizing meeting of APCWS. Dennis E. Frye Papers, APCWS Files, Western Maryland Room, Washington County Free Library, Hagerstown, Maryland.
103   Pfanz oral history and narrative, page 9.
104   Ibid.; Wenzel September 13 email.
105   Pohanka, September 6, 1987 minutes; Wenzel September 13 email.
106   Pohanka, September 6, 1987 minutes.
107   Gary W. Gallagher, speech on "The Birth of Modern Battlefield Preservation" at 2011 Civil War Trust Board of Trustees meeting, Chantilly, Va.; Accessed at http://www.civilwar.org/video/apcws-gallagher.html
108   Pohanka, September 6, 1987 minutes.
109   Text for APCWS brochure, November 1987, pages 2-3, Wenzel archive.
110   Pohanka, September 6, 1987 meeting.
111   Zenzen, Battling for Manassas, Chapter Nine, "Planned Mixed-Use Development, Accessed at https://www.nps.gov/parkhistory/online_books/mana/adhi9b.htm
112   Gary W. Gallagher oral history interview, Civil War Trust oral history project, February 20, 2012, Civil War Trust archives, Washington, D.C., page 6.
113   Krick oral history, page 9.
114   Gary W. Gallagher, undated letter to potential APCWS members. Wenzel archive.
115   Brian C. Pohanka, "Minutes of APCWS Meeting, January 16, 1988," Wenzel archive.
116   Ibid.
117   Ibid.
118   Ibid.
119   John P. Ackerly III oral history interview, Civil War Trust oral history project, March 11, 2012, Civil War Trust archives, Washington, D.C., pages 4-5.
120   Ibid.
121   Chris Calkins oral history interview, Civil War Trust oral history project, December 7, 2012, Civil War Trust archives, Washington, D.C., page 3.
122   Hall oral history, page 4.
123   Clark B. Hall follow-up conversation with the author, April 10, 2013.
124   Pohanka, January 16, 1988 minutes.
125   Hall April 10 follow-up conversation.
126   Cornelius F. Foote Jr and John F. Harris, "Huge Mall Planned at Manassas," *The Washington Post*, January 29, 1988.

CHAPTER THREE
127   Clint Schemmer, "It's War," and "Supervisors won't review mall plan," *Potomac News*, February 8, 1988.

128   Ibid.
129   Ibid.
130   Tersh Boasberg letter to Jody Powell, February 24, 1988, Clark B. Hall archive.
131   Francis F. Wilshin oral history interview conducted by S. Herbert Evison, June 29, 1971, National Park Service Oral History Project, NPS History Collection, Harpers Ferry Center, Harpers Ferry, W.Va. Page 12.
132   Wilshin oral history, pages 1-5
133   Ibid.
134   Wilshin oral history, page 12.
135   Ibid.
136   Wilshin oral history, pages 27-28.
137   Edwin C. Bearss oral history interview, conducted in 1992 by NPS historian Barry Mackintosh, from transcript shared with author by Mr. Bearss, pages 22-23.
138   Anne B. Snyder oral history interview conducted by Joan M. Zenzen, October 19, 1993, Manassas National Battlefield Park History Project, Manassas NBP, Manassas, Va. Page 7.
139   Snyder oral history, page 4.
140   Snyder oral history, page 1; Elbert Watson, "Annie got her musket," *World War II Times*, November 1989, page 6.
141   Snyder oral history, page 2.
142   Ibid.
143   James Burgess, "Investigation of Military Activity on Pageland Farm, 1861-1865," Manassas National Battlefield Park historical files, pages 2-4.
144   Anne B. Snyder letter to Pierre Thomas, *The Washington Post*, May 8, 1989, Anne B. Snyder files, Manassas National Battlefield Park, pages 1-2.
145   Ibid.
146   Ibid, page 3.
147   Zenzen, Battling For Manassas, Chapter Five, "Threatening the 'Very Heart' of the Park." Accessed at http://www.cr.nps.gov/history/online_books/mana/adhi5c.htm
148   Wilshin oral history, page 56.
149   Zenzen, Chapter Five. Accessed at: http://www.cr.nps.gov/history/online_books/mana/adhi5c.htm
150   Wilshin oral history, page 57.
151   Ibid.
152   Ibid.
153   Snyder oral history, pages 8-9.
154   Zenzen, Chapter Five. Accessed at http://www.cr.nps.gov/history/online_books/mana/adhi5c.htm
155   Wilshin oral history, pages 58-59.
156   Zenzen, Chapter Six, "Burial Ground for the Nation's Veterans." Accessed at http://www.cr.nps.gov/history/online_books/mana/adhi6b.htm
157   Ibid.
158   Ibid.
159   Ibid.
160   Wilshin oral history, pages 73-74.
161   Ibid.
162   Kenneth Bredemeier, "New Battle of Bull Run Threatens," *The Washington Post*, Panorama section, page 1.
163   Snyder interview, page 18.
164   Zenzen, Chapter Six, "Burial Ground."
165   Ibid.
166   Ibid; Author's interview with Ed Bearss, January 9, 2017.

167   Bearss January 9 interview.
168   "The Third Battle of Bull Run," *Open Space Action* magazine, September-October, 1969.
169   Snyder oral history, page 20.
170   Ibid.
171   Snyder oral history, page 14.
172   Snyder oral history, pages 19, 24, 27, 28, 30.
173   Ron Shaffer, "Amusement Park Site Set At Manassas," *The Washington Post*, February 15, 1973. page A-1.
174   William E. Welsh, "Following Soldiers into Battle," *The Washington Post*, May 4, 2001. Accessed at https://www.washingtonpost.com/archive/lifestyle/2001/05/04/following-soldiers-into-battle/415b2b2e-09e1-4ce5-83ec-0cbe5e0d459c/
175   Zenzen, Chapter Seven, "Great America in Manassas."
176   Ibid.
177   Ibid.
178   Ibid.
179   "Gainesville Curious," *Potomac News*, February 21, 1973, page A-2.
180   Snyder interview, page 37.
181   Zenzen, Chapter Seven.
182   Kathi Delay, "Park Questions Go Unanswered; Spokesman Fails to Show . . . " *Manassas Journal-Messenger*, February 26, 1973.
183   Ibid.
184   Herald Grandstaff, "Congressmen visit Battlefield Park," *Potomac News*, March 30, 1973.
185   Zenzen, Chapter Seven.
186   Ron Shaffer, "State Calls Marriott Park a Peril To All N. Virginia Development," *The Washington Post*, March 16, 1973, page A1.
187   Zenzen, Chapter Seven.
188   Ibid.
189   Ibid.
190   Ibid.
191   Lee Flor, "The Lady Fells a Giant," *Washington Star-News*, April 16, 1974.
192   Unbylined article, "Out-of-state letters protest Marriott park," *Potomac News*, January 30, 1974.
193   Ken Ringle, "Va. Park Wins Tie to I-66," *The Washington Post*, November 20, 1974, page C1.
194   Ibid.
195   Zenzen, Chapter Seven.
196   Ibid.
197   Jim Roberts, "Prince William Out as Park Site," *Richmond Times-Dispatch*, December 8, 1977, and William H. Jones, "Marriott Drops Its Plans for Va. Amusement Park," *The Washington Post*, March 2, 1978.
198   Zenzen, Chapter Eight.

CHAPTER FOUR
199   John T. Hazel, Jr., interview with author, February 7, 2017.
200   Zenzen, Battling For Manassas, Chapter Nine, "Seeking Partnerships," subchapter "Negotiations with Hazel/Peterson. Accessed at: http://www.cr.nps.gov/history/online_books/mana/adhi9c.htm
201   Ibid.
202   Joel Garreau, "Til Hazel, King of the New Frontier," *The Washington Post* Magazine, July 21, 1991, p 26. Accessed at https://www.washingtonpost.com/archive/lifestyle/

magazine/1991/07/21/til-hazel-king-of-the-new-frontier/6fe69465-631a-444f-a307-b6e19315d90d/?utm_term=.9e44f03eef67

203 Zenzen, Chapter Nine.

204 Hazel February 7 interview.

205 Zenzen, Chapter Nine.

206 Til Hazel February 7 interview; Til Hazel email to author, February 13, 2017

207 Hannah Hager (reporter) and Peter Arundel (producer), "The Virginians: John T. Hazel, Developer," *Loudoun Times-Mirror*, ARCOM Publishing, Inc., accessed on YouTube. https://www.youtube.com/watch?v=jUxwLUGMUlw

208 Hazel February 7 interview.

209 Ibid.

210 Garreau, "King of the New Frontier."

211 Ibid.

212 Ibid.

213 Snyder interview, page 45.

214 Edwin C. Bearss letter to Jerry Russell, December 31, 1986, NPS William Center file, Manassas National Battlefield Park.

215 Zenzen, Chapter Nine.

216 Christine Reid, "Sabers rattling in Manassas' 'Battle of the Mall,' *Richmond Times-Dispatch*, February 28, 1988.

217 Edward T. Hearn, "Reaction Mixed to New Mall," *Suburban Virginia Times*, Manassas, February 3, 1988.

218 Cornelius F. Foote Jr. and John F. Harris, "Huge Mall Planned at Manassas," *The Washington Post*, January 29, 1988, page A1

219 Zenzen, Chapter Nine.

220 Joel Garreau, "The Last Thing He Expected Was a Fight," *The Washington Post Magazine*, July 28, 1991, page 24.

221 Hazel February 7 interview.

222 Foote and Harris, "Huge Mall Planned . . ."

223 Jonathan Yardley, "The Shopping Mall & the Hallowed Ground," *The Washington Post*, February 1, 1988.

224 Edward T. Wenzel, Outline of Manassas/SBC events, document written for author.

225 Ibid.

226 Edward T. Wenzel interview with author, March 27, 2013.

227 Tersh Boasberg oral history interview, June 14, 2012, Civil War Trust oral history project, Civil War Trust archives, Washington, D.C., transcript page 8.

228 Clint Schemmer, "It's War," *Potomac News*, February 8, 1988. page A-7.

229 John Hennessy oral history interview, Civil War Trust oral history project, January 30, 2011, Civil War Trust archives, Washington, D.C., transcript pages 4- 5.

230 John F. Harris, "Manassas Mall Plan Pits Future Versus Past," *The Washington Post*, Metro, B1.

231 Edward T. Wenzel email to author, September 1, 2016; Hennessy oral history, page 5.

232 Boasberg oral history interview, pages 6-7.

233 Wenzel oral history, transcript page 30.

234 Boasberg oral history interview, page 7.

235 Boasberg oral history interview, page 8.

236 Kevin Maier, "Manassas: Once again a battlefield," *The Washington Times*, March 28, 1988.

237 Zenzen, Chapter 10.

238 Edward T. Hearn, "U.S. Should Take William Tract, Congressman Says," The *Journal Messenger*, Manassas, Va., February 25, 1988.

239 Hazel February 7 interview.

240   James A. Schaefer, Ph.D., letter to Save the Battlefield Coalition, March 1, 1988. From Anne D. Snyder excess files, Manassas National Battlefield Park.

241   Edward T. Wenzel email to author, February 8, 2017.

242   Benjamin Boley, Shea & Gardner, to Donald P. Hodel, Secretary of the Department of the Interior, March 3, 1988; and Benjamin Boley, Shea & Gardner, to Richard E. Lawson, Director, Department of Development Administration, Prince William County, Va., March 4, 1988; from Anne. D. Snyder excess files, Manassas National Battlefield Park.

243   Clint Schemmer, "Secretary of the Interior backs opposition to the mall," *Potomac News*, March 24, 1988.

244   Clint Schemmer, "Poll results a boost for mall opposition," *Potomac News*, April 13, 1988

245   Brad Coker oral history interview, Civil War Trust oral history project, Civil War Trust archives, Washington, D.C., transcript page 7-8.

246   Zenzen, Chapter 10.

247   Robert Mrazek oral history interview, Civil War Trust oral history project, May 21, 2012, Civil War Trust oral history project, Civil War Trust archives, Washington, D.C., transcript page 3.

248   Kevin Maier, "Developer vows to build mall no matter what," *The Washington Times*, May 5, 1988.

249   Ibid.

250   Mrazek oral history interview, transcript pages 5-6.

251   Maier, "Developer vows to build . . . "

252   Hazel interview, February 7.

253   Anne D. Snyder letter to Robert S. Noe Jr., County Executive, Prince William County, Virginia, May 10, 1988. From Anne D. Snyder excess files, Manassas National Battlefield Park, copy at Civil War Trust.

254   Robert S. Noe, Jr. County Executive, Prince William County, Va., letter to Anne D. Snyder, May 13, 1988. From Anne D. Snyder excess files, Manassas National Battlefield Park, copy at Civil War Trust.

255   Patrick Brennan, "Annie and Moses," memoir on William Center fight provided to author, October 24, 2016.

256   Ibid.

257   Ibid.

258   Ibid.

259   Ibid; Charlton Heston letter to Patrick Brennan, May 18, 1988, copy supplied to author.

260   Brennan, "Annie and Moses."

261   John F. Harris, "Wolf Joins Fray With Bill to Block William Center," *The Washington Post*, May 26, 1988.

262   Alan Fogg, "Mall developer counterattacks," *The Fairfax Journal*, June 17, 1988.

263   Mrazek oral history, transcript pages 3-4.

264   Anne D. Snyder, statement to House Subcommittee on Parks and Public Lands on H.R. 4526, from Anne D. Snyder excess files, Manassas National Battlefield Park, copy at Civil War Trust.

265   Garreau, "The Last Thing He Expected . . ." page 25.

266   "Mall Plans Dealt Another Blow," *The Washington Post*, July 13, 1988.

267   John F. Harris, "Manassas Purchase Backed by Warner; Preservation of Stuart's Hill Proposed," *The Washington Post*, July 17, 1988.

268   Hazel February 7 interview.

269   Hazel February 13 email.

270   Irma Peterson, "Day by day account of construction activity at William Center, as

noted by neighbors and recorded by Irma Peterson, June 23 thru December 2, 1988," pages 1-3. Anne D. Snyder papers, Manassas National Battlefield Park.

271   Kevin Maier, "Rapid march of construction alarms foes of Manassas mall," *The Washington Times*, August 2, 1988.

272   Hennessy oral history, page 24.

273   John F. Harris, "Battlefield Preservationists Win in House," *The Washington Post*, August 11, 1988.

274   Zenzen, Chapter 10.

275   Georgie Boge and Margie Holder Boge, *Paving Over the Past: A History and Guide to Civil War Battlefield Preservation*, (Washington, D.C., Island Press, 1993). page 5.

276   Mrazek oral history, transcript page 6.

277   Zenzen, Chapter 10, "Legislative Taking," Accessed at https://www.nps.gov/parkhistory/online_books/mana/adhi10e.htm; John F. Harris, "Manassas Preservationists Win a Last-Minute Hill Victory," *The Washington Post*, October 23, 1988.

278   Harris, "Manassas Preservationists Win . . ."

279   Peterson, "Day by day account of construction activity . . ." page 10.

280   Ibid.

281   Boasberg oral history, transcript page 9.

282   Zenzen, Chapter 10, "Was It Worth It?" Accessed at https://www.nps.gov/parkhistory/online_books/mana/adhi10f.htm

283   Civil War Trust Master Land Record, Civil War Trust archives, Washington, D.C.

284   Brennan, "Annie and Moses."

CHAPTER FIVE

285   Clark B. Hall oral history, transcript page 4.

286   Hall oral history, page 1.

287   Hall oral history, page 3.

288   Ibid.

289   Clark B. Hall interview with author, August 30, 2016.

290   A photograph and detailed information about the marker appear at www.markerhistory.com, specifically at http://www.markerhistory.com/opening-of-gettyburg-campaign-marker-f-13/

291   Hall oral history, page 4.

292   Clark B. Hall interview with author, February 5, 2015.

293   Ibid.

294   Ibid.

295   Hall Aug 30 interview.

296   A photograph and detailed information about the Fleetwood Hill markers appears at www.stonesentinels.com, specifically at http://www.stonesentinels.com/Brandy_Station/Battle_of_Brandy_Station-UDC.php. The date at the website is incorrect, as per "Civil War Battlefield Markers Unveiled," The Culpeper Exponent, August 12, 1926; from archives of Clark B. Hall.

297   Hall oral history, page 4.

298   Hall oral history, page 17.

299   Clark B. Hall, "The Battle of Brandy Station," from transcript of magazine article, page 16, Clark B. Hall archive.

300   Clark B. Hall interview with the author, April 10, 2013.

301   Ibid.

302   Ibid.

303   Clark B. Hall, Brandy Station Timeline, entry for February 11, 1988.

304   Clark B. Hall follow-up email to author, September 3, 2016.

305   Brian Pohanka, Minutes of the APCWS Board Meeting of May 15, 1988. Ed Wenzel archive.
306   Hall oral history, transcript page 14.
307   Ibid.
308   Clark B. Hall letter to Robert K. Krick, June 2, 1988, Hall archive.
309   Clark B. Hall, letter to the editor, *Culpeper Star-Exponent*, June 8, 1988. (Note: the same letter appeared in the *Culpeper News* on June 9, 1988).
310   Kathleen Hoffman, "Protection Group Eyes Brandy battlefield," *Culpeper News*, July 14, 1988.
311   "Willis Farm Sold to Out of State Company," *Culpeper News*, July 21, 1988.
312   E. L. Richardson, "Reflections on Lee Sammis Associates, Inc.", *Metropolitan Washington Business Properties* magazine. Page 8, 11.
313   Caroline Kane Kenna, "County Eyes Historic District Overlay Plan," *Culpeper News*, July 21, 1988.
314   Clark B. Hall email to author, November, 14, 2013.
315   Kenna, "County eyes," July 21, 1988.
316   "Californian Buys Spillman Land," *Culpeper News*, September 15, 1988.
317   Don Stockton, "Brandy Station Diary," entry for October 29, 1988. Hall archive.
318   Daryl Lease, "Some say trouble may be on horizon at Brandy Station," *The Free-Lance Star*, Fredericksburg, Virginia, November 12 1988.
319   Hall oral history, page 15; Christine Neuberger, "Brandy Station, Swords crossed again on battlefield," *Richmond* (Virginia) *Times-Dispatch*, November 13, 1988.
320   Ibid.
321   Neuberger, "Brandy Station, Swords crossed . . ."
322   "More Riverfront Land Sold to Californian," *Culpeper News*, November 10, 1988.
323   Hall, Timeline, page 2.
324   Clark B. Hall letter to Tersh Boasberg, January 3, 1989, Hall archive.
325   Boasberg oral history, transcript page 14.
326   Judith Bowman, "Sammis' plans revealed," *Culpeper Star-Exponent*, January 31, 1989.
327   Ibid.
328   Ibid.
329   Caroline Kane Kenna, "Sammis Unveils 5,000-Acre Elkwood Plans," *Culpeper News*, February 2, 1989.
330   Hall, Timeline, pages 3-4.
331   Paul Sullivan, "Battlefield eyed for designation as historic site," Fredericksburg *Free Lance-Star*, July 29, 1989.
332   Ana Valle, "Board rejects historic district study," *Culpeper Star-Exponent*, September 6, 1989; phone interview with Clark B. Hall, January 4, 2017.
333   Bryan Mitchell email to author, January 10, 2017.
334   Ibid.
335   Daryl Lease, "Battle over Brandy Station project drags on," Fredericksburg *Free Lance-Star*, September 20, 1989.
336   Christine Neuberger, "Complex proposed on battlefield," *Richmond Times-Dispatch*, October 6, 1989.
337   Mitchell January 10 email.
338   Ana Valle, "Supervisors plan 'business as usual,'" *Culpeper Star-Exponent*, November 10, 1989.
339   Ana Valle, "Sammis rezoning hearing continued,", November 10, 1989; "Extra time granted to study Sammis plan," January 12, 1990; "Supervisors want Sammis proposal," March 16, 1990, all from *Culpeper Star-Exponent*.
340   Ana Valle, "Sammis scenario," *Culpeper Star-Exponent*, April 14, 1990.
341   Ana Valle, "Planners reject Sammis plan," *Culpeper Star-Exponent*, May 11, 1990.

342 Brooke A. Masters and Alice Digilio, "Preservationists, Developers Battle Over Civil War Sites," *The Washington Post*, June 10, 1990.

343 Ibid.

344 Tersh Boasberg, "War and Remembrance: How to Save Our Civil War Sites," *The Washington Post*, Outlook section, April 8, 1990.

345 Edwin C. Bearss Civil War Trust oral history, transcript pages 1-2; Bearss 1992 NPS oral history, transcript pages 1-2.

346 Bearss Civil War Trust oral history, pages 8-10.

347 Ibid; Bearss 1992 NPS oral history, page 7.

348 Edwin C. Bearss interview with author, August 8, 2016.

349 Ibid.

350 Bearss August 8 interview.

351 Bearss 1992 oral history, page 13.

352 Bearss August 8 interview.

353 Brooke A. Masters, "U.S. Forms Plan to Save Battlefields," *The Washington Post*, July 20, 1990.

354 Kathleen Hoffman, "Cabinet Member Tours Brandy," *Culpeper News*, July 26, 1990.

355 Christine Neuberger, "Six Virginia battle sites on U.S. list," *Richmond Times-Dispatch*, July 21, 1990

356 Susan Montgomery, "Chamber supports Sammis rezoning," *Culpeper Star-Exponent*, August 22, 1990.

357 Editorial, "Approve Sammis' rezoning," *Culpeper Star-Exponent*, August 25, 1990.

358 Hall, Timeline.

359 Michael Zitz, "Culpeper: Past vs. the future," Fredericksburg *Free-Lance Star*, September 20, 1990.

360 Ibid.

361 Ibid.

362 Brooke A. Masters, "Battlefield Development Approved," *The Washington Post*, September 26, 1990.

363 Ana Valle, "Sammis rezoning approved," *Culpeper Star-Exponent*, Sept 25, 1990.

364 Ibid.

365 Christine Neuberger, "Suit targets Culpeper battlefield plan," *Richmond Times-Dispatch*, October 23, 1990.

366 A. Wilson Greene letter to Tersh Boasberg, October 16, 1990. Hall archive.

367 Ibid.

368 Vincent Vala, "Lawyers fire first shots in Brandy battle," *Culpeper Star-Exponent*, March 7, 1991.

369 "Civil War Sites Advisory Commission Report on the Nation's Civil War Battlefields," 1993 (updated 1997), Accessed at the National Park Service website: https://www.nps.gov/abpp/battles/tvii.htm

370 Daryl Lease, "Battle of Brandy Station continues," Fredericksburg *Free Lance-Star*, February 27, 1991.

371 Secretary of the Interior Manuel Lujan, Jr., letter to Jack E. Fincham, Chairman, Culpeper County Board of Supervisors, October 18, 1990. Hall archive.

372 Clark B. Hall interview, November 11, 2013.

373 Ibid.

374 Brooke A. Masters, "Battle Rejoined at Civil War Site in Virginia," *The Washington Post*, July 12, 1991.

CHAPTER SIX

375 Robert K. Krick, "Preliminary notes from diary on politicians and preservation," Robert K. Krick archive, page 1.

376   Krick, oral history, transcript page 3.
377   Mrazek oral history, transcript pages 4-5.
378   Krick oral history, page 7.
379   Krick oral history, page 18.
380   Mrazek oral history, pages 4-5.
381   Krick oral history, page 4.
382   Mrazek oral history, pages 7-8.
383   Krick oral history, page 5.
384   Ibid.
385   Robert K. Krick, "Krick thoughts on scope of H.R. 875 boundary," email to author, October 28, 2013.
386   Krick, "Preliminary notes . . ." page 1.
387   Ibid.
388   Krick oral history, page 4.
389   Krick, "Preliminary notes," page 2.
390   Robert K. Krick interview with the author, October 24, 2013.
391   Ibid.
392   Krick, "Preliminary notes . . ." page 6
393   Krick oral history, page 5.
394   Krick oral history, page 7.
395   Krick oral history, page 2.
396   Krick email, October 28.
397   Ibid.
398   Minutes of the APCWS Board Meeting, May 15, 1988, Ed Wenzel archive.
399   A. Wilson Greene oral history interview, Civil War Trust oral history project, June 21, 2011, Civil War Trust archives, Washington, D.C., transcript page 5.
400   APCWS May 15 minutes.
401   "Gilder Challenge Nets $117,000," *Hallowed Ground*, Vol. 2, No. 1, March 1989.
402   See photograph in APCWS scrapbook held by Civil War Trust, page 5.
403   Minutes of the APCWS Board of Directors meeting, November 13, 1988, page 1.
404   Minutes of the APCWS Board of Directors meeting, March 18, 1989, with attached "Goals and Objectives."
405   A. Wilson Greene e-mail to author, November 26, 2013.
406   "APCWS Acquires Land at Harris Farm Battle Site," *Hallowed Ground*, Vol. 2, No. 2, June 1989.
407   "Gilder Challenge Success Nets Big Bonus," *Hallowed Ground*, Vol. 3, No. 2, June 1990.
408   Facts gleaned from APCWS board minutes from its 1990 meetings, Robert K. Krick archive.
409   "APCWS Buys Bentonville, Hatcher's Run Battlefields," *Hallowed Ground*, Vol. 3, No. 3, September 1990; "APCWS Acquires McDowell Battlefield," *Hallowed Ground*, Vol. 3, No. 4, December 1990.
410   Ibid.
411   Michael J. Ybarra and Brooke A. Masters, "100,000-acre Gift Includes Key Battlefields," *The Washington Post*, July 2, 1990.
412   Williams most likely joined the APCWS board at its July 7, 1990 board meeting, but the meeting minutes were shown as missing in the early 1990s. He was first listed as a board member in the board meeting minutes of September 15. McPherson's appointment is shown in the board meeting minutes of May 3, 1991; Krick archive.
413   Minutes of the APCWS Board of Directors, November 17, 1990.
414   Facts gleaned from APCWS board minutes of 1991 meetings and other APCWS materials, Civil War Trust archive, Washington, DC.
415   Minutes of the APCWS Board of Directors meeting, July 20, 1991. Krick archive.

416   Civil War Trust Master Land Record, Civil War Trust archive, Washington, D.C.

417   Vincent Vala, "Landowners garner political support," *Culpeper Star-Exponent*, August 21. 1991.

418   Alice Menks, "Brandy Station: The Battle Wages On," letter to the editor, *The Washington Post*, October 20, 1992.

419   Ibid.

420   B.B. Mitchell III, "No Surrender at Brandy Station," *The Washington Post*, letters to the editor, October 4, 1992.

421   John F. Harris, "Pulling Up Stakes on Historical Claims," *The Washington Post*, February 9, 1992.

422   John F. Harris, "Wilder Signs Measure to Block Unwanted Historic Designation," *The Washington Post*, April 7, 1992.

423   Clark B. Hall email to author, September 3, 2016.

424   Clark B. Hall follow-up interview with the author, November 11, 2013; Hall email of September 3.

425   Ibid.

426   Ed Bearss interview, August 8, 2016; Tersh Boasberg interview, August 16, 2016.

427   Hall November 11 interview.

428   Sam Frazier memo to Lee Sammis regarding "Your visit next week," June 29, 1990, Clark B. Hall archive.

429   Lee Sammis memo to file, September 4, 1990, page 6, Hall archive.

430   "History of National Park Service Involvement," from 1991 Elkwood Downs document, Hall archive.

431   Michael Armm interview with author, February 9, 2017.

432   Hall September 3 email.

433   Ibid.

434   Bearss August 8 interview.

435   Ibid.

436   Boasberg August 16 interview.

437   Unbylined, "Preservationists beaten in effort to save battle site," Manassas, Virginia, *Journal-Messenger*, July 18, 1992.

438   Hall interview, November 11, 2013.

439   Hall oral history, transcript page 16.

440   Bill Miller, "Battlefield Designation Withdrawn," *The Washington Post*,   September 16, 1992.

CHAPTER SEVEN

441   Civil War Sites Advisory Commission Report on the Nation's Civil War Battlefields, Technical Volume One, Appendices, pages 2-7.

442   Ibid.

443   See http://www.ellisisland.org/EIinfo/about.asp

444   Ashlea Ebeling, "Battle Cry," *Forbes*, October 5, 1998. Accessed at http://www.forbes.com/forbes/1998/1005/6207078a.html

445   Carleton R. Bryant, "Civil War sites will be preserved," *The Washington Times*, May 14, 1991.

446   "Battlefield Fund Started," *The Washington Post*, May 14, 1991.

447   Frye oral history, transcript pages 14-15.

448   Chris Fordney, "Inside the Civil War Trust," *Civil War* magazine, March-April 1993, page 42.

449   Grae Baxter resume, Clark B. Hall archive.

450   The Civil War Battlefield Foundation Strategic Plan, March 24, 1992, pages 3, 8, Hall archive; Civil War Trust Board of Directors meeting minutes, June 26, 1992; Civil War Trust archives, Washington, D.C.

451   Lester "Ruff" Fant III oral history interview, Civil War Trust oral history project, August 30, 2012, Civil War Trust archives, Washington, D.C., page 4.

452   Christine Neuberger, "Battlefield action laid to trade-off," *Richmond Times-Dispatch*, September 16, 1992.

453   Edwin C. Bearss oral history interview conducted in 1992 by NPS historian Barry Mackintosh, from transcript shared by Mr. Bearss, page 81.

454   Ibid.

455   Brandy Station Foundation Bulletin, Autumn 1992, page 1.

456   Lorraine Woellert, "Uncivil Dispute - Battlefield fight rages on," *The Washington Times*, September 16, 1992.

457   Miller, "Battlefield Designation Withdrawn."

458   Clark B. Hall interview, November 11, 2013.

459   Ibid.

460   Ibid.

461   Tersh Boasberg, Memorandum Re: Meeting with Lee Sammis, September 23, 1992, pages 1-2. Hall archive.

462   Boasberg Memorandum, page 3.

463   Boasberg Memorandum, page 4.

464   J. Roderick Heller III letter to Jerry Russell, October 28, 1993, Hall archive.

465   Deborah Fitts, "Trust Acts at Harpers Ferry," and "Plans Hatching for Kentucky Battlefield," both in *Civil War Landscape*, the Quarterly Newsletter of the Civil War Trust, Vol. I, No. 2, Summer 1993.

466   Boasberg Memorandum, page 5.

467   "Some Sammis Property Advertised for Auction," *Culpeper News*, December 17, 1992.

468   Troy Elliott, "Elkwood Downs Bankruptcy Action Blamed on Lawsuit," *Culpeper News*, June 10, 1993.

469   Vincent Vala, "Seeking a Solution: How to recognize the battlefield," *Culpeper Star Exponent*, June 14, 1993.

470   Vincent Vala, "Elkwood Downs Files for Chapter 11 Protection," *Culpeper Star Exponent*, June 7, 1993.

471   Ibid.

472   Ibid.

473   Michael Armm interview with author, February 9, 2017.

474   Press Release, "Brandy Station Civil War Battlefield on Endangered Places List," National Trust for Historic Preservation, June 23, 1993. Hall archive.

475   Associated Press unbylined story, "Brandy Station Battlefield loses historic designation," Manassas, Virginia, *Journal-Messenger*, June 24, 1993.

476   Carol Innerst, "Civil War buffs seek funds to save battlefields," *The Washington Times*, July 13, 1993.

477   Ibid.

478   Ibid.

479   James Rowley, "A $93 million call to save battlefields," Associated Press story in *Fairfax Journal*, July 13, 1993.

480   Grae Baxter, "Brokering a Peace in the Battle Over Civil War Sites," *The Washington Post* editorial pages, July 18, 1993.

481   Tersh Boasberg letter to Grae Baxter, August 6, 1993. Hall archive.

482   Ibid.

483   Hall oral history, page 17.

484   Benton Ventures, Inc., press release, September 8, 1993, "World-Class Motorsports Complex." Hall archive.
485   Ibid.
486   Jerry Russell, Civil War Round Table Associates membership memo, September 1993, page 1. Hall archive.
487   Ted Byrd, "Racetrack plans move ahead at battlefield," Fredericksburg, Va., *Free-Lance Star*, September 9, 1993.
488   Civil War Trust, "Statement of Principles," undated document, about September 27, 1993, Hall archive.
489   Dale G. Morton, "Trust: Raceway not desirable for battlefield," *Culpeper Star-Exponent*, September 30, 1993.
490   Civil War Trust "Statement of Principles."
491   Hall interview, November 11, 2013.
492   Ibid.
493   Grae Baxter oral history interview, Civil War Trust oral history project, October 10, 2013, Civil War Trust archive, Washington, D.C.
494   J. Roderick Heller III oral history interview, Civil War Trust oral history project, October 10, 2013, Civil War Trust archive, Washington, D.C.
495   Annie Snyder letter to James R. Lazor, September 10, 1993, Hall archive.
496   Brian C. Pohanka letter to J. Roderick Heller III, September 30, 1993, Hall archive.
497   Jerry L. Russell letter to J. Roderick Heller III, December 6, 1993, Hall archive.
498   Howard A. Hillman letter to Jerry L. Russell, October 27, 1993, Hall archive.
499   Jerry L. Russell letter to Howard A. Hillman, December 10, 1993, Hall archive.
500   Tersh Boasberg letter to Rod Heller and Grae Baxter, January 10, 1994, Hall archive.
501   Grae Baxter letter to Jack E. Fincham, January 21, 1994, Hall archive.
502   Christine Neuberger, "Racing complex still faces many laps," *Richmond Times-Dispatch*, February 15, 1994.

CHAPTER EIGHT

503   Annie Snyder letter to Jerry Russell, January 19, 1994 (misdated 1993), Clark B. Hall archive.
504   Ibid.
505   Ibid.
506   Ibid.
507   Ibid.
508   Ibid.
509   Ibid.
510   William F. Powers and Marianne Kyriakos, "Disney Considering Prince William Site," *The Washington Post*, November 9, 1993; Kirstin Downey Grimsley and Kent Jenkins Jr., "Disney Theme Park Coming Here," *The Washington Post*, November 10, 1993.
511   Maria E. Odum and Spencer S. Hsu, "Disney Excites County," *The Washington Post*, November 10, 1993.
512   Powers and Kyriakos, "Disney Considering . . ."
513   Odum and Hsu, "Disney Excites . . ."
514   The Walt Disney Company, "Executive Summary of Rezoning Application For Disney's America," January 1994. Civil War Trust archive, Washington, D.C.
515   Ibid.
516   Michael Eisner, Work in Progress: Risking Failure, Surviving Success, (New York: Hyperion, 1998), page 319.
517   Eisner, page 324.
518   Steven C. Fehr, "In Disney's Grand Plan, Some See a Smoggy, Cloggy Transportation Mess," *The Washington Post*, November 12, 1993.

519   David S. Hilzenrath, "Disney's Land of Make-Believe," *The Washington Post*, November 12, 1993.
520   Eisner, page 322.
521   Larry Van Dyne, "Hit the Road, Mick," *The Washingtonian*, January, 1995, page 59-60.
522   Richard Moe, "Downside to 'Disney's America,'" *The Washington Post*, op-ed page, December 21, 1993.
523   Van Dyne, page 119.
524   Ibid.
525   Michael Siegel oral history interview, Civil War Trust oral history project, February 13, 2013, Civil War Trust archives, Washington, D.C., transcript page 5.
526   Siegel oral history, page 9.
527   Ibid.
528   Deborah Fitts, "The Disney Park Looms," *Civil War*, June 1994, page 19.
529   Minutes of the APCWS Board of Directors meeting, July 20, 1991, page 2, Robert K. Krick archive.
530   Ibid.
531   Minutes of the APCWS Board of Directors meeting, March 21, 1992, page 2, Krick archive.
532   Frye oral history, transcript page 17.
533   Greene oral history, June 21, 2011, transcript page 16.
534   Greene oral history, transcript page 11.
535   Minutes of the APCWS Board of Directors meeting, February 5, 1994, "Disney's America," page 3.
536   Greene oral history, transcript page 12.
537   APCWS Minutes, February 5, 1994, page 3.
538   Greene oral history, transcript page 17.
539   Fitts, "Disney Park Looms," page 18.
540   Ibid.
541   Ibid.
542   Tom Broadfoot letter to A. Wilson Greene, President, APCWS, March 18, 1994. Dennis E. Frye Papers, APCWS Files, Western Maryland Room, Washington County Free Library, Hagerstown, Maryland.
543   Fitts, "Disney Park Looms," page 16.
544   Ibid.
545   Gallagher oral history, transcript page 14.
546   Fitts, "Disney Park Looms," page 18.
547   Steve Miller (Disney) letter to Dennis Frye, March 25, 1994, including itinerary for APCWS visit. Frye Papers.
548   Frye oral history, transcript page 20.
549   Van Dyne, page 120.
550   Siegel interview, page 12.
551   Rebecca Bailey, "Leading Historians Organize Against Disney's America," *Civil War News*, June 1994.
552   Van Dyne, pages 121-122.
553   Minutes of the APCWS Board of Directors, meetings of November 6, 1993 and May 6, 1994. Krick archive.
554   Howard Coffin interview with author, February 20, 2013.
555   Minutes of the APCWS Board of Directors meeting, May 6, 1994, "Disney," page 1. Krick archive.
556   Greene oral history, page 18.
557   Ibid.
558   Minutes of Civil War Trust Board of Directors meeting, July 8, 1994, Civil War Trust archives, Washington, D.C.

559   William F. Powers, "Eisner Says Disney Won't Back Down," *The Washington Post*, June 14, 1994.
560   Van Dyne, page 122.
561   Eisner, page 308.
562   Eisner, pages 336-337.
563   Chris Miller oral history interview, Civil War Trust oral history project, July 24, 2012, Civil War Trust archives, Washington, D.C., transcript page 21.
564   Miller oral history, page 11.
565   Frye oral history, page 21; Ed Bearss interview with author, August 8, 2016.
566   Gallagher oral history, pages 12-13.
567   Gary W. Gallagher letter to A. Wilson Greene, May 10, 1994. Frye Papers.
568   Ibid.
569   Gallagher oral history, pages 12-13.
570   Frye oral history, page 21.
571   Minutes of the APCWS Board of Directors, meeting of August 20, 1994, page 3.
572   John P. "Jack" Ackerly III oral history interview, Civil War Trust oral history project, March 11, 2012, Civil War Trust archives, Washington, D.C., transcript page 6.
573   Minutes of the APCWS Board of Directors, meetings of February 5 and November 12, 1994. Krick archive.
574   John P. "Jack" Ackerly III letter to Carrington William, December 1, 1994. Frye Papers.
575   A. Wilson Greene resignation letter to Thomas W. Richards, December 5, 1994; Minutes of the APCWS Board of Directors, special meeting of December 10, 1994. Frye Papers.
576   Greene oral history, page 20.
577   APCWS Chairman Thomas W. Richards letter to Kathryn Jorgensen, managing editor of *The Civil War News*, January 20, 1995; Frye Papers.
578   A. Wilson Greene e-mail to author, November 27, 2013.
579   Dennis Frye email to author, January 9, 2017.
580   Statistics compiled from APCWS Board Meeting Minutes for April 22, 1990 (1,534 members); November 6, 1993 ("close to 6,000 members") and February 11, 1995 ("membership increased by 57 percent last year")
581   Civil War Trust Master Land Record, acquisitions and grants from 1990 through 1994; "Hallowed Ground Saved By APCWS" one-page flyer, Frye Papers.
582   A. Wilson Greene e-mail to author, November 29, 2013.

CHAPTER NINE

583   Deborah Fitts, "The Disney Park Looms," *Civil War*, June 1994, page 17.
584   Christine Neuberger, "Racing complex still faces many laps," *Richmond Times-Dispatch*, February 15, 1994.
585   Tersh Boasberg memorandum to APCWS President Will Greene, "End Game at Brandy Station," May 27, 1994, Clark B. Hall archive.
586   Tersh Boasberg letter to Jessica Strauss, April 19, 1994, copy from archive of Clark B. Hall.
587   Ibid.
588   Tersh Boasberg, "End Game at Brandy Station," memorandum to Will Greene, May 27, 1994, Hall archive.
589   Ibid.
590   Ibid.
591   Minutes of the Regular Meeting of the Board of Directors of APCWS, August 20, 1994, page 3, "Brandy Station Acquisition"; A. Wilson Greene, Memorandum – July Activities Update, August 3, 1994, Hall archive.

592   "Preservation Groups Make $5 Million Bid for Brandy Station Battlefield," *Brandy Station Foundation Bulletin*, August, 1994.

593   Christine Neuberger, "Battlefield Preservationists still hope to prevail," *Richmond Times-Dispatch*, July 21, 1994.

594   Martin Sipkoff, "Flank Attack," *Civil War Times Illustrated*, July/August 1994, p 60-61.

595   Tersh Boasberg "Update" memorandum to Will Greene, September 28, 1994, Hall archive; Tersh Boasberg interview with author, August 16, 2016.

596   Boasberg August 16 interview.

597   Ibid.

598   Ibid.

599   Ibid.

600   Ibid; Elizabeth Wilkerson, "Brandy Station decision delayed," *Richmond Times-Dispatch*, September 20, 1994.

601   Boasberg "Update" to Greene.

602   Gary Craig, "Golisano Backs Va. Track," *Rochester Times-Union*, September 21, 1994.

603   Ibid.

604   Clark B. Hall interview, November 11, 2013.

605   Tersh Boasberg letter to Bruce F. Williams, U.S. Army Corps of Engineers Norfolk District, May 26, 1994, archive of Clark B. Hall.

606   Tersh Boasberg letter to Richard Moe, October 31, 1994, Hall archive.

607   William H. Poore Jr. (Chief, Regulatory Branch, Norfolk District, Army Corps of Engineers) letter to Don Klima (Director, Eastern Office, Advisory Council on Historic Preservation), January 17, 1995, Hall archive.

608   Tersh Boasberg memorandum to Richard Nettler, February 2, 1995, Hall archive.

609   Don Klima letter to William H. Poore, February 15, 1995, Hall archive.

610   Frye oral history, transcript page 36; Frye became APCWS interim president in January 1994 and then resigned from the National Park Service on March 31, 1994 to become full-time APCWS president.

611   Richard B. Nettler, on behalf of the Brandy Station Foundation, letter to William H. Poore Jr., March 25, 1995.

612   Ibid; Richard B. Nettler letter to William H. Poore, Jr., April 3, 1995, Hall archive.

613   Hall November 11 interview.

614   Eric Nolan, "Lien filed on land for Brandy Station racetrack," *Culpeper Star-Exponent*, April 20, 1995.

615   Ibid.

616   Hall November 11 interview.

617   Eric Nolan, "Golisano pulls investment from racetrack," *Culpeper Star-Exponent*, April 27, 1995.

618   Ibid.

619   Jim Toler, "No truce yet in Culpeper," Fredericksburg *Free Lance-Star*, May 8, 1995.

620   Richard B. Nettler letter to Bruce Williams, Army Corp of Engineers, April 20, 1995, Hall archive.

621   Draft Memorandum of Agreement by Army Corps of Engineers, May 17, 1995, Hall archive.

622   Tersh Boasberg, Memorandum on purchase options for Brandy Station properties, June 1, 1995, Hall archive.

623   Eric Nolan, "Injunction filed against racetrack," *Culpeper Star-Exponent*, May 20, 1995.

624   Tersh Boasberg Memorandum to Dennis Frye/Bob Edmiston on William property, May 24, 1995. Hall archive.

625   Christine Neuberger, "Developer rejects group's offer for battlefield site," *Richmond Times-Dispatch*, June 3, 1995.

626   Ibid.
627   Eric Nolan, "More liens filed against Benton Ventures, Inc.," *Culpeper Star-Exponent*, June 28, 1995.
628   Theresa Knight, "Foundation Files Suit," *Culpeper News*, August 24, 1995.
629   Jim Toler, "Lawsuit filed over Brandy Station track," Fredericksburg *Free Lance-Star*, August 24, 1995.
630   Ibid.
631   Christine Neuberger, "Foreclosure move dims track prospects," *Richmond Times-Dispatch*, September 19, 1995.
632   Jim Toler, "Track unlikely to be built at Brandy Station," Fredericksburg *Free Lance-Star*, September 18, 1995.
633   Dennis E. Frye, "Success is Greatest Measure," Preservation News column, *The Civil War News*, February/March 1995.
634   Frye oral history, transcript page 37.
635   Ibid.
636   Ibid.
637   Frye oral history, transcript page 38.
638   Michael Armm interview with author, February 10, 2017.
639   Ibid; "Victory at Brandy," APCWS *Hallowed Ground* newsletter, November, 1995, Vol. 8, No. 4.; Hall archive.
640   Frye oral history, transcript page 39.
641   "Victory: Battlefield Property Purchased," *Brandy Station Foundation Bulletin*, October 1996.
642   Gallagher oral history, transcript page 19.
643   Frye oral history, transcript page 40.
644   Armm February 10 interview.
645   Jim Toler, "Peace comes at last to Brandy Station," Fredericksburg *Free Lance-Star*, September 13, 1996.
646   Ibid.
647   Deborah Fitts, "Ceremony Announces Brandy Sale; $100,000 Given in First Two Weeks," *The Civil War News*, October, 1996, page 65.
648   Ibid.
649   Hall oral history, transcript page 24.
650   Hall oral history, transcript page 24.
651   Armm February 10 interview.

CHAPTER TEN
652   Dennis E. Frye e-mail to author, March 28, 2014.
653   "Trust Acts at Harpers Ferry," *Civil War Landscape* (quarterly newsletter of the original Civil War Trust), Summer 1993, Vol 1, No. 2, page 1.
654   Dennis E. Frye e-mail to author, March 28, 2014.
655   Dennis E. Frye e-mail to author, February 11, 2014.
656   "Preservation Accomplishments," 1996 records of the original Civil War Trust, The Civil War Trust archives, Washington, D.C.
657   "American Battlefield Protection Foundation," section from minutes of the APCWS Board of Directors, meeting of May 3, 1991. Robert K. Krick archive.
658   Ibid.
659   "American Battlefield Protection Foundation," APCWS Board of Directors meeting minutes of July 20, 1991. Krick archive.
660   Civil War Trust Board of Directors meeting minutes of June 26, 1992, Civil War Trust archives, Washington, D.C.; "Civil War Trust," from APCWS Board of Directors meeting minutes of July 18, 1992. Krick archive.

661   "Civil War Trust," from the minutes of the APCWS Board of Directors, meetings of September 19, 1992, November 21, 1992 and January 30, 1993. Krick archive.

662   Minutes of the APCWS Board of Directors meeting for November 6, 1993. Krick archive.

663   Minutes of the APCWS Board of Directors meeting for February 5, 1994. Krick archive.

664   Frye oral history, transcript page 57.

665   Ibid.

666   Civil War Trust Fund Balance Sheet, December 31, 1994, Civil War Trust archive, Washington, D.C.

667   Dennis E. Frye, APCWS Facsimile cover sheet for message to Tom Richards, September 11, 1995, Dennis E. Frye Papers, APCWS Files, Western Maryland Room, Washington County Free Library, Hagerstown, Maryland.

668   Frye e-mail, March 28, 2014.

669   Grae Baxter, "The Civil War Battlefield Commemorative Coin Program: Countdown to 1995," Civil War Trust memorandum, June 10, 1994. Frye Papers.

670   Frank R. Wolf letter to Bruce Babbitt, February 27, 1995. Frye Papers.

671   Will Greene letter to Matt Andrews, December 8, 1994. Frye Papers.

672   Dennis E. Frye letter (draft) to Thomas J. Bliley, Jr., on or about July 10, 1995. Frye Papers.

673   Edgar M. Andrews III letter to Dennis E. Frye, July 6, 1995. Frye Papers.

674   Dennis E. Frye fax cover sheet note to Holly Robinson, July 11, 1995. Frye Papers.

675   Dennis E. Frye memo to John Haynes, July 12, 1995, Frye Papers.

676   Civil War Trust notice announcing acceptance of applications for preservation grants, postmarked July 17, 1995; Frank Wolf letter to J. Roderick Heller, July 17, 1995; "Loss of Third Winchester Battlefield Likely," APCWS press release, July 20, 1995; Christine Neuberger, "Winchester battlefield may become subdivision," *Richmond Times-Dispatch*, July 21, 1995. All from Frye Papers.

677   Thomas W. Richards confidential memo to APCWS Board of Trustees, August 2, 1995. Frye Papers.

678   Frye oral history, transcript pages 34, 60.

679   Dennis Frye memo to Tom Senter, August 7, 1995. Frye Papers.

680   Dennis Frye memo to Howard Coffin, "Civil War Trust issues," August 7, 1995; James M. Jeffords letter to J. Roderick Heller, August 11, 1995; Thomas J. Bliley letter to J. Roderick Heller, August 31, 1995. From Frye Papers.

681   J. Roderick Heller letter to James M. Jeffords, August 23, 1995. Frye Papers.

682   Jan Townsend letter to Edgar M. Andrews, August 15, 1995, Frye Papers.

683   Heller letter to Jeffords, August 23, 1995.

684   Thomas J. Bliley, Jr., letter to J. Roderick Heller, September 1, 1995; Dennis E. Frye letter to Edgar M. Andrews, September 5, 1995; Frye Papers.

685   Edgar M. Andrews III letter to Dennis E. Frye, September 8, 1995. Frye Papers.

686   Dennis E. Frye note on Fax cover sheet for Fax to Cameron O'Brion, September 11, 1995, Frye Papers.

687   Civil War Trust Third Winchester fundraising letter, undated. Frye Papers.

688   Dennis Frye interview with Bruce W. Kramer, March 29, 1996, transcript page 1. Frye Papers.

689   Dennis E. Frye, APCWS Fax cover sheet to Richards, September 11, 1995, Frye Papers.

690   Frye oral history interview, page 35.

691   O. James Lighthizer oral history interview, Civil War Trust oral history project, July 14, 2011 and May 3, 2012, Civil War Trust archives, Washington, D.C., transcript page 23.

692   Bearss Civil War Trust oral history interview, transcript page 25.

693   Edgar M. Andrews III, "The President's Perspective," *Civil War Landscape*, newsletter of the Civil War Trust, Fall 1995, page 2. Frye Papers.

694   Beth Delsher, "Surcharge raid must be stopped," *Coin World*, November 20, 1995.

695   Ibid.

696   Frye oral history, page 35.

697   Andrews, "President's Perspective."

698   Julie Fix Udani oral history interview, Civil War Trust oral history project, May 14, 2012, Civil War Trust archives, Washington, D.C., transcript pages 5-6.

699   Ibid.

700   Frye oral history, pages 56-57.

701   Minutes of the APCWS Board of Directors, meeting of April 25, 1996, Frye Papers. Tom Richards died in 2011.

702   Dennis E. Frye letter to Edgar M. Andrews III, December 15, 1995. Frye Papers.

703   Dennis E. Frye memorandum to Board of Trustees, Civil War Trust, December 18, 1995; Frye letter to Andrews of December 15, 1995; Frye Papers.

704   Edgar M. Andrews III membership letter to members of The Civil War Trust, undated (but has December 21,1995 Fax stamp). Frye Papers.

705   Dennis E. Frye interview with Bruce W. Kramer, March 29, 1996, page one. Frye Papers.

706   The Civil War Trust Preservation Accomplishments for 1996 (list of saved battlefields), from the records of the Civil War Trust, 1996, on file at The Civil War Trust, Washington, D.C.; "The Civil War Trust Grants $1.9 Million to Preserve Civil War Battlefields," press release, The Civil War Trust, January 30, 1996, Frye Papers.

707   Ibid.

708   Dennis E. Frye, "Special Announcement to Life Members/Color Bearers," letter from APCWS, October 12, 1995, Clark B. Hall archive; The Civil War Trust Board of Directors meeting minutes, November 2, 1995, Civil War Trust archive, Washington, D.C.

709   Michael D. Shear, "Rift Threatens Effort to Save Civil War Site," *The Washington Post*, March 10,1996. Frye Papers.

710   Ibid.

711   Ibid.

712   March 13, 1996 letter from APCWS Chairman Tom Richards to Meg Greenfield, Editorial Page Editor, *The Washington Post*, Frye Papers.

CHAPTER ELEVEN

713   Frederick J. Zavaglia interview with author, February 8, 2017.

714   Gregory M. LiCalzi, "Why a Financial Skeptic Became a Believer," *Hallowed Ground*, Summer 1999, Vol. 2, No. 3, page 2.

715   Gregory M. LiCalzi letter to Dennis E. Frye, February. 14, 1996, Dennis E. Frye Papers, APCWS Files, Western Maryland Room, Washington County Free Library, Hagerstown, Maryland.

716   Dennis E. Frye letter to Gregory M. LiCalzi, February 29, 1996, Frye Papers.

717   "NatWest proposal," included in documents for APCWS board meeting of April 25, 1996, Frye Papers.

718   Recommendation on agreement between APCWS and NatWest Bank for low interest bond financing, part of the APCWS board meeting package for meeting of April 25, 1996. Frye Papers.

719   LiCalzi, Skeptic to Believer, p. 20.

720   Frye oral history interview, transcript pages 40-41.

721   Gary W. Gallagher e-mail to author, June 3, 2014.

722   Gary W. Gallagher oral history interview, Civil War Trust oral history project, Civil War Trust archives, Washington, D.C., transcript page 17.

723 Gallagher oral history interview, transcript page 12.

724 Dennis E. Frye, "The New Hallowed Ground," *Hallowed Ground*, January. 1998, Vol. 1, No. 1, p. 2.

725 Dennis E. Frye email to author, October27, 2014. Jody Powell died in 2009.

726 Ibid.

727 Confidential Treasurer's Report for APCWS Board of Trustees, Review of July, 1995; August 17, 1995. Frye Papers.

728 Thomas W. Richards memo to Board of Trustees on Financial Reporting, January. 10, 1997. Frye Papers.

729 APCWS board meeting minutes, March 15, 1997, page 2; and April 27, 1997, page 3.

730 Frye oral history interview, page 53.

731 Dennis E. Frye, memo to Rebecca Rickey, Director of Administration, October. 29, 1996, "Documenting Tour of Duty Performance," APCWS Records 1996, Civil War Trust archives, Washington, D.C.

732 Ed Wenzel letter to A. Wilson Greene, executive director APCWS, January. 17, 1994, Ed Wenzel archive, with appended 2016 note from Wenzel.

733 Zavaglia February 8 interview.

734 Dana Shoaf oral history interview, Civil War Trust oral history project, Civil War Trust archives, Washington, D.C., transcript page 4; email from Dennis Frye to author, January. 11, 2017.

735 Ruth Hudspeth oral history interview, Civil War Trust oral history project, Civil War Trust archives, Washington, D.C., transcript page 5.

736 Frye oral history interview, page 45; List of Board of Trustees, APCWS, from 1998 APCWS records, Civil War Trust archives, Washington, D.C.

737 Frye oral history interview, page 46.

738 Henry E. Simpson oral history interview, Civil War Trust oral history project, Civil War Trust archives, Washington, D.C., transcript page 3.

739 Edwin C. Bearss oral history interview (first quote), Civil War Trust oral history project, transcript page 25; Ed Bearss interview, August 8, 2016 (second quote).

740 Alan E. Hoeweler, "Organization Report and Action" memo, April 22, 1998, From APCWS 1998 records, Civil War Trust archives, Washington, D.C.

741 Dennis Frye, "Personnel Policies and Procedures" memo to Fred Zavaglia, March 23, 1998, Frye Papers.

742 Ibid.

743 Hoeweler memo of April 22, 1998.

744 Treasurer's Report, APCWS Board Meeting of April 24, 1998, page 3. From APCWS 1998 records, archives of the Civil War Trust, Washington, D.C.

745 Minutes of the APCWS Board Meeting of April 24, 1998. From APCWS 1998 records, archives of the Civil War Trust, Washington, D.C.

746 Laura Ernde, "Chairman: Antietam Event hurt APCWS," *Hagerstown Morning Herald*, July 2, 1998. Frye Papers.

747 Ibid.

748 "The APCWS Whine List," editorial, *Hagerstown Herald-Mail*, July 6, 1998. Frye Papers.

749 Minutes of the Executive Committee of the APCWS Board of Directors, meeting of July 8, 1998, "Public Relations," APCWS 1998 records, archives of the Civil War Trust, Washington, D.C.

750 Dennis E. Frye email to Alan Hoeweler on "Press Communications," July 10, 1998; Frye memo to Hoeweler, "Discussion with Hagerstown newspaper editors," July 10, 1998. Frye Papers.

751 Dennis E. Frye, letter to the editor to Bob Maginnis, editorial page editor, *Hagerstown Herald-Mail*, July 7, 1998. Frye Papers.

752   Fred Zavaglia email to Dennis E. Frye, "Communications with the Press," July 10, 1998. Frye Papers.

753   Alan Hoeweler email to Dennis E. Frye, "Public Relations policy," July 13, 1998. Frye Papers.

754   Dennis E. Frye email to Alan Hoeweler, "Press Communications," July 10, 1998. Frye Papers.

755   Michael B. Wicklein letter to Alan Hoeweler, July 8, 1998; Hoeweler email to Frye, "What's going on?" July 13, 1998. Frye Papers.

756   Dennis E. Frye email to Alan Hoeweler, "What's going on response," July 14, 1998. Frye Papers.

757   Dennis E. Frye, resignation letter to Alan E. Howeler, July 23, 1998. Frye Papers.

758   Ibid; Alan Hoeweler letter to APCWS members announcing Frye resignation, August. 11, 1998. Frye Papers.

759   "Hallowed Ground Saved By APCWS," one-page, undated informational sheet issued by APCWS that includes saves through 1997. Frye Papers.

760   APCWS Debt Service, December. 31,1998, from APCWS 1998 records, Civil War Trust archives, Washington, D.C.

761   Robert Edmiston, "It's Business, As Usual," Message from Headquarters, *Hallowed Ground*, Spring 1999, Vol. 2, No. 2, page 2.

762   Daniel M. Laney interview with the author, November 7, 2014.

763   Hudspeth oral history interview, pages 6, 9.

764   Shoaf oral history interview, page 3,

765   Ibid.

766   Bonnie Repasi oral history interview, Civil War Trust oral history project, Civil War Trust archives, Washington, D.C., transcript page 5.

767   Edwin C. Bearss interview with author, August 8, 2016.

768   Elliot Gruber oral history interview, Civil War Trust oral history project, Civil War Trust archives, Washington, D.C., transcript page 6.

769   Minutes of the Board of Directors Meeting of the Civil War Trust, April 16, 1993. Civil War Trust archives, Washington, D.C.

770   Melissa Sadler oral history interview, Civil War Trust oral history project, Civil War Trust archives, Washington, D.C., from appendix added to interview, transcript page 11.

771   Repasi oral history interview, transcript page 7.

772   Gruber oral history interview, transcript pages 7-8.

773   "The Civil War Trust, Minutes of the Meeting of the Board of Directors," July 18, 1996 and November. 7, 1996. Civil War Trust archives, Washington, DC.

774   Repasi oral history, page 6.

775   Minutes of the Civil War Trust, 1997, various entries, Civil War Trust archives, Washington, D.C.

776   Minutes of the Civil War Trust, 1995-97, various entries; end-of-year financial statements, 1995 and 1996, Civil War Trust records of 1995, 1996 and 1997, Civil War Trust archives, Washington, D.C.

777   "Financials," Minutes of the Board of Directors of the Civil War Trust, May 2, 1996. Civil War Trust records for 1996, Civil War Trust archives, Washington, D.C.

778   Lester G. "Ruff" Fant oral history interview, Civil War Trust oral history project, Civil War Trust archives, Washington, D.C., transcript page 5.

779   Repasi oral history, page 7.

780   Gruber oral history, pages 2-3.

781   "Aged Payables," The Civil War Trust, as of October. 31,1997, Civil War Trust 1997 records, Civil War Trust archive, Washington, D.C.

782   Gruber oral history, page 3.

783   Ibid.

CHAPTER TWELVE

784   J. Roderick Heller, Memorandum on "The Civil War Trust-APCWS" potential merger, February. 2, 1995, Dennis E. Frye Papers, APCWS Files, Western Maryland Room, Washington County Free Library, Hagerstown, Maryland.

785   APCWS board meeting minutes, January 23, 1997; Civil War Trust board minutes, July 8, 1994. Civil War Trust archives, Washington, D.C.

786   John A. Farrell, "McMansionizing History," *The Washington Post*, Nov. 16, 2008. http://www.washingtonpost.com/wp-dyn/content/article/2008/11/07/AR2008110701937.html

787   Dennis E. Frye, "1997 Effort for Congressional Funding for Battlefield Acquisition," memorandum to Bob Zeller, December. 31, 2014.

788   Ibid. (Note: Frye memo of December 31, 2014 summarizes the funding effort and is appended by some 20 supporting documents, including correspondence, draft amendments, memos and emails).

789   Ibid.

790   Dennis E. Frye, handwritten Facsimile cover sheet to Jerry Russell, September. 22, 1997. Frye Papers.

791   Dennis Frye memorandum to John Haynes, "Review of LCWF Activities," July 15, 1998; Joby Warrick, "Administration Lists 100 Land Buys Worth $328 Million," *The Washington Post*, February. 2, 1998; Frye Papers.

792   Dennis E. Frye, memorandum to Elliot Gruber, "Battlefield Acquisition Priorities," February 10, 1998, Frye Papers.

793   Dennis E. Frye email to Bob Zeller, December 31, 2014, "Twenty years ago . . . "

794   Ibid; Elliot Gruber letter to Dennis E. Frye in response to memorandum, February 10 1998, Frye Papers.

795   John D. Haynes oral history interview, Civil War Trust oral history project, Civil War Trust archives, Washington, D.C., transcript pages 3, 4.

796   Lighthizer oral history interview, transcript pages 19, 20.

797   Fant oral history, transcript page 11.

798   Minutes of the Executive Committee of APCWS, "III – Discussion," April 3, 1998, Frye Papers.

799   Lighthizer oral history, page 18.

800   Ibid.

801   Frederick J. Zavaglia interview with author, February 8, 2017.

802   Minutes, APCWS Board of Directors meeting, April 30, 1998, page 7, Civil War Trust archives, Washington, D.C.

803   Simpson oral history interview, page 3.

804   Dennis E. Frye, memorandum to APCWS Board of Trustees, "Congressional Meeting on LCWF," May 26, 1998.

805   Ibid.

806   Frye oral history interview, transcript page 42.

807   Ibid.

808   Dennis E. Frye, memorandum to Alan Hoeweler," Land and Water Conservation Fund," November. 3, 1998. Frye Papers.

809   Ibid.

810   Alan E. Hoeweler email to Dennis E. Frye, November. 20, 1998, Frye Papers.

811   Dennis E. Frye interview with author, December 9, 2016.

812   Dennis E. Frye email to Dan Laney, January. 14, 1999, Frye Papers.; Frye December 9 interview.

813   Minutes, APCWS board meeting of November 14, 1998, "V-F- Old Business – Land and Water Conservation Fund." APCWS 1998 records, Civil War Trust archives, Washington, D.C.

814   Minutes, APCWS Board of Directors meeting, "VI. Old Business, E – Civil War Merger," November 14, 1998, APCWS 1998 records, Civil War Trust archives, Washington, D.C.

815   Minutes of the Civil War Trust board of directors, "Merger Talks," February 25, 1999. Civil War Trust 1999 records, Civil War Trust archives, Washington, D.C.

816   Haynes oral history interview, page 1.

817   Hudspeth oral history interview, page 10; Daniel M. Laney interview with author, November. 7, 2014.

818   Hudspeth oral history interview, pages 10-12.

819   Ibid.

820   Minutes of the meeting of the Civil War Trust Board of Directors, "General Business: Merger," May 21, 1999, Civil War Trust 1999 records, Civil War Trust archive, Washington, D.C.

821   Minutes of the executive committee of the APCWS Board of Trustees, June 2, 1999, page 4. APCWS 1999 records, Civil War Trust archives, Washington, D.C.

822   Ibid.

823   Ibid, page 8.

824   Ibid.

825   Ibid.

826   Ibid.

827   Ibid.

828   "A Letter from the Founders," *Hallowed Ground*, Winter 2000, Vol. 1, No. 1, page 5. Civil War Trust archives, Washington, D.C.

829   Lighthizer oral history, transcript page 2.

830   Henry E. Simpson letter to Frederick J. Zavaglia, July 23, 1999. APCWS 1999 records, Civil War Trust archives, Washington, D.C.

831   Robert K. Edmiston email to Frederick Zavaglia, "this and that," July 13, 1999. APCWS 1999 records, Civil War Trust archives, Washington, D.C.

832   Robert K. Edmiston emails to Alan Hoeweler, cc to Frederick Zavaglia, 3:47 p.m. and 5:10 p.m., July 14, 1999. APCWS 1999 records, Civil War Trust archives, Washington, D.C.

833   Laney November 7 interview.

834   Hudspeth oral history, page 12.

835   Dana Shoaf oral history interview, transcript page 4.

836   Hudspeth oral history, page 13.

837   Daniel M. Laney, cover letter to APCWS Merger Memorandum, July 14, 1999. APCWS 1999 records, Civil War Trust archives, Washington, D.C.

838   Zavaglia February. 8 interview.

839   Laney November 7 interview.

840   Edwin C. Bearss interview with author, August 8, 2016.

841   Frederick J. Zavaglia letter to Alan E. Hoeweler, July 25, 1999. APCWS 1999 records, Civil War Trust archives, Washington, D.C.

842   Frederick J. Zavaglia email to Robert Edmiston, September 21, 1999. APCWS 1999 records, Civil War Trust archives, Washington, D.C.

843   Minutes of the Civil War Trust board of directors meeting, September 19, 1999. Civil War Trust archives, Washington, D.C.

844   Robert Edmiston, handwritten notes of APCWS Board of Directors meeting, April 23, 1999, APCWS 1999 records, Civil War Trust archives, Washington, D.C.

845   Laney November 7 interview.

846   Minutes of the Final Meetings of the Civil War Trust and the Association for the Preservation of Civil War Sites, Inc., and the First Meeting of the Civil War Preservation Trust, November. 12, 1999.

847 Ibid.

848 Ibid.

849 Ibid.

850 Ibid.

851 Lighthizer oral history, page 1.

852 Lighthizer oral history, page 2.

853 Laney November 7 interview.

CHAPTER THIRTEEN

854 Lighthizer oral history, transcript page 4.

855 Frye oral history, transcript pages 57, 61, 62.

856 Ibid.

857 Ibid.

858 Hudspeth oral history, transcript pages 15-17.

859 Gruber oral history, transcript page 14.

860 Hudspeth oral history, transcript page 19.

861 Hudspeth oral history, transcript page 20.

862 Lighthizer oral history, transcript page 4.

863 Ibid; Hudspeth oral history, transcript page 21.

864 Lighthizer oral history, transcript pages 4-5.

865 Ibid.

866 Gruber oral history, transcript page 14.

867 Lighthizer oral history, transcript pages 4-5.

868 Ibid.

869 Hudspeth oral history, transcript page 20.

870 Dana Shoaf oral history, transcript page 7.

871 Ibid.

872 Shoaf oral history, transcript page 8.

873 Hudspeth oral history, transcript pages 20-21.

874 Lighthizer oral history, transcript pages 4-5.

875 Hudspeth oral history, transcript page 28

876 Gruber oral history, transcript page 18; Shoaf oral history, transcript pages 8-9.

877 Shoaf oral history, transcript pages 8-9.

878 Hudspeth oral history, transcript pages 28-29.

879 Robert Lee Hodge oral history interview, Civil War Trust oral history project, Civil War Trust archives, Washington, D.C., transcript pages 17-18.

880 Dennis Frye email to author, December 9, 2016.

881 *Hallowed Ground*, Winter 2000, Vol. 1, No. 1; Civil War Trust archives, Washington, DC.

882 Carrington Williams, "Joining Forces," A Letter from the Chairman, *Hallowed Ground*, Winter 2000, Vol. 1, No. 1, page 4.

883 Ibid.

884 "A Letter from the Founders" (page 5), and James Lighthizer, "Now We Are One," A Letter from the President (page 6), *Hallowed Ground*, Winter 2000, Vol. 1, No. 1.

885 "Trust Board Vows to Save 2,000 Acres in Year 2000," *Hallowed Ground*, Winter 2000, Vol. 1, No. 1, page 7.

886 Minutes of the Civil War Preservation Trust meeting of April 28, 2000, page 2, Civil War Trust archives, Washington, D.C.

887 Ibid.

888 Minutes of the Civil War Preservation Trust Board of Trustees meeting of October 20, 2000, page 2. Civil War Trust archives, Washington, D.C.,

889 CWPT Staff Roster, July 2002, from minutes of the Meeting of the Board of Trustees

of the Civil War Preservation Trust, Sept. 27, 2002; Minutes of the Civil War Preservation Trust meeting of the Board of Trustees, Oct. 20, 2000, page 2; Civil War Trust archives, Washington, D.C.

890   Jim Campi email to author, March 3, 2017.

891   David Duncan oral history interview, Civil War Trust oral history project, transcript pages 2-3.

892   Duncan oral history, page 3.

893   Duncan oral history, page 4.

894   Duncan oral history, page 5.

895   Ibid.

896   Minutes of the Civil War Preservation Trust Board of Trustees meeting of October 20, 2000, page 2. Civil War Trust archives, Washington, D.C.

897   Hudspeth oral history, pages 31.-32.

898   Hudspeth oral history, page 31.

899   Noah Mehrkam oral history interview, Civil War Trust oral history project, Civil War Trust archives, Washington, D.C., transcript page 5.

900   Civil War Trust Master Land Record, Civil War Trust, Washington, D.C.

901   Dr. Robert B. Moler, "Preserving Historical Land – a Neighborhood Steps Forward," Prince William Conservation Alliance, retrieved online at http://www.pwconserve.org/issues/davistract.html

902   Civil War Trust Master Land Record, Civil War Trust archive, Washington, D.C.

903   Robert K. Krick oral history interview, Civil War Trust oral history project, transcript pages 9-10

904   Krick oral history, page 15.

905   Lighthizer oral history, page 7.

906   Irvan Hess oral history interview, Civil War Trust oral history project, Civil War Trust archives, Washington, D.C., transcript page 3.

907   Lighthizer oral history, page 8.

908   Ibid.

909   Ibid.

910   Ibid.

911   Ibid.

912   Ibid.

913   Lighthizer oral history, pages 9-10.

914   Duncan oral history, page 8.

915   David Duncan email to author, September 26, 2016.

916   Lighthizer oral history, page 10.

917   Duncan September 26 email.

918   Lighthizer oral history, page 11.

919   Mehrkam oral history, page 9.

920   Civil War Trust Master Land Record.

921   Information gleaned from the American Battlefield Protection Plan website. https://www.nps.gov/abpp/index.htm

922   Civil War Trust Master Land Record.

923   Mehrkam oral history, pages 9 and 10.

924   Mehrkam oral history, page 10.

925   Ibid.

926   Ibid.

927   Jim Campi, "A Roar From the Portals of Hell," Civil War Trust webpage at http://www.civilwar.org/battlefields/bristoestation/bristoe-station-history-articles/bristoecampi.html

928   Mehrkam oral history, page 11; "Bristoe Station Battlefield," Prince William Conservation Alliance. http://www.pwconserve.org/issues/landuseplanning/bristoe/

929   Lighthizer May 23 interview.

930   Mehrkam oral history, page 11.

931   Ibid.

932   Ibid.

933   Lighthizer May 23 interview.

934   Ibid.

935   Mehrkam oral history, page 11.

936   Mehrkam oral history, page 17.

937   Jim Lighthizer interview with author, February 20, 2017; "Lawyer, Va. Del. Carrington Williams Dies," *The Washington Post*, August 7, 2002, accessed at https://www.washingtonpost.com/archive/local/2002/08/07/lawyer-va-del-carrington-williams-dies/f4d29db0-9f73-4ab3-ac4d-3a7de3158627/?utm_term=.04ce77bd0c4d

938   Lighthizer February 20 interview.

939   Lighthizer oral history, page 10.

940   Lighthizer oral history, page 11.

CHAPTER FOURTEEN

941   Minutes of the Meeting of the Board of Trustees of the Civil War Preservation Trust, January 23, 2002, p. 1. From Civil War Trust archives, Washington, D.C.

942   CWPT Staff Roster, July 2002, from minutes of the Meeting of the Board of Trustees of the Civil War Preservation Trust, September 27, 2002. From Civil War Trust archives, Washington, D.C.

943   "Congress Allocates $11 Million to Preserve America's Endangered Civil War Battlefields," Civil War Preservation Trust press release, October 11, 2001, from Civil War Trust archives, Washington, D.C.

944   Jim Campi oral history interview, Civil War Trust oral history project, transcript page 2.

945   The Civil War Sites Advisory Commission lists the Battle of Chancellorsville as occurring from April 30 to May 6, 1863, but the major action in the battle occurred on May 1-3.

946   "Needs Rezoning,", August 1, 2002, *Richmond Times-Dispatch*. Civil War Trust archives, Washington, D.C.

947   Ibid.

948   Campi oral history, page 10.

949   Eileen Mead, "Mullins Buys Ashley Farms," Fredericksburg, Virginia, *Free Lance-Star*, April 1, 1995.

950   Outer Connector Brochure for June 19, 2001 public hearing, Fredericksburg Area Metropolitan Planning Organization.

951   Spotsylvania County Planning Commission minutes, November 3, 1999, page 2; Betty Hayden Snyder, "Historic Spotsylvania farm for sale," Fredericksburg *Free Lance-Star*, October 4, 2001.

952   Betty Hayden Snyder, "Jury still out on plan for center," Fredericksburg *Free Lance-Star*, November25, 1999.

953   O. James Lighthizer oral history interview, Civil War Trust oral history project, transcript page 14.

954   Ibid.

955   Snyder, " . . . farm for sale," October 4, 2001.

956   Betty Hayden Snider and Elizabeth Pezzullo, "Park neighbor: 2,350 homes," Fredericksburg *Free Lance-Star*, June 25, 2002.

957   Ibid.

958   Ibid.
959   Campi oral history interview, transcript page 5.
960   Coalition Organizational Structure, December 11,2002, Coalition to Save Chancellorsville Battlefield, from files of Jim Campi, Civil War Trust, Washington, D.C.
961   Campi oral history interview, page 6.
962   Ibid.
963   Robert Lee Hodge oral history interview, page 17.
964   Campi oral history interview, page 6.
965   Elizabeth Pezzullo and Betty Hayden Snyder, "Rallying for a cause," Fredericksburg *Free Lance-Star*, August 1, 2002, pages 1 and 7.
966   Campi oral history interview, page 6.
967   John Hennessy oral history interview, transcript pages 12-13.
968   "Poll Indicates Local Oppositions to Chancellorsville Development," Civil War Interactive, August 30, 2002. Website no longer online. Copy of story in Civil War Trust archives, Washington, D.C.
969   John D. Mitchell and James Lighthizer, "Chancellorsville a battle site once again," op-ed "Comment" column, Fredericksburg *Free Lance-Star*, August 18, 2002, Civil War Trust archives, Washington, D.C.
970   Campi oral history interview, page 8.
971   Ibid.
972   "Election Results Provide Boost to Chancellorsville Preservation Hopes," Civil War Interactive, November 8, 2002. From Civil War Trust archives, Washington, D.C.
973   Betty Hayden Snider, "Panel endorses 'Town' plan," Fredericksburg *Free Lance-Star*, November 9, 2002; Phone interview with Jim Campi, February 9, 2015.
974   Ibid.
975   Campi February 9 phone interview.
976   Campi oral history interview, page 5.
977   Betty Hayden Snider, "Economist's numbers differ on proposed Town of Chancellorsville," Fredericksburg *Free Lance-Star*, December 5, 2002.
978   Betty Hayden Snider, "Lenwell quits board," Fredericksburg *Free Lance-Star*, November 27, 2002.
979   Spotsylvania County Board of Supervisors, Minutes of Meeting of December 10, 2002, page 13.
980   Larry Evans, "Soft touch at Town of Chancellorsville vigil pays off," Fredericksburg *Free Lance-Star*, January 22, 2003.
981   Ibid.
982   Ibid.
983   Ibid.
984   Ibid.
985   Ibid.
986   Spotsylvania County Board of Supervisors, Minutes of Meeting of January 14, 2003. page 22.
987   Campi oral history interview, pages 10-11.
988   "Developer Said to be Running 'Slick' Telemarketing Campaign," Statement issued by Coalition to Save Chancellorsville Battlefield, February 25, 2003; Kiran Krishnamurthy, "Town of Chancellorsville facing its foes," *Richmond Times-Dispatch*, March 23,2003, both Civil War Trust archives, Washington, D.C.
989   "Decision on battlefield development due Tuesday," Associated Press story, March 23, 2003; "Exactly who is the outsider?" undated flyer, Coalition to Save Chancellorsville Battlefield, both from Civil War Trust archives, Washington, D.C.
990   Michelle Boorstein, "Spotsylvania Rejects Building on Battlefield," *The Washington Post*, March 27, 2003.

991 Campi oral history interview, pages 13-14.

992 Ibid.

993 Betty Hayden Snider, "Mullins asks plenty for Route 3 farm," Fredericksburg *Free Lance-Star*, April 18, 2003.

994 Rusty Dennen, "Feds OK Mullins venture," Fredericksburg *Free Lance-Star*, October 22, 2003.

995 Betty Hayden Snider, "Growth foes oust veterans," Fredericksburg *Free Lance-Star*, November 5, 2003.

996 George Whitehurst, "Parties see hope in Mullins talks," Fredericksburg *Free Lance-Star*, August 27, 2004.

997 Deborah Fitts, "Housing Development Starts On Mullins Farm at Chancellorsville," *Civil War News*, July 2004.

998 "Dropping a hint: The Spotsylvania Board of Supervisors plays a little hardball to save more of the Chancellorsville battlefield," editorial in Fredericksburg *Free Lance-Star*, August 27, 2004, Civil War Trust archives, Washington, D.C.

999 Cathy Jett, "Building Community," Fredericksburg *Free Lance-Star*, September 30, 2004. Civil War Trust archives, Washington, D.C.; Campi phone interview, February 9.

1000 George Whitehurst, "Mullins battlefield deal is official," Fredericksburg *Free Lance-Star*, December 11, 2004.

1001 Ibid.

1002 Deborah Fitts, "More Good News at Chancellorsville as CWPT To Acquire Additional Land," *Civil War News*, January, 2006. Civil War Trust archive, Washington, D.C.

1003 Ibid.

1004 Campi oral history interview, page 7.

1005 Hennessy oral history interview, page 14.

1006 Ibid.

CHAPTER FIFTEEN

1007 Author's interview with William A. Frassanito, March 14, 2014.

1008 Ibid.

1009 Ibid.

1010 Ibid.

1011 Ibid.

1012 Ibid; Land Exchange between National Park Service/Gettysburg National Park and Gettysburg College: Hearing before the Environment, Energy and Natural Resources Subcommittee of the Committee on Government Operations, House of Representatives, One Hundred Third Congress, second session, May 9, 1994, transcript page 191. http://archive.org/stream/landexchangebetw00unit/landexchangebetw00unit_djvu.txt

1013 Ibid.

1014 Ibid.

1015 Ibid.

1016 Land Exchange hearing, transcript page 192.

1017 Land Exchange hearing, transcript pages 192-193.

1018 Land Exchange hearing, transcript page 191; Frassanito 2015 interview.

1019 Land Exchange hearing, transcript page 192; Follow-up telephone interview with William A Frassanito, April 16, 2015.

1020 Robert K. Krick interview with author, August 1, 2016.

1021 Frassanito 2014 interview.

1022 Ibid.

1023 Land exchange hearing, transcript page 22.

1024   Ibid.

1025   Ibid; "Gettysburg National Military Park During the World Wars," The Blog of Gettysburg National Military Park, post of July 26, 2013, as accessed at https://npsgnmp.wordpress.com/2013/07/26/gettysburg-national-military-park-during-the-world-wars/.

1026   Three monuments at the Gettysburg National Cemetery predate the Vincent and Taylor battlefield stones.

1027   Timothy B. Smith, The Golden Age of Battlefield Preservation, (Knoxville; University of Tennessee Press, 2008), p. 153.

1028   Smith, page 157; Amy Worden, "A Gettysburg battle plan: The Field as it once was," The Philadelphia Inquirer, June 24, 2013.

1029   Smith, page 169.

1030   http://civilwartalk.com/threads/things-that-arent-there-anymore-battlefield-gettysburg.76421/

1031   Garry E. Adelman email to author, February 23, 2015.

1032   Justin Lane, "Much-Derided Gettysburg Observation Tower Is Felled," New York Times, July 4, 2000.

1033   Wolfgang Saxon, "Thomas R. Ottenstein, 70; Built Belittled Tower at Gettysburg," New York Times obituary, August 5, 2000.

1034   Lane, " . . . Tower Is Felled."

1035   Ibid.

1036   "U.S. must pay $4 million for taking Gettysburg Tower," The Associated Press, May 1, 2006; Saxon, Ottenstein obituary.

1037   Adelman and Smith, page 85, from "The Grading of the Electric Railway, Star and Sentinel, May 9, 1893.

1038   Frassanito 2014 interview.

1039   Ibid.

1040   Land exchange hearing, transcript page 22.

1041   Land exchange hearing, transcript page 23.

1042   Ibid; Frassanito March 2014 interview.

1043   Frassanito 2014 interview.

1044   Land exchange hearing transcript.

1045   Land exchange hearing, transcript page 12.

1046   Land exchange hearing, transcript pages 161-162.

1047   Land exchange hearing, transcript page 125.

1048   Land exchange hearing, transcript page 110.

1049   Frassanito, April 16, 2015 interview.

1050   Land exchange hearing, transcript pages 192-193.

1051   Bearss Civil War Trust oral history interview, transcript pages 29-30.

1052   Ibid.

1053   Ed Bearss interview with author, August 8, 2016.

1054   Frassanito, April 16, 2015 interview; Land exchange hearing, transcript page 23.

1055   Ibid.

1056   Ibid.

1057   1991 minutes of the APCWS and Civil War Trust; Civil War Trust archives, Washington, D.C.; Frassanito April 15, 2015 interview.

1058   William A. Frassanito follow-up interview with author, April 30, 2015.

1059   Ibid.

1060   "Casino plan starts Gettysburg battle," by The Hartford Courant, as published in the Reading, Pennsylvania, Eagle, February 4, 2006.

1061   Ibid.

1062   Ibid.

1063   "Casino plan," *Hartford Courant*; David LeVan interview with author, March 4, 2017.

1064   Ibid.

1065   Ibid.

1066   Mark Berg interview with author, May 7, 2015.

1067   Ibid.

1068   Ibid.

1069   Jim and Susan Star Paddock oral history interview, Civil War Trust oral history project, transcript page 5.

1070   Paddock oral history interview, page 14.

1071   Ibid.

1072   Paddock oral history interview, page 15.

1073   Campi oral history interview, page 9.

1074   Jim Campi interview with author, April 15, 2015.

1075   Fox Butterfield, "Gettysburg Casino Plan Starts Whole New Battle," *New York Times*, June 27, 2005.

1076   Paddock oral history interview, pages 15-16.

1077   Ibid.

1078   Paddock oral history interview, pages 34-35.

1079   Staci L. George, "Casino foes hold candlelight vigil," *Gettysburg Times*, July 4, 2005. Civil War Trust archives, Washington, D.C.

1080   "Rendell stokes casino debate," *Gettysburg Times*, September 20, 2005. Civil War Trust archives, Washington, D.C.

1081   "Civil War Preservation Trust Praises Governor Rendell's Condemnation of Gettysburg Casino Proposal," Civil War Preservation Trust press release accessible at http://www.civilwar.org/aboutus/news/news-releases/2010-news/coalition-praises-rendell.html

1082   "No Casino Billboard Bought by CWPT," *Battlefield Journal*, Buckeystown, Md., November 1, 2005. Civil War Trust archives, Washington, D.C.; Mary Goundrey Koik correspondence with author, January 10, 2017.

1083   Charles Schillinger, "Survey: Pennsylvania voters don't want casino," Hanover, Pennsylvania, *Evening Sun*, November 15, 2005. Civil War Trust archives, Washington, D.C.

1084   Ibid.

1085   Ibid.

1086   Charles Schillinger, "Experts clash as slots report details emerge," Hanover, Pennsylvania, *Evening Sun*, December 25, 2005. Civil War Trust archives, Washington, D.C.

1087   Deborah Fitts, "Critics of Casino Say Opposition Is Growing," *Civil War News*, January, 2006.

1088   Kimberly Hefling, "Gettysburg among threatened war sites," The Associated Press as published in the *Cincinnati Enquirer*, March 4, 2006. Civil War Trust archives, Washington, D.C.

1089   Paddock oral history, page 18.

1090   LeVan March 4 interview.

1091   Campi oral history, page 7.

1092   Deborah Fitts, "Gettysburg Casino Opponents Gather . . ." *Civil War News*, December 2005, Civil War Trust archives, Washington, D.C.

1093   Kathi Schue, "GBPA Is Neutral On Casino," Letter to the Editor of *Civil War News*, June 2006. Civil War Trust archives, Washington, D.C.

1094   Jim Campi follow-up interview with author, April 15, 2015.

1095   Meg Bernhardt, "Trust's report assails casino application," Hanover, Pennsylvania, *Evening Sun*, April 4, 2006. Civil War Trust archives, Washington, D.C.

1096   Schillinger, "Experts clash . . . "

1097   Michael Siegel, "The Impact of a Large Casino on the Gettysburg Area, and Adams County, Pennsylvania; A Realistic Assessment," March 29, 2006; Bernhardt, "Trust's report . . . " Civil War Trust archives, Washington, D.C.

1098   LeVan March 4 interview.

1099   Frederick Kunkle, "In Gettysburg Casino Fight, 2 Visions for Tourism Collide," *The Washington Post*, April 6, 2006; Meg Bernhardt, "Debate continues over which side of slots issue has most support," Hanover, Pennsylvania, *Evening Sun*, May 18, 2006; Kathryn Jorgensen, "Gettysburg Casino Forces Pro & Con Are Working on Many Fronts," *Civil War News*, May 2006. Civil War Trust archives, Washington, D.C.

1100   Meg Bernhardt, "Casino gets zoning board approval," Hanover, Pennsylvania, *Evening Sun*, October 12, 2006. Civil War Trust archives, Washington, D.C.

1101   Meg Bernhardt, "Kicking back at casino zoning hearing," Hanover, Pennsylvania, *Evening Sun*, August 29, 2006. Civil War Trust archives, Washington, D.C.

1102   Meg Bernhardt, October 12, 2006 article.

1103   Paddock oral history interview, page 18.

1104   Richard Fellinger and Meg Bernhardt, "Crowd turns out for hearing," *Public Opinion*, Chambersburg, Pennsylvania, December 14, 2006. Civil War Trust archives, Washington, D.C.

1105   Meg Bernhardt, "Slots leave community divided," Hanover, Pennsylvania, *Evening Sun*, December 17, 2006; "Thank you and congratulations," Jim Campi email to CWPT, December 22, 2006. Civil War Trust archives, Washington, D.C.

1106   Marc Levy, "Pa. Awards License for Slot Machines," Associated Press as published in *The Washington Post*, December 20, 2006.

1107   Susan Star Paddock, "Gettysburg Casino still a bad idea," Hanover, Pennsylvania, *Evening Sun*, December 9, 2009.

1108   "Gaming Control Board Rejects Slots Parlor Near Gettysburg Battlefield," Civil War Preservation Trust press release, December 20, 2006. http://www.civilwar.org/aboutus/news/news-releases/2006-news/gaming-control-board-rejects.html

1109   See Doug Brouder and Yvonne Barton emails in "Congratulatory Notes" PDF in "Victory" file, "Casino I 2005-06" folder, Jim Campi files, Civil War Trust, Washington, D.C.

1110   Meg Barnhardt, "LeVan says no appear of slots decision," Hanover, Pennsylvania, *Evening Sun*, December 22, 2006.

CHAPTER SIXTEEN

1111   Julian Bibb interview with author, May 30, 2014.

1112   Ibid.

1113   Eric A. Jacobson and Richard A. Rupp, For Cause & For Country; Franklin, Tenn.: O'More Publishing, 2008. p. 297.

1114   Bibb May 30 interview.

1115   Ibid.

1116   Mary Pearce interview with author, May 29, 2015.

1117   Sam Huffman, "Franklin Battlefield Preservation Timeline," November 2014, copy in possession of author.

1118   Huffman timeline.

1119   Pearce May 29 interview.

1120   Huffman timeline.

1121   Ibid.

1122   Bibb May 30 interview.

1123   Sam Gant interview with author, August 11, 2014.

1124   Ibid.

1125   "Franklin Acquires Historic Land," March 1997 Save The Franklin Battlefield newsletter; "APCWS Assists Franklin Site," APCWS *Hallowed Ground*, January, 1997;

1126   "Early 1990s House on Carter's Hill Park to Be Saved: But Why?" Heritage Foundation of Franklin and Williamson County, Tenn., web article, May 19, 2014. Accessed at http://historicfranklin.com/carters-hill-park-saved-but-why/

1127   Save The Franklin Battlefield newsletter, January 2015. *www.franklin-stfb. org/2015Jan_STFBNewsletter.pdf*

1128   Laura Hill, "Dream plan debuts for Columbia Avenue," *Nashville Tennessean*, Williamson A.M. section, April 22, 1997.

1129   Kelly Gilfillan, "Structures will be moved, torn down for history-rich Civil War park," Franklin Home Page, March 5, 2014. Accessed at http://franklinhomepage.com/ structures-will-be-moved-torn-down-for-history-rich-civil-war-park/#.U2r-iCieZeE

1130   "Roper's Knob paid off," article from *Nashville Tennessean*, August 25, 1997, as excerpted in Save The Franklin Battlefield newsletter, September 1997.

1131   Save The Franklin Battlefield newsletter, June 2016. All STFB newsletters noted here were accessed at http://www.franklin-stfb.org/newsletter.html which features summaries and links of each newsletter from 1993 to present.

1132   Huffman timeline.

1133   Bibb May 30 interview.

1134   "Williamson County School Board Plans to Build New School Across from the Harrison House," Save The Franklin Battlefield newsletter, December, 2000.

1135   Mary Pearce interview with author, July 28, 2015.

1136   Ibid.

1137   Battle Ground Academy Timeline, accessed at http://www.battlegroundacademy.org/ Timeline

1138   "Preservationists protest building new schools close to historic sites," Article from "Williamson A.M." section of *Nashville Tennessean*, February 21, 2001, as excerpted in Save The Franklin Battlefield newsletter, March 2001.

1139   Save The Franklin Battlefield newsletter, April, 2001.

1140   "Top 10 Most Endangered Civil War Battlefields," 2001, Civil War Preservation Trust online archives, http://www.civilwar.org/history-under-siege/2001-history-under-siege.pdf

1141   Various newspaper excerpts as published in the Save The Franklin Battlefield newsletter, June, 2001.

1142   Ibid.

1143   Various newspaper excerpts as published in the Save The Franklin Battlefield newsletter, July, 2001.

1144   "Williamson County Residents Overwhelmingly Oppose Construction on Franklin Battlefield," Civil War Preservation Trust news release, online archive, http://www. civilwar.org/aboutus/news/news-releases/2001-news/williamson-county-residents. html

1145   "Critics say school board repeating Hood's folly," *Nashville Tennessean* article of July 18, 2001 as excerpted in Save The Franklin Battlefield newsletter, July 2001.

1146   Ed Ballam, "Battle of Franklin is lost, new school will be built," *Civil War News*, November 2001.

1147   Ibid.

1148   Save The Franklin Battlefield newsletter, August, 2001.

1149   Save The Franklin Battlefield newsletter, September, 2001.

1150   "Franklin Battlefield Among Most Endangered Civil War Sites in America," Civil War Preservation Trust news release, March 5, 2002. Accessed at http://www.civilwar.org/ aboutus/news/news-releases/2002-news/franklin-battlefield-among.html

1151   Jim Campi email to author, July 17, 2015.

1152   Campi oral history, page 15.
1153   Peggy Shaw, "Ben Stein lends name to preservation cause," *Nashville Tennessean*, March 19, 2002.
1154   Various newspaper excerpts as published in the Save The Franklin Battlefield newsletter, May, 2002.
1155   Campi oral history, page 15.
1156   Bibb May 30 interview.
1157   Pearce May 29 interview.
1158   Jim Lighthizer oral history, page 34; Save The Franklin Battlefield newsletter, March 2003.
1159   Pearce May 29 interview.
1160   Ibid.
1161   Save The Franklin Battlefield newsletter, April, 2003.
1162   Ibid.
1163   Save The Franklin Battlefield newsletter, May, 2003.
1164   Save The Franklin Battlefield newsletters, June and July, 2003.
1165   Save The Franklin Battlefield newsletter, June, 2003.
1166   Save The Franklin Battlefield newsletter, November 2003.
1167   Robert Hicks oral history interview, Civil War Trust oral history project, Civil War Trust archives, Washington, D.C., transcript page 1.
1168   Hicks oral history, pages 4-5.
1169   Hicks oral history, page 9; Lighthizer oral history page 34.
1170   Hicks oral history, page 23.
1171   Ibid.
1172   Hicks oral history, page 10.
1173   Ibid.
1174   J. Roderick Heller III oral history interview.
1175   Ibid.
1176   John McBryde, "Hellers played pivotal role in preservation of Carnton Plantation, Franklin," *Brentwood Home Page*, August 10, 2014. http://www.brentwoodhomepage.com/hellers-played-pivotal-role-in-preservation-of-carnton-plantation-franklin-cms-17112#.Vc0Y8PncgXx
1177   Heller oral history.
1178   Hicks oral history, page 13.
1179   Hicks oral history, pages 11 and 13.
1180   Mary Goundrey Koik email to author, December 14, 2016.
1181   Save The Franklin Battlefield newsletter, August 2004.
1182   Save The Franklin Battlefield newsletter, October 2004.
1183   Clint Confehr, "Franklin's Charge takes off," *Franklin Review Appeal*, August 22, 2004.
1184   Ibid.
1185   "Open letter to Amy Grant and Vince Gill," *Nashville Tennessean*, August 20, 2004, as reprinted by clipping service and on file at the Civil War Trust archives, Washington, D.C.
1186   "Franklin and Williamson County Residents Support Battlefield Preservation," Save The Franklin Battlefield newsletter, February, 2005.
1187   Save The Franklin Battlefield newsletter, December 2005; The Pizza Hut lot was initially named the Assault on the Cotton Gin Historic Park.
1188   Ibid; Civil War Trust Master Land Record, Civil War Trust, Washington, D.C.
1189   Hicks oral history, page 20.
1190   Hicks oral history, page 19.
1191   Campi oral history, page 17.
1192   Hicks oral history, pages 16 and 23.

1193   Save The Franklin Battlefield newsletter, June 2014 and January, 2015.
1194   Save The Franklin Battlefield newsletter June 2016 and August 2016.
1195   Pearce May 29 interview.
1196   Williamson County Parks and Recreation department, "Academy Park Project," accessed at http://www.wcparksandrec.com/facilities_and_parks/coming_soon!/index.php.
1197   Lighthizer oral history, page 35.

CHAPTER SEVENTEEN

1198   Frank O'Reilly, "The True Battle For Fredericksburg, Civil War Trust website, accessed at: http://www.civilwar.org/battlefields/fredericksburg/fredericksburg-history-articles/fredericksburgoreilly.html
1199   Robert K. Krick email to author, May 7, 2016.
1200   Ibid.
1201   Ibid.
1202   Jim Lighthizer interview with author, February 20, 2017.
1203   Krick May 7 email.
1204   Ibid.
1205   Kathryn Jorgensen, "Fredericksburg Farm Is for Sale; Preservationists Want To Save It," *Civil War News*, February/Mar. 2006.
1206   "Pierson Tract Meeting Update," email from Chris Allen, Civil War Trust, to Bob Krick, November 10, 2004. From the Civil War Trust archives.
1207   Laura Moyer, "Trust gets battle site," Fredericksburg, Virginia, *Free Lance-Star*, April 22, 2005, accessed at http://www.fredericksburg.com/local/trust-gets-battle-site/article_5eb2ae31-8068-504b-9e70-636c1c21688c.html
1208   Ibid.
1209   "Capitol Hill Reception" email from Vince Onorato to Jim Campi, March 13, 2005. From Civil War Trust archives, Washington, D.C.; Jim Campi email to author, March 3, 2017.
1210   Jim Campi email to author, July 17, 2015.
1211   Ibid.
1212   Deborah Fitts, "CWPT To Pay Record $12 Million For 205-Acre Slaughter Pen Farm," *Civil War News*, May 2006.
1213   Kathryn Jorgensen, "Fredericksburg Farm is for Sale; Preservationist Want to Save It," which includes the quote from the *Free Lance-Star*. Accessed at http://www.civilwarnews.com/archive/articles/fbgfarm.htm
1214   Tom Gilmore oral history interview, Civil War Trust oral history project, Civil War Trust archives, Washington, D.C., transcript page. 9
1215   Campi email, July 17, 2015.
1216   Gilmore oral history interview, page 10.
1217   Ronald Cogswell oral history interview, Civil War Trust oral history project, Civil War Trust archives, Washington, D.C., transcript page 18.
1218   Campi email, July 17, 2015.
1219   David Duncan oral history interview, transcript page 18.
1220   Cogswell oral history interview, page 17.
1221   Rusty Dennen, "Saving Slaughter Pen," Fredericksburg *Free Lance-Star*, March 29, 2006.
1222   Ibid.
1223   O. James Lighthizer, "Message From Headquarters," *Hallowed Ground*, Summer 2006, Vol 7, No. 2, page 2.
1224   Cogswell oral history interview, page 17. The ceremony noted in the narrative is the event of October 16, 2006, which is detailed later in the chapter.

1225   Gilmore oral history interview, pages 10-12.

1226   Ibid.

1227   Deborah Fitts, "$2 Million in Federal Money Goes to Slaughter Pen Farm," *Civil War News*, December 2006. https://www.civilwarnews.com/archive/articles/spennfitts.htm

1228   Gilmore oral history interview, page 13.

1229   Cogswell oral history interview, page 16.

1230   Gilmore oral history interview, page 11.

1231   John A. Farrell, "McMansionizing History," *The Washington Post Magazine*, November 16, 2008. Accessed at http://www.washingtonpost.com/wp-dyn/content/article/2008/11/07/AR2008110701937.html

1232   Gilmore oral history interview, page 11.

1233   Civil War Trust Master Land Record, Civil War Trust archives.

1234   Ibid.

1235   Blake Hallman oral history interview, Civil War Trust oral history project, Civil War Trust archives, Washington, D.C., transcript page 1.

1236   Ibid; Robert Behre, "Conversation led to conservation," *Post and Courier*, Charleston, S.C., February 3, 2006.

1237   Hallman oral history, page 3.

1238   Ibid.

1239   Ibid.

1240   "Historic Morris Island For Sale," Associated Press, January 28, 2005. As reprinted in The "Old Liner" Newsletter, Baltimore, Md., Civil War Round Table. http://bcwrt.nalweb.net/pages_02-05.PDF; "S.C.: Public Wants to Preserve Morris Island," Associated Press, February 24, 2005, as reprinted by *Realtor Magazine* online. Accessed at: http://www.realtor.org/RMODaily.nsf/pages/News2005022554?OpenDocument

1241   Ibid.

1242   Behre, "Conversation . . . "; Hallman oral history, page 4; "Historic Morris Island Battlefield Again Under Threat of Development," Civil War Trust press release, December 21, 2005. http://www.civilwar.org/aboutus/news/news-releases/2005-news/historic-morris-island.html

1243   "Agreement Will Protect Historic Morris Island," The Trust for Public Land press release, February 2, 2006. https://www.tpl.org/media-room/agreement-would-protect-historic-morris-island-sc

1244   Ibid.

1245   Hallman oral history, page 5.

1246   "Desecration of Harpers Ferry Battlefield," *Hallowed Ground*, Winter 2006, Vol. 7, No. 4. Pages 3-4

1247   Ibid.

1248   "Emergency Alert!" CWPT direct mail fundraising appeal in regard to Harpers Ferry desecration at School House Ridge, August 2006, Civil War Trust archives, Washington, D.C.

1249   "Harpers Ferry Desecrators Thwarted," *Hallowed Ground*, Winter 2007, Vol. 8, No. 4, pages 5-6; correspondence with Mary Goundrey Koik, December 14, 2016.

1250   Rob Hiassen, "Tragedy survived, then relived," *The Baltimore Sun*, January 21, 2007. Accessed at: http://articles.baltimoresun.com/2007-01-21/news/0701210034_1_conor-jim-lighthizer-five-hours

1251   Ibid.

1252   Ibid.

1253   Jim Lighthizer interview with author, February 20, 2017.

1254   Ibid.

1255   Ibid.

1256   Hiassen, "Tragedy survived."

1257   Farrell, "McMansionzing History."

1258   Duncan oral history, page 19.

1259   Ibid.

1260   "Interior Secretary Announces $2 million Grant for Slaughter Pen Farm, *Hallowed Ground*, Vol. 7, No. 4. Winter 2006, p.5; Correspondence with Mary Goundrey Koik, December 14, 2016.

1261   Kathryn Jorgensen email to author, December 4, 2015.

1262   Ibid.

1263   Clark B. Hall interview with author, December 3, 2015.

1264   Ibid.

1265   Ibid.

1266   Ibid.

1267   Kathryn Jorgensen, "Preservationist Deborah Fitts Dies at 63 . . ." *Civil War News*, August 2008.

1268   "Preservation Focus: Brandy Station, Va." *Hallowed Ground*, Spring 2000, p. 4.

1269   "Fleetwood Hill," email of Clark B. Hall to board members of Brandy Station Foundation, February 4, 2002. Clark B. Hall archive.

1270   Ibid.

1271   Ibid.

1272   Joseph A. Troilo letter to Rep. J. Kenneth Robinson, October 3, 1972, Hall archive.

1273   Ibid.

1274   Hall December 3 interview.

1275   Ibid.

1276   Clark B. Hall email to author, February 4, 2002.

1277   Ibid.

1278   Daralee Ota essay on Brian Pohanka, accessed at http://dragoon1st.tripod.com/cw/files/bcp_mem4.html

1279   Clark B. Hall, "A Chronicle of Endurance, Courage and Immortal Love," p. 3.

1280   Hall, "Chronicle," p. 9

1281   Hall interview, December 3, 2015.

1282   Deborah Fitts, "Brian Pohanka's Wife Will Carry on His Works," *Civil War News*, August 2005. http://www.civilwarnews.com/archive/articles/pohanka_wife.htm

1283   Hall, "Chronicle," p. 45.

1284   Hall interview, February 5, 2015.

1285   Hall interview, December 3, 2015.

1286   Ibid.

1287   Ibid.

1288   Tony Troilo interview, January 23, 2017.

1289   Ibid.

1290   Hall, "Chronicle," p. 5.

1291   Hall, "Chronicle," p. 87-88.

1292   Hall, "Chronicle," p. 297.

CHAPTER EIGHTEEN

1293   Dan McFarland, "Orange celebrates Walmart opening," Fredericksburg, Virginia, *Free Lance-Star*, July 10, 2013. Accessed at: http://www.fredericksburg.com/news/orange-celebrates-walmart-opening/article_dc923660-4964-579c-9c83-ae11f5d838e1.html

1294   Ibid.

1295   "New Walmart Supercenter Opens in Orange County," NBC29.com (Charlottesville, Va.). Accessed at: http://www.nbc29.com/story/22801504/new-wal-mart-supercenter-opens-in-orange-county

1296   "The Nerve Center of the Union Army at the Wilderness, May 5-7, 1864," brochure published by the Wilderness Battlefield Coalition, Civil War Trust archives, Washington, D.C.

1297 Most Endangered Battlefields, 2005 and 2006, *Hallowed Ground*, Spring 2005 and Spring 2006.

1298 "Update on the Wilderness," *Hallowed Ground*, Spring 2007, page 9.

1299 "Three Wins in the Wilderness: Orange County Holds Firm Against Development," *Hallowed Ground*, Winter 2007.

1300 "National Park Service Preserves 63 Acres at the Wilderness," *Hallowed Ground*, Spring 2008, page 6.

1301 "CWPT Announces 2008 Preservation Awards," *Hallowed Ground*, Summer 2008, page 6; "National Park Preserves . . . " *Hallowed Ground*, Spring 2008, page 6.

1302 "Trouble Brewing in the Wilderness," *Hallowed Ground*, Fall 2008, page 11.

1303 Ibid; also Robin Knepper, "Walmart Officials Meet in Orange," Fredericksburg *Free Lance-Star*, October 23, 2008. Accessed at: http://www.fredericksburg.com/local/wal-mart-officials-meet-in-orange/article_6ec85c29-7d30-5da6-913a-59c594f12d39.html

1304 Jim Campi interview with author, January 16, 2016.

1305 Ibid.

1306 Knepper, "Walmart officials . . . "

1307 "Vermont's stand," editorial, Fredericksburg *Free Lance-Star*, February 19, 2009. Accessed at: http://www.fredericksburg.com/opinioneditorial/vermont-s-stand/article_e126a6ac-7b33-5816-bfcb-ea78486abbea.html

1308 Ibid.

1309 Robin Knepper, "Wal-Mart survey shows support," Fredericksburg *Free Lance-Star*, February 19, 2009. http://www.fredericksburg.com/local/wal-mart-survey-shows-support/article_446140da-209f-54e4-bf61-87210c4e4772.html

1310 "Culpeper Star-Exponent Opposes Walmart," editorial of March 9, 2009 as reprinted on the No Wilderness Walmart blog, accessed at https://nowildernesswalmart.wordpress.com/2009/03/09/culpeper-star-exponent-opposes-walmart/ and "Wilderness Walmart and Congress," as well as "CWPT Most Endangered Battlefields," both on the No Wilderness Walmart blog accessed at https://nowildernesswalmart.wordpress.com/page/12/

1311 Robin Knepper, "Orange: No to Wilderness gateway study," Fredericksburg *Free Lance-Star*, April 16, 2009. Accessed at: http://www.fredericksburg.com/local/orange-no-to-wilderness-gateway-study/article_4d3436ef-f548-5ca4-af51-933ff2052dea.html

1312 Jim Campi January 16 interview.

1313 "Actor joins foes of Orange Wal-Mart," Fredericksburg *Free Lance-Star*, May 5, 2009. http://www.fredericksburg.com/local/actor-joins-foes-of-orange-wal-mart/article_fcb76de8-5726-546b-8733-fa2e5a9afa7d.html

1314 Ibid.

1315 Ibid.

1316 Miller oral history interview, transcript pages 15-17.

1317 "Planning Commission Recesses Until June 11" post of May 26, 2009; "Planning Commission Delays Decision" post of June 12, 2009," both on No Wilderness Walmart blog accessed at: https://nowildernesswalmart.wordpress.com.

1318 Robin Knepper, "Board Fires Rolfe," Fredericksburg *Free Lance-Star*, July 4, 2009. Accessed at: http://www.fredericksburg.com/local/board-fires-rolfe/article_38c267f8-038d-5e1e-a63e-e8367c5f3ec3.html

1319 "Planning Commission Votes in Favor of Walmart," Post of June 26, 2009, No Wilderness Walmart blog, accessed at https://nowildernesswalmart.wordpress.com/page/5/

1320 Campi January 16 interview.

1321   "Governor Kaine and Speaker Howell Urge Orange County to Move Walmart," and "Editorials push for compromise solution at Wilderness," both at No Wilderness Walmart blog, accessed at https://nowildernesswalmart.wordpress.com/page/4/

1322   "Board of Supervisors Public Hearing Rescheduled," No Wilderness Walmart blog. Accessed at: https://nowildernesswalmart.wordpress.com/

1323   Scott C. Boyd, "County Board Approves Walmart Special Permit at Wilderness," *Civil War News*, October 2009.

1324   Ibid.

1325   "Wilderness Walmart: Coalition Vows to Fight On," *Hallowed Ground*, Fall 2009, page 7.

1326   Ibid.

1327   Robin Knepper, "Walmart on its way," Fredericksburg *Free Lance-Star*, August 26, 2009. Accessed at: http://www.fredericksburg.com/local/walmart-on-its-way/article_011fb7f7-e106-5ed2-993e-c75ac13f8b39.html

1328   Ibid.

1329   Campi oral history interview, transcript page 14.

1330   "CWPT Supports Walmart Litigation," Civil War Preservation Trust press release, September 23, 2009. http://www.civilwar.org/aboutus/news/news-releases/2009-news/cwpt-supports-walmart-litigation.html; Robert Rosenbaum interview with author, January 11, 2016.

1331   Campi January 16 interview.

1332   Scott C. Boyd, "County Claims Wal-mart Opponents Lack Standing in Court," *Civil War News*, November 2009.

1333   Ibid.

1334   Ibid.

1335   Rosenbaum January 11 interview; Ron Cogswell oral history interview, transcript page 19-20.

1336   Rosenbaum January 11 interview.

1337   Michael Siegel oral history interview, transcript page 21.

1338   Rosenbaum January 11 interview.

1339   Ibid.

1340   Rosenbaum January 11 interview.

1341   Hannah Wever, "FoWB: Walmart okay, just no there!" *Orange County Review*, November 26, 2008. Accessed at: http://www.dailyprogress.com/orangenews/news/fowb-wal-mart-okay-just-not-there/article_62dba991-9648-5e1e-b040-bba6c2a78ba7.html

1342   Clint Schemmer, "State Criticizes Walmart Report," Fredericksburg *Free Lance-Star*, May 21, 2009. Accessed at: http://www.fredericksburg.com/local/state-criticizes-wal-mart-report/article_3bd38cfa-d3e4-569c-a00e-39da91730d10.html

1343   Ibid.

1344   Rosenbaum January 11 interview.

1345   Ibid.

1346   Clint Schemmer, "Historian Weighs in Against Walmart," Fredericksburg *Free Lance-Star*, October 13, 2010. Accessed at: http://www.fredericksburg.com/local/historian-weighs-in-against-walmart/article_1294cb5e-a44d-5921-a332-4079e6f2ef85.html

1347   Clint Schemmer, "Walmart Foes Get Reinforcements," Fredericksburg *Free Lance-Star*, January 28, 2010. Accessed at: http://www.fredericksburg.com/local/walmart-foes-get-reinforcements/article_22f1df20-5c4e-5434-bc17-769e4b51a624.html

1348   "Va. Battle over Walmart continues," *The Washington Post*, April 30, 2010. Accessed at: http://voices.washingtonpost.com/local-breaking-news/va-walmart-battle-continues.html; "Legal Wrangling Continues in Wilderness Walmart Case," *Hallowed Ground*, Fall 2010, page 6.

1349   Rosenbaum January 11 interview.

1350   Clint Schemmer, "Walmart Legal Fight Heats Up," Fredericksburg *Free Lance-Star*, October 19, 2010. Accessed at: http://www.fredericksburg.com/local/walmart-legal-fight-heats-up/article_1daef5cd-87d8-5a99-8fb1-1c4ae0224bca.html

1351   Rosenbaum January 11 interview.

1352   Brad Coker oral history interview, transcript page 13.

1353   Allison Brophy Champion, "County attorney: Walmart parcel not hallowed ground," *Culpeper Star-Exponent*, January 26, 2001, as published at http://www.newsadvance.com/rockingham_now/news/county-attorney-wal-mart-parcel-not-hallowed-ground/article_3ec2f05a-5150-5d2a-af6c-3b8cec863aaf.html

1354   Ibid.

1355   Rosenbaum January 11 interview.

1356   Ibid.

1357   Ibid.

1358   Ibid.

1359   Scott C. Boyd, "Walmart Drops Wilderness Project, To Buy Sites, Locate Store Elsewhere," *Civil War News*, February/March 2011.

1360   Ibid.

1361   Ibid.

1362   Ibid.

1363   Rosenbaum January 11 interview.

1364   "Orange County Disappointed with Walmart Decision," Press release of the Orange County, Va., Board of Supervisors, January 26, 2011. Accessed at Civil War Trust website at http://www.civilwar.org/take-action/speak-out/wilderness-walmart/orange-county-disappointed.html

1365   Ibid.

1366   "Winners of 2011 Preservation Awards Announced," *Hallowed Ground*, Vol. 12, No. 3, Fall 2001, page 15.

1367   "Wilderness Walmart Retrospective," undated article at Civil War Trust website, accessed at http://www.civilwar.org/take-action/speak-out/success-stories/wilderness-walmart-retrospective.html

1368   "Battlefield Coalition Unveils Finding of Year-long 'Wilderness Gateway Study," Press release of National Parks Conservation Association, April 13, 2012. https://www.npca.org/articles/685-battlefield-coalition-unveils-findings-of-year-long-wilderness-gateway

1369   Ibid.

1370   Jim Lighthizer oral history interview, transcript page 30.

1371   Jim Campi email to author, March 3, 2017.

CHAPTER NINETEEN

1372   "LeVan Property Easement," Gettysburg Foundation land preservation statement accessed at http://www.gettysburgfoundation.org/53; Jim Campi telephone interview with author, May 14, 2015.

1373   Campi May 14 interview.

1374   Ibid.

1375   "Casino Proposal Again Threatens Gettysburg," *Hallowed Ground*, Spring 2010, page 6.

1376   "Gettysburg Casino Controversy Nears Conclusion," *Hallowed Ground*, Winter 2010, page 6; Mary Goundrey Koik correspondence with author, January 10, 2017.

1377   Koik January 10 correspondence.

1378   James and Susan Paddock oral history interview, transcript page 24; Koik January 10 correspondence; David LeVan interview with author, March 4, 2017.

1379   "Vote on Controversial Gettysburg Casino Delayed," *Hallowed Ground*, Spring 2011, page 7; "Gaming Investors Roll Snake Eyes: Gettysburg Casino Defeated Again," *Hallowed Ground*, Summer 2011, page 6.

1380   "National Preservation Group Unveils New Name, Logo to Mark Beginning of Civil War Sesquicentennial" Civil War Trust news release. January 10, 2011. Accessed at http://www.civilwar.org/aboutus/news/news-releases/2011-news/civil-war-trust-announcement.html

1381   "History Unveils 'Give 150' Initiative to Mark Civil War Sesquicentennial," *Hallowed Ground*, Vol 12, No. 2, Summer 2011, page 9.

1382   Jim Lighthizer phone interview with author, November 1, 2016.

1383   *Hallowed Ground*, Summer 2012.

1384   Civil War Trust Master Land Record, Civil War Trust archives, Washington, D.C.

1385   "History Unveils 'Give 150' Initiative to Mark Civil War Sesquicentennial," *Hallowed Ground*, Vol 12, No. 2, Summer 2011, page 9.

1386   "For Shiloh Sesquicentennial, Major Preservation Victories," *Hallowed Ground*, Vol. 13, No. 2, Summer 2012, pages 4-5.

1387   Ibid.

1388   Ibid.

1389   Mary Goundrey Koik interview with author, January 20, 2017.

1390   Ibid.

1391   Civil War Trust Unveils Suite of Multimedia Offerings for 150th Anniversary of Battle of Antietam," Civil War Trust news release. September 13, 2012. Accessed at http://www.civilwar.org/aboutus/news/news-releases/2012-news/antietam-anniversary-tech.html

1392   *Campaign 150*, its progress and its ultimate success were covered in the Fall 2011, Winter 2014 and Summer 2015 issues of *Hallowed Ground*, among others.

1393   Ibid.

1394   Lighthizer November 1 interview.

1395   Civil War Trust Master Land Record.

1396   Lighthizer November 1 interview.

1397   Ibid.

1398   Timothy B. Smith, The Golden Age of Battlefield Preservation, (Knoxville; University of Tennessee Press, 2008), page 153.

1399   Smith, page 157.

1400   Smith, page 169.

1401   Jim Lighthizer telephone interview with author, November 17, 2016.

1402   Koik correspondence, January 10.

1403   Ibid.

1404   Elizabeth Smith, "Report from the Headquarters: A Reflection on the Lee's Headquarters Public Forum," *The Gettysburg Compiler*, October, 2015. Accessed at: https://gettysburgcompiler.com/2015/10/14/report-from-the-headquarters-a-reflection-on-the-lees-headquarters-public-forum/

1405   Civil War Trust Master Land Record, Civil War Trust archives, Washington, D.C.

1406   Lee's Headquarters Preservation Timeline, Civil War Trust website, accessed at: http://www.civilwar.org/battlefields/gettysburg/preservation/gettysburg-lees-headquarters.html

1407   Ibid.

1408   Ibid; Koik correspondence, January 10.

1409   Ibid.

1410   "Civil War Trust Announces Preservation and Restoration of General Lee's Headquarters at Gettysburg," Civil War Trust press release, October 28, 2016; http://www.civilwar.org/aboutus/news/news-releases/2016-news/announcing-lees-headquarters-restoration.html

1411   Lee's Headquarters timeline.

1412   Lighthizer November 17 interview.

1413   Lee's Headquarters timeline.

1414   Lighthizer November 17 interview.

1415   Ibid.

1416   Tony Troilo interview with author, January 23, 2017.

1417   Tony Troilo interview with author, February 25, 2017.

1418   Tony Troilo January 23 interview.

1419   Ibid.

1420   Emails of May 9, 2011 by Clark B. Hall to Jim Campi, other Civil War Trust staff members and the Brandy Station Foundation. From the records of Campi at The Civil War Trust, Washington, D.C.

1421   Email of May 11, 2011 by Clark B. Hall to Jim Campi, other Civil War Trust staff members. From the records of Campi at The Civil War Trust, Washington, D.C.

1422   Troilo January 23 interview.

1423   Ibid.

1424   Hall December 3, 2015 interview.

1425   Troilo January 23 interview.

1426   Hall December 3 interview.

1427   Ibid.

1428   Scott C. Boyd, "Agreement Reached on Restoration of Hill at Brandy Stations," *Civil War News*, January 2012, as accessed at the "Rantings of a Civil War Historian" blog by Eric Wittenburg, http://civilwarcavalry.com/?p=3101

1429   Boyd, *Civil War News*, January 2012.

1430   Troilo January 23 interview.

1431   Troilo February 25 interview.

1432   Ibid.

1433   Jeff Say, "Another victory on Fleetwood Hill," *Culpeper Star-Exponent*, December 20, 2102, as accessed at http://www.dailyprogress.com/starexponent/news/local_news/another-victory-on-fleetwood-hill/article_8eb4f41c-4af0-11e2-a40e-001a4bcf6878.html

1434   Clark B. Hall interviews with author, January 22, 2017 and February 6, 2015.

1435   Troilo January 23 interview.

CHAPTER TWENTY

1436   "90th Pennsylvania Volunteer Infantry Regiment," monument history at stonesentinels.com. Accessed at: http://antietam.stonesentinels.com/monuments/pennsylvania/90th-pennsylvania-volunteer-infantry-regiment/

1437   "Colonel Peter Lyle's Official Report of September 18, 1862 on South Mountain and Antietam," from the Official Records of the War of the Rebellion, Series 1, Vol. 19, Part 1, pages 265-266. As accessed at http://antietam.aotw.org/exhibit.php?exhibit_id=266; "The 90th Pennsylvania Infantry in the Cornfield: 'Solitary and alone, we gave and took our medicine,'" account of the 90th Pennsylvania at Antietam and in the Civil War as appearing in the "Antietam's Cornfield" blog. Accessed at: https://antietamscornfield.com/2016/06/18/the-90th-pennsylvania-infantry-in-the-cornfield-solitary-and-alone-we-gave-and-took-our-medicine/

1438   "Celebration at Antietam 'Epicenter,'" *Hallowed Ground*, Winter 2015. Page 4.

1439   Smith, Golden Age, pages 87, 103.

1440   "The Dunker Church," National Park Service website for Antietam National Battlefield. Accessed at: https://www.nps.gov/anti/learn/historyculture/dunkerchurch.htm

1441   Susan DeFord, "Historians Battle to Save Antietam," *The Washington Post*, Maryland Weekly section, August 8, 1988.

1442 Sherry Greenfield, "30 years later, Antietam preservation group is transforming battlefield to 1862," Hagerstown, Md., *Herald-Mail*, June 18, 2016. Accessed at: http://www.heraldmailmedia.com/news/local/years-later-antietam-preservation-group-is-transforming-battlefield-to/article_b1ecf2b4-359c-11e6-928f-a78541d1412d.html; Deb Reichmann, "Preservation Groups Winning Fight Over Antietam Farm," Associated Press story as it appeared in *The Washington Post*, November 13, 1993. Page F-12.

1443 DeFord, "Historians Battle . . ."; Public Law 86-438, April 22, 1960, accessed at http://uscode.house.gov/statutes/pl/86/438.pdf

1444 Dennis E. Frye interview with author, December 9, 2016.

1445 "Antietam battlefield unprotected; development could ruin historic site," *Potomac News*, March 4, 1988.

1446 Ibid.

1447 Ibid.

1448 "Foundation Buys, Donates Battlefield," Associated Press story as it appeared in *The Washington Post*, August 31, 1991; Deborah Fitts, "Antietam Park Acquires Farm, The Site of Union Assault," *Civil War News*, November, 1998, page 8.

1449 Eugene L. Meyer, "Antietam's Suspicious Summer," *The Washington Post*, September 4, 1989.

1450 P.J. Shuey, "Federal advisers get an earful," *The Frederick Post*, June 13, 1989.

1451 H. Grant Dehart email to author, June 2, 2016.

1452 Sherry Greenfield, "Life on the Battlefield," *Herald-Mail*, Hagerstown, Md., March 13, 2016. Accessed at: http://www.heraldmailmedia.com/news/local/life-on-antietam-battlefield/article_5332822a-e8a3-11e5-86ea-a3e84c630025.html; Philip C. Wilson obituary, *Herald-Mail*, Hagerstown, Md., April 21, 2014. Accessed at: http://www.heraldmailmedia.com/obituaries/philip-c-wilson/article_e415f9f2-c9ab-11e3-9a45-001a4bcf6878.html

1453 Ibid.

1454 Ibid.

1455 Ibid; Civil War Trust Master Land Record.

1456 Greenfield, "Life on the Battlefield."

1457 Antietam NPS ranger Keith Snyder interview with author, February 22, 2017.

1458 Civil War Trust Master Land Record.

1459 Snyder February 22 interview.

1460 Jim Lighthizer oral history interview, transcript page 38.

CHAPTER TWENTY-ONE

1461 "Civil War Trust Declares Victory in *Campaign 150*," *Hallowed Ground*, Summer 2015.

1462 "Civil War Trust Kicks Off *Campaign 1776*," *Hallowed Ground*, Winter 2014, page 4.

1463 Jim Campi interview with author, January 24, 2017.

1464 Ibid.

1465 Anne Levin, "Princeton Battlefield Focus of National Campaign," *Town Topics*, Princeton, N.J., Accessed at: http://www.towntopics.com/wordpress/2014/11/12/princeton-battlefield-focus-of-national-campaign/ Note: All issued of Princeton, New Jersey, newspapers, including *Town Topics* and *The Daily Princetonian*, are accessed at the Papers of Princeton website of Princeton University. Site at: http://library.princeton.edu/collections/papers-princeton

1466 "Victory at Princeton" website news release, *Campaign 1776*, a project of The Civil War Trust. Accessed at: http://www.campaign1776.org/battlefields/princeton/princeton-2014/

1467 Institute for Advanced Study "Mission and History," accessed at https://www.ias.edu/about/mission-history; IAS "Frequently Asked Questions," accessed at https://www.

ias.edu/about/faqs; Jim Campi correspondence with author, February 28 and March 3, 2017.

1468 George Washington letter to his brother, John, December 18, 1776, from the George Washington Papers; as presented by the Library of Congress and accessed at: http://www.loc.gov/teachers/classroommaterials/presentationsandactivities/presentations/timeline/amrev/north/plains.html

1469 William Myers, "An Open Letter to the Princeton Regional Planning Board," January 25, 2012. As accessed at: http://patch.com/new-jersey/princeton/an-open-letter-to-the-princeton-regional-planning-board

1470 "Historic Property Accepted by Edge," *Daily Princetonian*, October 21, 1946.

1471 "Open Space Commission Considers Weller Tract," *Town Topics*, October 23, 1969. (The "Weller tract" was on the park boundary opposite the one with Maxwell's Field, the site of the most recent preservation battle).

1472 "State May Want Land," *Town Topics*, November 6, 1969; "State to Reconsider," *Town Topics*, July 16, 1970.

1473 "Battle Is Won," *Town Topics*, February 22, 1973.

1474 G. I. Wolfe, "Town conservationists fight to save farmland," *Daily Princetonian*, September 29, 1983.

1475 Ibid.

1476 "Planning Board Will Review Institute's Plans For 400 to 600 Housing Units on Quaker Road," *Town Topics*, March, 16, 1983; "Town Conservationists Fight to Save Farmland," *Daily Princetonian*, September 29, 1983; Carolyn Connor letter to the editor, *Town Topics*, April 20, 1983; "Institute Drops Plans to Develop Quaker Road Land," *Town Topics*, March 14, 1984.

1477 "Last Chance for Public Input on Master Plan Will Come at Planning Board Meeting Thursday," *Town Topics*, July 12, 1989.

1478 "Institute Sues Planning Board Over Potential $10 Million Loss," *Town Topics*, January 17, 1990.

1479 Barbara Johnson, "Institute Woods & Lands Have Been Preserved Through an Historic Public-Private Partnership," *Town Topics*, April 2, 1997.

1480 "Faculty Housing Plan," Institute for Advanced Study website, accessed at https://www.ias.edu/about/campus-lands/faculty-housing-plans

1481 Rebecca Blackwell, "History Buffs Spar with Institute on Battlefield," *Town Topics*, February 26, 2003.

1482 Ibid.

1483 Jerry Hurwitz, "The Origins of the Princeton Battlefield Society and Its fight to prevent the desecration of the Princeton Battlefield by the Institute for Advanced Study," essay from the Civil War Trust archive, Washington, D.C.; "Review of Archaeological Studies at the Princeton Battlefield," overview compiled by the Civil War Trust, Civil War Trust archives, Washington, D.C.

1484 Ibid.

1485 Ibid.; Hurwitz essay.

1486 Anne Levin, "Institute and Preservationists Continue Fight," *Town Topics*, December 7, 2011.

1487 Anne Levin, "IAS Housing Plan Prevails, Opponents to Appeal," *Town Topics*, March 7, 2012, and "Battlefield Society Suit Filed to Block Plan for Institute Housing," April 11, 2012; Ellen Gilbert, "Trust Puts Battlefield on 'Endangered' List; Institute Defends Plans for Development," June 13, 2012; Anne Levin, "Battlefield Society Fires Another Round in Fight Against Institute Housing Plan," July 25, 2012. All from *Town Topics*.

1488 Ibid.

1489 "National Coalition Urges Institute for Advanced Study to Halt Destruction of Revolutionary War Battlefield at Princeton," *Campaign 1776* press release, March 4, 2016. http://www.campaign1776.org/about-us/news/national-coalition-urges.html

1490   Linda Song, "Battlefield Society to appeal Institute plans to build faculty housing," *The Daily Princetonian*, February 26, 2015. http://dailyprincetonian.com/ news/2015/02/battlefield-society-to-appeal-institute-plans-to-build-faculty-housing/

1491   Ibid., Plaintiff's Brief in Support of Appeal, undated from 2015, page 22, footnote 6, from the archives of the Civil War Trust, Washington, D.C.

1492   Annie Yang, "Institute for Advanced Study rejects offers to preserve historic battlefield," *The Daily Princetonian*, January 5, 2016. Accessed at: http:// dailyprincetonian.com/news/2016/01/institute-for-advanced-study-offers-to-preserve-historic-battlefield/; Annie Yang, "N.J. Supreme Court rejects appeal to halt Institute for Advanced Study construction," *The Daily Princetonian*, November 24, 2015. http://dailyprincetonian.com/news/2015/11/n-j-supreme-court-rejects-appeal-to-halt-institute-for-advanced-society-construction/; Lindsey Morrison, "Maxwell's Field, Where Washington Saved the Revolution, Is Threatened by Development," The Cultural Land Foundation, December 17, 2015. Accessed at: http://tclf.org/landslides/ maxwell%E2%80%99s-field-where-washington-saved-revolution-threatened-development

1493   George Will, "A battle to save Princeton battlefield," *The Washington Post*, April 8, 2016, Accessed at https://www.washingtonpost.com/opinions/a-battle-to-save-the-princeton-battlefield/2016/04/08/3d40e344-fce4-11e5-9140-e61d062438bb_story. html?utm_term=.b4afa94b3be3

1494   Jim Campi correspondence with author, March 3, 2017.

1495   Ibid.

1496   "Maxwell's Field Battlefield Preservation Plan," Civil War Trust document, November 11, 2106. Civil War Trust archive, Washington, D.C.

1497   Ibid.

1498   David Duncan interview with author, January 24, 2017.

1499   Jim Campi correspondence with author, February 28, 2017.

1500   "National Preservation Groups Announce Campaign to Protect and Study Parker's Revenge Battleground," *Campaign 1776* news release, June 12, 2015. Accessed at: http://www.campaign1776.org/about-us/news/announcement-at-parkers-revenge. html

1501   Cara Giaimo, "How a Team of Reenactors Helped Solve a Revolutionary War Mystery," Atlas Obscura, December 23, 2016. http://www.atlasobscura.com/articles/ how-a-team-of-reenactors-helped-solve-a-revolutionary-war-mystery

1502   June 12 news release.

1503   Ibid.

1504   Jason Urbanus, "Finding Parker's Reverge," *Archaeology* magazine, December 7, 2015. As accessed at: http://www.archaeology.org/issues/202-1601/trenches/3933-trenches-massachusetts-revolutionary-war-parker-s-revenge

1505   Ibid.

1506   "Archaeology Report Released on Parker's Revenge, November 14, 2016, National Park Service website, as accessed at: https://www.nps.gov/mima/learn/news/ archaeology-report-released-on-parkers-revenge.htm; Giaimo, "How a Team . . . "

1507   Ibid.

1508   Giamo, "How a Team . . . "

CHAPTER TWENTY-TWO

1509   Jim Lighthizer interview with author, May 23, 2016.

1510   Ibid.

1511   Ibid.

1512   Ibid.

1513   Ibid.

1514	Ibid.
1515	Ibid.
1516	Ibid.
1517	Civil War Trust Master Land Record.
1518	Ibid.
1519	Ibid.
1520	Gilmore oral history, page 6.
1521	Civil War Trust Master Land Record, Civil War Trust archives, Washington, D.C.
1522	"Civil War Trust Ownership – Fee and Easement," spreadsheet of Civil War Trust land records, Civil War Trust archives, Washington, D.C.
1523	Trust Deputy Director of Real Estate Kathy Robertson email to author, June 21, 2016.
1524	Gilmore oral history, transcript page 1.
1525	Gilmore oral history, transcript page 3.
1526	Ibid; Civil War Trust Master Land Record.
1527	Ibid.
1528	Gilmore oral history, page 7.
1529	Ibid; Gilmore oral history, page 16.
1530	Gilmore oral history, pages 21-22.
1531	Civil War Trust Master Land Record.
1532	Gilmore oral history, page 24.
1533	David Duncan oral history interview, page 7.
1534	Duncan oral history, pages 13-14.
1535	Duncan oral history, page 10.
1536	*Campaign 1776* mailer from Civil War Trust for Fort Ann and Sacket's Harbor, New York; January 27, 2017. Civil War Trust archives, Washington, D.C.
1537	Mehrkam oral history, page 18.
1538	Duncan oral history, pages 14-15.
1539	Ibid.
1540	"American Battlefield Protection Program FY 2016 Battlefield Land Acquisition Grants," accessed at National Park Service website at https://www.nps.gov/abpp/grants/FY2016BLAGAwardeeList.pdf
1541	Jim Campi correspondence with author, March 3, 2017.
1542	David Duncan interview with author, January 24, 2017.
1543	Ibid.
1544	Ibid.
1545	Jim Lighthizer and David Duncan joint interview with author, December 19, 2016; Duncan January 24 interview.
1546	Ibid.
1547	Ibid.
1548	Ibid.
1549	Garry Adelman interview with author, March 31, 2016.
1550	Ibid.
1551	Garry Adelman oral history interview, Civil War Trust oral history project, Civil War Trust archives, Washington, D.C., transcript page 1.
1552	Ibid.
1553	Garry Adelman "Webucation" email to author, March 15, 2016.
1554	Garry Adelman email to author, January 21, 2017.
1555	Ibid.
1556	Adelman March 15 email.
1557	Adelman January 21 email.
1558	Ibid.
1559	Ibid.

1560   Civil War Sites: The Official Guide to the Civil War Discovery Trail, published by the Civil War Trust, is available online at http://astore.amazon.com/civiwarprestr-20/detail/0762744359; Mary Goundrey Koik correspondence with author, January 10, 2017.

1561   APCWS Quarterly Report of Activities, First quarter of 1996. Dennis E. Frye Papers, APCWS Files, Western Maryland Room, Washington County Free Library, Hagerstown, Md.; *Hallowed Ground*, Spring 1997, Vol. 10, No. 1; page 10, and Summer 1997, Vol 10, No. 2, page 10. Minutes of the Meeting of the Board of Directors of the Civil War Trust, November 6, 1997, Civil War Trust archives, Washington, D.C.

1562   Rob Shenk oral history interview, Civil War Trust oral history project. Civil War Trust archives, Washington, D.C., transcript pages 2-3.

1563   Ibid.

1564   Ibid.

1565   Adelman January 21, 2017 email.

1566   Adelman March 15 email.

1567   Jim Lighthizer Interview with author, November 15, 2016.

1568   Jim Lighthizer interview with author, December 19, 2016.

1569   David Duncan email to author, January 25, 2017.

1570   Lighthizer December 19 interview.

1571   Duncan January 25 email.

1572   Ibid.

1573   Ibid.

1574   Ibid.

1575   Mary Munsell Abroe oral history interview, Civil War Trust oral history project, Civil War Trust archives, Washington, D.C., transcript page 5.

1576   Duncan January 24 interview.

1577   Campi March 3 correspondence.

1578   William W. Vodra oral history interview, Civil War Trust oral history project, Civil War Trust archives, Washington, D.C., transcript page 3.

1579   Vodra oral history, pages 5-6.

1580   Ibid.

1581   Jim Lighthizer Interview with author, November 28, 2016.

1582   Ibid.

1583   Ibid.

1584   Ibid; David Duncan email to author, November 29, 2016.

1585   Gary W. Gallagher interview with author, November 23, 2016.

1586   Ibid.

1587   Ibid.; Gary W. Gallagher email to author, November 23, 2016.

1588   Gallagher November 23 interview.

1589   Ibid.

1590   Ibid.

1591   List of Civil War Trust Board of Trustees, including biographical information, as posted at Trust website, http://www.civilwar.org/aboutus/meet-the-team/board.html

1592   Ibid.

1593   Gallagher November 23 interview.

1594   Ibid.

EPILOGUE

1595   Theodore Gerrish, Army Life: A Private's Reminiscences of the Civil War, (Portland: Hoyt, Fogg & Donham, 1882), pages 198-199.

1596   Ibid.

1597	"General Chamberlain's Address," *Dedication of the Twentieth Maine Monuments at Gettysburg*, Oct. 3, 1889, original program as printed in Maine at Gettysburg, (State of Maine, 1898), as accessed at http://www.joshualawrencechamberlain.com/maineatgettysburg.php
1598	Civil War Trust land acquisition statistics are as of early 2017.
1599	Ibid; p. 371.
1600	Gerrish, p. 198.
1601	Ibid.; Civil War Trust Master Land Record, Civil War Trust archives, Washington, D.C.
1602	Lighthizer oral history, transcript pages 16-17.
1603	Donald C. Pfanz, "A Brief History of the Origins of the Association for the Preservation of Civil War Sites," June, 2011 essay appended to Donald Pfanz oral history interview, Civil War Trust oral history project, page 9.
1604	John P. "Jack" Ackerly oral history, transcript page 15.
1605	Frederick Zavaglia interview with author, February 8, 2017.
1606	Bearss 2012 oral history interview, transcript page 32.
1607	Ibid.
1608	Karli Mauldin, "3 Projects to Watch in Franklin in 2016," *The Williamson Source*, Jan. 4, 2016. http://williamsonsource.com/3-projects-to-watch-in-franklin-tennessee-2016/
1609	Save The Franklin Battlefield newsletter, February 2017, accessed at http://www.franklin-stfb.org/2017Feb_STFBNewsletter.pdf; "Civil War Trust Lauds Tennessee Governor, Lawmakers for State Pioneering Battlefield Preservation Fund," Civil War Trust news release, February 7, 2017, accessed at http://www.civilwar.org/aboutus/news/news-releases/2017-news/tennessee-battlefield-preservation-fund.html
1610	David LeVan interview with author, March 5, 2017.
1611	Lillian Reed, "Don't see anyone with pitchforks: Casino plan faces first hurdle," York, Pennsylvania, *Daily Record*, February 2, 2017, accessed at http://www.ydr.com/story/news/2017/02/02/adams-co-casino-project-faces-zoning-hurdle/97403882/
1612	Tersh Boasberg oral history interview, transcript page 24.
1613	Tony Troilo interview with author, January 23, 2017
1614	Clark B. Hall interview with author, December 3, 2015.
1615	Ibid.
1616	Ibid.

Index

National Parks Conservation Association, 76, 253, 300–301, 346, *photo insert*
National Park Service (NPS), 11, 17, 18, 29, 41–42, 96, 99, 103, 107, 114–118, 121, 123–124, 196–197, 231–232, 300–301, 308–309, 319, 332–334, 339, 352, photo insert.
National Park Trust, 166
National Press Club, 144
National Register for Historic Places, 96, 103, 114–118, 121, 123–124, 308
National Trust for Historic Preservation, 76, 122, 127, 144, 230, 252–253, 300–301, 306, 309, 345–346
NationsBank, 182, 198, 200
The Nature Conservancy, 45, 143
NatWest, 181
Nau, John L., III, 319, 362, 365
Nelson, Nancy, 348
Nelson, Zann, 310
Neuberger, Christine, 123
New Hope Church, Georgia, 188
New Market Battlefield Park, Virginia, 113
New York Monument, 58
No Casino Gettysburg organization, 252–253, 255–256, 315
Noe, Robert, Jr., 79
Nolan, Alan T., 47
Noonan, Pat, 219–220
North Anna battlefield, Virginia, 46–47, 49
Northwest Outer Connector, Virginia, 229, 237
Northwest Prince William Citizens'Association (NWPW-CA), 72, 74
NVR, Inc. (NV Homes), 79

O
Oak Ridge Railroad Cut, Pennsylvania, 21, 241–244, 247–249
O'Connell, Libby, *photo insert*
O'Donnell, John, 242–243
Opinion polls, 77, 232–233, 254, 267–268, 274, 302
Orange County, Virginia, 299–312.
Orange Plank Road, Virginia, 108
Orange Turnpike, Virginia, 108, 227–229, 237–238
O'Reilly, Frank, 279
Orrock Farm, Virginia, 229
Ota, Daralee, 293
O'Toole, Jim, 123
Ottenstein, Thomas R., 246–247
Ox Hill Battlefield Park, Virginia, 35, 38.

P
Pacala, Mark, 141
Paddock, Jim, 252–253, 255
Paddock, Susan Star, 252–256, 316, *photo insert*
Palmito Ranch battlefield, Texas, 19
Pamplin, Robert B., Jr., 148
Pamplin Historical Park, Virginia, 148
Pandak, Sharon E., 309–310
Paramount Studios, 137
Parker, John, 348
Parker's Cross Roads battlefield, *photo insert*
Parker's Revenge battleground, Massachusetts, 347–349
Parris, Stan, 78, 80
Paul, William H., 329–330
Pearce, Mary, 260–261, 264–270, 276, 373
Pea Ridge National Military Park, Arkansas, 99
PEC. See Piedmont Environmental Council
Packham, Mary Ann, *photo insert*
Peebles Farm battlefield, Virginia, 19
Pegram, John, 113
Pennsylvania Gaming Control Board (PGCB), 253, 255
Pennsylvania Historical and Museum Commission, 322
Perryville, Kentucky, 286
Petersburg National Battlefield, Virginia, 17, 43, 112–113, 148, 353, 369, 371
Peterson, Irma, 82, 84
Peterson, Milt, 70, 84
Petitions, 61, 101, 252–253, 256, 315
Pfanz, Donald C., 17, 21, 41–47, 202, 370–371, *photo insert*
PGCB (Pennsylvania Gaming Control Board), 253, 255
Philadelphia Brigade Monument, Antietam, Maryland, 329, 332
Pickett's Charge, Pennsylvania, 244, 246–247
Piedmont Environmental Council (PEC), 138–139, 143, 301
Pierson, John W., 279–281
Pierson Farm, Virginia, 279–281
Planned mixed-use districts (PMDs), 53, 69, 73
Pleasonton, Alfred, 89
Poe, Ted, 302–304
Pohanka, Brian C., 17, 30–31, 34–38, 42–49, 72, 74, 76, 82, 90, 92, 97, 130–131, 142–143, 145, 202, 234–235, 293–294, 370, *photo insert*

Porter, Memory, 63–65
Port Hudson, Louisiana, 222
Port Republic battlefield, Virginia, 49, 112, 284–285
Powell, Jody, 75–76, 81, 135–136, 141, 183
Powell, Walter, 242, 248
Powell Tate (public relations firm), 135
Prairie Grove battlefield, Arkansas, 43
Preservation easements, 268, 280–281, 284, 333–334, 352–353
Preservation Pennsylvania, 252–253
Preservation Virginia, 301
Presque Isle Farm, Virginia, 93
Princeton battlefield, New Jersey, 340–349, *photo insert*
Princeton Battlefield Society, 343–344, 346
Princeton Battlefield State Park, New Jersey, 340, 343–344
Prince William County, Virginia, 41, 49, 53, 62, 64, 135–136, 143–144, 223Prince William League for the Protection of Natural Resources, 63–65
Protect Historic America, 144, 146, 151
Protests, 53, 57, 73–74, 84–85, 234, 253, 333–334
Public hearings, 74–75, 97, 101, 129, 242, 255–256, 304–306, 315–316
Pyne, Moses Taylor, 343

Q
Quaker Road, Princeton, New Jersey, 344
Quigley, Carroll, 100

R
Race tracks, 128–131, 151–159
Raines, Thaddeus P., Jr., 34
Rains, Craig, 311
Rankin, Betty, 75, 77, 136
Rappahannock Station battlefield, Virginia, 49
Reagan, Ronald, 80, 82, 84, 108, 121
Reams Station battlefield, Virginia, 49
Redding, Nick, 315–316, 319
Reed, Marvin, 344
Reenactments, 48, 97, 186–187, 323, 334–335, 349
Regula, Ralph, 196, 199
Relic hunters, 33–34
Rendell, Ed, 251, 253–254
Repasi, Bonnie, 189–192
Report on the Nation's Civil War Battlefields (CWSAC), 127, 221, 352, 363

"In great deeds something abides.
On great fields something stays. Forms change and pass;
bodies disappear; but spirits linger, to consecrate ground
for the vision-place of souls. Generations that know us
not...shall come to this deathless field,
to ponder and dream. . ."

—GEN. JOSHUA L. CHAMBERLAIN
Gettysburg, Pa., October 3, 1888

Perryville Battlefield State Historic Site
Perryville, Ky.